Advance Pra

MW00624654

FROM YAHWEH TO ZION

SIFTING & WINNOWING

BOOKS

Copyright © 2018
Sifting and Winnowing Books
POB 221, Lone Rock, WI 53556

Library of Congress Cataloging-in-Publication Data
From Yahweh to Zion: Three Thousand Years of Exile:
Jealous God, Chosen People, Promised Land . . .
Clash of Civilizations
By Laurent Guyénot,
Translated and edited by Kevin Barrett
ISBN 978-0-9961430-4-2

1. Judaism, History of. 2. Zionism 3. Old Testament, History of
4. Israel, History of

Cover design by Sandra Taylor, The Graphic Page
Illustration by Maria Comak

The translator-editor gratefully acknowledges proofreading and editing help by Chuck Millar and Cat McGuire.

FROM YAHWEH TO ZION:

THREE THOUSAND YEARS OF EXILE

Jealous God, Chosen People, Promised Land . . .
Clash of Civilizations

Laurent Guyénot

translated from French by
Kevin Barrett

CONTENTS

PREFACE

The book you are about to read is a major contribution not only to that overspecialized field known as the History of Religions, but also to its more generalized sibling, the History of Ideas. It is cultural critique of the first order. It is timely, of such relevance to current events as can hardly be overstated. And yet it could never be published by a major publishing house in any English-speaking country.

Why not? After all, in our Brave New World, destructive criticism of almost everything under the sun is permissible, if not encouraged or even required. Brutal, not particularly sophisticated attacks on Islam, Christianity, religion in general, the Pope, Mother Theresa, public decency, and indeed almost every traditional value are ubiquitous, regularly appearing in publishers' catalogues and bestseller lists, and assigned as required reading in universities and book clubs. How, in such an anything-goes atmosphere, can a scholarly interpretation of ideological history be so controversial as to be virtually unpublishable? How can a book about the history of the idea of God pose such problems in the year of our Lord 2018?

The answer is simple: This book traces the evolution of the concept of God through its relationship to Jewish tribal power. And the rulers of our Western world have made one thing abundantly clear: though God may be criticized, Jewish power must not be.

But what *is* Yahweh, the earliest known God of the Abrahamic monotheists and their descendants, if not an embodiment and representation of Jewish tribal power in general, and that of Jewish elites in particular? How can we think about what monotheism means in the era of the clash of civilizations without considering this foundational question?

In *From Yahweh to Zion*, Laurent Guyénot uncovers a mind-virus endemic to Judaism, yet present to greater or lesser degrees in Christianity and Islam as well: a conception of God that stubbornly clings to tribalism and all that it entails, rather than surrendering absolutely to universalism. This misconception of God as tribal shibboleth provides a powerful weapon in the ideological arsenals of unscrupulous elites, whether Jewish, Christian, or Muslim. And it may have mutated and hidden itself inside the secularist fundamentalisms that are substitute religions for the modern educated classes.

When an Iraqi Muslim bombs innocent civilians in a mosque or market, an American Christian flies a drone bomb into a wedding party in Afghanistan, or a secular French policeman forces a Muslim woman to remove her one-piece bathing suit, we may detect an atavistic tribalism driving the perpetrators of these acts to defile, subjugate, or destroy other peoples and their gods, as per the orders of the Old Testament god Yahweh. For though not all ethnocentric intolerance derives from Yahweh— such episodes have occurred in the histories of all peoples—the Yahwist cult has left its mark on the Jewish, Christian, and Islamic worlds, and thereby on the world at large, in an especially destructive way. Outbreaks of Old Testament fundamentalism have correlated with many of our worst conquests, subjugations, and genocides—from the Wars of Religion to the Native American holocaust to the settler colonial annihilations and subjugations of the peoples of Africa, Australia and New Zealand, and (more recently) Palestine. And in today's postreligious age—unofficially inaugurated by what National Medal of Science winner Lynn Margolis called the "most successful and most perverse publicity stunt in the history of public relations" on September 11, 2001—a hidden Yahwism seems to guide the hands of allegedly secular elites as they plot their new crusades.

Recognizing our own implication in such ideas and events can be difficult, even painful. But it may also be necessary. Having come to Islam in 1993, and adopted its revisionist account of Old Testament folklore and mythology as my own, I find Guyénot's critique of Yahwism disquieting and challenging. But I also find it useful, especially in understanding my coreligionists' lapses into tribalism and intolerance. ISIS, which lashes out at other religious approaches and their adherents as if they were false gods and idolaters, is a facile example. But many mainstream Muslims who would never dream of joining ISIS sometimes act as though fellow Muslims who take a slightly different path to God are *mushrikîn* (idol worshippers) rather than coreligionists and fellow human beings. The takfiris of ISIS and similar groups mirror the self-righteous, Yahwistic sides of ourselves.

Though Guyénot's argument could easily be caricatured as simplistically antimonotheistic and propolytheistic, I would not subscribe to that reading. Guyénot draws a portrait of Yahweh as psychopathic father whose war on idolatry amounts to an amoral, self-aggrandizing extinction of the other. Though such a reading may be largely warranted by the Old Testament and the Talmud, I don't think it applies to the monotheistic religions of Christianity or Islam, at least not to the same degree. And there are aspects of Biblical tradition that cut in the opposite direction, notably those highlighted by René Girard in numerous writings such as *The Scapegoat* (1986).

Girard suggests that monotheism's anti-idolatry impetus stems largely from its half-conscious understanding that polytheistic "religions" are, in the final analysis, cults of human sacrifice. Thus, according to the Girardian reading, the story of Abraham's near-sacrifice of his son is less about inculcating blind obedience to Yahweh than about ending the polytheistic pagan practice of sacrificing one's own children to the likes of Moloch. We could extend Girard's insight to encompass Muhammad's war on Meccan idolaters who buried their baby girls alive and sacrificed to monstrous gods around a defiled Kaaba in search of wealth and power for themselves and their cronies.

Such practices still exist, though they are no longer widespread. In today's North and West Africa, the practice of human sacrifice to gods or jinn by people seeking wealth and power continues on the margins of society, where it has been consigned by the reigning monotheism. Similar abominations apparently persist among so-called dark shamans in parts of Latin America as well as in the satanic cults of Europe and America. Such are the "idol worshippers" denigrated in the most reliable monotheistic scripture, in my view, the Holy Qur'an.

But if there is a positive or at least defensible side to monotheism's hostility to polytheism and idolatry, it does not form part of Guyénot's analysis in this book—which could be accused of one-sidedness in other ways as well. For example:

Where, one may ask, are the countless examples of noble, selfless Jewish behavior? What about all the wonderful Jewish high achievers in science and the arts? Where are the standard accounts of the endless gratuitous persecutions Jews have suffered everywhere they have settled? Is there not at least some truth to the stereotype of the Jew as eternal victim?

The answer to such objections is simple: Those stories have been endlessly told and retold in all the dominant media of the postwar West. Yet nowhere are they questioned; nowhere are alternative accounts proposed; nowhere are the viewpoints of those who found themselves in conflict with Jewish tribalism given fair consideration. Every historical conflict between Jews and goyim is assumed to be the fault of the goyim. If a man quarrels with everyone in his life—his neighbors, his boss, his coworkers, those he meets on the street—and then insists that all of those people are persecuting him for no reason whatsoever, few of us would take him at his word. Yet we unquestioningly accept such interpretations of interactions between Jewish and non-Jewish communities, whether due to lack of curiosity or fear: fear of being called names, of being socially ostracized, of possibly even being deprived of our livelihood.

It is long past time to stop fearing and start thinking. This book's task is to provide a plausible revisionist interpretation of critically important questions, not to echo conventional tropes in hopes of appearing "fair and balanced." By venturing boldly into forbidden territory, Laurent Guyénot forces us to think, freshly and critically, in a way that our culture habitually deems off-limits. A staunch antiracist, Guyénot makes it abundantly clear that he is critiquing ideas, not biology. And unlike much of the shrill, even hysterical "anti-Semitic" writing lurking in disreputable corners of the internet, this book is far less tendentious than the dominant discourse it critiques. Fair-minded yet unflinching, it is a magisterial work by an uncommonly erudite historian, and deserves the widest possible readership.

–Kevin Barrett

INTRODUCTION

"The destiny of the Jewish people appears to the historian as a paradoxical and incredible phenomenon, almost beyond comprehension. It is unique and without equivalent in the history of mankind," writes French author Alexandre Roudinesco.[1] Such commonplace assertions are hard to refute.

To explain what makes the Jewish people so special, and Jewish identity so enduring, without resorting to the notion of divine election, one has to agree that the Bible has played a major role. (I use the word "Bible" for the Jewish *Tanakh*, the Old Testament of the Christians.) Jews around the world have drawn from the Bible pride in their history and confidence in their destiny, no matter what hardship they may endure.

Whether Jewishness is defined as religious or ethnic, its roots are in the Bible. Therefore, its essence must be sought there. Whether he has read it or not, whether he judges it historical or mythical, every Jew ultimately bases his Jewishness on the Bible—or whatever he knows about the Bible. This venerable corpus—which includes the five "Books of Moses" (the Pentateuch, or Torah), the Historical Books, and the Prophets—constitutes the unshakable foundation of both Jewish religion and Jewish identity. (The Talmud is only a commentary on the Bible, and does not fundamentally alter its core ideology). From a religious viewpoint, the Bible preserves the memory and the essence of the Covenant with God that the believer internalizes. From an ethnic viewpoint, the Bible is the foundational collective memory of the Jewish people, and the pattern by which Jews interpret their whole subsequent history (the Dispersion, the Holocaust, the rebirth of Israel, and so on). Any nation is a narration, and what makes the Jewish nation special is ultimately what makes the biblical narration special. The Bible has always been the "portable fatherland" of the Diaspora Jews, as Heinrich Heine once put it. But it also became

---

[1] Alexandre Roudinesco, *Le Malheur d'Israël*, Éditions de Cluny, 1956, p. 7.

and has remained the heart of Israel, whose founders did not give it any other Constitution.

It is true that the earliest prophets of political Zionism— Moses Hess (*Rome and Jerusalem*, 1862), Leon Pinsker (*Auto-Emancipation*, 1882), and Theodor Herzl (*The Jewish State*, 1896)— did not draw their inspiration from the Bible, but rather from the great nationalist spirit that swept through Europe at the end of the nineteenth century. Pinsker and Herzl actually cared little whether the Jews colonized Palestine or any other region of the globe; the former considered land in North America, while the latter contemplated Argentina and later Uganda. More important still than nationalism, what drove these intellectual pioneers was the persistence of Judeophobia or anti-Semitism: Pinsker, who was from Odessa, converted to Zionism during the pogroms that followed the assassination of Alexander II; Herzl, at the height of the Dreyfus affair. Pinsker, a medical doctor, regarded Judeophobia as a hereditary and incurable "disease transmitted for two thousand years," and he characterized the Jews as "the people chosen for universal hatred."[2] The most recent manifestation of anti-Semitism in Nazi Germany was the justification for the creation of Israel in 1948. And it is still today one of the pillars of Jewish identity throughout the world, as documented in Yoav Shamir's excellent film *Defamation* (2009). Indeed, since the end of the 1960s the Holocaust has become the source of a new secular version of the Election—the belief that Jews are God's chosen people. Yet, as we shall see, the Holocaust resonates deeply with the Bible.

Fundamentally, as its very name indicates, Zionism is a biblically inspired project: Zion is a name used for Jerusalem by biblical prophets. Although officially a secular ideology, Zionism was, from the start, biblical to the core. Avigail Abarbanel makes the point in a text meant to explain to Israelis why she has given up her Israeli citizenship: "Let's say you did 'return home' as your myths say, that Palestine really was your ancestral home. But Palestine was fully populated when you started to covet it.

---

[2] Leon Pinsker, *Auto-Emancipation: An Appeal to His People by a Russian Jew*, 1882, on www.jewishvirtuallibrary.org/jsource/Zionism/pinsker.html.

In order to take it for yourself you have been following quite closely the biblical dictate to Joshua to just walk in and take everything. You killed, you expelled, you raped, you stole, you burned and destroyed and you replaced the population with your own people. I was always taught that the Zionist movement was largely non-religious (how you can be Jewish without Jewish religion is perplexing in itself). For a supposedly non-religious movement it's extraordinary how closely Zionism—your creator and your blueprint—has followed the Bible. Of course you never dare to critique the stories of the Bible. Not even the secular amongst you do that. None of my otherwise good teachers at my secular schools ever suggested that we question the morality of what Joshua did. If we were able to question it, the logical next step would have been to question Zionism, its crimes, and the rightness of the existence of our very own state. No, we couldn't be allowed to go that far. It was too dangerous. That would risk the precarious structure that held us in place."[3]

The founders of the Yishuv (Jewish communities settled in Palestine before 1947) and later the founders of the new State of Israel were steeped in the Bible. From their point of view, Zionism was the logical and necessary end of Yahwism. In *Ben-Gurion, Prophet of Fire* (1983), the biography of the man described as "the personification of the Zionist dream," Dan Kurzman entitles each chapter with a Bible quote. The preface begins like this: "The life of David Ben-Gurion is more than the story of an extraordinary man. It is the story of a biblical prophecy, an eternal dream. [...] Ben-Gurion was, in a modern sense, Moses, Joshua, Isaiah, a messiah who felt he was destined to create an exemplary Jewish state, a 'light unto the nations' that would help to redeem all mankind." For Ben-Gurion, Kurzman writes, the rebirth of Israel in 1948 "paralleled the Exodus from Egypt, the conquest of the land by Joshua, the Maccabean revolt." Yet Ben-Gurion had no religious inclination; he had never been to the synagogue, and ate pork for breakfast. He liked to say that "God did not choose Israel; Israel chose God," and he quoted

---

[3] Avigail Abarbanel, "Why I Left the Cult," October 8, 2016, on mondoweiss.net.

Joshua 24:22 to back it. According to the rabbi leading the Bible study group that he attended, Ben-Gurion "unconsciously believed he was blessed with a spark from Joshua's soul." He had been captivated by ancient history since his childhood, and changed his name David Grün to that of a Jewish general fighting the Romans. "There can be no worthwhile political or military education about Israel without profound knowledge of the Bible," he used to say.[4] He wrote in his diary in 1948, ten days after declaring independence, "We will break Transjordan [Jordan], bomb Amman and destroy its army, and then Syria falls, and if Egypt will still continue to fight—we will bombard Port Said, Alexandria and Cairo," then he adds: "This will be in revenge for what they (the Egyptians, the Aramis and Assyrians) did to our forefathers during biblical times."[5] Three days after the Israeli invasion of the Sinai in 1956, he declared before the Knesset that what was at stake was "the restoration of the kingdom of David and Solomon."[6]

Prophecy is part of the biblical mindset. In a statement published in the magazine *Look* on January 16, 1962, Ben-Gurion predicted that in the next twenty-five years: "All armies will be abolished, and there will be no more wars. In Jerusalem, the United Nations (a truly United Nations) will build a Shrine of the Prophets to serve the federated union of all continents; this will be the seat of the Supreme Court of Mankind, to settle all controversies among the federated continents, as prophesied by Isaiah."[7] That program is running late, but it has not changed. How could it? It is printed in Isaiah! Christians find hope in the prophecy that, one day, people "will hammer their swords into plowshares and their spears into sickles. Nations will not lift sword against nation, no longer will they learn how to make war" (Isaiah 2:4). But more important to Zionists are the previous verses, which describe these messianic times as a *Pax*

---

[4] Dan Kurzman, *Ben-Gurion, Prophet of Fire*, Touchstone, 1983, pp. 17–18, 22, 26–28.
[5] Ilan Pappe, *The Ethnic Cleansing of Palestine*, Oneworld Publications, 2007, p. 144.
[6] Israel Shahak, *Jewish History, Jewish Religion: The Weight of Three Thousand Years*, Pluto Press, 1994, p. 10.
[7] David Ben-Gurion and Amram Duchovny, *David Ben-Gurion, In His Own Words*, Fleet Press Corp., 1969, p. 116.

Judaica, when "all the nations" will pay tribute "to the mountain of Yahweh, to the house of the god of Jacob," when "the Law will issue from Zion and the word of Yahweh from Jerusalem," so that Yahweh will "judge between the nations and arbitrate between many peoples."

Ben-Gurion's attachment to the Bible was shared by almost every Zionist leader of his generation and the next. Moshe Dayan, the military hero of the 1967 Six-Day War, wrote a book entitled *Living with the Bible* (1978) in which he biblically justified the annexation of new territory. Even the nuclear policy of Israel has a biblical name: the Samson Option. On March 3, 2015, Prime Minister Benjamin Netanyahu dramatized in front of the American Congress his deep phobia of Iran by referring to the biblical book of Esther (the only Bible story that makes no mention of God). It is worth quoting the heart of his rhetorical appeal for a US strike against Iran: "We're an ancient people. In our nearly 4,000 years of history, many have tried repeatedly to destroy the Jewish people. Tomorrow night, on the Jewish holiday of Purim, we'll read the book of Esther. We'll read of a powerful Persian viceroy named Haman, who plotted to destroy the Jewish people some 2,500 years ago. But a courageous Jewish woman, Queen Esther, exposed the plot and gave the Jewish people the right to defend themselves against their enemies. The plot was foiled. Our people were saved. Today the Jewish people face another attempt by yet another Persian potentate to destroy us."[8] Netanyahu managed to schedule his address to the Congress on the eve of Purim, which celebrates the happy end of the book of Esther—the slaughter of 75,000 Persians, women and children included. This recent and typical speech by the head of the State of Israel is clear indication that the behavior of that nation on the international scene cannot be understood without a deep inquiry into the Bible's underlying ideology. Such is the main objective of this book.

---

[8] "The Complete Transcript of Netanyahu's Address to Congress," on www.washingtonpost.com.

The first three chapters probe the heart of the Hebrew Bible. They set out to extract its ideological substratum, unveiling the process by which Yahweh, through the voices of his priests, prophets, and scribes (the "cognitive elite")[9] shaped the vision and collective psychology of his chosen people. Christians have their own reading and particular conception of the Old Testament—a "religious," second-degree reading—that differs from the Jewish reading, and that impedes their understanding of Jewish identity. We must consider the biblical tradition in its original context in order to grasp its revolutionary and corrosive character.

Chapter 4 then examines the genesis of Christianity and its medieval evolution, while chapter 5 analyzes the evolution of the Jewish people in its relation to Christendom. The major turning point of this story is the expulsion of Sephardic Jews from the Iberian Peninsula in the fifteenth century, and their forced mass conversions to Christianity, followed by the pitiless hunt for the "false Christians" thus generated. These traumatic events radicalized Jewish anti-Christianity, and played a critical role in the upheaval of the old world, as Jewish historians alone have correctly apprehended. Chapters 6 through 9 shed light on world events from the nineteenth to the twenty-first centuries by focusing on the influence of Ashkenazi Jews in Central and Western Europe and then in North America. The "deep history" of networks, secret diplomacy, clandestine operations, psychological warfare, and propaganda reveals the decisive steps in this process, which launched a struggle for the soul and destiny of humanity. This book will highlight a "project" that has been ongoing for over a hundred years, marked by four world wars and culminating in the programmed destruction of the Arab-Muslim Middle East, the final installment. The two concluding chapters (10 and 11) provide a summary and synthesis, proposing theoretical models capable of handling the empirical data, and presenting a conception of history that

---

[9] This term, here borrowed from Gilad Atzmon, was first introduced by Richard Hernstein and Charles Murray in *The Bell Curve: Intelligence and Class Structure in American Life*, 1994.

recognizes the crucial role played by the Jewish people. These chapters, like the preceding ones, will rely mainly on Jewish authors, whose views on these questions are often much more relevant than those of conventional non-Jewish historians.

This book is a critical approach to "Jewishness" as a system of thought—a representation of the world and the self— essentially an idea. I am critiquing this idea by exposing its dangerous irrationality, nothing more. Even if it were as old as the world, any idea would deserve critique. Since the first victims of a toxic idea are the men and women who believe it, they are the first I wish to help liberate. Trying to understand Jewishness entails dealing with the nature of the Election, the Holocaust, and Israel, for they are the three "invisible walls" of the "Jewish prison," according to French journalist Jean Daniel's personal testimony.[10] If there is a moral judgment in the following pages, it is directed at the elite who have built this prison throughout the ages, and kept its key.

For today, just like yesterday, Jewishness is an identity shaped by the elite, as it has always been. The dominant ideology among world Jewry is, by definition, the ideology imposed by the dominant Jews, the cultural and religious elite intimately associated with the political and financial elite. "The evils of Israel are the evils of leadership," wrote Jewish publisher Samuel Roth in *Jews Must Live: An Account of the Persecution of the World by Israel on All the Frontiers of Civilization* (1934). He blames all the suffering of the Jews on "the stupendous hypocrisy and cruelty imposed upon us by our fatal leadership." "Beginning with the Lord God of Israel Himself, it was the successive leaders of Israel who one by one foregathered and guided the tragic career of the Jews—tragic to the Jews and no less tragic to the neighboring nations who have suffered them. [...] despite our faults, we would never have done so much damage to the world if it had not been for our genius for evil leadership."[11] This book will show that the submission of the Jewish people to the self-

---

[10] Jean Daniel, *La Prison juive. Humeurs et méditations d'un témoin*, Odile Jacob, 2003, p. 53.
[11] Samuel Roth, *Jews Must Live: An Account of the Persecution of the World by Israel on All the Frontiers of Civilization*, 1934, (archive.org).

proclaimed representatives of Yahweh—and to their ideology—
is the essence of biblical ethics. Even though the biblical
narrative itself presents the Hebrew people as often rebellious
and reverting to their "abominable" natural leaning toward
fraternization with their neighbors, Yahwist ideology, which
forbids intermarriage with the goyim, always seems to have the
final say.

Today, under the influence of a new elite, composed mostly
of sons and grandsons of rabbis, Jewishness tends to merge with
Zionism. Being Jewish had always been synonymous with being
part of "Israel," but now "Israel" has taken on a new meaning.
Jewish identity is no longer defined as belonging to a people or a
religion, but as loyalty to a particular Middle Eastern state. The
efforts of Jewish authorities to condemn anti-Zionism as a
disguise for anti-Semitism (Israel has become "the Jew of
nations," claims Paul Giniewski in *Antisionisme: le nouvel
antisémitisme*, 1973) are only the counterpart of their efforts to
convince all Jews that Zionism is a nonnegotiable part of their
Jewishness. When Rabbi Josy Eisenberg writes in an editorial for
the French magazine *L'Information juive*, "Except for a few
Jews—alas sometimes negationists—love for the State of Israel
is today the only common point of all Jews," he means it less as
an observation than as an injunction: each Jew is required to
love Israel or he will be deemed traitor to his own Jewish
identity, that is, a "self-hating Jew." At minimum, adds
Eisenberg, "there is today a moral imperative not to add our
voice to the detractors of Israel, and to always temper our
critiques."[12]

I do not ignore the fact that, like the ghettos of bygone days,
the "Jewish prison" has also been a refuge. As an even greater
paradox, it can be argued that the prison has incited great
creativity among the prisoners most determined to free
themselves; true freedom is, perhaps, only available through
escape. If so many Jews have left their mark on worldwide
cultural history, it is obviously not *in spite of* their Jewishness.
Instead it is often in an antagonistic relationship to it, or at least

---

[12] *Information juive* no. 297, January 2010, p. 4, on www.informationjuive.fr.

in a determined effort to move beyond it. These Jewish geniuses are very different from the communitarian elites, even though the latter try to appropriate and profit from the posthumous fame of the former. The archetypal example is Baruch Spinoza, excommunicated by the rabbis during his lifetime, now lionized as the greatest Jewish thinker. Almost without exception, the Jewish geniuses have been anticommunitarian, critical of Judaism, and, in the twentieth century, anti-Zionist. Today the Jewish mental prison consisting of victimization (Holocaust worship and fear of anti-Semitism) and guilt (blackmail-driven loyalty to Israel) has become so oppressive that those who wish to escape must first exhaust themselves breaking down the walls.

This book is, above all, the result of a sincere effort at cognitive empathy. I have read from a wide range of schools of thought, but among them I have given the greatest importance to Jewish writings. These have greatly influenced my vision of Jewish culture and its worldwide impact, leaving me today with the dispassionate conviction that Judaism and the Jewish people have been, throughout history, in their very antagonism to Gentile cultures, and sometimes in a brutal and tragic way, a dynamic factor of evolution. No Christian, indeed, could deny that fact without ignoring Jesus's background.

This book will deal with Judaism, the Jewish people, Jewish history, Jewishness, and Jewry (the Jewish community). I adopt for all these terms nominalist definitions, the only ones that suffer no objection: "A Jew is a person who considers him/herself a Jew and is so considered by others," to quote Raphael Patai.[13] Likewise, Jewishness is nothing but what Jews think of it. I am dealing with these notions exclusively from a cognitive viewpoint; my research is about beliefs, ideology, mental frameworks, and representations. For example, the fact that the majority of modern Jews define their Jewishness as ethnic rather than religious is, from the standpoint adopted here, a cognitive fact, nothing more. Whether genetic studies prove

---

[13] Raphael Patai, *The Jewish Mind*, Wayne State University Press, 1977 (books.google .com), p. 24.

them right or wrong is not the point, for ideology is independent from biology.

The thesis of this book is also independent from the question of the Bible's dating. That the majority of Jews and non-Jews think it is three thousand years old is just another cognitive fact. The nature of the Bible is in its content, not its age. Yet the historical context of its birth and growth, as informed by scholarly research, can be enlightening. Such is the subject of the first chapter.

Finally, the argument of this book is independent from the question of the existence of God—a question that presupposes a consensual definition of "God," an impossible task. Let it be said, however, that the author holds as self-evident that the Universe is endowed with Intelligence; for how could man, otherwise, be intelligent? Philosophers figured that out more than two thousand years ago.[14] The unfathomable mystery of that Cosmic Power of Truth and Love, without which human brotherhood is a vain idea, cannot be contained in a book or a set of dogmas. As for Yahweh, I consider him nothing more than the main character of a saga written by several generations of priests and scribes for their own advantage. Yet, as an idea cultivated in the collective psyche of millions of people for tens of centuries, it is certainly endowed with great spiritual power.

All Bible quotes are taken from the Catholic *New Jerusalem Bible*, which has not altered the divine name YHWH into "the Lord," as most other English translations have done for unscholarly reasons. I make only one alteration to this authoritative translation, for reasons that will be apparent later: I write "god" rather than "God" when the word is used as a noun rather than a name, as in "the god of Israel." For example, where the *NJB* arbitrarily differentiates "Chemosh, your god" from "Yahweh, our God" in Judges 11:24, I do not.

---

[14] e.g., Cicero, *On the Nature of the Gods* II, 6.

Chapter 1

THE PEOPLE OF SETH

> "If you faithfully obey the voice of
> Yahweh your God, by keeping and
> observing all his commandments, which
> I am laying down for you today, Yahweh
> your God will raise you higher than
> every other nation in the world."
>
> Deuteronomy 28:1

The Birth of Israel

The history of Israel, as recounted by mainstream historians, begins at the end of the tenth century BCE, when the Middle East was dominated by Assyria, whose capital was Assur. That is when the Omrides dynasty founded in northern Palestine a kingdom that took as its name Israel, and as its administrative capital Samaria. It was known in the Assyrian chronicles as the "House of Omri." Judea, in the south, was a backwards hinterland consisting of mountainous arid land inhabited by pastoral tribes that had only recently settled down. Religious life in Israel was certainly as diverse as in other parts of Syria. It was merely a local version of polytheism, which, across the known world, admitted the plurality of gods—some local, some national, others international or cosmic, all proceeding from or contained within the supreme god, referred to simply as El (God), or by majestic plural Elohim.

It is believed that a general by the name of Jehu first promoted the cult of his god Yahweh in the kingdom of Israel, after seizing the throne in 842 BCE.[1] Yahweh Sabaoth (Yahweh

---

[1] Ancient dates given in this book are those commonly admitted. They should be regarded as of relative value, since the chronological scale on which they are based has been seriously challenged and reduced by the so-called "revisionists of ancient history"; read Gunnar Heinsohn's paper on "The Restoration of Ancient History," on www.mikamar.biz/symposium/heinsohn.txt, and John Crowe's "The Revision of Ancient History – A Perspective," on www.sis-group.org.uk/ancient.htm.

of armies) seems to be the archaic name of this military god, which was carried in battle in a mobile ark (1 Samuel 4:4). He resembled Assur, the national and military god of the Assyrians, presented in Assyrian chronicles as the true king of the eponymous city-state, with the human ruler being only the vicegerent. Assur is a warrior god, who grants victory to his people and destroys the gods (i.e., temples and shrines) of conquered peoples.[2] This is also, as we shall see, the dominant feature of Yahweh.

In the middle of the eighth century, the Neo-Assyrian Empire embarked on a new round of political and commercial expansion, systematically destroying the cities that refused vassalage. Israel allied itself with Damascus against Assyria. Judea refused to join in this endeavor and stood under Assyrian protection. Israel was annihilated in 720 BCE. Jerusalem saw its population double in an influx of refugees who included priests bent on preserving their former national identity. Under their influence, a pan-Israelite ideology developed aiming to reconquer the North under the banner of Yahweh. The opportunity seemed to present itself with the weakening of Assyria during the reign of King Josiah (639–609), who tried to extend his control over the northern lands, and dreamed of making Jerusalem the center of a new empire.

In those ancient times, government propaganda took a religious form. And Yahweh is a vengeful god. He had defied Assur, was defeated by him, but continued to assert his superiority over his conqueror. The book of Isaiah, whose oldest strata was composed soon after the destruction of Israel by Assyria, is the founding document of that program: "Yahweh Sabaoth has sworn it, 'Yes, what I have planned will take place, what I have decided will be so: I shall break Assyria in my country, I shall trample on him on my mountains. Then his yoke will slip off them, his burden will slip from their shoulders. This is the decision taken in defiance of the whole world; this, the hand outstretched in defiance of all nations. Once Yahweh

---

[2] Jan Assmann, *Of God and Gods: Egypt, Israel, and the Rise of Monotheism*, University of Wisconsin Press, 2008, p. 44.

Sabaoth has decided, who will stop him? Once he stretches out his hand, who can withdraw it?'" (14:24–27).

The book of Isaiah would be expanded during several centuries, without deviating from the initial plan, which was to make Zion the new center of the world: "It will happen in the final days that the mountain of Yahweh's house will rise higher than the mountains and tower above the heights. Then all the nations will stream to it. [...] For the Law will issue from Zion and the word of Yahweh from Jerusalem" (2:2–3). Kings, Yahweh assures his people, "will fall prostrate before you, faces to the ground, and lick the dust at your feet" (49:23), whereas "I shall make your oppressors eat their own flesh, they will be as drunk on their own blood as on new wine. And all humanity will know that I am Yahweh, your Saviour, your redeemer, the Mighty One of Jacob" (49:26). "For the nation and kingdom that will not serve you will perish, and the nations will be utterly destroyed" (60:12).

Yahweh held his people solely responsible for his defeat by Assur: they have failed him by their religious pluralism, likened to a betrayal of their holy alliance. In fact, according to the biblical chroniclers, it was Yahweh himself who led Assur against the Israeli people to punish them for their apostasy. Judah, on the contrary, saw its own survival as the sign of Yahweh's favor: Judah thus earned the birthright over Israel, as Jacob had over Esau. This theme was probably introduced into the biblical narrative at the time of Josiah, by weaving together traditions from the North (Israel) and from the South (Judea). Northern legends, for example, glorified the ancient king Saul, while southern folklore honored David, the shepherd turned honorable bandit. In the resulting story, the tension between Saul and David is resolved in favor of the latter when Saul says to David, who once served him: "Now I know that you will indeed reign and that the sovereignty in Israel will pass into your hands" (1 Samuel 24:21). God establishes on David an eternal dynasty (2 Samuel 7:12–16) and his son Solomon reigns over an empire.

Despite two centuries of fruitless searching, archaeologists have come to admit that the magnificent Kingdom of Solomon has no more reality than Arthur's Camelot. At the supposed time of Solomon, Jerusalem was only a large village, while Samaria hosted a palace. The myth of Solomon probably started as a fantasy mirror image of Josiah's political project, designed to strengthen the claims of prophet-priests that a new David (Josiah) would restore the empire of Solomon. The game of mirrors thus created between mythical past and prophetic future is a masterpiece of political propaganda.[3]

Josiah's expansionist scheme was thwarted by Egypt, which also hoped to take advantage of the weakening of Assyria. After Josiah's death in battle against the Egyptian army, the days of Judah were numbered. The books of Kings tell us that several of his sons reigned briefly, first as vassals of Egypt, then of Babylon. When the last of them rebelled against King Nebuchadnezzar II, the latter retaliated by besieging and finally burning Jerusalem in 588 BCE, deporting some of its elites (the book of Jeremiah 52:30 advances the plausible figure of 4,600 people); another group found refuge in Egypt. The exiles enjoyed broad autonomy in Babylon, and some even acquired wealth and influence. Speaking on behalf of Yahweh from Egypt, the priest-prophet Jeremiah wrote to the exiles: "Work for the good of the city to which I have exiled you; pray to Yahweh on its behalf, since on its welfare yours depends" (Jeremiah 29:7). But twenty chapters later, Jeremiah announced the "vengeance of the Lord" on the Babylonians and called on their Persian enemies to "slaughter and curse with destruction every last one of them" (50:21). In the same spirit, the author of Psalm 137:8 writes: "Daughter of Babel, doomed to destruction, [...] a blessing on anyone who seizes your babies and shatters them against a rock!" The reason for this violent shift in Yahweh's sentiment was that the situation had changed: in 555 BCE, a prince named Nabonad seized power in Babylon. He made war against the Persian king Cyrus (Koresch) and allied with the king of Egypt Amasis. There is evidence that the Judean exiles sided with the Persians, according to Jewish historian Heinrich Graetz: "Did any of the Judean favorites at

---

[3] Israel Finkelstein and Neil Adher Silberman, *David and Solomon: In Search of the Bible's Sacred Kings and the Roots of the Western Tradition*, S&S International, 2007.

the Babylonian court, or any of the converted heathens open secret negotiations with Cyrus? The kindness shown later on to the Judeans by the Persian warrior, and their persecution by Nabonad, led to the supposition that such was the case."[4]

When the Persians conquered Babylon in 539 BCE, some of the exiles and their descendants (42,360 people with their 7,337 servants and 200 male and female singers, according to Ezra 2:64–67) returned to Jerusalem under the protection of King Cyrus, with the project of rebuilding the Temple in Jerusalem. For his gentleness, Cyrus is bestowed the title of God's "Anointed" (*Mashiah*) in Isaiah 45:1, Yahweh (or his influential devotees) having "grasped [him] by his right hand, to make the nations bow before him." In 458 BCE, eighty years after the return of the first exiles, Ezra, proud descendant of a line of Yahwist priests, went from Babylon to Jerusalem, accompanied by some 1,500 followers. Carrying with him an amplified version of the Torah, Ezra called himself the "Secretary of the Law of the God of heaven" (Ezra 7:21), mandated by the king of Persia. He was soon joined by Nehemiah, a Persian court official of Judean origin.

Ezra the Proto-Zionist

Chapter 22 of the second book of Kings tells how Deuteronomy, the heart of the biblical canon, was "discovered" during the reign of Josiah. It was during renovation work in the Temple that the high priest Hilkiah found a "scroll of the Law (Torah)" that he identified as having been written by Moses himself. Historians interpret this narrative as a legend fabricated by priests to pass their new law (Deuteronomy) as the mere reenactment of an old law. Therefore, according to the most conservative biblical science, Deuteronomy dates to the age of Josiah around 625 BCE. The story of its discovery is a pious fraud. From the same period come most of the six historical books following Deuteronomy (Joshua, Judges, Samuel I and II, Kings I and II), which recount the history of Israel from Moses

---

[4] Heinrich Graetz, *History of the Jews*, Jewish Publication Society of America, 1891 (archive.org), vol. 1, p. 343.

to Josiah. They form what is known as "Deuteronomic history," as they are cast in the same ideological mold as Deuteronomy—what I more simply call Yahwism.

But this dating is now being challenged. According to Philip Davies, a representative of the "minimalist" school, the "reform of Josiah" is itself "bound to be regarded as a pious legend, just about possible perhaps, but extremely improbable." Indeed, it is hardly conceivable that Deuteronomy was written in a monarchy, let alone under the authority of a king, because it is a law code adapted to a theocracy, a country ruled by priests. The entire Deuteronomic history minimizes the royal function, which it depicts as having been only grudgingly granted by Yahweh to the Hebrews: "It is not you they have rejected but me," Yahweh complains to Samuel when the Hebrews ask for a king (1 Samuel 8:7). The idea that a king would sponsor a priestly code of law limiting his power, to which he would then submit voluntarily, makes no sense. On the other hand, the Deuteronomic ideology perfectly corresponds to the regime that Ezra and Nehemiah wanted to impose: the reign of a caste of priests, with a weak king or no king at all. This does not mean that all the contents of the Bible were invented in this period. There was an aggregation of oral and written materials: chronicles and legends of kings, warriors, and holy men, as well as religious and secular songs, visions, and prophecies. But "the *ideological structure* of the biblical literature can only be explained in the last analysis as a product of the Persian period," the time when Ezra drafted his project of reconquest.[5]

The tale of the "discovery" of the "Law of Moses" in the Temple under Josiah is a double deception. This Torah supposedly written by Moses, abandoned and then revived two centuries later by Josiah, then becoming obsolete again as the country was ravaged, then finally returned by Ezra to a people who, it seems, no longer remembered it—this Torah had in fact never been known or applied before Ezra, but was invented by

---

5 Philip Davies, *In Search of "Ancient Israel": A Study in Biblical Origins,* Journal of the Study of the Old Testament, 1992, pp. 41, 94.

him and the Levitical families who intended to make it the instrument of their new power over the Palestinian population.

The biblical text was designed to establish Ezra's legitimacy based on Moses the mythical ancestor, as well as Josiah the last king before the Exile. It is built on a *mise en abîme* that goes like this: First, Moses receives from Yahweh the Law (of Deuteronomy) and urges the Hebrew people to "faithfully obey the voice of Yahweh your God, by keeping and observing all his commandments" (Deuteronomy 28:1–20). Secondly, Josiah receives from the high priest that same "Book of the Law," the "Law of Moses" (that had once fallen from the sky but now emerges from the dust), and summons "the whole populace, high and low" to hear it being read (2 Kings 23:2). Thirdly, Ezra brings back from Babylon this very "Book of the Law of Moses" and summons the families of the settlers to read it to them "from dawn till noon" (Nehemiah 8:1–3).

The first two episodes are mythical, only the third is historical. For a historian critical of his sources, the only near-certainty is that, around 458 BCE, a clan claiming to issue from a lineage of Yahwistic Judean priests and installed in Babylon won from the Persians the right to establish a semi-autonomous state in Palestine; and that in order to dominate the local population, they developed a version of history presenting themselves as legitimate heirs of an ancient tradition.

Historians of recent training admit that the Pentateuch incorporates traditions older than the Exile and Return, but they downgrade their importance. The conquest of Canaan by Joshua, for example, is seen as a mythical projection of the reconquest of Canaan by the Jews of Babylon, designed to give Ezra the image of a new Moses or Joshua. Indeed, what the Lord required of the Hebrews during the conquest of Canaan under Moses and Joshua is exactly what Ezra and Nehemiah required of the Judeo-Babylonians colonizing Palestine concerning their relations with the "people of the land," an expression recurring in the books of Ezra and Nehemiah to denote the population of Judea over which the Babylonian settlers intended to reign. These indigenous people, who believed themselves rightful inhabitants of the country, were declared "foreigners" in the inverted view of history imposed by the Persian-backed settlers, and explicitly identified with the peoples fought by Joshua in bygone days.

Ezra complains that the exiles who settled back in Palestine before him "have been unfaithful" to Yahweh "by marrying foreign women from the people of the country" (Ezra 10:2), these people with "disgusting practices" (9:14). He requires that all the perpetrators repudiate their foreign wives and the children born of them. The fact that the prohibition of intermarriage by Ezra is the faithful echo of the one formulated in Deuteronomy, and that the mixed marriages condemned by Ezra are reminiscent of those blamed on the Hebrew people in the books of Numbers and Kings, must be interpreted in reverse, according to the new historians, since much of the Pentateuch and all the Deuteronomic literature were written to support the theocratic project of Ezra.

The book of Ezra says that when the settlers from Babylon wanted to (re)build the Temple, they first found themselves in "fear of the people of the country" (3:3). These latter are referred to as "the enemies of Judah and Benjamin" when they proposed to the exiles: "Let us help you build, for we resort to your god as you do and we have been sacrificing to him since the time of Esarhaddon king of Assyria, who brought us here" (4:2). This language actually reflects the gaze of the exiles on the locals, whom they considered the descendants of Assyrian colonists practicing an illegitimate version of the Hebrew religion, polluted by idolatry—a view justified in the second book of Kings (17:23–41) by the assertion that all of Israel was deported by the Assyrians (the famous twelve lost tribes). But current historians, informed by the Assyrian archives, estimate that only 20 percent of the population of the kingdom of Samaria was deported. Clinging to this prejudice, the exiles rejected the indigenous proposal: "It is out of the question that you should join us in building a temple for our god. We shall build for Yahweh, god of Israel, on our own, as King Cyrus king of Persia has commanded us." Conflict ensued: "The people of the country then set about demoralizing the people of Judah and deterring them from building" (Ezra 4:3–4).

Through additional arrogance, these "people of Judah" (the settlers) who scorned the "people of the country" (indigenous

Judeans) were not content merely to declare themselves the only ones worthy of the name of Judah. They also usurped the prestigious name of Israel, which previously had only meant the former northern kingdom.

Like the conquest of Canaan by Joshua, the journey of Abraham from Mesopotamia to Palestine, prompted by Yahweh's commitment "to give you this country as your possession" (Genesis 15:7), seems written as a model for the (re)conquest of Palestine by the exiles in Babylon. Abraham was in fact unknown among pre-exilic prophets.[6] Other episodes of Genesis, like the Tower of Babel (chapter 11), cannot have been written prior to the fall of Babylon. The same is true of the Garden of Eden, since the Hebrew word *Pardès* (from which "Paradise" derives) is of Persian origin.

Other episodes betray a xenophobia that fits well with the spirit of the conquest of Ezra. For example, the curious story in which the three sons of Noah, at the initiative of the youngest, Cham, "cover the nakedness" of their father (Genesis 9:18–29), contains the thinly veiled idea that Ham, the ancestor of the Canaanites, had sex with his dead-drunk father. Noah cursed him when "he learned what his youngest son had done to him." This is probably an etiological account of the impurity attributed to the Canaanites—the narrative equivalent of an obscene insult tossed in their direction to justify their enslavement: "Accursed be Canaan, he shall be his brothers' meanest slave."[7]

The explanation also applies to the history of the two daughters of Lot (Abraham's nephew), who, after being virtually delivered to the Sodomites by their father (Genesis 19:8), got him drunk and seduced him, thereby conceiving Moab and Ben-Ammi, ancestors of the Moabites and Ammonites (Genesis 19:31–38). On the other hand, Judah's fornication with his daughter-in-law Tamar, dressed as a prostitute (Genesis 38), is depicted as the God-blessed action that produced the tribe of Judah.

---

[6] Mario Liverani, *La Bible et l'invention de l'histoire*, Gallimard, 2012, pp. 354–355.

[7] André Pichot, *Aux origines des théories raciales, de la Bible à Darwin*, Flammarion, 2008, pp. 67–95.

Hasmonean Literary Production

The books of Ezra and Nehemiah base the authority for the reforms of their eponymous heroes on edicts supposedly issued by Persian sovereigns. "Yahweh roused the spirit of Cyrus king of Persia to issue a proclamation and to have it publicly displayed throughout his kingdom: 'Cyrus king of Persia says this, Yahweh, the God of heaven, has given me all the kingdoms of the earth and has appointed me to build him a temple in Jerusalem, in Judah.'" (Ezra 1:1–2). The book of Ezra then reproduces a contrary edict of the next emperor, Xerxes, prompted by a warning from locals against the danger of allowing the exiles to rebuild the walls of Jerusalem: "this city is a rebellious city, the bane of kings and provinces, and […] sedition has been stirred up there from ancient times" (4:15). The Judeans countered by writing to the next king of Persia, Darius, to invite him to search the archives of Babylon for the edict of Cyrus. This was found at Ectabane, and summarized in a new edict of Darius authorizing the rebuilding of the temple, and ordering gigantic burnt offerings financed by "the royal revenue." Darius warned that "if anyone disobeys this order, a beam is to be torn from his house, he is to be impaled on it and his house is to be reduced to a rubbish-heap for his offense" (6:11).

Then it is Artaxerxes who, by a new edict, is supposed to have granted Ezra authority to lead "all members of the people of Israel in my kingdom, including their priests and Levites, who freely choose to go to Jerusalem," and to rule over "the whole people of Trans-Euphrates [territories west to the Euphrates], that is, for all who know the Law of your God; and you are to teach it to those who do not know it. And on anyone who will not comply with the Law of your God and the Law of the king let sentence be swiftly executed, whether it be death, banishment, fine or imprisonment." Thus ends what is presented as "the text of the document which King Artaxerxes gave to Ezra" (7:11–26).

The edicts of Cyrus, Darius, and Artaxerxes are fake. No historian believes them authentic. The fraud is almost transparent in the first case, which was supposedly lost and then found. As for the edict of Artaxerxes, it is even more incredible. However, it is unlikely that writing under Persian rule, Jews would have produced false edicts, even in Hebrew. This leads to the plausible theory that the books of Ezra and Nehemiah, in their present form, were written after the end of the Persian rule over Judea. This brings us to the Hellenistic period, which followed the conquest of Alexander the Great in 333 BCE.

Large Jewish communities were living in Egypt at that time. Some date back to the Babylonian conquest, when refugees settled there by the thousands, counting among them the prophet Jeremiah. As in Babylon, the Jews supported the Persian conquest of Egypt, and obtained under Persian rule privileged status as intermediaries between the ruling elite and the population. In 332, true to their strategy, they welcomed the new conqueror, Alexander the Macedonian, who accorded them special rights. To encourage immigration to his new capital, Alexander went so far as to grant the Jews the same privileges as the Hellenes who formed the ruling elite. This privileged status, alongside the legendary ability of Jews to enrich themselves, naturally aroused the jealousy of the natives; Jewish historian Flavius Josephus reports in his *War of the Jews* (II.18.7) that there was in Alexandria "perpetual sedition" of the Gentiles (Greeks and Egyptians) against the privileged Jews, which intensified in the second half of the second century BCE.

After Alexander's death, his generals fought among themselves over his conquests. Around 300 BCE, Ptolemy Soter reigned as Pharaoh of Egypt and its dependencies, which included Judea, while Seleucus received almost the whole of Asia, including Persia and Upper Syria. But a century later, Judea fell to the house of the Seleucids. Hellenistic culture, born of the love affair of Greece and Egypt, then permeated the entire Middle East. The use of Greek spread from Asia to Egypt, although Aramaic, from which Hebrew and Arabic derive, remained the lingua franca in Judea and Mesopotamia.

However, in and around Judea, the assimilationist trend was being fought by an identity movement. In the second century, the tension heightened between the Jews who embraced Hellenism and those who rejected it. In 167 BCE, the decision of the Seleucid king Antiochus Epiphanes to end Jewish exclusiveness by dedicating the Temple to Zeus Olympios provoked the revolt of part of the population of Judea, led by Judas Maccabeus and his brothers.

The Maccabean chronicle stigmatizes all those who advocated assimilation: "It was then that there emerged from Israel a set of renegades who led many people astray. 'Come,' they said, 'let us ally ourselves with the gentiles surrounding us, for since we separated ourselves from them many misfortunes have overtaken us.' This proposal proved acceptable, and a number of the people eagerly approached the king, who authorized them to practice the gentiles' observances." And so they "abandoned the holy covenant, submitting to gentile rule as willing slaves of impiety" (1 Maccabees 1:11–15), to the point of marrying outside their community. When Antiochus imposed his "royal prescriptions," "many Israelites chose to accept his religion, sacrificing to idols and profaning the Sabbath" (1:43). As a consequence, the Maccabees "organized themselves into an armed force, striking down the sinners in their anger, and the renegades in their fury" (2:44). These quotations show that the Maccabean revolution was really a civil war led by the *Ioudaismoi* against the *Hellenismoi* (in the terms of 2 Maccabees 2:21, 4:13, and 14:38); the former longed for their integration into the global culture, while the latter saw such integration as tantamount to apostasy.[8]

Taking advantage of the disintegration of the Seleucid state, the Maccabees seized effective control of Judea. They established a fundamentalist regime based on the book of Leviticus, written shortly before. While neither of Levitic nor of Davidic lineage, they usurped the function of high priest (in 152 BCE) and king (in 104 BCE), forming the Hasmonean dynasty that lasted until the conquest of Jerusalem by the Roman general Pompey in 63 BCE. The Hasmoneans launched a vast enterprise of conquest, absorbing not only Samaria, but Galilee in the north, Idumea in the south and Moabitide in the east, imposing circumcision there. Galilee and Idumea were converted to the

---

8 Norman Cantor, *The Sacred Chain: The History of the Jews*, Harper Perennial, 1995, pp. 55–61.

centralized cult of Yahweh in Jerusalem, probably by hardy
Judean settlers. But the Samaritans, who considered themselves
the true Israelites, refused to forsake their temple of Mount
Gerizim for the Jerusalem one. During the Maccabean war, they
had already remained loyal to Antiochus and provided him with
an army (1 Maccabees 3:10). Hyrcanus destroyed their temples
and sanctuaries.

The *Book of Jubilees*, a text of Hasmonean propaganda,
reaffirms the supranational destiny of Israel, based on Yahweh's
promise to Abraham: "I am Yahweh who created the heaven
and the earth, and I will increase you and multiply you
exceedingly, and kings shall come forth from you, and they shall
judge everywhere wherever the foot of the sons of men has
trodden. And I will give to your seed all the earth which is under
heaven, and they shall judge all the nations according to their
desires, and after that they shall get possession of the whole
earth and inherit it forever" (32:18–19).

Although the Maccabees' revolt was accompanied by the
rejection of everything Greek, their descendants unrestrainedly
adopted Greek culture and customs, which led them, in turn, to
be hated by nationalists, represented then by ultra-legalistic
Pharisees (*Parushim* in Hebrew, meaning the "Separated," which
could also be translated as "Puritans"). In 89 BCE, if we are to
believe Josephus, the Hasmonean king Alexander Janneus, after
taking a rebellious city, "did one of the most barbarous actions
in the world to [the Pharisees]; for as he was feasting with his
concubines, in the sight of all the city, he ordered about eight
hundred of them to be crucified; and while they were living, he
ordered the throats of their children and wives to be cut before
their eyes" (*Jewish Antiquities* XIII.14).

It was under the authority of the Hasmoneans that the
biblical canon was established. The two books of Chronicles,
which incorporate the content of the books of Kings, are dated
from this period. Opinions vary on the importance of the
Hasmonean influence on the final version of the Pentateuch, the
historical books and the Prophets. But all historians date from
this period a large number of peripheral books, written in Greek
for the most part. This is of course the case with the two books
of Maccabees, hagiographies in honor of the founding martyrs.

The book of Jonah, whose hero is sent to the Assyrian city of Nineveh to convert its inhabitants, also dates to the time of the Hasmoneans and their efforts at mass conversion. Some texts from this period appear to be efforts at syncretism between Greek wisdom and Yahwism, such as the book of Wisdom or Ecclesiasticus (Sirach). Others are actual frauds, such as the book of Baruch, which presents itself as a letter from the prophet Jeremiah to the exiles in Babylon.

The book of Daniel introduced the new genre of backdated prophetic visions and dreams, which contributed to the prestige of the Jewish scriptures among unsuspecting Gentiles. Flavius Josephus relates in his *Jewish Antiquities* that Alexander the Great was impressed when, in Jerusalem, he was given a book that announced that a Greek would destroy the Persian empire. In reality, the book did not yet exist, and Alexander had never set foot in Jerusalem.

The narrative part of the book of Daniel was inspired by a novelistic genre in vogue in the Hellenistic world. Young Daniel, selected from the Judean exiles to be educated by the chief eunuch of King Nebuchadnezzar, proves capable of interpreting the dreams of the king. He decrypts the premonitory announcement of the fall of Babylon, as well as the collapses of the Persian and Macedonian kingdoms, and predicts with amazing clarity the reign of Antiochus Epiphanes—a contemporary at the time of writing. Impressed, Nebuchadnezzar falls at the feet of Daniel and says: "Your god is indeed the God of gods, the Master of kings" (2:47).

We may compare this to the third book of the Sibylline Oracles, a Jewish-Alexandrian fraud composed in the middle of the second century BCE, which makes the oracle of Delphi glorify the Jewish people; it did not impress the pagan Greeks, but would later be taken seriously by the fathers of the Christian church. The *Letter of Aristeas to Philocrates* is another crypto-Jewish text from the Hellenistic period, written by an Alexandrian Jew pretending to be a Greek in order to sing the praises of Judaism. He recounts, in the style of legend, the Greek translation of the Pentateuch (the Septuagint), which Pharaoh Ptolemy II Philadelphus had ordered and sponsored in person. From reading the translation, Ptolemy supposedly swooned in ecstasy before such Jewish wisdom, exclaiming that it "comes from God." (Josephus takes up this legend in the twelfth book of his *Jewish Antiquities*).

The books of Tobit, Judith, and Esther belong to the same romance genre as that of Daniel. The heroes are smart Jews who, having reached the rank of courtier, use their influence to benefit their community. The author of the book of Esther was probably inspired by the book of Ezra to invent an even more fantastical decree than the false edict of Cyrus. It is issued by King Ahasuerus (Xerxes), under the influence of the high court official Haman, vexed by the insolence of the Jew Mordecai, and sent to the governors of 127 provinces. It is thus formulated in the Greek version of Esther: "Among all the nations in the world there is scattered a certain hostile people, who have laws contrary to those of every nation and continually disregard the ordinances of kings, so that the unifying of the kingdom that we honorably intend cannot be brought about. We understand that this people, and it alone, stands constantly in opposition to every nation, perversely following a strange manner of life and laws, and is ill-disposed to our government, doing all the harm they can so that our kingdom may not attain stability. Therefore we have decreed that those indicated to you in the letters written by Haman, who is in charge of affairs and is our second father, shall all—wives and children included—be utterly destroyed by the swords of their enemies, without pity or restraint, on the fourteenth day of the twelfth month, Adar, of this present year, so that those who have long been hostile and remain so may in a single day go down in violence to Hades, and leave our government completely secure and untroubled hereafter" (3:13c–13g).

Needless to say, though the issues raised by Xerxes fairly reflect the complaints that we find expressed against Jews in other Hellenistic sources, the proposed "final solution" is a fiction: no known decree, no ancient chronicle, nor any other evidence exists that any sovereign has ever contemplated the solution of the extermination of the Jews. But the motif serves to celebrate the salvific action of the heroine Esther, Mordecai's niece, who shares the king's bed without revealing that she is Jewish. (The rabbinical tradition says that Esther was not only

Mordecai's niece, but also his wife, whom he would have somehow slipped into the bed of the sovereign as did Abraham in Egypt with his half-sister and wife Sarah).

Convinced by Esther's charm, the king cancels the order to kill the Jews and instead hangs Haman and his ten sons on the gallows Haman had raised for Mordecai and his sons. Since a royal decree cannot be canceled, Esther convinces Ahasuerus to issue a new decree by which he gives the Jews "permission to destroy, slaughter and annihilate any armed force of any people or province that might attack them, together with their women and children, and to plunder their possessions" (8:11). And thus do the Jews massacre 75,000 people. Throughout the land, "there was joy and gladness among the Jews, with feasting and holiday-making. Of the country's population many became Jews, since now the Jews were feared" (8:17).

Every year the Jews celebrate the happy ending of this imaginary story by the feast of Purim, one month before Easter. Until the Middle Ages, they used to hang or burn effigies of Haman. Since all enemies of the Jews were then assimilated to Christians, Haman was identified with Christ and often put on a cross rather than a gibbet.[9]

Scholarly research in "form criticism" has shown that the "romance of Joseph," which occupies the last chapters of Genesis (37–50), belongs to the same genre as the novels of Tobit, Esther, and Daniel, and dates from the same period. To flee famine, the 70 members of the tribe of Jacob come from Canaan with their flocks to settle in the land of Goshen, northeast of Egypt. They are nomadic herders, and "the Egyptians have a horror of all shepherds" (Genesis 46:34). Joseph, a member of the tribe, is sold by his brothers to the Ishmaelites, then becomes a slave to Potiphar, a eunuch of Pharaoh. Thanks to his gift of dream interpretation (like Daniel) and his organizational abilities, Joseph wins the trust of the Pharaoh and becomes his chancellor (41:40). Having pardoned his brothers, he encourages the members of his tribe and

---

[9] Elliott Horowitz, *Reckless Rites: Purim and the Legacy of Jewish Violence*, Princeton University Press, 2006, pp. 56, 17–18.

obtains for them "land holdings in Egypt, in the best part of the country, the region of Rameses." Responsible for managing the national grain reserves, he stores large amounts during the years of plenty; and then, when famine strikes, he negotiates a high price for the monopolized grain and thus "accumulated all the money to be found in Egypt and Canaan." The following year, having created a monetary shortage, he forces the peasants to relinquish their herds in exchange for grain: "Hand over your livestock and I shall issue you food in exchange for your livestock, if your money has come to an end." One year later, the peasants have nothing left "except our bodies and our land," and so have to beg, then sell themselves in order to survive: "Take us and our land in exchange for food, and we with our land will become Pharaoh's serfs; only give us seed, so that we can survive and not die and the land not revert to desert!" (47:11–19). Thus it was that the Hebrews, after settling in Egypt, "acquired property there; they were fruitful and grew very numerous" (47:27).

The basic plots of the stories of Joseph, Esther, and Daniel share much in common: Joseph advises the King of Egypt, Daniel the King of Babylon, and Esther the King of Persia. Both the stories of Joseph and Esther focus on the influence that can be exercised for the benefit of the Jewish people, by a member of the Jewish community infiltrated into the heart of power. Joseph has ascended to the position of the king's advisor by his ability to interpret dreams; while Esther, the niece of an official "attached to the Royal Court," was introduced into the harem of the Persian king, where she seduces and steers him. Joseph is the prototype of the court Jew who, having risen to a position of public responsibility thanks to his practical intelligence, promotes his tribe at the expense of the people he pretends to serve while actually ruining and enslaving them by grabbing their money and putting them in debt. For all this, he is blessed by Yahweh and held up as an example.

The situation described in the Joseph novel is consistent with the Hellenistic period. The rulers of Egypt at the time, having adopted the title of pharaoh and some of the accompanying customs, were Greek, not Egyptian; they did not speak the language of Egyptian peasants, an alien and exploited

people. Jews, however, had been familiar to them for centuries.
A secondary argument in favor of a Hellenistic dating of the
Joseph story is its resemblance to the story of another Joseph
that the historian Flavius Josephus situates at the time of the
Ptolemies (*Jewish Antiquities* XII.4). This Joseph, a man "of great
reputation among the people of Jerusalem, for gravity, prudence,
and justice," was appointed as Judea's tax collector by Ptolemy
after promising to bring back double the tax revenues of his
competitors. "The king was pleased to hear that offer; and,
because it augmented his revenues, said he would confirm the
sale of the taxes to him." Joseph fulfilled his contract by
murdering several prominent citizens and confiscating their
property. He became extremely rich and was thus able to help
his coreligionists. Therefore, concludes the historian, Joseph
"was a good man, and of great magnanimity; and brought the
Jews out of a state of poverty and meanness, to one that was
more splendid." The proximity of the two Joseph narratives
suggests that they derive from the same matrix.

When reflecting on biblical literature, it is important to
understand that it is not a product of the "Jewish people." The
romantic illusion that people create their national mythology has
been debunked; a literature that gains national status is always
the product of an intellectual elite patronized by a political elite.
It is today admitted that the heart of the biblical corpus, with its
code of laws and its "history of Israel," is the work of a small
group of skillful priestly scribes. They produced much of the
Bible in Babylon, while jealously preserving their pedigree
records, intermarrying (often between cousins or uncle and
niece), and making circumcision a distinctive sign (it was not
practiced in Mesopotamia).[10] They developed a highly effective
strategy to survive and thrive by infiltrating spheres of power.
Even if the stories of Joseph, Daniel, and Esther are postexilic,
they convey the same culture of exile inscribed from the
beginning in the genetic code of Judaism. After having probably
helped the conquest of Babylon by the Persians, the Judean

---

[10] Niels Peter Lemche, *The Israelites in History and Tradition,* John Knox Press, 1998,
p. 122.

exiles obtained new high offices at the Persian court, as well as military and financial support for their theocratic project in Palestine. The Torah is the instrument crafted by these master propagandists to subjugate and control the Palestinian population.

By writing a book purporting to cover the whole history of mankind, from the creation of the world to its apocalyptic end, and a history rolled out by the hand of the Creator, the priest-scribes assured their book a millennial success; they made it "the Book" *par excellence*. They gave it, moreover, a semblance of unbeatable seniority by pretending it was written by a Moses who had to be situated in the thirteenth century BCE. Several Alexandrian Jewish authors even attempted (with little success) to bluff the Greeks about the age of the Torah, insisting that Homer, Hesiod, Pythagoras, Socrates, and Plato had been inspired by Moses. This is the case with Aristobulus of Paneas in his *Explanations of the Scripture of Moses* (around 170 BCE) or with Artapanos in *On the Jews*, where he presents Joseph (son of Jacob) and Moses as the "first inventors" who taught the Egyptians everything they knew, from astronomy and agriculture to philosophy and religion.[11] The same extravagant claims appear in *The Wisdom of Salomon*, composed in Egypt in the late first century BCE, then in Philo of Alexandria two centuries later. They would again be taken up by Flavius Josephus in Roman times. Yet no Greek or Latin text from a non-Jew offers any evidence that these claims ever impressed the pagans. In reality, the Hebrew Bible is much more recent than is commonly believed. With the exception of some later additions, its final redaction probably dates from the Hellenistic period, a time of great literary production. It is therefore roughly contemporary with its Greek version, known as the Septuagint.

The high antiquity of the Jewish people itself was contested as early as the first century CE by Greek scholars, notably the Hellenized Egyptian Apion, whose work is lost but known through the rebuttal of Flavius Josephus. Flavius says he has

---

[11] Mélèze Modrzejewski, *The Jews of Egypt, From Rameses II to Emperor Hadrian*, Princeton University Press, 1995, p. 66.

written his *Against Apion* against those who "will not believe
what I have written concerning the antiquity of our nation, while
they take it for a plain sign that our nation is of a late date,
because they are not so much as vouchsafed a bare mention by
the most famous historiographers among the Grecians" (I,1).

Kenites, Midianites, and Arabs

An interesting hypothesis on the identity building of the early
Hebrews has been drawn from the Genesis story of the
primordial brothers Cain and Abel. Cain, the elder and a
cultivator, saw his sacrificial offering ignored by Yahweh, who
preferred the offering of the younger Abel, a shepherd. This
provoked the murderous jealousy of Cain, who felt cheated of
his birthright. Yahweh cursed Cain for his fratricide (aggravated
by his denial): "Listen! Your brother's blood is crying out to me
from the ground. Now be cursed and banned from the ground
that has opened its mouth to receive your brother's blood at
your hands. When you till the ground it will no longer yield up
its strength to you. A restless wanderer you will be on earth"
(4:9–12). But Yahweh's curse is mitigated by a special
protection: "'Whoever kills Cain will suffer a sevenfold
vengeance.' So Yahweh put a mark on Cain, so that no one
coming across him would kill him" (4:15).

In this form, the story resembles an etiological legend,
intended to explain the origin of a nomadic lifestyle through the
original sin of an ancestor. What nomadic people, unfit for
agriculture, was described by the original legend? And what does
the famous "mark of Cain" mean? The scholar Hyam Maccoby
has an answer: The name of Cain (*Qayin* in Hebrew) is identical
to the name of the tribe of Kenites, and also means "smith" or
"iron-worker." Such tribes of blacksmiths are well attested in
ancient times; they were nomads because their skills were
required over a very wide area. They were also often known for
their mastery of the art of music. Finally, they were often the
object of superstitious fears, because the art of metalworking is
associated with magic.

The descendants of Cain are described in Genesis 4:19–24
as nomads living in tents, inventors of ironwork, makers of

metallic musical instruments, and marked by a magical protection making it perilous to attack them (according to a possible interpretation of the "mark of Cain"). Moreover, the biblical narrative retains the trace of a special covenant between the Israelites and the Kenites, who are the only foreign people presented in benevolent terms. Saul spares them when he exterminates the Amalekites among whom they dwell: "Go away, leave your homes among the Amalekites, in case I destroy you with them—you acted with faithful love towards all the Israelites when they were coming up from Egypt" (1 Samuel 15:6). Moses's father-in-law is described as a Kenite (or "Cain") in Judges 1:16, where we learn that "The sons of Hobab the Kenite, father-in-law of Moses, marched up with the sons of Judah from the City of Palm Trees into the desert of Judah lying in the Negeb of Arad, where they went and settled among the people." This may echo a common origin of Israelites and Kenites, or at least a closeness based on a shared status of migrants and wanderers. According to Maccoby, many biblical stories are borrowed from Kenite traditions.[12]

The curse of Cain has parallels in the traditions of other nomadic peoples. Yuri Slezkine remarks that before the modern era, some ethnic groups of wanderers conceived their mode of existence "as divine punishment for an original transgression." For example: "Of the many legends accounting for the Gypsy predicament, one claims that Adam and Eve were so fruitful that they decided to hide some of their children from God, who became angry and condemned the ones he could not see to eternal homelessness. Other explanations include punishment for incest or refusal of hospitality, but the most common one blames the Gypsies for forging the nails used to crucify Jesus."[13] Since nomadism is deeply embedded in the Hebrews' collective memory, should we then seek the secret source of the wandering of the Jewish people in a "Cain complex" dating back to a primordial fratricide, like Freud seeking the key to the

---

[12] Hyam Maccoby, *The Sacred Executioner: Human Sacrifice and the Legacy of Guilt*, Thames & Hudson, 1982, pp. 13–51.
[13] Yuri Slezkine, *The Jewish Century*, Princeton University Press, 2004, pp. 22-23.

human psyche in a universal Oedipus complex dating back to a primordial parricide (*Totem and Taboo*, 1913)? Such an enterprise would be equally speculative.

The Bible does not clearly distinguish between the Kenites and the Midianites, but suggests that the former are a tribe among the latter. Hohab, Moses's father-in-law, is called a Kenite in the book of Judges, but named "Hobab son of Reuel the Midianite" in Numbers (10:29). The same father-in-law is identified as a Midianite "priest" (*kohen*) in Exodus, and named Reuel (Exodus 2:18), then Jethro (3:1). In that Exodus story, when Moses flees Egypt "into Midianite territory" (2:15), he is hosted by Jethro who eventually gives him his daughter Zipporah, with whom Moses will have two sons. It is while grazing his father-in-law's flocks that Moses finds himself near Mount Horeb, "to the far side of the desert" (3:1). There he meets Yahweh, the god of Abraham, for the first time, and is told (by Yahweh) that Mount Horeb is "holy ground." Later, his Midianite wife appeases Yahweh, who wants to kill Moses, by circumcising their son with a flint, so that Yahweh "let him go" (4:24-26). In chapter 18 of the same Book of Exodus, after having led his people from Egypt across the Red Sea, and established his camp in the desert, Moses is met by Jethro, who rejoices over the miracles accomplished by his son-in-law. Then Jethro "offered a burnt offering and other sacrifices to God; and Aaron and all the elders of Israel came and ate with Moses' father-in-law in the presence of God" (18:12).

Assuming this story to be archaic, some scholars, beginning with Eduard Meyer in 1906, have argued that the cult of Yahweh originated with the Midianites, and was passed on to Moses, the son-in-law of a Midianite priest who, it is implied, had seven daughters but no son.[14] The Bible even hints at Jethro's role in crafting the first Constitution of the Hebrews. Jethro says to Moses: "Now listen to the advice I am going to give you, and God be with you! Your task is to represent the people to God, to lay their cases before God, and to teach them the statutes and laws, and show them the way they ought to

---

[14] Karl Budde, *Religion of Israel to the Exile*, Lowrie Press, 2008.

follow and how they ought to behave. At the same time, from the people at large choose capable and God-fearing men, men who are trustworthy and incorruptible, and put them in charge as heads of thousands, hundreds, fifties and tens, and make them the people's permanent judges. They will refer all important matters to you, but all minor matters they will decide themselves, so making things easier for you by sharing the burden with you. If you do this—and may God so command you—you will be able to stand the strain, and all these people will go home satisfied." Moses took his father-in-law's advice and did just as he said. Moses chose capable men from all Israel and put them in charge of the people as heads of thousands, hundreds, fifties and tens. (Exodus 18:19-25).

"Yahweh came from Sinai," the Bible says (Deuteronomy 33:2 and Psalms 68:18). It is there that Moses first encounters Yahweh, who orders him to go back to Egypt and free his people; it is there that Moses brings them back; and it is from there that, two years later, on Yahweh's order again, he sets off with them towards Canaan. And Sinai, with its Mount Sinai or Mount Horeb, is located in the land of the Midianites, which Greek authors place unanimously in northwest Arabia, on the eastern shore of the Gulf of Aqaba, and not in the Egyptian peninsula which bears this name since the Church placed it there, apparently under Constantine. Even Paul the Apostle knew that "Sinai is a mountain in Arabia" (Galatians 4,25).

Explorer Charles Beke was among the first to place Mount Horeb in Arabia (*Sinai in Arabia and of Midian*, 1878). This thesis has gained the support of a growing number of scholars, including Hershel Shanks, editor of the *Biblical Archaeology Review*, and Frank Moore Cross, Hebrew professor at Harvard. The precise location of Mount Horeb/Sinai can be deduced from phenomena witnessed by the Hebrews there: "Now at daybreak two days later, there were peals of thunder and flashes of lightning, dense cloud on the mountain and a very loud trumpet blast; and, in the camp, all the people trembled. Then Moses led the people out of the camp to meet God; and they took their stand at the bottom of the mountain. Mount Sinai was entirely wrapped in smoke, because Yahweh had descended on it in the form of fire. The smoke rose like smoke from a furnace and the whole mountain shook violently. Louder and louder grew the trumpeting. Moses spoke, and God answered him in the thunder" (Exodus 19:16-19). If Mount Horeb shakes, rumbles, smokes and spits fire like a volcano, then it should be a volcano, as Beke was the first to remark (*Mount Sinai a Volcano*, 1873). Northwest Arabia, where Midian is located, happens to be a volcanic area, unlike the Egyptian Sinai; volcanic activity was still documented there in the Middle Ages.[15] Among the most likely candidates is Jabal al-Lawz, whose summit consists of metamorphic rocks.[16]

These geographic considerations point to an Arab origin of Mosaic Yahwism. This in turn may explain why tribalism and nomadism are so entrenched in the Judaic tradition. Genesis 25 says that Midianites are descendants of Abraham, just like the Ishmaelites. Midianites and Ishmaelites are actually confused in Genesis 37, where we read that "Midianite merchants sold Joseph to the Ishmaelites" who "took Joseph to Egypt" (37:28), then that "the Midianites had sold him in Egypt" (37:36). The Bible actually gives Abraham as common ancestor to the Midianites, the Kenites, the Moabites, the Edomites, and the Amalekites, all predominantly nomadic peoples whose arid lands are situated between Arabia and Judea. Islamic tradition teaches that Abraham came from Arabia and died there, and some scholars consider this tradition as possibly older than the biblical tale of Abraham coming from Mesopotamia. At the time of Muhammad (early 7th century) powerful "Jewish tribes" were living in the Hejaz, although we know nothing of their particular brand of Judaism. According to Islamic tradition, they had been living there since the time of Moses.[17] Orientalist David Samuel Margoliouth remarks that these tribes and some of their members bore recognizably Arab names rather than Jewish ones. Many Hebrew names, including Yahweh itself, come from

---

[15] Colin Humphreys, *The Miracles of Exodus: A Scientist's Discovery of the Extraordinary Natural Causes of the Biblical Stories*, HarperOne, 2003.

[16] Larry Williams, *The Mount Sinai Myth*, Wynwood Press, 1990; Howard Blum *The Gold of Exodus: The Discovery of the True Mount Sinai*, Simon & Schuster, 1998.

[17] Gordon D. Newby, *A History of the Jews of Arabia*, University of South Carolina Press, 2009.

Arabic, according to Margoliouth, who also claims that the book of Job, among other stories in the biblical canon, "ostensibly comes from Arabia."[18]

The origin of the Hebrews among the nomadic population of northern Arabia is consistent with the most likely etymology of their name, as deriving from the Accadian term *Habiru*. This word is attested as far back as the fourteenth century BCE on the Egyptian Amarna tablets, to designate nomadic wanderers or refugees from the East, often with the negative connotation of disruption of public order.[19] In the Bible, the Israelites are called "Hebrews" only by Egyptians (14 times in Exodus) and Philistines (8 times in 1 Samuel). In Exodus 1-15, the term is applied to Jacob's tribe settling in Egypt. Yahweh is designated there as "the god of Israel" but is presented as "the god of the Hebrews" to Pharaoh (7:17). But *habiru* is also employed with the vulgar meaning of "bandits," "thieves," or "robbers" in Isaiah 1:23 and Hosea 6:9.[20]

If we follow Midianite-Kenite theory,[21] Yahwism turns out to be the religion of an unstable confederation of proto-Arab tribes who, perhaps after returning to Midian from a period of exploitation under Egyptian rule, set out to conquer lower Syria, a land "flowing with milk and honey" (Numbers 13:27). Canaan was then a prosperous and urbanized region, unlike the poorer lands of its southern fringe. Its inhabitants, whom the Bible portrays as detestable idolaters, were members of a technologically and culturally advanced civilization, organized in city-states, struggling to maintain independence from the more powerful states in Egypt and Mesopotamia.

We need not conclude that the religion of the ancient Hebrews was identical to that of the Midianites. It was, rather, a new form of it, and Moses deserves credit for its novelty. What Moses brought to Yahweh is mobility. The Midianite Yahweh

---

[18] David Samuel Margoliouth, *Relations Between Arabs and Israelites Prior to the Rise of Islam: The Schweich Lectures 1921*, Oxford UP, 1924 (archive.org).
[19] Karl Budde, *Religion of Israel to the Exile*, Putnam's Sons, 1899 (archive.org), pp. 5-11.
[20] Niels Peter Lemche, *The Israelites in History and Tradition, op. cit.*, pp. 58-60.
[21] As recently propounded by Swiss scholar Thomas Römer in his lectures in the Collège de France, 2011–2012, on www.college-de-france.fr/.

was a topical god, inseparable and almost indistinguishable from his sacred mountain, from whence he thundered publicly and spoke privately. Yahweh cannot leave Mount Horeb, and therefore proposes to Moses to "send an angel to precede you, to guard you as you go and bring you to the place that I have prepared" (Exodus 23:20). However, two chapters later, he has changed his mind and asks Moses to make for him, out of the precious materials stolen from the Egyptians, a luxurious gold plated tent, the detailed specifications of which are given in Exodus, chapters 25 to 31. Henceforth, it is in this "Tabernacle" that Yahweh will reside, and that Moses will talk to him "face to face, as a man talks to his friend" (33:11). Moses has delocalized Yahweh, and his successors finally settled him on a throne in Jerusalem.

From the Exodus narrative, two different stages can be identified in the story of Yahweh and his people. First, Yahweh asks Moses to bring them from Egypt to Sinai: "After you have led the people out of Egypt, you will worship God on this mountain" (3:12). At this stage, Yahweh says nothing of conquering Canaan. Moses must simply declare to the Israelites that he is sent by "the god of your ancestors" (3:16) to guide them to Midian. The implication here is that their ancestors are from Midian, just like Yahweh.

It is only two years after settling in Midian that Moses receives a new order to bring them to Canaan. It is hard to resist the hypothesis that the real motivation for this massive migration (603,550 males over twenty years old, not counting the Levites, according to Numbers 1:44) was overpopulation and scarcity of natural resources. It is then that Canaan becomes the Promised Land. Moses tried to recruit his father-in-law: "You know where we can camp in the desert, and so you will be our eyes. If you come with us, we shall share with you whatever blessings Yahweh gives us" (Numbers 10:31-32). Jethro seems to have refused, and the Midianites who did not join the expedition later became the Hebrews' most hated enemies, as recounted in Numbers 31.

Cain and Abel as mirror images of Seth and Osiris

The biblical story of Cain and Abel seems adapted from the Kenites' legend of their primal ancestor, the fratricide Cain, but with the addition of a crucial element: a third son of Adam and Eve, named Seth, granted by God to replace Abel after his death. The fact that this third son was added as an afterthought is evidenced by a comparison between Seth's and Cain's progenies. The names of Cain and four of his five descendants are reproduced with little change in five of the seven descendants of Seth (compare Genesis 4:17–18 and 5:6–32). Clearly a scribe has copied the progeny of Cain and pasted it to Seth.

Seth happens to be also the name of an Egyptian god, the younger brother of Osiris. Strangely enough, the story of Cain and Abel bears a striking resemblance to the story of Osiris and Seth, whose most detailed rendering has been provided by Plutarch in the first century CE. Like Cain and Abel, Osiris and Seth are born of a primordial couple, together with their two sisters Isis and Nephthys, whom they respectively marry.[22] Osiris, the elder, receives from his divine father the fertile soil of the Nile Valley, and teaches agriculture to its inhabitants, while his sister-wife Isis teaches them to make bread. Seth, the youngest, has to settle for the barren deserts surrounding the river valley. Jealous of God's favor and men's worship that his brother receives, Seth decides to eliminate him. Employing a ruse, he locks Osiris in a coffin, seals it, and throws it into the Nile. Isis finds the body of her husband and hides it. Seth discovers the hiding place and cuts up the body into fourteen pieces that he scatters across the land of Egypt. Isis searches patiently and finds all the pieces except the penis, which she replaces with a simulacrum. The body is then reconstituted by Nout, the mother of Osiris, who "tied the bones of her son back together, put his heart back in his body, and set his head where it belonged." Then the body is embalmed by Anubis, the jackal-headed god, and brought back to life by Thoth, the prince of

---

[22] For a good overview, read Bojana Mojsov, *Osiris: Death and Afterlife of a God*, Wiley-Blackwell, 2005.

magic, thanks to the lamentations of Isis. She then conceives, with the revived Osiris, a son, Horus, whom she hides in the great Delta reed beds to escape the homicidal schemes of his uncle. Warned by his mother, Horus escapes an attempted rape by Seth. He returns as an adult to complete the deliverance of Osiris by taking vengeance on Seth, which has the effect, in the words of a litany of Horus to his father, of "driving out the evil attached to [Osiris]" and "killing his suffering." Horus, however, cannot destroy Seth, who continues to covet the throne of Egypt. Their dispute is finally brought before the court of the gods, who then split Egypt between Seth and Horus (Upper and Lower Egypts), before changing their minds and banishing Seth to give the entirety of both lands to Horus. The struggle turns out to be endless: repeatedly beaten and chained, Seth is released periodically from his chains to once again seize the advantage.

The myth of Osiris lends itself to multiple interpretations. Fundamentally, says Plutarch, the enemy brothers represent "two contrary principles, two rival powers" in perpetual struggle throughout creation. In the Cosmic Soul, explains Plutarch, "All that is good, is Osiris; and in earth and wind and water and the heavens and stars, that which is ordered, established, and healthy, as evidenced by season, temperature, and cycles of revolution, is the efflux of Osiris and his reflected image." That is why, at the time of Plutarch, Osiris merged with the sun god Ra, whose regular course maintained the stability of the world. By contrast, "that part of the soul which is impressionable, impulsive, irrational and truculent, and in the bodily part what is destructible, diseased and disorderly, as evidenced by abnormal seasons and temperatures, and by obscurations of the sun and disappearances of the moon," bears the mark of Seth (Plutarch, *Isis and Osiris* 49).

During this period, the myth of Osiris became an object of fascination far beyond the borders of Egypt, resonating with dualistic religious views from Persia and Mesopotamia. Seth represented the destructive principle par excellence. On the earthly plane, Osiris is the Nile river and Isis the soil fertilized by it, and the cyclical floods of the Nile are symbolically equivalent to the death and resurrection of Osiris, while a poor flood, leading to drought and famine, was one of the disasters wrought by Seth, the god of the desert. The peasants of the Nile Valley placed themselves under the protection of Osiris and Isis, while Seth was perceived as the god of foreigners and nomads, be they shepherds, hunters, caravan merchants, or invaders.

There is an obvious symmetry between the Egyptian myth of Osiris and Seth, and the biblical story of Cain and Abel. Cain, the elder, is sedentary and cultivates fertile lands like Osiris, while Abel, the younger, is a nomadic shepherd inhabiting arid lands like Seth. Yet the biblical god acts opposite to the Egyptian pantheon: he upsets the social order by favoring the younger brother, thus provoking the elder's legitimate sense of unfairness. As in a mirror image of the Egyptian myth, the Bible has the elder brother kill his younger brother.

The epilogue added to the Cain-Abel story reinforces the symmetry. Like Osiris, the murdered Abel gets a new life of some kind, when Yahweh grants to Adam and Eve "another offspring, in place of Abel." And this third son, a substitute or alter ego of the second, is named Seth (Genesis 4:25). This homonymy cannot be a coincidence, but rather strong evidence that the Cain-Abel story, in the form that has come down to us, is dependent on the Osiris-Seth myth. This fits the hypothesis of a biblical redaction in the Hellenistic period. The Yahwist scribes have deliberately reversed the Egyptian myth, by shifting the good role to the younger brother Abel, and naming his resurrected alter-ego after the Egyptian god Seth. Must we conclude that the Levites, motivated by their incurable Egyptophobia, have chosen to redeem the mortal enemy of Egypt's national god and identify with him? We are encouraged in this conclusion by the many other biblical stories built on the inversion of Egyptian ones that we shall encounter further on.

Adding additional support to that exegetic interpretation, we find that the Hellenistic Egyptians did ascribe to the Jews a sympathy for Seth, which fueled their Judeophobia. According to Plutarch, some Egyptians believed that, after having been banned from Egypt by the gods, Seth wandered in Palestine where he fathered two sons, *Hierosolymos* and *Youdaios*, that is, "Jerusalem" and "Judah." In other words, these Egyptians saw the Jews as "sons of Seth." There was also a persistent rumor in the Greco-Roman world that in their temple in Jerusalem, the

Jews worshiped a golden donkey's head, the donkey being the animal symbol of Seth. A contemporary of Plutarch, the Roman author Apion, accredited that rumor, which Jewish historian Flavius Josephus, for his part, denied in his treatise *Against Apion*. Tacitus also mentioned it in his *Histories*, while noting that Roman general Pompey found no donkey's head when entering the Holy of Holies in 63 BCE.

Labeling the Jews as worshippers or descendants of Seth may have been an expression of anti-Semitism (to use an anachronistic term). But it is not without historical basis. In the first century CE, Flavius Josephus, relying on the History of Egypt written by the Egyptian Manetho three centuries earlier, identifies the Hebrews with the Hyksos, a confederation of nomadic warriors from Palestine, who reigned over Lower and Middle Egypt for more than a century before being repelled. Josephus estimates that the 480,000 Hyksos fleeing Egypt back to their ancestors' homeland in Palestine were none other than the twelve Israelite tribes. These Hyksos distinguished themselves by the exclusive worship of Seth. Their King Apophis, reads a slightly later papyrus, "chose for his lord the god Seth. He did not worship any other deity in the whole land except Seth."[23] The Hyksos seem to have considered Seth as a jealous god, since they "destroyed the temples of the gods," according to Manetho quoted by Josephus. The Hyksos' tyrannical and brutal government left Egyptians with traumatic memories. Unlike Flavius, Manetho had not identified the Hyksos with the Jews but had simply mentioned that, before being expelled from Egypt as lepers, the Jews had settled in Avaris, the former capital of the Hyksos, consecrated to Seth.

Osirism versus Judaism

The Pentateuch gives us the Jewish viewpoint on Egyptian religion, a viewpoint that Christians have inherited with the Book. To understand the Egyptian viewpoint on Jewish religion, let us delve more deeply into the significance of the Osiris myth, which can be regarded as the cornerstone of Egyptian

---

[23] Papyrus Sallier 1, quoted in Jan Assmann, *Of God and Gods, op. cit.*, p. 48.

civilization from the beginning of the first millennium BCE. When he visited Egypt in 450 BCE, Herodotus noted that "Egyptians do not all worship the same gods, except for Isis and Osiris; these two all without distinction worship" (*Histories* II.17). Until the triumph of Christianity, no other myth contributed more to shaping the spirit of the inhabitants of the Nile Valley, from peasants to pharaohs. On it was crystallized the national identity of the world's oldest state, as well as individuals' metaphysical hopes in the most afterlife-oriented civilization ever.

From a strictly narrative viewpoint, the basic plot of the myth follows a universal pattern, best known in the story of Hamlet adapted by Shakespeare from a Scandinavian legend: Osiris is King Hamlet, murdered treacherously by his brother, and Horus is his son, the young prince Hamlet junior, commissioned by the ghost of his father to avenge the killing. Seth is the exact equivalent of the treacherous Claudius, the archetypal villain, whose thirst for power is uninhibited by any moral conscience—what we today would call a sociopath or psychopath. Seth, however, remains in the Egyptian imagination an eternal principle, whose final disappearance no eschatology can foresee. He is the necessary opponent, the destabilizing principle without which humanity would be immobile. Without Seth, there can be no resurrection of Osiris; without a fight against evil, there can be no heroic sacrifice.

The legend of Osiris is a myth of love as much as a myth of resurrection. Both themes are intimately linked in this timeless story of love triumphing over death—the only love story worth telling. It combines the Hamlet plot with another universal scheme that folklorists label by the title of its best-known version, "Beauty and the Beast." In the tale of "Hamlet," it is revenge carried out by the son on earth that soothes the spirit of the dead (and heals his injury), while in the tale type "Beauty and the Beast" it is the sacrificial love of a woman that heals the heart of the dead (and breaks the spell that had been put on him).[24] Isis was both wife and sister (the "soul mate") of Osiris, but by giving him life, she also becomes his mother, encapsulating the feminine ideal in its entirety. The myth of Osiris is thus fertile with an imagination that does not restrict Eros to a sexual or even emotional register, but opens onto the spiritual and the universal. Love that triumphs over death is the supreme idea of the relationship between Osiris and Isis. Seth, on the other hand, is portrayed as a debased pervert, as manifested in his attempted rape of Horus.

For the Egyptians, Osiris is the principle of harmony that binds the human community. He brings together all the tribes of Egypt around the nation's sacred kingship. According to myth, for each of the scattered pieces of the body of Osiris she found, Isis conducted local funeral rites and so left a "tomb of Osiris" in each township. Thus was realized the consubstantial union of the land of Egypt and the body of Osiris. The annual festival of Osiris at Abydos was a celebration of civil peace and national unity against all invaders. Seth, by contrast, was synonymous with "domination and violence," says Plutarch. He was the god of discord and civil war—the master of *fitna* in Qur'anic terms, or a kind of *diabolos* in the etymological sense of "divider." For the Egyptians, German Egyptologist Jan Assmann writes, "The gods are social beings, living and acting in 'constellations'; a lonely god would be devoid of any power of personality and would have no impact on the great project of maintaining the world."[25] Seth is the exception that proves the rule: he was a pariah among the gods, who excluded him from their board of directors for disturbing the divine order. His "theophobic" nature agreed with the exclusivity of worship established by the Hyksos, who banished the other religions from the public sphere, adding religious persecution to political oppression.

After the defeat of Seth, Horus inherited the title of king of the world and received the *ka* of his father—the vital generational principle that lingers on Earth, as opposed to the *ba*

---

[24] Laurent Guyénot, *La Mort féerique. Anthropologie du merveilleux,* Gallimard, 2011, p. 318.
[25] Jan Assmann, *Of God and Gods, op. cit.,* p. 47.

which is the individual soul leaving this world. Horus, the falcon-king, then reigned over the Egyptians through the pharaoh, who was his incarnation on earth. But it is to Osiris that the royalty of the Other World returned. One of the ideas implicit in the myth is that Osiris reigns over the Hereafter, while the earthly world is the land of perpetual struggle between his son Horus and Seth. As long as Horus governs, which is to say when the state is in the hands of worthy representatives of Osiris's values, Seth is under control. But whenever Seth takes over the management of the world, lies and violence prevail.

While Horus rules over mortals, kingship of the otherworld goes to Osiris. Osiris is opposed to Seth like resurrection is opposed to annihilation; both form the double face of death. Funerary rites of embalming, a ritual reconstitution of the body, find their mythical expression in the reassembly of Osiris's body. Osiris presides over the judgment of the dead and attracts the purified souls, as Plutarch explains: "When these souls are set free and migrate into the realm of the invisible and the unseen, the dispassionate and the pure, then this god [Osiris] becomes their leader and king, since it is on him that they are bound to be dependent in their insatiate contemplation and yearning for that beauty which is for men unutterable and indescribable" (*Isis and Osiris* 78). On a personal level, Osiris personifies the virtues, making hearts light and enabling favorable judgments. Seth, conversely, embodies all the vices that prohibit access to immortality: murder, lying, stealing, greed, adultery, homosexuality, blasphemy, and rebellion against parents.

What does all this have to do with Yahweh? Was Yahweh, the god who led the Hebrews out of Egypt, related in any way to the Egyptian Seth, the god of strangers, refugees and nomads, banned from Egypt by his peers? After all, the Torah tells us that Yahweh was formerly known as *El Shaddai* (Genesis 17:1, Exodus 6:2–3), a Semitic name translatable as "the destroyer god" (from *el*, "god," and *shadad*, "destroy"), an appropriate surname for Seth.

Despite all these similarities, there is no conclusive evidence of a historical link between the cults of Seth and Yahweh. However, it is possible to show that the Egyptians who believed that the Jews had the ass-headed god Seth as their divinity or ancestor, had legitimate reasons to do so. They were simply following the universal practice of translating foreign gods into their own pantheon on the basis of functional resemblances. Indeed, from the point of view of Egyptian metaphysics, the god of the Jews betrays a Sethian character. Yahweh is Seth on an archetypal or paradigmatic level. Such is the thesis we will defend in the following chapters, thereby offering, in certain respects, an Egyptian outlook on the Jewish question.

Yahweh is Seth, first of all, to the extent that he shares the dominant trait of his character, murderous jealousy: "Yahweh's name is the Jealous One" (Exodus 34:14). As the next chapter shows, Yahweh manifests toward all his fellows an implacable hatred that characterizes him as a sociopath among the gods, very much like Seth. At a time when the pantheons of the world demonstrated courtesy, hospitality, and even fraternity, allowing peoples to recognize each other as living under the same heavens, Yahweh taught the Hebrews contempt for the deities of their neighbors—making them, in the eyes of these neighbors, a threat to the cosmic and social order. It will be shown in chapter 2 that the exclusive monotheism demanded by Yahweh (or "monoyahwism," as Jan Assmann calls it) is a degraded imitation of that inclusive monotheism toward which all the wisdoms of the world converge by affirming the fundamental unity of all gods. In Canaan, Yahweh's hatred rages especially against Baal, who is somewhat the equivalent of Osiris: the great universal god, especially honored as an agrarian deity by cultivators, though despised by nomads. Yahweh also attacks Asherah, the Great Divine Mother adored throughout the Middle East under various names, and assimilated to Isis in the Hellenistic period.

Yahweh is also Seth (the anti-Osiris) in his denial of life after death, as I argue in chapter 3. The Hebrew Bible differs from all religious traditions of Antiquity by the inability of its authors to conceive of an afterlife beyond sleep in the humid darkness of Sheol: "For dust you are and to dust you shall return" (Genesis 3:19), without any soul worthy of the name. Yahweh does not care about the dead, whom he "remembers no more" (Psalms 88:6). The Torah constantly identifies individuals with their genetic origin; the only afterlife it offers is through offspring.

When Abraham contemplates the starry sky, he does not see spiritualized souls, as do the Egyptians, but the image of his future earthly offspring (Genesis 15:5; 22:17). Only generation allows man to survive; therefore, only the people as a whole is eternal. Here is the explanation for the asymmetry between the myth of Osiris and its biblical inversion: there is no resurrection for Abel, as Seth-Yahweh is the god of death, not resurrection. There is no Other World for the good dead in the Torah: the Yahwist scribes have borrowed Paradise, the land of blessed immortality, from neighboring cultures, but shifted it to the beginning of the story, then closed access to it forever. The originality of the Bible, as we shall see, is often merely the inversion of motifs from other cultures (Egyptian, Canaanite, Babylonian, Persian, and Greek).

If the Hebrew Bible is heavily tainted with Egyptophobia, Egyptian traditions were themselves strongly Judeophobic. The Egyptians of the Hellenistic period knew the Exodus story of how the Hebrews escaped from Egypt after "despoiling" the Egyptians of "silver and golden jewelry, and clothing" that had been entrusted to them as loan guarantees (12:35–36). But they had another version of how the Jews left Egypt: The Jews did not flee Egypt but rather were expelled by royal decree. The earliest known example of that alternative Exodus is found in Hecataeus of Abdera's *Aegyptiaca*, written around 300 BCE: "When in ancient times a pestilence arose in Egypt, the common people ascribed their troubles to the workings of a divine agency; for indeed with many strangers of all sorts dwelling in their midst and practicing different rites of religion and sacrifice, their own traditional observances in honor of the gods had fallen into disuse. Hence the natives of the land surmised that unless they removed the foreigners, their troubles would never be resolved. At once, therefore, the aliens were driven from the country." The greatest number went to Judea under the guidance of Moses. "The sacrifices that he established differ from those of other nations, as does their way of living, for as a result of their own expulsion from Egypt he introduced a way of life which was somewhat unsocial and hostile to foreigners."[26]

Another Egyptian version of the Exodus appeared shortly after that of Hecateus in the writing of Manetho, quoted at length by Flavius Josephus in *Against Apion*. In it Jews are no longer just held responsible for epidemics and other ills by their disregard for the gods, but are themselves contagious lepers, and expelled as such. The same rumor was repeated by several authors. In the first century CE, Pompeius Trogus connects the theme of contagion with that of the legendary antisocial behavior (*amixia*) of the Jews. He adds—as an echo of Exodus—that Moses, before being expelled, "carried off by stealth the sacred utensils of the Egyptians, who, trying to recover them by force of arms, were compelled by tempests to return home." Later, "as they remembered that they had been driven from Egypt for fear of spreading infection, [the Jews] took care, in order that they might not become odious, from the same cause, to their neighbors, to have no communication with strangers; a rule which, from having been adopted on that particular occasion, gradually became a religious institution" (*Philippic Histories*).[27]

The Roman historian Tacitus stands by this version, which he claims is agreed upon by "most authorities." After being expelled as lepers (victims of "a wasting disease which caused bodily disfigurement"), the Jews, under Moses's guidance, adopted a sort of anti-religion. Tacitus writes: "Among the Jews all things are profane that we hold sacred; on the other hand they regard as permissible what seems to us immoral." They show a "stubborn loyalty and ready benevolence towards brother Jews. But the rest of the world they confront with the hatred reserved for enemies. [...] Those who come over to their religion adopt the practice [of circumcision], and have this lesson first instilled into them, to despise all gods, to disown

---

[26] Peter Schäfer, *Judeophobia: Attitudes Toward the Jews in the Ancient World*, Harvard University Press, 1998, pp. 15–16.

[27] *Jewish Life and Thought Among Greeks and Romans: Primary Readings*, ed. and introduced by Louis Feldman and Meyer Reinhold, Augsburg Fortress, 1996, pp. 356, 385.

their country, and set at naught parents, children, and brethren" (*Histories* V.3–5).

Common sense tells us that this slanderous story of the Jews' origin as Egyptian lepers is an aggravated expression of the account reported by Hecataeus, which makes them foreigners, not lepers. It is not difficult to see how, in the Egyptian mind, foreigners and wanderers (*habiru*) who do not respect the Egyptian gods could turn into vectors of disease. In an edict by Emperor Claudius dated 41 CE, it is the spirit of civil war fomented by the Alexandrian Jews that is compared to "a public sickness" infecting the whole Roman world (*oikoumene*).[28]

---

[28] Joseph Mélèze Modrzejewski, *The Jews of Egypt, op. cit.*, p. 183.

Chapter 2

THE THEOCLASTIC GOD

> "Anyone who has intercourse with an animal will be put to death. Anyone who sacrifices to other gods will be put under the curse of destruction."
>
> Exodus 22:18–19

Jealousy and Narcissistic Hubris

"Yahweh's name is the Jealous One" (Exodus 34:14). The Torah emphasizes jealousy as his main personality trait, calling him "the Jealous One" repeatedly (Exodus 20:5, Deuteronomy 4:24, 5:9, and 6:15). What Yahweh demands from his people above anything else is exclusivity of worship. But that is not all. He also demands that all his neighbors' shrines be utterly destroyed: "Tear down their altars, smash their standing-stones, cut down their sacred poles and burn their idols" (Deuteronomy 7:5). Thus spoke Yahweh, otherwise known as *El Shaddai*, "the destroyer god" (Exodus 6:3).

After the destruction of the northern kingdom of Israel by Assyria, Yahwist priests and prophets who had sought refuge in Jerusalem held the Israelites responsible for their country's defeat: they "provoked Yahweh's anger" by "sacrificing on all the high places like the nations which Yahweh had expelled for them," and by "serving idols" (2 Kings 17:11–12). Israel's divine election had now passed to the smaller kingdom of Judah, whose survival depended on respecting the exclusivity of Yahweh's cult and of Jerusalem's Temple, and on destroying any trace of rival cults and holy places.

The second book of Kings judges David's heirs on the unique criterion of obedience to that precept. Hezekiah is praised for having done "what Yahweh regards as right," namely abolishing the "high places" (2 Kings 18:3–4). On the other hand, his son Manasseh is blamed for having done "what is displeasing to Yahweh, copying the disgusting practices of the

nations whom Yahweh had dispossessed for the Israelites. He
rebuilt the high places that his father Hezekiah had destroyed,
he set up altars to Baal and made a sacred pole [an *Ashera*], as
Ahab king of Israel had done, he worshiped the whole array of
heaven and served it. [...] He built altars to the whole array of
heaven in the two courts of the Temple of Yahweh" (2 Kings
21:2–5). Manasseh's son Amon is no better. Josiah, however,
proves worthy of his great-great-grandfather Hezekiah,
removing from the temple "all the cult objects which had been
made for Baal, Asherah and the whole array of heaven. [...] He
exterminated the spurious priests whom the kings of Judah had
appointed and who offered sacrifice on the high places, in the
towns of Judah and the neighborhood of Jerusalem; also those
who offered sacrifice to Baal, to the sun, the moon, the
constellations and the whole array of heaven" (2 Kings 23:4–5).
In Samaria, over which he regained partial control, Josiah
ordered the sanctuary of Bethel destroyed, and "All the priests
of the high places who were there he slaughtered on the altars,
and on those altars burned human bones" (2 Kings 23:20). In
other words, Josiah is zealously faithful to the Law of Moses.

For the Egyptians, gods are social beings, who collaborate in
the management of the cosmos. The harmony of this world,
including human affairs, depends on good cooperation between
the gods.[1] Hebrew theology, on the other hand, promotes the
war of one god against all others. Yahweh feels a deep aversion
toward all other gods and goddesses. His obsession is to
preserve his people from any influence from other divine beings,
and to make it his "personal possession" and "a kingdom of
priests" devoted to his cult (Exodus 19:5–6). The Jealous One is
possessive: "I shall set you apart from all these peoples, for you
to be mine" (Leviticus 20:26). It is for their arrogant contempt
of their neighbors' religious practices that the Jews were
perceived everywhere as a "race hated by the gods" (Tacitus,
Histories V.3).

---

[1] Jan Assmann, "Seth the Iconoclast," in *Of God and Gods: Egypt, Israel, and the Rise of
Monotheism*, University of Wisconsin Press, 2008, pp. 28–52, 46.

In the ancient world, respecting the variety of the gods was the basis of international relationships. From the third millennium BCE onward, nations built their mutual trust on their capacity to match their gods; in this way, they knew they were living under the same heaven. "Contracts with other states," explains Egyptologist Jan Assmann, "had to be sealed by oath, and the gods to whom this oath was sworn had to be compatible. Tables of divine equivalences were thus drawn up that eventually correlated up to six different pantheons." This translatability of the gods relied on a standardization of their cosmic functions: the sun god of one country, for example, was assumed to be the same as the sun god of another. Polytheism as a cultural system used a "translational technique," says Assmann, and in this respect, it "represents a major cultural achievement." By standardizing the cosmic function of each god, it made the divine world of one particular group compatible with the divine world of another group. "Religion functioned as a medium of communication, not elimination and exclusion. The principle of the translatability of divine names helped to overcome the primitive ethnocentrism of the tribal religions, to establish relations between cultures, and to make these cultures more transparent to each other."[2] This was how the Greek and Egyptian deities merged into a Greco-Egyptian syncretism: Osiris took on the traits of Hades, as well as Asclepius and Dionysus.

Yahweh, however, could not be matched up with any other god, and his priests forbade doing so. "Whereas polytheism, or rather 'cosmotheism,' rendered different cultures mutually transparent and compatible, the new counter-religion [Yahwism] blocked intercultural translatability."[3] And when the Lord directs his people, "You will make no pact with them or with their gods" (Exodus 23:32), or "Do not utter the names of their gods, do not swear by them, do not serve them and do not bow down

---

[2] Jan Assmann, *The Price of Monotheism,* Stanford University Press, 2009, kindle, k. 255, 322–324.
[3] Jan Assmann, *Moses the Egyptian: The Memory of Egypt in Western Monotheism,* Harvard University Press, 1998, p. 3.

to them" (Joshua 23:7), he is in effect preventing any relationship of trust with the neighboring peoples.

The polytheisms of the great civilizations, Assmann emphasizes, are cosmotheisms, insofar as the gods, among other functions, form the organic body of the world. Such a conception naturally leads to a form of inclusive or convergent monotheism, compatible with polytheism: all gods are one, as the cosmos is one. The notion of the unity of the divine realm naturally connects with the notion of a supreme god, creator of heaven and earth, enthroned atop a hierarchy of deities emanating from him—a concept familiar to Plato, Aristotle, Seneca, and most ancient philosophers. The Yahwist priests, in a competitive mood, would also develop their own monotheism; but it was an exclusive and revolutionary monotheism, the exact opposite of the inclusive and evolutionary monotheism of neighboring peoples, and it led to the same result only in appearance.

To understand how this biblical monotheism came about, it is necessary to know that in the oldest strata of the Bible, Yahweh is a national, ethnic god, not the supreme God of the Universe. The Israelites revered Yahweh as the Assyrians worshiped their god Ashur and credited him with their military victories: "For all peoples go forward, each in the name of its god (*elohim*), while we go forward in the name of Yahweh our God for ever and ever" (Micah 4:5). "I am the god of your ancestors, the god of Abraham, the god of Isaac and the god of Jacob," Yahweh says to Moses (Exodus 3:6). Then Yahweh mandates Moses to say to his people: "Yahweh, the god of your ancestors, has appeared to me," and to urge them to talk to Pharaoh in the name of "Yahweh, the god of the Hebrews" (3:16–18). "This is what Yahweh, god [*elohim*] of Israel, says, Let my people go," Moses and Aaron say to Pharaoh (5:1). The Hebrews chant after the miracle of the Red Sea engulfing Pharaoh and his army, "Yahweh, who is like you, majestic in sanctity, who like you among the gods [*elim*]?" (15:11).[4] And in Canaan, a Hebrew chief declares to his defeated enemy: "Will

---

[4] See also Psalms 89:7.

you not keep as your possession whatever Chemosh, your god, has given you? And, just the same, we shall keep as ours whatever Yahweh our god has given us, to inherit from those who were before us!" (Judges 11:24).[5] In all these verses, Yahweh is an ethnic or national god among others.

Yahweh's superiority over other gods presupposes the existence of these other gods. One story in particular deserves to be mentioned here: After the Philistines had captured the Ark of the defeated Israelites, they "put it in the temple of Dagon, setting it down beside Dagon" (1 Samuel 5:2). The next day, they found the broken statue of Dagon. Yahweh then afflicted the inhabitants of two Philistine cities, Ashdod and Gat, with a proliferation of rats and an epidemic of tumors. The Philistines then ordered their priests to return the Ark to the Israelites, along with a penitential offering of "five golden tumours and five golden rats." "So make models of your tumours and models of your rats ravaging the territory, and pay honor to the god of Israel. Then perhaps he will stop oppressing you, your gods and your country" (6:4–5).

We repeat: At this stage, Yahweh was not the creator of the universe, but an ethnic god among many, demonstrating his superiority over all other gods and demanding the exclusive worship of the Israelites. The term "monolatry" has been coined to describe this rare form of polytheism that presupposes the existence of a plurality of gods but prohibits the worship of all except one. This is the meaning of the first commandments given to Moses: "I am Yahweh your God who brought you out of Egypt, where you lived as slaves. You shall have no other gods to rival me" (Exodus 20:2–3). David's understanding of Yahweh's blessing in 2 Samuel 7:23–26, if read without monotheistic spectacles, also points to a covenant between *a* god and *a* people: "Is there another people on earth like your people, like Israel, whom a god proceeded to redeem, to make them his people and to make a name for himself by performing great and terrible things on their behalf, by driving out nations and their gods before his people? For you constituted your

---

[5] Jean Soler, *Qui est Dieu?*, Éditions de Fallois, 2012, pp. 12–17, 33–37.

people Israel your own people for ever and you, Yahweh, became their god. Now, god Yahweh, may the promise which you have made for your servant and for his family stand firm forever as you have said, so that your name will be exalted for ever and people will say, 'Israel's god is Yahweh Sabaoth.'"

It was only during the Babylonian exile that Yahweh, deprived of the temple where he had previously sat between two cherubim, began to claim to have created the universe himself. After banning all trade with other gods and declaring Yahweh more powerful than they, the Yahwist priests and prophets would claim that these other gods simply did not exist. And if Yahweh was the only real god, then he must have been the creator and master of the universe. The exterminating fury of the deicide god thus reached its logical conclusion, since denying the existence of other gods condemns them to nothingness.

This evolution from monolatry to monotheism was retro-projected to the time of King Hezekiah in the following curious story. Having destroyed the northern kingdom, the Assyrian king threatens Hezekiah in these words: "Do not let your god on whom you are relying deceive you with the promise: 'Jerusalem will not fall into the king of Assyria's clutches' [...] Did the gods of the nations whom my ancestors devastated save them?" Hezekiah then goes up to the Jerusalem Temple and offers the following prayer: "Yahweh Sabaoth, god of Israel, enthroned on the winged creatures, you alone are God of all the kingdoms of the world, you made heaven and earth. [...] It is true, Yahweh, that the kings of Assyria have destroyed the nations, they have thrown their gods on the fire, for these were not gods but human artifacts—wood and stone—and hence they have destroyed them. But now, Yahweh our god, save us from his clutches, I beg you, and let all the kingdoms of the world know that you alone are God, Yahweh" (2 Kings 19:10–19). In response to this prayer, "the angel of Yahweh went out and struck down a hundred and eighty-five thousand men in the Assyrian camp," then struck their king by the hand of his sons (19:35–37). Pure fiction: the Assyrian annals tell us that in reality, Hezekiah paid tribute to the Assyrian king. But the lesson of the story, for critical readers, is that a prayer sufficed to annihilate all other gods and promote Yahweh from the status of national god to that of universal God.

Of course, the universal God, Father of all men, was known in Samaria and Judea much before Yahweh was introduced there. The Bible itself tells how Abraham was initiated by Melchizedek, king of Salem (Jerusalem's former name), "a priest of God Most High [...], Creator of heaven and earth" (Genesis 14:18-20). The High God was commonly called El, meaning "God" (from which derives the Arabic name Allah). So the trick was to merge Yahweh with El; in the post-exilic strata of the Torah, the two names become interchangeable. Historical-critical scholars have long noted that biblical passages referring to Yahweh belong to southern traditions (Judea), while the traditions of the North (Israel or Samaria) designated the creator simply as "El" or "Elohim." This indicates that it was in Judah that Yahweh usurped the majesty of El, who was thus declared residing in the Jerusalem Temple, to be worshiped nowhere else. From this point of view, Yahwism is a conspiracy against the true God.

In the biblical story, Baal is the most formidable rival of Yahweh. To justify the eradication of Baal worship in Canaan, Yahwist scribes present him as a foreign god imported by Jezebel, the Phoenician wife of Ahab (1 Kings 16:31–32). But he was actually the traditional god of the land. Baal was for the Canaanites what Osiris was for the Egyptians: both fertility god and lord of the dead. Baal is actually the equivalent for "Lord" in Aramaic (as well as for the Greek *Kyrios* and the Hebrew *Adonai*). The term is often used in the plural to designate the deities at large, including the deified dead. But in all of ancient Syria, Baal Shamem, the "Heavenly Lord," refers to the supreme God, understood as including all the manifestations of the divine.[6] It is ironic that Yahweh, originally a minor tribal god, should rival the great Baal for the status of supreme God.

In the cycles of Elijah and Elisha, Elijah challenges 450 prophets of Baal to conjure lightning upon the burnt offering of

---

[6] Norman Habel, *Yahweh Versus Baal: A Conflict of Religious Cultures*, Bookman Associates, 1964, p. 41.

a bull: "You must call on the name of your god, and I shall call
on the name of Yahweh; the god who answers with fire, is God
indeed." The prophets of Baal exhaust themselves by shouting
to their god, performing "their hobbling dance," and gashing
themselves with swords and spears, with no result, while
Yahweh sets fire to Elijah's bull after Elijah has drenched it with
twelve jars of water to raise the challenge. People then fall on
their faces and scream "Yahweh is God!" Then, on Elijah's
order, they seize all the prophets of Baal, and Elijah slaughters
them (1 Kings 18). Let us appreciate the significance of this
battle of the gods, which is still awaiting its Hollywood
adaptation. It perfectly illustrates how, to arrive at monotheism,
Yahwism takes the diametrically opposite path from other
cultures of the same period: Rather than reaching
philosophically the notion of the unity of all gods under a
universal Godhead, the Yahwists pursued the outright negation
of other gods and the extermination of their priests. In this
process, theology and anthropology are inseparable. It is insofar
as the national god of the Jews managed to establish himself as
the "one God" of humanity that the Jewish people would be
able to style themselves as the "chosen people."

For a Greek, writes historian Joseph Mélèze Modrzejewski,
"monotheism can only be the subject of philosophical
speculation and not of religious practice, polytheistic by
definition." Therefore, when the Greeks discovered the Jews in
Egypt after Alexander's conquest, a misunderstanding took
place, nurtured by Jewish intellectuals themselves. Because they
worshiped only one god and claimed for him the title of
universal creator, the Jews gained for themselves a reputation as
a "people of philosophers"—while the Egyptians, for their part,
accused them of "atheism." Around 315 BCE, Theophrastus of
Eresus, disciple of Aristotle, called the Jews "philosophers by
birth," while mentioning that they "now sacrifice live victims
according to their old mode of sacrifice," that is, by burning

completely their animal offerings (the original meaning of "holocaust").[7]

The misunderstanding became a public scandal in 167, when Antiochos IV dedicated the temple in Jerusalem to Zeus Olympios (the supreme god). He was expressing the idea that Yahweh was another name of Zeus. But the revolt led by the Jewish Maccabees proved that in their eyes, Yahweh remained primarily the god of the Jews, and only incidentally the supreme God. In other words, Jewish monotheism is really a supremacism and not a universalism.

More than a misunderstanding, it is an ambiguity inherent to Judaism and its relationship to Gentiles. That is apparent in the Edict of Persian king Cyrus according to the book of Ezra: "Yahweh, the God of heaven, has given me all the kingdoms of the earth and has appointed me to build him a Temple in Jerusalem, in Judah. Whoever among you belongs to the full tally of his people, may his God be with him! Let him go up to Jerusalem, in Judah, and build the Temple of Yahweh, the god of Israel, who is the god in Jerusalem" (1:2–3). So, Cyrus speaks in the name of "the God of heaven" while authorizing the Judean exiles to build a temple to "Yahweh, the god of Israel […] the god in Jerusalem."

We understand that both phrases refer to the same God, but the duality is significant. We find it again in the edict authorizing the second wave of return. It is now Artaxerxes, "king of kings," addressing "the priest Ezra, Secretary of the Law of *the God of heaven*," to ask him to offer a gigantic holocaust "to *the god of Israel* who resides in Jerusalem" (7:12–15). We later find twice the expression "God of heaven" interspersed with seven references to "your God," that is to say, the God of Ezra and Israel (and keep in mind that capitalization here is a convention of modern translators). The phrase "God of heaven" appears one more time in the book of Ezra, and it is, again, in an edict of a Persian king: Darius confirms the edict of Cyrus and recommends that the Israelites "may offer sacrifices acceptable

---

[7] Joseph Mélèze Modrzejewski, *The Jews of Egypt, From Rameses II to Emperor Hadrian*, Princeton University Press, 1995, pp. 48–49.

to the God of heaven and pray for the life of the king and his sons" (6:10). Elsewhere the book of Ezra only refers to the "God of Israel" (four times), "Yahweh, the God of your fathers" (once), and "our God" (ten times). In other words, according to the author of the book of Ezra, only the kings of Persia imagine that Yahweh is "the God of heaven"—a common designation of the universal god Ahura Mazda among the Persians—while for the Jews, Yahweh is merely their god, the "god of Israel," the god of their fathers, in short, a tribal god.

The same principle can be observed in the book of Daniel, when Nebuchadnezzar, impressed by the gifts of Daniel's oracle, prostrates himself and exclaims: "Your god is indeed the God of gods, the Master of kings" (Daniel 2:47). These passages (in which the god of the Jews becomes, in the eyes of the goyim, the God of the Universe) reveal the real secret of Judaism, the key to its relationship to universalism and Gentiles: for the Jews, Yahweh is the god of the Jews, while Gentiles are led to believe that he is the supreme and only God. "In the heart of any pious Jew, God is a Jew," confirms Maurice Samuel in *You Gentiles* (1924).[8]

Finally, note that the monotheism of the Torah is untempered by dualism. There is no trace in the Torah of a cosmic struggle between two principles, as in the myth of Osiris or in Persian Zoroastrianism. The fundamental tension is not between good and evil, but between Yahweh and the other gods. The snake (Nachash) tempting Eve in the Garden of Eden disappears forever from the Bible after that: it has no ontological consistency. The "devil" (*diabolos* in Greek) will make his appearance in the Gospels, and "Lucifer" later still, based on a tendentious exegesis of Isaiah 14:12 in the Latin translation (Vulgate). As for "the satan," it appears to be borrowed from a Sumerian legal word meaning the "accuser," and it never occurs as a proper name in the Pentateuch (Torah). "Satan" is the

---

[8] Maurice Samuel, *You Gentiles*, New York, 1924 (archive.org), pp. 74–75.

prosecution lawyer in Zechariah 3:1 and in the book of Job.[9] In the Old Testament, when he personifies a destructive principle, Satan is hard to distinguish from Yahweh himself. Thus, in 2 Samuel 24, Yahweh incites David to abuse his power, while in the same episode recounted by 1 Chronicles 21, the role is given to Satan. One reads in the latter narrative that "Satan took his stand against Israel" (21:1), that "God [...] punished Israel" (21:7), that "the angel of Yahweh wreaks havoc throughout the territory of Israel" (21:12) and that "Yahweh unleashed an epidemic on Israel" (21:14). Ultimately, it is always God who strikes not only the enemies of Israel, but also Israel itself when it proves unworthy of him. It is he who triggers wars, epidemics, and plagues of every imaginable sort; he uses alternately Israel to destroy the nations (as a "mace," Jeremiah 51:20), and the nations to destroy Israel. Yahweh is the source of both good and evil. (It follows logically, according to some kabbalistic schools, that one can serve him through evil as well as through good.)

The relationship between man and the biblical god is purely contractual and legalistic. According to the Egyptologist Jan Assmann, the idea that God could dictate his laws to men is an innovation of the Bible. In Egypt and elsewhere in the ancient world, the law was not the responsibility of the gods, but of men. It stemmed from human consensus, and its application was based on human judgment. The law therefore had no divine or eternal character: "No 'pagan' religion made the law its chief concern."

The Mosaic law, for its part, fell from heaven already engraved in stone. "Monotheism's achievement was not to have introduced law and justice, but to have transferred them from the earth and human experience, as the source of the law, to heaven and the divine will. By 'theologizing' justice, that is, by placing justice in god's hands, monotheism elevates it to the status of religious truth."[10] From the Egyptian point of view, attributing the decrees of law to a divine revelation is a

---

[9] Samuel Noah Kramer, *History Begins at Sumer,* University of Pennsylvania Press, 1988, pp. 144–150.
[10] Jan Assmann, *The Price of Monotheism, op. cit.,* k. 698.

perversion of religion and a distortion of law, which normally draws its source and legitimacy from human experience. The Yahwist priests stripped man of this fundamental responsibility, in order to deify law and history. According to the great Jewish thinker Yeshayahu Leibowitz, "The Torah does not recognize moral imperatives stemming from knowledge of natural reality or from awareness of man's duty to his fellow man. All it recognizes are Mitzvot, divine imperatives."[11] The hundreds of *mitzvot* ("commandments") are an end in themselves, not a way to a higher moral consciousness. In fact, according to Gilad Atzmon, Jewish legalism stifles genuine ethical judgment, for "ethical people don't need 'commandments' to know that murder or theft are wrong."[12] Jesus expressed the same view when he accused the Pharisees of preventing people from entering the Kingdom of God with their Law (Matthew 13).

It can be remarked that elevating the law, a human construction, to the level of a divine command, has contributed to making Jews unassimilable. This is what Zionist author Jakob Klatzkin, an admirer of Spinoza, once pointed out in the journal *Der Jude,* 1916: "Only the Jewish Code rules our life. Whenever other laws are forced upon us we regard them as dire oppression and constantly dodge them. We form in ourselves a closed juridical and business corporation. A strong wall built by us separates us from the people of the lands in which we live—and behind that wall is a Jewish State."[13] Jewish historian Bernard Lazare likewise remarked that all the peoples conquered by the Romans submitted without difficulty to the laws of their conquerors, because laws and religions were clearly separated in their cultures. Only the Jews resisted assimilation, because Mosaic laws are religious by nature, and suffer no compromise.[14]

---

[11] Yeshayahu Leibowitz, *Judaism, Human Values and the Jewish State,* Harvard University Press, 1995, p. 18.

[12] www.gilad.co.uk/writings/on-idfs-failure-and-jewish-ethics.html.

[13] Quoted in Robert Edward Edmondson, *The Jewish System Indicted by the Documentary Record,* 1937 (archive.org), p. 15.

[14] Bernard Lazare, *L'Antisémitisme, son histoire et ses causes* (1894), Kontre Kulture, 2011, p. 12.

No Goddess for Yahweh

Neither is there is any trace in Yahwist metaphysics of gender complementarity. According to the Bible, Yahweh needed no female deity to create the world—in a curious manner, hanging the sun in the sky three days and three nights only after declaring "let there be light" (Genesis 1:3–19). Yahweh is a god without history, without genealogy, without wife or mother or children; and therefore without mythology. Yet archeologists have found in the ruins of Kuntillet Ajrud (the Sinai Peninsula) inscriptions dating from the eighth century BCE, asking the blessing of "Yahweh and his Asherah," suggesting that the Hebrews of that time had not yet excluded the Great Goddess from their religion.

The discovery of the cuneiform tablets of Ugarit (in modern Syria) has helped us understand the importance of the goddess Asherah in the Semitic cultures of the ancient Middle East. Asherah was the consort of El, the sky god and father of the gods, but she also appears as his mother, while her children Baal and Anath are also a couple. According to Raphael Patai, author of *The Hebrew Goddess*, "For about six centuries [...], that is to say, down to the destruction of Jerusalem by Nebuchadnezzar in 586 BCE, the Hebrews worshiped Asherah (and next to her also other, originally Canaanite, gods and goddesses) in most places and times."[15] Only in the Yahwism of the Exile, which triumphed with the reform of Ezra, was Asherah removed successfully. Yahweh's repulsion for Asherah is matched only by his hatred of Baal. We find the name of Asherah forty times in the Old Testament, either to designate and curse the goddess, or to designate her symbol in the form of "sacred poles" that the Yahwist kings strove to destroy.

We are now so used to the idea of a Creator who is male, single, and alone, that we have trouble imagining the spiritual void this implies from the point of view of ancient polytheism. The Bible tells that Hebrews often rebelled against this misogynous theology of their priests, and worshiped Asherah as

---

15 Raphael Patai, *The Hebrew Goddess*, 3rd ed., Wayne State University Press, 1990, p. 34.

"Queen of Heaven," to the dismay of the prophet Jeremiah (7:18). After the destruction of Jerusalem by Babylon, the book of Jeremiah tells us, Judean refugees in Egypt wondered if it was not their neglect of the Great Goddess, rather than of Yahweh, that was responsible for their misfortune, and they turned toward her with fervor. Jeremiah called them back to order by threatening that Yahweh would exterminate them (chapter 44).

The Great Goddess is known in the Middle East under multiple identities. Under the name of Ishtar, she is the "Queen of all the inhabited places, who keeps the people in order," according to a Mesopotamian anthem.[16] In the Hellenistic period, Asherah and Ishtar were still assimilated to the Egyptian Isis, while Isis was enriched in turn with attributes of Demeter, Artemis, and Aphrodite, to which the Romans added Diana and Venus. Isis became for the Greeks the "myrionyme" goddess ("of ten thousand names"). In the Hellenistic synthesis that combined ancient Egyptian religion with Greek philosophy, the worship of the goddess Isis took precedence over that of her husband-brother Osiris. It radiated from Alexandria across the eastern edge of the Mediterranean basin. Isis became the symbol of Hellenistic civilization and its ambition to encompass all cultures.[17] "You are, by yourself, all other goddesses invoked by all peoples," said Isidoros addressing Isis. "You, the unique, who are all," said the dedication of a worshiper from Capua. And in Apuleius's novel *The Golden Ass,* the goddess Isis calls herself "Queen of Heaven" and says: "My name, my divinity is adored throughout all the world in diverse manners, in variable customs and in many names."[18]

How can Yahweh, a male god who tolerates no female counterpart, help men grasp the mystery of womanhood? Yahwism reduces the divine to the masculine, and ignores the most universal and mysterious of all human experiences: the complementarity of genders. In the Garden of Eden, natural law itself is reversed when the woman is declared to have come out

---

[16] Gérard Chaliand, *Les Voix du Sacré*, Robert Laffont, 1992, p. 32.

[17] Jean-Pierre Chevillot, *D'Isis au Christ: Aux sources hellénistiques du christianisme*, L'Harmattan, 2010, kindle, k. 27–33.

[18] Françoise Dunand, *Isis, mère des dieux*, Actes Sud, 2008, p. 232.

of the man, rather than the reverse. If the function of myths is to express in narrative form universal truths, are we not here dealing with an anti-myth? Historical exegesis has long understood that the biblical story of the transgression of the first couple was meant as a polemical attack on Eastern traditions that exalt sexuality as a holy experience and a divine encounter, through initiatory or marriage rites. These rites have long been misrepresented in Western traditions by the calumnious rumor of "sacred prostitution." The lack of any "metaphysics of sex" in Judeo-Christian culture has led to a judgment of obscenity passed on the whole iconography of *hieros gamos* in Asian sacred art.[19] In Genesis, the first sexual act of Adam and Eve (of which the consumption of the forbidden fruit is the obvious metaphor) is the source of all evil, the "original sin" in Augustinian terms. No transcendence, no positive value whatsoever is attached to it, since even the knowledge that it is supposed to grant is denied.

On this ground, Yahwism is an anti-Osirism, since the myth of Osiris and Isis magnifies the power of love over death. The Egyptian myth has parallels in countless myths and tales foreign to Judaism and Christianity, in which a lost soul, a victim of a bad death (Osiris) is saved in the afterlife by the sacrificial love of his soul mate (Isis).[20] This type of mythical imagination is totally foreign to the Bible. No biblical narrative encourages Jews to conceive of sexuality as anything other than a natural function. The paucity of Jewish reflection on the supernatural power of human love can be contrasted with the rich traditions of India, where the erotic and the sacred go together. See for example how the Creator Brahma creates Dawn, radiant of youth and vitality, and himself succumbs to her charms, according to the Kalika Purana. One of the lessons of these myths of Hieros Gamos, according to Indologist Heinrich Zimmer, is that a man may find his own soul by adoring a woman, and vice versa.[21]

---

[19] Stehanie Lynn Budin, *The Myth of Sacred Prostitution in Antiquity*, Cambridge University Press, 2009.

[20] Laurent Guyénot, *La Mort féerique. Anthropologie du merveilleux (XIIᵉ-XVᵉ siècle)*, Gallimard, 2011.

[21] Heinrich Zimmer, *The King and the Corpse: Tales of the Soul's Conquest of Evil*, 1948.

Yahwism, for its part, only values marriage from the perspective of creating lineages and communities. The only major exception is the Song of Songs—which only found a place in the Hebrew corpus in the first century CE due to an allegorical interpretation of Rabbi Akiva unrelated to its original inspiration. In reality, the Song of Songs is merely a poetic evocation of youthful love, probably of non-Jewish origin, whose carnal eroticism does not rise beyond comparison with drunkenness. The divine is never mentioned.[22]

From Deicide to Genocide

The ancient peoples readily admitted that they all worshiped the same Great Goddess under different names. The cult of the Mother Goddess is undoubtedly the most international and the most likely to bring different peoples together; all men can recognize themselves as the son of one universal Mother. Motherhood is pacifying. It is also, perhaps, less discriminating than fatherhood, and it seems that the concept of chosen people would make less sense in a world embraced by the Queen of Heaven than in a world controlled by the one Yahweh. But the exclusively male character of Yahweh and his refusal to share power with a goddess are not the only factors involved. It is the chronic jealousy of Yahweh, not just his misogyny, on which the xenophobia of biblical Israel is founded. We have seen that the ancient peoples always ensured that their gods were compatible or on good terms, making cultural and economic relations possible.

The authors of Deuteronomy were aware of the widespread idea that national gods were all under the authority of the Supreme Creator. But they altered it in typical fashion: "When the Most High (*Elyown*) gave the nations each their heritage, when he partitioned out the human race, he assigned the boundaries of nations according to the number of the children of God, but Yahweh's portion was his people, Jacob was to be the measure of his inheritance" (32:8–9). In other words, among all nations, the very Father of humankind has picked one for

---

[22] Jean Soler, *Qui est Dieu?, op. cit.*, p. 23.

himself, leaving the others under the care of lesser gods (angelic powers, for such is here the accepted meaning of "children of God"). That is the ultimate source of Jewish pride: "Of all the peoples on earth, you have been chosen by Yahweh your God to be his own people" (7:6). And this people of his, Yahweh naturally wants to "raise higher than every other nation in the world" (28:1). Although he implicitly admits being the Father of all other national gods, he feels for them only a murderous hatred.

The essence of monotheistic Yahwism, which is a secondary development of tribalistic Yahwism, is the exclusive alliance between the universal Creator and a peculiar people, in order to make it "a people that dwells on its own, not to be reckoned among other nations" (Numbers 23:9). Its specificity is less in the affirmation of a unique God than in the affirmation of a unique people. The one God is the side of the coin shown to the goy to remind him his eternal debt to the "inventors of monotheism"; but the other side, the concept of chosen people, is what binds the Jewish community together, so that one can give up God without abandoning the exceptionality of the Jewish people.

And so, even while claiming to be the Creator of the universe and humanity, Yahweh remains a national, chauvinist god; that is the basis for the dissonance between tribalism and universalism that has brought up the "Jewish question" throughout the ages. In fact, the Jewish conception of Yahweh parallels the historical process, for in the development of Yahwism, it is not the Creator of the Universe who became the god of Israel, but rather the god of Israel who became the Creator of the Universe. And so for the Jews, Yahweh is primarily the god of Jews, and secondarily the Creator of the Universe; whereas Christians, deceived by the biblical narrative, see things the other way around.

Having chosen for himself a single tribe among all the peoples, using unknown criteria, Yahweh plans on making of them not a guide, but a bane for the rest of humanity: "Today and henceforth, I shall fill the peoples under all heavens with fear and terror of you; whoever hears word of your approach will tremble and writhe in anguish because of you"

(Deuteronomy 2:25). The biblical stories are there to dramatize the message. Let us mention a few, taken from the cycles of Jacob, Moses, and David, all carrying the same trademark.

Shechem, the son of Hamor, king of the Canaanite town of Shechem, "fell in love with [Jacob's daughter Dinah] and tried to win her heart," then "seized her and forced her to sleep with him." Jacob's sons "were outraged and infuriated that Shechem had insulted Israel by sleeping with Jacob's daughter—a thing totally unacceptable. Hamor reasoned with them as follows, 'My son Shechem's heart is set on your daughter. Please allow her to marry him. Intermarry with us; give us your daughters and take our daughters for yourselves. We can live together, and the country will be open to you, for you to live in, and move about in, and acquire holdings.' Then Shechem addressed the girl's father and brothers, 'Grant me this favour, and I will give you whatever you ask. Demand as high a bride-price from me as you please, and I will pay as much as you ask. Only let me marry the girl.'" Jacob's sons then "gave Shechem and his father Hamor a crafty answer," demanding that "you become like us by circumcising all your males. Then we will give you our daughters, taking yours for ourselves; and we will stay with you to make one nation." Hamor, trusting the good intentions of Jacob's tribe, convinced all his male subjects to be circumcised. "Now on the third day, when the men were still in pain, Jacob's two sons Simeon and Levi, Dinah's brothers, each took his sword and advanced unopposed against the town and slaughtered all the males. They killed Hamor and his son Shechem with the sword, removed Dinah from Shechem's house and came away. When Jacob's other sons came on the slain, they pillaged the town in reprisal for the dishonoring of their sister. They seized their flocks, cattle, donkeys, everything else in the town and in the countryside, and all their possessions. They took all their children and wives captive and looted everything to be found in the houses" (Genesis 34:1–29).

Second example: In Moses's time, when the kings of Heshbon and Bashan wanted to prevent the Hebrews from entering their territory, the Hebrews "captured all his towns and laid all these towns under the curse of destruction: men, women and children, we left no survivors except the livestock which we took as our booty, and the spoils of the captured towns" (Deuteronomy 2:34–35).

That is nothing compared to what King David did to the people of Rabba, after having sacked their town and "carried off great quantities of booty": "And he brought forth the people that were therein, and put them under saws, and under harrows of iron, and under axes of iron, and made them pass through the brickkiln: and thus did he unto all the cities of the children of Ammon. And David and all the people returned unto Jerusalem" (2 Samuel 12:31). The episode is repeated in 1 Chronicles 20:3: "And he brought forth the people that were therein, and cut them with saws, and with harrows of iron, and with axes. Even so dealt David with all the cities of the children of Ammon."

I have quoted here from the King James Revised Version. Significantly, this episode has been fraudulently retranslated after 1946. We now read in the Revised Standard Version: "And he brought forth the people who were in it, and set them to labor with saws and iron picks and iron axes, and made them toil at the brickkilns." And in the Catholic New Jerusalem Bible: "And he expelled its inhabitants, setting them to work with saws, iron picks and iron axes, employing them at brickmaking." This new rendering makes the story politically correct, but highly improbable, since iron tools were never needed to make bricks—certainly not axes, picks and saws—but made deadly weapons that no victor in his right mind would distribute to the men he had just vanquished.

The war code established by Yahweh makes a distinction between the cities outside and those within the territory given to his people. In the former, "you will put the whole male population to the sword. But the women, children, livestock and whatever the town contains by way of spoil, you may take for yourselves as booty. You will feed on the spoils of the enemies whom Yahweh your God has handed over to you." In the nearby foreign towns, on the other hand, "you must not spare the life of any living thing," men and women, young and old, children and babies, and even livestock, "so that they may not teach you to do all the detestable things which they do to honor their gods" (Deuteronomy 20:13–18). So, in Jericho, "They enforced the curse of destruction on everyone in the city: men and women, young and old, including the oxen, the sheep and the donkeys, slaughtering them all" (Joshua 6:21).

The city of Ai met the same fate. Its inhabitants were all slaughtered, twelve thousand of them, "until not one was left alive and none to flee. [...] When Israel had finished killing all the inhabitants of Ai in the open ground, and in the desert where they had pursued them, and when every single one had fallen to the sword, all Israel returned to Ai and slaughtered its remaining population" (8:22–25). Women were not spared. "For booty, Israel took only the cattle and the spoils of this town" (8:27). In the whole land, Joshua "left not one survivor and put every living thing under the curse of destruction, as Yahweh, god of Israel, had commanded" (10:40).

Likewise for the nomadic tribe of Amalekites, the first enemy the Hebrews faced during the Exodus from Egypt and Canaan. In a cynically paradoxical formulation, Yahweh asked Moses: "Write this down in a book to commemorate it, and repeat it over to Joshua, for I shall blot out all memory of Amalek under heaven" (Exodus 17:14). The idea is repeated in Deuteronomy 25:19: "When Yahweh your God has granted you peace from all the enemies surrounding you, in the country given you by Yahweh your God to own as your heritage, you must blot out the memory of Amalek under heaven. Do not forget."

The mission fell to Saul in 1 Samuel 15: "I intend to punish what Amalek did to Israel—laying a trap for him on the way as he was coming up from Egypt. Now, go and crush Amalek; put him under the curse of destruction with all that he possesses. Do not spare him, but kill man and woman, babe and suckling, ox and sheep, camel and donkey." Thus spoke Yahweh Sabaoth, the divinely spiteful, by way of the prophet Samuel. Since Saul spared King Agag "with the best of the sheep and cattle, the fatlings and lambs," Yahweh repudiates him: "I regret having made Saul king, since he has broken his allegiance to me and not carried out my orders." Yahweh withdrew Saul's kingship and Samuel "butchered" Agag ("hewed Agag in pieces," in the *Revised Standard Version*, faithfully translating the Hebrew verb *shsf*).

Despite this theoretically perfect biblical genocide, the Jews never ceased to identify their enemies with Amalekites. Flavius Josephus, writing for the Romans, recognizes them in the Arabs of Idumea. Later, Amalek came to be associated, like his grandfather Esau, with Rome and therefore, from the fourth century onward, with Christianity. The villain of the book of Esther, Haman, is referred to repeatedly as an Agagite, that is, a descendant of the Amalekite king Agag. That is why the hanging of Haman and his ten sons and the massacre of 75,000 Persians are often conflated in Jewish tradition with the extermination of the Amalekites and the brutal execution of their king. The Torah reading on the morning of Purim is taken from the account of the battle against the Amalekites, which ends with the conclusion that "Yahweh will be at war with Amalek generation after generation" (Exodus 17:16).[23]

When the people, under Moses's guidance, settled temporarily in the country of Moab (or Midian) in Transjordania, some married Moabite women, who "invited them to the sacrifices of their gods" (Numbers 25:2). Such abomination required "the vengeance of Yahweh on Midian." (The peoples of Moab and Midian seem here conflated). And so, instructed by Yahweh as always, Moses formed an army and ordered them to "put every [Midianite] male to death." However, the soldiers were guilty of taking "the Midianite women and their little ones captive," instead of slaughtering them. Moses "was enraged with the officers of the army" and rebuked them: "Why have you spared the life of all the women? They were the very ones who [...] caused the Israelites to be unfaithful to Yahweh. [...] So kill all the male children and kill all the women who have ever slept with a man; but spare the lives of the young girls who have never slept with a man, and keep them for yourselves." At the end of the day, "The spoils, the remainder of the booty captured by the soldiers, came to six hundred and seventy-five thousand sheep and goats, seventy-two thousand head of cattle, sixty-one thousand donkeys, and in

---

[23] Elliott Horowitz, *Reckless Rites: Purim and the Legacy of Jewish Violence*, Princeton University Press, 2006, pp. 122–125, 4.

persons, women who had never slept with a man, thirty-two
thousand in all," not to mention "gold, silver, bronze, iron, tin
and lead" (Numbers 31:3–31).

And we would be in error if we believed that the message of
the prophets, most of whom were priests, softens the violence
of the historical books: "For this is the Day of Lord Yahweh
Sabaoth, a day of vengeance when he takes revenge on his foes:
The sword will devour until gorged, until drunk with their
blood," foresees Jeremiah as reprisals against Babylon. For
Yahweh promises through him "an end of all the nations where
I have driven you," which includes Egypt (Jeremiah 46:10–28).
"Yahweh's sword is gorged with blood, it is greasy with fat,"
says Isaiah, on the occasion of "a great slaughter in the land of
Edom" (Isaiah 34:6).

Zechariah prophesies that Yahweh will fight "all the
nations" allied against Israel. In a single day, the whole earth will
become a desert, with the exception of Jerusalem, which will
"stand high in her place." Zechariah seems to have envisioned
what God could do with nuclear weapons: "And this is the
plague with which Yahweh will strike all the nations who have
fought against Jerusalem; their flesh will rot while they are still
standing on their feet; their eyes will rot in their sockets; their
tongues will rot in their mouths." It is only after the carnage that
the world will finally find peace, providing they worship
Yahweh; then "the wealth of all the surrounding nations will be
heaped together: gold, silver, clothing, in vast quantity. [...]
After this, all the survivors of all the nations which have
attacked Jerusalem will come up year after year to worship the
King, Yahweh Sabaoth, and to keep the feast of Shelters. Should
one of the races of the world fail to come up to Jerusalem to
worship the King, Yahweh Sabaoth, there will be no rain for
that one" (Zechariah 14).

The prophetic dream of Israel—nightmare of the nations—
is very clearly a supremacist and imperial project. There is
indeed, in Isaiah, the hope of world peace, when the peoples of
the earth "will hammer their swords into ploughshares and their
spears into sickles. Nation will not lift sword against nation, no
longer will they learn how to make war" (Isaiah 2:4). But that
day will only come when all nations pay homage to Zion. In

those glorious days, says Yahweh to his people in Second Isaiah, kings "will fall prostrate before you, faces to the ground, and lick the dust at your feet," whereas Israel's oppressors will "eat their own flesh [and] will be as drunk on their own blood" (49:23–26); "For the nation and kingdom that will not serve you will perish, and the nations will be utterly destroyed" (60:12); "Strangers will come forward to feed your flocks, foreigners be your ploughmen and vinedressers; but you will be called 'priests of Yahweh' and be addressed as 'ministers of our God.' You will feed on the wealth of nations, you will supplant them in their glory" (61:5–6); "You will suck the milk of nations, you will suck the wealth of kings" (60:16).

Certainly all these past and future genocides perpetrated in the name of Yahweh are imaginary, but the psychological effect produced by their accumulation ad nauseam on the chosen people is not, especially since some are commemorated ritually. It is to celebrate the massacre of seventy-five thousand Persians slaughtered by the Jews in one day that Mordecai, the secondary hero of the book of Esther, "a man held in respect among the Jews, esteemed by thousands of his brothers, a man who sought the good of his people and cared for the welfare of his entire race" (10:3), establishes Purim, a month before Easter. Emmanuel Levinas would have us believe that "Jewish consciousness, formed precisely through contact with this moral hardness, has learned the absolute horror of blood."[24] It's a bit like claiming that the virtual violence of video games will eventually make our children less violent. Was it not on the day of Purim, February 25th, 1994, that Baruch Goldstein massacred with a submachine gun twenty-nine pious Muslims at the tomb of Abraham? Has his grave not become a place of pilgrimage for Orthodox Jews?[25]

---

[24] Emmanuel Levinas, *Difficile Liberté,* quoted in Hervé Ryssen, *Les Espérances planétariennes,* Éditions Baskerville, 2005, p. 308.
[25] Hervé Ryssen, *Les Espérances planétariennes, op. cit.,* p. 301.

The Plunder of the Nations

"Feeding on the wealth of the nations" is the destiny of the Jewish nation, says the prophet (Isaiah 61:6). It is also the way it was first created, for plundering is the essence of the conquest of Canaan, according to Deuteronomy 6:10–12: "When Yahweh has brought you into the country which he swore to your ancestors Abraham, Isaac and Jacob that he would give you, with great and prosperous cities you have not built, with houses full of good things you have not provided, with wells you have not dug, with vineyards and olive trees you have not planted, and then, when you have eaten as much as you want, be careful you do not forget Yahweh who has brought you out of Egypt, out of the place of slave-labor."

Gentiles, Canaanites, or others are no different from their belongings in Yahweh's eyes, and can therefore become the property of Hebrews. "The male and female slaves you have will come from the nations around you; from these you may purchase male and female slaves. As slaves, you may also purchase the children of aliens resident among you, and also members of their families living with you who have been born on your soil; and they will become your property, and you may leave them as a legacy to your sons after you as their perpetual possession. These you may have for slaves; but you will not oppress your brother-Israelites" (Leviticus 25:44–46). Note that, from the historian's point of view, the prohibition proves the practice (there is no need to legislate on something that doesn't exist), and the story of Joseph illustrates that a Jew sold as slave by other Jews was not inconceivable.

While waiting for the fulfillment of their imperial destiny, the chosen people can, even more effectively, exercise their incomparable mastery of monetary mechanisms. One of the revolutionary contributions of biblical religion in the world is the transformation of money from a means of exchange to a means of power and even war. In every civilization that has reached the stage of monetary trade, lending at interest, which makes money a commodity in itself, was seen as a moral perversion and a social danger. Aristotle condemns usury in his *Politics* as the "most unnatural" activity because it gives money the ability to produce itself out of nothing, and thereby take on a quasi-spiritual, supernatural character. Around the same time, Deuteronomy prohibited the practice, but only between Jews: "You may demand interest on a loan to a foreigner, but you must not demand interest from your brother" (23:21).[26] During the Jubilee, every seven years, any creditor must remit his Jewish neighbor's debt. But not the stranger's: "A foreigner you may exploit, but you must remit whatever claim you have on your brother" (15:3). As far as we know, the Yahwist priests were the first to conceive of enslaving entire nations through debt: "If Yahweh your God blesses you as he has promised, you will be creditors to many nations but debtors to none; you will rule over many nations, and be ruled by none" (15:6).

The story of Joseph bringing the Egyptian peasants into debt bondage confirms that the enrichment of Jews by Gentile debt is a biblical ideal. This story is deeply immoral, but quite central in the saga of the chosen people; it guarantees divine blessing on all abuses of power practiced against foreigners. It also illustrates a lesson that Jews have effectively applied throughout their history, from medieval Europe to eighteenth century Russia: the ability to grab money through a monopoly on lending at interest is greatly increased if one first receives from the state authority to collect taxes. The lesson is repeated in the similar story that Flavius Josephus situates in the Hellenistic period (already mentioned in our previous chapter). "As difficult as it may be for the modern reader to accept," remarks Lawrence Wills, "we actually have before us hero legends concerning tax farmers, as if we were reading the Robin Hood legend told from the Sheriff of Nottingham's perspective."[27]

The story of Joseph, and those of Esther and Daniel, offer as Jewish heroes characters who have reached the rank of kings' advisers and intermediaries in the oppression of peoples; the heroes make use of such positions to promote their community.

---

[26] Also Exodus 22:24 and Leviticus 25:35–37.
[27] Lawrence Wills, *Jew in the Court of the Foreign King: Ancient Jewish Court Legends*, Cornell University Press, 1995, p. 189.

The court Jews mentioned in the Bible most often occupy the functions of cupbearer or eunuch, that is, purveyors of wine and women. Second Kings 20:18 informs us that some Judeans served as "eunuchs in the palace of the king of Babylon," eunuchs being generally attached to the harem. "How often," remarks Heinrich Graetz, "have these guardians of the harem, these servants of their master's whims, become in turn masters of their master."[28] If there is one thing possible to a guardian of the harem, it is to introduce the woman of his choice into the prince's bed, as did Mordecai, "attached to the Chancellery" with "two royal eunuchs," with Esther, his niece and perhaps spouse (Esther 2:21).

The Levitic Tyranny

The first victims of Yahweh's violence are the chosen people themselves. Deuteronomy orders the stoning of any parent, son, brother, or wife who "tries secretly to seduce you, saying, 'Let us go and serve other gods,' unknown to you or your ancestors before you. [...] you must show him no pity, you must not spare him or conceal his guilt. No, you must kill him, your hand must strike the first blow in putting him to death and the hands of the rest of the people following. You must stone him to death, since he has tried to divert you from Yahweh your God" (13:7–11). Worse still, if "in one of the towns which Yahweh your God has given you for a home, there are men, scoundrels from your own stock, who have led their fellow-citizens astray, saying, 'Let us go and serve other gods,' hitherto unknown to you [...], you must put the inhabitants of that town to the sword; you must lay it under the curse of destruction—the town and everything in it. You must pile up all its loot in the public square and burn the town and all its loot, offering it all to Yahweh your God. It is to be a ruin for all time, and never rebuilt." For that is "what is right in the eyes of Yahweh your God" (13:13–19).

---

[28] Heinrich Graetz, *History of the Jews,* Jewish Publication Society of America, 1891 (archive.org), vol.1, p. 331.

When some Jews beyond the control of Moses ate with the Moabites, joined in their religious cults, and took women from among them, "Yahweh said to Moses, 'Take all the leaders of the people. Impale them facing the sun, for Yahweh, to deflect his burning anger from Israel'" (Numbers 25:4). When a Hebrew had the gall to appear before Moses with his Midianite wife, Phinehas, grandson of Aaron, "seized a lance, followed the Israelite into the alcove, and there ran them both through, the Israelite and the woman, through the stomach." Yahweh congratulated him for having "the same zeal as I have," and, as a reward, gave "to him and his descendants after him, [...] the priesthood for ever" that is, "the right to perform the ritual of expiation for the Israelites" (25:11–13). Is it not extraordinary that the founding of the Aaronic priesthood (reclaimed by Ezra and the high priests he installed in power) is thus based on a double murder blessed by Yahweh?

The overarching theme of the Bible is the relationship between Yahweh and his people. But according to a critical reading, the Bible is actually the history of the relationship between *the priestly elite speaking for Yahweh* and the Jewish people, who are sometimes submissive, and sometimes rebellious to authority. The Bible itself shows that it is the priests that prevented the Jewish people from establishing any form of alliance with the surrounding peoples, and pushed them to genocidal violence against their neighbors. In the tragedy of Shechem summarized above (Genesis 34:1–29), it is Levi, embodying the priestly authority, who incites the massacre, while Jacob condemns it. Prophets, who claim to have a direct line with God, are priests or spokesmen of priests.

The power of the Levitical elites over the people is based on a system of interpretation of national history that is formidably infallible: whenever misfortune strikes, it is always the fault of the people (or the king) who did not obey God's law (and its priestly guarantors) with enough fervor. After the destruction of Israel by the Assyrian army, the priests base their authority over the kingdom of Judea by proclaiming that Yahweh deprived Israel of victory because the Israelites had betrayed his alliance by "sacrificing on all the high places in the manner of the nations which Yahweh had expelled before them," and

"worshiping idols" (2 Kings 17:11–12). The Assyrian army itself
is "the rod of my anger" (Isaiah 10.5). The argument is the same
after the destruction of Jerusalem by Babylon. The national
tragedy does not imply a superiority of the foreign gods over
Yahweh, which would encourage their adoption. Rather, it is
Yahweh himself who used the Babylonians, after the Assyrians,
to punish the people who betrayed him. The only remedy for
disaster: strengthened loyalty to Yahweh.

The Yahwist lesson is always the same. Each time the
Hebrews begin to sympathize with other nations to the point of
mingling with their religious life (social life being inseparable
from worship), Yahweh punishes them by sending against them
… other nations. The hand of friendship held out by others is a
death trap. He whose friendship you seek is your worst enemy.
This principle in Yahwist ideology encloses the Jewish people in
a cognitive vicious circle, preventing them from learning the
only sensible lesson from their experience: that contacts
promote cultural understanding between peoples, while refusal
of contact generates hostility. According to the Bible, the chosen
people have obligations only toward Yahweh, never toward their
neighbors. And when those neighbors are hostile, their
complaints are irrelevant, since ultimately it is always Yahweh
who sends them against his people when he has decided to
punish them. For two thousand years, Jews have been
constantly reminded by their elites that the persecutions they
suffer are not the result of offensive behavior against Gentiles,
but rather their efforts to live with them in harmony—efforts
that amount to infidelity to God and to their vocation as "a
people apart."

From time to time the people rebel against this devastating
logic. After the capture of Jerusalem by Babylon, Judean
refugees in Egypt, suddenly freed from the Levitical yoke, decide
to worship Ishtar, the "Queen of Heaven," saying that it was
perhaps for having neglected her that their country had been
ravaged. This provokes the wrath of Jeremiah, who, in the name
of Yahweh, threatens them with extermination (Jeremiah 44).
Likewise, doubts gnaw at some communities after the
destruction of Jerusalem by the Romans in 70 CE, as evidenced
by the Jewish literature of this period: "The world which was

made on account of us abides; but we, on account of whom it was made, vanish," some complain in *The Apocalypse of Baruch* (14:19). Or: "If, as you say, you created the world for us, why do not we have what is ours?" (IV Ezra 6:59). Many Jews of Alexandria, Ephesus, and Rome rushed through the exit door offered by Christianity.

The history of the Jews, of course, cannot be reduced to a struggle between the elites and the people; the people are divided, sometimes to the point of civil war, while the elite is ever-changing and subject to rivalries. Nonetheless, the tension between an elite legislating forever in the name of God, and a refractory people, is the fundamental dialectic tension in Jewish history because it is the heart of Jewish collective memory preserved in the Bible. It is inscribed in Jewishness, and internalized by the Jewish community to this day. Every Jew is constantly pressed to identify with the ruling elites, yet resists these elites to some extent. Since biblical times, common sense often prevails among the Jews known as "assimilationists"—the internal enemies of Yahwism. But the mobilizing power of the Yahwist ideology tirelessly triumphs, and with each disaster or threat of disaster, the people lets itself be convinced *en masse* to retreat into its mental fortress. The few dissenting voices are stigmatized as emanating from Jews contaminated by "self-hatred."

Endogamy and Monotheism

When two peoples become neighbors, they face a choice between war and marriage. In the ancient world, marriage required the mutual adoption of each other's gods, or at least their cohabitation in the same household. To marry a woman of another people not only binds one to her relatives, but to her gods as well. This does not pose a problem to the extent that the gods are social beings who tolerate each other. But the god of the Hebrews is a jealous god, who tolerates no other. Yahweh therefore always imposes the choice of war. The command of strict endogamy is justified in the Bible by strict monotheism, and foreign women are held primarily responsible for the apostasy of their husbands; worse, they transmit their gods and religious rites to their children. At the first conquest of Canaan, it was forbidden to marry one's children to the natives, "for your son would be seduced from following me into serving other gods; the wrath of Yahweh would blaze out against you and he would instantly destroy you" (Deuteronomy 7:3–4). To prevent religious contagion, Moses orders, in the name of Yahweh, the extermination of all living beings without distinction in certain conquered towns "so that they may not teach you to do all the detestable things which they do to honor their gods" (20:18). Similarly, during the return from the Exile, on learning that the "survivors" had resorted to the abomination of mixed marriages, and that "the holy race has been contaminated by the people of the country," Ezra makes them promise to "send away all the foreign wives and their children" (Ezra 9:2; 10:3).

Since the alliance between Yahweh and his chosen people is comparable to a marriage, mixed marriages and foreign cults are both considered forms of adultery or prostitution. To worship other gods is like having sex with a foreigner. To dramatize this idea, the prophet Hosea marries a prostitute, "as Yahweh loves the Israelites although they turn to other gods" (Hosea 3:1). Conversely, as Niels Lemche writes, "Intermingling with foreign women means playing with foreign gods, which is the same as breaking the covenant relationship."[29] Keeping the blood pure of any foreign influence is the core of the covenant with Yahweh. When some Hebrews take wives from Moab, it is described, in biblical terms, as: "The people gave themselves over to prostitution with Moabite women. These invited them to the sacrifices of their gods, and the people ate and bowed down before their gods" (Numbers 25:1–2). Moses/Yahweh orders the impalement of the chiefs of the guilty tribes, then the extermination of all Midianites, with the exception of "young girls who have never slept with a man, and keep them for yourselves" (31:18). For the prohibition of intermarriage does not apply to rape and sexual slavery; the well-known principle that Jewishness is transmitted by the mother was originally

---

[29] Niels Peter Lemche, *The Israelites in History and Tradition*, John Knox Press, 1998, p. 110.

prescribed to keep the bastards of these unions from polluting the community.

For a king to marry a foreign princess is a political act that seals an alliance between the kingdoms. Even this is condemned by Yahwists scribes, although in the case of Solomon, the sentence is ambiguous since the seven hundred wives and three hundred concubines attributed to this fictional king, which make him the world champion in all categories, are a sign of his vast influence. However, his foreign wives, "who offered incense and sacrifice to their gods" (1 Kings 11:8), were held responsible for the decline of Solomon and his kingdom when he was old. "His wives swayed his heart to other gods" (11:4), including "Astarte the goddess of the Sidonians, Chemosh the god of Moab, Milcom the god of the Ammonites" (11:33). Similarly, the king of Israel, Ahab son of Omri, is the most despised of the northern kings because he took to wife Jezebel, a Phoenician princess and worshiper of Baal. Under her influence, Ahab "proceeded to serve Baal and worship him. He erected an altar to him in the temple of Baal which he built in Samaria. Ahab also put up a sacred pole [an *Ashera*] and committed other crimes as well, provoking the anger of Yahweh, god of Israel, more than all the kings of Israel his predecessors" (1 Kings 16:31–33).

The command of endogamy is so highly valued in the Bible that it even trumps the prohibition of incest as understood by most cultures. Abraham marries his half-sister Sarah, his father's daughter (and prefers her son to that of his concubine). This allows him, when he goes to Egypt, to pretend that his wife is his sister, so the Pharaoh can requisition her as a concubine, offering Abraham in exchange "flocks, oxen, donkeys, men and women slaves, she-donkeys and camels" (Genesis 12:16). Abraham renews the strategy in the land of Negev. When the king Abimelech learns the truth and confronts Abraham, who responds: "Anyway, she really is my sister, my father's daughter though not my mother's, besides being my wife." Then Abimelech gave back to Abraham his wife, together with "sheep, cattle, men and women slaves" (20:12–14).

This second narrative suffers from improbability insofar as Sara is already old. It is actually a duplicate of the same story told later about Isaac, whose young wife Rebecca was coveted by the same Abimelech, thinking she was Isaac's sister. Seeing through a window "Isaac caressing Rebekah," Abimelech accuses Isaac of misleading him: "What a thing to do to us! One of the people might easily have slept with your wife. We should have incurred guilt, thanks to you" (26:10). It is hard to resist the impression that Isaac, in imitation of his father, uses his wife to extract from these highly moral Philistines a ransom as a debt of honor. The scheme is not unlike the story of Esther, a secret Jew and niece—as well as wife according to some readings—of the influential Jew Mordecai, who uses her to favorably dispose the Persian king toward the Jewish community.

Isaac is less endogamous than his father Abraham, whose marriage to a half-sister remains an isolated case. Isaac receives an Egyptian wife in his youth, but his heirs are the children he will have with Rebecca, the daughter of his cousin Bethuel (whose mother, Milcah, had married his uncle Nahor, according to Genesis 11:29). Rebecca, horrified at the idea that her son Jacob should marry outside of the family, sends him to her brother Laban so he can marry one of Laban's daughters, i.e., his cousin. Jacob marries both Leah and Rachel (Genesis 28). The case of Esau, Jacob's older brother, appears similar: He offends his parents by marrying two Hittite women ("These were a bitter disappointment to Isaac and Rebekah" 26:35), then broadens his efforts and takes to wife his cousin Mahalath, the daughter of his uncle Ishmael (28:9). However, Ishmael is himself of impure lineage, being the son of Abraham and his Egyptian handmaid Hagar. So Esau is excluded from the chosen people and is the ancestor of the Edomites (Genesis 36). This genealogy can only have been invented by a caste of Babylonian exiles carrying inbreeding to an extreme. At the time of the Second Temple that followed their return, marriages between uncle and niece were highly valued, especially among families of priests, who were obsessed with the purity of their blood.

Endogamy is also a characteristic feature of Jewish novels written in the Persian and Hellenistic periods. Let us recall how Tobiah, the son of Tobit, marries his "closest relative," the daughter of his uncle. The angel Raphael informs him that her father Raguel "has no right whatever to refuse you or to betroth her to anyone else. That would be asking for death, as prescribed in the Book of Moses, once he is aware that kinship gives you the pre-eminent right to marry his daughter" (Tobit 6:13).

The puritan revolution of the Maccabees emphasized strict endogamy and, in keeping with Deuteronomic tradition, viewed intermarriage as idolatry. The *Book of Jubilees*, a book of the Hasmonean period, proclaims: "And if there is any man who wishes in Israel to give his daughter or his sister to any man who is of the seed of the Gentiles he shall surely die, and they shall stone him with stones; for he has wrought shame in Israel; and they shall burn the woman with fire, because she has dishonored the name of the house of her father, and she shall be rooted out of Yisrael" (30:7).

It is true that during that same period, Judaism experienced a period of expansion during which many people were converted. In 125 BCE John Hyrcanus conquered the land of Edom and, according to Flavius Josephus, "subdued all the Edomites, and permitted them to stay in that country, if they would circumcise their genitals, and make use of the laws of the Jews; [...] at which time therefore this befell them, that they were hereafter no other than Jews" (*Jewish Antiquities* XIII.9). His son Aristobulus, nicknamed Philhellene, annexed Galilee in 104 BCE, then occupied mostly by Itureans, uniting Itureans to Edomites "by the bond of the circumcision of their genitals" (XIII.11). Alexander Jannaeus, brother and heir of Aristobulus, was less successful in his attempt to convert the Hellenistic cities of Samaria, Gaza, and Pela in Transjordan; so he "slew the inhabitants of Gaza; yet they were not of cowardly hearts, but opposed those that came to slay them, and slew as many of the Jews" (XIII.13). These policies of forced conversions came from Hellenized rulers viewed as "godless" by contemporary pious Jews. Moreover, they did not contradict the principle of inbreeding, because the converted Jews were still considered second-class, while native Jewish society remained hostile to their marital integration, especially among the elites.

Modern Jewish historians writing for Gentiles have spread the idea that ancient Judaism was a proselytizing faith, but this idea is based on a misinterpretation of the data. Ancient Jewish chronicles have not retained the name of even a single missionary, and Jewish literature on the conversion of the Gentiles is limited to the one that will take place at the end of time, when the world will recognize the superiority of the Jews. The evidence does, however, confirm the existence of "Judaizers" who approached Jewish communities and attended their meetings; all belonged to the elite, so that if they were to marry within the Jewish community, they would play a particular role. Yet even this practice was condemned by Orthodox rabbis. At the end of the second century, Rabbi Hiyya the Great comments: "Do not have faith in a proselyte until twenty-four generations have passed, because the inherent evil is still within him."[30]

---

[30] Quoted in Kevin MacDonald, *A People That Shall Dwell Alone: Judaism as a Group Evolutionary Strategy*, Praeger, 1994, kindle 2013, k. 3122–3231.

Chapter 3

THE PRINCE OF THIS WORLD

> "I shall shake all the nations, and the
> treasures of all the nations will flow in,
> and I shall fill this Temple with glory,
> says Yahweh Sabaoth. Mine is the silver,
> mine the gold! Yahweh Sabaoth declares."
>
> Haggai 2:7–8

Death and Culture in the Antique World

The Bible is a collection of disparate, stylistically varied texts from various epochs. Consequently, the biblical notions concerning the fate of the deceased in the hereafter are multiple, heterogeneous, and generally difficult to reconcile. There is nevertheless a fundamental Yahwist conception, of which the others are only deviations: the Hebrew Bible does not grant man any form of afterlife worthy of the name: man is dust and returns to dust (Genesis 3:19). "My spirit cannot be indefinitely responsible for human beings, who are only flesh" (Genesis 6:3). Yahweh has nothing to do with the dead "whom you remember no more, cut off as they are from your protection" (Psalms 88:5). Genesis 2:7 plays on the semantic link between man, *adam,* and earth, *adamah* : "Elohim shaped *adam,* dust of *adamah.*"

Admittedly this denial of the afterlife in Yahwist literature is not absolute: there is Sheol. The Bible uses this term to designate a dark and damp region underground, where the dead, good as well as bad, subsist only as impotent shadows in an unconscious sleep. While Sheol represents a subterranean place, it is above all a negative concept that approaches the idea of nothingness (unthinkable by definition); death in Sheol is virtual annihilation. In fact, the term appears only five times in the Pentateuch: four times in Genesis, as a conventional name for death,[1] and once in Numbers, concerning Korah and two

---

[1] Genesis 37:35; 42:38; 44:29; 44:31.

hundred and fifty notables, "renowned men" who rebelled against the authority of Moses and Aaron: "The ground split apart under their feet, the earth opened its mouth and swallowed them, their families, all Korah's people and all their property. They went down alive to Sheol with all their belongings. The earth closed over them and they disappeared in the middle of the community" (Numbers 16:31–33). The term here has only a narrative function, since no subterranean afterlife is granted to these men after their living burial.

Some will object that the Torah has two terms to designate the immortal spirit: *nephesh* and *ruah*. This is a misunderstanding. The Hebrew word *nephesh* is translated in the Septuagint by the Greek *psyche*, and in English by "soul." But in reality it designates a "living being," that is to say, a body that life has not yet left; it sometimes translates simply as "life." The term is intimately related to blood in the food prohibitions of Leviticus 17. "According to the primeval Jewish view," writes Jewish historian Josef Kastein, "the blood was the seat of the soul," which is why it is forbidden to consume the blood of animals. The Hebrew word *ruah*, translated as *pneuma* in the Septuagint, and generally as "spirit" in English, means "wind," "breath," "respiration," and thus also designates life. Thus there is no notion of immortal soul in the formula of Genesis 2:7: "Yahweh God shaped man from the soil of the ground and blew the breath of life [*ruah*] into his nostrils, and man became a living being [*nephesh*]."

The metaphysical materialism of the biblical worldview is overlooked or denied by Reform Judaism, and mentioning it is now considered bad manners. But such was not the case a century ago, when Sigmund Freud wrote in *Moses and Monotheism* (1939) about the Egyptians: "No other people of antiquity has done so much to deny death, has made such careful provision for an after-life [...]. The early Jewish religion, on the other hand, had entirely relinquished immortality; the possibility of an existence after death was never mentioned in any place."[2]

---

2 Sigmund Freud, *Moses and Monotheism*, Hogarth Press, 1939 (archive.org), pp. 33-34.

From the Egyptian point of view, such a denial of life after death makes Yahwism an anti-Osirian religion, that is to say, a Sethian anti-religion. To understand this, we must consider the details of the death and resurrection of Osiris, related by Plutarch. Osiris is the first king of Egypt. Scheming to take his place, his younger brother Seth discreetly takes the measure of his body and commands the making of a sumptuously decorated coffin. Through deceit he induces Osiris to lie down, closes the lid, seals it with lead, and throws the coffin into the Nile, which carries Osiris as far as the Mediterranean. Isis, aided by her sister Nephthys, goes in search of her husband's coffin. After many attempts, she discovers the body, which she brings back to Egypt and hides. Seth discovers the hiding place and cuts the body into fourteen pieces, which he disseminates throughout the land of Egypt. The faithful Isis then transforms herself into a kite and sets off in search of the scattered limbs of her husband. She finds all the pieces except one: his virile member, which had been eaten by fish. Isis makes a simulacrum to replace it, reconstitutes the body, and brings it back to life through lamentations and prayers.

The story of Osiris is a funerary myth; it conveys a vision of the destiny of man after death. Seth is the personification of death in its destructive corporeal aspect, while Osiris is the personification of the spiritual victory over death. As the first king and first death in history, Osiris is also the king of the dead. Each Pharaoh inherits his destiny and, when he dies, becomes Osiris, king of the Other World, even as his son inherits the royal throne on earth, corresponding to the role of Horus. In texts carved on the inner walls of the pyramids, which are nothing more than gigantic and sophisticated burial mounds, the divinities of the Egyptian pantheon are grouped around their sovereign, Osiris, to assist him in his new life in the grave. The dead pharaoh inherits royalty in the Other World: "May you rise up, protected and provided for like a god, equipped with the attributes of Osiris on the throne of the First of the Occidentals, to do what he did among the glorified, imperishable stars."[3]

---

[3] Jan Assmann, *Mort et Au-delà dans l'Égypte ancienne*, Rocher, 2003, pp. 87, 186.

Progressively, these royal texts became more democratic. The Texts of the Sarcophagi, placed in the coffins of the notables of the Middle Kingdom, were inspired by them. Then in the New Kingdom appeared the Books of the Dead, papyri placed in the tombs of ordinary deceased. They describe Osiris sitting in the Hall of Judgment, surrounded by an arena of divine judges. A scale was placed before the deceased in order to carry out the weighing of his heart; the other plate of the scale was occupied by the pen of Maat, goddess of Truth and Immutable Justice. If the balance weighed against him, the dead man's soul was forever excluded from eternal happiness. All justified souls were admitted into the community of gods and spirits, modeled on the pattern of earthly society. Osiris, we must note, does not judge the dead; he only presides over their judgment. The conscience of each one is his own judge. From the Middle Kingdom onward, as documented by Bojana Mojsov, Osiris "was the voice that spoke to every heart, the undisputed sovereign of the dead whom everyone had to encounter when the hour had struck. As a god who shared human suffering and death, Osiris would know the human heart and understand the trials and tribulations of earthly life."[4] While Osiris reigns over the dead, Isis takes care of the living, and assists them on their final journey, provided they have been initiated.

The motif of the missing and then reconstituted penis indicates that Osiris belongs to mankind, yet is an exception to the rule that the dead do not procreate. Though dead, Osiris conceives Horus with Isis. Osiris is an exceptional and paradigmatic dead man. The same is true of most of the mythical characters held to rule over the Other World: they come from the world of the living, they are the divine deceased. In the Sumerian epic of Gilgamesh, the mythical king who quested for immortality during his lifetime was promoted to "Grand Judge of the Dead" after his death.[5] In India, Yama is the first man who "has traveled to heavenly heights [...] and

---

[4] Bojana Mojsov, *Osiris: Death and Afterlife of a God,* Wiley-Blackwell, 2005, p. 46.
[5] Jean Bottéro, *L'Épopée de Gilgamesh, le grand homme qui ne voulait pas mourir,* Gallimard, 1992, p. 34.

shows the way to the multitude," according to the Rig-Veda (X.14). In Greece, Dionysus, who is the same figure as Osiris according to Herodotus (II.41), passed through the human experience of birth, suffering, and violent death before becoming a divinity of death, whose worship aims to ensure a good afterlife. Odin, the Germanic god of the dead, is described by the Scandinavian mythographers as a magician warrior who, having died hanging from a tree, became "Lord of the Dead," reigning in Valhalla over "all men who perish by arms."[6] One could multiply the examples of heroes or mythical earthly kings who have become kings of the dead, generally after a sacrificial death.[7] But none has had a radiance comparable to Osiris, probably because no great civilization was as preoccupied with death as Egypt.

The Egyptian vision of the afterlife exerted great influence on surrounding civilizations. Greek authors readily admitted this debt, and Herodotus even knew that the cults celebrated at Eleusis were of Egyptian origins.[8] Hellenism, which radiated outward from Alexandria beginning in the third century BCE, owes much to Osirism, as does the later phenomenon of Neoplatonism. The "mysteries of Osiris," an initiatic cult described by Iamblichus about 320 CE, competed with Christianity in popularity. Apuleius, a second-century Roman author of Berber origin, gives us an encrypted summary in his loosely autobiographical novel *Metamorphoses (or The Golden Ass)*. Pursuing an interest in magic, the hero, Lucius, is turned into an ass—the symbol of Seth, symbolizing a world of crime and debauchery. By praying to the "divine Mother" Isis, he recovers his human shape. He then devotes his life to the goddess and is initiated into her Mysteries, described as "a voluntary death" by which one can be "born again." Isis promises Lucius a happy afterlife, "when, having passed through the allotted space of your life, you descend to the realms beneath," and, "dwelling in the Elysian fields, (you) shall frequently adore me whom you

---

[6] Snorri Sturluson, *Histoire des rois de Norvège, première partie*, Gallimard, 2000, pp. 61–63.

[7] Bruce Lincoln, *Death, War, and Sacrifice: Studies in Ideology and Practice*, University of Chicago Press, 1991.

[8] George Foucart, *Les mystères d'Éleusis*, Picard, 1914 (archive.org), pp. 46, 253.

now see, and shall there behold me shining amidst the darkness of Acheron."

According to an ancient theory that had fallen out of favor but is now returning to the forefront of religious anthropology, man's struggle against death is the source of religious rituals and myths.[9] For the Egyptologist Jan Assmann, "death is the origin and cradle of culture," for culture is the effort of man to survive death, individually and collectively. Its first achievements were devoted to representations of immortality and to symbolic exchanges between the world of the living and the world of the dead.[10] According to the most reasonable hypothesis, prehistoric cave art was a means of communicating with the underworld of the dead. Prehistoric megaliths, the earliest stone architecture, were also houses for the dead; and images were probably first fashioned to memorialize the dead. Art stems from the desire to make visible the invisible. It is in this light that we must understand the Deuteronomic prohibition: "You shall not make yourself a carved image or any likeness of anything in heaven above or on earth beneath or in the waters under the earth" (Exodus 20:4).

Drama, epic, and myths are also born from funerary rites and the need to keep the dead alive. The majority of myths and folktales have as their central theme the bond between a mortal and an invisible power. This is why the highest ideal of love is found in myths of the Other World. The myth of Orpheus and Eurydice, associated with the Greek mystical current of Orphism, structurally resembles the myth of Osiris and Isis: Orpheus the king, driven to despair by the death of his beloved wife, travels through hell to find her, rescue her, and bring her back to life; in the version popularized by Virgil and Ovid, he fails. In the myth of Demeter and Persephone, a mother goes in search of her daughter who has been abducted by Hades, but only succeeds in bringing her back for part of the year. Love that survives death, and to some extent triumphs over it, is one

---

[9] e.g., Numa-Denis Fustel de Coulanges, *The Ancient City: A Study of the Religion, Law, and Institutions of Greece and Rome* (1864), Dover, 2012.
[10] Jan Assmann, *Mort et Au-delà dans l'Égypte ancienne*, Rocher, 2003, p. 17.

of the most prized narrative themes of ancient culture; it takes many forms, ranging from sacred myths to ghost stories (one of which, narrated around 130 CE by Phlegon of Tralles, inspired Goethe's ballad "The Bride of Corinth").

Biblical Materialism

Unlike the Egyptian, Babylonian, Persian, Greek, or Roman traditions, the Hebrew religion is hostile to any imaginary form of the hereafter. In the Hebrew Bible, one would search in vain for the idea that the dying man will meet his Creator: the life of each of the patriarchs ends simply by mentioning their place of burial. About Jacob, it is said that, "breathing his last, he was gathered to his people" (Genesis 49:33), but nothing suggests here anything more than a conventional euphemism. Jacob, in any case, does not join Yahweh. In fact, Yahweh does not seem to reside in any other place than the earthly Jerusalem Temple. Reflecting a Sethian vision of life and death, the Judaic tradition knows nothing of the funerary myths so popular in other cultures, whose heroes explore the Other World.

Hope of a better life and fear of divine retribution in the hereafter are absent from the Bible. When, in Isaiah 38, King Hezekiah "fell ill and was at the point of death," he supplicates Yahweh to lengthen his physical life, not to welcome his spirit. "I have heard your prayer and seen your tears," Yahweh answers. "I shall cure you: in three days' time you will go up to the Temple of Yahweh. I shall add fifteen years to your life" (38:5). The Song of Hezekiah that follows clearly states that Sheol holds no promise of any real life and that it is not even under the rule of Yahweh. Once dead, Hezekiah laments, "I shall never see Yahweh again in the land of the living." "For Sheol cannot praise you, nor Death celebrate you; those who go down to the pit can hope no longer in your constancy. The living, the living are the ones who praise you, as I do today" (38:11–19).

We note in passing that biblical materialism goes together with the absence of any transcendent conception of the complementarity of the sexes. In the Bible, the male-female relationship is entirely absorbed in the conjugal and the parental, that is, the social realm. Yahweh does not say to Adam and Eve, "Let love open your hearts and unite your souls," nor anything of the kind, but instead, "Be fruitful, multiply, fill the earth and subdue it" (Genesis 1:28). Such an implicit devaluation of Eros, elsewhere celebrated as potentially magical, initiatory, or mystical, puts a damper on one of the most beautiful promises of the human experience. This is in turn, of course, related to the injunction of endogamy, since the transcendence of Eros is one of the foundations of exogamy. Consanguinity is not conducive to rapturous infatuation.

The so-called polytheistic peoples place their fundamental hopes in an otherworldly Promised Land. It may be represented as a remote island, a high mountain, a subterranean or underwater world, but the point is that it is not accessible to mortals, to fleshly beings, except for the handful of mythical heroes who have ventured there and come back alive. This otherworldly Paradise is often endowed with a miraculous spring or a "tree of life," that provides eternal life and youth. It is Mag Mell, "the Plain of Happiness" where we remain young and beautiful, in Irish mythology; or the "World of the Living, where there is no death, no lack, no sin."[11] No such hope is given by Yahweh to his people. The Promised Land of the Jews is an accessible geographical place situated between the Nile and the Euphrates; it is a destiny that is exclusively terrestrial and collective. Yahwism has focused all his people's hope on this earth, where, obviously, neither milk nor honey really flows. After the Jealous God and the Chosen People, the Promised Land is the third pillar of biblical Judaism.

In fact, the Yahwist scribes have taken the universal mythic theme of the blessed afterlife for the virtuous dead and turned it on its head; they have transferred this paradise (*Pardès*, the Garden) and its tree of life, the future hope of each man, into a past lost forever for all mankind. And there they have staged the drama introducing into the world the double scourge of death and labor; for death in their eyes bears no promise, and labor

---

[11] Laurent Guyénot, *La Mort féerique. Anthropologie du merveilleux (XIIe-XVe siècle)*, Gallimard, 2011, p. 155.

produces no spiritual merit. It is only in punishment of his transgression in the Garden that Yahweh declares to Adam: "By the sweat of your face will you earn your food, until you return to the ground, as you were taken from it. For dust you are and to dust you shall return" (Genesis 3:19). By the same spirit of contradiction, the serpent, associated throughout the Near East with the chthonian divinities but also with revealed or intuitive knowledge (the *gnosis* of the Greeks), is likewise the object of an inversion: when it offers to the first humans the means of acquiring knowledge and to "be like gods" (Genesis 3:5), it borrows the language of initiatory mysteries; but the Bible presents the serpent as a liar.

Yahweh is hardly a god, if we define a god as a creature of the Other World. He is heard strolling in the Garden of Eden (Genesis 3:8), but that's because the Garden is an earthly place, just like the Promised Land. Yahweh is more a king than a god, which is precisely why the biblical Levites are always in conflict with the Judean and Israeli kings. According to the Levites, Yahweh alone, ideally, should be king (an invisible king speaking through his appointed ministers); human kings are tolerated as long as they strictly conform to Yahweh's will (that is, to the Levites' command).

The Yahwist denial of the afterlife is linked to the Egyptophobia that permeates the Torah. But it is also historically linked to the rejection of Baal, who was for the inhabitants of Syria what Osiris was for the Egyptians: both god of fertility and lord of the dead. This is why the persistence of the cult of Baal is associated in the Bible with necromancy: "The history of the ancient Israelite conceptions of afterlife is closely related to the struggle between Yahwism and Baalism," Klass Spronk explains. The absence of any speculation on the afterlife in the Hebrew Bible is due "to the fear of becoming entangled in the Canaanite religious ideas about life and death."[12]

Nevertheless, these religious ideas seem very much alive among Hebrews resisting Levitical orthodoxy. It is said that the

---

[12] Klass Spronk, *Beatific Afterlife in Ancient Israel and in the Ancient Near East,* Verlag Butzon & Bercker, 1986, pp. 344–345.

Israelites worshiped and offered sacrifices to a bronze serpent called Nehushtan, supposedly built by Moses, until Hezekiah "smashed" it (2 Kings 18:4). "They committed themselves to serve Baal-Peor, and ate sacrifices made to lifeless gods," we read in Psalm 106:28. The prophet Isaiah condemns those who "consult ghosts and wizards that whisper and mutter" or "the dead on behalf of the living" (8:19). Yahweh chastises his people for "constantly provoking me to my face by sacrificing in gardens, burning incense on bricks, living in tombs, spending the night in dark corners" (65:3–4). Deuteronomy expressly forbids the activity of "soothsayer, augur or sorcerer, weaver of spells, consulter of ghosts or mediums, or necromancer. For anyone who does these things is detestable to Yahweh your God" (18:11–12). Leviticus confirms: "Do not have recourse to the spirits of the dead or to magicians; they will defile you. I, Yahweh, am your God" (19:31). Whoever breaks this rule must be put to death (20:6–7 and 27).[13] In the eyes of the historian, the prohibition proves the practice; all these passages leave no doubt about the reality of the cults of the dead condemned in derogatory terms by the priests and prophets of Yahweh. These practices included offerings of food to the dead, incubation on graves, and other means of communicating with the hereafter.

According to a likely etymology, "religion" (from Latin *religare*, "to bind") serves to bind man to the transcendent. It holds him upright by pulling him heavenward. Man therefore exists in vertical tension between the natural and supernatural worlds, between his biological destiny (survival through progeny) and his spiritual destiny (survival through death). Yahweh is the god who cut this vertical bond and turned man's attention exclusively toward the material world. This fundamentally materialistic nature of ancient Hebraism has often been pointed out by historians of religion: the rewards promised by Yahweh to those who "fear" him are entirely material—to be "full of days," to have numerous offspring and a great fortune. Man's only survival is through generation, or blood descent,

---

[13] Deuteronomy 26:14 is also generally interpreted as a condemnation of offerings to the dead. Read Susan Niditch, *Ancient Israelite Religion*, Oxford University Press, 1997.

according to the Torah. This explains the asymmetry between the myth of Osiris and its biblical reflection in the story of Cain and Abel: it is not Abel's soul that suffers, but rather his blood "crying out to God from the ground" (Genesis 4:10). Nor is there any resurrection, since Seth-Yahweh is the god of death—meaning annihilation, not resurrection. Therefore the assassinated Abel must be "replaced" by a third offspring of Adam and Eve.

Circumcision reinforces this primacy of the physical. God said to Abraham: "You for your part must keep my covenant, you and your descendants after you, generation after generation. This is my covenant which you must keep between myself and you, and your descendants after you: every one of your males must be circumcised. You must circumcise the flesh of your foreskin, and that will be the sign of the covenant between myself and you. As soon as he is eight days old, every one of your males, generation after generation, must be circumcised, including slaves born within the household or bought from a foreigner not of your descent. Whether born within the household or bought, they must be circumcised. My covenant must be marked in your flesh as a covenant in perpetuity. The uncircumcised male, whose foreskin has not been circumcised—that person must be cut off from his people: he has broken my covenant" (Genesis 17:9–14). Circumcision, as "the sign of the covenant," perfectly symbolizes the unspiritual nature of Yahwism. As a mark in the flesh somehow transmitted from father to son, it is like a superimposed genetic trait, a Yahwist gene. Spinoza was on the mark when he wrote: "I attribute such value to the sign of circumcision, that it is the only thing that I esteem capable of assuring an eternal existence to this nation."

Certainly, in the Hellenistic period, Greek dualism infiltrated the so-called Jewish "wisdom literature," which features the voice of Sophia, sometimes assimilated to the Logos. Thus, the Book of Wisdom, written in Greek in Alexandria in the first century BCE, asserts that "God created human beings to be immortal," and criticizes those who "do not believe in a reward for blameless souls" (2:22–23). But such texts are the exceptions confirming the rule. They form part of the brief parenthesis of Hellenistic Judaism, which was vigorously repressed by

Talmudism and would only be saved from oblivion by Christian copyists. And even within this Hellenistic Judaism, the materialist viewpoint prevailed. According to Ecclesiastes, "The living are at least aware that they are going to die, but the dead know nothing whatever. No more wages for them, since their memory is forgotten. [...] there is neither achievement, nor planning, nor science, nor wisdom in Sheol where you are going" (9:5–10). In fact, "the fate of humans and the fate of animals is the same: as the one dies, so the other dies; both have the selfsame breath. The human is in no way better off than the animal—since all is futile. Everything goes to the same place, everything comes from the dust, everything returns to the dust" (3:19–20).

The book of Job conveys the same message: there will be no hoped-for consolation when Job's suffering finally ends. "If man once dead could live again, I would wait in hope, every day of my suffering, for my relief to come" (Job 14:14).[14] Alas! "There is always hope for a tree: when felled, it can start its life again; its shoots continue to sprout. [...]. But a human being? He dies, and dead he remains, breathes his last, and then where is he? [...] A human being, once laid to rest, will never rise again, the heavens will wear out before he wakes up, or before he is roused from his sleep" (14:7–12). As the only reward for his fidelity to Yahweh, Job gets a 140 year reprieve on earth, numerous offspring, "fourteen thousand sheep, six thousand camels, a thousand yoke of oxen and a thousand she-donkeys" (42:12).

It is true that between the first century BCE and the first century CE, the idea of the "resurrection" of the dead made its entry into Maccabean literature, written in Greek for the greater glory of the Hasmonean dynasty founded by the Maccabees. The Greek word *anistanai* literally means "to rise, awaken, get up," and *anastasis* means awakening. It is therefore the opposite of "to lie down/fall asleep," the conventional Hebrew euphemism evoking the death of kings ("he fell asleep with his ancestors," 1 Kings 14:31, 15:24, and 16:6, or 2 Kings 14:29),

---

[14] According to a more accurate translation than the *Jerusalem Bible*, too ambiguous here.

while the Greek texts prefer *koimao*, also "fall asleep" (as in the case of the stoned Stenus of Acts 7:60). The notion of resurrection was applied to the horribly tortured martyrs of the resistance against the Seleucid emperor Antiochus. Then it was extended to all mankind and postponed till the end of time in the book of Daniel: "Of those who are sleeping in the Land of Dust, many will awaken, some to everlasting life, some to shame and everlasting disgrace. Those who are wise will shine as brightly as the expanse of the heavens, and those who have instructed many in uprightness, as bright as stars for all eternity" (12:2–3). Such a vision is taken directly from the Greco-Roman ideal of the hero, right down to its vocabulary. The transfiguration of the good dead into a "body of light" is a common religious motif in Hellenistic culture and beyond. But the rabbinic imagination will mostly ignore that aspect, and rather stick to the idea of the coming back to life of the physical corpse out of its tomb, with its limbs reconstituted. In such a grossly materialistic expectation, there is no need, and hardly any space, for an immortal soul. Besides, even the resurrection at the end of the world has always remained somewhat marginal within the rabbinic tradition, which accepts the authority of the book of Daniel, but rejects the books of Maccabees. In the twelfth century, the great Maimonides evokes the "resurrection of the dead" at the end of time, in the last of his thirteen articles of faith, but this belief has never been developed in the Talmud.

Eventually, by another of these inversions, which are the trademark of Judaism, after the birth of Christianity, Talmudic rabbinism adopted by imitation the belief in the immortality of the soul, but in a restrictive form: only Jews have a divine soul, the soul of Gentiles being "equivalent to that of animals" (*Midrasch Schir Haschirim*). If "God created the *akums* [non-Jews] in the form of men" rather than beasts, says the Talmud, it is "in honor of the Jews. The akums were created only to serve the Jews day and night without being able to leave their service. It would not be appropriate for a Jew to be served by an animal; instead, it should be by an animal with a human form" (*Sepher*

Midrasch Talpioth).[15] There were always Jewish scholars to defend
the immortality of the soul in a less polemical form, but they still
borrowed it from Christianity. Here is what Jewish historian
Heinrich Graetz said of one of them, Joseph Albo, a native of
Soria in Spain in the first half of the fifteenth century: "It is a
remarkable fact that Albo, who thought that he was developing
his religio-philosophical system exclusively in the native spirit of
Judaism, placed at its head a principle of indubitably Christian
origin; so powerfully do surroundings affect even those who
exert themselves to throw off such influence. The religious
philosopher of Soria propounded as his fundamental idea that
salvation was the whole aim of man in this life, and that Judaism
strongly emphasized this aspect of religion." On the other hand,
Albo is fully Jewish when he gives obedience to 613 religious
prescriptions as a recipe for eternal happiness.[16]

Finally, when in the eighteenth century Moses Mendelssohn
defended belief in the immortality of the soul—a necessary
condition for the elevation of humanity according to him—he
would in no way rely on the Jewish tradition. Instead he
produced a dialogue in the style of Plato, entitled *Phaedo or the
Immortality of the Soul* (1767).

Biblical versus Heroic Cultures

One of the most important aspects of man's relationship to his
dead is hero worship. No better definition has been given of the
hero than Lewis Farnell's: "The hero in the Greek religious
sense is a person whose virtue, influence, or personality was so
powerful in his lifetime or through the peculiar circumstances of
his death that his spirit after death is regarded as of supernatural
power, claiming to be reverenced and propitiated."[17] Basically, a
hero is a man to whom a community acknowledges its debt, and
worshipping the hero is the way it pays off its debt. There are as
many types of heroes as types of debts. A heroic cult can be

---

[15] André Gaillard, *Les Racines judaïques de l'antisémtisme,* AMG Éditions, 2012, p. 69.
[16] Heinrich Graetz, *History of the Jews,* Jewish Publication Society of America, 1891
(archive.org), vol. 4, p. 240.
[17] Lewis Richard Farnell, *Greek Hero Cults and Ideas of Immortality* (1921) Adamant
Media Co., 2005, p. 343.

born directly from popular fervor or from an official institution, such as the oracle of Delphi in Greece or the Senate in Rome.

Greece is the heroic civilization par excellence. Heroic cults can be traced back to the birth of the *polis* in the eighth century. They persisted during the Hellenistic period and continued thereafter.[18] At the time the Gospels were written, Carla Antonaccio writes, Greece was "saturated with heroes."[19] And it was not just Greece: the divinized dead exist in all traditional cultures, and certainly throughout the Mediterranean.

Heroes embody their societies' contradictions and traumas, and open the way for transcending them. Every heroic legend affirms human freedom in its dialectical relationship with divine power. Heroism is a humanism insofar as it glorifies the man who surpasses his limits, transgresses the established human rules, and sometimes even goes so far as to defy the gods. That is why the heroic is intimately linked to the tragic. But heroism is also the affirmation of the presence of the divine in the human, which is why the heroic paradigm is the cloth from which myth is woven. By the will of the gods, the hero has escaped death-as-annihilation, and various versions of his legend present different narrative representations of that victory: resurrection (he "wakes up" after falling "asleep"); transfiguration (his body is supernaturally transformed); or simply ascension (he is miraculously transported to the hereafter). The mythic vision is always paradoxical, since it affirms that the dead are alive.

The heroic ideology implies that certain beings are not only the children of their parents, but also possess something extra, a supplement of soul, that comes to them from a special bond with divinity. This bond is often understood as adoptive: the hero is the twice-born man whose second birth is by the grace of a god. But the legendary process, working backwards, often brings the miraculous back to the conception of the hero. His connection with the divinity, which distinguishes him from ordinary men, is then imagined as genetic: it is the god himself

---

[18] Christopher Jones, *New Heroes in Antiquity: From Achilles to Antinoos*, Harvard University Press, 2010.
[19] Carla Antonaccio, *An Archaeology of Ancestors: Tomb Cult and Hero Cult in Early Greece*, Rowman and Littlefield, 1995, p. 1.

who conceived the hero with a mortal. The term "son of god" thus becomes a synonym of "demigod" in Greek mythography since Hesiod. Myth-making can go one step further and make the hero a god temporarily descended among men.

Quite logically, the Hebrew Bible ignores the religious concept of the immortal hero, with a single exception: Elijah, who is seen by his disciple Elisha carried in a "chariot of fire drawn by horses of fire" and "ascending to the heavens in a whirlwind," to never reappear again (2 Kings 2:11). But the classical motif of the hero transfigured by death, resplendent with light, is here clearly atrophied, a mere fossil or residue of heroic ideology covered by biblical antiheroism.

We also find traces of a belief in immortality in the mention of a cult on Samuel's tomb, to which Saul resorts, in order to have the prophet's ghost "rise from the earth" and "disclose the future" (1 Samuel 28:3–19). This episode recalls Ulysses conjuring up the spirit of the clairvoyant Tiresias in the *Odyssey* (Song XI). But the biblical author has covered this story with reprobation: not only has Saul already been condemned by Yahweh at this stage, but the priestess attached to the tomb of Samuel (pejoratively termed a sorceress) only bends to his demand against her will.

It is significant that both Elijah and Samuel are heroes from the northern kingdom of Israel. The tomb of Samuel in Shiloh was a famous place of worship and pilgrimage. All the burial places of the judges mentioned in the book of Judges, whose references hint at their importance as religious sanctuaries, are also located in the North.[20] Samaria also hosts Joseph's tomb, as well as the well of Jacob known to Jesus (John 4:6), located precisely where Jacob's bones were buried according to Joshua 24:32. This is evidence that before the usurpation of Israel's cultural heritage by the Yahwist priests of Judea, the people of Israel worshiped their heroic dead, and that such rites still survived in the North despite prohibition by the Jerusalem priesthood.

---

[20] Mario Liverani, *Israel's History and the History of Israel*, Routledge, 2007, p. 410.

There are also in the Bible residual stories of heroes being conceived by gods. The most obvious case is the *nephilim* of Genesis 6, those giants conceived by the "sons of the gods" with the "daughters of men." Who are "the heroes of the past, those famous men"? This passage is evidently an echo of the "fortunate heroes" mentioned by Hesiod in *Works and Days* (172). What is therefore significant is that the passage seems written expressly to deny their immortality, since Yahweh reacts to these hybrid unions by proclaiming: "My spirit cannot be indefinitely responsible for human beings, who are only flesh; let the time allowed each be a hundred and twenty years" (6:3).

The biblical redactors integrated other legendary narratives of supernaturally conceived heroes, but they did so in a demythologized and satirical fashion. One example is the story of Samson—another hero of the North—a sort of Hercules capable of defeating a thousand men with the "jawbone of a donkey" (Judges 15:15). An "angel of Yahweh" announces to Samson's future mother, the wife of Manoah: "You are barren and have had no child, but you are going to conceive and give birth to a son." The wife goes to find her husband to tell him of this visit from a "man of God [...] who looked like the Angel of God, so majestic was he." Suspicious as any husband would be in such circumstances, Manoah asks to see the stranger, and when his wife, visited again, calls him to introduce him to her visitor, Manoah asks him: "Are you the man who spoke to this woman?" ("speaking" sounds like a euphemism). Manoah then invites him to share a meal, "for Manoah did not know that this was the Angel of Yahweh" (13:3–15).

The conception of Isaac, son of Abraham and Sarah, is strangely similar. Again, it is hard to resist the impression that we are dealing here with a parody of Greek nativities of demigods. Abraham is sitting near his tent in the middle of the day when he saw a noble man and his two companions standing by. He greets them respectfully: "'My lord,' he said, 'if I find favour with you, please do not pass your servant by. Let me have a little water brought, and you can wash your feet and have a rest under the tree. Let me fetch a little bread and you can refresh yourselves before going further, now that you have come in your servant's direction.' They replied, 'Do as you say.'

Abraham hurried to the tent and said to Sarah, 'Quick, knead three measures of our best flour and make loaves.' Then, running to the herd, Abraham took a fine and tender calf and gave it to the servant, who hurried to prepare it. Then taking curds, milk and the calf which had been prepared, he laid all before them, and they ate while he remained standing near them under the tree. 'Where is your wife Sarah?' they asked him. 'She is in the tent,' he replied. Then his guest said, 'I shall come back to you next year, and then your wife Sarah will have a son'" (Genesis 18:1–10).

We see here Abraham offering hospitality to a powerful man, and the man proposing to return the favor by conceiving with Sarah a son for Abraham, knowing the couple to be sterile. Such a reading is not far-fetched, since a little further, Judah asks his son Onan to sleep with his sister-in-law Tamar "to maintain your brother's line" (Genesis 38:8). It is only later in Isaac's conception story that the guest is identified with Yahweh, and his companions with "angels" (*malachim*): "Yahweh treated Sarah as he had said, and did what he had promised her. Sarah conceived and bore Abraham a son in his old age, at the time God had promised" (21:1–2).

Meanwhile, the very same two "angels" were sent to Sodom and received hospitality from Lot, Abraham's nephew. Hearing of it, "the men of Sodom, both young and old, all the people without exception" wanted to seize them, saying to Lot: "Send them out to us so that we can have intercourse with them" (19:4–5). To which Lot answered: "Look, I have two daughters who are virgins. I am ready to send them out to you, for you to treat as you please, but do nothing to these men since they are now under the protection of my roof" (19:8). It is hard to decide whether we should read this story as an obscene parody of the belief in angels and spirits. It is strange in any case that the heroic motif of the fertile union of a god with a mortal is associated with a story of angels targeted for sodomy.

In conclusion, the biblical scribes strongly disliked the heroic ideology that grants the noble dead a blessed immortality and a role in enhancing the welfare of their community. Yahwist religion erased this ideology from ancient legends, but not to the point of making it undetectable by historical criticism. Contrary to a widespread idea, the denial of the individual soul in the Hebrew Bible is not an archaism dating back to a stage when men had not yet developed this concept. On the contrary, it is a revolutionary ideology, aggressively set against a universal belief that is probably as old as humanity, judging by funerary archeology. Critical analysis of the biblical legends proves that the Yahwist editors deliberately eliminated every notion of heroic immortality from the traditions that they appropriated from the ancient kingdom of Israel. This is easily seen in the account of Abel's death, when Yahweh says to Cain, "Listen! Your brother's blood is crying out to me from the ground" (Genesis 4:10). Spilled blood crying for vengeance is metaphorical, but the metaphor is not the product of poetic skill; rather, it is a distortion of the common motif of the murdered soul crying for vengeance. Abel has no soul, no eternal spirit; his blood is all that is left of him. Therefore, it must be his blood that cries out.

Biblical antiheroism is profoundly antihumanist. The heroic imagination, while admitting the communion of the human with the divine, grants man great freedom in relation to the gods. Heroes are the authors of their own accomplishments, whether as warriors, conquerors, legislators, builders, or simply thinkers. But the Moses of Exodus, the perfect man according to Yahwism, takes no initiative; he merely repeats slavishly what Yahweh tells him (like Abraham, who does not object to the divine order to sacrifice his son). Far from drawing from his own wisdom the laws that he gives to his people, Moses contents himself with receiving them from Yahweh already engraved in stone. (His only contribution, in fact, is to break the tablets).

The materialism inherent in Judaism has profound consequences in Jewish mentality. Among these consequences, Karl Marx identifies the immoderate pursuit of financial power: "Money is the jealous god of Israel, in face of which no other god may exist. Money degrades all the gods of man—and turns them into commodities."[21] By their perfection of usury, which

---

[21] Karl Marx, *On the Jewish Question*, 1843, on www.marxists.org/archive

has now resulted in the transformation of money into debt and its complete dematerialization, Jews have somehow endowed money with a virtually supernatural power. It is as if the spiritual world in which the Jew does not believe has been replaced by a spiritual world of his own making: a spiritualization of matter that is actually an inverted spiritual world, since instead of linking man to heaven, it chains him to earth. Jewish political adviser Jacques Attali, who credits the Jewish people with making money "the single and universal instrument of exchange, just as he makes his God the unique and universal instrument of transcendence," also points out that in Hebrew, "currency" (*DaMim*) is the same word as "blood" (*DaM*, plural *DaMim*), and rejoices in this "dangerous and luminous proximity."[22]

The Eternal People

The heroic ideology implies that man, at his best, is not merely the fruit of his parents; his soul is partly extragenetic. Blood and soul are different things. But Judaism sacralizes genetics above everything else. And so it is the entire chosen people, acting "as one man" (Judges 20:1), who is somehow heroized in the Bible. It is significant that the name "Israel" is both that of a person (Jacob) and of the people who descend from him.

The Hebrew Bible binds the individual to his collective racial origin rather than to his personal spiritual destiny. The immortality that is denied the individual is reinvested entirely on the collective: only the people is eternal. ("I instituted an eternal people" Isaiah 44:7). This is why endogamy assumes the character of a sacred law, the transgression of which merits death. "There is in the fate of the race, as in the Semitic character, a fixedness, a stability, an immortality that strike the mind," writes Isaac Kadmi-Cohen in *Nomads: An Essay on the Jewish Soul* (1929). The author describes Judaism (more generally "Semitic religions") as "the spiritualization that deifies the race, *jus sanguinis* [blood law]." Through Yahweh, therefore, it is the people who are deified: "Thus divinity in Judaism is contained in the exaltation of the entity represented by the race ... It is

---

[22] Jacques Attali, *Les Juifs, le monde et l'argent*, Fayard, 2002, p. 36.

therefore in this exclusive love, in this jealousy, one might say, of the race that the deep meaning of Semitism is concentrated and that its ideal character appears."[23]

Through the beginning of the twentieth century, many Jewish thinkers likewise understood Judaism as a kind of tribal soul. The American rabbi Harry Waton, writing in his *A Program for Jews and Humanity* in 1939, summarized this analysis quite well: "Jehovah differs from all other gods. All other gods dwell in heaven. For this reason, all other religions are concerned about heaven, and they promise all reward in heaven after death. For this reason, all other religions negate the earth and the material world and are indifferent to the well-being and progress of mankind on this earth. But Jehovah comes down from heaven to dwell on this earth and to embody himself in mankind. For this reason, Judaism concerns itself only about this earth and promises all reward right here on this earth." "Hebrew religion, in fact, was intensely materialistic and it is precisely this that gave it persistent and effective reality." "The Bible speaks of an immortality right here on earth. In what consists this immortality? It consists in this: the soul continues to live and function through the children and grandchildren and the people descending from them. Hence, when a man dies, his soul is gathered to his people. Abraham, Isaac, Jacob, Moses, and all the rest continue to live in the Jewish people, and in due time they will live in the whole human race. This was the immortality of the Jewish people, and it was known to the Jews all the time." "The Jews that have a deeper understanding of Judaism know that the only immortality there is for the Jew is the immortality in the Jewish people. Each Jew continues to live in the Jewish people, and he will continue to live so long as the Jewish people will live."[24]

The purity of blood, that is, of lineage, is the great preoccupation of Deuteronomic legislators and historians. It has been pointed out that blood plays the same role with the ancient

[23] Isaac Kadmi-Cohen, *Nomades: Essai sur l'âme juive*, Felix Alcan, 1929 (archive.org), pp. 115, 98, 143, 27–28.
[24] Harry Waton, *A Program for the Jews and an Answer to All Anti-Semites: A Program for Humanity*, 1939 (archive.org), pp. 52, 125, 132.

Hebrews as language among the Greeks. For the Greeks, the archetypal figure of the foreigner is the barbarian, an onomatopoeia designating those whose language is incomprehensible; whereas in biblical history, apart from the history of the Tower of Babel, everyone seems to speak the same language. There is almost no mention of any interpreters. The only exception is when Aaron makes himself the interpreter of Moses to his people; but he does this not because Moses, brought up in the royal palace, does not speak Hebrew, but only because he is "slow and hesitant of speech" (Exodus 4:10).[25] Today, even if language has taken on a specific identity function in modern Israel, it is always blood that prevails.

Ultimately, since eternity is granted only to the people as a race, it is as if the Jews were united by a collective, ethnic, genetic soul. Thus it is said that a Jew's soul is the Jewish people. Or should this collective soul be named Yahweh? Maurice Samuel writes in *You Gentiles* (1924): "The feeling in the Jew, even in the free-thinking Jew like myself, is that to be one with his people is to be thereby admitted to the power of enjoying the infinite. I might say, of ourselves: 'We and God grew up together.'"[26] Likewise, Harry Waton writes: "The Jews should realize that Jehovah no longer dwells in heaven, but he dwells in us right here on earth."[27] This is reminiscent of the anthropological truth of religion as set forth by Ludwig Feuerbach in *The Essence of Christianity* (1841), according to which God is the objectified human essence: "The consciousness of God is the self-consciousness of man."[28] Feuerbach was concerning himself with Christianity and its universal God, but his insight can also be applied to Judaism and its supremacist God. The profound truth of Judaism is that Yahweh is objectified Jewishness.

The Jewish people is haunted by its past, totally absorbed in it. That is the basis of its incomparable resistance to dissolution. It is inhabited by a unique destiny, and each Jew carries within

---

[25] Niels Peter Lemche, *The Israelites in History and Tradition*, John Knox Press, 1998, p. 111.
[26] Maurice Samuel, *You Gentiles*, New York, 1924 (archive.org), pp. 74–75.
[27] Harry Waton, *A Program for the Jews, op. cit.*, p. 148.
[28] Ludwig Feuerbach, *L'Essence du christianisme* (1841), François Maspéro, 1973, p. 129.

himself a portion of that destiny. From an Osirian or spiritual point of view, the explanation for this peculiarity is the denial of the survival of the individual soul. The Jewish people's collective character displays a form of monomania resembling the folkloric vision of dead men who haunt this world, stuck in their past earthly life, because, refusing the possibility of an afterlife, they do not even know that they have passed through death.

And yet, what appears horribly missing from Yahwism is at the same time its source of strength. For the individual has only a few decades to accomplish his destiny, while a whole people has centuries, even millennia. Thus can Jeremiah reassure the exiles of Babylon that in seven generations they will return to Jerusalem. Seven generations in the history of a people is not unlike seven years in the life of a man. While the goy awaits his hour on a scale of a century, the chosen people see much further. This explains the peculiar development of Jewish thought called "apocalyptic eschatology," compared to which the hope of an individual future life is referred to as "minor eschatology." The transfiguration that, in Greek culture, refers to the fate of the individual after his death, becomes in the Jewish apocalyptic literature of the intertestamental period (between the second century BCE and the second century CE) applied to the whole Jewish people, symbolized by the heavenly Jerusalem.

Many modern Jewish thinkers have identified this feature of Jewish religion as the source of its incomparable strength. For Moses Hess (*Rome and Jerusalem: The Last National Question*, 1862), the father of modern Jewish nationalism, "Jewish religion is, above all, Jewish patriotism." "Nothing is more foreign to the spirit of Judaism than the idea of the salvation of the individual which, according to the modern conception, is the corner-stone of religion." The essence of Judaism is "the vivid belief in the continuity of the spirit in human history." This brilliant idea, "which is one of the fairest blossoms of Judaism," is not, according to Hess, derived from a denial of individual immortality. On the contrary, it "has, in the course of ages, shrunk to the belief in the atomistic immortality of the individual soul; and thus, torn from its roots and trunk, has withered and decayed."[29]

On this point Hess is mistaken, but only in part, for it is probably true that an exclusively individual conception of immortality tends to weaken the group spirit, and that before the great universalist religions (Christianity, Buddhism, Islam), the notion of individual immortality was not completely separated from the idea of a spiritual attachment of man to his clan (a clan soul). From that point of view, Christianity's strictly individual notion of the soul (a new soul deposited by God in each new body) can be viewed as a cognitive limit: it sheds no light on the ancestral depths of the psyche.

The emphasis on the individual eternal soul (eternal even in hell) is also unconducive to a holistic vision of human destiny. Socialists of religious inclination, such as Jean Jaurès, have pointed out this weakness. In his view, there can be no purely individual salvation, because each man's soul is linked to all other souls.[30] This dialectic of individual versus collective soul is well encapsulated by Jim Casy in John Steinbeck's masterpiece *The Grapes of Wrath*. Casy, a disillusioned preacher, finds a new faith in humanity through social activism. He takes comfort in the idea that, "Maybe all men got one big soul ever'body's a part of."[31] This narrowness of the Western concept of the soul, which may be the ultimate source of Western individualism, is best perceived in contrast with Buddhist philosophy, which asserts the impermanence and interconnectedness of all individual souls.

---

[29] Moses Hess, *Rome and Jerusalem: A Study in Jewish Nationalism*, 1918 (archive.org), pp. 48, 64–65.
[30] Henri Guillemin, *L'arrière-pensée de Jaurès*, Gallimard, 1966.
[31] John Steinbeck, *The Grapes of Wrath* (1939), Penguin Classics, 2000, p. 26.

Chapter 4

THE LAST HERO

"Next, taking him to a very high mountain, the devil showed him all the kingdoms of the world and their splendour. And he said to him, 'I will give you all these, if you fall at my feet and do me homage.' Then Jesus replied, 'Away with you, Satan!'"

Matthew 4:8–10

Jews, Greeks, and Romans

In 63 BCE, the general Pompeius annexed Syria to the Roman Empire. He took advantage of a rivalry between the two sons of the Hasmonean king John Hyrcan I to integrate Judea, Samaria, and Galilee into the province of Syria. Hyrcan II was maintained at the head of a reduced territory and downgraded from king to ethnarch, while his pro-Roman counselor, an Idumean (Edomite) by the name of Antipater, was accorded special powers. After the fall of Pompeius, Hyrcan II and Antipater pledged allegiance to Caesar. In 47 BCE, Antipater was made governor of all Judea.

Thus began the "century of Herod," from the name of Antipater's son who took the title of king of Judea in 37 BCE. Herod the Great, as he would be called, reigned for 40 years as a "friend"—that is, client—of Rome. He equipped the country with roads, ports, bridges, aqueducts, racetracks, and amphitheaters. But his biggest project was dedicated to the national religion: the construction of a gigantic temple, completed in 64 CE under his great-grandson and destroyed soon after by Titus's army in 70. After Herod's death in 4 CE, his sons Antipas and Aristobulus reigned in Galilee and Samaria, while the Romans placed Judea under the rule of a Roman governor, the position occupied by Pontius Pilate from 26 to 37.

Herod's reign was a period of relative peace and prosperity. Roman authority and cultural influence in Judea were tolerated,

as were Roman offerings to the Temple, aimed at making
Yahweh favorable to the emperor. But at Herod's death, the
fundamentalist movement, which had been kept in check,
regained momentum. Riots broke out whenever Roman
paganism intruded into the Holy City, as when Pilate introduced
military banners with the emperor's effigies (Flavius Josephus,
Jewish Antiquities XVIII.3).

Members of the priestly class (high priests and Sadducees),
who already formed the core of the Hasmonean party and
remained a powerful hereditary class under the Herodians, used
their capacity to mobilize crowds in their power struggles. Many
were ready to conspire for the restoration of a true theocracy
independent from Rome. Under their leadership, the Sadducee
Eleazar, son of the high priest who defied Roman power by
opposing the daily sacrifices offered in the Temple in the name
and at the expense of the emperor, launched an armed rebellion
in 66. The war ended in 70 when Roman legions under the
command of Titus besieged, plundered, and destroyed Jerusalem
and its Temple, and then other strongholds of the insurgents.
The last, Masada, fell in 73.

When the rebellion broke out against Rome, the Samaritans
remained loyal to the Romans and provided support. Under the
Hasmoneans, they had resisted circumcision and conversion to
the Jerusalem-centered cult. After Herod's death, open
hostilities broke out again between Judeans and Samaritans.
Galilean Jews who had to cross Samaria on their way to
Jerusalem were in hostile territory, and many skirmishes
resulted. However, Galilee itself was far from completely
submissive to religious centralism: in the middle of the first
century CE, Jerusalemites still referred to it as "Galilee of the
nations" (Matthew 4:15). Hellenistic cults flourished in the
Galilean cities of Sepphoris and Magdala, where Jews were a
minority.

The progressive degradation of the relationship between
Rome and Jerusalem followed a parallel course in the rest of the
empire. Under the Hasmoneans and until the end of Herod the
Great's reign, the Diaspora Jews were faithful allies of the
Romans, and treated as such. In Alexandria as in Judea, Jews
who had supported Caesar against the Greeks were rewarded

with increased privileges. The same was true in all the Greek eastern cities that fell under Roman control. Jews enjoyed freedom of cult, judicial autonomy, discharge from any obligation on the Sabbath, exemption from military service, low taxation, and exemption from compulsory emperor worship (a mere civil formality as a token of loyalty). Moreover, they were allowed to collect funds and send them to the Jerusalem Temple bureaucracy.[1]

This situation inevitably fostered resentment from the Greeks who enjoyed none of these privileges, though they were recognized as Roman citizens. Many governors of Greek cities preferred facing penalties rather than implementing the imperial measures in favor of Jews. The famous lawyer Cicero gives us a glimpse of these tensions in his plea *Pro Flaco* (59 CE). His client, Lucius Valerius Flaccus, governor of Asia, had prevented the Jewish communities under his jurisdiction from sending their annual contributions to Jerusalem. These contributions had been seized in several cities, to the satisfaction of non-Jewish residents. Cicero defended Flaccus's measure as economically wise.

In Alexandria, where the Jews composed up to one-third of the population, the Jews' preferential treatment caused much unrest. Historian Michael Grant writes: "The Greeks nursed many long-standing grudges against the huge local Jewish community—religious, racial, economic and social alike. But what they objected to most of all was that the Jews collaborated so willingly with the Roman authorities. For the Greeks, disillusioned after half a century of Roman rule, had now produced a party of extreme anti-Roman nationalists. Being anti-Roman, they were strongly anti-Jewish as well—influenced still further in this direction by the native Egyptians, who were known to exceed all other peoples in the hatred they felt for the Jews."[2] Following anti-Jewish riots in 38, Jews and Greeks from Alexandria each sent a delegation to Rome to settle their differences. They were briefly received by Caligula, then by his

---

[1] Michael Grant, *Jews in the Roman World,* Weidenfeld & Nicolson, 2011, pp. 58–61.
[2] Michael Grant, *Jews in the Roman World, op. cit.,* p. 121.

successor Claudius. The Jewish delegation was headed by Philo, who gives his account in *Legatio ad Gaium*. Isidoros, representing the Alexandrian Greeks, stated about the Jews in front of the emperor Claudius: "I accuse them of trying to stir up the entire world." Claudius was much better disposed toward Jews than Caligula, who had challenged Jewish separatism by ordering that his statue be erected in Jerusalem's Temple, but had died before his order could be executed. For having insinuated that Claudius's court was filled with Jews, Isidoros was condemned to death.[3]

Nevertheless, the edict issued by Claudius after the arbitration hearing concluded that, if Jews continued to sow dissent and "to agitate for more privileges than they formerly possessed, [...] I will by all means take vengeance on them as fomenters of what is a general plague infecting the whole world." This edict was followed by another addressed to all the Jewish communities of the empire, asking them not to "behave with contempt towards the gods of other peoples."[4] Finally, after more outbreaks of violence between Greeks and Jews, the Romans turned against the Jews, and, from 115 to 117, the Greeks themselves joined with their Roman conquerors in the violent repression that stamped out the Jewish community of Alexandria, of which no more is heard.

Jesus, Rome, and Jerusalem

For obvious reasons, the aforementioned context is crucial for understanding the birth of the "Jesus movement" in Palestine from the year 30, and its development in Syria and Egypt after 70. If we are to believe the Gospels, Jesus was Galilean like most if not all of his early disciples, and it was in Galilee and neighboring Syrian towns that his reputation first spread. For that reason alone, his reception in Jerusalem was predictable. He was neither a Judean Jew nor an orthodox Jew, and was probably not even perceived as an ethnic Jew; he was *a marginal*

---

[3] Quoted in Joseph Mélèze Modrzejewski, *The Jews of Egypt, From Rameses II to Emperor Hadrian*, Princeton University Press, 1995, p. 178.
[4] Quoted in Michael Grant, *Jews in the Roman World, op. cit.,* pp. 134–135.

Jew, to quote John Meier's recent three-volume biography.[5] Jesus was a former disciple of John the Baptist, whose movement was active in Samaria and Transjordania. Jesus's harsh criticism of the Temple cult must also be considered as akin to the Samaritans' politico-religious worldview. In the Gospel of John, the use of the term *oi Ioudaioi* (71 times) to designate Jesus's enemies is generally regarded as meaning "Judeans."[6] By contrast, the same author puts Jesus in friendly contact with the Samaritans, although, normally, "Jews, of course, do not associate with Samaritans" (John 4:9). When Jesus talks to a Samaritan woman at Jacob's well, she mentions the bone of contention between Samaritans and Judeans: "Our fathers worshiped on this mountain, though you say that Jerusalem is the place where one ought to worship." In response, Jesus announces reconciliation: "Believe me, woman, the hour is coming when you will worship the Father neither on this mountain nor in Jerusalem. [...] But the hour is coming—indeed is already here—when true worshippers will worship the Father in spirit and truth" (4:20–23). Hearing this, the Samaritans hail him as "the Savior of the world" (4:42). On the other hand, the Jerusalem authorities condemn him in these terms: "Are we not right in saying that you are a Samaritan and possessed by a devil?" (8:48). In the Gospel of Luke, Jesus challenges the Jerusalemites' ethnic and religious chauvinism with his parable of the "good Samaritan" who acted more morally than a priest and a Levite (Luke 10:29–37). In brief, Jesus was not a Samaritan, but he was certainly reaching out to the Samaritans, and deeply critical of the Judeans' hostility to them. In that sense, he was already a peacemaker.

What can be said about Jesus's attitude toward the Romans? For two centuries, mainstream historians have depicted the tragic story of Jesus as an episode in the struggle between Jews and Romans. But their critical exegesis of the Gospels focused on the Jewishness of Jesus and on the responsibility of the

---

[5] John Meier, *A Marginal Jew: Rethinking the Historical Jesus*, 3 vols, Doubleday, 1993–2001.

[6] Gerald Caron, *Qui sont les Juifs de l'Évangile de Jean?*, Bellarmin, 1997, pp. 30–33.

Romans for his execution cannot change the fact that the four canonical Gospel writers present the Jews (Pharisees, Sadducees, Herodians, and Judeans in general) rather than the Romans as Jesus's mortal enemies. The synoptic account is unambiguous. During the great Easter festival at Jerusalem, "the chief priests and the scribes were looking for a way to arrest Jesus by some trick and have him put to death," but they decided "it must not be during the festivities, or there will be a disturbance among the people" (Mark 14:1–2). They corrupted one of his followers, Judas Iscariot, who told them where to find him, and they had him arrested in the middle of the night by "a number of men armed with swords and clubs" (14:43). Then, "all the chief priests and the elders and the scribes assembled" (14:53) in order to find against him, by false testimonies, a chief accuser to report to the Romans, for they had no legal right to execute him themselves. Under the pretext that he had claimed to be "Messiah," they delivered him, chained, to the Roman authorities, as a seditious would-be "king of the Jews." Pontius Pilate found no basis in this accusation; although not known for his leniency, he was reluctant to condemn Jesus, "for he realized it was out of jealousy that the chief priests had handed Jesus over" (Mark 15:10). When Pilate addressed "the crowd," proposing to release him, it was "the chief priests" (members of the powerful priestly families) who "incited the crowd to demand that he should release Barabbas for them instead" (15:11).

So even though it is Pilate who, "after having Jesus scourged, handed him over to be crucified" (15:15), the Gospel narrative clearly defines the range of responsibilities. The Jewish elite wanted Jesus dead but, having no legal right to execute him, they incited the crowd against him and compelled Pilate to convict him. This justifies the shortcut used by Paul when he writes that the Jews "put the Lord Jesus to death" (1 Thessalonians 2:15), or when Peter speaks to the Sanhedrin of "Jesus Christ the Nazarene, whom you crucified" (Acts 4:10), or says to the Jews gathered in Jerusalem, "this man [...] you took and had crucified and killed by men outside the Law" (2:23).

This New Testament narrative has been challenged by modern historical criticism. The evangelists, we are told, were eager to please Rome, and therefore portrayed their Christ as innocent of the crimes for which he was crucified, and blamed the Jews for having turned the Romans against him. For the same reason, these modern critics allege, the evangelists also cleared Pilate of the miscarriage of justice by inventing the scene in which he proposes to release Jesus and then washes his hands. According to this interpretation, the evangelists, and Paul even more so, founded Christian anti-Semitism on a historical lie. In *Who Killed Jesus?*, for example, John Dominic Crossan writes for the purpose of "exposing the roots of anti-Semitism in the Gospel story of the death of Jesus."[7]

The thesis is not entirely specious. It is undeniable that the Gospel narrative exonerates Jesus of all sedition against Rome, and in so doing also exonerates Pilate, perhaps excessively, from any hostility toward Jesus. (An apocryphal tradition expands on Matthew 27:19 to give Pilate the wife "Saint Procula" and claims that Pilate himself converted.)

The scene where Pilate offers the crowd a choice between Jesus and Barabbas is hardly credible to historians. One is tempted to explain it by the rewriting of an original narrative in which Jesus and Barabbas were one; indeed, Barabbas means "son of the Father" in Aramaic—Abba is the expression Jesus used to address his God, for example in Mark 14:36. Additionally, some manuscripts designate him as "Jesus Barabbas."[8] So according to a plausible hypothesis, the crowd really clamored in vain for the liberation of Jesus, but a secondary editor transformed the scene by duplicating "Jesus son of God" into Jesus *and* Barabbas. The same editor nevertheless absolved the "crowd" from responsibility by declaring that it was manipulated by the "high priests."

In any case, the main responsibility for the death of Jesus is still imputed to the priestly elites of Jerusalem. Matthew, it is true, incriminates the entire people, who together shoulder the whole responsibility for the murder of Christ: "Let his blood be

[7] John Dominic Crossan, *Who Killed Jesus? Exposing the Roots of Anti-Semitism in the Gospel Story of the Death of Jesus*, Harper San Francisco, 1995.
[8] Keith Elliott and Ian Moir, *Manuscripts and the Text of the New Testament*, T&T Clark, 1995, p. 65.

on us and on our children" (27:25); and there is undoubtedly a clear Judeophobic trend in the Gospel of Mark—a trend that is all the more significant because Matthew deeply Judaized the message of Christ, as we shall see.

Historical-critical analysis of the Gospels is a perfectly legitimate field of scientific inquiry. It submits the Gospels to the same tests of credibility as any other historical source, with the added advantage of having four interdependent versions (three if we limit ourselves to the Synoptic Gospels, Mark, Matthew, and Luke), which enables us to separate the successive layers of redactions. It is clear that the Gospel of Mark is the oldest and has served as the basis of the two other Synoptic Gospels. But it is also believed that its lost first version (the hypothetical *Urmarkus* or Proto-Mark) has been revised in an attempt to harmonize it with Matthew.[9] Given this complex redactional history of the Gospels, it is legitimate to question their historical reliability. The question, regarding Jesus's crucifixion, is whether the evangelists' story of a Jewish conspiracy against Jesus is basically true, or whether it is a cover-up of the Romans' responsibility. We have to choose between two theories: a "conspiracy theory" today considered anti-Semitic (though the evangelists were themselves Jewish), and a politically correct revisionist theory that shifts the blame entirely to the Romans—thereby implicitly admitting that Jesus was the seditious anti-Roman agitator that the Jerusalem priests said he was.

From a historical point of view, the evangelists' narrative is perfectly plausible in its broad outlines. It offers no obvious reasons to turn it on its head. Neither the conspiracy of the local elite nor the treason of Judas are implausible; on the contrary, they seem quite realistic. Paul himself twice fell victim to the same methods. It was the Jews who, at Corinth, seized him and dragged him before the proconsul Gallion under the accusation: "This individual is trying to persuade people to worship God in a manner contrary to the Law." Gallion washed his hands of the affair after the manner of Pilate, but did not yield to Jewish

---

[9] Marie-Émile Boismard, *L'Évangile de Marc, sa préhistoire*, Gabalda, 1994.

pressure: "Listen, you Jews. If this were a misdemeanour or a crime, it would be in order for me to listen to your plea; but if it is only quibbles about words and names, and about your own Law, then you must deal with it yourselves—I have no intention of making legal decisions about these things" (Acts 18:12–14).

An even closer approximation to Jesus's situation took place when Paul arrived in Jerusalem after his third voyage in Asia: "Some Jews from Asia caught sight of him in the Temple and stirred up the crowd and seized him" (Acts 21:27). When the Roman tribune Claudius Lysias intervened, the crowd loudly demanded that Paul be put to death. But the tribune excused himself from the case and "gave orders for a meeting of the chief priests and the entire Sanhedrin; then he brought Paul down and set him in front of them" (22:30). He then withdrew Paul and surrounded him with Roman guards. But forty conspirators convinced the Sanhedrin to ask the tribune for the right to question Paul again, secretly intending to kill him. The tribune learned of their intention and had Paul escorted to Caesarea with a letter for the governor of Syria, Felix, in which he explained: "I found that the accusation concerned disputed points of their Law, but that there was no charge deserving death or imprisonment" (23:29).

The high priests also went to Caesarea with a lawyer named Tertullus to plead their cause against Paul: "We have found this man a perfect pest; he stirs up trouble among Jews the world over and is a ringleader of the Nazarene sect" (24:5). Felix dismissed them and "gave orders to the centurion that Paul should be kept under arrest but free from restriction, and that none of his own people should be prevented from seeing to his needs" (24:23). Paul, as a Roman citizen, "appealed to Caesar" (25:11), and Felix's successor, Festus, granted him the right to be taken to Rome to plead before the emperor. He first gave Paul an opportunity to plead his case to King Agrippa II. After having heard it, Festus and Agrippa deliberated: "'This man is doing nothing that deserves death or imprisonment.' And Agrippa remarked to Festus, 'The man could have been set free if he had not appealed to Caesar'" (26:31–32). And so Paul was escorted to Rome, and the Acts of the Apostles tell us no more.

Not being a Roman citizen, Jesus did not receive the same consideration as Paul. Aside from this difference, the methods used against Paul and against Jesus were the same. Unless we challenge the credibility of Paul's story, there is no reason to challenge that of Jesus. It is all the more credible that it corresponds to a situation that was often repeated in the first two centuries of our era. According to the testimonies of Tertullian, Justin, Origen, and Eusebius, it was the Jews who incited the Romans to persecute Christians, denouncing them with slanderous accusations, such as allegedly eating children slaughtered in nocturnal gatherings: "The Jews were behind all the persecutions of the Christians. They wandered through the country everywhere hating and undermining the Christian faith," affirms Saint Justin around 116 CE. *The Martyrdom of Polycarp* (second century) underlines the importance of the Jewish participation in the persecution of the Christians of Smyrna.[10] It seems therefore very likely that Jesus was a victim of the same methods.

Moreover, to suppose that the evangelists have falsified this aspect of the biography of Jesus obliges us to suppose that they have totally distorted the meaning of his message. For never, according to the Gospel stories, did Jesus attack the Romans or the authority of Rome. When the Pharisees and Herodians questioned him, hoping to trap him, on what he thought of the tax exacted by Rome, Jesus showed them the portrait of the emperor on a Roman coin and replied: "Pay Caesar what belongs to Caesar—and God what belongs to God" (Mark 12:17), which was a way of distancing himself from the protest against Roman taxation. In this scene, it is actually the Jewish authorities who conspire against Jesus by searching for a pretext for denouncing him to the Romans. The scene is as credible as Jesus's reply was memorable.

This episode may be profitably compared to another, also having money as its central theme: Jesus's overthrowing the stalls of the money-changers and merchants of the Temple,

---

[10] Martin Peltier, *L'Antichristianisme juif. L'enseignement de la haine*, Diffusion Internationale Édition, 2014, pp. 38–49.

accusing them of transforming the Temple "into a bandits' den" (Mark 11:17). The money-changers' business consisted of converting the various coins into the only coinage authorized to purchase the sacrificial animals and to pay the religious tax: the half-shekel. This highly lucrative financial traffic profited from money trading as well as usury, and gave rise to many abuses. Thus the only time Jesus behaved violently was not against the Romans and their taxes, but against the financial practices of the Jews. And it is again "the chief priests and the scribes" who, seeing this, "tried to find some way of doing away with him; they were afraid of him because the people were carried away by his teaching" (11:18).

To understand the context, one must know that the earliest safe-deposit banks known in history were religious temples, because they were well guarded and therefore safe. Philo of Alexandria, a contemporary of Jesus whose brother Alexander was director of customs and banker of the king of Judea, evoked such a "temple deposit" in his book *Against Flaccus*.[11] As the only authorized (and obligatory) place of religious sacrifice in Judea, the Jerusalem Temple had become, by the time of Jesus, a massive money magnet. But Yahweh's vocation of amassing riches had begun long before that: "All the silver and all the gold, everything made of bronze or iron, will be consecrated to Yahweh and put in his treasury" (Joshua 6:19). In a very real sense, it is as much the bank as the Temple that symbolically destroys Jesus. His message was often directed against the love of money that festered in the Jewish society of his time: "How hard it is for those who have riches to enter the kingdom of God" (Mark 10:23); "But store up treasures for yourselves in heaven, where neither moth nor woodworm destroys them and thieves cannot break in and steal. For wherever your treasure is, there will your heart be too" (Matthew 6:20–21). The idea of "storing up treasures in heaven" is totally foreign to Yahwism, as is the idea of "saving one's life while losing it" (Matthew 16:25).

---

[11] Joseph Mélèze Modrzejewski, *The Jews of Egypt, op. cit.*, p. 169.

The message of Jesus was also directed against the obsessive legalism of the Pharisees, the founding fathers of rabbinical Judaism. Jesus's vision of the reign of God among men is the opposite of both the reign of money and the rule of law; it is the reign of the Spirit descended among men, and unconditionally welcomed by them. His disciples later explained that his death was necessary for him to send down the Holy Spirit (Paraclete), more or less confused with the risen Christ who had become "a life-giving spirit" (1 Corinthians 15:45). But it is unlikely that Jesus would have rested this hope on his own sacrifice. The Holy Spirit was for him a reality blossoming in the hearts of men, to be realized socially in a conviviality that breaks down the barriers erected in the name of purity by the Law: "What goes into the mouth does not make anyone unclean; it is what comes out of the mouth that makes someone unclean" (Matthew 15:11).

To conclude, the number one enemy of Christ is Judaism, in its sacerdotal-financial, Pharisaical-Puritanical, and anti-Roman zealot components (in that order). An abundance of evidence concurs in confirming that Jesus was the victim of a conspiracy of the Jewish elites in Jerusalem, arranged through lying witnesses and quotations taken out of context (Matthew 26:59–61) to use the Romans to eliminate a pacifist opposed to anti-Roman and anti-Samaritan chauvinism (see Luke 10:29–37). In denouncing Jesus as an enemy of Rome, these Jewish elites implicitly pledged their loyalty to the Roman authorities with a Machiavellian hypocrisy. But at the same time, having the Romans crucify a beloved prophet of the people meant exacerbating the anti-Roman sentiment that Jesus had tried to appease. In their arrogant confidence in Yahweh, they would eventually draw upon themselves the destruction that Jesus foresaw. Two centuries of biased historical criticism cannot erase this Gospel truth.

Anastasis

Christ is, in many ways, the culmination of the Greco-Roman heroic ideal: Jesus's birth, life, death, and resurrection are perfect manifestations of the heroic paradigm. And it is quite natural:

the Gospels were written in Greek in one of the urban crossroads of Hellenistic civilization—Antioch, Rome, or Alexandria. And as we can imagine from the New Testament, the worship of Jesus instituted by his disciples "in remembrance of [him]" (Luke 22:19) is essentially a heroic cult of the Greek type. A generation of exegetes immersed themselves in the Hebrew tradition in search of antecedents for the idea of the salvific death of Christ; they found only the obscure "suffering servant" passage of Isaiah 53.[12] The Greco-Roman antecedents, on the other hand, are legion: The sacrificial death of a man who then breaths his spirit into his community is the essential idea of heroic religiosity. Of the founding hero of Rome, Romulus, Livy tells us that after he was put to death by the senators, the Romans "began to cheer Romulus, like a god born of a god, the king and the father of the city, imploring his protection, so that he should always protect its children with his benevolent favor." The heroizing of Romulus was encouraged by his apparition to a certain Proculus Julius, to whom he said: "Go and tell the Romans that the gods of heaven desire my Rome to become the capital of the world." (*History of Rome* I.16).

To compare the worship of Jesus with the cults of the Greco-Roman heroes is nothing new; the resemblance was obvious to the first Christians, as well as to their adversaries. Saint Justin, a Christian intellectual from a pagan family, conceded it: by saying that Jesus "was begotten without any carnal act, that he was crucified, that he died, and that after rising from the dead he ascended to heaven, we admit nothing stranger than the history of those beings whom you call sons of Zeus." The difference, Justin insists, is that the story of Jesus is truthful, while those of the pagan demigods are lies invented by demons to "sow in the minds of men the suspicion that the things predicted of Christ were a fable like those related by the poets."[13] To set Jesus apart from the heroes by placing him

---

[12] Sam Williams, *Jesus' Death as Saving Event: Background of a Concept*, Scholars Press for Harvard Theological Review, 1975.
[13] I *Apologies* V.3, quoted in Martin Hengel, *La Crucifixion dans l'Antiquité et la folie du message de la croix*, Cerf, 1981, p. 13.

above them, out of competition, was the main concern of the
first apologists.

Jesus is not the only Christian hero, he is merely the first.
The cults of the saints, which mobilized Christian devotion in
late antiquity and the Middle Ages, represent the prolongation of
the heroic culture of classical antiquity. Until the tenth century,
their cults were mainly spontaneous local manifestations of
popular piety, centered on tombs or martyrs' relics. The cults of
the Christian saints developed parallel to the declining vestiges
of pagan heroic cults throughout late antiquity, as Christopher
Jones shows in his masterful book on Greco-Roman heroic
religiosity. Many of the venerated tombs were those of men who
did not die for their Christian faith; some were described as
brigands by the authorities. Augustine himself conceded that
only an "ecclesiastical form of expression" prevented the holy
martyrs from being described as heroes (*The City of God* X.21).[14]
More than a century ago, Stefan Czarnowski demonstrated that
saints belong to the hero category: "They bring together, in fact,
the essential features. They are glorified men, who by their acts
or by their death have merited a privileged position between the
elect. The faithful live in communion with them. They see in the
saints their advocates with God."[15] The cult of the saints, being
strongly attached to their shrines, allowed communities to
preserve a certain autonomy in their religious life. With it,
Christianity successfully subverted Yahwist monotheism, whose
tribal-universal god demands above all the extermination of any
religious particularism.

As for Christ himself, the title of "hero" is not applied to
him in the Gospels. In Mark, Jesus is simply declared "son of
God": twice by a voice from heaven (1:11 and 9:7); twice by
demons (3:11 and 5:7), who elsewhere called him "the Holy One
of God" (1:24); and once by a centurion seeing Jesus expire
(15:39). Mark gives the expression "son of God" an "adoptive"
meaning: Jesus becomes the son of God by the descent of the

---

[14] Christopher Jones, *New Heroes in Antiquity: From Achilles to Antinoos*, Harvard
University Press, 2009, p. 84.
[15] Stefan Czarnowski, *Le Culte des héros et ses conditions sociales*, Félix Alcan, 1919, p. 27.

Holy Spirit during his baptism. Mark knows nothing of any alleged virginal conception. The fact that Matthew and Luke reinforce the heroic pattern with their narratives of the Nativity, which give the term "son of God" a sense of "conception" (Jesus is conceived by the Holy Spirit descending on Mary), proves that they also understood the term "son of God" in Hellenic terms.

As for the motif of heroic immortality, it is also perfectly recognizable in the Gospel of Mark, although the notion of "resurrection" deserves some clarification. The Greek term *anastasis*, as we have already said, literally means "rising," and opposes "lying down," which is a metaphor for death. *Anastasis* is thus the awakening after the sleep of death. The term can be understood in the sense of a physical return to life, but this is not the meaning that comes to a Hellenized spirit like Paul of Tarsus, who, to answer the question "how are dead people raised," distinguishes "celestial bodies" from "terrestrial bodies," and explains: "What is sown is a natural body, and what is raised is a spiritual body" (1 Corinthians 15:35–44). The New Testament use of *anastasis* implies a metaphorical conception of death as sleep, which forms the narrative framework of many myths and tales in all the folklores of the world. Subsequent Christian doctrine introduced the absurdity of physical resurrection, directly derived from Jewish materialism, and reinforced at the end of the Middle Ages by the iconography of decaying corpses emerging from tombs.

Jesus himself clearly expressed his conception of *anastasis* when he was questioned by Sadducees hoping to confront him with contradictions in the doctrine. They presented him with the theoretical case of seven brothers successively married to the same woman (Mark 12:18–27). The Sadducees, faithful to the Torah, did not believe in any form of life after death, and opposed the Pharisaic conception of resurrection, born of Maccabean literature. But Jesus refuted both Pharisees and Sadducees, clearly expressing a spiritualist conception of the resurrection conforming to the most common Hellenistic view: "For when they rise from the dead, [...] they are like the angels in heaven." Then he added a very personal exegesis of the Torah: "Now about the dead rising again, have you never read in the Book of Moses, in the passage about the bush, how God spoke to him and said: I am the God of Abraham, the God of Isaac and the God of Jacob? He is God, not of the dead, but of the living. You are very much mistaken" (Mark 12:25–27). The aphorism "Yahweh is a god of the living not the dead" usually expressed the Yahwist rejection of any form of worship of the dead. But Jesus reversed its meaning to support the idea that Abraham, Isaac, and Jacob were alive, that is, partaking of the angelic life that awaits man after death.

There is no reason to suppose that Jesus expected for himself any other type of resurrection than this. But what of his disciples? How did they understand and describe the *anastasis* of Jesus? Consider first how Paul, our oldest source, explains to the believers of Corinth: "The tradition I handed on to you in the first place, a tradition which I had myself received, was that Christ died for our sins, in accordance with the scriptures, and that he was buried; and that on the third day, he was raised to life, in accordance with the scriptures; and that he appeared to Cephas; and later to the Twelve; and next he appeared to more than five hundred of the brothers at the same time, most of whom are still with us, though some have fallen asleep; then he appeared to James, and then to all the apostles. Last of all he appeared to me too" (1 Corinthians 15:3–8). Paul uses the Greek term *ôphthê* to "appear" or "to be seen," here clearly referring to a supernatural vision. He makes no distinction between the apparitions of the risen Jesus to the disciples and his own experience, which is described in Acts 9:3 as "a light from heaven [that] shone all round him," accompanied by a voice.

Things are more complex in the Gospels, where we must take into account the different editorial layers, using the most well-founded hypotheses of "source criticism," which recognizes Mark's priority and the existence of a proto-Mark. In its primitive version, the Gospel of Mark was probably content with this: "Having risen in the morning on the first day of the week, he appeared first to Mary of Magdala from whom he had cast out seven devils. She then went to those who had been his companions, and who were mourning and in tears, and told them. But they did not believe her when they heard her say that he was alive and that she had seen him. After this, he showed himself under another form to two of them as they were on their way into the country. These went back and told the others, who did not believe them either. Lastly, he showed himself to the Eleven themselves while they were at table. He reproached them for their incredulity and obstinacy, because they had refused to believe those who had seen him after he had risen" (Mark 16:9–14).

The preceding passage, Mark 16:1–8, gives a different account, actually borrowed and edited from Matthew 28:1–10: Mary Magdalene and one other woman (two in Mark) go to the tomb. "And suddenly there was a violent earthquake, for an angel of the Lord, descending from heaven, came and rolled away the stone and sat on it. His face was like lightning, his robe white as snow" (Matthew 28:2–3). The angel told them: "He is not here, for he has risen, as he said he would. Come and see the place where he lay, then go quickly and tell his disciples, 'He has risen from the dead and now he is going ahead of you to Galilee; that is where you will see him.' Look! I have told you" (28:6–7). Then, as they left the tomb, they saw Jesus "coming to meet them," and heard him tell them the very same message: "Do not be afraid; go and tell my brothers that they must leave for Galilee; there they will see me" (28:9–10). We detect within this narrative a duplication: An editor rewrote the scene to distinguish the "angel of the Lord" from Jesus, who were one in the original narrative, the angel of the Lord being none other than the ascended spirit of Christ. The angel is the encrypted form of the spirit of Christ, reminiscent of Jesus's own statement that, when one rises from the dead, one is like "angels in heaven."

There is reason to believe that the motifs of the rolled stone and the empty tomb, which "materialize" an originally purely spiritual apparition, are motifs invented by Matthew and later added in Mark. Paul, whose epistles are older than the Gospels, makes no allusion to the empty tomb. This tendency to transform the supernatural appearances of Christ into a physical resurrection of his corpse was further strengthened by Luke, in which the resurrected Christ himself undertakes to combat what is now heresy: "See by my hands and my feet that it is I myself.

Touch me and see for yourselves; a ghost has no flesh and bones as you can see I have" (Luke 24:39). Here the Maccabean conception of the resurrection of the martyrs has overcome the primitive spiritualist conception of proto-Mark and Paul.

This primitive conception, henceforth designated "Gnostic," was fought by the faction that, after long controversies and with the support of imperial power, eventually determined the doctrinal basis of the Church of Rome and controlled its canon. The first Alexandrian church, in any case, was certainly Gnostic. (The only two Christians of Alexandria known before the end of the second century were the Gnostics Basilides and Valentinus.)[16] It is now generally accepted, following Walter Bauer and Robert Moore, that heresy precedes orthodoxy on the historical timeline. Church orthodoxy is not a pure doctrine from which heresies deviate, but a construction completed in the fourth century on the ruins of those Christian currents it excluded by declaring them heresies.[17]

The oldest known Gnostic texts are the Coptic papyrus codices discovered in 1945 in Nag Hammadi in Egypt, dating from 350–400 but translating Greek texts probably going back to 140. One of them, the *Letter of Peter to Philip*, tells that after Jesus's death, the disciples were praying on Mont Olive when "a great light appeared, so that the mountain shone from the sight of him who had appeared. And a voice called out to them saying 'Listen … I am Jesus Christ, who is with you forever.'" In another Gnostic text, *The Wisdom of Jesus Christ*, the disciples were likewise gathered on a mountain after Jesus's death, when "then there appeared to them the Redeemer, not in his original form but in the invisible spirit. But his appearance was the appearance of a great angel of light."[18]

These accounts resemble those of the Transfiguration in Mark 9. Critical exegetes have long suspected that the Transfiguration was, in the primitive narrative (Proto-Mark), a

---

[16] Joseph Mélèze Modrzejewski, *The Jews of Egypt*, op. cit., p. 228.

[17] Walter Bauer, *Orthodoxy and Heresy in Earliest Christianity* (1934), Sigler Press, 1996; Robert I. Moore, *The Formation of a Persecuting Society: Power and Deviance in Western Europe, 950–1250*, Blackwell Publishing, 1987.

[18] Elaine Pagels, *The Gnostic Gospels*, Weidenfeld & Nicolson, 1979, p. 16.

scene of Resurrection, which was then shifted before the Crucifixion, perhaps in the context of the struggle against Gnosticism.[19] According to this hypothesis, it was originally the risen Jesus (transfigured by death into dazzling whiteness) who appeared together with Moses and Elijah and disappeared with them. But in the version we now have, Peter, James, and John were praying with Jesus on a mountain, when "in their presence he was transfigured: his clothes became brilliantly white, whiter than any earthly bleacher could make them. Elijah appeared to them with Moses; and they were talking to Jesus." Peter addressed Jesus. "Then suddenly, when they looked round, they saw no one with them any more but only Jesus" (Mark 9:2–8). A discussion follows in which Jesus asks the three apostles not to talk about their vision until he "rises from the dead." Why this request? Is this an awkward way for the editor who shifted the narrative to hide his fraud and explain why no one had heard about the Transfiguration story before? In doing so, he betrays the fact that Transfiguration and Resurrection were initially one.

The hypothesis of a post-Easter apparition of the risen Christ shifted before Easter and applied to the earthly Jesus can also be applied to the brief narrative where the disciples saw Jesus walking on the waters and "thought it was a ghost and cried out" (Mark 6:49). The result is a story that, since time immemorial, offers itself to ridicule—less so in the version of Mark, it is true, than in the elaboration of Matthew (14:22–33), in which Peter imitates Jesus and takes a few steps on the waters himself, before sinking for lack of faith.

If I have dwelled on these points of critical exegesis, it is not for the pleasure of deconstructing the conventional Gospel narrative, but to show that the earliest legend of Jesus, which belonged to a Greek spiritualist and heroic paradigm, underwent a materialistic transformation or Judaization. Other cases will be examined later. The suppression of the so-called Gnostic faith, and the imposition of a creed affirming that Jesus physically exited his tomb, can hardly be considered a minor detail in the religious history of our civilization.

---

[19] Simon Légasse, *L'Évangile de Marc*, Le Cerf, 1997, vol. 2, pp. 535–536.

The Return of Osiris and Isis

The historian of religions cannot help but notice that the crucified and risen Christ is equivalent to Osiris dismembered and resurrected. This parallel, first made by Gerald Massey in *The Natural Genesis* (1883), in no way undermines the historical truth of Jesus's life, since, as Carl Jung argued in *Answer to Job*, mythic patterns are embodied in real lives. The mythical equivalence of Christ and Osiris must be considered as a primordial factor in the success of Christianity in the Greco-Roman world. Christianity's encounter with the philosophical currents of Alexandria (especially Neo-Platonism) only accentuated this Osirian character. The cult of Osiris and Isis had spread throughout the Mediterranean basin since the beginning of the first millennium BCE, absorbing a large number of other cults on its way. Its encounter and fusion with Christian worship is therefore exceptional only in the fact that it was Christ who absorbed Osiris, and not the other way around.

Another remarkable case of a hero whose worship was superimposed on that of Osiris is that of Antinous, a young man beloved by the emperor Hadrian, who died in the Nile in the year 130 CE. His death was immediately interpreted as a sacrificial act to appease the Nile, whose catastrophic floods in the last two years were threatening Egypt with famine. Some also said that Antinous had cut short his life to prolong the life of the suffering emperor. The cult of Antinous, assimilated to a new avatar of Osiris, spread from Egypt throughout the empire with the encouragement of Hadrian, notwithstanding the horrified protests of the Christians. It involved mysteries, games, and oracles; and a tablet found in Antinopolis, the city founded in his honor, shows him as a "divinity of the dead" (*nekyodaimon*). Although it seems to have been welcomed with enthusiasm in the Near East, the cult of Antinous declined soon after the death of Hadrian. Historians have held that Antinous was the lover (*eromenos*) of Hadrian, and his worship the mere caprice of a grieving emperor. But this interpretation derives both from the Christian slanders and from the *Historia Augusta*, a Roman chronicle today considered a forgery. What is certain is that Antinous was perceived and honored as the incarnation of an ideal of human perfection; his face and his body, sculpted in thousands of copies, became the canon of youthful beauty in the Greco-Roman world.[20]

Christianity's Osirian root is the best-kept secret of church historians. That Christ is, to some extent, the mythical double of Osiris, and that the overwhelming success of his cult is largely due to this resemblance, have always been embarrassing facts for the Church. For this reason, the importance of the cult of Osiris in the Greco-Roman world has long been underestimated. Yet, on the margins of clerical culture, there is evidence that the myth of Osiris and his kinship with the legend of Christ was still known in the Middle Ages. The proof is none other than *Le Conte du Graal* (or *Roman de Perceval*) by Chrétien de Troyes, a roman à clef with multiple levels of meaning written around 1180. One finds there the undeniable trace of the story of Osiris, Horus, and Seth, incarnated respectively by the Fisher King, Perceval, and Chevalier Vermeil.[21]

If Osiris gradually took on the features of Christ during the first centuries of our era, Isis, his sister-wife, continued her career in the form of the Virgin Mary, whose worship was sanctioned in the fourth century by the Council of Ephesus. Indeed, Isis had been called "the mother of god" (*Theotokos*) centuries before the term was applied to Mary in Egypt and Syria.[22] During the Hellenistic period, Isis had in fact taken the ascendancy over Osiris. Already assimilated in the Near East to Ishtar, Asherah, or Astarte, she had been syncretically enriched by the attributes of Demeter, Artemis, and Aphrodite, to which the Romans added Diana and Venus. Numerous place names testify to her importance in Gaul; the very name of Paris could derive from Bar-Isis, namely the "Mount of Isis," the old name of the Sainte-Geneviève hill.[23]

---

[20] Royston Lambert, *Beloved and God: The Story of Hadrian and Antinous*, Phoenix Giant, 1984 ; Christopher Jones, *New Heroes in Antiquity*, op. cit., pp. 75–83.

[21] Silvestro Fiore, "Les origines orientales de la légende du Graal," *Cahiers de civilisation médiévale* 10 (1967), pp. 207–219.

[22] Bojana Mojsov, *Osiris: Death and Afterlife of a God*, Wiley-Blackwell, 2005, p. 116.

[23] F. Pommerol, "Origine du culte des Vierges Noires," *Bulletin de la Société d'anthropologie de Paris*, 1901, vol. 2, pp. 83–88, on www.persee.fr.

The cult of Isis is associated with that of Horus, known to the Greeks as Harpocrates (a transcription of the Egyptian *Har pa khrad*, "Horus the child"). Horus is conceived miraculously (from a supernatural father) at the spring equinox, at the time of harvest and, like the baby Jesus, is born every year at the winter solstice, to revive the Light. The birth of the divine child is, in both cases, inscribed in a history of salvation, a victory over evil and death. Isis hid Horus to protect him from the evil uncle whom he was destined to overthrow, just as Mary hid Jesus—in Egypt precisely—to save him from King Herod, who was determined to get rid of "the infant king of the Jews" (Matthew 2:2). The birth of Horus announces the defeat of Seth, who reigned on earth since he killed Osiris. Isis is often represented in a majestic position holding the young Horus on her lap, sometimes suckling him, and her representations are difficult to distinguish from those of the Virgin suckling the infant Jesus in the first Christian art, which were modeled after them.[24] Many representations of Isis were reassigned to the Virgin Mary and worshiped under her name during the Middle Ages. Such is the case with the famous Black Virgins produced between the eleventh and thirteenth centuries in the western Mediterranean basin. (There are nearly two hundred in the south of France).

The cult of Isis survived until the High Middle Ages, especially in the rural world (the term *paganus* means "peasant"). Only in the twelfth century was it totally supplanted by the cult of the Virgin Mary, who suddenly assumed an overwhelming place in Christian liturgy, as the mediator between Christ and his church. Bernard de Clairvaux (1090–1153) was the main promoter of this new piety, which served to Christianize all sanctuaries once dedicated to Isis, including innumerable holy wells. He coined the expression "Our Lady" ("Notre Dame"), or rather applied it to Mary for the first time, as well as other titles such as "Queen of Heaven." All Cistercian monasteries founded under his tutelage were dedicated to Our Lady, and all the Gothic cathedrals from then on were consecrated to her.

---

[24] Françoise Dunand, *Isis, mère des dieux*, Actes Sud, 2008, pp. 280–286.

Isis is above all the wife of Osiris, and the texts of her lamentations of mourning, which bring Osiris back to life, played an important part in the Isiac ceremonies: "O beautiful adolescent suddenly departed, vigorous young man for whom it was not the season, come back to us in your first form."[25] It is said that when Osiris died, Isis was so desperate that her flood of tears caused the Nile to flood, which is why the summer night when the warning signs of the flood appear is called the "Night of Tears."[26] Likewise, the Mary of late antiquity sheds tears as she clings to the foot of the cross. "I am overwhelmed by love, and cannot endure having to stay in the room, when you are on the wood of the cross," writes Romanos the Melodist in a hymn to Mary in the sixth century. At the end of the Middle Ages, the theme of *Mater Dolorosa* and the Latin poem *Stabat Mater* expressed a widespread devotion to Mary, promoted in particular by the Franciscan order.

Mary is like the second Eve standing by the side of the second Adam, an idea illustrated on many church tympans where Mary and Jesus sit side by side. However, strictly speaking, the Virgin Mary is not the bride of Christ, and the conjugal love that binds Isis to Osiris is absent from Christian mythology. Not only is Mary's virginity her most holy attribute, but the very idea that Jesus might have loved a woman in the flesh is anathema to Christian doctrine. Yet, isn't it remarkable that, among the three temptations of Jesus in the desert (Matthew 4:1–11), none is related to sexuality, which suggests that it had not yet been "demonized" at the time of the writing of the Gospels. The Gospel story shows Jesus surrounded by women who passionately admired him, and it is to Mary of Magdala, a follower of the first hour, that the resurrected Jesus first appeared (Mark 16:9). This is strangely reminiscent of the folktale motif of the departed young man appearing *post-mortem* to the love of his life—or, for that matter, of Osiris mourned, buried, and resurrected by his sister-lover Isis. Such tales are, of course, out of place in Christian tradition; they are the raw

---

[25] Claire Lalouette, *Contes et récits de l'Égypte ancienne*, Flammarion, 1995, p. 110.
[26] Bojana Mojsov, *Osiris, op. cit.*, p. 16.

materials of medieval romance and courtly poetry, whose authors, as Denis de Rougemont has correctly observed (*L'Amour et l'Occident*, 1938), have sometimes self-consciously served an alternative religion.

The Return of Yahweh

Resurrectionism, in the sense of a material conception of *anastasis* (with body emerging from the grave) is of Maccabean and Pharisaical inspiration; it is contrary both to the preaching of Jesus and to the outlook of the first known author of his legend (proto-Mark), who adopted a Hellenistic view of life after death ("like angels in heaven"). Can we therefore call this doctrine, enshrined in dogma, a "Judaization" of the Gospel message? This might seem paradoxical, since Jesus was Jewish; we are used to seeing things in reverse. We hear about the "paganization" of primitive Christianity, when the community of "Jewish Christians" (Jews admitting the messiahship of Jesus) was gradually supplanted by the "pagan Christians" (pagans converted by Paul and his emulators). But the point of view I have adopted here is that the original message of Christ, although destined for the Jews, broke with institutional Judaism (Pharisee as well as Sadducee), and was closer to spiritualist conceptions widespread in the Hellenistic world, including among Hellenized Jews.

There is another fundamental element of the Christian imagination that deserves to be seen as a Judaization of the message of Christ: apocalypticism. The scholarly consensus today rejects the authenticity of the apocalyptic prophecies attributed to Jesus in the Gospels, because they are contradictory to the hope of the Reign of God that typifies Jesus's message.[27] Jesus even seems to have openly criticized apocalyptic expectations: "The coming of the kingdom of God does not admit of observation and there will be no one to say, 'Look, it is here! Look, it is there!' For look, the kingdom of God is among you" (Luke 17:20–21). Jesus was aiming for a social transformation inspired by the Spirit of the Father and

---

[27] See for example James Charlesworth, *Jesus within Judaism*, SPCK, 1989.

the radical ethics of his Sermon on the Mount, not a supernatural and cataclysmic mutation of the world. Nothing expresses better the gradual maturation of the Reign than the "organic" parables of Jesus in Mark, recognized as having the highest claim to authenticity: "What can we say that the kingdom is like? What parable can we find for it? It is like a mustard seed which, at the time of its sowing, is the smallest of all the seeds on earth. Yet once it is sown it grows into the biggest shrub of them all and puts out big branches so that the birds of the air can shelter in its shade" (Mark 4:30–32). These birds may be a metaphor for angels or celestial spirits that dwell among men when they live fraternally. This parable, and other similar images, are found in the *Gospel of Thomas*, a text preserved in a Coptic (Egyptian) version and today considered as old as the canonical Gospels, but rejected from the canon because of its "Gnosticizing" tendencies.

It was mainly Matthew, followed by Luke, who reintroduced the apocalyptic into the message of Jesus. (It is also in Matthew alone that Jesus says, "I was sent only to the lost sheep of the House of Israel" 15:24). Mark's only apocalyptic passage in chapter 13 is a condensation of apocalyptic imagery from the books of Daniel, Isaiah, and Ezekiel, henceforth repeated in many Christian writings.[28] This is the only time that Jesus uses such apocalyptic imagery, and the length of this *logion* contrasts with the usual brevity of the words of Jesus in Mark; the passage is therefore unanimously considered a late addition.

The most important apocalyptic text of the Christian tradition, known as the book of Revelation, is not only foreign to the message of the earthly Jesus, but is today regarded as of non-Christian origin, for its central part (from 4:1 to 22:15) refers neither to Jesus nor to any Christian theme evidenced elsewhere. Only the prologue (including the letters to the seven churches in Asia) and the epilogue are ostensibly Christian, and they are attached to the body of the text by easily identifiable editorial transitions (not to mention the double signature of "John" in 22:8 and "Jesus" in 22:16). The book of Revelation

---

[28] Acts 2:19–20, 2 Thessalonians 1:7, 2 Peter 3:7, Revelation 1:7 and 8:10–12.

takes up in part the animal symbolism of Daniel (the two monstrous beasts and the dragon of chapter 13, followed by the lamb of chapter 14) and displays a ferocious hatred of Rome, as well as of those who sympathize with Hellenism: "To anyone who proves victorious, and keeps working for me until the end, I will give the authority over the nations which I myself have been given by my Father, to rule them with an iron scepter and shatter them like so many pots" (2:26–27).

We may therefore look at the apocalyptic current as the result of a re-Judaization of the Gospel message, under the influence of a turn of mind foreign to Jesus. This is a relevant observation for our time, for we shall see that apocalypticism has distorted so-called "evangelical" Christianity to the point of transforming it into an objective ally of American-Zionist militarism. How can we not think of an atomic war when reading, in Revelation 19:11–20, how the angel "called Trustworthy and True," with eyes like "flames of fire" and a cloak "soaked in blood," will smite the earth? "From his mouth came a sharp sword with which to strike the nations"; he will then invite the birds to "eat the flesh of kings, and the flesh of great generals and heroes, the flesh of horses and their riders and of all kinds of people, citizens and slaves, small and great alike" at "God's great feast."

More important still in the evolution of Christianity was the adoption of the Tanakh, the Hebrew Bible, into its canon. What has Christ to do with Yahweh? How can we think of Yahweh as the Father (*Abba*) that Jesus knew? How should we interpret the fundamentally anti-Jewish dimension of the Gospels, whose supreme expression is the accusation hurled by Jesus at the "Jews" (meaning the mob as well as the political and religious elite): "You are of the devil, your father, and it is the desires of your father you want to accomplish. He was a murderer from the beginning" (John 8:44). Who is this *diabolos* who wants to murder Christ, if not Yahweh-Seth? Is not this Yahweh who promises his people, in exchange for their submission, domination over the nations of the world (Deuteronomy 28:1) the very Devil who offers Jesus the exact same bargain (Matthew 4:8-10)? The so-called Gnostic Christians were well aware of the problem. They held Yahweh as an evil demiurge who had enslaved men through terror and deceitful promises of material well-being, while the loving God of Christ came to liberate them through "knowledge" (*gnosis*, a term indicating a deeper transformation of the self than a mere intellectual understanding). Yahweh, they believed, is the Prince of this world, while Christos came from heaven to rescue them.

Unfortunately, radical Gnostics, while they recognized Yahweh as evil, did not contest his claim of having created the world; and so they held the physical world inherently evil. This paradoxical position led them to take the side of the serpent of Genesis, which was like vindicating Baal, but which has passed, in the Christian confusion, as the mark of Satanism. The Gnostic text *The Testimony of Truth* rewrites the story of the Garden of Eden from the point of view of the serpent, presented as the principle of divine wisdom. He convinces Adam and Eve to partake of knowledge (*gnosis*), while the Demiurge tries to keep them away from it by threatening them with death.[29]

A more moderate form of Gnosticism almost prevailed in Rome at the beginning of the second century under the authority of Marcion, a Christian of Stoic culture who had assembled the first Christian canon (limited to a short version of Luke's Gospel without the Nativity, and ten epistles of Paul). "Marcion's heretical tradition has invaded the whole world," Tertullian warned in his book (*Against Marcion* V.19).[30] It was in reaction to Marcion that the competing group, known today as the "Great Church," created its own canon including the Hebrew Bible. In the sixteenth century, the Council of Trent declared the Old and New Testaments as being of equal divine authority and as part of a single book. In many ways, Christians today take the Old Testament more seriously than the Jews, who do not give it the status of a divine revelation. Unfortunately, by admitting the Old Testament into its canon, the Church has placed itself in a dilemma that would, in the long run, destroy its credibility: how to reconcile Yahweh and Christ, when they are

---

[29] Elaine Pagels, *The Gnostic Gospels, op. cit.*, pp. 17–18.
[30] Walter Bauer, *Orthodoxie et hérésie au début du christianisme* (1934), *op. cit.*, p. 51.

opposites like Osiris and Seth? Having adopted and sanctified the Old Testament, the Church had to forbid the people from reading it, lest they grow ashamed of the God they are asked to worship. Its free access in vernacular languages in the fifteenth century marked the beginning of dechristianization.

The Old Testament was to become the Trojan horse of Yahwism within Christianity. By enhancing its status, the reformers of the sixteenth and seventeenth centuries launched an irreversible return to Judaism. For this reason, some Catholics call Protestantism "Old Testamentism." That is overly simplistic: it was the bishops of the first centuries who opted for the adoption of the Hebrew Bible into the canon. Later the "reforming" popes of the eleventh to thirteenth centuries relied heavily on it to mobilize the crusaders. Be that as it may, the Judaization of Christianity, to which Protestantism made a decisive but not exclusive contribution, paved the way for the anti-Christianism of the Enlightenment. Voltaire, for example, denigrated the Christian God by citing the Old Testament: "Never was common sense attacked with so much indecency and fury" (*Sermon of the Fifty*).

The purpose of this chapter is not to quarrel with the Christian canon or dogmas, but simply to understand the extent to which Christianity is the child of Yahwism. It must be noted, for example, that it carries within its genes an exclusivism that derives directly from the ideology of the jealous god: it was not enough that Jesus was a son of god, or even that he was the son of the only God; he had to be the only son of the only God. And since, according to Yahwist dogma, only God can be the object of a cult, it was finally necessary that Jesus be God. The Council of Constantinople, summoned by the emperor Theodosius in 381, proclaimed Jesus "the only begotten Son of God, born of the Father before all the centuries, a light born of the Light, true God born of the true God, begotten not created, consubstantial (*homoousios*) to the Father, by whom everything was created."[31] Thus exclusive monotheism, which had produced in Judaism the monstrous idea of a law-making God,

[31] Richard Rubenstein, *Le Jour où Jésus devint Dieu,* La Découverte, 2004, p. 256.

produced in Christianity another poison: dogmatism, that is, the legal obligation to believe in absurdities. Contrary to common opinion, it is not by virtue of its Hellenistic heritage that Christian dogma came to declare the crucified Galilean and the Divine Creator nearly identical; for among the Greeks a hero has never been confounded with the supreme God. It is, rather, the exclusivist obsession inherited from Judaism that finally erased the distinction between the Son and the Father.

And yet, paradoxically, it was the deification of Jesus, not only in mythical and liturgical discourses but also in logical discourse, which allowed medieval Christianity to largely emancipate itself from Yahwism, at least until the printing press and the Reformation reintroduced the Old Testament. For it was only by becoming God himself that Jesus was able to eclipse Yahweh. But to eclipse Yahweh was not to destroy him. And if Christianity can be seen as a victory of Osirism over Yahwism, from another point of view it is a Judaized form of Osirism.

The Miracle of Constantine

What can explain the success of Christianity? Its merits, first of all. From the beginning, the cult of Christ was a popular religion, which quickly overflowed the narrow circle of a Jewish sect to arouse contagious enthusiasm among the non-Jewish subjects of the empire. This enthusiasm stemmed not only from the new cult's powerful Osirian resonances, but also from its revolutionary dimension; not only from its links with tradition, but also its modernity. Christ was the hero of the oppressed of the Roman Empire. To the people subjected to the unprecedented physical violence of the empire, it brought the consolation of a spiritual victory: the promise of a kingdom that is not of this world, but one that the humble can experience in this life.

But the success of Christianity is also undoubtedly linked to its way of posing and responding to the "Jewish question" at a time when the influence of the Jews on the affairs of the empire was becoming a major concern. The Gospels denounce the corruption of Jewish society and religion by money, as well as the ability of Jewish elites to crush their enemies using political pressure, while controlling crowds. Christ is the heroic figure opposed to excessive Jewish power. These are the two major virtues of original Christianity: by sharing the passion of Christ, the Christian frees himself from the joint power of Rome and Jerusalem.

This popular enthusiasm for Eucharistic worship, however, does not explain the political triumph of the Church. The true "miracle" of Christianity, it has been said, was the "conversion" of the Roman emperor Constantine in 312. His favor granted to the Church transformed a persecuted sect into a powerful institution that soon began persecuting all competing cults. Why did one Roman emperor favor, and another (Theodosius in 395) elevate to the rank of state religion, a cult glorifying a man crucified by the Romans as a bandit, while forbidding its faithful to express their loyalty to the emperor through the customary civic worship? An explanation for this turning point is given by the authorized biographer of Constantine, Eusebius of Caesarea: Constantine supposedly received a vision, then a military victory under the sign of Christ. But it is hardly convincing. Historians doubt whether Constantine really became a Christian, for he maintained and renovated pagan religious traditions (including a cult of *Sol Invictus*) and retained the religious title of Pontifex Maximus (literally "the great bridge builder" between gods and men). So why did Constantine legalize Christianity? We must suppose that he saw in Christ a new version of Osiris, and in the cult of martyrs a new heroic, popular, and nonmartial religiosity.

But he may have had another motivation. Several sources attribute to him, before his support for Christianity, a virulent Judeophobia, and the opinion that "the Jews, who had spread everywhere, actually hoped to become masters of the Roman world."[32] His antipathy to "this disgraceful sect" is therefore more likely a cause than a consequence of his benevolence toward Christianity. Constantine was in this matter merely the heir of his predecessors—who all had to answer the grievances of their subjects against the Jews—before he even heard of Christianity. Tiberius (14–37) had expelled the Jews from Rome

---

[32] Michael Grant, *The Jews in the Roman World*, Charles Scribner's Sons, 1973, pp. 283–284.

in 19 CE. Claudius (41–54) had renewed the operation (as mentioned in Acts 18:2). Hadrian (117–138), who had to suppress the revolt of Simon Bar Kokhba in Palestine, forbade circumcision and once again expelled the Jews. Only Nero and Trajan were favorable to the Jews. In the absence of another convincing explanation, it is therefore natural to suppose that by favoring Christianity, Emperor Constantine and his successors (with the exception of the ephemeral Julian the Apostate, Christianophobic and Judaeophile) hoped to solve the thorny "Jewish question" with which all empires from Babylon onward had been confronted. Did not the Church pretend to be the gate of salvation for the Jews, and had it not been so for thousands of Jews?

For there to be a door, there must be a wall, and it was indeed at this time that Christianity and Judaism completed their separation. Constantine actually forbade Christians to go through the door in the other direction. An edict of 329 punished every Christian who converted or reconverted to Judaism. Another, in 335, prohibited Jews from circumcising their Christian slaves. In 353, his son Constantius II decreed the expropriation of every Christian who had become a Jew. [33]

For the Jews, the door became more and more narrow as the doctors of the Church, seized with dogmatic hubris, turned Jesus into God. Jews were asked to relinquish whatever common sense they had to convert to the Christian creed. To this must be added the Judeophobia of the Great Church under imperial protection. The Talmud was the Jews' response to the appropriation by Christians of their heritage. It transformed rabbinic Judaism into a fundamentally anti-Christian religion. Christianity and Talmudism were both born from the ashes of the old biblical religion after the crises of the first two centuries CE, which saw the destruction of Jerusalem in 70 and the expulsion of its Jewish population in 135. Both reached their discernible outlines only in the fourth century, and both pretended to reform ancient Judaism, but in opposite directions and in vicious competition: Talmudism, emerging from the

---

[33] Amon Linder, *The Jews in Roman Imperial Legislation*, Wayne State University Press, 1987.

Pharisaical current, exacerbated the purificationist, ritualistic, legalistic, and separatist tendencies; while Christianity opposed it and, under the inspiration of Paul, rejected circumcision and the Mosaic law as a whole. Christianity must be regarded as the elder of the two—as Osiris is the elder of Seth—insofar as it exercised more influence over its competitor than it received. The great Jewish scholar Jacob Neusner goes so far as to write that "Judaism as we know it was born in the encounter with triumphant Christianity."[34] Rabbinic orthodoxy, which became the new cement holding the Jewish community together, hardened in the rejection of Christianity and its growing influence. At the beginning of the second century, a ritual prayer was introduced into synagogues to curse the *mînim* or "sectaries," a term referring particularly to Christians.

The Levitical Vatican

One must bear in mind that, after the fourth century, the Roman Empire was centered in Constantinople, not Rome. The Italian city had plunged into irreversible decadence. It had ceased to be the imperial capital by 286, having been replaced by Milan, then by Ravenna. The common representation of the "Eastern Roman Empire" as the continuation of the empire founded in the Latium, whose capital had simply been transferred to the Bosphorus, is a misleading viewpoint inherited from Western historiography. Modern Byzantine studies rather insist on the essential differences between the Greek-speaking Byzantine civilization and that of imperial Rome, which was a vague and distant memory at the end of the first millennium CE. Scholars describe the Byzantine Empire (which actually called itself a kingdom, *basileia,* ruled by a king, *basileus*) as a commonwealth, that is, "the supra-national idea of an association of Christian peoples, to which the emperor and the 'ecumenical patriarch' of Constantinople provided a symbolic

---

[34] Jacob Neusner, *Judaism and Christianity in the Age of Constantine: History, Messiah, Israel, and the Initial Confrontation,* University of Chicago Press, 1987, p. ix.

leadership—even if each of these peoples was fully independent politically and economically."[35]

Unlike Rome, Constantinople was Christian by birth. Its foundation is inseparable from the adoption of Christianity by its founder Constantine the Great. The two major centers of outreach of the Christian faith were Antioch and Alexandria, but it was around Constantinople that the unity of the Church was forged, at the so-called "ecumenical" councils (the *Œkumene* meant the civilized world placed under the authority of the *basileus*), whose participants were exclusively oriental: no Latin bishop was present at the Council of Constantinople in 381. From the sixth century on, the patriarch of Constantinople was the keeper of orthodoxy, but the emperor was nevertheless the protector of all Christian communities within the commonwealth, many of which rejected the orthodox creed.

The emperor also maintained good relations with the Shiite Fatimid caliphate of Egypt, which had conquered Jerusalem and lower Syria from the Abbasids in the 960s. Many Christian churches operated freely on their territory, and there was a great Shiite mosque in Constantinople. Destabilization came from the common enemy of the Byzantines and Fatimids: the Seljuq Turks. But final destruction emerged, unexpectedly, from the West, in the form of the Frankish crusaders, a new species of mercenaries paid in spiritual currency and looting by the Roman church.

The global power of the Roman popes, and their amazing capacity to mobilize the Western warrior class, had grown in the tenth century when German king Otto I had made alliance with the local ruling family of the Latium, the counts of Tusculum, who had by then established a hereditary right on the bishopric of Rome, but who exerted no authority beyond the Latium. The Roman pope (from the Greek *papa*, a Greek word that had hitherto been applied respectfully to every bishop) and the German emperor thus cofounded the Holy Roman Empire, in

---

[35] Dimitri Obolensky, *The Byzantine Commonwealth: Eastern Europe, 500–1453*, Praeger, 1971, quoted in John Meyendorff, *Byzantium and the Rise of Russia*, Cambridge University Press, 1981, p. 2.

imitation and as a challenge to the patriarch and the *basileus* of Constantinople. In the next two centuries, the power of the popes continued to grow, through constant struggle with the German emperors, especially those of the Hohenstaufen dynasty. The popes resorted to their newly invented psychological weapon of excommunication, which could be used to undermine any sovereign's authority. In the middle of the eleventh century, triumphant popes developed a radical political vision of their own universal empire, best summarized by the *Dictatus Papae*, a series of 27 statements by Pope Gregory VII, which included the following claims:

"1. That the Roman church was founded by God alone. 2. That the Roman pontiff alone can with right be called universal. 3. That he alone can depose or reinstate bishops. [...] 8. That he alone may use the imperial insignia. 9. That of the pope alone all princes shall kiss the feet. 10. That his name alone shall be spoken in the churches. 11. That his title [Pope] is unique in the world. 12. That it may be permitted to him to depose emperors. [...] 19. That he himself may be judged by no one. [...] 22. That the Roman church has never erred; nor will it err to all eternity, the Scripture bearing witness. 23. That the Roman pontiff, if he have been canonically ordained, is undoubtedly made holy by the merits of St. Peter. [...] 27. That he may absolve subjects from their fealty to wicked men."

In their attempt to establish this new world order, the Gregorian reformers employed an army of legists who elaborated a new canonical legal system to supersede customary feudal laws. Almost all popes between 1100 and 1300 were jurists, and they transformed the papacy into a huge international judicial machine.[36] The "Donation of Constantine," a forgery made in a pontifical scriptorium, constitutes the centerpiece of the legal basis they needed for their formidable claims. By this document, the Emperor Constantine supposedly transferred his authority over the western regions of the empire

---

[36] John Meyendorff and Aristeides Papadakis, *The Christian East and the Rise of the Papacy*, St. Vladimir's Seminary Press, 1994, p. 211.

to Pope Sylvester I, making the pope the supreme sovereign of all western kings.

The false donation also bestowed on the papacy "supremacy over the four principal sees, Alexandria, Antioch, Jerusalem and Constantinople, as also over all the churches of God in the whole earth." So it also served in the pope's struggle with the patriarch of Constantinople, which ultimately led to the Great Schism of 1054. Other arguments used in support of the pope's pretense at world supremacy included the claim to be sitting on the throne of Saint Peter, Christ's first disciple, supposed to have been martyred in Rome. The origin of this tradition is disputed; the New Testament says nothing of Peter's travel to Rome, and assumes that Peter simply remained the head of the Jerusalem church. And the earliest sources mentioning Peter's presence in Rome, the writings of Peter's supposed immediate successor Clement of Rome, are today recognized as forgeries.

There is something Levitical in the papal authoritarian legalism of the Gregorian Reform, its fraudulent international law, and its transformation of articles of faith into binding laws. The whole theocratic papal ideology appears to be directly inspired by the political project of the Deuteronomic school: a world order placed under the supreme authority of a caste of priests. The Roman church's vision of sin, penance, and salvation is likewise legalistic, but also monetary in essence, in sharp contrast to the original conception of the Greek fathers that stressed man's potential for deification (*theosis*), rather than his need to extirpate himself from sin.[37] With his associates, Pope Gregory VII, a former financier (born Hildebrand, a family of bankers to this day) turned the Church into an institution of spiritual credit. Their accounting conception of sin would lead to the traffic of indulgences, which would later revolt Martin Luther and launch the Reformation.

The Schism of 1054 was the starting point of a geopolitical offensive that started with the pope's support of the conquest of southern Italy and Sicily in 1061 by the troops of Norman

---

[37] Read John Meyendorff, *Byzantine Theology: Historical Trends and Doctrinal Themes*, Fordham University Press, 1974.

warrior Robert Guiscard, and developed into the crusades. In the last decade of the eleventh century, Pope Urban II found an innovative method of colonizing the Near East: the militarized pilgrimage. The spiritual reward traditionally promised to the unarmed pilgrim was now granted to the heavily armed killer of heathens, in addition to the promise of plunder. The crusades were the direct outcome of the Gregorian Reform: by imposing himself as the sovereign of kings, who were therefore made his vassals, the pope claimed for himself the right to order them to make war under his supreme command. Thus the papal authority, after having repressed private wars in Western Europe in the tenth century under the movement of the "Peace of God," started a world war that would last two centuries in the Holy Land and environs. After having proclaimed that even tournaments were a mortal sin, and that dying in the course of one of those festive chivalric jousts would send you straight to hell, the Vatican declared that dying in its allegedly holy wars would erase all your sins and propel you to heaven.

Until recently, it was believed that the crusades were a response to a desperate call for help from Byzantine Emperor Alexios Komnenos, because this is how Western contemporary chroniclers such as Ekkehard of Aura and Bernold of St Blasien presented it. The emperor sent an embassy to Rome, writes Ekkehard, and "deplored his inability to defend the churches of the east. He beseeched the pope to call to his aid, if that were possible, the entire west." This is today considered a grossly misleading picture of the tone and nature of Alexios's request, backed by forgeries such as a doctored version of a letter to the count of Flanders, in which Alexios purportedly confessed his powerlessness against the Turks and humbly begged for rescue. In fact, the emperor was in no desperate situation, and his request was just for mercenaries to fight under his command; the Byzantines had always drawn in warriors from foreign nations to serve under their banner in return for imperial largesse. An army of crusaders under the order of a papal legate was never what Alexios had called for, and Byzantines were deeply worried and suspicious when they saw it coming. "Alexios and his advisers saw the approaching crusade not as the arrival of long-awaited allies but rather as a potential threat to the *Oikoumene*," writes Jonathan Harris. They feared that the liberation of the Holy Sepulcher was a mere pretext for some sinister plot against Constantinople.[38]

The Holy City had recently been taken from the Egyptian Fatimids by the intolerant Seljuq Turks. The news of the Turks' desecration of the tomb of Christ, and semi-imaginary stories of their cruel treatment of Christians, served to inflame the Western population, and masses set off toward Jerusalem under the slogan "avenge Jesus." Some realized along the way that they did not need to go to the Orient, "while we have right here, before our eyes, the Jews," in the words of chronicler Raoul Glaber.[39] When they reached Jerusalem, the Holy City had just been reconquered by the Fatimids, who immediately promised to restore the rights of Christians and offered to the crusaders' leaders an alliance against the Seljuqs. The crusaders rejected the offer. Inspired by the biblical story of Jericho (Joshua 6), they started with a procession around the walls of Jerusalem, led by priests praying and singing at the top of their voices, before dashing forward against the walls, expecting a miracle. Then, resorting to their sophisticated siege machinery, they entered the city on July 15, 1099, and committed a mass slaughter. "In the temple and portico of Solomon [the al-Aqsa Mosque]," writes chronicler Raymond of Aguilers, "men rode in blood up to their knees and the bridle reins. Indeed, it was a just and splendid judgment of God, that this place should be filled with the blood of the unbelievers, since it had suffered so long from their blasphemies."[40] This unheard of massacre left a traumatic memory in the Muslim world, from which the Christian-Muslim relationship would never recover.[41]

The crusaders succeeded in establishing four new Christian states in Syria and Palestine, which formed the basis of a Western presence that was to endure until 1291: the kingdom of Jerusalem, ruled by Frankish knight Godfrey of Bouillon, then

---

[38] Jonathan Harris, *Byzantium and the Crusades*, Hambledon Continuum, 2003, p. 56.

[39] Jean Flori, *Pierre l'Ermite et la Première Croisade*, Fayard, 1999, pp. 266–267.

[40] Raymond d'Aguilers, *Histoire des Francs qui prirent Jérusalem. Chronique de la première croisade*, Les Perséides, 2004, p. 165.

[41] Read Amin Maalouf, *The Crusades Through Arab Eyes*, Schocken, 1989.

by his brother Baldwin of Boulogne, who took on the title of king; the principality of Antioch, seized by the Norman Bohemond of Tarento (son of the above mentioned Robert Guiscard) who refused to honor his promise to hand it over to the Byzantine emperor; the county of Edessa, formed by Baldwin of Boulogne; and the county of Tripoli, conquered by Raymond of Toulouse.

At the end of the twelfth century, Jerusalem having been recovered by Saladin (in conditions of humanity that contrast sharply with the capture of Jerusalem by the crusaders in 1099), Pope Innocent III solemnly proclaimed a new crusade, the fourth in modern numbering. This time, the Byzantines' fear of a hidden agenda proved fully justified. Instead of going to Jerusalem via Alexandria, as officially announced, the Frankish knights, financed by the Venetians, moved toward Constantinople. The huge army of the crusaders penetrated into the city in April 1204 and sacked it during three days. "Since the creation of this world, such great wealth had neither been seen nor conquered," marveled the chronicler Robert de Clari.[42] Palaces, churches, monasteries, and libraries were systematically pillaged. "Nuns were ravished in their convents. [...] Wounded women and children lay dying in the streets. For three days the ghastly scenes of pillage and bloodshed continued, till the huge and beautiful city was a shambles."[43]

After having appropriated the best residences in the city, the conquerors elected and crowned as new emperor of Constantinople the Frank Baldwin of Flanders, and as new patriarch the Venetian Thomas Morosini, who imposed the exclusive religious authority of Rome. As for the great mosque of Constantinople, it was burnt down by the crusaders—and the fire spread to a third of the city. Innocent III immediately placed the new emperor under his protection, and commanded that the crusading army stay to protect Constantinople from any attempt by the Byzantines to retake the city, rather than fulfill their

---

[42] Robert de Clari, *La Conquête de Constantinople,* Champion Classiques, 2004, p. 171.
[43] Steven Runciman, *A History of the Crusades, vol. 3: The Kingdom of Acre and the Later Crusades* (1954), Penguin Classics, 2016, p. 123.

original vow to liberate Jerusalem. "Surely, this was done by the Lord and is wondrous in our eyes. This is truly a change done by the right hand of the Most High, in which the right hand of the Lord manifested power so that he might exalt the most holy Roman Church while He returns the daughter to the mother, the part to the whole and the member to the head."[44]

The new Franco-Latin Empire built on the smoking ruins of Constantinople lasted only half a century. The Byzantines, entrenched in Nicaea (Iznik), slowly regained part of their ancient territory, and, in 1261, under the command of Michael VIII Palaiologos, chased the Franks and Latins from Constantinople. But the city they took back was but the shadow of its own past glory: the Greek population had been slaughtered or had fled, the churches and the monasteries had been profaned, the palaces were in ruins, and international trade had come to a stop.

Moreover, as soon as news arrived that Constantinople had "fallen," Pope Urban IV ordered that a new crusade be preached throughout Europe to retake Constantinople, promising that those who joined the expedition would enjoy the same remission of sin granted to those who went to the Holy Land.[45] There were few volunteers. But in 1281 again, Pope Martin IV encouraged the project of Charles of Anjou (brother of King Louis IX) to take back Constantinople and establish a new Catholic empire. It failed.

But Byzantine civilization had been fatally weakened. It collapsed a century and a half later, after one thousand years of existence, when the Ottoman Sultan Mehmet II took Constantinople in 1453. All specialists admit that the Fourth Crusade had inflicted on Byzantium a mortal wound, and exhausted its capacity to resist the Muslim expansion. The renowned medieval historian Steven Runciman wrote: "There was never a greater crime against humanity than the Fourth Crusade. Not only did it cause the destruction or dispersal of all

---

[44] Innocent III, paraphrased by Jonathan Harris, *Byzantium and the Crusades*, Hambledon Continuum, 2003, p. xiii.
[45] Jonathan Harris, *Byzantium and the Crusades, op. cit.*, p. 50.

the treasures of the past that Byzantium had devotedly stored, and the mortal wounding of a civilization that was still active and great; but it was also an act of gigantic political folly. It brought no help to the Christians in Palestine. Instead it robbed them of potential helpers. And it upset the whole defense of Christendom."[46] The crusades had also contributed to the fall of the Shiite caliphate of Egypt, a prosperous and tolerant civilization that had been on friendly terms with Eastern Christians, ultimately furthering the domination of the Sunni Turks with their more radical brand of Islam.

However, for the West, and Italy in particular, the sack of Constantinople kicked off astounding economic growth, fed initially by the vast quantities of plundered gold. In the early thirteenth century the first gold coins appeared in the West, where only silver coinage had been previously issued (except in Sicily and Spain).[47] The cultural benefits of the Fourth Crusade were also impressive: in subsequent years, whole libraries were pillaged, which Greek-speaking scholars would then start to translate into Latin. This was how most of the Ancient Greek heritage, which had been preserved by Constantinople, reached Europe—and not through the Arabs, as has been wrongly imagined.[48] The rise of pre-Renaissance humanism and classical studies in Italy was a direct result of the Fourth Crusade.[49] And when the last bearers of Constantinople's high culture fled Ottoman rule in the fifteenth century, they contributed to the blooming of the Italian Renaissance. Throughout this period, the notion of *Translatio Imperii* promoted by the Roman church, that is, the claim of a translation of Roman civilization from West to East in Constantine's time, disguised the very real translation of Byzantine culture from East to West that had started in the late twelfth century and lasted through the fifteenth century.

---

[46] Steven Runciman, *A History of the Crusades*, vol. 3, *op. cit.*, p. 130.

[47] Edwin Hunt, *The Medieval Super-Companies: A Study of the Peruzzi Company of Florence*, Cambridge University Press, 1994.

[48] Sylvain Gouguenheim, *Aristote au mont Saint-Michel. Les racines grecques de l'Europe chrétienne*, Seuil, 2008.

[49] Steven Runciman, *A History of the Crusades*, vol. 3, *op. cit.*, p. 391.

In the final analysis, there is something Sethian in the fratricide committed by Rome against Constantinople by the trickery of the crusades, and in Rome's determination to erase the memory of her defrauded and murdered elder sister. Yet like Osiris, Byzantium has been resurrected. Her spirit moved to the far northeast, in the great plains of Russia. As John Meyendorff tells it in *Byzantium and the Rise of Russia*: "Since the adoption of Christianity as the state religion of the Kievan principality (988), the influence of Byzantine civilization upon Russia became the determining factor of Russian civilization."[50] At the end of the tenth century, Russian king Vladimir the Great received baptism and married a sister of Byzantine emperor Basil II, and his son Iaroslav made Orthodox Christianity the religion of his subjects. The Greek alphabet was adapted to the Slavic tongue by Byzantine monks. During the schism of 1054 and throughout the vanishing years of Byzantium, Russia remained faithful to Constantinople's religious leadership, and to this day still carries its spiritual legacy, as symbolized by the Byzantine double-headed eagle on the Russian flag.

---

[50] John Meyendorff, *Byzantium and the Rise of Russia, op. cit.*, p. 10.

Chapter 5

THE WANDERING CRYPTO-JEW

> "Rebekah took her elder son Esau's best clothes, which she had at home, and dressed her younger son Jacob in them. [...] Jacob said to his father, 'I am Esau your first-born.'"
>
> Genesis 27:15–19

The Jews and Europe in the Middle Ages

The rise of European Jewish communities in the Middle Ages is shrouded in mystery, as are many other aspects of medieval civilization until the twelfth century. What emerges from the chronicles most clearly is the fact that, although excluded from Christian society, Jews had a virtual monopoly on the practice of lending at interest—an economic power that the Church denied Christians for moral reasons. By contrast, the practice of usury as a weapon of domination over "the nations" is promoted by the laws of Deuteronomy (15:6), by the "heroic" legends in the Hebrew Bible (Joseph in Egypt), by the Talmud, and even by Maimonides, now considered the greatest Jewish thinker of the Middle Ages.

The interest rates imposed on the rural poor generally were around 65 percent and could reach more than 150 percent. In France, they were legally capped at 43 percent in 1206. Under such conditions, usurious lending did not stimulate economic development. On the contrary, it led to the impoverishment of ordinary people and the enrichment of a financier class. Debt often put farmers in a desperate situation, forcing them to sell themselves into virtual slavery. Throughout medieval Europe, from France to Russia passing through Germany and Poland, the Jews were hated; they were perennial victims of popular anger for their ruthless usury, alongside their aggressive commercial practices such as client-hunting, predatory pricing, and other violations of the codes of the guilds and corporations from which they were excluded.[1] Even the bourgeois would complain about these practices and petition or even pay princes to put an end to them.

Kings and princes, however, granted Jewish usurers protection whenever Judeophobia arose among the people. The tax on interest made Jews an important source of contributions to the royal treasury. Additionally, the kings and princes would themselves fall under the control of the moneylenders. Indeed, usury allowed Jews, operating in a network, to concentrate in their hands an ever-greater share of the money supply. Jews became the king's creditors whenever he ran out of money, especially in wartime. It was these Jewish bankers, says Abraham Léon, who "allowed the kings to maintain the costly armies of mercenaries that begin to replace the undisciplined hordes of the nobility."[2]

The powerful used Jews as intermediaries for collecting taxes, in kind and in cash. "Tax farming" and lending at interest are activities that combine into a formidable power, since it is often taxes that force producers into debt. Occupying powers have always been able to count on the collaboration of the Jews as an intermediate class to exploit, and force into submission, the population of the occupied country; such was already the case in Egypt under Persian rule in the fifth century BCE, and again under the Ptolemies. Jewish elites, it seems, felt no solidarity with oppressed people, but remained loyal to the monarch who granted them privileged status and protected them from the vengeful mob.

England offers a good illustration of this phenomenon. The first Jews, mostly from Rouen, arrived there with William the Conqueror in 1066.[3] They were soon in all major cities of England, serving as intermediaries between the new elite and the Norman Anglo-Saxon population. The king and his barons, who had decimated and replaced the Anglo-Saxon nobility, granted

---

[1] Werner Sombart, *The Jews and Modern Capitalism* (1911) Batoche Books, 2001.
[2] Abraham Léon, *La Conception matérialiste de la question juive* (1942), Kontre Kulture, 2013, p. 109.
[3] Norman Golb, *The Jews in Medieval Normandy: A Social and Intellectual History*, Cambridge University Press, 1998.

the Jews a monopoly on tax collection, which at the time was a profession akin to racketeering under royal protection. According to historian Edward Freeman, a specialist in the Norman Conquest, "They came as the king's special men, or more truly as his special chattels, strangers alike to the Church and the commonwealth, but strong in the protection of a master who commonly found it his interest to protect them against all others. Hated, feared, and loathed, but far too deeply feared to be scorned or oppressed, they stalked defiantly among the people of the land, on whose wants they throve, safe from harm or insult, save now and then, when popular wrath burst all bounds, when their proud mansions and fortified quarters could shelter them no longer from raging crowds who were eager to wash out their debts in the blood of their creditors."[4]

Despite these violent episodes, the economic clout of the Jews quickly rose. The king became obliged to his Jewish bankers and made them his advisers. In the second half of the twelfth century, Henry II owed the Jewish financier Aaron of Lincoln alone a sum equivalent to the kingdom's annual budget. Aaron died as the richest man in England, but the king then seized his property.

Sometimes popular resentment and the Church's pressure reached a critical point, forcing the king to expel the Jews, not without demanding financial compensation from the bourgeois and/or confiscating some of the Jews' money. The Jews were first expelled from the Kingdom of France (at the time hardly bigger than today's Ile de France) in 1182, their property confiscated by Philip Augustus. Many took refuge in Flanders and Alsace. The latter, under Count Philippe, achieved such prosperity that the king grew jealous, to the point of recalling the Jews in 1198. The Jewish financiers were in fact weaving international networks; they knew how to make themselves indispensable by stoking princely rivalries.

Throughout the Middle Ages, the Church continued to condemn Jewish usury for its damage to the social fabric. The

---

[4] Edward Freeman, *The Reign of William Rufus and the Accession of Henry the First*, Clarendon Press, 1882, vol. 1, pp. 160–161.

issue was central to the Fourth Lateran Council convened in 1215 by Innocent III. Five edicts issued by the council concerned the Jews, two of them condemning the usurers' abusive practice of appropriating the properties of defaulting debtors. Decree 67 of the council said: "The more Christians are restrained from the practice of usury, the more are they oppressed in this manner by the treachery of the Jews, so that in a short time they exhaust the resources of the Christians. Wishing, therefore, in this matter to protect the Christians against cruel oppression by the Jews, we ordain in this decree that if in future, under any pretext, Jews extort from Christians oppressive and excessive interest, the society of Christians shall be denied them until they have made suitable satisfaction for their excesses." The pope complained that the Jews extort "not only usury, but usury on the usury," that is to say, compound interest (on a second loan contracted by a debtor to pay a first loan).

Of course, throughout the thirteenth century, some Christians were also in the moneylending business despite the religious prohibition. In his *Divine Comedy* (begun in 1306), the Italian poet Dante would reserve for them one of the spheres of the most infamous of the nine concentric regions of hell, alongside sodomites, because like them they do violence to "the natural order" through sterile activity.

The edict of Innocent III had only a limited immediate effect, but under the reign of the son of Philip Augustus, Louis VIII (1223–1226), and especially his grandson Louis IX, also known as Saint Louis (1226–1270), the status of the Jews was marked by the growing influence of the Church—though the interests of the Crown were not forgotten. In 1223 a decree prohibited interest on loans made by Jews and asked the nobility to accept repayment of principal on behalf of the Jews. But this decree had to be republished in 1230, which proves that it was very imperfectly applied. Saint Louis was distinguished by his commitment to fully liberate France from Jewish usury, beginning by breaking the royal treasury's dependence on the Jews. His contemporary and biographer William of Chartres depicts his concern "that the Jews should not oppress Christians by usury, and they shall not be authorized to engage, under the shelter of my protection, in such activities and infect my country by their poison."[5] In 1234, Louis IX freed his subjects from one-third of their debts to Jews, and ordered that the same share be returned to those who had already repaid their loans. Additionally, he prohibited imprisoning Christians or selling their property to pay off debts owed to Jews. In 1240, Jean I, duke of Brittany, expelled all Jews and released all his subjects from all debts, mortgages, or pledges contracted with them.

In 1306, Louis IX's grandson Philip the Fair arrested and exiled the Jews, seizing their properties including the debts they held, without even doing the service to his subjects of freeing them from those debts. According to estimates, one hundred thousand Jews were exiled under harsh conditions. Philip had hitherto exploited the wealth of the Jews; he had imposed on them a new tax in 1292 and, three years later, seized their property, giving them eight days to redeem it. But in 1306, with his treasury empty, he decided to kill the goose that laid the golden eggs. Given that the kingdom had expanded since the first expulsion under Philip Augustus, the Jews were compelled to flee even further away. Many probably ended their journey in Poland, together with the German Yiddish-speaking Jews, called Ashkenaz (the Hebrew name for Germany). Since the thirteenth century, in fact, Poland constituted a *Paradisus Judeorum* and attracted several waves of Jews fleeing restrictions and persecutions. Beginning in 1264, the Statute on Jewish Liberties granted them the right to self-governance.

By the seventeenth century Poland, then the largest country in Europe, hosted the majority of the world's Jews. Various theories have been put forward to explain the extraordinary population growth of this community. Some researchers cite a possible conversion of the Khazar kingdom (in present Kazakhstan) in the early ninth century,[6] but the evidence is very thin, and the absence of any trace of Turkish influence in

---

[5] Kevin MacDonald, *A People That Shall Dwell Alone: Judaism as a Group Evolutionary Strategy*, Praeger, 1994, kindle 2013, k. 7218–26.

[6] Arthur Koestler, *The Thirteenth Tribe: The Khazar Empire and Its Heritage*, Hutchinson, 1976.

Yiddish makes this a risky hypothesis.[7] In fact, it was after the Middle Ages that the Polish Jewish population seems to have exploded, thanks in large part to a widespread practice of early marriage. Between 1340 and 1772 the Jewish population of Poland grew 75 times larger, going from about 10 thousand to 750 thousand.[8]

In England, Edward I prohibited Jewish usury in 1275, then banished the Jews (about 16,000 people) from his kingdom in 1290 by his decree on The Statutes of Jewry: "Forasmuch as the King hath seen that divers evils and the disinheriting of good men of his land have happened by the usuries which the Jews have made in time past, and that divers sins have followed thereupon albeit that he and his ancestors have received much benefit from the Jewish people in all times past, nevertheless, for the honor of God and the common benefit of the people the King hath ordained and established, that from henceforth no Jew shall lend anything at usury either upon land, or upon rent or upon other thing." Most of the expelled Jews emigrated to the big commercial capitals of Europe. To circumvent laws that restricted their commercial and political activity, many took the opportunity to nominally convert to Christianity. A significant number moved to Venice, which was already home to a large and prosperous Jewish colony, and became the banking capital of Europe. Some would return later to London in Christian disguise.

Truth be told, the Roman Catholic Church's attitude toward moneylending and banking was ambivalent. The crusade spawned a huge increase in banking activity, since it required mortgages, interest-bearing loans, and bills of exchange at a scale previously unknown. Such activity became the specialty of the Knights Templar (the Poor Knights of Christ of the Order of the Temple of Solomon, by their full name), founded in the early twelfth century by nine soldier-monks from Troyes—a city with an influential Jewish community. Taking as their insignia

---

[7] For a refutation of the Khazar hypothesis, read Shaul Stampfer, 'Did the Khazars convert to Judaism,"*Jewish Social Studies*, vol. 19-3, spring/summer 2013, on the net.
[8] Iwo Cyprian Pogonowski, *Jews in Poland: A Documentary History; the Rise of the Jews as a Nation from Congressus Judaicus in Poland to the Knesset in Israel,* Hippocrene Books, 1993, pp. 13–14.

the seal of Solomon (or Star of David) in the middle of the Cross Pattée (footed cross) the Templars were heavily influenced by the trade and finance of the Jews. In an 1139 bull, Pope Innocent II granted them exemption from paying tithes (church tax), full use of tithes they collected, and the right to keep any kind of booty seized in the Holy Land from conquered Saracens.

The Templars invented modern banking. They issued the check or money order called the "letter of credit" and their command posts served as safe-deposit boxes for kings and wealthy individuals. They provided transportation of funds secured by their reputation and warrior tradition. They also acted as officers to recover debts or safeguard property under litigation. The prohibition of usury was circumvented by "reciprocal gifts." By seizing their debtors' assets at death, they appropriated, in the middle of the thirteenth century, part of France's territory and formed a state within the state. When French king Philip the Fair targeted the Jewish financial networks in 1306, he simultaneously attacked the Templars, who were an essential link in these networks.

The "Jewish question" became complicated in Europe when the Talmud became known to Christians. Written in Hebrew, it had been carefully concealed from public view, actually containing the statement: "The goyim who seek to discover the secrets of the Law of Israel commit a crime that calls for the death penalty" (Sanhedrin 59a). It was in 1236 that Nicolas Donin, a converted Jew who became a Dominican monk, gained an audience with Pope Gregory IX to convince him of the blasphemous character of the Talmud, which presents Christ as the illegitimate son of a Roman soldier and a prostitute (Sanhedrin 106a), capable of miracles only by sorcery, and not risen but "sent to hell, where he was punished by being boiled in excrement" (Gittin 56b).[9] A *disputatio* (debate on the public square lasting sometimes several months) was organized in Paris in the presence of Blanche of Castile, between Donin and Rabbi Yehiel, during which the latter failed to convince his audience

---

[9] Peter Schäfer, *Jesus in the Talmud*, Princeton University Press, 2007, pp. 82–93.

that the Talmud was talking about another Jesus and another Mary. Following these exchanges, Gregory IX publicly condemned the Talmud as "the first cause that keeps the Jews stubborn in their perfidy." In 1242, more than 10,000 volumes were burned. Judaism stopped being perceived as the religion of the Old Testament, and began to be viewed as a threat to public order, since the Talmud preaches violence and deception against Christians.[10]

In the twelfth century, the prayer of Kol Nidre, solemnly declaimed three times the day before Yom Kippur, the holiday of forgiveness, was already in use in all Jewish communities, Sephardic as well as Ashkenazi: "All vows, obligations, oaths or anathemas, pledges of all names, which we shall have vowed, sworn, devoted or bound ourselves to, from this day of atonement (whose arrival we hope for in happiness) to the next, we repent, aforehand, of them all, they shall be deemed absolved, forgiven, annulled, void and made of no effect; they shall not be binding nor have any power; the vows shall not be reckoned vows, the obligations shall not be reckoned obligatory, nor the oaths considered as oaths."[11] For Jewish author Samuel Roth, this yearly ceremony in which every Jew, young and old, absolved himself before God of all his lies, perjuries, and betrayals of trust against Gentiles, has largely contributed to the Jews' moral corruption for a millennium: "Can it be doubted what a fearful influence for evil this must exert on his character as a citizen and as a human being?" (*Jews Must Live*, 1934).[12] This practice creates, among other things, unlimited tolerance for apostasy, since it declares Christian baptism inoperative. With each wave of expulsions, many Jewish families chose conversion rather than exile, while continuing to "Judaize" discreetly or covertly. The fifth edict of the Fourth Lateran Council (1215) concerns the problem of crypto-Jews, that is to say, insincere converts.

---

[10] Michael Jones, *The Jewish Revolutionary Spirit and Its Impact on World History*, Fidelity Press, 2008, pp. 118–123.

[11] Yirmiyahu Yovel, *L'Aventure marrane. Judaïsme et modernité*, Seuil, 2011, p. 395.

[12] Samuel Roth, *Jews Must Live: An account of the persecution of the world by Israel on all the frontiers of civilization*, 1934 (archive.org), ch. IX.

The situation of Jews in the Middle Ages cannot be understood simply by examining their relationships with Christians; that external aspect is secondary to the internal structure of the community itself, whose most salient characteristic was the oppression by the "doctors of the law" on the masses of Jews in order to preserve them from any outside influence. The Talmud, conceived as "a wall around the Torah," allowed the rabbis to "stand guard over the guard itself," according to the Talmudic expression.[13] Though Moses Maimonides attempted to reconcile faith and Aristotelian science in the *Guide for the Perplexed* (*Moreh Neboukhim*), his effort was violently rejected at the time, and his disciples ostracized, by community elites. "In 1232, Rabbi Solomon of Montpellier hurled anathemas [complete exclusion from the community, often leading to death] against all those who would read the *Moreh Neboukhim* or engage in scientific and philosophical studies," reports the Jewish historian Bernard Lazare, who gave a vivid portrayal of medieval Jewish communities. "These miserable Jews, whom the whole world tormented for their faith, persecuted their own coreligionists more fiercely, more bitterly, than they had ever been persecuted. Those accused of indifference were condemned to the worst tortures; blasphemers had their tongues cut off; Jewish women who had relations with Christians were condemned to be disfigured, and their noses were removed." Rationalists resisted, but they were an isolated minority. "As for the mass of Jews, they had completely fallen under the yoke of the obscurantists. They were now separated from the world, every horizon closed, with nothing left to nourish their minds but futile talmudic commentaries, idle and mediocre discussions on the law; they were enclosed and stifled by ceremonial practices, like mummies swaddled by their bands: their directors and guides had locked them in the narrowest and most abominable of dungeons. From there emerged a fearful bewilderment, a terrible decay, a collapse of intellectualism, a

---

[13] Isaac Kadmi-Cohen, *Nomades: Essai sur l'âme juive*, Felix Alcan, 1929 (archive.org), p. 145.

compression of the brain that rendered them unfit to conceive any idea."[14]

Forced Conversions in Spain and Portugal

While the Ashkenazi Jews of Eastern Europe were living in complete cultural isolation, Sephardic Jews from the Iberian Peninsula were preparing to exercise a decisive influence on European affairs. Documented from the fifth century onward, this community flourished under the rule of Muslims, whose conquest they facilitated during the eighth century. Muslim Andalusia was a highly cultured society with a relatively peaceful coexistence between Muslims, Jews, and Christians. Many Jews exiled from France took refuge there between the twelfth and fourteenth centuries, but Catholic Spain also received them. It is estimated that in the kingdom of Aragon in 1294, 22 percent of tax revenues were levied on the Jews, who made up only 3 percent of the population.

The situation of the Jews was particularly favorable in Castile during the reign of King Peter I (1350–1369), known as Peter the Cruel: "Don Pedro was, indeed, so surrounded by Jews, that his enemies reproached his court for its Jewish character," writes Heinrich Graetz. The treasurer and advisor to the king, Samuel Ha-Levi, was a particularly powerful figure. Graetz relates his dubious role in the failure of Peter's marriage with the very Catholic Blanche de Bourbon, a descendant of St. Louis, and in the civil war that followed. While his ministers were negotiating his marriage, the king fell in love with a certain Maria de Padilla. Samuel, and with him all the Jews of Spain, sided with Maria. "The reason assigned was that Blanche, having observed with displeasure the influence possessed by Samuel and other Jews at her husband's court, and the honors and distinctions enjoyed by them, had made the firm resolve, which she even commenced to put into execution, to compass the fall of the more prominent Jews, and obtain the banishment of the whole of the Jewish population from Spain. She made no secret of her aversion to

---

[14] Bernard Lazare, *L'Antisémitisme, son histoire et ses causes* (1894), Kontre Kulture, 2011, pp. 71–73.

the Jews, but, on the contrary, expressed it openly. For this reason, it is stated, the Jewish courtiers took up a position of antagonism to the queen, and, on their part, lost no opportunity of increasing Don Pedro's dislike for her. If Blanche de Bourbon really fostered such anti-Jewish feelings, and circumstances certainly seem to bear out this view, then the Jews were compelled in self-defense to prevent the queen from acquiring any ascendency, declare themselves for the Padilla party, and support it with all the means in their power." The scheme was successful. "Samuel Abulafia, by the wisdom of his counsels, his able financial administration, and his zeal for the cause of Maria de Padilla, continued to rise in the favor of the king. His power was greater than that of the grandees of the realm. His wealth was princely, and eighty black slaves served in his palace." Peter would ultimately poison his wife Blanche, but only after putting Samuel to death and confiscating his fortune. He was excommunicated by the pope and perished in the civil war against his brother Henry of Trastamara, backed by the famous Bertrand du Guesclin.[15] But the power of the Jews decreased only temporarily. In 1371, the citizens complained in a petition to the new king of Castile that they controlled the cities.

At the end of the fourteenth century, episodic clashes throughout Spain degenerated into massacres. On June 9, 1391, a crowd gripped by a frenzy of killing and looting invaded the vast Jewish district of Seville. Jews could only escape it by taking refuge in churches and undergoing baptism. Violence spread like wildfire in Castile, then under the authority of a weak king, and from there to the entire Iberian Peninsula. The estimated number of victims in one year amounted to approximately fifty thousand deaths and tens of thousands of converts.

In the early fifteenth century, tensions continued to mount. The years 1412–1415 were marked by a new round of collective conversions: many were forced, but some were voluntary, with motives ranging from opportunism to sincere religious conviction (due to the preaching of the Dominican monk

---

[15] Heinrich Graetz, *History of the Jews,* Jewish Publication Society of America, 1891 (archive.org), vol. 4, pp. 116–119.

Vincent Ferrer in particular).[16] In a quarter century (1391–1415), pressures, threats, and sermons made over a hundred thousand converts. Although church and Spanish law prohibited forced baptisms in theory, it still held those forced conversions legally irreversible.

Freed from the restrictions imposed on Jews, these converts, called "New Christians," *conversos*, or *marranos*, experienced a meteoric socio-economic ascension. In the words of historian of Marranism Yirmiyahu Yovel: "*Conversos* rushed into Christian society and infiltrated most of its interstices. After one or two generations, they were in the councils of Castile and Aragon, exercising the functions of royal counselors and administrators, commanding the army and navy, and occupying all ecclesiastical offices from parish priest to bishop and cardinal. Those who wanted to keep a secret Jewish aspect of their identity would sometimes seek refuge in Catholic monasteries. The *conversos* were priests and soldiers, politicians and professors, judges and theologians, writers, poets and legal advisors—and of course, as in the past, doctors, accountants and high-flying merchants. Some allied themselves by marriage to the greatest families of Spanish nobility [. . .] Their ascent and penetration in society were of astonishing magnitude and speed."[17]

This rise of the New Christians naturally generated hostility among ethnic Christians (called by contrast "Old Christians"). The former group not only practiced strict endogamy for the most part, sometimes within blood ties prohibited by the Church (marriage between first cousins or between uncle and niece),[18] but also continued to "Judaize": "Many converts," writes Yirmiyahu Yovel, "effectively tried to keep—in the privacy of their homes and their clandestine behavior—a form of Jewish identity. They secretly observed some Jewish rituals, refrained as much as possible from eating forbidden foods, practiced silent prayer, murmured old formulas and Jewish blessings, and taught their children that they would be saved by

---

[16] Nathan Wachtel, *Entre Moïse et Jésus. Études marranes (XVᵉ-XIXᵉ siècle)*, CNRS éditions, 2013, p. 9.
[17] Yirmiyahu Yovel, *L'Aventure marrane, op. cit.*, pp. 119–120.
[18] Kevin MacDonald, *A People That Shall Dwell Alone, op. cit.*, k. 3337–39.

the Law of Moses and not by that of Christ; they considered themselves captives in the 'land of idolatry' and awaited their own Messiah." Many met secretly and developed codes and verbal masks. The biblical figure of Esther, the clandestine Jew, was particularly popular among the Judaizers; subsequent generations of Marranos would pray to "Saint Esther."[19]

Anti-Marrano violence erupted in Toledo from 1449 until the 1470s, and spread to Andalusia. To eradicate crypto-Judaism, King Ferdinand of Aragon and Queen Isabella of Castile established the Spanish Inquisition, whose first courts opened in 1480 in Seville. Not only did the Inquisition have no jurisdiction over the Jews, it sometimes received denunciations from Jews who despised or were jealous of *conversos*. Pedro de la Caballeria, the son of a convert who had attained high ecclesiastical office and had even negotiated the marriage of Isabella and Ferdinand, was tried posthumously as a secret Jew; he had reportedly told a Jewish neighbor who reproached him about his conversion : "Silence, fool! Could I, as a Jew, ever have risen higher than a rabbinical post? But now, see, I am one of the chief councilors (*jurado*) of the city. For the sake of the little hanged man (Jesus), I am accorded every honor, and I issue orders and decrees to the whole city of Saragossa. Who hinders me—if I choose—from fasting on Yom Kippur and keeping your festivals and all the rest? When I was a Jew I dared not walk as far as this (i.e. beyond the prescribed limits of a Sabbath day's walk) but now I do as I please."[20]

Upon completion of the Reconquista in 1492, Ferdinand and Isabella took drastic measures. With the Alhambra Decree, they ordered the final expulsion of Jews who refused to convert. The explicit motivation given for such drastic measures is the bad influence that Jews have on their converted brethren: "You well know that in our dominion, there are certain bad Christians that judaised and committed apostasy against our Holy Catholic faith, much of it the cause of communications between Jews and Christians. [...] These Jews instruct these Christians in the

---

[19] Yirmiyahu Yovel, *L'Aventure marrane, op. cit.*, pp. 149–151.
[20] Léon Poliakov, *Histoire de l'antisémitisme* (1981), tome 1, Seuil, 1991, p. 157.

ceremonies and observances of their Law, circumcising their children, […]." Believing that "the true remedy of such damages and difficulties lay in the severing of all communications between the said Jews," the king and queen of Spain had first ordered, in 1480, "that the Jews be separated from the cities and towns of our domains and that they be given separate quarters." That proved insufficient, and Jews have kept "trying by whatever manner to subvert our holy Catholic faith and trying to draw faithful Christians away from their beliefs."

The estimated number of Jews expelled from Spain varies among historians; Yovel sets the minimum figure at 120,000, out of a total of about 160,000 Spanish Jews of whom 40,000 chose baptism. Approximately 80,000 of the expelled accepted the paying offer of temporary asylum proffered by John II in Portugal, with the others settling in the south of France or Italy, Algeria or Morocco, Turkey or northern Germany (Hamburg), and in the Netherlands.

As in every episode of this type, the Jews who chose exile rather than apostasy were more committed to their faith and their community, and they took with them a deep resentment against Catholicism. The case of Isaac Abravanel (1437–1508) is emblematic: born in Lisbon to a rich and powerful family, he had derived great profits from his business ventures and became, thanks to his ability to lend huge amounts of money, the bagman of Ferdinand and Isabella. In 1492, he chose exile and took refuge in Italy, where he served the king of Naples and the Venetian Republic. The idea of Israel taking revenge against Edom/Esau (code names for Rome and the Church) is central to the exegeses he published after leaving Spain. For example, the book of Daniel means, according to him, "that at the precise moment the Lord takes vengeance on the nations, Israel will then go from darkness to light and out of bondage," and "nothing will survive of the house of Esau." "Indeed, any deliverance promised Israel is associated with the fall of Edom."[21]

---

[21] Jean-Christophe Attias, *Isaac Abravanel, la mémoire et l'espérance*, Cerf, 1992, pp. 140, 111, 269, 276.

The expulsion of Jews from Spain had tripled their number in Portugal, where they grew overnight from 4 percent to almost 12 percent, out of a total population of one million. The Jews quickly came to dominate economic life there. But in 1496, as part of a matrimonial alliance with Spain that would unify the peninsula, the king of Portugal Manuel I aligned with Spanish Jewish policy. He required a massive conversion of the Jews but—in an unheard-of move—prevented them from leaving the kingdom because he did not want to deprive himself of their financial manna. However, he guaranteed them that no investigation would be conducted into their religious life during a transitional period of twenty years (a guarantee renewed in 1512 and again in 1524). Portugal now had a population consisting of about 12 percent New Christians, concentrated in the cities where they represented as much as a quarter to a third of the population. Historian of the crypto-Jews Nathan Wachtel notes that "this was how, under a regime of relative tolerance, the New Christians in Portugal learned and perfected the art of leading a double life: apparently Christian on the outside, while privately given to observing (however imperfectly) the celebrations and rites of the Jewish religion."[22] In Portugal, as in Spain earlier, popular hostility was not slow to manifest itself in massacres like the one in Lisbon in 1506, which caused several hundreds or even thousands of deaths. Consequently, King Manuel eventually allowed the Marranos to leave the kingdom in 1507 and let them engage in international trade.

In 1540, the new Portuguese king João III introduced the Inquisition following the Spanish model. But the crypto-Judaism of the Portuguese Marranos was much more committed and durable than its nearly-extinct counterpart in Spain. There were three main reasons for this. First, the Portuguese Marranos descended mainly from Spanish Jews who had rejected the alternative of apostasy in 1492. Secondly, they had only converted under the threat of death, being denied the alternate possibility of leaving Portugal. And thirdly, by 1540, they had already Judaized for almost half a century with relative impunity.

----

[22] Nathan Wachtel, *Entre Moïse et Jésus, op. cit.*, p. 27.

The Portuguese Inquisition was horribly efficient, torturing and burning alive tens of thousands of Judaizers, tracking them down all over Europe and even in the colonies of the New World for harmless beliefs and practices. In light of these events, the papal bull of Clement VIII in 1593, *Caeca et Obdurata*, took on a sadly ironic dimension when it denounced "the blind and unfeeling perfidy of the Jews," which "does not recognize the mercy toward them of the Church that patiently awaits their conversion."

Judaizing Marranos developed signs of mutual recognition. "Being Marrano means being affiliated with a vast secret society of protection and assistance," wrote Léon Poliakow.[23] The secret, explains Nathan Wachtel, "became an essential component of religious fervor itself," and "definitively marked what we may call the Marrano lifestyle: secrecy exalted as a value in itself, a sign of eminent virtue." The Marranos developed discrete signs for recognizing each other: "an allusion, an ambiguous expression, or just a word spoken in a certain way (such as 'believer' or 'faithful' or 'good Christian' meant to be understood ironically). A gesture, a smile, or a glance often sufficed." By necessity, the Marranos did not reveal their true religion to their children until adolescence; teenagers were then stunned to learn that everything they had been taught before (Jesus Christ, the Virgin Mary, the Trinity, saints) was false, and that salvation was not found in the "law of Jesus" but in that of Moses. Thus did Marranism introduce a practice of converting Christians to crypto-Judaism.[24]

Among other negative effects, forced conversions and the Inquisition put a stop to sincere conversion. Voluntary converts were amalgamated with forced converts, and like them were considered suspect in the eyes of the Old Christians; if they maintained links with their Jewish relatives, or kept their aversion to pork, they risked torture, destruction, and death.

Why, under such circumstances, would anyone convert, considering that the Inquisition had no jurisdiction over the

---

[23] Léon Poliakow, *Histoire de l'antisémitisme* (1981), *op. cit.*
[24] Nathan Wachtel, *Entre Moïse et Jésus op. cit.*, pp. 188, 187, 113.

unconverted Jews? It is likely that without the Inquisition, Marranism would have influenced Judaism as well as Christianity and served as a bridge between the two. But syncretism, which is a form of religious miscegenation, was persecuted until the early eighteenth century. Accused at this time of Judaizing in Rio de Janeiro, Theresa Paes de Jesus, from a Marrano family, excused herself: "I thought Jesus Christ was the same person as Moses, [. . .] he was the king of the Jews worshiped by Jews and Christians." For this confession she was burned at the stake. The Inquisition crystallized, among a core group of Marranos, a deeply internalized hatred of Catholicism, which led to such sacrilegious practices as the flagellation of Christ.[25] This resentment, combined with a battle-hardened practice of concealment, infiltration, and secret intelligence networks, helped transform European Judaism into an ever-more-formidable anti-Christian force.

Throughout the sixteenth century, the Marranos migrated to nations with Jewish communities, but were not allowed to officially join them. Many, feeling as foreign to one religion as the other, lost their faith. But their rejection of Jewish religion was not a rejection of Jewishness. On the contrary: beginning in the fifteenth century, a heightened racial pride emerged among the New Christians, in direct contradiction to the Christian concept that, among the baptized, "there is neither Jew nor Greek" (Galatians 3:28). Having been forced to change their religion, the Marranos minimized the importance of religion and interpreted their Jewishness in racial terms, allowing them to view themselves as fundamentally Jewish, and only incidentally Christian. It was the Marranos who, inspired by the Talmud, disseminated the first racist theories: in 1655 Isaac La Peyrère, a Marrano from Bordeaux, claimed in his treatise *Præadamitæ* that Adam is the ancestor of the Jewish race, while other breeds are derived from a pre-Adamic humanity, devoid of soul. In an earlier book, *Du rappel des Juifs* (1643), La Peyrère had already evoked a fundamental difference in biological makeup between Jews and Gentiles, while conceding that the difference is less

---

[25] Nathan Wachtel, *Entre Moïse et Jésus, op. cit.*, pp. 210, 128–130.

than that between the bodies of beasts and men's bodies because only the latter are "capable of resurrection and immortality"; however, "the bodies of Jews are capable of more Grace and Glory than the bodies of the Gentiles."[26]

Far from blending in with Christian society, New Christians socialized and married only among themselves, continued to practice usury, and still served as intermediaries between the elite and the masses of Old Christians, only with increased freedom and legitimacy. This behavior was the determining factor in the transformation of religiously based Judeophobia into the racial Judeophobia that would later be called "anti-Semitism"; the 1449 anti-Jewish revolt against the *conversos* of Toledo marked the turning point. Until then, both the Church and the people recognized that a Jewish convert to Christianity was not a Jew but a Christian. But conversion, which had reinforced the racial paradigm among New Christians, triggered a backlash among Spanish Old Christians: they too began to exalt their race. The ideology of "pure blood" became a central value of the *hidalgo* nobility, and resulted in the *limpieza de sangre* (purity of blood) statutes of 1449 denying the *conversos* access to certain occupations. According to historian Americo Castro, this Spanish purity-of-blood ideology was basically a reaction to, and a mirror image of, Jewish racism. Yet it was milder: one could hardly find among Spaniards the equivalent of this certificate established in 1300 by a rabbi, guaranteeing after investigation that two young candidates for marriage "were of pure descent, without any family taint, and that they could intermarry with the most honored families in Israel; for there had been no admixture of impure blood in the paternal or maternal antecedents and their collateral relatives."[27]

---

[26] Quoted in André Pichot, *Aux origines des théories raciales, de la Bible à Darwin,* Flammarion, 2008, pp. 52–66.

[27] Americo Castro, *The Spaniards: An Introduction to Their History,* University of California Press, 1971, p. 75.

The Marrano Dispersion

Part of the Marrano community never left Portugal, and in the early twentieth century, ethnographers were able to document remnant Marrano communities that had maintained their secret customs for more than five centuries, oblivious to their specific historical ties with the Jews of the world. For example, the village of Belmonte, a Marrano community discovered around 1920, officially converted to Judaism in 1985, under the guidance of the American Rabbi Joshua Stampfer.[28]

But a larger number of Portuguese Marranos spread around the world beginning in 1507, when they were first allowed to trade internationally. Some crossed the Pyrenees to reach Bayonne and Bordeaux, others settled in Northern Europe or in the Mediterranean basin, while others sailed to Lima in South America, or Goa in India. "From the mid-seventeenth century onward," summarizes Yovel, "the Marranos created a worldwide network of Spanish-Portuguese establishments, a kind of archipelago of islands where they interacted to some degree with their surroundings, bringing with them their languages, their cultures, their Iberian customs, their skills and trade networks along with the restlessness and split identity that was their own special characteristic." The conversos quickly became first-class international businessmen, confidently exchanging bank notes and IOUs. They "created the first pre-modern, albeit fragmented, model of economic globalization" and "soon began to rise to the forefront of international trade, virtually monopolizing the market for certain commodities, such as sugar, to participate to a lesser degree in trading spices, rare woods, tea, coffee, and the transportation of slaves."[29] Their strength lay not only in their network of solidarity, but also in their great mobility, with wealthy families always ready to respond to constraints or opportunities by a new exile.

---

[28] David Canelo, *The Last Crypto-Jews of Portugal: The Story and History of Belmonte's Judeo Community*, Stampfer, 1990. Watch the documentary by Stan Neumann and Frederick Brenner, "The Last Marranos," 1991.

[29] Yirmiyahu Yovel *L'Aventure marrane, op. cit.*, pp. 479, 483, 347.

Fleeing the Inquisition, many Marranos took refuge in the Ottoman Empire, particularly in the city of Thessaloniki, where they were free to practice their religion. They converted nominally to Islam in large numbers during the seventeenth century, following the example of Sabbatai Zevi, the Kabbalist and self-styled messiah, forming the Dönmeh community, whose numbers were assessed at more than one million in the early twentieth century. In 1550, the French King Henri II allowed "merchants and other Portuguese called New Christians" to settle in Bordeaux, granting them privileges that allowed them to acquire great wealth in maritime trade, including the slave trade.[30] In Venice, Portuguese Marranos settled in the early sixteenth century. By the middle of the seventeenth century "they attained the hegemony in local affairs," according to Cecil Roth.[31] It is worth mentioning that the first edition of the Babylonian Talmud was printed in Venice in 1520. From 1512 onward, an even larger Marrano community settled in the Netherlands, then under Spanish rule. Antwerp became their capital and emerged as a booming economic center. Calvinist uprisings led to the independence of the United Provinces in 1579. When, in 1585, Philip II of Spain temporarily retook Antwerp, Jews and Calvinists transferred their businesses to Amsterdam. In the seventeenth century, the Jewish community of Amsterdam, called the "New Jerusalem of the North," was composed largely of conversos who had returned to Judaism. Ashkenazi Jews also flocked to Amsterdam after the pogroms in Poland and Ukraine in 1648. Many of these Jews and crypto-Jews eventually would join the "New Amsterdam," later renamed New York.

When circumstances permitted, the Marranos returned to Judaism. But if it benefitted their affairs, they could also re-don the Christian mask when travelling back to Spain, Portugal, or in the Iberian colonies. Many made use of two names: a Hebrew name within the Jewish community, and a Spanish or Portuguese name in international affairs. A notable example is

---

[30] Bernard Lazare, *L'Antisémitisme, son histoire et ses causes, op. cit.*, p. 91.
[31] Cecil Roth, *A History of the Marranos* (1932), Meridian Books, 1959, p. 84.

Moshe Curie, one of the wealthiest Marranos of Amsterdam, who signed his bills, powers, and IOUs with the name Jeronimo Nunes da Costa.[32] Thus the sixteenth and seventeenth centuries "saw the return of Marrano emigrants to Judaism, a return that did not only occur in the Ottoman Empire, a traditional refuge for Jews, but also in European cities like Venice, Ferrara, Hamburg, Amsterdam and London. Jewish communities also reappeared, barely concealed, in prohibited areas such as Spanish Flanders and the Bordeaux region, where authorities had good business reasons to close their eyes. This led to the phenomenon of 'New Jews,' ex-New Christians who returned to the religion of their ancestors."[33]

The distinction between Jew and crypto-Jew gradually became baseless. The term "Portuguese" came to designate the Sephardic Jews exiled in Christian masks, whether or not they retained the mask. "The same commercial network," writes Yovel, "could contain secret Judaizers in Seville or Mexico, assimilated Catholics in Antwerp or Toulouse, officially declared Jews in London or Curacao, perhaps even a dissident converted to Calvinism, alongside all kinds of undecided Marranos, agnostics and freethinkers."[34] Nathan Wachtel adds: "Quasi-global dispersion, transcontinental and transoceanic solidarity: these huge networks linking New Christians in Lisbon, Antwerp or Mexico, and the Jews of Livorno, Amsterdam or Constantinople, had a remarkable character, something new at this dawn of modernity, which was to join together tens of thousands of people who did not officially profess the same religious faith, yet shared the feeling of belonging to the same community, designated by the lapidary phrase: the *Nação*."[35] It is significant that the term "nation," which comes from the Latin *natio*, "birth," was applied to the international community of Marranos before it came to designate any other "peoples." It may be said that the idea of "nation" is a crypto-Jewish contribution to the Christian West.

---

[32] Nathan Wachtel, *Entre Moïse et Jésus, op. cit.*, pp. 27, 35.
[33] Yirmiyahu Yovel, *L'Aventure marrane, op. cit.*, p. 488.
[34] Yirmiyahu Yovel, *L'Aventure marrane, op. cit.*, p. 484.
[35] Nathan Wachtel, *La Foi du souvenir. Labyrinthes Marranes*, Seuil, 2001, p. 26.

Firmly established in all major European ports, the Marranos played the leading role in the commercial and colonial expansion of sixteenth- to eighteenth-century Europe. Their networks were not only the link between the maritime empires of the Spanish, Portuguese, Dutch, French, and English, but also took on a global dimension, connecting Asia, Africa, Europe, and America. Portuguese Marranos mastered large-scale trade, on the routes to the East Indies as well as the newly opened sea routes to the "West Indies," meaning the American continent. Christopher Columbus—who left Spain during the same month that the decree of expulsion of the Jews was declared—was himself Marrano, according to a thesis defended by several Jewish historians, including Cecil Roth, author of an authoritative history of Marranism: "That epoch-making expedition of 1492 was as a matter of fact very largely a Jewish, or rather a Marrano, enterprise. There are grounds for believing that Columbus was himself a member of a New Christian family."[36] Christopher Columbus, we may recall, was the author of a genocide-by-forced-labor of Caribbean populations, island after island. In 1495, he sent the first shipments of Indian slaves to Spain: "Let us in the name of the Holy Trinity, go on sending all the slaves that can be sold," he wrote. Others were enslaved in their own lands for the extraction of the gold that Columbus intended to send back to his sponsors. Each Haitian above the age of thirteen was required to bring in a quota of gold, and those who failed had their hands cut off. The hell imposed on these populations resulted in the first known mass suicides. The population was decimated in two generations. The unspeakable cruelty of Columbus and his men was documented by the priest Bartolome de las Casas.

In the wake of Columbus, the Marranos became the main catalysts of the new spirit of colonial expansion, from Mexico to Peru and from the Caribbean to Brazil. Beginning in 1569, the Inquisition's courts were introduced in the Americas to hunt

---

[36] Cecil Roth, *A History of the Marranos, op. cit.*, p. 106. The thesis was expounded by Simon Wiesenthal in *Sails of Hope: The Secret Mission of Christopher Columbus*, MacMillan, 1973.

Judaizing Marranos, who then found a relatively mild situation in Brazil, where inquisitorial activity remained moderate until the very end of the seventeenth century. They developed in particular the cultivation of sugar cane, as explained by Nathan Wachtel: "The cultivation of sugar cane and sugar manufacturing require complex technology, abundant capital and extensive trade networks: at every successive stage of the sugar trade, the New Christians played a prominent role."[37] The Marranos of Latin America, who formed an "underground America," would also master the cultivation and commerce of cocoa, tobacco, and coffee—all addictive products that Europeans would grow heavily dependent upon in less than a century. The Inquisition of Lima in 1636 worried about the near monopoly of Portuguese Marranos in all branches of trade: "They achieved such mastery over trade that everything, from brocade to sackcloth, and from diamonds to cumin, passed through their hands." And the Bishop of Puebla, Juan de Palafox, wrote in 1641: "They have so much power, not only in this city but also inland, that they can threaten the security of the kingdom."[38]

No international trade escaped them, and in time of war, they traded with enemy countries equally. Naturally, said Wachtel, "the traffic of African slaves [. . .] was virtually controlled at the end of the sixteenth century and the first half of the seventeenth, by the networks of the Marrano diaspora," all beneficiaries of *asientos* (exclusive contracts granted by the Crown) being Portuguese businessmen. Some were at the same time priests, like Diego Lopez de Lisboa in the first decade of the seventeenth century.[39] Note that, out of a little over nine million slaves imported to the Americas between 1519 and 1867, eight million were in Brazil and the Caribbean, where the traffic was in the hands of Marranos. The conditions were much harder there than in North America; the majority of slaves died young without founding families. Jewish justification of this traffic,

---

[37] Nathan Wachtel, *La Foi du souvenir, op. cit.*, p. 20
[38] Quoted in Nathan Wachtel, *Entre Moïse et Jésus, op. cit.*, pp. 168, 171–172.
[39] Nathan Wachtel, *La Foi du souvenir, op. cit.*, pp. 14, 24–25, and *Entre Moïse et Jésus, op. cit.*, p. 183.

inspired by the Hebrew Bible, was voiced by Jacob ben Isaac
Achkenazi de Janow in his *Commentary on the Torah* in the early
seventeenth century: Blacks were descended from Ham, the
youngest son of Noah, who was cursed by the Lord with these
words: "Accursed be Canaan, he shall be his brothers' meanest
slave" (Genesis 9:25).[40] It is fair to mention that Pope Paul III
proclaimed in 1537 his bull *Sublimus Dei* prohibiting slavery of
American Indians and all other peoples, denouncing such
practices as directly inspired by "the enemy of mankind."

In the nineteenth century, traces of the Marranos were
gradually lost. After the annexation of half of Mexico by the
United States in 1848, the crypto-Jews who became US
citizens, now enjoying freedom of religion (Jews had been
officially banned in Mexico until then), seldom opted for a
return to Judaism. They preferred Presbyterianism, a
compromise that allowed them access to the Old Testament. At
least until the 1960s, some families in New Mexico and Texas
still kept the memory of their secret Jewish heritage.[41] Surveys
have revealed isolated pockets of Marranos in Brazil until the
end of the twentieth century, with some of them solemnly
returning to Judaism. In May 1997, on the five-hundredth
anniversary of the forced conversion of the Portuguese in 1497,
the first "National Congress of Marrano Jews" was held in
Recife, Brazil.

Marranos and the Church

Many Marranos were monks or priests, and some rose to
important ecclesiastical positions in the Catholic Church. The
question of their sincerity is often difficult to determine. From
the sixteenth century, the monastic order of Saint Jerome, and
especially the Monastery of Our Lady of Guadalupe, were
known for attracting Judaizing Marranos. One prominent friar,
Hernando de Talavera, was the confessor of Isabella the

---

[40] André Pichot, *Aux origines des théories raciales, op. cit.*, pp. 67–95.
[41] Stanley Hordes, *To the End of the Earth: A History of the Crypto-Jews of New Mexico*,
Columbia University Press, 2005; Richard Santos, *Silent Heritage: The Sephardim and the
Colonization of the Spanish North American Frontier, 1492–1600*, New Sepharad Press,
2000.

Catholic. Crypto-Jews were actually suspected of becoming the confessors of Old Christians in order to learn their secrets. Fray Vicente Rocamoro, confessor to Anne-Marie (daughter of Philip III of Spain and future empress) suddenly disappeared, then reappeared in 1643 in the Jewish community of Amsterdam under the name of Isaac de Rocamora.[42]

Conversely, there were unquestionably sincere converts among the Marranos, who found in Jesus the model of the Jew emancipated from Mosaic Law. St. Teresa of Avila, for example, came from a Marrano family. It was said that some of these sincere converts nonetheless brought into the Church a Jewish spirit: Ignatius of Loyola, founder of the Society of Jesus, was from a Marrano family, and many historians have noted that the Jesuit order owes much to the spirit of Jewish networking. The Inquisitor Tomas de Torquemada and his assistant Diego Daza, the most cruel persecutors of the "false Christians," were Marranos. In general, the question of sincerity is impossible to decide, as conversions may lead to virtual split personalities. We must also take into account that a Marrano could feel Christian by religion and Jewish by blood.

A good example is Solomon Halevi, chief rabbi of Burgos, who converted in 1390 or 1391, taking the name of Pablo de Santa Maria, becoming Bishop of Burgos in 1416. His sincerity seems beyond doubt, since he spoke harshly of the Jews, whom he accused of plotting to control Spain. As a bishop, he forced them to wear a badge to distinguish them from Christians. Yet he did not hesitate to proudly display his "Levitical" heritage.

After Halevi's death in 1435, his son Alonso Cartagena succeeded him as bishop of Burgos. A prolific writer like his father, he strove to mitigate the breach between the Old and New Testaments: "The strength of the Gospel is in the Law, and the foundation of the Law is the principle of the Gospel." The result, for Cartagena, was that the conversion of Jews to Christianity is not really a conversion, but simply a deeper understanding of their historical role: a converted Jew was a better Christian because he did not really convert but rather

---

[42] Yirmiyahu Yovel, *L'Aventure marrane, op. cit.,* pp. 185–191.

deepened his faith, while the Gentiles first had to get rid of their false pagan beliefs in coming to Christ. Alonso held Jewishness superior from the racial perspective: it was because of their superior genetic heritage that Jews were chosen, not only to give birth to Christ, but to be a natural aristocracy of humanity. The Jews embodied Israel in flesh and spirit at the same time; it was really the Jews, in a way, who were the "Old Christians."[43]

About 270 years after Nicholas Donin had persuaded the pope to take action against the Talmud, another converted Jew, Joseph Pfefferkorn, embarked on a similar crusade. A native of Moravia who had converted ("withdrawn from the filthy and pestilential mire of the Jews") in 1504 with his family, he abandoned the practice of usury and took the name of Johannes. He traveled through the German-speaking countries to preach conversion to the Jews, and wrote several books, including *The Mirror of the Jews* and *The Enemy of the Jews*, to "prevent the damage which the mangy dogs [Jews] do to Christian power in both the spiritual and worldly sphere." He denounced, for example, the way Jews were ruining farmers through usury and expropriation of their lands, their efforts to morally corrupt Christians, and the revolutionary spirit of the Jews, who "pray for revenge against the whole Christian Church and especially against the Roman Empire, so that it should be broken and destroyed." Supported by the Dominicans and the Franciscans, Pfefferkorn received from Emperor Maximilian I the right to confiscate Jewish books, examine them, and destroy those deemed hostile to the Christian faith. But a Jewish delegation successfully argued that the subject should first be discussed by a committee.

Johannes Reuchlin, the greatest humanist scholar of his time after Erasmus, defended the Jews.[44] Reuchlin immersed himself in Jewish writings and published in 1506 *De rudimentis Hebraicis*, the first Hebrew grammar by a non-Jew. He was interested in Kabbalah, which he combined with Neoplatonic magic in his

[43] Yirmiyahu Yovel, *L'Aventure marrane*, *op. cit.*, pp. 96–98, 141–143; Nathan Wachtel, *Entre Moïse et Jésus*, *op. cit.*, pp. 54–65.
[44] Michael Jones, *The Jewish Revolutionary Spirit*, *op. cit.*, pp. 225–255. Bernard Lazare, *L'Antisémitisme, son histoire et ses causes* (1894), Kontre Kulture, 2011, p. 101.

book *De verbo mirifico* (*The Magic Word*). Kabbalah is an outgrowth of Talmudism particularly popular in Marrano circles. Its founding text, the *Zohar* (*Book of Splendor*), presents itself as having been written in the second century CE by Simeon bar Yochai Rabbi, hidden in a cave, and fortuitously rediscovered in the thirteenth century by Moses de Leon in a market of Spain. Needless to say, academic research ascribes authorship to Moses de Leon himself; the book's antiquity is factitious. The basic principle of Kabbalah is the sacralization of the Hebrew language: since it is the language of God, by which God created the world, it follows that the knowledge of sacred words and their numeric meanings (associated with angelic powers) grants a demiurgic power to the kabbalist.

Reuchlin defended the Talmud and Kabbalah before the emperor, against the Dominicans. He considered these Jewish books "the speech and the most sacred words of God." His erudition, aided by the corruption of certain officials, managed to overturn the imperial order to destroy Jewish books. The debate continued for more than a decade in the universities, motivating many books in both camps. In 1517, Reuchlin published *De arte caballistica*, dedicated to Pope Leo X. In 1533, Cornelius Agrippa, inspired by Reuchlin, published *De occulta philosophia*. Thus did kabbalistic occult inspiration take root in the Christian West. Humanist thinkers, opposed to the Christian foundations of their society, sided with Reuchlin and campaigned against the Dominicans. They counted among their ranks such Marranos as Fernando de Rojas, author of the famous *Celestine* (1499). Pope Leo X (1513–1521) took the side of Reuchlin, who dedicated his *De arte caballistica* to him in 1517. Leo X, whose real name was Giovanni Médici, came from the powerful Florentine family of the Medici, a "race of usurers" according to Machiavelli, owners of the most important bank in Europe, founded in 1397.[45] The Medicis were closely linked to the Abravanel clan, and favored the immigration into Tuscany of Jews from Spain and the Balkans. Leo X made the papacy

---

[45] Jacques Heers, *La Naissance du capitalisme au Moyen Âge. Changeurs, usuriers et grands financiers*, Perrin, 2012, p. 105.

hated by his immoderate use of indulgences to fill the coffers of the Vatican.

Let us take a brief detour to discuss the Kabbalah, emphasizing its role in the birth of Zionism, through prophecies of the return of the Jews to Palestine, notably in the *Zohar*. Though the Kabbalah was born in Spain in the thirteenth century and spread, under a veil of secrecy, in Italy and Germany in the fourteenth century, it was at the end of the fifteenth century that it became an important part of Judaism, especially among crypto-Jews, who found in its occult dimension a resonance with their own hidden condition. The expulsion of the Jews from Spain in 1492 triggered a great craze for Kabbalah, while accentuating its double messianic-apocalyptic dimension.[46]

The Marranos found themselves better placed than the unconverted Jews to influence the Church with regard to kabbalistic prophecies. Thus, Solomon Molcho (1500–1532), born in Portugal to a Marrano family, rose to the post of royal secretary in the High Court of Justice, met the Pope, and tried to convince him to form an army of Marranos and attack the Ottoman Empire in order to liberate Palestine for the Jews. According to historian Youssef Hindi, Molcho "was the first to have concretely established Zionism's political strategy towards Christians, with the aim of using them to bring the Jews back to the Holy Land [. . .] persuading them to embrace Jewish messianic designs as their own."[47]

The controversy of Reuchlin led to an unquestionable victory of Judaism over Christianity, and it was the starting point of the Reformation. According to Heinrich Graetz, "We can boldly assert that the war for and against the Talmud aroused German consciousness, and created a public opinion, without which the Reformation, like many other efforts, would have died in the hour of birth, or, perhaps, would never have been born at all."[48] Luther took the side of Reuchlin, joining the ranks of his

---

[46] Gershom Scholem, *La Kabbale, op. cit.*, pp. 137–142.
[47] Youssef Hindi, *Occident et Islam. Sources et genèse messianiques du sionisme*, Sigest, 2015, pp. 42–46.
[48] Heinrich Graetz, *History of the Jews, op. cit.*, vol. 4, p. 423.

continued struggle by writing *Sola Scriptura*, the pillar of his Reformation, and promoting the study of Hebrew. Most disciples of Reuchlin became Lutherans. Luther was initially very friendly toward Jews, publishing in 1523 a pamphlet titled *That Jesus Christ Was Born a Jew*. In it he blamed "the popes, bishops, sophists, and monks—the crude asses' heads" for being unable to convert the Jews: "If I had been a Jew and had seen such dolts and blockheads govern and teach the Christian faith, I would sooner have become a hog than a Christian." Hoping to do better, he wrote: "The Jews are of the lineage of Christ. We are aliens and in-laws; they are blood relatives, cousins, and brothers of our Lord. Therefore, if one is to boast of flesh and blood, the Jews are actually nearer to Christ than we are." But after much disappointment, Luther had second thoughts. In *On the Jews and Their Lies*, written a few years before his death, he deemed them so corrupted by deadly sins as to be almost unredeemable, and especially resented their economic prosperity: "They are nothing but thieves and robbers who daily eat no morsel and wear no thread of clothing which they have not stolen and pilfered from us by means of their accursed usury." Luther recognized, in particular, the evil influence of the book of Esther, "which so well fits their bloodthirsty, vengeful, murderous greed and hope."[49]

Luther's turning against the Jews was also a turning against the spirit of the Old Testament, whose deleterious influence Luther had seen in the peasant revolt led by Thomas Muntzer, with whom he disengaged. Speaking to members of the Allstedt alliance in April 1525, Muntzer exhorted them to massacre: "Do not be merciful, even though Esau offers you good words [Genesis 33:4]. Pay no heed to the lamentations of the godless. They will bid you in a friendly manner, cry and plead like children. Do not let yourselves be merciful, as God commanded through Moses [Deuteronomy 7:1–5]." In 1538 Luther wrote a polemic charge *Against the Sabbatarians*, those Christians who insisted upon following the Old Testament command to

---

[49] Elliott Horowitz, *Reckless Rites: Purim and the Legacy of Jewish Violence*, Princeton University Press, 2006, p. 12.

worship on the Sabbath, and whom Luther suspected to be infiltrated by Jews.[50]

Since its appearance, the Protestant Reformation has been seen by Catholics as effecting a return to Judaism under the influence of Jews and Marranos. Its contempt for saints and destruction of the Marian cult, in particular, are an indirect attack against Christ. If the Jews shunned the Reformation, this was not the case for crypto-Jews, who saw it as a way to leave the Church and gain easier access to the Hebrew Bible. The role of the Marranos was particularly important in the Calvinist movement, which not only brought back the God of the Old Testament, but also condoned moneymaking and usury. During his lifetime, Calvin was already suspected of having Marrano origin. His name, spelled Jehan Cauvin, plausibly derives from Cauin, a French version of Coen. Calvin wrote commentaries on the entire Old Testament and perfectly mastered Hebrew, which he learned from rabbis. He heaped praise on the Jewish people: pure knowledge of God comes from them, as did the Messiah. His obsession with the law, and his belief that idolatry should be eradicated by military force, have their roots in the Old Testament, as does his obsession with purity. Calvin writes in his commentary on Psalm 119: "Where did Our Lord Jesus Christ and his apostles draw their doctrine, if not Moses? And when we peel off all the layers, we find that the Gospel is simply an exhibition of what Moses had already said." The Covenant of God with the Jewish people is irrevocable because "no promise of God can be undone." The new covenant is indistinguishable from the first: "The covenant made with the ancient Fathers, in its substance and truth, is so similar to ours, that we can call them one. The only difference is the order in which they were given."

According to the famous thesis of Max Weber in *The Protestant Ethic and the Spirit of Capitalism* (1905), the Calvinists were the main architects of global capitalism. Werner Sombart opposed him, in *The Jews and Modern Capitalism* (1911), with the

---

[50] Jason Martin, "An Abandonment of Hope: Martin Luther and the Jews," biblicalstudies.org.uk/pdf/churchman/107-04_331.pdf.

thesis that this role must be credited to the Jews. The history of Marranism, of which neither Weber nor Sombart had sufficient knowledge, reconciles both theses, since Calvinism is, in its origin and spirit, a form of crypto-Judaism.

Assimilation or Dissimulation?

Crypto-Judaism as a form of resistance to exile and discrimination should logically have disappeared with the European reforms culminating in the Emancipation of the Jews in the second half of the eighteenth century. These reforms, which put an end to discrimination against Jews, began shortly before the French Revolution. They supported the aspiration of the Jews of Europe to participate in the European Enlightenment (*Haskalah*), following the example of Moses Mendelssohn (1729–1786). By a decree of May 30, 1806, shortly after his coronation, Napoleon convened a meeting in Paris of representatives of the Jews of France, Italy, and Holland, and posed them twelve questions to test the compatibility of Jewish worship with French citizenship. In appearance, the operation was successful: the "Reform Judaism" that took shape shortly thereafter was defined as a religion alongside Catholicism or Protestantism. This assimilationist strategy offered an illusion to the Gentiles for about a century, but generated strong resistance within the Jewish community: by assimilating and becoming just another religion in a world won over to humanism, was Judaism not making itself vulnerable to the same forces of disintegration that were undermining Christianity? And above all, did not assimilation make inevitable the spread of mixed marriages that eventually could lead to the disappearance of the Jewish community?

For many humanist Jews, who did not attend synagogue and abhorred the Talmud, Judaism had little appeal as a religion. Was not the logical outcome of assimilation the conversion to the majority religion of the host nation, whether Catholic or Protestant? Such reasoning led half of the Jews of Berlin to convert to Christianity in the late eighteenth and early nineteenth century, according to the estimate of Heinrich Graetz. Very few of these conversions obeyed strictly religious motivations. Some seem to have had social integration as their main objective, as exemplified by those Jews who had their children baptized while remaining themselves Jews. Others may have been motivated by a sincere love of European culture. But in many cases these conversions were followed by disillusionment—and a reinforcement of the racial conception of Jewishness.

Heinrich Heine (1797–1856) is the most famous example. Converted to Lutheranism in 1825, he conceived of baptism as the "entrance ticket to European civilization." But he complained of still being considered a Jew by the Germans (and so preferred living in France, where he was regarded as German). Just a few years after his conversion, his writings exhibited a very negative attitude toward Christianity, described as "a gloomy, sanguinary religion for criminals" that repressed sensuality. At the end of his life he regretted his baptism, which had brought him no benefit, and stated in his final book *Romanzero*: "I make no secret of my Judaism, to which I have not returned, because I have not left it."[51]

It is therefore not surprising that in the eyes of many non-Jewish Europeans, these Jewish converts still appeared to be crypto-Jews; they continued to be called Taufjuden ("baptized Jews") in Germany. Even the new strictly religious definition of "Jews" was seen as a subtle form of crypto-Judaism, because in practice, Jews retained a solidarity that went beyond that of Christians and seemed to outweigh their status as citizens of their host nation. Endogamy, in particular, remained very strong among the rich Jewish bourgeoisie, whose family bonds were intertwined with commercial ties. Judeophobia fed on this sociological reality, and, in a vicious circle of misunderstanding, reinforced the feeling among Jews that their efforts to assimilate were in vain.

To all these factors must be added the awakening of nationalism on the ruins of the Napoleonic empire. In the second half of the nineteenth century, religion tended to give

---

[51] Quoted in Kevin MacDonald, *Separation and Its Discontents: Toward an Evolutionary Theory of Anti-Semitism*, Praeger, 1998, kindle 2013, k. 4732–4877.

way again to ethnicity (race, the people) in the definition of
Jewishness. Moritz Hess, after twenty years of efforts to
assimilate (and a marriage with a non-Jew) underwent a true
conversion. He changed his name to Moses and published *Rome
and Jerusalem* (1862). The assimilation that he had previously
believed in now appeared to him as a way of lying to oneself,
while reconnecting with his "Jewish nationality" meant
rediscovering an unalterable truth: "A thought which I believed
to be buried forever in my heart, has been revived in me anew.
It is the thought of my nationality, which is inseparably
connected with the ancestral heritage and the memories of the
Holy Land, the Eternal City." According to Hess, the efforts of
the Jews to merge with a nationality other than their own are
doomed to failure. "We shall always remain strangers among the
nations," and "the Jew in exile who denies his nationality will
never earn the respect of the nations among whom he dwells."
For "the Jews are something more than mere 'followers of a
religion,' namely, they are a race brotherhood, a nation."[52] Hess
was influenced by Heinrich Graetz's *History of the Jews* (published
in German in 1853), and in turn influenced the Austro-
Hungarian Theodor Herzl, whose *Jewish State* (1896) would
become the Zionist manifesto. The movement in favor of a land
for the Jews met the movement aimed at resurrecting the
Hebrew language, led by Eliezer Ben-Yehuda, which became the
second pillar of the Zionist project.

Officially, the reformed rabbis were anti-Zionists. On the
occasion of their 1885 Pittsburgh Conference, they issued the
following statement: "We consider ourselves no longer a nation,
but a religion community, and therefore expect neither a return
to Palestine, nor the restoration of a sacrificial worship under
the Sons of Aaron, or of any of the laws concerning the Jewish
State."[53] Yet this theoretical rejection of nationalism was largely
eclipsed by a very widespread messianic theory in Reform
Judaism, whose spokesman was the famous German-American

---

[52] Moses Hess, *Rome and Jerusalem: A Study in Jewish Nationalism*, 1918 (archive.org),
pp. 43, 74, 71.
[53] Quoted in Alfred Lilienthal, *What Price Israel?* (1953), 50th Anniversary Edition,
Infinity Publishing, 2003, p. 14.

rabbi Kaufmann Kohler. A star of the Pittsburgh Conference, Kohler argued that by renouncing the expectation of an individual Messiah, "Reform Judaism has thus accepted the belief that Israel, the suffering Messiah of the centuries, shall at the end of days become the triumphant Messiah of the nations."[54] One can see in this neo-messianism a form of super-nationalism through which Reform Judaism contributed, paradoxically, to the rise of the very Zionism that it claimed to disavow.

It must be emphasized that at the beginning of the twentieth century, the majority of Jews living in Germany for many generations remained indifferent to the Zionist call, and that assimilation continued unabated. This is why one might think that the "Jewish question" would have been resolved, in the long run, by the complete assimilation of the majority of Western European Jews, had it not been for a great upheaval in this community: the emergence on the historical stage of Ashkenazi Jews from Eastern Europe. Their immigration began in Germany and the Netherlands after the partition of Poland in 1772, expanded throughout the nineteenth century, and became massive in 1880. Until then, the Jews of Western Europe, of Hispanic descent (Sephardim) for the most part, were almost unaware of the existence of millions of Polish and Russian Jews. They found it difficult to adjust to the influx of these extremely poor Jews of Talmudic culture, Yiddish-speaking, living in isolation, practicing backward customs, and so numerous that within a century they would supplant the Sephardim. These Ashkenazi Jews from the shtetl of Eastern European Yiddishland had, for generations, been considered foreigners in their host nation, and even as a state within the state, subject to their own laws and representatives. It was these Ashkenazi immigrants who reversed assimilationism, stimulating a new movement of contraction toward ethnic-racial identity. After Herzl's death in 1905 and even at the Zionist Congress in 1903, they took over the Zionist movement.

---

[54] Kaufmnann Kohler, *Jewish Theology, Systematically and Historically Considered*, Macmillan, 1918 (www.gutenberg.org), p. 290.

Chapter 6

THE IMPERIAL MATRIX

> "Thus says Yahweh to his anointed one, to Cyrus whom, he says, I have grasped by his right hand, to make the nations bow before him and to disarm kings: [...] It is for the sake of my servant Jacob and of Israel my chosen one, that I have called you by your name, have given you a title though you do not know me. [...] Though you do not know me, I have armed you."
>
> Isaiah 45:1–5

The Two Sides of Albion

The influence of the Marranos in England began under Henry VIII (1509–1547). It initially coincided with that of the Venetians, who, in the 1530s, gained the upper hand over the king's government by heavily indebting it. The moneylenders also played a crucial role in Henry's matrimonial life, favoring his divorce from his first wife Catherine of Aragon, daughter of Ferdinand of Aragon and Isabella of Castile. The rupture of the king's marriage foreshadowed that of the Spain-England alliance he had sealed, as well as his schism with the Catholic Church. Francesco Zorzi, a Franciscan monk from Venice, conversant in Hebrew and a collector of rabbinical and kabbalistic works, advised Henry VIII in his request for a divorce between 1527 and 1533. Another influential advisor was Thomas Cromwell, an obscure adventurer who, after serving rich merchants in Venice, returned to England, managed important affairs for the Church, and was elected to Parliament in 1523, becoming "chief minister" in 1532. Having gained the confidence of Henry VIII, he encouraged him to become the new Constantine by founding the Anglican Church, then became his business agent for the confiscation of church property, which he largely diverted for his own profit. Thomas Cromwell was surely a creature of the Venetian Marranos, if he was not a Marrano himself.

Under Henry VIII, England became the stronghold of antipopeism, and its rivalry against powerful Catholic Spain was exacerbated. With his wife Isabella of Portugal, the king of Spain Charles I, grandson of Ferdinand and Isabella, governed a vast empire including the Netherlands, the kingdom of Naples, and the Habsburg possessions, as well as many colonies. When he was elected emperor of Germany in 1519 under the name of Charles V, he became the most powerful Christian monarch of the first half of the sixteenth century. His eldest son Philip II succeeded him (1556–1598). Raised in the fervor of the Spanish court, Philip II was the leader of the Counter-Reformation and dreamed of reconciling Christianity around the Roman church. Because of his marriage to the Catholic Mary Tudor (daughter of Henry VIII and his first wife Catherine of Aragon), Philip became consort king of England when Mary ascended to the throne in 1554. Mary strove to restore Catholicism, but after only a four-year reign, she was decapitated and replaced by her half-sister Elizabeth. The latter opposed the Catholic Church and initiated a hostile policy toward Spain, encouraging piracy against Spanish shipping. In 1588, Philip II launched a disastrous war against England, which resulted in the rout of his "invincible Armada" and augured the end of Spanish hegemony.

England sought to undermine Spain's control over its seventeen provinces in the Netherlands, including Belgium, Nord-Pas-de-Calais, and part of Picardy. It benefited from the support of many crypto-Jews converted to Calvinism. According to Jewish historian and journalist Lucien Wolf, "the Marranos in Antwerp had taken an active part in the Reformation movement, and had given up their mask of Catholicism for a not less hollow pretense of Calvinism. [...] The simulation of Calvinism brought them new friends, who, like them, were enemies of Rome, Spain and the Inquisition. [...] Moreover, it was a form of Christianity which came nearer to their own simple Judaism."[1] Deeply involved in the development of printing in Antwerp and Amsterdam, these Calvinist Marranos actively contributed to the propaganda against Philip II, Spain, and Catholicism. In 1566 they triggered a revolt in Antwerp that spread to all the cities of Holland. In one year, 4,000 priests, monks, and nuns were killed, 12,000 nuns driven out of their convents, thousands of churches desecrated and ransacked, and countless monasteries destroyed with their libraries. Many Spanish contemporaries, like the poet Francisco de Quevedo (1580–1645), discerned a Jewish conspiracy at the source of these revolts and the concurrent decline of Spain.[2] The revolts led to the independence of the United Provinces in 1579 (which Spain did not recognize until 1648). When Philip II temporarily took over Antwerp in 1585, Jews, Marranos, and Calvinists transferred their economic activity to Amsterdam. Many returned to Judaism, even bringing with them certain Calvinists of non-Jewish origin.

During the reign of Elizabeth (1558–1603), although the Jews remained officially banned in the kingdom, many of them penetrated into the higher spheres of the state under an (often perfunctory) Anglican or Calvinist disguise. Under the double Marrano/Puritan influence, the Hebrew vogue spread through the aristocracy. A Judeophilic climate prevailed in the court of Elizabeth. Jewish and Christian Hebraists were sought after, producing in 1611 the translation known as the *King James Bible*.

The Kabbalah, one of the Trojan horses of Judaism in European Christianity, also gained adherents among English nobles and intellectuals, and gave birth to a prolific literature. The Hebraist John Dee was the most important promoter of occultism in the Elizabethan period. When in 1558 Queen Elizabeth acceded to the throne, Dee became her close personal adviser in science and astrology, to the point of fixing the date of her coronation. Dee may have inspired playwright Christopher Marlowe's main character in his tragic story of

---

[1] Lucien Wolf, *Report on the "Marranos" or Crypto-Jews of Portugal*, Anglo-Jewish Association, 1926.
[2] Henry Kamen, *The Spanish Inquisition: A Historical Revision*, Yale University Press, 1998, p. 31.

Doctor Faustus, a man who sells his soul to the devil to satisfy his greed for knowledge.

Elizabethan theater, the flagship of the English Renaissance, reflects the hostility of the people and part of the aristocracy against the economic and cultural influence of the Jews. One alleged prototype for William Shakespeare's Shylock in *The Merchant of Venice* was the Calvinist Jew Rodrigo Lopez, a personal doctor of Queen Elizabeth who was hanged for attempting to poison her. Barabbas, the main character of *The Jew of Malta* by Christopher Marlowe, holds his colossal fortune as evidence of the superiority of Judaism over Christianity. After the governor of Malta confiscates his house and gives it to nuns, Barabbas persuades his daughter to become a nun, retrieve his money that is hidden in the house, and seize the opportunity to poison the nuns. Barabbas sometimes allies himself with the Christians, sometimes with the Turks, with the aim of destroying them both in the end: "Thus, loving neither, will I live with both, making a profit of my policy; And he from whom my most advantage comes shall be my friend. This is the life we Jews are used to lead" (V, 3).

Seth and Osiris, it seems, vied for the soul of Elizabethan England. While crypto-Jewish puritanism spread its grip, making its way down from the top thanks to its usurious power, British culture produced the masterpieces of Shakespeare, whose spirit is so little Protestant that he was suspected of being a crypto-Catholic, notably for his ideas on the afterlife.[3] Shakespeare's most cherished gift to European culture is undoubtedly his tragedy *Romeo and Juliet*, a work of youth that, despite some blunders, surpasses the novel of *Tristan and Iseult* as a mythic depiction of passionate love. The love that strikes Romeo and Juliet like a thunderbolt has the power of a mystical experience: it is a meeting of the divine in the other, which makes the lovers' souls blossom and reveals them to themselves. Their love shatters family and social loyalties: "Deny thy father and refuse thy name," Juliet asks, "And I'll no longer be a Capulet" (II, 2).

---

[3] Stephen Greenblatt, *Hamlet in Purgatory*, Princeton University Press, 2001.

Death becomes the only desirable alternative to the possibility of living this love in this life, for love contains in itself the certainty that it will triumph over death. The double suicide of the lovers is a heroic death, a "martyrdom" of true love, a redemptive sacrifice that triumphs over the social violence that incited it. Seeing the bodies of their children, the Capulets and Montagues decide to end their vendetta. Like Christians before the crucified Christ, they repent of having murdered the noblest of human creatures: man and woman united in true love. In the final scenes of the play, they promise to raise gilded statues of their children placed side by side in the (henceforth pacified) city of Verona.

Romeo and Juliet is the ultimate myth of exogamy, exalting the supernatural power of love that transcends the clan and abolishes war. Though fictitious, *Romeo and Juliet* has attained the status of a sacred, meta-Christian myth that reintroduces into the Western imagination a mythology of eros transcended by the underlying figure of Christ. It suffuses English Romanticism— which, not surprisingly, Moses Hess judges "decadent," preferring Jewish novels, since "the Jews alone had the good sense to subordinate sexual to maternal love."[4]

The Triumph of Puritanism

Many Marranos, after having transited through Holland, immigrated to England in the years 1630–1650, mixing in with the Calvinist refugees. At the beginning of the century there were about a hundred Marranos among the more prosperous families of London, and by 1650 they possessed a twelfth of all English commerce.[5] These Marranos retained the Portuguese nationality and their rallying point was the home of the Portuguese ambassador, the Marrano Antonio De Souza. One of them was Fernandez Carvajal (1590–1659), whose commercial activities, extending from Brazil to the Levant (Near East), and from wine to gunpowder, brought an average 100,000

---

[4] Moses Hess, *Rome and Jerusalem: A Study in Jewish Nationalism*, 1918 (archive.org), pp. 82, 86.
[5] Cecil Roth, *A History of the Marranos* (1932), Meridian Books, 1959, p. 100.

pounds per year back to England. Carvajal was the first Portuguese to obtain the status of "denizen," which granted practically the same rights as citizenship. In 1650, when the war between England and Portugal erupted, his ships were exempted from seizure.

Cecil Roth explains: "The religious developments of the seventeenth century brought to its climax an unmistakable philo-semitic tendency in certain English circles. Puritanism represented above all a return to the Bible, and this automatically fostered a more favourable frame of mind towards the people of the Old Testament." And so, "Though the Jews were still jealously excluded from England, there was no country in which the Hebraic spirit was so deeply rooted or so universally spread."[6] In other words, Puritanism was a kind of Judeo-Protestantism. Some Puritans went so far as to consider the Levitical laws as still in force; they circumcised their children and scrupulously respected the Sabbath. Under Charles I (1625–1649), writes Isaac d'Israeli, "it seemed that religion chiefly consisted of Sabbatarian rigours; and that a British senate had been transformed into a company of Hebrew Rabbins."[7]

At the end of the Thirty Years War in 1648, the Treaty of Westphalia put an end to the Spanish dream of universal Catholic monarchy. The Counter-Reformation was contained, and the independence of the Netherlands recognized. The Jews could now practice their religion in broad daylight. At the same time, the antimonarchical revolution of the Puritans, led by Oliver Cromwell (kin to the Thomas Cromwell mentioned above), triumphed in England after a civil war that the Puritans, bent on re-enacting the experience of the people of Israel, viewed as a holy war aimed at establishing a biblical type of theocracy on British soil. Cromwell enjoyed the support of many Marranos: Fernandez Carvajal, the main financier of the revolutionary army, put at Cromwell's disposal his network of spies based in Holland. Antimonarchical propaganda in England

---

[6] Cecil Roth, *A History of the Jews in England* (1941), Clarendon Press, 1964, p. 148.
[7] Isaac Disraeli, *Commentaries on the Life and Reign of Charles the First, King of England*, 2 vols., 1851, quoted in Archibald Maule Ramsay, *The Nameless War*, 1952 (archive.org).

was largely dependent on the Dutch press, from whence thousands of tracts clandestinely crossed the Channel. After signing the death warrant against King Charles I in 1649 (the act was drafted by a certain Isaac Dorislaus from Leiden), Cromwell rose to the summit of the ephemeral Commonwealth of England to reign as Lord Protector from 1653 until his death in 1658. He conquered Catholic Ireland in 1649 and engaged there in a quasi-genocidal repression.

The famous Dutch rabbi Menasseh Ben Israel (born in Madeira of Portuguese Marrano parents who returned to Judaism in Amsterdam) played a decisive role in the final stage of Judaization in England. He took the lead in lobbying for the readmission of Jews in England, that is, the liberation of the crypto-Jews from their pseudo-Christianity. A petition was presented to Parliament in 1648 (the Cartwright Petition). In December 1655, Ben Israel met Cromwell and, one year later, dedicated his book *Justice for the Jews* to him. In his earlier work *The Hope of Israel*, published both in Latin and English, he included among his arguments in favor of the return of the Jews to England the idea that their presence would fulfill the prophecy of Deuteronomy 28:64: "Yahweh will scatter you throughout every people, from one end of the earth to the other." "I conceived," writes Menasseh, "that by the *end of the earth* might be understood this *Island*." In other words, the Last Days long awaited by the Puritans would not take place until the Jewish Diaspora reached England. Others supported this argument by asserting that "England" means "angel-land, angel of the earth." Menasseh also asserted that the Last Days imply, among the prophecies to be fulfilled, the return of the Jews "into their own land."[8] Thus the opening of the frontiers of England to the Jews was conceived as a prelude to their reconquest of Palestine—an idea which had also made its way in England since the publication in 1621 of Sir Henry Finch's *The World's Great Restauration, or Calling of the Jews.*[9]

---

[8] *Menasseh ben Israel's mission to Oliver Cromwell, being a reprint of the pamphlets published by Menasseh ben Israel to promote the re-admission of the Jews to England 1649–1656*, ed. by Lucien Wolf, Macmillan & Co., 1901 (archive.org), p. xvi.

[9] Cecil Roth, *A History of the Jews in England, op. cit.*, p. 150.

Due to strong resistance, the banishment of the Jews was not officially lifted before 1690, after the Second English Revolution, but from the early seventeenth century onward it was no longer applied. When England again entered into war with Spain in 1655, and declared her intention to seize on her territory all Spanish or Portuguese property, the Marrano merchants declared themselves to belong to the "Hebrew nation," and placed themselves under the protection of Cromwell. Many Marranos openly returned to Judaism, while others preferred to maintain nominal Christianity, which had become less binding. Jewish and crypto-Jewish immigration (the distinction was by now insignificant) grew rapidly.[10] During the next century, several waves of Ashkenazi immigration joined these Jews and Marranos of Sephardic origin.

During their civil war against the royalist Anglicans, the Puritans saw themselves as Israel exiled among the Egyptians, and used the image of the Exodus as a rallying cry. For them, Cromwell was not only Moses leading the people out of Egypt, but also Joshua exterminating the Canaanites.[11] In reality, the Puritan revolution was more like that of the Maccabees (who had themselves rewritten the story of Moses and Joshua to their advantage). Puritan England was exalted as a new Israel, though this did not deprive the Jews of their privileged status. It was often asserted that the new Chosen People must help the old Chosen People return to their original homeland as a prelude to their conversion at the Second Coming of Christ. Jews enjoyed such prestige in seventeenth-century England that authors vied with each other to prove that the English were the direct descendants of the Jews in general and the famous ten lost tribes of Israel in particular. This strange theory, called British Israelism or Anglo-Israelism, originated in *The Rights of the Kingdom* (1646), a plea for regicide written by John Sadler, private secretary of Oliver Cromwell, Hebraist and friend of Menasseh Ben Israel. This line of thought remained influential until the

---

[10] Daniel Lindenberg, *Destins Marranes. L'identité juive en question*, Hachettes, 1997, pp. 47–93.
[11] John Hale, "England *as* Israel in Milton's Writings," *Early Modern Literary Studies*, 2.2 (1996), pp. 31–54, on purl.oclc.org/emls/02-2/halemil2.html.

Victorian era. In the 1790s Richard Brothers planned to reveal their Jewishness to Jews "hidden" among the English and to lead them, like a new Moses, to their eternal promised land of Canaan.

Another Judeomaniacal theory was born at the time of Cromwell: a certain Antonio de Montezinos returned from America claiming to have identified descendants of the ten lost tribes of Israel. The theory ran rampant in England thanks to a book by Thomas Thorowgood, *Jews in America, or the Probability that the Indians are Jews* (1648). Ben Israel made it his own in his 1650 book *The Hope of Israel*, and asked Lord Protector Cromwell for support in sending Jews to re-Judaize the Sioux and Comanches.[12]

Finally, Freemasonry, born in the British Isles at the beginning of the eighteenth century, was strongly influenced by the philo-Semitism that prevailed among the English aristocracy and bourgeoisie. Masonic jargon, symbolism, and mythology drew heavily from the Torah, the Talmud, and the Kabbalah. Other intellectual streams were, of course, involved in the birth of Freemasonry: philosophical clubs indebted to the humanists of the sixteenth century such as Erasmus, struggling to escape persecution and to promote religious peace by following the path of a "natural religion" emancipated from dogmas and revelations. The Irish John Toland played an important role with his posthumous *Pantheisticon* published in 1720. It describes the rules and rites of a society of enlightened thinkers who meet secretly to discuss philosophy and search for esoteric truths.[13] Jewish lore was transplanted into this tradition in the Grand Lodge of England, which adopted in 1723 Anderson's Constitution and its kabbalistic mumbo-jumbo. In 1730, initiation rites were enriched with the legend of Hiram, a character barely mentioned in the biblical story of the building of Solomon's temple (1 Kings 7:13), transformed by kabbalist-masonic imagination into the architect killed by three

---

[12] Tudor Parfitt, *The Lost Tribes of Israel: The History of a Myth*, Weidenfeld & Nicolson, 2002; Cecil Roth, *A History of the Jews in England, op. cit.*, p. 155.
[13] Albert Lantoine, *Un précurseur de la franc-maçonnerie. John Toland (1670–1722), suivi de la traduction française du Pantheisticon de John Toland*, Éditions E. Nourry, 1927.

companions bent on stealing the secret password—a story that suspiciously resembles the Talmudic fable of Jesus entering the Holy of Holies to steal the sacred word. Against such evidence of Jewish influence on Freemasonry, some have objected that, until the end of the eighteenth century, Jews were officially excluded from the lodges. But not the Marranos. It is these crypto-Jews, who had a long experience in secret gatherings, secret means of recognition (handshakes, code words, etc.), and initiation ceremonies, who progressively infiltrated and Judaized Freemasonry. We know, for example, of the influence of Portuguese kabbalist Martinez Paschalis, founder in 1754 of the Order of Cohens, later transformed by his disciples into the Martinist Order. Father Joseph Lémann, a converted Jew, saw in this Masonic order "the prefiguration of an actual liaison between Judaism and secret societies."[14] The influence of crypto-Jews explains in part why, according to the encyclical of Pope Leo XIII in 1884, Freemasonry aims to "completely ruin the religious and social discipline that was born of Christian institutions."

From the time of Cromwell can also be traced the birth of a complex of anthropological and sociological ideas that reached maturity in the Victorian era and then radiated throughout the West. This trend was propelled by Thomas Hobbes, author of the famous *Leviathan* (1651). Hobbes was a Puritan, but his religious ideas are so typically Jewish that many have speculated on his Marrano origin. For example, Hobbes reduces the Christian faith to the assertion that "Jesus is the Messiah," and defends a political vision of a Messiah who owes everything to the Old Testament. Like Maimonides, he sees the coming of the Messiah (in his case, the return of Christ) as the coming of a new Moses. For Hobbes, "the Kingdom of God was first instituted by the ministry of Moses over the Jews," since at that time, "God alone is king"; the misfortunes of Israel began with Samuel, the first king of the Hebrews, installed on the throne

---

[14] L'Abbé Joseph Lémann, *L'Entrée des Israélites dans la société française et les États chrétiens,* 3ᵉ éd., 1886, p. 351.

against the advice of Yahweh.[15] Whether or not Hobbes was of crypto-Jewish origin, his philosophical materialism is compatible with Judaism and not with Christianity: "The universe is corporeal; all that is real is material, and what is not material is not real." Hobbes breaks with the political tradition inherited from Aristotle (and renewed by Thomas Aquinas), according to which man is a naturally political being. For Hobbes, man is sociable not by nature, but by necessity. Driven mainly by the instinct of self-preservation and living permanently in the anguished fear of violent death, "man is a wolf for man" in the state of nature, and human relations are summarized as "war of all against all." In order to avoid extinction, mankind invents social order, which is a contract between individuals by which everyone transfers his natural rights to a sovereign. The political conception of Hobbes, and its anthropological underpinning, had an immense impact on later "contractualist" republican philosophers of the Enlightenment.

In the wake of Hobbes came Bernard Mandeville, born of Huguenot parents in Holland, and settled in London in 1693. In 1714, he published *The Fable of the Bees; or, Private Vices, Publick Benefits,* which argues that vice is the indispensable motive that produces a society of luxury, while virtue is of no use, and even detrimental to public prosperity.

After Hobbes and Mandeville came Adam Smith, the great theorist of mercantile liberalism. In *The Wealth of Nations* (1776)—a title strangely echoing Isaiah 61:6—Smith substituted the Market for the Sovereign of Hobbes. Postulating, like Hobbes, that the human being is motivated exclusively by his own profit, he wagered nevertheless that in a society of free competition, the sum of individual selfishness is enough to create a just society: "Every individual [...] intends only his own gain, and he is in this, as in many other cases, led by an invisible hand to promote an end which was no part of his intention." This "invisible hand" (an expression borrowed from Mandeville) is, in reality, that of the god Mammon reigning over a world

---

[15] Robert Kraynak, "The Idea of the Messiah in the Theology of Thomas Hobbes," *Jewish Political Studies Review,* Fall 1992, on jcpa.org.

totally subject to the mercantile spirit. Karl Marx, born in a
converted Jewish family, and of English economic formation,
well understood that the reign of money inaugurated by the
liberalism of Smith represents the ultimate and hidden triumph
of Judaism. "What is the secular basis of Judaism? Practical
need, self-interest. What is the worldly religion of the Jew?
Huckstering. What is his worldly God? Money." For Marx,
money is the force of alienation par excellence: "Money is the
estranged essence of man's work and man's existence, and this
alien essence dominates him, and he worships it." Therefore, the
only real emancipation of the Jews would be if Jews
emancipated themselves from money. "The Jew has
emancipated himself in a Jewish manner, not only because he
has acquired financial power, but also because, through him and
also apart from him, money has become a world power and the
practical Jewish spirit has become the practical spirit of the
Christian nations. The Jews have emancipated themselves
insofar as the Christians have become Jews. [...] The Jew is
perpetually created by civil society from its own entrails. [...]
The god of the Jews has become secularized and has become
the god of the world."[16] In other words, Judaism had conquered
Christianity from within.

Beginning in the seventeenth century, it was the Jews who
made London the world's foremost financial center, on the
model of Amsterdam. The death of Cromwell in 1657 was
followed by the restoration of Charles II, son of Charles I, who
was succeeded by his brother James II, Catholic and pro-French,
later overthrown by the Glorious Revolution (1688–89) that
brought to power his son-in-law William III of Orange, with the
help of the Huguenots of Amsterdam. William of Orange,
responsible to his bankers, authorized them to found the Bank
of England in 1694. He granted the Bank a monopoly on the
issue of money, that is to say, on the public debt, ordering the
British Treasury to borrow 1,250,000 pounds from his bankers.

The Bank of England is in essence a cartel of private
bankers, who have the exclusive privilege of granting the

---

[16] Karl Marx, *On the Jewish Question*, 1843, on www.marxists.org/archive.

government interest-bearing loans guaranteed by taxes. This institution was the first of its kind. (Napoleon created the Bank of France on the same model in 1800). The Bank of England laid the foundations for the financial domination of the world by the usurers of the City of London.

The Rothschild saga began in Germany, when Mayer Amschel Bauer (1744–1812) transformed his father's pawn shop into a bank, adopted the name of Rothschild, and became the manager of the fortune of William I, elector of Hesse-Cassel. Rothschild sent each of his five sons to create or head a subsidiary of the family bank in London, Paris, Vienna, Naples, and Frankfurt. Inter-branch marriages enabled the family to maintain control, diversify its banking activities and increase its financial capacity by participating in the development of mining and railroads during the nineteenth century. Nathan Mayer Rothschild (1777–1836), founder of the English branch, profited greatly by financing the English war against Napoleon. Through audacious manipulations during the Battle of Waterloo in June 1815, he multiplied his fortune by twenty in a few days by buying up for pennies on the dollar the same shares whose prices he had previously caused to collapse by falsely broadcasting indications that England had lost the battle, at a time when, with the exception of his agents, nobody knew the outcome. Thus did Nathan Rothschild gain control of the Bank of England.[17]

The influence of Puritanism on many aspects of British society, and in particular on its commercialism, naturally extended to the United States, which lacked any ingrained culture capable of stemming it. In American national mythology, everything began with the first colony founded by the Mayflower "Pilgrim Fathers" in 1620 in Massachusetts. They were Puritans who defined themselves as the new chosen people fleeing from Egypt (Anglican England) and settling in the Promised Land. Twenty thousand others followed them

---

[17] Ignatius Balla, *The Romance of the Rothschilds*, Londres, 1913 (a book attacked by the Rothschilds in a slander appeal that they lost), quoted in Eustace Mullins, *The Secrets of the Federal Reserve* (1952), and in Hongbing Song, *The Currency Wars*, 2007.

between 1629 and 1640. They multiplied at an impressive rate, doubling in each generation for two centuries: there were one hundred thousand in 1700, more than one million in 1800, six million in 1900, and more than sixteen million in 1988.[18] Puritanism is the matrix that, through several transformations and mutations, produced American "evangelical" Christianity. One of its most curious emanations is the Mormon Church, which today has more than six million followers. Mormonism was founded in 1830 by a certain Joseph Smith, who claimed to have received from an angel an ancient book engraved on gold plates, written by prophets of Jewish origin who lived on the American continent between 600 BCE and 420 CE. The Book of Mormon takes up the Judeomaniacal theory of the Jewish origin of Native Americans.

The Disraeli Enigma

A few decades after the end of the Napoleonic wars, Europe once again entered a period of global conflict, from which it would not extricate itself for a century. In 1853 the Crimean War broke out between Russia and the Ottoman Empire, the latter receiving the aid of France and the United Kingdom. The war ended in 1856 with the Treaty of Paris, which aimed at limiting Russian expansionism for the benefit of the Ottoman Empire. Twenty years later, in 1877, Tsar Alexander II of Russia, declaring himself protector of the Christians, went to war once more against the Ottomans, who had drowned the Serb uprising in the bloodbath of 1875, and likewise the Bulgarian uprising the following year. With the Russians at the gates of Constantinople, the Ottomans were forced to grant independence to many of the people they previously dominated. By the Treaty of San Stefano, signed in 1878, the Tsar founded the autonomous principalities of Bulgaria, Serbia, and Romania, and amputated the Ottoman Empire of territories populated by Georgians and Armenians. The Sultan was also forced to

---

[18] David Hackett Fischer, *Albion's Seed: Four British Folkways in America,* Oxford University Press, 1989, p. 17.

commit to ensuring the safety of Christian subjects who remained under his authority.

This treaty, however, displeased Britain and Austria-Hungary, both hostile to the expansion of Russian influence. England was especially unhappy, since Alexander II undertook the conquest of territories in Central Asia, where the English owned many colonies. In 1878, England and Austria-Hungary convened the Congress of Berlin, which resulted in the Berlin Treaty, canceling that of San Stefano. The independence of the Christian states of the Balkans was replaced by a gradual and conditional emancipation. Russian conquests were relinquished and Armenia was returned, for the most part, to the Ottoman Empire. The independent principalities of the Balkans were fragmented into weak, rivalrous, and ethnically divided small states, and part of Bulgaria was put back under Ottoman vassalage. This territorial redistribution (the prototype of future "balkanizations") elicited profound nationalist resentments that helped spark the First World War, as well as the Armenian genocide with its 1,200,000 victims.

The Treaty of Berlin's main objective was to save what could be saved from a weakening Ottoman Empire in order to counter pan-Slavism and Russian influence. England, the first maritime power, wanted to prevent Russia from getting closer to the Bosphorus. The British obtained the right to use Cyprus as a naval base, while protecting the colonial roads and monitoring the Suez Canal. Thus was launched the so-called "Great Game" for colonial rule in Asia, which, for the British Empire, entailed containing Russian expansion, and leading in particular to the creation of Afghanistan as a buffer state. (The same policy would be promoted by Zbigniew Brzezinski 120 years later, this time on behalf of American hegemony.)

There are several ways to interpret this historical episode that carries the seed of all the tragedies of the twentieth century, several possible viewpoints about the forces shaping history at this crucial time. But in the end, history is made by men, and it can be understood only if one identifies the main protagonists. One name stands out among the instigators of this pivotal era's British imperial policy: Benjamin Disraeli (1804–1881), prime minister under Queen Victoria from 1868 to 1869, and again from 1874 to 1880. Disraeli was the man who made the takeover of the Suez Canal by England possible in 1875, through funding from his friend Lionel Rothschild, son of Nathan (in an operation that at the same time consolidated the Rothschilds' control over the Bank of England).

Disraeli has been called the true inventor of British imperialism, since it was he who, by introducing the Royal Titles Act in 1876, had Queen Victoria proclaimed Empress of India by Parliament. What is more, Disraeli was the main inspiration for the 1884–1885 Berlin Congress, where the Europeans carved up Africa. Lastly, Disraeli can be considered one of the forerunners of Zionism. Well before Theodor Herzl, Disraeli tried to add the "restoration of Israel" to the Berlin Congress's agenda, hoping to convince the Sultan to concede Palestine as an autonomous province. Zionism was for him an old dream: soon after a trip to the Middle East at the age of twenty-six, Disraeli published his first novel, *The Wondrous Tale of Alroy*, and made his hero, an influential Jew of the Middle Ages, say: "My wish is a national existence which we have not. My wish is the Land of Promise and Jerusalem and the Temple, all we forfeited, all we have yearned after, all for which we have fought, our beauteous country, our holy creed, our simple manners, and our ancient customs."

Disraeli wrote these lines even before the beginnings of biblical archeology; it was not until 1841, after a trip to Palestine, that Edward Robinson published his *Biblical Researches in Palestine*. The first excavations of the Palestine Exploration Fund sponsored by Queen Victoria began in 1867. However, wealthy British Jews had taken an interest in Palestine long before that. Disraeli's interest was influenced by that of his neighbor and friend of forty years, Moses Montefiore, like him of Sephardic origin, and like him closely related to the Rothschilds. (Montefiore married Judith Cohen, the sister-in-law of Nathan Mayer Rothschild). After a trip to Palestine in 1827, Montefiore devoted his immense resources to helping his coreligionists in the Holy Land, notably by buying land and building housing.

Disraeli hailed from a family of Marranos (crypto-Jews of Portuguese origin) converted back to Judaism in Venice. His grandfather had moved to London in 1748. Benjamin was baptized at the age of thirteen, when his father, Isaac D'Israeli, converted to Anglican Christianity together with all his family. Isaac D'Israeli is the author of a book called *The Genius of Judaism* (in response to Chateaubriand's *The Genius of Christianity*), in which he glorifies the unique qualities of the Jewish people, but blames Talmudic rabbis for "sealing up the national mind of their people" and "corrupting the simplicity of their antique creed." As for many other Jews of the time, conversion for D'Israeli was above all opportunistic: until the beginning of the nineteenth century, administrative careers remained closed to the Jews. A law of 1740 had authorized their naturalization, but it had provoked popular riots and was repealed in 1753. Many influential Jews, such as City banker Sampson Gideon, then opted for nominal conversion for their children.[19]

Benjamin Disraeli received baptism almost at the same time as Heinrich Heine. Like Heine, Disraeli embodied the contradictions and drama of assimilated Jews in the late nineteenth century, who aspired to assimilation to the point that they wanted to personify all the virtues and values of European nations, but whose conversion to an already devitalized Christianity could only be a source of disappointment. Such conversions were often followed by an even stronger, more tormented attachment to their Jewishness, felt as a racial rather than a religious identity: Disraeli defined himself as "Anglican of Jewish race." For Hannah Arendt, Disraeli is a "race fanatic" who, in his first novel *Alroy* (1833), "evolved a plan for a Jewish Empire in which Jews would rule as a strictly separated class." In his other novel *Coningsby* (1844), he "unfolded a fantastic scheme according to which Jewish money dominates the rise and fall of courts and empires and rules supreme in diplomacy."

This idea "became the pivot of his political philosophy."[20] The character Sidonia, who appears in *Coningsby* and in his two later novels, *Sybil* (1845) and *Tancred* (1847), is a fictional avatar of his author, or rather, according to his biographer Robert

---

[19] Cecil Roth, *A History of the Marranos, op. cit.*, p. 148.
[20] Hannah Arendt, *The Origins of Totalitarianism*, vol. 1: *Antisemitism*, Meridian Books, 1958, pp. 309–310.

Blake, "a cross between Lionel de Rothschild and Disraeli himself."[21] He is descended from a noble family of Aragon, whose eminent members included an archbishop and a grand inquisitor, who nevertheless secretly adhered to the Judaism of their ancestors. The father of Sidonia, like Nathan the father of Lionel de Rothschild, "made a large fortune by military contracts, and supplying the commissariat of the different armies" during the Napoleonic wars. Then, having settled in London, he "staked all he was worth on the Waterloo loan; and the event made him one of the greatest capitalists in Europe."

Sidonia attended at the age of seventeen the princely courts of which he was the creditor, and became an expert in the arcana of power. "The secret history of the world was his pastime. His great pleasure was to contrast the hidden motive, with the public pretext, of transactions." To his protégé Coningsby, he confided that everywhere he traveled he saw, behind the monarchs and heads of state, Jewish advisers, and concluded: "So you see, my dear Coningsby, the world is governed by very different personages from what is imagined by those who are not behind the scenes." Disraeli himself, according to Robert Blake, "was addicted to conspiracy."

Sidonia, like Disraeli, is passionate about his race: "The race is everything; There is no other truth." He refuses to marry a non-Jewess because "No earthly consideration would ever induce him to impair that purity of race on which he prides himself." The term "race" at the time had an imprecise meaning that sometimes extended to what is now called ethnicity. However, Disraeli insists in *Endymion* (1880), his last novel, on the idea that "language and religion do not make a race—there is only one thing that makes a race, and that is blood." He also writes: "No man will treat with indifference the principle of race. It is the key of history."

In a nonfictional work (*Lord George Bentinck: A Political Biography*, 1852), Disraeli wrote that Jews "are a living and the most striking evidence of the falsity of that pernicious doctrine of modern times, the natural equality of man. [...] the natural

---

[21] Robert Blake, *Disraeli* (1966), Faber Finds, 2010, p. 202.

equality of man now in vogue, and taking the form of cosmopolitan fraternity, is a principle which, were it possible to act on it, would deteriorate the great races and destroy all the genius of the world. [...] The native tendency of the Jewish race, who are justly proud of their blood, is against the doctrine of the equality of man."[22]

Disraeli is clearly on the same wavelength as Moses Hess. His Jewish supremacism was complicated by discrimination between Jews, since Sephardim and Ashkenazim were "two races among the Hebrews," the first being "the superior race" (an idea already expressed by his father in his *Genius of Judaism*).[23]

What was Disraeli's motivation behind the foreign policy he imparted to the British Empire? Did he believe the fate of the British was to conquer the world? Or, remembering how Ezra and Nehemiah exploited Persian authority, did he see the British Empire as the instrument for the Jewish nation's fulfillment of its destiny—in other words, as Zionism's mule? In mooring the Suez Canal (dug between 1859 and 1869 by French Ferdinand de Lesseps) to British interests, does he simply seek to outdo the French, or is he laying the foundation for the future alliance between Israel and the Anglo-American Empire? Indeed, Disraeli could henceforth argue that a Jewish autonomous government in Palestine would be quite capable of defending British economic interests in the region. This would be Chaim Weizmann's pitch to the British thirty years later: "Jewish Palestine would be a safeguard to England, in particular in respect to the Suez Canal."[24]

Thus, Disraeli is truly the one who, with the help of Lionel Rothschild, laid the first stone of the new Jewish state. When in 1956 Israel invaded the Sinai to take control of the canal, she did it by again promising Britain to return the control of the canal that had been nationalized by Nasser. And what of Disraeli's Russophobia, to which, some say, he converted Queen Victoria?

---

[22] Benjamin Disraeli, *Lord George Bentinck*, Archibald, 1852 (archive.org), p. 496.

[23] Repeated by his friend Lord Stanley, as quoted in Todd Endelman, *The Self-Fashioning of Disraeli (1818–1851)*, eds. Charles Richmond and Paul Smith, Cambridge University Press, 1998, pp. 106–130.

[24] Chaim Weizmann, *Trial and Error*, Harper & Brothers, 1949, p. 192.

Is it imperial geostrategy, or the old Jewish enmity against the last Christian kingdom, where 70 percent of the world's Jews (recently emancipated by Alexander II, but victims of recurrent pogroms) still lived?

No one can answer these questions with certainty; perhaps Disraeli could not himself. His contemporaries, however, pondered them. Disraeli's open hostility to Russia and his defense of the Turks, whose massacres of the Serbs and Bulgarians were well known, gave rise to theories of a Jewish conspiracy. William Ewart Gladstone, a longtime opponent of Disraeli and himself prime minister several times (1868–1874, 1880–1885, 1886, and 1892–1894), declared that Disraeli "was holding British foreign policy hostage to his Jewish sympathies, and that he was more interested in relieving the anguish of Jews in Russia and Turkey than in any British interests." The newspaper *The Truth* of November 22, 1877, alluding to the intimacy of Disraeli with the Rothschilds suspected "a tacit conspiracy [...] on the part of a considerable number of Anglo-Hebrews, to drag us into a war on behalf of the Turks." It was remembered, moreover, that in a speech in the Commons gallery in 1847, Disraeli had demanded the admission of Jews to eligible functions, on the grounds that "the Jewish mind exercises a vast influence on the affairs of Europe." Some complained about the influence of Disraeli on Queen Victoria— an influence he explained to a friend in these terms: "Everyone likes flattery, and when it comes to Royalty you should lay it on with a trowel."[25]

The queen, it must be said, was already, like much of the aristocracy, under the spell of a fashionable theory assigning an Israelite origin to the Anglo-Saxons. This theory appeared under Oliver Cromwell and was renewed in 1840 by Pastor John Wilson with his *Lectures on Ancient Israel and the Israelitish Origin of the Modern Nations of Europe*. Edward Hine brought it back in 1870 in *The English Nation Identified with the Lost Israel*, where he derives the word "Saxon" from "Isaac's sons." This theory offered biblical justification to British colonialism, and even to

---

[25] Stanley Weintraub, *Disraeli: A Biography*, Hamish Hamilton, 1993, pp. 579, 547.

the genocide of colonized peoples (new Canaanites) by the British Empire (new Israel).[26] Happy to believe that her noble lineage descended from King David, the queen had her sons circumcised, a custom that has continued to this day. There was some truth in the British elite's sense of their Jewishness, for during the sixteenth and seventeenth centuries, many matrimonial unions had united rich Jewish families with the old destitute landed aristocracy, to the extent that, according to Hilaire Belloc's estimate, "with the opening of the twentieth century those of the great territorial English families in which there was no Jewish blood were the exception."[27]

The Disraeli case is illuminating because the questions raised about him are the same as those that arise today on the relationship between the United States and the Zionist network—questions that divide even the most respected observers. Which, of the Anglo-American Empire and international Jewry, steers the other? Is Israel the bridgehead of the United States in the Middle East, or is the United States, as Zbigniew Brzezinski once insinuated, the "mule" of Israel?[28] Is the dog wagging its tail, or the tail wagging the dog? Answering this question for the half century preceding the First World War helps answer the same question in contemporary times, because the symbiotic relationship between Israel and the empire grew up during that period.

The answer depends on one's point of view. The Zionists naturally have an interest in promoting the view that Israel serves Anglo-American interests, rather than the reverse. Disraeli argued in front of the British Parliament that a Jewish Palestine would be in the interest of British colonialism. But this argument is deceptive. Jewish Zionists have always seen things from the other end of the telescope, and one can hardly believe that Disraeli did not secretly share their view. When the hero of his *Tancred* (1847), a Jew who has been promoted Lord

---

[26] André Pichot, *Aux origines des théories raciales, de la Bible à Darwin,* Flammarion, 2008, pp. 124–143, 319.
[27] Hilaire Belloc, *The Jews,* Constable & Co., 1922 (archive.org), p. 223.
[28] YouTube, "Brzezinski: US won't follow Israel like a stupid mule." (www.youtube .com/watch?v=ifEGiJ2ZxDM).

Beaconsfield, glorifies the British Empire in these words: "We wish to conquer the world, led by angels, in order to bring man to happiness, under divine sovereignty," who lies behind this ambiguous "we"?

When a British Jew such as Disraeli says "we," there is always a possible double sense. And the ambiguity is always strategic, for a large part of the Anglo-Saxon industrial, political, and cultural elite shared a common belief in the British Empire's global mission to civilize the world. Cecil Rhodes (1853–1902), who gave his name to two African countries, Rhodesia and Northern Rhodesia (now Zimbabwe and Zambia), was an ardent propagandist for world government by the "British race." According to Carroll Quigley, in 1891 Rhodes founded a secret society devoted to this cause, which was later developed by his friend Lord Alfred Milner, and known since 1909 as the Round Table or the Rhodes-Milner Group. Lord Salisbury, minister of foreign affairs in the Disraeli cabinet (1878–1880), then prime minister in 1885, was a member of this secret society, according to Quigley, as was Lord Nathan Rothschild.[29]

Many other connections could be evoked to illustrate that, from the mid-nineteenth century onward, British imperialism and Zionism have been intimately intertwined. As historical movements, they seem to have been born simultaneously, like the twins Esau and Jacob. But meta-historical reflection on this question must take into account two important facts: first, the roots of the British Empire do not go back beyond the seventeenth century, whereas those of Zionism go back more than two millennia; and secondly, the British Empire declined after the First World War, whereas Zionism was launched toward continuing success. For these two reasons, the thesis that Zionism is a by-product of British imperialism seems to me unsustainable.

The question of the relationship between Albion and Zion is also related to that of the relationship between legal and occult power, and in particular the measure of the real power of the

---

[29] Carroll Quigley, *The Anglo-American Establishment, From Rhodes to Cliveden* (1949), Books In Focus, 1981.

Rothschild dynasty over British policy. There is little question, for example, that without the Rothschilds, Great Britain would never have gained control of the Suez Canal, which was the cornerstone of the empire in the Middle East, and sealed its alliance with Zionism. The Rothschilds never sought political office, preferring the less visible but much greater financial power; there is no question that Disraeli's power was really the Rothschilds'. Nevertheless, matrimonial alliances with the political elite could also be helpful: Lord Archibald Primrose, secretary of state for foreign affairs in 1886 and from 1892 to 1894, and prime minister in 1894–1895, was Mayer Amschel de Rothschild's son-in-law.

Concerning the relationship between the Rothschilds and Zionism, it is interesting to learn from Theodor Herzl's diaries that the glorious founder of Zionism envisioned the future Jewish state as an "aristocratic republic" ("I am against democracy") with, at its head, "the first Prince Rothschild." Quoting from his long tirade exhorting the Rothschilds to redeem their evil power through the Zionist project: "I don't know whether all governments already realize what an international menace your World House constitutes. Without you no wars can be waged, and if peace is to be concluded, people are all the more dependent on you. For the year 1895 the military expenses of the five Great Powers have been estimated at four billion francs, and their actual peacetime military strength at 2,800,000 men. And these military forces, which are unparalleled in history, you command financially, regardless of the conflicting desires of the nations. [...] And your accursed wealth is still growing. Everywhere it increases more rapidly than the national wealth of the countries in which you reside. Therefore this increase takes place only at the expense of the national prosperity, even though you yourselves may be the most decent persons in the world. For that reason, the Jewish State from the outset will not tolerate your alarming wealth, which would stifle our economic and political freedom. [...] But if you do go with us, we shall enrich you one last time more. And we shall make you big beyond the dreams of the modest founder of your House and even of his proudest grand-children. [...] We shall make you big, because we shall take our first

elected ruler from your House. That is the shining beacon which
we shall place atop the finished Eiffel Tower of your fortune. In
history it will seem as though that had been the object of the
entire edifice."[30] As Richard Wagner once said (*Judaism in Music*,
1850), however, the Rothschilds preferred to remain "the Jews
of the Kings" rather than "the Kings of the Jews."

The Gestation of Zionism

Disraeli was not the inventor of Zionism. The idea of a return of
the Jews to Palestine was already circulating before he came to
power. An article in the London *Times* of August 17, 1840,
shortly before the Crimean War, already suggested: "The minds
of Jews have been earnestly directed towards Palestine, and that
in anticipation of a reconstruction of the Jewish state many are
prepared to avail themselves of the facilities which events may
afford to return to the land of their fathers." And: "It is for the
Christian philanthropists and enlightened statesmen of Europe
to consider whether this remarkable people does not present
materials which, when collected and brought into fusion under
national institutions might not be advantageously employed for
the interests of civilization in the East."[31]

Nevertheless, it was Disraeli who gave the first concrete
impulse to the historical movement that was to culminate, less
than a century later, in the creation of Israel. Through his policy
and his access to Rothschild money, Disraeli undoubtedly sowed
the seeds of what later became the Zionist project of
colonization of Palestine by the Jews. If it was too soon to make
this project an openly avowed issue, this was primarily because
the population destined to populate the new country was not yet
available. Russian Jews were no more attracted to Palestine than
European Jews; indeed, they hardly knew where it was.
Emancipated since 1855 by Tsar Alexander II, who had given
them free access to the university, Russian Jews aspired only to

---

[30] *The Complete Diaries of Theodor Herzl*, edited by Raphael Patai, Herzl Press & Thomas
Yoseloff, 1960, vol. 1, pp. 163–170.

[31] Jill Duchess of Hamilton, *God, Guns and Israel: Britain, the First World War and the Jews
in the Holy City*, History Press, 2013, k. 1731–52.

migrate to Europe and the United States. Pogroms, including the one in Odessa that lasted three days in 1871, did not convince them of the necessity to establish their own state. It was only after the assassination of Alexander II in 1881 that the increased violence against them made some sensitive to the call of Leon Pinsker in his booklet *Auto-Emancipation: An Appeal to his People by a Russian Jew* published in 1882. As a precursor of Herzl, Pinsker called for "the national regeneration of the Jews," "the creation of a Jewish nationality, of a people living upon its own soil, the auto-emancipation of the Jews; their return to the ranks of the nations by the acquisition of a Jewish homeland."[32]

It was also in 1881, the year of Disraeli's death, that Baron Edmond de Rothschild, from the Parisian branch, started to buy land in Palestine and funded the installation of Jewish settlers, especially in Tel Aviv. More than twelve thousand acres of land were bought, and more than forty colonies were founded under the aegis of his *Palestine Jewish Colonization Association* (PICA). His son James later continued this philanthropic investment. Yesterday hailed as "the Father of the Yishuv," Edmond is honored on Israeli currency today.

Furthermore, in his efforts to influence world affairs, proto-Zionist Disraeli did not yet have at his disposal a sufficiently tightly knit international network that would act in concert. The international Jewish organizations such as B'nai B'rith (Hebrew for "the sons of the Alliance") founded in New York in 1843, or the Universal Israelite Alliance, founded in France in 1860 by Isaac Moses Aaron (also known as Adolphe) Crémieux, felt that Israel was doing very well as a diasporic nation. At this point they had no designs on Palestine.

It was the Austro-Hungarian Jew Theodor Herzl who is regarded as the historical founder of Zionism, not only by his book *The Jewish State* (1896), but also by his indefatigable public relations work, which helped win a large number of influential Jewish personalities to the Zionist cause. Far more than a manifesto, his book is a program, almost a manual. Like Disraeli, Herzl first turned to the Ottoman Empire for help: "If His

---

[32] On www.jewishvirtuallibrary.org/jsource/Zionism/pinsker.html.

Majesty the Sultan were to give us Palestine, we could in return undertake to regulate the whole finances of Turkey. We should there form a portion of a rampart of Europe against Asia, an outpost of civilization as opposed to barbarism."[33] Herzl approached Sultan Abdul Hamid with this offer through emissaries (as reported in his journal, June 9, 1896): "Let the Sultan give us that piece of land, and in return we shall set his house in order, straighten out his finances, and influence public opinion all over the world in his favor." In other words, he promised to devote to the service of Ottoman Turkey the two Jewish weapons par excellence: the bank and the press. The Sultan categorically and repeatedly rejected all offers, saying, as reported in Herzl's journal, June 19: "I cannot sell even a foot of land, for it does not belong to me, but to my people. [...] Let the Jews save their billions. [...] When my Empire is partitioned, they may get Palestine for nothing. But only our corpse will be divided. I will not agree to vivisection." As he had already done at the Berlin Congress, the Sultan opposed any Jewish mass immigration to Palestine. Four years later, after many more attempts, Herzl concluded (June 4, 1900): "At present I can see only one more plan: See to it that Turkey's difficulties increase; wage a personal campaign against the Sultan, possibly seek contact with the exiled princes and the Young Turks; and, at the same time, by intensifying Jewish Socialist activities stir up the desire among the European governments to exert pressure on Turkey to take in the Jews."[34] Yet Herzl still managed to obtain a personal audience with the Sultan in May 1901.

Although nothing emerged from this interview, Herzl used the diplomatic coup as a stepping stone for his negotiations in Europe. Pulling out all the stops, he went to St. Petersburg in 1903 (soon after the first pogrom of Kishinev) and was received by the finance and interior ministers, to whom he hawked Zionism as a solution to the problem of revolutionary subversion. Undoubtedly armed with the same argument, Herzl

---

[33] Theodor Herzl, *The Jewish State*, on www.jewishvirtuallibrary.org.
[34] *The Complete Diaries of Theodor Herzl, op. cit.*, vol. 1, pp. 362–363, 378–379, and vol. 3, p. 960.

met Kaiser Wilhelm II in 1898, presenting Zionism as a means of diverting the Jews from communism. However, Herzl already understood that "The center of gravity has shifted to England," as he noted during a trip to England in November 1895.[35] In the second sentence quoted above from *The Jewish State*, Herzl implicitly referred to Russia's containment policy when he presented his future Jewish state in Palestine as "an element of the wall against Asia." It was a call directed at England. Like Disraeli, Herzl sold his project to the British as an integral part of their colonial-imperial policy. That is why in 1903, having established close contact with Joseph Chamberlain, secretary of state for the colonies, Herzl received from the British government an offer to facilitate a large Jewish settlement, with autonomous government, in present-day Uganda. The offer was presented to the sixth Zionist Congress in Basel in 1903, and rejected at the seventh congress in 1906. (Herzl died between the two).

A quarter century after Disraeli had saved the Ottoman Empire, the Sultan's opposition stymied all hope of acquiring Palestine; it was thus necessary that the Ottoman Empire disappear and the cards be redistributed. Herzl understood that "the division of Turkey means a world war."[36] His partner Max Nordau, a speaker with incomparable prophetic talent, made before the 1903 Zionist Congress a famous prophecy of the upcoming war whence "a free and Jewish Palestine" would emerge. (In the 1911 congress, he would make another prophecy: that the European governments were preparing the "complete annihilation for six million [Jewish] people."[37])

Writing in 1938, Jewish historian Benzion Netanyahu (father of the later prime minister) summarized the feverish anticipation of this great cataclysm in the Zionist community. As is always the case in Jewish historiography, all eyes were fixed on the fate of the chosen people with complete indifference to the collateral

---

[35] Benzion Netanyahu, *The Founding Fathers of Zionism* (1938), Balfour Books, 2012, k. 2575.

[36] Theodor Herzl, *Zionism*, state edition, 1937, p. 65, quoted in Benzion Netanyahu, *The Founding Fathers of Zionism, op. cit.*, k. 1456–9.

[37] Quoted in Ben Hecht, *Perfidy*, 1961 (www.hirhome.com), p. 224.

victims: "The great moment came, as he prophesied, bound together with the storm of a world war, and bearing in its wings an exterminating attack on world Jewry, which began with the massacre of the Jews of Ukraine (during the Russian Civil War) and continues to spread to the present day. Herzl's political activity resulted in the fact that the Jews, whom he had united in a political organization, were recognized as a political entity, and that their aspirations [...] became part of the international political system. Indeed, due to the war, those aspirations had become so important that the major powers turned to the Zionists."[38]

Shortly before the outbreak of the World War, in 1908, the sultanate itself would be destroyed from within by the secular revolution of the Young Turks, a movement described by T. E. Lawrence as "50% crypto-Jewish and 95% freemasonic," and, according to Rabbi Joachim Prinz, led by "ardent 'doennmehs'," that is, crypto-Jews who, though nominally Muslims, "had as their real prophet Shabtai Zvi, the Messiah of Smyrna" (*The Secret Jews*, 1973).[39] After having attracted Armenians to their revolution with the promise of political autonomy, the Young Turks, once in power, suppressed their nationalist aspirations by the extermination in 1915–16 of 1,200,000 of this ancient and vibrant people whom rabbinic tradition assimilated to the Amalekites of the Bible.[40]

There is no consensus on the main causes of the Great War, which killed eight million soldiers and left twenty million disabled, while killing and wounding even larger numbers of civilians. The decision of Kaiser Wilhelm II to build a military fleet capable of defying British naval supremacy is often cited as the major factor. However, as historian Patrick Buchanan has clearly shown, this decision was merely the result of a deterioration in the relationship between England and Germany,

---

[38] Benzion Netanyahu, *The Founding Fathers of Zionism, op. cit.*, k. 1614–20.

[39] Joachim Prinz, *The Secret Jews,* Random House, 1973, p. 122; Wayne Madsen, "The Dönmeh: The Middle East's Most Whispered Secret (Part I)," *Strategic Culture Foundation*, October 25, 2011, on www.strategic-culture.org.

[40] Elliott Horowitz, *Reckless Rites: Purim and the Legacy of Jewish Violence,* Princeton University Press, 2006, pp. 122–125.

a diplomatic breakdown for which England was primarily responsible. The German Kaiser, the grandson of Queen Victoria and therefore the nephew of King Edward VII, was deeply attached to this relationship, and his foreign policy was animated by a vision that he summed up at the funeral of his grandmother in 1901: "I believe that the two Teutonic nations will, bit by bit, learn to know each other better, and that they will stand together to help in keeping the peace of the world. We ought to form an Anglo-Germanic alliance, you to keep the seas, while we would be responsible for the land; with such an alliance not a mouse could stir in Europe without our permission."

The Kaiser was particularly anxious not to impinge on England's colonial ambitions. But he was repeatedly humiliated by his uncle and the British government, who never understood the interest of a strong and friendly Germany. From this point of view, the deep causes of the First World War were intimately linked with the cultural and political developments in England that we have just described: Puritan Judeomania on the one hand, and imperial hubris on the other. The first undoubtedly caused the British elite to lose any sense of ethnic and civilizational solidarity with the Germanic nation, while the latter made it blind to the interest of maintaining a balance with Germany.

Since history is written by the victors, the vanquished are always wrong, and blamed for starting the war. However, a growing number of revisionist historians believe that Great Britain carried the heaviest responsibility for triggering this mechanized butchery.[41] The British press played its part with anti-German propaganda, no newspaper more so than the *Times*, the most influential press organ with the ruling class, which made its owner Lord Northcliffe, according to some, the most powerful man of his time. Under pressure from him, a Ministry of Ammunition was created in 1915 and entrusted to David

---

[41] Read also Niall Ferguson, *The Pity of War (1914–1918)*, Penguin Books, 2009, and Gerry Docherty and Jim MacGregor, *Hidden History: The Secret Origins of the First World War*, Mainstream Publishing, 2013.

Lloyd George, the same Lloyd George who became prime minister in 1917 and named Northcliffe director of propaganda. Lloyd George and Northcliffe were both members of the Rhodes-Milner Group vaunting the grandiose vision of British "race" and empire. Lord Balfour was also the nephew of Lord Salisbury, from whom he inherited the post of prime minister in 1902.[42] In the United States, the same anti-German propaganda was relayed by the *New York Times*, as this article by Rudyard Kipling, published on May 14, 1916, illustrates: "One thing that we must get into our thick heads is that wherever the German— man or woman—gets a suitable culture to thrive in he or she means death and loss to civilized people, precisely as germs of any disease suffered to multiply mean death or loss to mankind. [. . .] As far as we are concerned the German is typhoid or plague—*Pestis Teutonicus*, if you like."[43]

The Balfour-Rothschild Declaration

The Zionists were divided, according to their country of residence, on which side to support during the war. The most active current was led by Chaim Weizmann, Jew of Belarusian origin who became a British citizen in 1910, and who envisioned a British victory. Weizmann was elected president of the Zionist Federation of Great Britain in 1917, then president of the World Zionist Organization (founded by Herzl) in 1920, ending his career as Israel's first president from 1948 until his death in 1952. During the war Weizmann was a chemist known for his contribution to the war effort, and simultaneously the most influential Zionist lobbyist, with direct access to Prime Minister David Lloyd George (1916 to 1922) and his foreign minister Arthur Balfour, who had already received him in 1906.

On the same side were the Jews of the new Yishuv (the community of Jewish settlers since 1882), who organized resistance against the Ottoman Empire. In 1917, Zeev

---

[42] Carroll Quigley, *The Anglo-American Establishment, op. cit.*, pp. 16–17, 142.
[43] Quoted in Don Heddesheimer, *The First Holocaust: Jewish Fund Raising Campaigns With Holocaust Claims During and After World War One*, Theses & Dissertations Press, 2003 (archive.org), p. 38.

(Vladimir) Jabotinsky, a Jew from Odessa, succeeded in convincing the British to form three Jewish battalions to fight the Turks in the Jordan Valley. This "Jewish Legion" was officially dissolved in 1919, but in reality was recycled in the underground Haganah (*Tzva Haganah le-Yisra'el*, or "Defense Forces of Israel"), which in 1948 formed the embryo of the regular Israeli army.

In October 1916, England was on the brink of defeat. The submarines invented by the Germans had given them a decisive advantage, wreaking considerable havoc on the supplies of the Allies. Germany proposed a just peace, based on a return to pre-war conditions without compensation or redress. It was then that anti-Zionist Prime Minister Herbert Asquith was dismissed from power following a press campaign and replaced by David Lloyd George, who appointed Arthur Balfour as foreign minister. Lloyd George and Balfour were Christians influenced by dispensationalism in favor of Zionism.

Arthur Balfour signed a letter dated November 2, 1917, addressed to Lord Lionel Walter Rothschild, president of the Zionist Federation (and grandson of Baron Lionel de Rothschild, financier of the Suez Canal under the influence of Disraeli) stating that his government would "view with favour the establishment in Palestine of a national home for the Jewish people, and will use their best endeavors to facilitate the achievement of this object." The letter went on to say that it is "clearly understood that nothing shall be done which may prejudice the civil and religious rights of existing non-Jewish communities in Palestine, or the rights and political status enjoyed by Jews in any other country." Note that the "political rights" of Palestinian Arabs (who comprised 92 percent of the population) were not taken into consideration, unlike those of Jews all over the world. Six weeks after the Balfour Declaration, the newspapers reported the triumphal entry of General Edmund Allenby into Jerusalem; the credit for the conquest was almost wholly due to the assistance of the Arabs, over a hundred thousand strong, to whom the promise of autonomy had been made by England in 1915.

It is now known that this "Balfour Declaration," the first official decree offered to Zionism, was the result of long negotiations. The first version proposed that "Palestine should be reconstituted as the National Home of the Jewish people." The final version was deliberately ambiguous, which allowed Lloyd George to claim in 1938 that "National Home" simply meant "some form of British, American or other protectorate to give Jews a real center of national culture." According to a report of the Palestine Royal Commission of 1937, Lloyd George explained the deal in those terms: "Zionist leaders gave us a definite promise that, if the Allies committed themselves to giving facilities for the establishment of a national home for the Jews in Palestine, they would do their best to rally Jewish sentiment and support throughout the world to the Allied cause. They kept their word."[44] Churchill himself declared during the House of Commons debate on the Palestine Mandate, on July 4, 1922: "Pledges and promises were made during the War, and they were made not only on the merits, though I think the merits are considerable. They were made because it was considered they would be of value to us in our struggle to win the War. It was considered that the support which the Jews could give us all over the world, and particularly in the United States, and also in Russia, would be a definite palpable advantage." When on March 12, 1937, Churchill was called before the Palestine Royal Commission, he repeated the argument: "I insist upon loyalty and upon the good faith of England to the Jews, to which I attach the most enormous importance, because we gained great advantages in the War. We did not adopt Zionism entirely out of altruistic love of starting a Zionist colony: It was a matter of great importance to this country. It was a potent factor on public opinion in America and we are bound by honour…"[45]

The United States had proclaimed its neutrality in August 1914, the day of Great Britain's declaration of war against Germany. President Woodrow Wilson was re-elected in 1916 on the slogan "He saved us from the war" and the promise to

---

[44] Alfred Lilienthal, *What Price Israel?* (1953), Infinity Publishing, 2003, pp. 21, 18.
[45] Martin Gilbert, *Churchill and the Jews: A Lifelong Friendship*, Henry Holt & Company, 2007, kindle ed.

continue in that direction. On April 2, 1917, he declared to Congress that the United States was in a state of war and announced that the objective of the war was "to establish a new international order." Why did Wilson reverse course and renege on his promises? At the approach of the war, a little more than thirty years after Disraeli's death, an extremely efficient Zionist network had been set up across the two sides of the Atlantic. Nahum Sokolow, a stakeholder in these deep politics, testifies to this in his *History of Zionism*: "Between London, New York, and Washington there was constant communication, either by telegraph, or by personal visit, and as a result there was perfect unity among the Zionists of both hemispheres."

Among the architects of the secret diplomacy leading to the Balfour Declaration, Nahum Sokolow praises very specifically "the beneficent personal influence of the Honorable Louis D. Brandeis, Judge of the Supreme Court."[46] Louis Brandeis (1856–1941), descended from a Frankist family (adepts of kabbalist Jacob Frank), had been appointed to the highest level of the judiciary in 1916 by President Wilson, at the demand of Wall Street lawyer Samuel Untermeyer who, as rumor has it, blackmailed Wilson with letters to his mistress Mrs. Mary Allen Peck.[47] Untermeyer would become president of the *Keren Hayesod* (Hebrew for "The Foundation Fund"), a fundraising organization established at the London World Zionist Conference in 1920, to provide resources for the Zionist movement. Brandeis was, with Untermeyer, one of the most powerful Zionist schemers, exercising an unparalleled influence on the White House. Brandeis established a formidable tandem with his protégé Felix Frankfurter, who would be his successor in exerting influence on Roosevelt. "Working together over a period of 25 years, they placed a network of disciples in positions of influence, and labored diligently for the enactment

---

[46] Nahum Sokolow, *History of Zionism (1600–1918)*, vol. 2, 1919, pp. 79–80, quoted in Alison Weir, *Against Our Better Judgment: The Hidden History of How the U.S. Was Used to Create Israel*, 2014, k. 387–475.

[47] Gene Smith, *When the Cheering Stopped: The Last Years of Woodrow Wilson*, William Morrow & Co., 1964, pp. 20–23.

of their desired programs," writes Bruce Allen Murphy in *The Brandeis/Frankfurter Connection*.[48]

Brandeis and Frankfurter belonged to a secret society dedicated to the Zionist cause and named the *Parushim* (Hebrew for "Pharisees" or "Separated"). Sarah Schmidt, professor of Jewish history at the Hebrew University of Jerusalem, described the society as "a secret underground guerilla force determined to influence the course of events in a quiet, anonymous way." At the initiation ceremony, each new member received for instructions: "Until our purpose shall be accomplished, you will be fellow of a brotherhood whose bond you will regard as greater than any other in your life—dearer than that of family, of school, of nation. By entering this brotherhood, you become a self-dedicated soldier in the army of Zion." The insider responded by vowing: "Before this council, in the name of all that I hold dear and holy, I hereby vow myself, my life, my fortune, and my honor to the restoration of the Jewish nation. [...] I pledge myself utterly to guard and to obey and to keep secret the laws and the labor of the fellowship, its existence and its aims. Amen."[49]

The influence of Judge Brandeis on Wilson was only one element of a complex system of influence. One of its transmission belts was the closest advisor to the President, Edward Mandell House, known as Colonel House even though he never served in the army. According to his biographer, House said of Brandeis: "His mind and mine agree on most of the questions." Wilson declared: "Mr. House is my second personality. He is my self. His thoughts and mine are one." Colonel House's second name was taken from a Jewish merchant from Houston, one of the most intimate friends of his father, who was of Dutch descent and changed his name from Huis to House upon emigrating to the United States. His brother-in-law, Dr. Sidney Mezes, was Jewish. House perhaps

---

[48] Bruce Allen Murphy, *The Brandeis/Frankfurter Connection: The Secret Political Activities of Two Supreme Court Justices*, Oxford University Press, 1982, p. 10.
[49] Sarah Schmidt, "The 'Parushim': A Secret Episode in American Zionist History," *American Jewish Historical Quarterly* 65, no. 2, December 1975, pp. 121–139, on ifamericansknew.org/history/parushim.html.

belonged to those descendants of the Marranos who maintained a secret attachment to Judaism.

Be that as it may, House's role in favor of the hidden powers was decisive on more than one occasion, including the ratification of the Federal Reserve Act (discreetly passed by Congress on December 23, 1913), which placed the American currency under the control of a bankers' cartel: "The Schiff, Warburg, Kahn, Rockefeller and Morgan families placed their trust in House. When the Federal Reserve legislation finally took definitive form, House was the intermediary between the White House and the financiers." House published an anonymous novel in 1912 entitled *Philip Dru: Administrator*, whose hero Selwyn is the avatar of the author (he resides at Mandell House). He is assisted by a "high priest of finance" named John Thor, whose "influence in all commercial America was absolute." Thor reads backwards Roth (which makes one think of the Rothschilds), but the banker who in reality weighed most on the presidency of Wilson, in concert with House, was Bernard Baruch, who was appointed in 1916 to the head of the Advisory Commission of the Council of National Defense, then chairman of the War Industries Board, and was the key man in the American mobilization for war. He did not exaggerate when he declared before a select congressional committee, "I probably had more power than perhaps any other man did in the war."[50]

It is easy to imagine how President Wilson, an idealistic and naive scholar, was manipulated to drag America into war. But the hidden counselors' grip on the president is only one aspect of the power that Zionism began to acquire over American foreign and military policy. Another important aspect is the manipulation of public opinion. It should be emphasized that while the overwhelming majority of Americans were opposed to entry into the war until 1917, American Jews who had been integrated for several generations were no exception. Among them, Zionism had only very limited and discreet support. They believed that Israel was doing very well in the form of a nation

---

[50] Robert Edward Edmondson, *The Jewish System Indicted by the Documentary Record*, 1937 (archive.org), p. 9.

scattered throughout the world; they feared that the creation of a Jewish state would attract a suspicion of "double loyalty" to their community; and they had no desire to emigrate to Palestine. Reform Judaism, the most visible current in the United States, had not officially denied its status as a religion or affirmed any nationalist aspiration. Chaim Weizmann explains in his autobiography that in order to obtain financial contributions from certain wealthy Jews, it was necessary to deceive them by evoking a "Jewish cultural home" (a university) in Palestine rather than a state: "To them the university-to-be in Jerusalem was philanthropy, which did not compromise them; to us it was nationalist renaissance. They would give—with disclaimers; we would accept—with reservations."[51] Moreover, the majority of American Jews from the old German and Dutch immigrants were rather favorable to Germany in the European conflict.

The entry of the United States into the war was the result of a series of coordinated actions behind the scenes by a highly structured and powerful transatlantic network, including a core of bankers (some linked to the Rothschilds) and some influential newspaper directors, with those of the *New York Times* and the *Washington Post* playing major roles. One key player was Walter Lippmann, one of the most influential American journalists until after the Second World War. Lippmann was one of the craftsmen of the Committee on Public Information, the government agency charged in April 1917 with responsibility for war propaganda. Another leading thinker of the committee was Edward Bernays, Freud's nephew (both by his father and mother), considered the first propaganda theorist with his book *Propaganda* (1928), which begins as follows: "The conscious and intelligent manipulation of the organized habits and opinions of the masses is an important element in democratic society. Those who manipulate this unseen mechanism of society constitute an invisible government which is the true ruling power of our country. [...] Propaganda is the executive arm of the invisible government."

---

[51] Quoted in Alan Hart, *Zionism: The Real Enemy of the Jews*, vol. 1, *op. cit.*, p. 117.

Militant Zionism was widespread among the recent Jewish immigrants from Eastern Europe: between 1881 and 1920, nearly three million of them entered the United States legally (one million between 1897 and 1915). Established mainly in the large cities of the East, mostly poor but resourceful, they formed, from the beginning of the First World War, the majority of American Jews. Their influence on American society was still weak but would grow rapidly, thanks to their strong investment in the press and later in the cinema. At the beginning of the century, they had a hundred publications in English, Yiddish, and other languages. The Zionists could count on a large part of this press to mobilize the Jewish population in favor of war.

The Treaty of Versailles

After the defeat of Germany, the great powers met in Paris for the peace conference that began in January 1919 and closed in August 1920. The Treaty of Versailles, under the headline of "Minority Treaties," placed Palestine under the provisional authority of the British, whose "mandate" included the terms of the Balfour Declaration, namely the creation of a "Jewish national home." Making clear to the world that this was only the first stone of a much more ambitious edifice, Chaim Weizmann declared before the conference: "The Bible is our mandate."

Emile Joseph Dillon, author of *The Inside Story of the Peace Conference* (1920) wrote: "Of all the collectivities whose interests were furthered at the Conference, the Jews had perhaps the most resourceful and certainly the most influential exponents. There were Jews from Palestine, from Poland, Russia, the Ukraine, Rumania, Greece, Britain, Holland, and Belgium; but the largest and most brilliant contingent was sent by the United States."[52] Among the many Jewish advisers representing the United States was Bernard Baruch, a member of the Supreme Economic Council. Another was Lucien Wolf, of whom Israel Zangwill wrote: "The Minority Treaties were the touchstone of

---

[52] Emile Joseph Dillon, *The Inside Story of the Peace Conference* (1920), Harper & Brothers, Kindle 2011, k. 180–90.

the League of Nations, that essentially Jewish aspiration. And the man behind the Minority Treaties was Lucien Wolf."[53]

The British government appointed Herbert Samuel, a Jew, as high commissioner for Palestine. The British mandate over Palestine was rightly perceived as a betrayal by the Arabs, who had revolted against the Turks in 1916 at the instigation of the British, weighing decisively on the outcome of the war. After holding a General National Syrian Congress in Damascus on July 2, 1919, they voted in favor of a United Syria with a constitutional monarchy that would include the territories currently occupied by Syria, Lebanon, Jordan, and Palestine. But when the decisions of the conference concerning the partition of the lands of the Ottoman Empire were made public, Syria was divided into three spheres of influence, while the future of Palestine remained suspended, vulnerable to Zionist ambitions. In his classic book *The Seven Pillars of Wisdom*, T. E. Lawrence, the famous British officer who had organized the Arab forces, acknowledged that the Arabs were betrayed, having revolted against the Turks based "on false hopes." "If I had been an honorable adviser, I would have sent my men [Arabs] home and not let them risk their lives for such stuff."[54]

President Wilson had been persuaded to lead his country into war by the prospect of establishing, atop the heaps of corpses, a new world order of lasting peace based on the general disarmament of nations. His dream was enshrined in the Covenant of the League of Nations, signed June 28, 1919, and placed in the preamble of the Treaty of Versailles. The charter emphasized the need for general disarmament and provided for its implementation by a Disarmament Council in article 8: "The members of the Society recognize that the maintenance of peace requires the reduction of national armaments to the minimum compatible with national security and with the implementation of international obligations imposed by a joint action. The Council, taking into account the geographical situation and the

---

[53] *The Jewish Guardian*, June 11, 1920, quoted in H. A. Gwynne, *The Cause of World Unrest*, Putnam's Sons, 1920 (archive.org), p. xxix.
[54] Alan Hart, *Zionism: The Real Enemy of the Jews*, vol. 1, *op. cit.*, pp. 85–87.

special conditions of each State, shall prepare the plans for such reduction, in the light of the examination and decision of the various governments." It was in this international perspective that "in order to make possible the preparation of a general limitation of armaments of all nations," the Treaty of Versailles forbade Germany to rearm. The American Senate refused to ratify the US accession to the very League of Nations that had been Wilson's fondest wish, and no country chose to set an example by reducing its armaments.

Another problem, highlighted by Niall Ferguson in *The Pity of War*, is that "the League of Nations was not simply to guarantee the territorial integrity of its member states but could accommodate future territorial adjustments 'pursuant to the principle of self-determination.'" But the Treaty of Versailles had excluded from the Reich about twenty million Germans, who now found themselves Polish—not counting the Germans in Alsace-Lorraine and the Soviet Union.[55] When, taking note of this double hypocrisy, Hitler withdrew from the Conference of Disarmament and the League of Nations in October 1933 and committed to the remilitarization of Germany, his action was approved by 95 percent of Germans in a plebiscite.

In 1914, Germany had the most flourishing culture in Europe and the most competitive industry in the world, qualitatively and quantitatively. The Treaty of Versailles imposed on it an astronomical debt of 132 billion gold marks, the catastrophic consequences of which were foreseeable. Renowned economist John Maynard Keynes warned against such an attempt at "reducing Germany to servitude for a generation": "If we aim deliberately at the impoverishment of Central Europe, vengeance, I dare predict, will not limp. Nothing can then delay for very long that final civil war between the forces of Reaction and the despairing convulsions of Revolution, before which the horrors of the late German war will fade into nothing, and which will destroy, whoever is victor, the civilization and the progress of our generation."[56]

---

[55] Niall Ferguson, *The Pity of War, op. cit.*, k. 9756–66.
[56] John M. Keynes, *The Economic Consequences of the Peace*, 1919, on gutenberg.org.

In the First World War, when the Ottoman Empire was the enemy of the British, Russia was allied with the United Kingdom and France through a complex set of alliances (the Triple Entente). But the Tsar had to face major revolutionary movements. In February 1917, he was forced to abdicate before the provisional government of Aleksandr Kerensky. Kerensky yielded to British intimidation and decided to keep Russia in the war, an unpopular decision that seriously weakened him. That is when, on April 16, 1917, to get Russia out of the war, the Germans sent back home thirty-two exiled Bolsheviks including Lenin, soon joined by two hundred Mensheviks, and financed their propaganda organ, *Pravda*, in exchange for their promise to withdraw from the war if they seized power. A year later, they signed with Leon Trotsky (Bronstein by his real name) the Treaty of Brest-Litovsk, which ended the Eastern Front.

Thus, while the English were bringing America into war by supporting a Jewish movement (Zionism), the Germans managed to get Russia out of the war by supporting another Jewish movement (Bolshevism). Robert Wilton, the *Times* correspondent in Russia until 1920, writes in *The Last Days of the Romanovs*: "The Germans knew what they were doing when they sent Lenin's pack of Jews into Russia. They chose them as agents of destruction. Why? Because the Jews were not Russians and to them the destruction of Russia was all in the way of business, revolutionary or financial. The whole record of Bolshevism in Russia is indelibly impressed with the stamp of alien invasion." The Bolshevik regime was predominantly Jewish from its inception. The Central Committee, which exercised supreme power, consisted of nine Jews and three Russians (Lenin was counted among the Russians, although his maternal grandfather, born Srul [Israel], was Jewish). Among the names of 556 high officials of the Bolshevik state officially published in 1918–1919, 458 were identifiable as Jews, according to Robert Wilton.[57]

---

[57] Robert Wilton, *The Last Days of the Romanovs*, George H. Doran Co., 1920 (archive.org), pp. 392–393.

Chapter 7

THE BIRTH PANGS OF ZION

> "The country which you are about to possess is a polluted country, polluted by the people of the country and their disgusting practices, which have filled it with their filth from end to end. Hence you are not to give your daughters in marriage to their sons, or let their daughters marry your sons, or ever concern yourselves about peace or good relations with them, if you want to grow stronger, to live off the fat of the land and bequeath it to your sons forever."
>
> Ezra 9:11–12

Marxism and Zionism

By defining itself as a religion and officially renouncing any national or ethnic claim, Reform Judaism of the nineteenth century made itself vulnerable to the general decline of religious piety that also affected Christianity. Many emancipated Jews rejected not only the ethnic-national conception of Judaism, but also its religious conception. Some converted to Christianity, less to change their religion than to break with their inheritance and better assimilate. This was the case with Heinrich Heine in 1825. It was also the case a year earlier with Herschel Levi, who baptized his whole family and changed his name to Heinrich Marx. His son Karl was then six years old. Twenty years later, Karl Marx displayed a virulent hostility to Judaism, which he saw as the source of the capitalist spirit.

However, in a notable and widely noted paradox, the humanism of Marx remains imprinted with the very Judaism he execrated. Marx's vision of world revolution painfully giving birth to the new world seems haunted by Hebrew messianism. In his *Manifesto of the Communist Party* cosigned by Friedrich Engels in 1848, the Communists "openly proclaim that their goals cannot be reached except through the violent overthrow of the entire social order of the past." The proletariat, composed at that time of disinherited and uprooted peasants, became a new "chosen people" guiding humanity toward happiness. According to the Jewish journalist Bernard Lazare, the Jewish traditional denial of the spiritual world is the source of Marx's philosophical materialism, in the name of which he ousted Gospel-friendly brands of socialism: "Having no hope of future compensation, the Jew could not resign himself to the misfortunes of life. [. . .] To the scourges that struck him, he replied neither by the fatalism of the Muslim, nor by the resignation of the Christian: he answered by revolt."[1]

It should be pointed out, however, that revolutions are not a Jewish specialty—the Jews have been more often the victims than the instigators of revolutions. According to the more detailed analysis of Hilaire Belloc, leader of the English "distributist" current, Marxism proves its filiation with Judaism by its determination to destroy three things valued by Europeans and traditionally despised by Jews: (non-Jewish) patriotism, (Christian) religion, and (landed) property.[2] The first point is symptomatic of the failure of Jewish assimilation, since the aim of assimilation was to make Jews national citizens and not "citizens of the world," that is, stateless internationalists. Marx's internationalism is blind to the patriotic feeling of the working classes, and reproduces Jewish hostility to nations and nationalisms of all kinds.

It is not the revolutionary spirit of the nineteenth century that is Jewish, but the Marxist ideology that gradually took control of it by merciless elimination of its competitors, derided as "nationalist," "utopian," "or "petit-bourgeois"—as Marx called Pierre-Joseph Proudhon, while shamelessly plagiarizing his work. Mikhail Bakunin, another member of the First International ousted by Marx, attributed Marx's attachment to the state to his Jewishness, pointing out that the state is always the protector and best customer of the bankers: "What can

---

[1] Bernard Lazare, *L'Antisémitisme, son histoire et ses causes* (1894), Kontre Kulture, 2011, p. 173.
[2] Hilaire Belloc, *The Jews*, Constable & Co., 1922 (archive.org), pp. 167–185.

Communism and the High Bank have in common? Ah! It is that Marx's communism wants the powerful centralization of the State, and where there is a centralization of the State, there must necessarily be today a Central Bank of the State, and where such a Central Bank exists, the parasite nation of the Jews, speculating on the work of the people, will always find a way to exist."[3]

Marxism, at bottom, is still a Jewish response to Judaism. It is a crypto-Judaism that doesn't know itself. And it is precisely because he had not left the mental matrix of Judaism that Marx was incapable of recognizing its real nature: "Let us not look for the secret of the Jew in his religion, but let us look for the secret of his religion in the real Jew."[4] This thesis, taken up by the Marxist Abraham Léon who sees the Jews as a social class (*un peuple-classe*),[5] is a decoy insofar as it underestimates, as belonging to the "superstructure" of Jewish society, what is rather its deep ideological foundation: the Jews are, foremost, an idea (*un peuple-idée*).

The journalist Moritz Hess had long shared the vision of his friend Karl Marx. He even published calumnies against Bakunin after the General Congress of the International in Basel (September 5–12, 1869), accusing him of being an *agent provocateur* of the Russian government and of working "in the interest of pan-Slavism."[6] Yet seven years earlier he signed his book *Rome and Jerusalem* under the name of Moses Hess. Hess is a precursor of Zionism, convinced that "the race war was more important than class struggle" in history. Marx and Hess have something in common: they both broke with religion. But while in Marx this was a divorce from Judaism (symbolized by his baptism), in Hess it was, on the contrary, a return to Judaism seen as an ethnic identity and no longer as a religion. Marxism is, in some way, an extreme extension of assimilation (a fusion of Judaism into humanism), while Zionism is an extreme reaction against assimilation (the return of Judaism to nationalism).

---

[3] Michel Bakounine, "Aux compagnons de la Fédération des sections internationales du Jura," 1872, quoted in Henri Arvon, *Les Juifs et l'Idéologie*, PUF, 1978, p. 50.

[4] Karl Marx, *On the Jewish Question*, 1843, on www.marxists.org/archive.

[5] Abraham Léon, *La Conception matérialiste de la question juive* (1946), Kontre Kulture, 2013.

[6] Read Bakounine's answer, "Aux citoyens rédacteurs du *Réveil*," on Wikisource.org.

Hess's book *Rome and Jerusalem* (1862) had little immediate echo. Only after the outbreak of the Dreyfus affair in 1894 could a substantial portion of the European Jewish community be convinced of the failure of assimilation and the incurability of anti-Semitism—despite the fact that the mobilization of the Dreyfusards in 1899 and the final rehabilitation of Dreyfus in 1906 could logically lead to the opposite conclusion. The Dreyfus affair was what launched Zionism, by converting Theodor Herzl and Max Nordau, cofounders of the World Zionist Organization. Herzl writes in his Journal: "Anti-Semitism is a propelling force which, like the wave of the future, will bring Jews into the promised land. [...] Anti-Semitism has grown and continues to grow—and so do I."[7]

The term "anti-Semitism" was introduced by Wilhelm Marr, founder of the League of Anti-Semites (*Antisemitische-Liga*) in 1879 and journalist with the newspaper *Antisemitische Hefte*. It is based on an abuse of the word "Semite" forged by linguists for the purpose of language classification, just like its "Aryan" counterpart. Anti-Semitism designates a modern form of Judeophobia based on an ethnic conception of Jewishness, rather than the religious conception of traditional Christianity. It is therefore a mirror image of Jewish nationalism that, precisely at this moment, got rid of the religious definition of Jewishness to adopt an ethnic definition.

Until the end of the nineteenth century, the majority of Jews living in Germany for several generations remained as indifferent to the Zionist appeal as to the revolutionary appeal, cherishing above all their social success. It was among the Ashkenazi Jews who lived in Russian territory or had emigrated to Germany and Austria-Hungary that these movements would become tidal waves. These eastern European Jews formed the revolutionary vanguard that in March 1848 arose in the German Confederation and other regions under the domination of the Austrian Empire and the Kingdom of Prussia. It was among them also that in 1882, the appeal of the doctor Leon Pinsker of Odessa for the Jews' "return to the ranks of the nations by the

---

[7] Alfred M. Lowenthal, *Diaries of Theodore Herzl*, Grosset & Dunlop, 1962, p. 7.

acquisition of a Jewish homeland" was taken up. At the seventh World Zionist Congress (1905), young Jews from Poland and Russia took the lead. Among them were Chaim Weizmann and Nahum Sokolow, who later in London became key figures behind the Balfour Declaration. In 1922, as president of the Zionist Executive Committee, Sokolow made a strikingly prophetic declaration: "Jerusalem some day will become the capital of the world's peace."[8] As for Weizmann, he remained until 1948 one of the most energetic promoters of Zionism in England and the United States, and ended his life as the first president of the State of Israel.

At the end of the nineteenth century, conversion to communism or Zionism among the newly emancipated Ashkenazi Jews was associated with the rejection of the Talmud. But the split led to two divergent options and two visions of history. Chaim Weizmann recounts in his autobiography (*Trial and Error*, 1949) that Jews in Russia in the early twentieth century were divided, sometimes within single families, between revolutionary communists and revolutionary Zionists. These divisions, however, were relative and changeable; not only were the pioneers of Zionism often Marxist, but many communist Jews became ardent Zionists throughout the twentieth century. The borderline was all the more vague as the powerful General Jewish Labour Bund in Lithuania, Poland, and Russia, better known as the Bund, inscribed in its revolutionary agenda the right of the Jews to found a secular Yiddish-speaking nation. Moreover, some financiers in Europe and America supported the two movements jointly, to make them the two jaws of the same pincers that would clutch Europe: Jacob Schiff, one of the richest American bankers of the time, financed Herzl and Lenin simultaneously.

---

[8] "Says Jews of World will back League," *New York Times*, August 28, 1922, on query.nytimes.com.

Russia and the Jews

Before analyzing the impact of Zionism and communism in Europe during what Yuri Slezkine calls "the Jewish century,"[9] we need to look back at the history of the Jews of Eastern Europe. From the sixteenth to twentieth centuries, the Jewish community in Poland was the largest in the world. Its origin remains difficult to explain, but immigration from the Rhine countries at the end of the Middle Ages is the most plausible hypothesis. In the seventeenth century, Poland was governed by an oligarchy that concentrated all the wealth in its hands, and relied on the Jews for the exploitation of the peasants. Totally unassimilated, speaking Yiddish and hardly any Polish, the Jews lived under the control of their own administrative and judicial system, the *kahal*, which maintained the cohesion of the community by prohibiting competition among its members. But the Jews were also important players in the national economy. They were the landowners' administrators and tax collectors. As legal middlemen in the grain trade, they manipulated prices at will. Their complicity in the oppression of the peasant masses by the nobility inevitably generated resentments that were expressed in explosions of violence. When the Cossacks led by Bogdan Chmielnicki revolted against the Polish nobles in 1648, the Jews were the first to be massacred.[10]

After the annexation of part of Poland by Russia between 1772 and 1795, these Ashkenazi Jews lived mainly in Russia, cantoned in their "Pale of Settlement." They numbered six hundred thousand on the eve of the first partition (1772), and nearly six million by 1897.[11] At the beginning of the nineteenth century, most still spoke neither Polish nor Russian. In 1801 a memoir written by the senator and writer Gabriel Romanovich Derjavin for Tsar Paul I after an observation mission in the Pale of Settlement, revealed that a majority of Jews made their living

---

[9] Yuri Slezkine, *The Jewish Century*, Princeton University Press, 2004.

[10] Alexandre Soljénitsyne, *Deux siècles ensemble (1795–1995)*, tome I: *Juifs et Russes avant la Révolution*, Fayard, 2003, pp. 26–36.

[11] Iwo Cyprian Pogonowski, *Jews in Poland: A Documentary History*, Hippocrene Books, 1993, pp. 13–15.

from the manufacture and sale of vodka, to which they were granted exclusive rights by the Polish nobility. By combining this activity with their second specialty, lending money at interest (i.e., selling alcohol on credit), they encouraged alcoholism among the peasants and indebted them to the point of ruin: "The Jews out of greed were exploiting the drinking problems of the peasants to cheat them out of their grain, in order to turn the grain into vodka, and as a result were causing famine." Derjavin also denounced the Polish landowners, who did not administer their properties directly but instead used Jewish tenants: "Many greedy farmers ruin the peasants through back-breaking labors and impositions, and render them bereft of land or family." Several efforts were made to put an end to this situation, but the lack of continuity in the policy of the successive tsars rendered them ineffective. A parallel policy of encouraging Jews to become farmers, through the granting of fertile lands, material, and animals, also failed and was abandoned in 1866.[12]

Tsar Alexander II (1855–1881), who emancipated the serfs in 1861, also abolished most of the restrictions imposed on the Jews and facilitated their access to Russian education. Between 1876 and 1883, the proportion of Jews in the universities increased considerably. Emancipated and educated, many young Jewish intellectuals became revolutionaries. While rejecting the Talmudism of their parents, they inherited their hatred of Christian and peasant Russia, while the Tsar remained in their eyes an avatar of Pharaoh. The assassination of Alexander II in March 1881, by a group of anarchists including Jews, triggered violent pogroms. Noting that more than 40 percent of law and medicine students at Kharkov and Odessa universities were Jewish, the new Tsar imposed a *numerus clausus*, which only reinforced the sense of injustice and revolutionary spirit among Jewish youth.[13]

[12] Alexandre Soljénitsyne, *Deux siècles ensemble*, tome I, *op. cit.*, pp. 50–54, 154.
[13] Erich Haberer, *Jews and Revolution in Nineteenth-century Russia*, Cambridge University Press, 1995, pp. 253–254.

The revolutionary forces that forced Tsar Nicholas II to abdicate in February 1917 were far from being exclusively Jewish. There was great discontent in all underprivileged classes, especially among the peasants. However, both opponents and advocates of Bolshevism have noted the high proportion of Jews among the Bolsheviks who overturned the February Revolution and Aleksandr Kerensky's provisional government by their own October Revolution.[14] Jewish historian Angelo Rappoport wrote in his seminal work: "The Jews in Russia, in their total mass, were responsible for the Revolution."[15] Winston Churchill wrote in a famous article in the *Illustrated Sunday Herald* published February 8, 1920: "There is no need to exaggerate the part played in the creation of Bolshevism and in the actual bringing about of the Russian Revolution by these international and for the most part atheistical Jews. It is certainly a very great one; it probably outweighs all others." In this article titled "Zionism versus Bolshevism: A struggle for the soul of the Jewish people," Churchill sided with the Zionist cause, referring to Bolshevism as "this world-wide conspiracy for the overthrow of civilization."[16]

On the other side, the official gazette of Hungarian Jewry *Egyenlöség* (Equality) proclaimed: "Jewish intellect and knowledge, Jewish courage and love of peace saved Russia and perhaps the whole world. Never has world historical mission of Jewry shone so brightly as in Russia. Trotsky's words prove that the Biblical and prophetic Jewish spirit of Isaiah and Micah, the great peace-makers, with that of the Talmudic Elders, is inspiring the leaders of Russia to-day."[17] The September 10, 1920 edition of *The American Hebrew* magazine pompously bragged: "The Bolshevik Revolution eliminated the most brutal dictatorship in history. This great achievement, destined to

---

[14] Read Alexandre Soljénitsyne, *Deux siècles ensemble (1795–1995)*, tome II: *Juifs et Russes pendant la période soviétique*, Fayard, 2003.

[15] Angelo Solomon Rappoport, *The Pioneers of the Russian Revolution*, Brentano's, 1919 (archive.org), p. 250.

[16] On en.wikisource.org/wiki/Zionism_versus_Bolshevism.

[17] Louis Marschalko, *The World Conquerors: The Real War Criminals*, 1958 (archive.org), p. 50.

figure in history as one of the overshadowing results of the World War, was largely the product of Jewish thinking, Jewish discontent, Jewish effort to reconstruct."[18] "Jewish financing" should be added to the list, for the Bolshevik Revolution was largely financed by Wall Street bankers such as Jacob Schiff, who gloated: "The Russian revolution is possibly the most important event in Jewish history since the race was brought out of slavery."[19]

The *American Hebrew* had also published, October 31, 1919, an article titled "The Crucifixion of Jews Must Stop!" warning of "this threatened holocaust of human life" on "six millions" of European Jews, who "are being whirled toward the grave by a cruel and relentless fate," "six million men and women [a figure repeated seven times in one page] are dying from lack of the necessaries of life [...] through the awful tyranny of war and a bigoted lust for Jewish blood."[20] "Jewish blood" here refers to the Russian civil war, when the counter-revolutionary struggle of the Russian and Ukrainian peasants gave rise to anti-Jewish pogroms (6,000 victims in 1919). The *New York Times* also distinguished itself in postwar propaganda designed to convince readers that the Jews had been the main victims of the First World War. In the *New York Times* of September 29, 1919, Felix Warburg, chairman of the Joint Distribution Committee of American Funds for Jewish War Sufferers (founded in 1914 and still in existence with the shortened name of American Jewish Joint Distribution Committee), wrote that the Jews "were the worst sufferers in the war." "The successive blows of contending armies have all but broken the back of European Jewry and have reduced to tragically unbelievable poverty,

---

[18] Michael Jones, *The Jewish Revolutionary Spirit and Its Impact on World History*, Fidelity Press, 2008, p. 747.

[19] Bertie Charles Forbes, *Men Who Are Making America*, 1917 (archive.org), p. 334; Antony Sutton, *Wall Street and the Bolshevik Revolution* (1976), Clairview Books, 2011.

[20] Read on en.wikipedia.org/wiki/The_American_Hebrew. See other similar press articles on YouTube, "'Six million Jews' reference in ten newspapers between 1915–1938."

starvation and disease about 6,000,000 souls, or half the Jewish population of the earth."[21]

Despite the many Russian pseudonyms adopted by the officers of the Bolshevik system, Russians were well aware that they had been conquered by a foreign people. A 1926 Agitprop report to the Central Committee secretariat expresses concern about a wave of anti-Semitism resulting from "the sense that the Soviet regime patronizes the Jews, that it is 'the Jewish government,' that the Jews cause unemployment, housing shortages, college admissions problems, price rises, and commercial speculation—this sense is instilled in the workers by all the hostile elements." Repression of this "bourgeois anti-Semitism" was all the more brutal in that, as Yuri Slezkine notes, "the Soviet secret police—the regime's sacred center, known after 1934 as the NKVD—was one of the most Jewish of all Soviet institutions. [...] Out of twenty NKVD directorates, twelve (60 percent, including State Security, Police, Labor Camps, and Resettlement [deportation]) were headed by officers who identified themselves as ethnic Jews. The most exclusive and sensitive of all NKVD agencies, the Main Directorate for State Security, consisted of ten departments: seven of them [...] were run by immigrants from the former Pale of Settlement."[22] Robert Wilton, a Moscow correspondent for the London *Times* for seventeen years, provided precise indications as to the proportion of Jews among Bolshevik apparatchiks as early as 1920. The Central Committee of the Bolshevik Party, which exercised supreme power, included 9 Jews and 3 Russians. (Lenin was counted among the Russians, although his maternal grandfather, born Srul [Israel], was Jewish). All the Central Committees of the parties represented included 41 identifiable Jews out of 61 members. The Council of People's Commissars comprised 17 Jews out of 22 members. Among the names of

---

[21] Quoted in Don Heddesheimer, *The First Holocaust: Jewish Fund Raising Campaigns With Holocaust Claims During and After World War One*, Theses & Dissertations Press, 2003 (archive.org), pp. 47, 106.

[22] Yuri Slezkine, *The Jewish Century*, *op. cit.*, k. 4453 and 4275.

556 high officials of the Bolshevik State officially published in 1918–1919, 458 were identifiable as Jews.[23]

The Bolshevik Revolution pulled the rug out from under the Zionist propaganda machine, which had hitherto been based on reports of the Russian pogroms, amplified by the Western press. On March 25, 1906, the *New York Times* could evoke the fate of "Russia's 6,000,000 Jews": "the Russian Government's studied policy for the 'solution' of the Jewish question is systematic and murderous extermination." But such alarmist propaganda was no longer possible in 1917, since one of the first measures taken by the Bolsheviks was a law criminalizing anti-Semitism. The Russian Civil War did provide some space for a new narrative: on July 20, 1921, during the Russian Civil War, the same *New York Times* could still publish the headline "Massacre Threatens All Jews as Soviet Power Wanes. Russia's 6,000,000 Jews are facing extermination."[24] A few years later, Chaim Weizmann, who had used the pogroms of Russia as a diplomatic lever in 1917, was forced to contradict himself: "Nothing can be more superficial and nothing can be more wrong than that the sufferings of Russian Jewry ever were the cause of Zionism. The fundamental cause of Zionism has been, and is, the ineradicable national striving of Jewry to have a home of its own—a national center, a national home with a national Jewish life."[25] Only when Hitler's coming to power posed a new threat to the Jews, could Jewish suffering become again the main argument for the creation of Israel.

Ironically, the Jewish character of the Bolshevik Revolution was one of the main causes of the German anti-Semitism that brought Hitler to power. The Red Terror was a very close threat to the Germans. In 1918 there was a Bolshevik Revolution in Bavaria led by the Jew Kurt Eisner, who had established a short-lived Bavarian Soviet Republic. "What is most essential in National Socialism," according to German historian Ernst Nolte, "is its relation to Marxism, particularly to communism, in

---

[23] Douglas Reed, *The Controversy of Zion* (1956), Dolphin Press, 1978, pp. 342–346.
[24] Benton Bradberry, *The Myth of German Villainy*, Authorhouse, 2012, p. 198.
[25] Chaim Weizmann, *Trial and Error*, Harper and Brothers, 1949, p. 201.

the form it took through the Bolshevik victory during the Russian Revolution."[26] It is often forgotten that in 1933, when Hitler came to power, the Soviets had just committed genocidal massacres followed by organized famine in Ukraine, at the gates of Germany, killing nearly eight million people, or one-third of the population. This crime against humanity, carried out by a predominantly Jewish NKVD, would never be mentioned in the Nuremberg trials, and still today is hardly ever discussed. (When in 2009, Ukraine opened a tribunal to prosecute the crime, Aleksandr Feldman, the chairman of the Ukrainian Jewish Committee, forced the cancellation of the proceedings on the pretext that it would constitute an incitement to hatred, since the names of almost all the Soviet officers charged were Jewish.)[27]

The second enemy designated by Hitler was international finance, which was responsible for the depression of the 1930s. Banking was heavily dominated by Jews. In Berlin before the First World War, thirty private banks out of fifty belonged to Jewish families, and the proportion increased after the war.[28] Thus, many Germans equated the horrors of Bolshevism with a Jewish plot, and the dominant position of the Jews in the capitalist economy—the revolution and the bank—were the two crucibles of Nazi anti-Semitism. This reminds us of Theodor Herzl's assessment of the root of anti-Semitism: "When we sink, we become a revolutionary proletariat, the subordinate officers of all revolutionary parties; and at the same time, when we rise, there rises also our terrible power of the purse."[29] To all this was added the well-known role of the Jews in the defeat and annihilation of Germany at the end of the First World War, as the English Zionist Samuel Landman acknowledged in a 1936 memoir: "The fact that it was Jewish help that brought the USA into the War on the side of the Allies has rankled ever since in German—especially Nazi—minds, and has contributed in no

---

[26] Ernst Nolte, *La Guerre civile européenne: National-socialisme et bolchevisme (1917–1945)* (1989), Perrin, 2011, p. 39.
[27] Vladimir Matveyev, "Jewish group objects to 'Great Famine' case," June 15, 2009, on www.jta.org.
[28] Yuri Slezkine, *The Jewish Century, op. cit.,* k. 846.
[29] Theodor Herzl, *The Jewish State,* on www.jewishvirtuallibrary.org.

small measure to the prominence which anti-Semitism occupies in the Nazi programme."[30]

Of course, "the Jews" of Germany were not responsible for the intrigues of a handful of elites in the circles of power. These elites, however, claim to speak in the name of the Jews, and derive some of their power from this claim of representing their people. They pretend to speak for the community, while, to its misfortune, the silent majority of the Jews is taken hostage. Thus, as early as the 1920s, Judeophobia spread in Germany, hindering the process of assimilation of even the most German-speaking Jews. The case of Theodor Lessing is exemplary: from a family whose Judaism was no more than a remnant, he departed still further from the Jewish community in 1899 and married a young woman of the Prussian aristocracy. But his in-laws refused to meet their Jewish son-in-law, and he returned to the Jewish faith, henceforth with an ethnic conception of Jewishness. He expressed his rejection of assimilation in *Jewish Self-Hatred*, published in Berlin in 1930. Lessing psychologically analyzes the tragic journey of certain Jews who have broken with their Jewishness, while curiously avoiding the question of his own narcissistic wound that led him to break with his desire for assimilation.

Zionism and Nazism

German Judeophobia was radicalized by the racialist theories of the time and turned into an extremely virulent anti-Semitism. Jewish intellectuals largely contributed to this ideological climate. *The Struggle of the Races (Der Rassenkampf)* published in 1883 by Ludwig Gumplowicz, a Jew from Cracow and professor of political science in Graz for twenty years, had a considerable influence on Germanic racism: "The perpetual struggle of the races is the law of history, while 'perpetual peace' is only the dream of the idealists," he wrote. According to Gumplowicz, individuals of the same race are interconnected by "syngeneic feelings" that make them "seek to act as a single factor in the

---

[30] Samuel Landman, *Great Britain, the Jews and Palestine: How America Was Dragged into World War One by the Zionist Lobby*, 1936, p. 6, on desip.igc.org/1939sLandman.htm.

struggle for domination."[31] The term "race" at the time had a rather vague meaning, synonymous with "people," and Gumplowicz, who expressed no particular sympathy for the Jews, included in the formation of syngeneic feeling not only consanguinity, but also education, language, religion, custom, and law. But the theoreticians of Jewish nationalism developed a narrower conception of race, which would directly influence, through mimetic rivalry, the ideology of the Aryan race. Recall that for Benjamin Disraeli, "language and religion do not make a race—there is only one thing that makes a race, and that is blood" (*Endymion*, 1880). As early as 1862, Moses Hess had emphasized the purity of his race: "The Jewish race is one of the primary races of mankind that has retained its integrity, in spite of the continual change of its climatic environment, and the Jewish type has conserved its purity through the centuries." "The Jewish type is indestructible." Therefore, "a Jew belongs to his race and consequently also to Judaism, in spite of the fact that he or his ancestors have become apostates."[32] The editor of *Jewish World*, Lucien Wolf, an influential historian and politician, insisted on the racial definition of Jewishness. He proclaimed the racial superiority of the Jews in an influential 1884 article titled "What is Judaism? A Question of To-Day": "It is too little known that the Jews are as a race really superior, physically, mentally, and morally, to the people among whom they dwell."[33]

Thus, in nineteenth- to twentieth-century Germany, Jewish racism precedes Aryan racism, just as in sixteenth- to seventeenth-century Spain the Marranos' pride in their blood had provoked a reaction: the Iberian statutes of "purity of blood." The parallel was made by Yitzhak Fritz Baer in *Galut*, published in Berlin in 1936. In both cases, we have Jewish communities suddenly emancipated (by baptism between 1391

---

[31] Ludwig Gumplowicz, *La Lutte des races. Recherches sociologiques*, Guillaumin, 1893 (archive.org), pp. 261, 242.

[32] Moses Hess, *Rome and Jerusalem: A Study in Jewish Nationalism*, 1918 (archive.org), pp. 59, 61, 98.

[33] Daniel Langton, "Jewish evolutionary perspectives on Judaism, antisemitism, and race science in late nineteenth-century England: a comparative study of Lucien Wolf and Joseph Jacobs," *Jewish Historical Studies*, vol. 46, 2014, pp. 37–73, on www.escholar.manchester.ac.uk.

and 1497, by European laws between the end of the eighteenth century and early nineteenth century), who rapidly acquire an economic, political, and cultural power disproportionate to their number, and who express racial pride offensive to the Gentiles, generating in the latter a hostility that turns into "race war."[34] "A Jew brought up among Germans may assume German custom, German words. He may be wholly imbued with that German fluid but the nucleus of his spiritual structure will always remain Jewish, because his blood, his body, his physical-racial type are Jewish. [...] A preservation of national integrity is impossible except by a preservation of racial purity." These words were not written by Adolf Hitler in *Mein Kampf*, but twenty years earlier, in 1904, by the Zionist Zeev (Vladimir) Jabotinsky in his "Letter on Autonomy."[35] At the time of Hitler's accession to power in 1933, the Jewish community had been subjected to racial indoctrination of the völkisch type for half a century, especially from the Zionists. It was the Jew Haim Arlosoroff who, after the First World War, invented the term *Volkssozialismus* as the ideology of the Zionist party *Hapoel Hatzair* ("Young Workers").[36]

It is therefore not surprising that Zionist and anti-assimilationist Jews were in favor of the Nuremberg laws, which prohibited marriages between Jews and Germans in the Reich. Joachim Prinz, a Zionist ideologist of German Jewry, who became president of the American Jewish Congress (1958–1966), writes in his book *Wir Juden* ("We the Jews") published in Berlin in 1934: "We want assimilation to be replaced by a new law: the declaration of belonging to the Jewish nation and the Jewish race. A state built upon the principle of the purity of nation and race can only be honored and respected by a Jew who declares his belonging to his own kind. [...] For only he who honors his own breed and his own blood can have an

---

[34] Nathan Wachtel, *Entre Moïse et Jésus. Études marranes (XVᵉ-XIXᵉ siècle)*, CNRS éditions, 2013, pp. 40–42.

[35] Lenni Brenner, *51 Documents: Zionist Collaboration with the Nazis*, Barricade Books, 2002, pp. 7–20.

[36] Walter Laqueur, *A History of Zionism: From the French Revolution to the Establishment of the State of Israel*, Fine Communications, 1997, p. 476.

attitude of honor towards the national will of other nations."[37]
Prinz left Germany in 1937 and immediately justified himself in
an article for the journal *Young Zionist* titled "Zionism under the
Nazi Government": "The government announced very solemnly
that there was no country in the world which tried to solve the
Jewish problem as seriously as did Germany. Solution of the
Jewish question? It was our Zionist dream! We never denied the
existence of the Jewish question! Dissimilation? It was our own
appeal!"[38]

The relationship between Nazism and Judaism was well
known in Jewish circles of the 1930s. No one expressed it better
than the American rabbi Harry Waton in a book published in
1939 by the Committee for the Preservation of the Jews, *A
Program for the Jews*: "Nazism is an imitation of Judaism; Nazism
adopted the principles and ideas of Judaism with which to
destroy Judaism and the Jews." "The Nazi philosophy starts out
with the postulate: The blood of a race determines the nature,
course of evolution and the destiny of that race. [...] whether
consciously or not, the Nazis took this theory from the Bible
itself." Waton goes further still: "Hitler's declaration that the
Jewish consciousness is poison to the Aryan races is the deepest
insight that the Western world has yet achieved in its own
nature; and his capacity to realize this is the proof of his genius
as well as the secret of his power and of the curious fascination
which his personality exerts. [...] it is not the practical power or
wealth of the Jews that he fears, but the character of the Jewish
mind. [...] It is the hidden penetration of the Jewish spirit into
the Gentile mind that is the danger; and it is a danger because
the 'Aryan' mind cannot resist it, but must succumb."[39] Waton,
in fact, misunderstands Hitler's real views on Jewishness, which,
in private, were less racist than his own: "We use the term
Jewish race," Hitler wrote to a friend, "merely for reasons of
linguistic convenience, for in the real sense of the word, and

---

[37] Quoted in Israel Shahak, *Jewish History, Jewish Religion: The Weight of Three Thousand Years*, Pluto Press, 1994, p. 86.
[38] Quoted in Lenni Brenner, *Zionism in the Age of Dictators*, Lawrence Hill & Co., 1983.
[39] Harry Waton, *A Program for the Jews and an Answer to All Anti-Semites: A Program for Humanity*, 1939 (archive.org), pp. 54, 64–67, 200.

from a genetic point of view there is no Jewish race. [...] The Jewish race is above all a community of the spirit."[40]

Nazism and Zionism shared more than one ideological foundation; they had as their common enemy the assimilationist Jew. They also had a common goal: the emigration of Jews from Germany. Reinhardt Heydrich, chief of the SS Security Service, wrote in 1935 in *Das Schwarze Korps,* the official SS journal: "We must separate Jewry into two categories: the Zionists and those who favour being assimilated. The Zionists adhere to a strict racial position and by emigrating to Palestine they are helping to build their own Jewish state. [...] The time cannot be far distant when Palestine will again be able to accept its sons who have been lost to it for over a thousand years. Our good wishes together with our official good will go with them."[41] It would be exaggerating to say that Hitler was ideologically a Zionist, for he had written in *Mein Kampf* in 1923: "For while Zionism tries to make the other part of the world believe that the national self-consciousness of the Jew finds satisfaction in the creation of a Palestinian State, the Jews again most slyly dupe the stupid goyim. They have no thought of building up a Jewish State in Palestine, so that they might inhabit it, but they only want a central organization of their international world cheating, endowed with prerogatives, withdrawn from the seizure of others: a refuge for convicted rascals and a high school for future rogues."[42] Nevertheless, the Nazis were largely favorable to the project originally formulated by Herzl, who had boasted in his diary: "I believe I have found the solution of the Jewish Question. Not *a* solution, but *the* solution, the only one," repeating further that Zionism was "the only possible, final, and successful solution of the Jewish Question."[43] The first Zionist association inspired by Herzl's book, the *National-jüdische*

---

[40] Letter to Martin Bormann dated February 3, 1945, quoted in Gunnar Heinsohn, "What makes the Holocaust a uniquely unique genocide?," *Journal of Genocide Research,* November 2000, pp. 411–413, on migs.concordia.ca.

[41] Quoted in Heinz Höhne, *The Order of the Death's Head: The Story of Hitler's SS,* Penguin Books, 2001, p. 133.

[42] Adolf Hitler, *Mein Kampf,* Reynal & Hitchcock, 1941 (archive.org), pp. 447–448.

[43] *The Complete Diaries of Theodor Herzl,* edited by Raphael Patai, Herzl Press & Thomas Yoseloff, 1960, vol. 1, p. 118.

Vereinigung Köln, declared as its goal in 1897: "The Final Solution
of the Jewish Question lies therefore in the establishment of the
Jewish State."[44]

The Nazis naturally wholeheartedly supported Jewish
emigration to Palestine. In the spring of 1933, Baron Leopold
Itz von Mildenstein, one of the earliest SS officers, spent six
months in Palestine in the company of Zionist Kurt Tuchler.
On his return, he wrote for *Angriff* (a journal founded by Joseph
Goebbels) a series of twelve articles expressing great admiration
for the pioneering spirit of Zionist Jews. It is not surprising,
therefore, that when in 1933, the *American Jewish Congress*
declared economic war on Germany and organized the boycott
of German products, the Zionist Federation of Germany
addressed a memorandum to "the New German State" (dated
June, 21) condemning the boycott, and expressing sympathy for
the Nazi ideology: "Our acknowledgment of Jewish nationality
provides for a clear and sincere relationship to the German
people and its national and racial realities. Precisely because we
do not wish to falsify these fundamentals, because we, too, are
against mixed marriage and are for maintaining the purity of the
Jewish group and reject any trespasses in the cultural domain."
"The realization of Zionism could only be hurt by resentment of
Jews abroad against the German development. Boycott
propaganda—such as is currently being carried on against
Germany in many ways—is in essence un-Zionist."[45]

As Hannah Arendt has shown in her controversial book
Eichmann in Jerusalem (1963), Nazi policy was pro-Zionist until
1938, and "all leading positions in the Nazi-appointed
'Reichsvereinigung' [compulsory organization of all Jews in Nazi
Germany] were held by Zionists." This created "a situation in
which the non-selected majority of Jews inevitably found
themselves confronted with two enemies—the Nazi authorities
and the Jewish authorities." Arendt was the first Jewish
intellectual to unveil one of the Zionists' darkest secrets, which

---

[44] Isaiah Friedman, *Germany, Turkey, and Zionism 1897–1918,* Transaction Publishers,
1998, p. 17.
[45] Lucy Dawidowicz, *A Holocaust Reader,* Behrman House, 1976, pp. 150–155.

has been since abundantly documented (e.g., by Tom Segev in *The Seventh Million*): "There existed in those first years a mutually highly satisfactory agreement between the Nazi authorities and the Jewish Agency for Palestine—a '*Haavarah*', or Transfer Agreement, which provided that an emigrant to Palestine could transfer his money there in German goods and exchange them for pounds upon arrival. It was soon the only legal way for a Jew to take his money with him. The alternative was the establishment of a blocked account, which could be liquidated abroad only at a loss of between fifty and ninety-five percent). The result was that in the thirties, when American Jewry took great pains to organize a boycott of German merchandise, Palestine, of all places, was swamped with all kinds of 'goods made in Germany'."[46] Some sixty thousand wealthy Jews benefited from this *Haavara Agreement*, making a decisive contribution to the Jewish colonization of Palestine.

This collaboration between Ben-Gurion's Jewish Agency and Hitler's Nazi government started in 1933 and ended officially in 1938 with Great Britain's entry into the war. But the Lehi or Stern Gang, a dissident faction of the terrorist Irgun, led by future head of state Yitzhak Shamir, continued to bet on the Germans. In a document dated January 11, 1941, it recognized that "The evacuation of the Jewish masses from Europe is a precondition for solving the Jewish question," envisioning "the establishment of the historical Jewish state on a national and totalitarian basis, and bound by treaty with the German Reich," and, with that aim, "offers to actively take part in the war on Germany's side." The talks came to an end with the arrest by the British authorities of several Lehi members, including Yitzhak Shamir, for "terrorism and collaboration with the Nazi enemy."[47]

In London and Washington, of course, the Zionist movement, led by Chaim Weizmann, supported the economic war against Germany. Weizmann revived the winning strategy of

[46] Hannah Arendt, *Eichmann in Jerusalem: A Report on the Banality of Evil*, Penguin, 2006, pp. 136–138.
[47] Alan Hart, *Zionism: The Real Enemy of the Jews*, vol. 1: *The False Messiah*, Clarity Press, 2009, pp. 211–213.

the First World War, attempting to monetize Jewish influence in England to bring the United States into the war. In a letter to Churchill dated September 10, 1941, he wrote: "I have spent months in America, traveling up and down the country [...]. There is only one big ethnic group which is willing to stand, to a man, for Great Britain, and a policy of 'all-out-aid' for her: the five million American Jews. [...] It has been repeatedly acknowledged by British Statesmen that it was the Jews who, in the last war, effectively helped to tip the scales in America in favour of Great Britain. They are keen to do it—and may do it—again.."[48]

The *quid pro quo* for this Jewish influence was the formation of an official "Jewish Army" among the Allied troops. This "Jewish Army" was an idea of Vladimir Jabotinsky, who had already suggested it to the British in 1917 and made it public again in 1940 in his book *The War and the Jew*.[49] The purpose, of course, was to use this official Jewish army after the war as an argument for the foundation of Israel, for whoever has an army must necessarily have a state. The failure of this claim did not prevent the founders of the Jewish state from inscribing in their Declaration of Independence in 1948: "In the Second World War, the Jewish community of this country contributed its full share to the struggle of the freedom- and peace-loving nations against the forces of Nazi wickedness and, by the blood of its soldiers and its war effort, gained the right to be reckoned among the peoples who founded the United Nations."

In fact, the Zionists clashed with the British, not the Germans, in their efforts to increase the Jewish population in Palestine. Jewish immigration consistently surpassed British quotas, and accelerated with the rise of Nazism: from 82,000 colonists for the period 1924–1931 to 217,000 for the period 1932–1938. In 1939, when the Germans invaded Poland, the population of Palestine was already one-third Jewish. The British government then issued a White Paper limiting Jewish

---

[48] David Irving, *Churchill's War*, vol. 2: *Triumph in Adversity*, Focal Point Publications, 2001, pp. 76–77.
[49] Vladimir Jabotinsky, *The War and the Jew*, Dial Press, 1942 (archive.org).

immigration to 75,000 for the next five years. This provoked not only a strong protest from Ben-Gurion's Jewish Agency, but also the mobilization of military groups (Haganah, and its offshoot the Irgun) against the British authorities in Palestine.[50]

An example: In November 1940, the British prevented three vessels chartered by the Central Bureau for Jewish Emigration (under the supervision of Adolf Eichmann), carrying 3,600 Jews from Nazi-occupied areas, from landing at the port of Haifa. On November 25, while the British were transferring these illegal immigrants to their ship, the Patria, with the intention of provisionally taking them to Mauritius, the Haganah sank the ship, drowning 267 of the 1,800 Jewish passengers already on board. The Haganah claimed that the passengers themselves had scuttled their ship, preferring death to the prospect of not being able to debark in the promised land. Then, forced to admit responsibility, the Hagana pleaded a mistake: the intention supposedly was simply to damage the ship and prevent the departure of the refugees.

English opposition prevented Hitler from considering the transfer of all Jews from Europe to Palestine, especially since he had always hoped for an alliance with England against the Soviet Union: "In Europe there are only two possible allies for Germany, England and Italy, for the whole of the future," he wrote in 1923 in *Mein Kampf*. Moreover, Hitler did not want to alienate the Arab States, which were hostile to the Judaization of Palestine. On the other hand, the British and American Zionists hampered President Roosevelt's efforts to find solutions to the Jewish refugee crisis by convening the Evian Conference in July 1938 (*International Conference on Political and Economic Problems Caused by the Expulsion of Jews from the Reich*). Weizmann had declared at the Zionist Congress in London in 1937: "The hopes of Europe's six million Jews are centered on emigration." But, considering emigration only to Palestine, he added: "From the depths of the tragedy I want to save two million young people. [...] The old will pass. [...] Only the branch of the young shall

---

[50] Alan Hart, *Zionism*, vol. 1, *op. cit.*, pp. 115–116, 155–159.

survive…"[51] Ben-Gurion protested against the plan to open all borders to the persecuted Jews on the pretext that "pity will take over and the energy of the people will be channeled to save Jews from various countries. Zionism will be removed from the agenda not only in public opinion in Great Britain and the United States, but elsewhere in Jewish public opinion. If we allow the separation of the refugee problem from the problem of Palestine, we will endanger the existence of Zionism."[52] The failure of the Evian Conference, by preventing the escape of German Jews, made war inevitable: the hundred deaths of "The Night of Broken Glass" (November 9–10, 1938), a pogrom triggered by the assassination of a German diplomat in Paris by a young Polish Jew, provided Roosevelt a pretext to formally impose a complete economic embargo on Germany, recall his ambassador from Berlin, and announce the construction of ten thousand planes. When war broke out, there remained in Germany about 275,000 Jews who, for want of a visa, were unable to emigrate.

In May 1940, Heinrich Himmler drafted a project for Hitler: "A great emigration of all the Jews to a colony in Africa or elsewhere." He affirmed his "inner conviction" that it was necessary "to reject as contrary to the Germanic spirit and as impossible the Bolshevik method of physical extermination of a people" (a method demonstrated by the Ukrainian genocide of 1932–33, which left more than seven million dead). According to the French historian Florent Brayard, this is "a particularly important document to gauge the Nazi projects," which proves that there was at that time "no determined genocidal perspective." After the armistice with France, the territorial solution envisaged was Madagascar—an underpopulated and almost unexploited French colony. The Madagascar Plan envisioned deporting one million European Jews every year over four years. The plan was postponed until after the hoped-for victory against England, since its realization required mastery

---

[51] Rabbi Moshe Shonfeld, *Holocaust Victims Accuse: Documents and Testimony of Jewish War Criminals*, Bnei Yeshivos, 1977 (netureikartaru.com/Holocaust_Victims_Accuse.pdf), p. 25.
[52] Alan Hart, *Zionism*, vol. 1, *op. cit.*, p. 164.

of the seas. After the opening of the Eastern Front in 1941, it gave way to the plan of mass deportation to the concentration camps of Poland.

Hitler's Prophecy

In the absence of a written document, historians are still debating the date when the expression "final solution," borrowed from German Zionists who meant mass emigration to Palestine, would have become a Nazi code word for "extermination." Brayard hypothesizes that between 1941 and 1942, "The final solution of the Jewish question," the systematic murder of all European Jews, was conceived and implemented in absolute secrecy, or at least the greatest possible. But he notes that in Joseph Goebbels' diary, until October 1943 Hitler's close friend was persuaded that the fate of the deported Jews, once the war was over, would be expulsion to the east of Germany and its annexed territories.[53]

Given that in January 1942 the project of exterminating the Jews, through forced labor, sterilization and/or outright elimination, was adopted by Hitler and some of his entourage, one of the key questions historians must elucidate is that of the ideological gestation of this project. In an earlier work on the *"Final Solution of the Jewish Question"* Florent Brayard rightly emphasizes a famous prophecy announced by Hitler from the Reichstag tribune on January 30, 1939. After recalling that he had often been a prophet, as when he predicted his own rise to power, Hitler added: "I want to be a prophet again: If international Jewish finance inside and outside Europe were to once again cast peoples into World War, the result would not be the Bolshevization of the world, and thus the victory of Judaism, but the annihilation of the Jewish race in Europe." This "prophetic warning to Jewry!" as the headline of *Völkische Beobachter* put it the following day, was widely distributed and discussed, and extracts were inserted in a revised version of the propaganda film *The Wandering Jew*. This "prophecy" was a warning to England and France, who nevertheless entered the

---

[53] Florent Brayard, *Auschwitz. Enquête sur un complot nazi*, Seuil, 2012, pp. 34, 254–256.

war on September 3, 1939. Hitler renewed his threat on January 30, 1941, mainly for the United States. The *New York Times*, which the Nazis held as the leader of the "Jewish press," responded to Hitler's speech with an article that was tantamount to challenging him to act on his word: "There is not a single precedent to prove he will either keep a promise or fulfill a threat. If there is any guarantee in his record, in fact, it is that the one thing he will not do is the thing he says he will do."[54]

The United States entered the war in December under the pretext of the Japanese attack on Pearl Harbor. It was on December 12, 1941, that Hitler made the following remarks during a long speech, which we know from the notes taken by Goebbels and transcribed in his diary: "As far as the Jewish question is concerned, the Führer is determined to make a blank slate. He prophesized to the Jews that they would suffer destruction if they provoked another world war. It was not just empty words. World war is here, so the destruction of the Jews must be the necessary consequence." Historians like Christopher Browning believe that if one were to specify the moment when Hitler and his entourage rallied to the idea of exterminating all the Jews of Europe, it was just after the US entry into the war. Hitler's prophecy was the key to this development, not only among the elite of the Reich but also in German public opinion. For this prophecy, recalled Brayard, "was an object of recurring attention in Nazi propaganda, which, at certain key moments, never ceased to repeat it." Beginning in 1942, many Nazi dignitaries referred to it, in private or in public, to call for the destruction of European Jewry. Nazi Germany was, as it were, contaminated by that prophetic spirit that, already in the biblical tradition, nourished genocidal projects. "By launching his prophecy, Hitler had thus constituted a singular and constraining discursive space. True, this prophecy could be mobilized for propaganda purposes, but at the time of its realization, its internal logic determined the forms that this use might take. Moreover, in choosing to reiterate it, Hitler had put at stake his

---

[54] Jeffrey Herf, *The Jewish Enemy – Nazi Propaganda During World War II and the Holocaust*, Harvard University Press, 2008.

very status as a prophet, the oracular power of his word, the specific nature of his power: It was not possible, with the world war having come, that the prophecy should not come true. [. . .] Indeed, this constraint was sufficient to initiate a phase of radicalization of the anti-Jewish policy."[55] What this analysis conceals is the cynical role of the Allies and their press, who pretended not to take seriously this prophecy of the Holocaust, while at the same time taunting Hitler with it—taunts that were clearly driven by the Jewish elite, and that in a sense caught Hitler in the trap of his own prophecy.

"Judea Declares War on Germany"

History, as written by the victors, is merely the continuation of war propaganda. Writing history is "the last battle," to quote the title of the book by David Irving on the Nuremberg trials.[56] Ironically, the statutes of this International Military Tribunal, which included a prohibition against the defense evoking *Tu Quoque* ("You also")—a principle of law allowing the accused to return the accusation to the accuser (in this case, war crimes, crimes against peace and against humanity)—are dated August 8, 1945, precisely between the atomic bombings of Hiroshima and Nagasaki. This was already making a mockery of justice. On top of that, it is a well-established fact that the confessions of several convicted Nazi officers were obtained under torture. This is the case for Rudolf Höss, commander of Auschwitz from 1940 to 1943. According to the British sergeant Bernard Clarke, who captured him, "It took three days [of beating and sleep deprivation] to get a coherent statement out of him."[57] His deposition, which refers to three million deaths at Auschwitz under his responsibility, is today recognized as grossly exaggerated. There are many other proven cases of confessions extracted under torture and blackmail by the prosecution in Nuremberg: Maurice Bardèche, a survivor of the Nazi camps,

---

[55] Florent Brayard, *La « Solution Finale de la Question Juive ». La technique, le temps et les catégories de la décision*, Fayard, 2004, pp. 380–381, 396–399, and 16–21.
[56] David Irving, *Nuremberg: The Last Battle*, Focal Point, 1996.
[57] Quoted in Rupert Butler, *Legions of Death*, Hamlyn Publishing, 1983, pp. 236–238.

assembled a number of them in 1950 in *Nuremberg II or Les Faux-Monnayeurs*.[58] Like the Paris Conference in 1919, the Nuremberg trials were influenced by a staff composed of a majority of Jews (more than two thirds according to Hungarian journalist Louis Marchalko). Benton Bradberry writes in *The Myth of German Villainy* that the trials were "permeated throughout with an atmosphere of Jewish vengeance seeking," and remarks that the tens of Nazi leaders who were condemned to death were hanged on Purim day (October 16, 1946), the Jewish holiday celebrating the hanging of the ten sons of Haman.[59] For the new Levitic elite, writing history always means writing the history of Israel. And writing the history of Israel always means reproducing biblical history.

Authentic historical work consists of revising official history. This presupposes the re-assessment, in the chain of causes and effects, of the story from the side of the vanquished. The limited scope of this chapter permits us to recall only a few factors that contributed to launching the Germans—and not just some high Nazi officials—into a state of murderous rage against Jews. We have already mentioned the Germans' perception of the role of the Jews in the Bolshevik Revolution at the gates of Germany on the one hand, and in Germany's defeat and economic collapse after the First World War on the other. These factors partly explain the rise of Hitler, whose Judeophobia was clearly displayed in *Mein Kampf*. At the outbreak of war with England in 1939, the Nazis tried to convince the German people that the war had been willed and orchestrated by the Jews. A few hours before his suicide, Hitler wrote again: "It is untrue that I or anyone else in Germany wanted war in 1939. It was wanted and provoked solely by international statesmen either of Jewish origin or working for Jewish interests."[60]

Some evidence supports this claim. Indeed, on March 24, 1933, less than two months after the appointment of Hitler as Chancellor of the Reich, the British *Daily Express* published a

[58] Maurice Bardèche, *Nuremberg*, Kontre Kulture, 2016, p. 271–360.
[59] Benton Bradberry, *The Myth of German Villainy*, Authorhouse, 2012, p. 6.
[60] Adolf Hitler, in his political testament written April 29, 1945, the day before his suicide, on www.historylearningsite.co.uk.

front page article entitled "Judea Declares War on Germany. Jews of All the World Unite in Action." The article proclaimed: "The Israeli people around the world declare economic and financial war against Germany. Fourteen million Jews dispersed throughout the world have banded together as one man to declare war on the German persecutors of their co-religionists."

This campaign was supported by the majority of Jewish representative bodies and coordinated by influential Zionist lawyer Samuel Untermeyer. In a radio speech reproduced by the *New York Times* on August 7, 1933, Untermeyer called for "a holy war" against "medieval Hitlerland," "a war that must be waged unremittingly," by "the economic boycott against all German goods, shipping and services. [...] we will undermine the Hitler regime and bring the German people to their senses by destroying their export trade on which their very existence depends." Untermeyer called "traitor to their race" all Jews who refused to join this boycott. He had no doubt that Jews, who had overcome persecution "from time immemorial," would once again prevail. "For the Jews are the aristocrats of the world."[61] Joining with Samuel Untermeyer in calling for an economic war against Germany, Bernard Baruch promoted preparations for actual war, as he proudly asserted in his autobiography: "I emphasised that the defeat of Germany and Japan and their elimination from world trade would give Britain a tremendous opportunity to swell her foreign commerce in both volume and profit."[62]

Five days after the *Daily Express* article, Hitler publicly announced a counter-boycott of Jewish businesses in Germany as "merely a defensive measure exclusively directed toward Jewry in Germany," and warned that international Jewry's war on Germany would negatively affect German Jews. Goebbels broadcast a speech two days later explicitly warning that the attacks of international Jewry against Germany would rebound against German Jews.[63] Jeffrey Herf, who cites these two

---

[61] These articles are easily found on the Internet.
[62] Bernard Baruch, *Baruch: The Public Years*, Holt, Rinehart and Winston, 1960, p. 347.
[63] Jeffrey Herf, *The Jewish Enemy, op. cit.*

speeches, fails to point out that they came in response to a declaration of war, accompanied by unfounded accusations, by American Jewish elites. This dishonest presentation is characteristic of mainstream historians of the Holocaust. Herf asserts that the Nazi leaders sincerely believed in the "Jewish conspiracy" they denounced, but fails to specify what their objective reasons for believing it were, so as to present their Judeophobia as a symptom of paranoia.

Behind the struggle against anti-Semitism was a more fundamental hostility against any form of nationalism, as plainly expressed by Solomon Freehof in *Race, Nation or Religion: Three Questions Jews Must Answer* (1935): "What stands in our way everywhere in the world is Modern Nationalism. That is our chief enemy. We are on the side of Liberalism against Nationalism. That is our only safety." The daily Chicago newspaper *The Sentinel,* reporting a finding of the Central Conference of American Rabbis on September 24, 1936, wrote: "Nationalism is a danger for the Jewish people. Today, as in all epochs of history, it is proved that Jews cannot live in powerful states where a high national culture has developed."[64]

In September 1939, as Great Britain declared war on Germany, the World Jewish Congress declared that international Jewry had already waged an economic war and now stood by Great Britain against Germany. The mobilization of American Jews against Germany intensified. In early 1941 appeared the 96–page booklet by Jewish American businessman Theodore Kaufman, *Germany Must Perish.* Suggesting as "a final solution" that "Germany be policed forever by an international armed force," the author concludes: "There is, in fine, no other solution except one: That Germany must perish forever from this earth." He proposes that "the extinction of the German nation and the total eradication from the earth, of all her people" be achieved by sterilizing all German males under sixty, and females under forty-five, which could be done in less than a month by about twenty thousand surgeons. "Accordingly in the

---

[64] Quoted in Robert Edward Edmondson, *The Jewish System Indicted by the Documentary Record,* 1937 (archive.org), p. 14.

span of two generations, […] the elimination of Germanism and its carriers, will have been an accomplished fact."[65]

Interviewed by the *Canadian Jewish Chronicle*, Kaufman speaks of the Jews' "mission" to guide humankind toward "perpetual peace"; thanks to them, "slowly but surely the world will develop into a paradise"; but for the moment, "let us sterilize all Germans and wars of world domination will come to an end!"[66] German Minister of Propaganda Joseph Goebbels had a translation of Kaufman's book massively printed and read on the radio, as a way to show the German people what awaited them if they showed signs of weakness. By further asserting that German Jews were of his opinion, Kaufman provided the Nazis with a pretext for stigmatizing Jews by the Yellow Star (September 1941) and their deportation as enemies of the nation.[67]

Jeffrey Herf claims that Kaufman's book had no impact except in Nazi propaganda. That is not the case. It was reviewed positively in the *New York Times* and the *Washington Post*. In 1944, it would be commented upon by Louis Nizer in his very influential book *What to Do with Germany?* (highly praised by Harry Truman). Nizer rejected Kaufman's solution as exaggerated, but recommended the death penalty for 150,000 Germans, and "labor battalions" for hundreds of thousands more.[68] The same year, celebrated Hollywood screenwriter Ben Hecht wrote in his *Guide for the Bedeviled*: "A cancer flourishes in the body of the world and in its mind and soul, and […] this cancerous thing is Germany, Germanism, and Germans."[69]

Louis Marschalko cites a few more well-published Jewish authors advocating a "final solution" for the "German question": Leon Dodd, who in *How Many World Wars* (New York, 1942), proclaims that no Germany and no German race

---

[65] Theodore Kaufman, *Germany Must Perish*, Argyle Press, 1941 (archive.org), p. 30.

[66] "'Hitler Will Be Nothing But a Rosebud,' Says the Author of 'Germany Must Perish'," *The Canadian Jewish Chronicle*, September 26, 1941, quoted in Brandon Martinez, *Grand Deceptions: Zionist Intrigue in the 20th and 21st Centuries*, Progressive Press, 2014, kindle, k. 226.

[67] Florent Brayard, *Auschwitz, op. cit.*, pp. 42–43.

[68] Louis Nizer, *What to do with Germany?*, Brentano's, 1944 (archive.org), pp. 98–107.

[69] Ben Hecht, *A Guide for the Bedeviled*, Charles Scribner's Sons, 1944, p. 120.

must be left after the war; Charles Heartman, who in *There Must Be No Germany After This War* (New York, 1942), also demands the physical extermination of the German people; Einzig Palil, who in *Can We Win the Peace?* (London, 1942), demanded the dismembering of Germany and the total demolition of German industry; Ivor Duncan, who in the March, 1942, issue of *Zentral Europa Observer*, demanded the sterilization of forty million Germans, estimating the total cost at five million pounds sterling.[70]

While in 1942 and 1943 the chances of a German victory diminished, various events fed the Nazi propaganda mill and convinced the Germans that surrender was not an option. In the spring of 1943 German soldiers discovered the bodies of more than 4,500 Polish officers shot in the head by the Soviet NKVD in the spring of 1940 in the forest of Katyn (in Poland near the Belarusian border). Later other mass graves were discovered, raising the number of members of the Polish elite so executed by the Soviets in 1940 to more than 25,000. The Nazis denounced this "Judeo-Bolshevik" massacre, but the Soviets denied their responsibility and claimed that the massacre was perpetrated by the Nazis during their advance in 1941. The Germans then called on an international commission and the Red Cross, both of which confirmed Soviet guilt. But these conclusions were ignored by the Allies and the Western press. Jewish neurologist Richard Brickner exploited the lie of German guilt in a book published in 1943 under the title *Is Germany Incurable?* He intended to show that "the national group we call Germany behaves and has long behaved startlingly like an individual involved in a dangerous mental trend," which he characterized as "the real murder-psychosis," involving megalomania and "the paranoid's conviction of his own a priori world-shaking importance, of the supreme value and significance of his every act and thought."[71] Despite evidence against the Soviets, the Nuremberg Tribunal declared the Nazis guilty of the Katyn massacre, just as it ignored Soviet

---

[70] Louis Marschalko, *The World Conquerors, op. cit.*, p. 105.
[71] Richard Brickner, *Is Germany Incurable?*, J. B. Lippincott Co., 1943, pp. 30, 56, 163.

responsibility for the deaths of more than 440,000 Poles (according to recent estimates) between September 1939 and June 1941, murdered with the aim of eliminating "social classes that were hostile to communism."

Shortly after the Normandy landings, Roosevelt and Churchill discussed the future of Germany at the Second Quebec Conference of September 11, 1944, and signed a project developed under the leadership of Jewish-Americans Henry Morgenthau Jr., the Secretary of the Treasury, and his assistant Harry Dexter White. This "Morgenthau Plan," entitled *Suggested Post-Surrender Program for Germany, or Program to Prevent Germany from Starting a World War III*, "is looking forward to converting Germany into a country primarily agricultural and pastoral in its character," by dismantling and transporting to Allied nations "all industrial plants and equipment not destroyed by military action," while calling for "forced German labor outside Germany." The revelation of this insane plan by the *Wall Street Journal* (September 23, 1944) helped push the Nazis into a desperate fight-to-the-death mentality, and suggested to Henry Stimson, US Secretary of War, this commentary: "It is Semitism gone wild for vengeance and, if it is ultimately carried out (I can't believe that it will be), it as sure as fate will lay the seeds for another war in the next generation."[72] The plan was abandoned in 1946 because of the Soviet threat. Germany needed to become a bulwark against communism, and would therefore be entitled to the Marshall Plan. But until then, the Germans experienced a "peace" more infernal than all wars: destruction and plunder, organized famine, mass rapes, and the deportation of millions of slaves to the Soviet Union, most of whom would never return. According to James Bacque, more than nine million Germans died as a result of Allied starvation and expulsion policies in the first five years after the war.[73] According to Jewish author John Sack, Jews played a major part

---

[72] Quoted in David Irving, *Nuremberg: The Last Battle, op. cit.*, p. 20.
[73] James Bacque, *Crimes and Mercies: The Fate of German Civilians Under Allied Occupation, 1944–1950*, Little, Brown & Company, 1997 (archive.org). Read also the report by Ralph Franklin Keeling, *Gruesome Harvest: The Costly Attempt to Exterminate the People of Germany*, Institute of American Economics, 1947.

in the massive cruelty perpetrated on the 200,000 German
civilians parked in over a thousand concentration camps in
Poland, "many of them starved, beaten and tortured." On the
basis of many documented cases, he claims that "more than
60,000 died at the hands of a largely Jewish-run security
organization," and lays the blame primarily on Zionist Jews.[74]

It is well known that Roosevelt's conduct of the war,
beginning with his decision to involve the United States, was
influenced by his being greatly weakened physically and largely
captive to his advisers. He was much influenced by his wife
Eleanor Roosevelt, who had communist sympathies and a very
favorable opinion of Stalin.[75] At the Yalta Conference he was
constantly assisted by a State Department official by the name of
Alger Hiss, a former protégé of Felix Frankfurter, whom he
would later appoint as the first Secretary-General of the United
Nations. In 1948, thanks to the efforts of Richard Nixon (then a
member of the House Un-American Activities Committee), Hiss
was convicted of espionage for the Soviets. The Soviet archives
made public in the 1990s confirmed his guilt.

Among the gray eminences behind Roosevelt were many
Jewish personalities. In addition to Henry Morgenthau Jr. at the
Treasury, we must mention the banker Bernard Baruch, already
very influential under Wilson, and Felix Frankfurter, successor
of Louis Brandeis to the Supreme Court. According to Curtis
Dall, son-in-law of Roosevelt: "Mr. Baruch, as top man, raised
most of the campaign and expense money; Mr. Frankfurter
approved, directly or obliquely, most of the important
governmental appointments. They were, without doubt, the
'Gold Dust Twins.'"[76]

Curtis Dall has also revealed a secret diplomatic channel
demonstrating that the White House harbored a strong desire to
prolong the war: on the one hand to deprive Germany of any

---

[74] John Sack, *An Eye for an Eye: The Untold Story of Jewish Revenge Against Germans in 1945*, Basic Books, 1993.

[75] Beata de Robien, "Eleanor Roosevelt, une femme influente sous influence," *La Nouvelle Revue d'Histoire*, n⁰ 69, November-December 2013, pp. 21–24.

[76] Curtis Dall, *FDR: My Exploited Father-in-Law*, Christian Crusade Publications, 1968, p. 69.

possibility of escaping her programmed destruction; and on the other, to give the USSR time to invade Central Europe. Soon after Roosevelt and Churchill agreed in Casablanca in January 1943 to demand "unconditional surrender" from Germany, George Earle, the American ambassador to Bulgaria who served as special emissary to the Balkans from his base in Istanbul in neutral Turkey, was contacted by Admiral Wilhelm Canaris, head of the German intelligence service. Canaris explained that if President Roosevelt made it clear that he would accept an "honorable surrender," the German generals, many of whom were hostile to Hitler's suicidal policy, would deliver Hitler to international justice and put the German army at the disposal of US forces to ally against the USSR, the true enemy of Western civilization, and protect Central Europe from Soviet assault. Earle then met the German ambassador Fritz von Papen, a fervent Catholic and anti-Hitlerian, then Baron Kurt von Lersner, another German dignitary. Convinced of both the sincerity of the Germans and of Stalin's determination to conquer Europe, Earle thrice sent an urgent message to Roosevelt by diplomatic and military channels inviting him to seize this unexpected opportunity. The only response Earle finally received from Roosevelt was an order to defer to the commander-in-chief in Europe, General Eisenhower. This killed the initiative of the German anti-Nazi dignitaries, who were executed by Hitler after their vain attempts to assassinate him on July 20, 1944.[77]

Eisenhower, as it turned out, was instructed to leave Central Europe—where most of the population only wanted to surrender to American troops—undefended against Stalin's invasion. He could have used General Alexander's allied forces in Italy to occupy Eastern Europe and the Balkans before they passed from Hitler's yoke to that of the Red Army. The allied armies would then have freed Berlin entirely and would have reached Vienna, Budapest, and Prague, while the Soviet state would have been kept within the natural frontiers of Russia. Instead, Italian troops were used for a landing on the French

---

[77] Curtis Dall, *FDR: My Exploited Father-in-Law, op. cit.,* pp. 146–157.

Mediterranean coast, complementary to the main landing in Normandy, which brought no decisive military advantage. General Mark Clark, who in 1943 commanded the American forces in Italy, saw in this strategy "one of the outstanding political mistakes of the war."[78] Moreover, Eisenhower restrained General Patton's enthusiasm, forcing him to stop a hundred kilometers before Berlin, and on March 28, 1945, he sent a "personal message for Marshal Stalin" to inform him of it. Patton nevertheless took Vienna against Eisenhower's orders.

Thus the Second World War was completed with the determined aim of laying the foundations of a new conflict in Europe. The Atlantic Charter of August 14, 1941, had declared that the United States and Great Britain "wish to see sovereign rights and self government restored to those who have been forcibly deprived of them," and "hope to see established a peace which will afford to all nations the means of dwelling in safety within their own boundaries." This referred first of all to Poland, whose joint invasion by the Nazis and the Soviets had justified the Allies' entry into the war. Yet the result of the Second World War was not to liberate Poland and the other Eastern European peoples, but to hand them over to the Soviet dictatorship. This situation did not result from any failure by the United States, but on the contrary from the secret will of the powers that controlled the White House.

Many other proofs exist of the secret complicity of the United States in the capture of Central Europe by the Soviets. During 1942, large quantities of uranium, cadmium, and heavy water thorium, aluminum tubes, and copper wiring (all materials required for the creation of a nuclear reactor) were sent to the Soviet government from an air base in Great Falls, Montana, established specifically for this purpose. This incredible high-tech military smuggling, organized from the White House, is known through the publication of notes taken by Captain George Racey Jordan, who participated in the delivery of these cargoes, which included many other kinds of industrial equipment (*From Major Jordan's Diaries*, 1952). This secret

---

[78] Douglas Reed, *The Controversy of Zion* (1956), Dolphin Press, 1978, p. 370.

assistance to the Soviets was supervised by Harry Hopkins, who had been placed in the White House by Bernard Baruch. Also delivered to Moscow were duplicates of United States Treasury plates, together with tons of paper and gallons of the appropriate ink for printing unlimited quantities of dollar bills.[79] The transfers were supervised by Harry Dexter White, a protégé of Henry Morgenthau Jr. and a liaison officer between the Treasury and the State Department, who was also the principal US official at the Bretton Woods conference in 1944 and closely associated with the founding of the International Monetary Fund. Born Weit Magilewski of Lithuanian Jewish parents, White was charged with espionage on behalf of the Soviets, alongside Alger Hiss, following the denunciation of another repentant spy, Whittaker Chambers.

In 1941 Hitler had made the bold bet that England would at least accept a truce to allow Germany to defeat the Soviet Union. He had reason to believe it. Since 1917 Churchill had not ceased to present Bolshevism as the worst scourge of mankind. "Bolshevism is not a policy; it is a disease," he said in the House of Commons on May 29, 1919, adding that "it is not a creed; it is a pestilence." He prescribed gas as "the right medicine for the Bolshevist." Later in the same year, on November 6, he compared the Germans sending Lenin back to Russia as sending "a phial containing a culture of typhoid or cholera to be poured into the water supply of a great city." And he declared: "Of all the tyrannies in history, the Bolshevist tyranny is the worst, the most destructive, and the most degrading. It is sheer humbug to pretend that it is not far worse than German militarism." But twenty years later, on September 3, 1939, the same Churchill declared in the House of Commons: "We are fighting to save the whole world from the pestilence of Nazi tyranny and in defense of all that is most sacred to man." And, whereas he had, in 1919, recommended to Lloyd George to "Feed Germany; fight Bolshevism; make Germany fight Bolshevism," in 1939 he denounced Chamberlain's refusal to initiate a *rapprochement* with

---

[79] Curtis Dall, *FDR: My Exploited Father-in-Law, op. cit.*, p. 112; Douglas Reed, *The Controversy of Zion, op. cit.*, pp. 362–366.

the Soviet Union.[80] Nevertheless, Hitler was betting on Churchill's self-interest when in May 1941 he parachuted his closest associate Rudolf Hess into Scotland with a mission to secretly inform the British government of his imminent offensive against the USSR and to propose a peace treaty. Hess was captured, Churchill refused to hear him, imprisoned him until the end of the war, then refused to release him as a prisoner of war and sentenced him in perpetuity for "conspiracy and crime against peace."[81]

The very first day of Hitler's Operation Barbarossa, June 22, 1941, Churchill spoke on the BBC to explain that Nazism was worse than communism: "The Nazi regime is indistinguishable from the worst features of Communism. It is devoid of all theme and principle except appetite and racial domination. It excels all forms of human wickedness in the efficiency of its cruelty and ferocious aggression." The British government, Churchill went on to say, has "but one aim and one single, irrevocable purpose. We are resolved to destroy Hitler and every vestige of the Nazi regime." And so, "any man or state who fights on against Nazidom will have our aid. That is our policy and that is our declaration. It follows, therefore, that we shall give whatever help we can to Russia and the Russian people." Suddenly, Churchill stopped speaking of the Soviet Union, but of the "Russian people": "The cause of any Russian fighting for his hearth and home is the cause of free men and free peoples in every quarter of the globe. Let us learn the lessons already taught by such cruel experience. Let us redouble our exertions, and strike with united strength while life and power remain."[82]

In a text dictated on February 4, 1945, and included in his *Political Testament,* Hitler analyzed Churchill's refusal. According to him, Churchill should have understood England's need to "come to terms with me," in order to preserve the "balance of power" and maintain Europe's independence from the "two giants, the United States and Russia"; "When I attacked

---

[80] Antoine Capet, "'The Creeds of the Devil': Churchill between the Two Totalitarianisms, 1917–1945," on www.winstonchurchill.org.

[81] David Irving, *Hess: The Missing Years, 1941–45,* Macmillan, 1987.

[82] "Alliance with Russia," on www.winstonchurchill.org.

eastwards and lanced the communist abscess, I hoped thereby to rekindle a spark of common sense in the minds of the Western Powers. I gave them the chance, without lifting a finger, of making a contribution to an act of catharsis, in which they could have safely left the task of disinfecting the West in our hands alone. [...] I had underestimated the power of Jewish domination over Churchill's England."[83] What Hitler could not understand was that, behind the scenes of Anglo-American power, it had been decided not only that Nazi Germany was a worse enemy than the USSR, but that the USSR was not an enemy to be defeated at all. In fact, the leadership had decided to deliver half of Europe to Stalin.

"An old Zionist like [Churchill]"

Another thing that Hitler could not know is how deeply Churchill was committed to helping Weizmann make the war the springboard for the foundation of Israel. It was only after his retirement that Churchill confessed. He declared publicly, on the fourth anniversary of the independence of Israel, that he had been "a Zionist from the days of the Balfour Declaration," and he wrote to US President Eisenhower in 1956: "I am, of course, a Zionist, and have been ever since the Balfour Declaration."[84]

Churchill's Zionism helps explain how the Balfour Declaration became such a cornerstone of British policy. Churchill had always claimed that the intention of the Balfour Declaration was that Palestine might in the course of time become "an overwhelmingly Jewish State." In his 1920 article "Zionism versus Bolshevism" he had already affirmed the British Government's responsibility "of securing for the Jewish race all over the world a home and a centre of national life. [...] if, as may well happen, there should be created in our own lifetime by the banks of the Jordan a Jewish State under the protection of the British Crown, which might comprise three or four millions of Jews, an event would have occurred in the

[83] *Political Testament of Adolf Hitler*, on archive.org.
[84] Unless mentioned otherwise, this section is based on Martin Gilbert, *Churchill and the Jews: A Lifelong Friendship*, Henry Holt & Company, 2007, kindle ed.

history of the world which would, from every point of view, be beneficial, and would be especially in harmony with the truest interests of the British Empire."

In 1922, as Under-Secretary of State for the Colonies, Churchill issued a White Paper crafted to reassure the Arabs, whose apprehensions, it said, "are partly based upon exaggerated interpretations of the meaning of the [Balfour] Declaration." By "a Jewish National Home in Palestine," the Declaration "does not mean a Jewish government to dominate Arabs. [...] We cannot tolerate the expropriation of one set of people by another." Yet that White Paper imposed no limitation to Jewish immigration in Palestine, nor to the purchase of lands by Jews, which were the great concerns of the Arabs. It simply said, in terms alarmingly vague: "For the fulfillment of this policy it is necessary that the Jewish community in Palestine should be able to increase its numbers by immigration. This immigration cannot be so great in volume as to exceed whatever may be the economic capacity of the country at the time to absorb new arrivals. [...] Hitherto the immigration has fulfilled these conditions." Moreover, if Churchill's White Paper said that Jews will not rule over Arabs, it could be understood to mean that they will rule in a land free of Arabs. It was, therefore, carte blanche for the Zionist plan.

In 1939, a new Labour majority undermined Churchill's influence in Parliament. A new White Paper was voted for by a large majority, which limited Jewish immigration to 75,000 for the next five years, with the stated purpose of preserving an Arab majority in Palestine. This was a serious reversal of policy regarding Zionism: The 1939 White Paper was unequivocally against letting Palestine become a Jewish State. This provoked not only a strong protest from Ben-Gurion's Jewish Agency, but also the mobilization of military groups (Haganah, and its offshoot the Irgun) against the British authorities in Palestine.[85]

Churchill fought relentlessly against this 1939 White Paper, which he regarded as a betrayal of Great Britain's commitment to the Balfour Declaration. His thoughts, he would say in 1942,

---

[85] Alan Hart, *Zionism*, vol. 1, *op. cit.*, pp. 115–116, 155–159.

were "99 per cent identical" with Weizmann's. He had often consulted him in private meetings since 1919. In May 1939, the new White Paper was debated in the House of Commons. Churchill invited Weizmann to his London apartment to go over his speech and, as Weizmann recalled in his memoirs, "he asked me if I had any changes to suggest." In 1951, Churchill would refer to himself, in a letter to Weizmann, as "an old Zionist like me."

In the words of Martin Gilbert, author of *Churchill and the Jews: A Lifelong Friendship* (who also documents Churchill's intimate family ties with the Rothschilds and other Jewish bankers), Churchill "refused to allow the 1939 White Paper, despite its passage into law by an overwhelming majority of Members of Parliament, to come into effect. This was certainly unconstitutional." In December 1939, as Weizmann was planning a trip to the USA, the Foreign Office sent a telegram to the British Ambassador in the USA reiterating the guidelines of the new White Paper. Churchill protested to his War Cabinet colleagues that this would undermine Weizmann's endeavor "to bring United States opinion as far as he possibly can on to our side." In a memorandum that he wrote for the War Cabinet on Christmas Day 1939, he expressed his opposition to the restrictions on Jewish immigration to Palestine by reminding his Cabinet colleagues that: "it was not for light or sentimental reasons that Lord Balfour and the Government of 1917 made the promises to the Zionists which have been the cause of so much subsequent discussion. The influence of American Jewry was rated then as a factor of the highest importance, and we did not feel ourselves in such a strong position as to be able to treat it with indifference. [...] when the future is full of measureless uncertainties, I should have thought it was more necessary, even than in November 1917, to conciliate American Jewry and enlist their aid in combating isolationist and indeed anti-British tendencies in the United States." In another memorandum dated 19 May 1941, Churchill expressed his hope for the establishment after the war of a "Jewish State of Western Palestine" with the fullest rights for immigration and development, and with provision "for expansion in the desert regions to the southwards which they would gradually reclaim."[86]

In 1945, Churchill was defeated by a Labour majority. The new Prime Minister, Clement Attlee, appointed Ernest Bevin, a man not well disposed toward Zionism, as Foreign Secretary. Churchill understood that the new British government would stick by the 1939 White Paper, and that the hopes of Zionism now rested on the USA. He then argued for the UK to give up on "a responsibility which we are failing to discharge and which in the process is covering us with blood and shame," and to return the Mandate to the United Nations. As soon as the British handed the Mandate back to the UN, the Zionists declared the founding of the State of Israel, which the US and the Soviet Union immediately recognized. Churchill urged the British Government to do the same. In 1955, he even supported a suggestion by James de Rothschild that Israel, the nation that had founded itself by ousting Great Britain from Palestine by terrorism, should now be admitted to the British Commonwealth: "It would be a wonderful thing," he said during a lunch at Buckingham Palace. "So many people want to leave us; it might be the turning of the tide."

Birth of the "Jewish State"

The fate of Palestine was not on the agenda of the Yalta Conference (February 1945); Franklin Roosevelt wanted to discuss it first with King Ibn Saud of Arabia. He did so immediately after the conference, from February 12 to 14, 1945, aboard the cruiser USS Quincy. Ibn Saud expressed his fears about the consequences of US support for the Zionists and Roosevelt gave him his word, confirmed by a letter dated April 5, that he "would take no action, in my capacity as Chief of the Executive Branch of this Government, which might prove hostile to the Arab people." In describing his meeting with Ibn Saud, Roosevelt told Congress: "On the problem of Arabia," he said, "I learned more about that whole problem—the Moslem

---

[86] Martin Gilbert, "Winston Churchill and the foundation of Israel," May 2, 2016, www.martingilbert.com/blog/winston-churchill-and-the-foundation-of-israel/

problem, the Jewish problem—by talking with Ibn Saud for five minutes than I could have learned in the exchange of two or three dozen letters."[87]

Roosevelt died on April 12. "If Roosevelt had not died, there might not have been a Jewish state," has commented Nahum Goldmann, one of Zionism's most influential representatives with Ben-Gurion and Weizmann. (He was president of the World Jewish Congress and the World Zionist Organization from 1956 to 1968.) "Our great luck was that Roosevelt was replaced by Harry Truman, who was a simple and upright man. He said, 'My friends are Jews; the Jews want the partition, so I am giving it to them.'"[88] David Niles, Roosevelt's assistant "for minorities" (i.e., for the Jews), expressed the same feeling to Stephen Isaacs: "Had Roosevelt lived, Israel would probably not have become a state."[89] Niles, one of the few FDR advisors retained by Truman, was the gray eminence of Zionism in the White House. It was he who, behind Truman's back but on his behalf, orchestrated the campaign of intimidation and corruption that obtained a two-thirds majority in favor of the 1947 Partition Plan at the General Assembly of the United Nations.[90]

In his *Memoirs* published in 1956, Truman commented—in eloquent but somewhat hypocritical terms—on the circumstances of the vote: "The facts were that not only were there pressure movements around the United Nations unlike anything that had been seen there before but that the White House, too, was subjected to a constant barrage. I do not think I ever had as much pressure and propaganda aimed at the White House as I had in this instance. The persistence of a few of the extreme Zionist leaders—actuated by political motives and engaging in political threats—disturbed and annoyed me. Some

---

[87] Martin Gilbert, *Churchill and the Jews, op. cit.*, k. 3705–53.

[88] Nahum Goldmann, *Le Paradoxe juif. Conversations en français avec Léon Abramowicz,* Stock, 1976 (archive.org), pp. 17–18.

[89] Stephen Isaacs, *Jews and American Politics,* Doubleday, 1974, p. 244.

[90] Alfred Lilienthal, *What Price Israel?* (1953), Infinity Publishing, 2003, p. 50.

were even suggesting that we pressure sovereign nations into favorable votes in the General Assembly."[91]

In December 1945, a few months after Roosevelt's death, Truman publicly expressed his aversion to the idea of a "Jewish state": "The Palestine Government [...] should be the Government of the people of Palestine, irrespective of race, creed or color."[92] However, on May 15, 1948, Truman recognized the State of Israel ten minutes after the announcement of its unilateral proclamation. This decision went against the recommendations of his secretary of state George Marshall, his defense secretary James Forrestal and all his advisers, as well as British Foreign Minister Ernest Benin. Moreover, it betrayed the spirit of the Quincy Pact. How was Truman "turned around"? Based on documents revealed by the Truman Library in 2003, an article in the *Jewish World Review* entitled "Truman did it to save his own skin" shows that his recognition of the Jewish state was strongly advised by his campaign director Clark Clifford, with the aim of securing the famous "Jewish vote" (a half-fiction cleverly maintained by the Zionist elites to increase their power) but also in exchange for campaign funding. Truman's patron Abraham Feinberg, president of the Americans for Haganah Incorporated, which raised money for the Jewish militia against the Arabs, made no secret of having funded the Truman campaign in recorded testimony for the Truman Library in 1973.[93]

On May 28, 1949, a year after his recognition of the Jewish state—and six days after the alleged suicide of US Secretary of Defense James Forrestal, who more than anyone else had tried to deter Truman from recognizing Israel—Truman expressed in a letter to the government of Ben-Gurion his "deep disappointment at the Israeli refusal to make any of the desired concessions on refugees and boundaries." He demanded Israel's

---

[91] Harry Truman, *Years of Trial and Hope*, vol. 2, Doubleday, 1956 (archive.org), p. 158.
[92] Alfred Lilienthal, *What Price Israel?, op. cit.*, pp. xix–xx.
[93] Sidney Zion, "Truman did it to save his own skin," *Jewish World Review*, July 21, 2003, quoted in Alfred Lilienthal, *What Price Israel?, op. cit.*, pp. xix–xx; Richard McKinzie, "Abraham Feinberg Oral History Interview," Truman Library, August 23, 1973, on www.trumanlibrary.org/oralhist/feinberg.htm.

withdrawal to the borders of the UN Partition Plan and, in a pathetic plea revealing his helplessness, warned that if Israel pursued this path, "the U.S. will regretfully be forced to the conclusion that a revision of its attitude toward Israel has become unavoidable." Ten days later Truman received an answer indicating that "The war has proved the indispensability to the survival of Israel of certain vital areas not comprised originally in the share of the Jewish state." As for the Palestinian refugees, they were "members of an aggressor group defeated in a war of its own making."[94]

Truman should have known as early as 1947 that Israel, founded as a "Jewish State" on the "Land of Israel" by its Declaration of Independence, would not be content with the borders granted by the UN Partition Resolution of November 29, 1947. Many of the "founding fathers" of Israel rejected the Partition in the name of the sacred principle of "The Sanctity of the Indivisibility of the Land," to quote from Menachem Begin: "The dismembering of our homeland was illegal. It will never be recognized. The signature of institutions and individuals on the dissection contract is totally invalid." Ben-Gurion signed the resolution in November, but only after having warned, in May, that "We want the Land of Israel in its entirety," and before declaring in December that the boundaries assigned to Israel by the resolution were "not final."[95]

Ben-Gurion's government later refrained from such a politically damaging public stance, but it surfaced again in the euphoria of the 1967 conquest. According to Yitzhak Tabenkin, a founding father of Zionism from the 1930s, "The goal of our entire project was then, and remains: a Greater Israel within its natural and ancient borders; from the Mediterranean to the desert and from Lebanon to the Dead Sea—as the reborn homeland of the entire Jewish people. This is the original Zionist ideal." It was advocated as public policy by dozens of prominent Israelis who wrote and signed the document "For a

---

[94] Alan Hart, *Zionism: The Real Enemy of the Jews*, vol. 2: *David Becomes Goliath*, Clarity Press, 2013, p. 92.
[95] Norman Finkelstein, *Knowing Too Much: Why the American Romance with Israel Is Coming to an End*, OR Books, 2012, p. 278.

Greater Israel" published in September 1967.[96] Israel has not yet, to this day, endowed itself with a constitution, which would oblige it to define its borders, that is to say, what it means by "the land of Israel."

By defining itself as a "Jewish state," Israel also included racial discrimination in its birth certificate. A constitutional law was passed in 1985 to prohibit political parties from opposing this principle.[97] Just five years after the end of the Second World War, Israel adopted the Law of Return that prevented the 1948 Palestinian refugees from returning to their villages. As Haim Cohen, former judge of the Supreme Court of Israel, remarked: "The bitter irony of fate decreed that the same biological and racist argument extended by the Nazis, and which inspired the inflammatory laws of Nuremberg, serve as the basis for the official definition of Jewishness in the bosom of the state of Israel."[98]

Even before its birth, it was clear that Israel would carry in its genes, not only colonialist expansion and racial discrimination, but also terrorism, trademarked by the "false flag" strategy. The Irgun, a right-wing militia founded in 1931 as an offshoot of the Haganah, on the ideological basis of Jabotinsky's Revisionist Zionism, whose leaders included future prime minister Menachem Begin, carried out dozens of bombings and other attacks against Palestinian and British targets between 1937 and 1948 (when it was integrated into the newly created Israeli army). Its most high-profile attack was the bombing of the King David Hotel in Jerusalem on July 22, 1946. The hotel was the British administrative and military headquarters. Six Irgun terrorists dressed as Arabs entered the building and deposited around the central pillar 225 kilograms of TNT hidden in milk cans, while other militiamen were spreading explosives along the access roads to the hotel to prevent the

---

[96] Noam Chomsky, *The Fateful Triangle: The United States, Israel and the Palestinians*, South End Press, 1983, p. 161; Idith Zertal, *Israel's Holocaust and the Politics of Nationhood*, Cambridge University Press, 2005, pp. 186–190.

[97] Israel Shahak, *Jewish History, Jewish Religion, op. cit.*, p. 22.

[98] Quoted in Joseph Badi, *Fundamental Laws of the State of Israel*, Twayne Publishers, 1960, p. 156.

arrival of rescuers. The stratagem failed when a British officer grew suspicious and intervened; a shooting ensued. The commandos fled and detonated the explosives, killing ninety-two people, twenty-eight of them British and fifteen Jewish.

In his 1951 autobiography, Menachem (Volfovitz) Begin, former leader of the Irgun and founder of the Herut, forerunner of today's Likud Party, vaunted the importance of his terrorist actions for the founding of the Zionist state. In his autobiography *The Revolt*, Menachem Begin brags about "the military victory at Deir Yassin," because the news of this slaughter of 254 villagers (mostly unarmed men, women, and children) immediately led to the "maddened, uncontrollable stampede of 635,000 Arabs. [...] The political and economic significance of this development can hardly be overestimated."[99]

"Irgun was from the beginning organized on the strictly conspiratorial lines of a terrorist underground movement," writes disillusioned Zionist Arthur Koestler. As for the members of the Lehi (also known as the Stern Gang), a splinter group of the Irgun founded by Avraham Stern in 1940, which would subsequently be led by another future Israeli prime minister, Yitzhak Shamir, they "were believers in unrestricted and indiscriminate terror."[100] On November 6, 1944, members of Lehi (otherwise known as the Stern Gang) assassinated Lord Moyne, the British resident minister in the Middle East, for his anti-Zionist positions. (The bodies of his murderers, executed in Egypt, were later exchanged for twenty Arab prisoners and buried at the "monument of heroes" in Jerusalem.) On September 17, 1948, the same terrorist group murdered in Jerusalem Count Folke Bernadotte, a Swedish diplomat appointed United Nations mediator in Palestine. He had just submitted his report A/648, which described "large-scale Zionist plundering and destruction of villages," and concluded that the "return of the Arab refugees rooted in this land for centuries" was necessary. His assassin, Nathan Friedman-Yellin,

---

[99] Menachem Begin, *The Revolt: Story of the Irgun,* Henry Schuman, 1951, quoted in Alfred Lilienthal, *What Price Israel?, op. cit.*, p. 81.
[100] Arthur Koestler, "The Rise of Terrorism," in *Promise and Fulfilment – Palestine 1917–1949,* Macmillan, 1949.

was arrested, convicted, and then amnestied; in 1960 he was elected to the Knesset.[101]

The "Human Material"

Anti-Zionist rabbi Moshe Shonfeld claimed that the Zionists had, during World War II, knowingly aggravated the Holocaust, as a necessary founding sacrifice for their Jewish state. Relying on numerous testimonies, he thus summarized the politics of the Zionist leaders: "The shedding of Jewish blood in the Diaspora is necessary in order for us to demand the establishment of a 'Jewish' state before a peace commission. Money will be sent to save a group of 'chalutzim' (pioneers), while the remainder of Czech Jewry must resign itself to annihilation in the Auschwitz crematoria." In other words, "The Zionist leaders saw the spilt Jewish blood of the holocaust as grease for the wheels of the Jewish national state."[102]

In 1948, when international recognition was achieved, Israel's goal was twofold: territorial expansion through annexation and ethnic cleansing of Arab territories, and demographic expansion through mass immigration. The first objective required that tensions be maintained in order to provide pretexts for the enlargement of borders by force. As for the immigrants needed to colonize the conquered territories, they would be acquired by whatever means might be necessary. In the 1940s, the first "human material" (to use Theodor Herzl's own phrase from *The Jewish State*) came from the Jewish "refugees" who had fled or been deported during the war.

We have seen how behind the scenes, the Zionists opposed refugees being welcomed anywhere other than Palestine, in accordance with the principle enunciated by Ben-Gurion in 1935: "We must give a Zionist response to the catastrophe faced by German Jewry—to turn this disaster into an opportunity to develop our country." Again on December 8, 1942, Ben-Gurion declared at the Mapai general assembly: "It is the job of Zionism

---

[101] Alan Hart, *Zionism*, vol. 2, *op. cit.*, p. 90; Roger Garaudy, *Les Mythes fondateurs de la politique israélienne*, La Vieille Taupe, 1995, p. 153.
[102] Rabbi Moshe Shonfeld, *Holocaust Victims Accuse, op. cit.*, pp. 28, 24.

not to save the remnant of Israel in Europe but rather to save the land of Israel for the Jewish people and the Yishuw."[103] Early in 1944, Roosevelt recommenced opening the borders of allied countries to Jewish refugees, but his efforts again clashed with the opposition of Jewish representative elites. When Morris Ernst, sent by Roosevelt to London to discuss the project, returned with British agreement to welcome 150,000 refugees, Roosevelt was satisfied: "150,000 to England—150,000 to match that in the United States—pick up 200,000 or 300,000 elsewhere and we can start with half a million of these oppressed people." But a week later, Roosevelt announced to Ernst the abandonment of the project "because the dominant vocal Jewish leadership of America won't stand for it." The Zionists "know they can raise vast sums for Palestine by saying to donors, 'There is no other place for this poor Jew to go.' But if there is a world political asylum, they cannot raise their money." Incredulous, Ernst made the rounds of his Jewish contacts. He wrote in his memoirs that "active Jewish leaders decried, sneered and then attacked me as if I were a traitor. At one dinner party I was openly accused of furthering this plan of freer immigration [into the US] in order to undermine political Zionism."[104]

Truman's efforts were similarly hampered. Rabbi Philip Bernstein, who was in 1946 adviser on Jewish affairs to the US high commissioner in Germany, testified in 1950 in the *Yiddish Bulletin* that he had lied to the president by making him believe that the overwhelming majority of Jewish refugees wanted to settle in Palestine. In reality, they wanted either to return where they came from or to emigrate to the United States. Rabbi Abraham Klausner, chaplain and "father figure" at the Dachau concentration camp after its liberation in April 1945, wrote in a report of May 2, 1948, to the American Jewish Conference: "I am convinced that the people must be forced to go to Palestine. They are neither prepared to understand their own position nor the promises of the future. [...] It must be borne in mind that

---

[103] Quoted in Tom Segev, *The Seventh Million: The Israelis and the Holocaust*, Hill and Wang, 1993, pp. 27, 129.
[104] John Mulhall, *America and the Founding of Israel: An Investigation of the Morality of America's Role*, Deshon, 1995, p. 109.

we are dealing with a sick people. They are not to be asked, but to be told, what to do." The means of "forcing" them to emigrate into Palestine against their will included propaganda (rumors of pogroms in the United States), harassment, and confiscation of food.[105]

The operation was a success: between 1945 and 1952, nearly one million Jews settled in the territories evacuated by the Palestinians. Until 1948, this still had to be done in violation of British rule. But it could be done with the approval of world public opinion, provided the right symbols were mobilized. And what more powerful symbol than the Exodus, the eternally recyclable myth of the Jewish people in desperate search of its Promised Land? On July 11, 1947, 4,500 refugees from Displaced Persons camps in Germany, selected by the organization in charge of Zionist clandestine immigration (Mossad Le'aliyah Beth) and smuggled to the south of France, embarked from there for Palestine, aboard a vessel that, at sea, was renamed *Exodus 1947* in order to attract more media attention. The British prevented the ship from landing. Three refugees were killed and dozens were wounded in the violent clashes. The British returned the refugees to their French port of origin, but the French government, headed by Léon Blum, agreed with the Zionists to prevent them from disembarking. They were finally sent back to Germany, which generated worldwide sympathy for them and protests against the British.[106]

The victims of Nazism were not the only ones "convinced" to immigrate to Israel. The Zionists also coveted the Jews of the Arab countries, especially those of Iraq—descendants of the millennial community of Babylon—who were unwilling to emigrate. The chief rabbi of Iraq, Khedourin Sassoon, spiritual leader of his community for forty-eight years, declared in 1950: "Iraqi Jews will be forever against Zionism. Jews and Arabs have enjoyed the same rights and privileges for 1000 years and do not regard themselves as a distinctive separate part of this nation."[107]

---

[105] Alfred Lilienthal, *What Price Israel?, op. cit.*, pp. 148–150.
[106] Idith Zertal, *Israel's Holocaust and the Politics of Nationhood,* Cambridge University Press, 2005, pp. 44–51.
[107] Quoted in Alfred Lilienthal, *What Price Israel?, op. cit.*, p. 151.

The Zionists then used a method that they later perfected: the faking of anti-Semitic acts. Between 1950 and 1951, the city of Baghdad was hit by a series of explosions targeting Iraqi Jews, causing deaths, injuries, and material damage. These bombings, blamed on Arab nationalists, spread fear in the Jewish community. On the very night of the first attack, Zionist tracts were already circulating, enjoining "all the tribe of Zion living in Babylon" to make its Aliyah. An Iraqi court later convicted about 20 people for these bombings. All were members of the secret Iraqi Zionist organization. Approximately 125,000 Jews had meanwhile left Iraq for Israel.[108] These new Israelis of Iraqi origin soon complained of discrimination. One of them, Naeim Giladi, testified in his book of the racism which then prevailed among the Ashkenazi toward the Jews of the Middle East and Africa (descendants of converted Berbers or Sephardic Jews exiled in the sixteenth century) and who were subjected to aggressive eugenic measures.[109]

The Eastern European Ashkenazim nevertheless remained the main reservoir of Jews coveted by the Zionist state. Since they were in the Soviet Union or its satellites, their immigration was subject to Stalin's goodwill.

The USSR and Israel

Until 1947, the historic founders of Israel had skillfully exploited the rivalry between the US and Soviet empires in order to persuade each of them to support the UN Partition Plan (and bring with them the countries in their respective spheres of influence) by offering to both parties the prospect of a strategic alliance in the Middle East. Truman's support for the creation of a Jewish state was unsurprising, but Stalin's was unexpected. Using newly uncovered documents from Russian archives, Laurent Rucker shows, in *Moscow's Surprise*, that Soviet support resulted from years of secret diplomatic dealings that started in

---

[108] Naeim Giladi, *Ben-Gurion's Scandals: How the Haganah and Mossad Eliminated Jews* (1992), Dandelion Books, 2003.
[109] Ella Shohat, *Le Sionisme du point de vue de ses victimes juives : Les juifs orientaux en Israël*, La Fabrique, 2006.

January 1941 in London, when Ivan Maisky, Moscow's ambassador to London, met with Chaim Weizmann, then in November with Ben-Gurion, who was on his way to the United States. On that occasion, Maisky stated to Ben-Gurion, "You are going to America. You will render us a great service if you will impress upon people there the urgency of helping us; we need tanks, guns, planes—as many as possible, and above all, as soon as possible." In 1943, Maisky was transferred to Moscow to prepare for the future peace conferences, and stopped in Palestine on the way, to meet with Ben-Gurion. From that time, writes Rucker, "contact between Soviet and Zionist representatives intensified as plans for the postwar order were formulated." In return for Zionist help in securing US military support for the Soviet Union in 1941–1943, the Soviet Union would provide "political, military, and demographic support for the Zionist movement" from 1947 to 1949.[110]

When recognizing the Jewish state on May 14, 1948, Stalin hoped that Israel would lean on the Soviet side in the Cold War that was looming, for the Israeli Labor Party, the founding and majority party, was collectivist. Therefore Israel obtained from the Soviets the armaments that enabled it to fight the Arab countries hostile to the new state in 1948, even while the United States was respecting the UN arms embargo. The weapons came from Czechoslovakia, where the great Skoda arsenal had passed from the Nazis to the Communists. Without these weapons, it is likely that the State of Israel would not have survived. Moreover, more than two hundred thousand Jews, mainly from Poland, but also from Romania, Hungary, and Bulgaria, were allowed to emigrate to Palestine, after the British withdrawal, during the years 1948–1952.

Stalin, however, was not long in noticing the double game Israel was playing in asking for American support. Moreover, he was concerned about the unexpected and overwhelming enthusiasm of the Soviet Jews for Israel and their massive demand for emigration. When Golda Meir (born Mabovitch in

---

[110] Laurent Rucker, *Moscow's Surprise: The Soviet-Israeli Alliance of 1947–1949,* Cold War International History Project, Working Paper #46, on www.cwihp.org, pp. 1–4.

Kiev) moved to Moscow as the first ambassador of the State of Israel, five months after the official foundation of the Jewish state, her arrival aroused a suspicious enthusiasm among the Russian Jewish population: fifty thousand Jews went to the synagogue on the Saturday following her arrival. Golda Meir missed no occasion to remind Russian Jews that their current country of residence was not their true home, and "every one of her public appearances was accompanied by a demonstration of Soviet Jewish identification with Israel," writes Yuri Slezkine.[111]

Stalin was also concerned about the loyalty of Soviet Jews in the war against America, where many had relatives.[112] He began to repress the resurgence of Jewish nationalism in November 1948, arresting the leaders of the influential Anti-Fascist Jewish Committee, and closing many Jewish institutions in the country. On January 15, 1953, nine doctors, including seven Jews, were accused by Stalin of conspiracy to poison him. This affair of the "Jewish doctors" caused an uproar in the West. "Stalin will succeed where Hitler failed," predicted *Commentary,* press organ of the *American Jewish Committee.* "He will finally wipe out the Jews of Central and Eastern Europe. [...] The parallel with the policy of Nazi extermination is almost complete."[113] On February 11, the USSR broke off diplomatic relations with Israel. It was in this context that Stalin died suddenly, on the morning of March 6, 1953, at the age of seventy-four, officially of a cerebral hemorrhage, but more likely of poisoning. A month later, the "Jewish doctors" were released.

The 1950s were marked by the disaffection of many European Communists, some of whom converted to Trotskyism. Their denunciation of Soviet anti-Semitism pushed into oblivion the strong involvement of Jews in the Red Terror. Thus, for example, Annie Kriegel left the French Communist Party in 1956 to devote herself to writing a critical history of communism. In 1982 she founded the journal *Communisme* with

---

[111] Yuri Slezkine, *The Jewish Century, op. cit.,* k. 5197.

[112] Kevin MacDonald, *Separation and Its Discontents: Toward an Evolutionary Theory of Anti-Semitism,* Praeger, 1998, kindle 2013, k. 2503–10.

[113] Quoted in Norman Finkelstein, *The Holocaust Industry: Reflections on the Exploitation of Jewish Suffering,* Verso, 2014, p. 20.

Stéphane Courtois, who, after her death, directed the publication of *The Black Book of Communism: Crimes, Terror, Repression* (1997), which sold over a million copies worldwide. That volume succeeds in exposing the crimes of Communism (80 million deaths) without ever mentioning the Jewish component of the Communist forces in Europe.

Nasser, the Useful Enemy

In the United States, after Truman's two terms, General Dwight Eisenhower was elected president in November 1952. Although he had previously been a member of Roosevelt's Democratic Party, he ran on the Republican ticket, at the invitation of a faction that wanted to block the natural leader of the Republican Party—Robert Taft, a senator who had protested against Roosevelt's military and economic support to the USSR. In 1948, Taft had also courageously denounced the Nuremberg trials, which in his view violated the basic principles of justice. Taft then opposed the formation of NATO in 1949; Eisenhower, in contrast, had just been appointed first commander-in-chief of this military alliance. "Ike" would become the president of the Cold War, and his two inaugural addresses (January 1953 and 1957) were entirely devoted to this subject. Eisenhower was the first of a long series of American presidents who would mention his support of Israel during election campaigns: "The state of Israel is democracy's outpost in the Middle East and every American who loves liberty must join the effort to make secure forever the future of this newest member in the family of nations" (October 16, 1952).[114]

In 1948, the Arab countries had proven totally unfit to confront the Israeli intruder due to their dissensions, corruptions, and betrayals. But in 1952, a more formidable enemy stood against Israel in the person of Colonel Gamal Abdel Nasser, who took power in Egypt and soon became a hero of Arab nationalism and, even more dangerously, pan-Arabism. Nasser's willingness to recognize Israel within the

---

[114] "Eisenhower Says Israel is Democracy's Outpost in Middle East," October 6, 1952, on www.jta.org.

borders of the Partition made him an even more formidable obstacle to the secret project of Israeli expansionism. Israeli hawks reacted with a new, highly confrontational policy aimed at creating pretexts for attacking Egypt and conquering new lands, while discrediting Nasser in the eyes of the West so as to prevent any alliance between Egypt and the West. If Nasser—the founder of a secular democratic state—allied with the Americans, they would apply irresistible diplomatic and economic pressure forcing Israel to accept peace on a territorial basis deemed insufficient by the Zionists. The Zionist strategy thus was to ensure that Israel was perceived in Washington, London, and Paris as the only reliable bastion of anti-communism in the Middle East, while simultaneously portraying Nasser's Egypt as a communist ally. The Cold War was the indispensable context for achieving these objectives, which is why a climate of anti-communist paranoia had to be maintained among the American people and elite. Zionist propaganda did not hesitate to demonize Nasser by comparing him to Hitler: Ben-Gurion called him a "fascist dictator" while Menachem Begin insisted that he was surrounded by Nazi emissaries.[115]

Nasser's priority in 1952 was to ensure that the British withdrew from the Suez Canal in 1956, as provided for by the agreement passed twenty years earlier. He needed this diplomatic victory to obtain sufficient credibility in the eyes of his people to weaken his internal enemy, the Muslim Brotherhood, and thus be in a position to negotiate with Israel. Israel's hawks therefore decided to prevent this historic turn, with the aim of keeping Egypt cast as an enemy of the West. In the summer of 1954, four days before British Secretary of State for War Anthony Head traveled to Cairo to prepare for the withdrawal, Egyptian Jews trained in Israel committed several false flag bomb attacks against British targets, designed to be blamed on the Muslim Brotherhood. Dan Kurzman, Ben-Gurion's hagiographer, sums up the logic of this psychological operation: "Why not blow up American and British property in Egypt ? Washington and London would think Nasser couldn't

---

[115] Tom Segev, *The Seventh Million, op. cit.*, p. 227.

control the extremist Moslem Brotherhood or the Communists. And if he cracked down on them, all the better. They would retaliate and there would be no end to violence in Egypt. Would Britain leave the strategic Suez Canal to a nation in flames? Would America let it? Presumably not."[116]

Operation Susannah, the second confirmed case of false flag terrorism in modern history, failed due to the arrest of one of the bombers, leading to the apprehension of twelve other Israeli agents. The scandal came to be known as the "Lavon Affair," named after the minister of defense Pinhas Lavon who took the blame. The goal, in the words of the head of Israeli military intelligence Benjamin Givli, was "to break the West's confidence in the existing [Egyptian] regime."[117] The scandal was played down in the Israeli and US media, and it was not until 2005 that the Israeli state recognized its responsibility. In the 1950s, however, Israel exploited the incident by making its population believe that innocent Israeli agents had been victims of Egyptian anti-Semitism.[118]

Moshe Sharett, minister of foreign affairs from 1948 to 1956 and prime minister from 1954 to 1955 (who grew up in contact with the Arabs and knew their language and culture, unlike the Ashkenazi who constituted the majority of the government) advocated moderate Zionism and respect for international law. He was opposed by Ben-Gurion's hawks, who conceived of the Arabs as a primitive enemy that had to be crushed purely by force.[119] This clan, Sharett wrote regretfully in his newspaper in 1955, wanted "to set the Middle East on fire," "to frighten the West into supporting Israel's aims," and thus "raises terrorism to the level of a sacred principle." Sharett included in this condemnation Pinhas Lavon and Moshe Dayan, as well as Shimon Peres, who would eventually become president of Israel at the age of 84.[120]

---

[116] Dan Kurzman, *Ben-Gurion, Prophet of Fire,* Touchstone, 1983, p. 372.

[117] Quoted in Noam Chomsky, *The Fateful Triangle, op. cit.,* p. 467.

[118] Alan Hart, *Zionism: The Real Enemy of the Jews,* vol. 2, *op. cit.,* p. 118.

[119] Alan Hart, *Zionism: The Real Enemy of the Jews,* vol. 2, *op. cit.,* page 117.

[120] Livia Rokach, *Israel's Sacred Terrorism: A Study Based on Moshe Sharett's Personal Diary and Other Documents,* Association of Arab-American University Graduates, 1986, pp. 42–49.

There were no limits to what the Israeli hawks would do to sabotage the dialogue between Sharrett and Nasser and to prevent a lasting entente between Israel and Egypt. Using the pretext of the death of an Israeli during an infiltration operation by Palestinians—on land stolen from them—Ariel Sharon attacked Gaza on February 28, 1955, forcing Nasser to break off negotiations with Sharrett and driving the latter to resign. The hawks returned to power. Paradoxically, it was the Israeli attack on Gaza that caused the outburst of indignation necessary for the formation of a Palestinian nationalist movement: "The Israelis probably saved us from extinction with that attack," said Yasser Arafat.[121] The creation of Fatah (Palestine Liberation Movement) in 1958 complicated Nasser's task, but, recognizing Arafat's determination and political intelligence, as well as his uncontested leadership in the eyes of his people, Nasser became his protector and main supporter.

As a result of the Gaza attack, Nasser decided to arm Egypt appropriately, realizing that his only chance of peace rested on his ability to respond to Israel's attacks. He therefore endeavored to convince the United States and Great Britain to sell arms to him, but rejected the condition imposed on him by Secretary of State John Foster Dulles to engage in a formal alliance with the United States that would be unacceptable in the eyes of his people. Although ideologically anti-communist, Nasser was finally compelled to accept the competing offer from the Soviets, which was generous and theoretically unconditional. In September 1955 he signed a contract with the USSR for the purchase of arms through Czechoslovakia. It set off an intense Zionist campaign to discredit Nasser, in the eyes of the West, as a danger to the stability of the Middle East and, conversely, to present Israel as the only reliable ally in the region. On February 14, 1956, Ben-Gurion sent an open letter to Eisenhower, disseminated throughout the American Jewish community, demanding US arms aid for Israel.

On July 19, 1956, a month after the British withdrawal from Suez, the US government canceled financing for the Aswan

---

[121] Alan Hart, *Zionism: The Real Enemy of the Jews*, vol. 2, *op. cit.*, p. 164.

Grand Dam, instantly destroying Nasser's most ambitious project for modernizing Egypt. In response, Nasser nationalized the canal on July 26, compensating the shareholders. In October, the British and French signed the "Protocol of Sèvres," a secret agreement with Israel to take back the Canal Zone from Nasser and, if possible, overthrow him. (France correctly saw Nasser as an ally of Algerian nationalists of the FLN.) The Machiavellian plan was as follows: Israel would attack Egypt and occupy the Sinai Peninsula; Britain and France would threaten to intervene, demanding that each side withdraw from the combat zone, while proposing an armistice that would be unacceptable to Nasser since it would leave Israeli troops inside Egypt. Nasser would have no choice but to refuse the ultimatum, and English and French troops could then launch a seemingly justifiable invasion.

The offensive began on October 29, 1956, with the Israelis, British, and French counting on the fact that Eisenhower was busy with his re-election campaign. Khrushchev vigorously protested and threatened to send troops against Israel. Eisenhower took Khrushchev seriously, and made the right choice by joining his protest, while publicly blaming the British and the French rather than the Israelis. (Ike's popularity was such that no press campaign could prevent his re-election.) Israel withdrew from the Sinai, and an international peacekeeping force was stationed in Sharm El Sheikh until 1967.

Israel drew two lessons for the future: first, to arrange to never again appear as the aggressor, for the United States could not tolerate it; and second, to build a stronger influence over US domestic policy and place a more conciliatory man in the White House.

Chapter 8

THE INVISIBLE COUP

> "I, Yahweh your God, am a jealous god and I punish a parent's fault in the children, the grandchildren, and the great-grandchildren among those who hate me."
>
> Exodus 20:5

John F. Kennedy, the Lobby, and the Bomb

In the 1960 presidential elections, Vice President Richard Nixon was in line to become Eisenhower's successor. He was not regarded as a friend of Israel, and has even been suspected of anti-Semitism, on the basis of recently declassified White House recordings. On the Democrats' side, the Zionist lobby threw their support to Lyndon Johnson, a longtime ally. As the Senate majority leader in 1957, Johnson had strongly protested against UN sanctions aimed at forcing Israel to retreat from the Sinai, with a letter to Secretary of State John Foster Dulles published in the *New York Times* (February 20, 1957).[1] But John Kennedy won the primaries.

Kennedy was worse than Nixon for the Zionists. His Irish Catholic background was already a bad omen, and his father, while ambassador in London, had supported Neville Chamberlain's appeasement policy toward Hitler. In September 1960, the *Herut*, Menachem Begin's political party, voiced concerns about whether Joe Kennedy "did not inject some poisonous drops of anti-Semitism in the minds of his children, including his son John's."[2] Referring to the traditionally Democratic "Jewish vote," the author asks: "How can the future of Israel (sic) be entrusted to these men who might come to

---

[1] Louis Bloomfield, *Egypt, Israel, and the Gulf of Aqaba*, Carswell, 1957, p. 152.
[2] Alan Hart, *Zionism: The Real Enemy of the Jews*, vol. 2: *David Becomes Goliath*, Clarity Press, 2013, p. 252.

power thanks to Jewish votes, strange and paradoxical as this may seem." In his Pulitzer prize-winning book *Profiles in Courage* (1956), Kennedy had declared his admiration for Senator Robert Taft, who by calling the Nuremberg trials a shameful parody of justice had sacrificed his political career, including his chances for the presidency, rather than build it on hypocrisy. Worse, as a senator, Kennedy had expressed sympathy for the Palestinian refugees, whose camps he had visited in 1956.[3]

Kennedy came to power at a time when the dismantling of the French, British, and Belgian colonial empires had led to the independence of twenty new African states. As a senator and while campaigning for the presidency, he had urged Washington to "recognize the force of Arab nationalism" so as to "channel it along constructive lines." "Call it nationalism, call it anti-colonialism, call it what you will, Africa is going through a revolution. [...] The word is out—and spreading like wildfire in nearly a thousand languages and dialects—that it is no longer necessary to remain forever poor or forever in bondage."[4] Kennedy felt no sympathy for Israel's anachronistic colonial adventure, but great admiration for Gamal Abdel Nasser, the hero of Arab nationalism. Nasser was perceived by the Zionist leaders as the greatest obstacle to their secret expansionist agenda, especially because of his willingness to recognize Israel within the 1948 Partition borders.

As soon as it became clear that Kennedy would beat Johnson in the Democratic primaries, Zionists pressured him to pick Johnson as his running mate, rather than Adlai Stevenson, another unlucky contender for the presidential ticket, who was the preferred choice of the Kennedy team. (Kennedy would name Stevenson Ambassador to the U.N. instead). "You know, we had never considered Lyndon," Kennedy once apologized to his assistant Hyman Raskin, "but I was left with no choice [...] those bastards were trying to frame me. They threatened me

---

[3] Alan Hart, *Zionism: The Real Enemy of the Jews*, vol. 2: *David Becomes Goliath*, Clarity Press, 2009, pp. 251–252.
[4] Arthur Schlesinger, *A Thousand Days: John Kennedy in the White House* (1965), Mariner Books, 2002, p. 554.

with problems and I don't need more problems."[5] It is on record, thanks to Kennedy insider Arthur Schlesinger (*A Thousand Days*, 1965), that it was in fact Philip Graham and Joseph Alsop, respectively publisher and columnist of the *Washington Post*, both strong supporters of Israel, who convinced Kennedy to take Johnson on his ticket, in a closed door conversation.[6] Schlesinger doesn't reveal Graham and Alsop's arguments, and states that Kennedy's final decision "defies historical reconstruction"—a curious statement for a historian so well informed, which can only be explained by Schlesinger's refusal throughout his 872 pages to come to grips with Kennedy's Middle East policy and his battle with Zionism. Alan Hart has convincingly filled in the blanks: both Graham and Alsop were strongly pro-Israel as well as pro-Johnson, and both could exert a huge influence on public opinion. So "Kennedy was forced by Israel's supporters to take Johnson as his vice-presidential running mate."[7] Why would the Zionists want Johnson as vice-president, rather than keep him as Senate majority leader, a better position for blocking anti-Israel legislation? It can only be because they saw the vice-presidency as a step to the presidency. And the sooner, the better.

After the Press came the Bank: John Kennedy soon received a visit from Zionist financier Abraham Feinberg (who had already financed Truman in exchange for the recognition of Israel), who said to him, as Kennedy reported to his friend Charles Bartlett: "We know your campaign is in trouble. We're willing to pay your bills if you'll let us have control of your Middle East policy." Bartlett recalls that Kennedy was deeply upset and swore that, "if he ever did get to be President, he was going to do something about it."[8] Thanks to his father's fortune, Kennedy was relatively independent, but not to the point of being able to reject Feinberg's offer. And so, after naming

---

[5] Phillip Nelson, *LBJ: The Mastermind of JFK's Assassination*, XLibris, 2010, p. 320.

[6] Arthur Schlesinger, *A Thousand Days*, op. cit., p. 56; Alan Hart, *Zionism*, vol. 2, op. cit., p. 257.

[7] Alan Hart, *Zionism*, vol. 2: op. cit., p. 257.

[8] Seymour Hersh, *The Samson Option: Israel's Nuclear Arsenal and American Foreign Policy*, Random House, 1991, pp. 94–97.

Johnson as vice-president, he appointed Myer Feldman as his special counsel on the Middle East. Born of Jewish Ukrainian immigrants, Feldman was known as "a behind-the-scenes liaison to Israel," and often met with Israel's Prime Minister Ben-Gurion and Foreign Secretary Golda Meir, as the *New York Times* candidly remembers him.[9]

From 1962 to 1963, JFK submitted seven bills in an effort to reform the Congressional campaign finance system. All of them were defeated by the influential groups they sought to curtail. Meanwhile, with the support of the attorney general Robert Kennedy, Senator William Fulbright, chairman of the Committee on Foreign Relations, conducted an audit on the American Zionist Council (precursor of AIPAC), the concluding report of which recommended that it be registered as a "foreign agent" and therefore subject to the obligations defined by the Foreign Agents Registration Act of 1938, which would considerably limit its influence.[10]

The Zionists' worst fears proved justified. Historian Philip Muehlenbeck writes: "While the Eisenhower administration had sought to isolate Nasser and reduce his influence through building up Saudi Arabia's King Saud as a conservative rival to the Egyptian president, the Kennedy administration pursued the exact opposite strategy."[11] During his first months in the White House, Kennedy committed himself in letters to Nasser and other Arab heads of state to supporting UN Resolution 194 for the right of return of Palestinian refugees. Former Undersecretary of State George Ball noted in his book, *The Passionate Attachment* (1992), that Ben-Gurion reacted with "a letter to the Israeli ambassador in Washington, intended to be circulated among Jewish-American leaders, in which he stated: 'Israel will regard this plan as a more serious danger to her existence than all the threats of the Arab dictators and Kings, than all the Arab armies, than all of Nasser's missiles and his

---

[9] Douglas Martin, "Myer Feldman, 92, Adviser to President Kennedy, Dies," *New York Times*, March 3, 2007, on www.nytimes.com.
[10] The Israel Lobby Archive, www.irmep.org/ila/forrel/.
[11] Philip Muehlenbeck, *Betting on the Africans: John F. Kennedy's Courting of African Nationalist Leaders*, Oxford UP, 2012.

Soviet MIGs. [...] Israel will fight against this implementation down to the last man."[12]

But the greatest danger that Kennedy represented to Israel was his determination to stop its nuclear weapons program. By the early 1950s, David Ben-Gurion, both prime minister and defense minister, had entrusted Shimon Peres to nudge Israel toward the secret manufacture of atomic bombs, by diverting materials from the cooperation program Atoms for Peace, launched naively by Eisenhower, and by organizing industrial espionage and smuggling. Kennedy had made nuclear disarmament one of his grand missions on the international level. He had announced it at the General Assembly of the United Nation on September 25, 1961, with a powerful speech declaring his "intention to challenge the Soviet Union, not to an arms race, but to a peace race—to advance together step by step, stage by stage, until general and complete disarmament has been achieved." The challenge had been well received by Nikita Khrushchev, and the first step was taken on August 5, 1963, with the signature of the first international Test Ban Treaty. In 1963, with only four countries in possession of nuclear weapons, nuclear disarmament was an achievable goal, and Kennedy was determined not to let this opportunity pass. "I am haunted by the feeling that by 1970, unless we are successful, there may be ten nuclear powers instead of four, and by 1975, fifteen or twenty," he said prophetically during his press conference on March 21, 1963.[13]

Israel, however, was just as determined in its secret race to be the first and only country in the Middle East with the bomb. Informed by the CIA in 1960 of the military aim pursued at the Dimona complex in the Negev desert, Kennedy did his utmost to force Israel to renounce it. He replaced CIA Director Allen Dulles by John McCone, who had, as Eisenhower's chairman of the Atomic Energy Commission (AEC), leaked to the *New York Times* the truth about Israel's Dimona project; the story was

---

[12] Quoted in George and Douglas Ball, *The Passionate Attachment: America's Involvement With Israel, 1947 to the Present*, W.W. Norton & Co., 1992, p. 51.
[13] Audio file on JFK Library: www.jfklibrary.org/Asset-Viewer/Archives/JFKWHA-169.aspx.

printed on December 19, 1960, weeks before Kennedy was to take office. As Alan Hart writes, "there can be no doubt that Kennedy's determination to stop Israel developing its own nuclear bomb was the prime factor in his decision to appoint McCone."[14] Then Kennedy urged Ben-Gurion to allow regular inspections of Dimona, first verbally in New York in 1961, and later through more and more insistent letters. In the last one, cabled June 15, 1963, to the Israeli ambassador with instructions to hand it personally to Ben-Gurion, Kennedy demanded Ben-Gurion's agreement for an immediate visit followed by regular visits every six months, otherwise "this Government's commitment to and support of Israel could be seriously jeopardized."[15] The result was unexpected: Ben-Gurion avoided receiving the letter by announcing his resignation on June 16. As soon as the new prime minister Levi Eshkol took office, Kennedy sent him a similar letter, dated July 5, 1963, to no avail. Did Ben-Gurion resign in order to move into the shadows of the deep state? Eleven days later, his words showed the same commitment to provide Israel with the bomb: "I do not know of any other nation whose neighbors declare that they wish to terminate it, and not only declare, but prepare for it by all means available to them. [...] Our numbers are small, and there is no chance that we could compare ourselves with America's 180 million, or with any Arab neighboring state. There is one thing, however, in which we are not inferior to any other people in the world—this is the Jewish brain. And the Jewish brain does not disappoint; Jewish science does not disappoint. [...] I am confident [...] that science is able to provide us with the weapons that will serve the peace and deter our enemies."[16]

The secret showdown between Kennedy and Ben-Gurion on the nuclear question was revealed by two books: Seymour Hersh's *The Samson Option* in 1991, then Avner Cohen's *Israel and the Bomb* in 1998. The Israeli newspaper *Haaretz* published a

---

[14] Alan Hart, *Zionism: The Real Enemy of the Jews*, vol. 2: *David Becomes Goliath*, Clarity Press, 2009, p. 273.

[15] Warren Bass, *Support Any Friend: Kennedy's Middle East and the Making of the US-Israel Alliance*, 2003, p. 219.

[16] Avner Cohen, *Israel and the Bomb*, Columbia University Press, 1998, p. 13.

review of Cohen's book on February 5, 1999, which reads: "The murder of American President John F. Kennedy brought to an abrupt end the massive pressure being applied by the US administration on the government of Israel to discontinue the nuclear program. Cohen demonstrates at length the pressures applied by Kennedy on Ben-Gurion. He brings the fascinating exchange of letters between the two, in which Kennedy makes it quite clear to [Ben-Gurion] that he [JFK] will under no circumstances agree to Israel becoming a nuclear state. The book implied that, had Kennedy remained alive, it is doubtful whether Israel would today have a nuclear option."[17] The subject has been taken up by Michael Karpin in 2007, in *The Bomb in the Basement*. Karpin writes: "Kennedy placed the limitation of the nuclear arms race at the center of American foreign policy. In his judgment the United States, as the leader of the free world, was responsible for restricting the proliferation of nuclear weapons. Kennedy displayed great determination in his fight for disarmament and nuclear nonproliferation. Israel's nuclear enterprise was in direct contradiction with the principles of his policy."[18]

Who Killed Kennedy?

Kennedy was assassinated on November 22, 1963, in Dallas, Texas, at 12:30 p.m. One hour later, Lee Harvey Oswald was apprehended. The same day, Americans heard on television: "The assassin of President Kennedy is an admitted Marxist who spent three years in Russia trying to renounce his US citizenship." "After changing his mind and returning to the United States last year, Oswald became a sympathizer of the Cuban prime minister, Fidel Castro."[19] But quickly Oswald's Soviet and Cuban connections were forgotten and he was presented to the public as the sole assassin. The FBI confirmed

---

[17] Michael Collins Piper, *False Flags: Template for Terror*, American Free Press, 2013, pp. 54–55.
[18] Michael Karpin, *The Bomb in the Basement: How Israel Went Nuclear and What That Means for the World*, Simon & Schuster, 2007, p. 180.
[19] As read by Fidel Castro in his November 23 speech, on educationforum.ipbhost .com/index.php?showtopic=18765.

it, and after a mock investigation by a presidential commission, this became official truth. Assuming this theory is a lie (as about 75 percent of Americans today believe), and that Oswald was in fact "just a patsy" as he publicly claimed, the quest for the real culprits must logically start by investigating the man who shot Oswald to death at point-blank range two days later, while Oswald was being transferred from the Dallas Police station (where he had been interrogated for two days while no one made a recording or took notes) to the Dallas County jail. Oswald's assassin is known as Jack Ruby, but few people know that his real name was Jacob Leon Rubenstein, that he was the son of Jewish Polish immigrants, and that, asked by the Warren Commission how he had been allowed into the Police Station, he claimed he had been translating for Israeli reporters. (Ruby spoke Yiddish, but what Israeli reporter in the US could possibly need a Yiddish translator?)

Ruby was a member of the Jewish underworld, and a friend of Los Angeles gangster Mickey Cohen, whom he had known and idolized since 1946. Cohen was the successor of the famed Benjamin Siegelbaum, a.k.a. Bugsy Siegel, one of the bosses of Murder Incorporated. Cohen was infatuated with the Zionist cause, to which he had been introduced by Hollywood script writer Ben Hecht, as he explained in his memoirs: "Now I got so engrossed with Israel that I actually pushed aside a lot of my activities and done nothing but what was involved with this Irgun war." What kept him so busy, he goes on to explain, was stealing surplus weapons coming back from Europe after WWII and sending them to the Irgun.[20] Like Ben Hecht, Mickey Cohen was in contact with Menachem Begin, the former Irgun chief, with whom he even "spent a lot of time," according to Gary Wean, former detective sergeant for the Los Angeles Police Department. (Incidentally, Wean claims that Cohen, who specialized in sexually compromising Hollywood stars for the purpose of blackmail, was responsible for pushing Marilyn

---

[20] Mickey Cohen, *In My Own Words*, Prentice-Hall, 1975, pp. 91–92.

Monroe into Kennedy's bed.)[21] The major godfather to whom Cohen was accountable was Meyer Suchowljansky, known as Lansky, himself a dedicated Zionist and a generous donor to the Anti-Defamation League. (His granddaughter Mira Lansky Boland would become an ADL official.) So there is a direct line connecting Jack Ruby, via Mickey Cohen, to the Israeli terrorist ring, and in particular to Menachem Begin, a specialist in false flag terror. We also know that Ruby phoned Al Gruber, a Mickey Cohen associate, just after Oswald's arrest; no doubt he received then "an offer he couldn't refuse," as they say in the underworld.[22] As Gail Raven, a former girlfriend of Ruby and nightclub dancer in his Carousel Club, once said: "He had no choice. [...] Jack had bosses, just like everyone else."[23] To top it all, Ruby's defense lawyer William Kunstler wrote in his memoirs that Ruby told him he had killed Oswald "for the Jews," and Ruby's rabbi Hillel Silverman received the same confession when visiting Ruby in jail.[24] According to a declassified US State Department document, Israeli Foreign Minister Golda Meir reacted to the news that Ruby had just killed Oswald with this sentence: "Ruby is alive, Oy vaaboy if we get caught!"[25]

Jack Ruby was also linked to Lyndon Johnson. Former Nixon operative Roger Stone said in an interview with the *Daily Caller* that in November 1963, upon seeing Ruby on television, "Nixon said, 'The damn thing is, I knew this Jack Ruby. Murray [Chotiner] brought him to me in 1947, said he was one of 'Johnson's boys' and that LBJ wanted us to hire him as an informant to the [House Un-American Activities] Committee. We did.' I think Nixon immediately recognized that LBJ was

---

[21] Brad Lewis, *Hollywood's Celebrity Gangster: The Incredible Life and Times of Mickey Cohen*, Amazon, 2009, pp. 56, 265–266, 287.

[22] Michael Collins Piper, *Final Judgment: The Missing Link in the JFK Assassination Conspiracy*, American Free Press, 6th ed., ebook 2005, pp. 133–155, 226.

[23] jfkfacts.org/assassination/news/ex-flame-says-jack-ruby-had-no-choice-but-to-kill-oswald/.

[24] William Kunstler, *My Life as a Radical Lawyer*, Carol Publishing, 1994, p. 158; Steve North, "Lee Harvey Oswald's Killer 'Jack Ruby' Came From Strong Jewish Background," *The Forward*, November 17, 2013, on forward.com.

[25] Alan Hart, *Zionism*, vol. 2, *op. cit.*, p. 279.

using one his operatives to do 'clean up' work on the murder of John Kennedy."[26] That Ruby acted on Johnson's orders is a likely explanation of Ruby's odd statements to the Warren Commission: "If you don't take me back to Washington tonight to give me a chance to prove to the President that I am not guilty, then you will see the most tragic thing that will ever happen." Ruby made himself clearer: "There will be a certain tragic occurrence happening if you don't take my testimony and somehow vindicate me so my people don't suffer because of what I have done." He feared that his act would be used "to create some falsehood about some of the Jewish faith," but added that "maybe something can be saved [...], if our President, Lyndon Johnson, knew the truth from me."[27] Ruby seems to have wanted to send through the Commission a message to Johnson, or rather a warning that he might spill the beans about Israel's involvement if Johnson did not intervene in his favor. We get the impression that Ruby expected Johnson to pardon him—just as in 1952 Johnson had managed, through corruption of the judge and threats to the jury, to keep his personal hitman Mac Wallace out of jail, with only a five-year suspended sentence, despite his conviction for first-degree murder, which is normally a sure ticket to death row in Texas.[28] Ruby's sense of betrayal would explain why in 1965, sentenced to life in prison, Ruby implicitly accused Johnson of Kennedy's murder in a press conference: "If [Adlai Stevenson] was Vice-President there would never have been an assassination of our beloved President Kennedy."[29]

Ruby's statement to the Warren Commission was leaked to journalist Dorothy Kilgallen and published in the *New York Journal American,* August 18–20, 1964. Kilgallen also interviewed Jack Ruby and boasted afterwards of being about to "break the real story" and publish "the biggest scoop of the century" in a book titled *Murder One.* The book was never published: Kilgallen

---

[26] Patrick Howley, "Why Jack Ruby was probably part of the Kennedy conspiracy," *Daily Caller,* March 14, 2014, on dailycaller.com.

[27] Read Ruby's deposition on jfkmurdersolved.com/ruby.htm.

[28] Phillip Nelson, *LBJ: The Mastermind, op. cit.,* pp. 271–80.

[29] See on YouTube, "Jack Ruby Talks."

was found dead of an overdose of barbiturates and alcohol on November 8, 1965.[30] As for Ruby, he died from a rapidly spreading cancer in 1967.

Kennedy's death propelled Johnson to become head of state and, in the atmosphere of national crisis thus created, enabled him to bully both justice and the press while achieving his life's ambition. Many Americans immediately suspected Johnson's involvement in the assassination, especially after the publication in 1964 of a book by James Evetts Haley, *A Texan Looks at Lyndon*, which portrayed Johnson as deeply corrupt. According to his biographer Robert Caro, Johnson was a man thirsting "for power in its most naked form, for power not to improve the lives of others, but to manipulate and dominate them, to bend them to his will [...], a hunger so fierce and consuming that no consideration of morality or ethics, no cost to himself—or to anyone else—could stand before it."[31] Throughout the years, a considerable amount of evidence has accumulated indicating that Johnson, alongside complicit Texas authorities, masterminded Kennedy's assassination. This thesis is highly convincing.[32]

Complicity among high-ranking Navy officers is also certain. President Kennedy was pronounced dead at Parkland Hospital in Dallas, but his body was literally stolen at gunpoint from the appointed coroner, Earl Rose, and the autopsy was performed at Bethesda Naval Hospital in Washington by an inexperienced military doctor (James Humes), flanked by senior officers and federal agents. The autopsy report stated that the fatal bullet had entered the back of the skull, contradicting testimony of twenty-one members of the Dallas hospital staff who saw two entry bullet-wounds on the front of Kennedy's body. Dr. Charles Crenshaw, for example, divulged in 1992: "From the damage I saw, there was no doubt in my mind that the bullet had entered his head through the front"—an account that exonerates

---

[30] David Talbot, *Brothers: The Hidden History of the Kennedy Years*, Simon & Schuster, 2007, pp. 262–263.

[31] Quoted in Phillip Nelson, *LBJ: The Mastermind, op. cit.*, p. 17.

[32] Latest book following this line of inquiry: Roger Stone, *The Man Who Killed Kennedy: The Case Against LBJ*, Skyhorse, 2013.

Oswald, who was behind the president at the time of the shooting.[33]

Navy involvement links directly to Johnson, who had many shady business partners there. The Navy secretary appointed by Kennedy in January 1961 was Texan John Connally, who had obtained that position at the insistence of Johnson. When Connally resigned eleven months later to run for the Texas governorship, Johnson convinced Kennedy to name another of his Texan friends, Fred Korth. Connally and Korth were both closely associated with the Texas-based company General Dynamics, which was close to bankruptcy in 1961. Korth, who had been president of GD's main bank, Continental National Bank, was forced to resign in November 1963, weeks before the Dallas coup, after the Justice Department implicated him in a fraud involving a $7 billion contract for the construction of 1,700 TFX military aircraft by General Dynamics (the biggest arms contract ever at this time). Johnson's personal secretary, Bobby Baker ("my strong right arm," as he liked to call him), was charged in the same case, and one of Baker's associates, Don Reynolds, was testifying against him on November 22 before the Senate Rules Committee. He attested to having seen Baker with a suitcase containing $100,000 in kickbacks intended for Johnson, and further claimed to have been offered bribes for his silence.[34]

Because of this mounting scandal and other suspicions of corruption, Kennedy was determined to change vice-presidents for his upcoming reelection campaign, as part of "making government service an honorable career," as he had confided to his longtime personal secretary Evelyn Lincoln.[35] While in Dallas the day before the president's visit for the Soda Bottlers' Convention (as business attorney for Pepsi-Cola), Nixon publicized the rumor of Johnson's removal, as the *Dallas Morning News* reported on November 22: "Nixon Predicts JFK May

---

[33] James Douglass, *JFK and the Unspeakable: Why He Died and Why It Matters*, Touchstone, 2008, p. 300.

[34] Read articles "John Connally" and "Fred Korth" on spartacus-educational.com.

[35] Phillip Nelson, *LBJ: The Mastermind, op. cit.*, p. 372.

Drop Johnson." Instead, Johnson became president that very day.

From the moment he became president while Kennedy's body was still warm, Johnson used all the weight of his newly acquired authority to kill the investigation and impose the necessity of selling to the public the "lone gunman" theory. In order to do that, he didn't try to convince people around him that this was the truth; rather, he claimed it was a matter of national security. Instead of playing down the importance of evidence linking Oswald to the USSR and communist Cuba, he dramatized its highly explosive nature, capable of igniting a new world war—a nuclear one. Hours after Oswald was arrested, Johnson insisted that all federal and state bodies quickly deny any rumor of foreign conspiracy and assert that Oswald had acted alone. Dallas District Attorney Henry Wade, Texas Attorney General Waggoner Carr, and Police Chief Jesse Curry all received phone calls from Johnson's aide Cliff Carter (Johnson's flunky ever since he had helped him steal his first Senate election in 1948), issued directly from Air Force One and then the White House. According to Wade, "[Carter] said that President Johnson felt any word of a conspiracy—some plot by foreign nations—to kill President Kennedy would shake our nation to its foundations. [...] Washington's word to me was that it would hurt foreign relations if I alleged conspiracy, whether I could prove it or not. I was just to charge Oswald with plain murder and go for the death penalty. Johnson had Cliff Carter call me three or four times that weekend."

Johnson continued to raise the specter of nuclear war to silence the "rumors" of a communist conspiracy: "40 million American lives hung in the balance," he kept repeating.[36] Johnson used the same argument to direct the hand of the members of the Warren Commission formed on November 29 to appease public suspicion of a government cover-up. "We've got to be taking this out of the arena where they're testifying that Khrushchev and Castro did this and did that and check us into a war that can kill 40 million Americans in an hour," he

---

36 Phillip Nelson, *LBJ: The Mastermind, op. cit.*, p. 513–514, 619.

explained to Senator Richard Russell in a telephone conversation on November 29, persuading him to join the commission.[37]

The man who played the key role in fabricating the government lie purveyed by the commission was Arlen Specter, the inventor of what came to be called the "magic bullet" theory: a single bullet supposed to have caused seven wounds to Kennedy and John Connally, who was sitting in front of him in the limousine, and later found in pristine condition on a gurney in Parkland Memorial Hospital in Dallas. Specter was still defending his theory in his 2000 autobiography entitled, with an ironic touch of chutzpah, *Passion for Truth*. At his death in 2012, Specter, the son of Russian Jewish immigrants, was officially mourned by the Israeli government as "an unswerving defender of the Jewish State," and by AIPAC, as "a leading architect of the congressional bond between our country and Israel."[38]

Many other Israeli *sayanim* can be identified in the story. (*Sayanim* is a term for Mossad assistants recruited from the Jewish Diaspora to help with operations outside Israel.) JFK's trip to Dallas, being officially non-political, was sponsored by a powerful business group known as the Dallas Citizens Council, dominated by Julius Schepps, "a wholesale liquor distributor, member of every synagogue in town, and de facto leader of the Jewish community," as described by Bryan Edward Stone in *The Chosen Folks: Jews on the Frontiers of Texas*.[39] As Stone makes clear (after Natalie Ornish in *Pioneer Jewish Texans*, 1989[40]), wealthy Jews were highly influential in Texas, contrary to the popular image. Among other influential figures was advertising executive and PR man Sam Bloom, who chaired the "host committee" inviting Kennedy. According to former British intelligence officer Colonel John Hughes-Wilson, it was Bloom who "suggested that the police make Oswald accessible to the press.

---

[37] On YouTube, "Phone call: Lyndon Johnson & Richard Russell."

[38] Natasha Mozgovaya, "Prominent Jewish-American politician Arlen Specter dies at 82," *Haaretz*, October 14, 2012, on www.haaretz.com.

[39] Bryan Edward Stone, *The Chosen Folks: Jews on the Frontiers of Texas*, University of Texas Press, 2010, p. 200.

[40] Natalie Ornish, *Pioneer Jewish Texans*, The Texas A&M University Press, 2011.

He also suggested—against the explicit advice of the local FBI—that they move the alleged assassin from the Dallas police station to the Dallas County Jail in order to give the newsmen a good story and pictures. Dallas FBI agent James Hosty always believed that Bloom and Ruby were in cahoots; when the police later searched Ruby's home, they found a slip of paper with Bloom's name, address and telephone number on it."[41]

The Hijacked Conspiracy

I cannot, in the scope of this chapter, tackle all the questions raised by Kennedy's assassination, nor mention all the hypotheses explored for fifty years.[42] What must be clarified here is Oswald's precise role in the plot. The real nature of his communist connections is unclear and probably ambivalent. Many testimonies from close friends and relatives indicate that Oswald had sincere sympathies for Marxism and for Castro's regime in Cuba, but there is also evidence that, on his return from the USSR in June 1962, he was hired by the FBI for undercover work in communist circles. It ultimately makes little difference; what is clear is that Oswald's communist connections were carefully monitored and recorded—for example, he was twice filmed handing out leaflets for the pro-Castro Fair Play for Cuba Committee in New Orleans—in order to be used on November 22, 1963, as his motive for shooting the president.

This raises the hypothesis that the assassination of Kennedy was designed as a false flag attack, meant to provide a false pretense for invading Cuba and overthrowing Castro, but that Johnson thwarted the second part of the plan. This is the thesis put forward by the majority of Kennedy conspiracy theorists, or at least by the most visible ones, such as James Douglass in *JFK and the Unspeakable* (2008): Kennedy, they say, fell victim to a plot by the anti-communist far-right in the military-intelligence complex with accomplices in the community of Cuban exiles.

---

[41] John Hughes-Wilson, *JFK-An American Coup d'État: The Truth Behind the Kennedy Assassination,* John Blake, 2014.
[42] Read my earlier book *JFK–9/11,* Progressive Press, 2014. My interpretation has changed on minor details.

James Douglass and like-minded researchers do indeed demonstrate convincingly that Kennedy was in conflict with the old guard of the CIA and the Pentagon, since he had spoiled the Bay of Pigs operation (April 1961) by refusing to involve US military units. Worse, he had negotiated a peaceful outcome to the Cuban Missile Crisis with Nikita Khrushchev (October 1962) by pledging to dismantle the American missiles in Turkey in exchange for the withdrawal of Soviet missiles in Cuba.

Some of those researchers never attempt to explain why, if the Dallas shooting was staged as a pretense for invading Cuba, that invasion never took place. Those who address the question, like James Douglass, credit Johnson with preventing the invasion. Johnson, we are led to understand, had nothing to do with the assassination plot, and thwarted the plotters' ultimate aim to start World War III. This is to ignore the huge amount of evidence gathered against Johnson for fifty years. It also begs another question: if Johnson resisted the hawks' pressure to invade Cuba, why did he escalate the Vietnam War? In late 1963, Kennedy had decided to evacuate all US military personnel in Vietnam (who amounted to only 15,000 "military advisors"). On November 11, he signed directive NSAM-263 for the removal of "1,000 U.S. military personnel by the end of 1963," in anticipation for withdrawing "by the end of 1965 [...] the bulk of U.S. personnel."[43] On November 21, the day before his fatal visit to Texas, he expressed his resolution to his assistant press secretary Malcolm Kilduff, after reading a report on the latest casualties: "After I come back from Texas, that's going to change. There's no reason for us to lose another man over there. Vietnam is not worth another American life."[44]

On November 26, the day after Kennedy's funeral, Johnson buried the NSAM-263 directive and replaced it with another, NSAM-273, which required the military to develop a plan "for the United States to begin carrying the war north," including "different levels of possible increased activity," and "military operations up to a line up to 50 kilometers inside Laos"—which

---

[43] On JFK Library, www.jfklibrary.org/
[44] Phillip Nelson, *LBJ: The Mastermind, op. cit.*, p. 638.

violated the 1962 Geneva Accords on the neutrality of Laos.[45] Johnson's decision regarding Vietnam was a clear betrayal of Kennedy's earlier policy, and the amazing expediency of his change of policy suggests premeditation. It has also been discovered that, in the weeks preceding the Kennedy assassination, Johnson and his business partners had invested heavily in the aircraft manufacturer Ling-Temco-Vought (LTV), founded by a close acquaintance of Johnson, James Ling, and headquartered in Dallas. In January 1964, LTV was to become one of the Pentagon's biggest arms suppliers for the Vietnam War.[46]

In my analysis, authors arguing for a conspiracy hatched within the US military-industrial-intelligence complex (let's call it the inside job thesis) prove convincingly that the leadership in the CIA and the Pentagon was desperately trying to start a war against Castro, and that they were prepared to deceive the president in order to do that. But they fail to demonstrate that they were prepared to assassinate the president: there is a huge difference between setting up a secret operation behind the president's back and committing high treason by murdering their own president.

One solution to the problem has been provided by the already-mentioned Gary Wean in his book *There's a Fish in the Courthouse* (1987), quoted by Michael Piper in his groundbreaking *Final Judgment*. Relying on a well-informed source in Dallas (identified as Republican Senator John Tower in his 1996 second edition), Wean raises the possibility that the Dallas coup was "a double-cross of fantastic dimensions," in which a failed assassination attempt staged by the CIA was hijacked by what he names the Mishpucka (Hebrew for "the Family"), the Russian Jewish Mafia, whose evil power reaching into the highest spheres Wean has been investigating for years in California. The Mishpucka wanted Kennedy dead and turned the operation into a successful assassination, then escaped investigation by hiding behind the CIA's scheme. JFK

---

[45] LBJ Library: www.lbjlib.utexas.edu/johnson/archives.hom/nsams/nsam273.asp.
[46] Joan Mellen, *A Farewell to Justice,* Potomac Books, 2007.

researcher Dick Russell has independently added weight to that theory by interviewing Cuban exiles who believe they were manipulated (*The Man Who Knew Too Much*, 1992).

The assumption is that the CIA and their Cuban exile associates intended to spare Kennedy's life but force him to retaliate against Castro. It was a false flag operation: Oswald, the patsy, had been groomed with the "legend" of a pro-Castro communist activist, to be sold to the public by news media on the day of the assassination. According to what Tower told Wean, "There was to be an attempt on the life of President Kennedy so 'realistic' that its failure would be looked upon as nothing less than a miracle. Footprints would lead right to Castro's doorstep, a trail that the rankest amateur could not lose."

Israel had no interest in Cuba but wanted Kennedy dead. So did Johnson. So they hijacked the operation, probably by providing the real snipers on the grassy knoll. The national security state was too deeply involved to be able to protest, and had to go along with its original plan to blame Oswald, knowing that if they tried to expose Israel's coup, they would be the first to be exposed.[47]

Several researchers have independently reached the same conclusion that a fake assassination attempt by CIA-led Cuban exiles was turned into a real assassination by a third party, but few succeeded—or, more probably, dared—to name that third party. They are mentioned by the late Michael Collins Piper. One of them was former CIA contract agent Robert Morrow in his 1976 novelized version of events, *Betrayal*. Another was longtime independent investigator Scott Thompson, who alleged that Howard Hunt was coordinating the fraudulent assassination attempt, but notes that "it remains unclear to this day who intervened into the dummy assassination set-up and turned it into the real thing." Veteran JFK investigator Dick Russell, in *The Man Who Knew Too Much*, has also pondered the possibility

---

[47] Michael Collins Piper, *Final Judgment: The Missing Link in the JFK Assassination Conspiracy*, American Free Press, 6th ed., 2005, pp. 290–297; *False Flags: Template for Terror*, American Free Press, 2013, p. 81; and Ch. 44 of Gary Wean, *There's a Fish in the Courthouse*, Casitas, 1987, www.kenrahn.com/JFK/Critical_Summaries/Articles/Wean_Chap_44.html.

that the CIA's relationship with Oswald was "usurped by another group," and noted: "Many people in the CIA had reasons to cover up their own relationship to Oswald, even if this had nothing to do with an assassination conspiracy. [...] what cannot be overlooked is that a third force was aware of the counterspy web [surrounding Oswald] and seized on it to their own advantage."[48]

Whether or not the CIA was implicated in a fake assassination attempt on Kennedy is, after all, secondary—for a person's or an organization's vulnerability to blackmail is proportional to the number of illegal activities he or it wants to keep secret, and no organization has more dirty secrets to hide than the CIA. By its privileged access to the media, the Zionist network had plenty of means of keeping the agency on the defensive.

The Mossad had also placed its mole, James Jesus Angleton, in a key position inside the CIA. Angleton was both the Mossad liaison for the CIA, as head of the CIA "Israel Office," and the chief of counterintelligence since 1954, which allowed him to conduct massive domestic spying on American citizens in collaboration with the Anti-Defamation League (ADL). Angleton played a key role in the cover-up after Kennedy's assassination as liaison between the CIA and the Warren Commission. But many prominent JFK investigators contend that Angleton also played a key role in setting up Oswald as the patsy in the first place. Professor John Newman writes in *Oswald and the CIA*: "In my view, whoever Oswald's direct handler or handlers were, we must now seriously consider the possibility that Angleton was probably their general manager. No one else in the Agency had the access, the authority, and the diabolically ingenious mind to manage this sophisticated plot. No one else had the means necessary to plant the WWIII virus in Oswald's files and keep it dormant for six weeks until the president's assassination. Whoever was ultimately responsible for the decision to kill Kennedy, their reach extended into the national intelligence apparatus to such a degree that they could call upon

---

[48] Michael Collins Piper, *False Flags, op. cit.*, pp. 85–87.

a person who knew its inner secrets and workings so well that he could design a failsafe mechanism into the fabric of the plot. The only person who could ensure a national security cover-up of an apparent counterintelligence nightmare was the head of counterintelligence."[49]

What Newman fails to notice, however, is that Angleton was more Mossad than CIA. He is actually the ultimate source of the conspiracy trail linking the CIA to the JFK assassination, by initiating and then leaking a secret CIA memorandum dated 1966 and intended for recently nominated CIA director Richard Helms, saying that CIA agent Howard Hunt was in Dallas on November 22, 1963, and that an alibi for him to be elsewhere "ought to be considered." This memo was given to the House Select Committee on Assassinations (HSCA), and simultaneously to reporters Joe Trento and Jacquie Powers, who reported it in the *Sunday News Journal,* on August 20, 1978. Trento subsequently revealed to JFK assassination investigator Dick Russell that it was Angleton himself who leaked the memo. Michael Collins Piper, who connected the dots, writes: "It is my contention that Angleton's conspiratorial activities in regard to the JFK assassination—including his singular involvement in circulating the 'Hunt in Dallas' story—unquestionably stem from Angleton's link to Israel and its role in the JFK assassination conspiracy."[50] Angleton's links to Israel were such that, according to his latest biographer, Michael Howard Holzman, "after his death, not one but two monuments to Angleton were dedicated at memorial services in Israel" during ceremonies attended by chiefs of Israeli intelligence and even a future prime minister.[51] Another biographer, Tom Mangold, states: "Angleton's closest professional friends overseas […] came from the Mossad and […] he was held in immense esteem

---

[49] Cited in Michael Collins Piper, *False Flags, op. cit.,* p. 78.
[50] Michael Collins Piper, *False Flags, op. cit.,* pp. 67–77.
[51] Michael Howard Holzman, *James Jesus Angleton, the CIA, and the Craft of Counterintelligence,* University of Massachusetts Press, 2008, p. 153.

by his Israeli colleagues and by the state of Israel, which was to award him profound honors after his death."[52]

The theory that the conspiracy trail leading to the anti-communist far right in Kennedy's assassination was planted deliberately by Israel's *sayanim* can explain a number of oddities in some of the clues. How else can we reasonably explain, for example, the full-page advertisement printed in the *Dallas Morning News* of November 22, bordered in black like a funeral notice and carrying the ironic bold headline "WELCOME, MR. KENNEDY TO DALLAS...," that accused the president of having betrayed the Cubans now "living in slavery"?[53] The veiled threat was authored by a nonexistent American Fact-Finding Committee.

How can any serious investigator take this at face value, and believe that a right-wing group planning to assassinate Kennedy in Dallas on November 22 would sign their crime in such a way, while at the same time trying to blame it on the communists? Yet this is exactly what most "inside job" theorists do. What they usually fail to mention is that the announcement was paid and even signed by a certain Bernard Weissman, a Jewish American who had moved to Dallas no sooner than the 4th of November, and who had been seen on the 14th in Jack Ruby's strip-tease bar the Carousel Club, in a two-hour meeting also attended by J. D. Tippit, the police officer who would be shot to death one hour after Kennedy, supposedly also by Oswald while resisting arrest.[54] The *Dallas Morning News* advertisement was not the only sign conspicuously posted to point to the anti-communist far right: on the same day, an infamous poster could be seen in the streets of Dallas, with Kennedy's photo under the headline "WANTED FOR TREASON."

While it massively supported the government thesis of the lone gunman, the mainstream media subtly fed suspicions directed at the CIA. For maximal efficiency, the expectation of a CIA coup was even planted into public opinion before the

---

[52] Tom Mangold, *Cold Warrior: James Jesus Angleton, the CIA's Master Spy Hunter*, Simon & Schuster, 1991.

[53] James Douglass, *JFK and the Unspeakable, op. cit.*, p. 361.

[54] "Bernard Weissman" on jfk.hood.edu and spartacus-educational.com.

assassination. This was done on October 2 with an article in the *Washington Daily News*, by an obscure Saigon correspondent named Richard Starnes, picked up the next day by the *New York Times*'s chief Washington correspondent Arthur Krock. The article denounced the CIA's "unrestrained thirst for power" and quoted an unnamed "very high official" who claimed that the White House could not control the CIA, and that: "If the United States ever experiences an attempt at a coup to overthrow the Government, it will come from the CIA and not the Pentagon. The agency represents a tremendous power and total unaccountability to anyone."[55] In such a way, the *New York Times* was planting a sign, a month and a half before the Dallas killing, pointing to the CIA as the most likely instigator of the upcoming coup. Most Kennedy researchers take this sign at face value, and even suggest that Kennedy had himself leaked his worries to the press as a warning to Americans. This, in spite of the fact that Kennedy "was so disturbed" by the article that he brought it up in the National Security Council the same day, asking advice about how to respond. "Kennedy decided to say nothing about the article, but it had shaken him," comments James Douglass.[56]

One month after Kennedy's assassination, it was the turn of the *Washington Post* to use a very similar trick, by publishing an op-ed signed by Harry Truman, in which the former president said he was "disturbed by the way CIA has been diverted from its original assignment. It has become an operational and at times a policy-making arm of the government." "I never had any thought when I set up the CIA that it would be injected into peacetime cloak and dagger operations," at the point of becoming across the globe "a symbol of sinister and mysterious foreign intrigue [...] there are now some searching questions that need to be answered."[57]

---

[55] "Assassination studies Kennedy knew a coup was coming," on YouTube.

[56] James Douglass, *JFK and the Unspeakable, op. cit.*, pp. 12–13 and 186–196; See also on educationforum.ipbhost.com/index.php?showtopic=7534.

[57] "Harry Truman Writes: Limit CIA Role to Intelligence," *Washington Post*, December 22, 1963, quoted in Mark Lane, *Last Word: My Indictment of the CIA in the Murder of JFK*, Skyhorse Publishing, 2011, p. 246.

Truman was hinting at the CIA's role in toppling foreign governments and assassinating elected leaders abroad. But given the timing of his article, one month to the day after Dallas, it could only be understood by anyone with ears to hear, and at least subliminally by the rest, as an indictment of the CIA in the Kennedy assassination. This article, widely reprinted in the 1970s after the creation of the Church Committee and the House Select Committee on Assassinations, is regarded as Truman's whistleblowing. Yet its *mea culpa* style is completely unlike Truman, and it was in fact not written by Truman, but by his longtime assistant and ghostwriter, David Noyes. Truman probably never saw it prior to its publication in the *Washington Post*'s morning edition, but he (and not the CIA) may be responsible for its deletion from the afternoon print runs.[58] Noyes's role as Truman's ghostwriter is documented in Sidney Krasnoff's book, *Truman and Noyes: Story of a President's Alter Ego* (Jonathan Stuart Press, 1997), which the publisher advertises as "an EXTRAORDINARY story of the relationship between a Missouri born Baptist, with no formal education beyond high school & a Russian born Jew with an eighth grade education."[59]

In the 70s, the mainstream media and publishing houses again played a major role in steering conspiracy theorists toward the CIA trail, while avoiding any hint of Israeli involvement. One major contributor to that effort was A. J. Weberman, with his 1975 book *Coup d'État in America: The CIA and the Assassination of John F. Kennedy*, co-authored by Michael Canfield. According to the New York *Jewish Daily Forward* (December 28, 2012), Weberman had "immigrated to Israel in 1959 and has dual American-Israeli citizenship," and is "a close associate of Jewish Defense Organization founder Mordechai Levy, whose fringe group is a spin-off of the late Rabbi Meir Kahane's militant right-wing Jewish Defense League." Weberman acknowledged Richard Perle's assistance in his investigation.[60] The Weberman-Canfield book contributed to the momentum

---

58 Thomas Troy, "Truman on CIA," September 22, 1993, on www.cia.gov.
59 Sidney Krasnoff, *Truman and Noyes: Story of a President's Alter Ego,* Jonathan Stuart Press, 1997, publisher's presentation.
60 Michael Collins Piper, *False Flags, op. cit.,* p. 67.

that led the House Select Committee on Assassinations (HSCA) to reinvestigate in 1976 the murders of JFK and Dr. Martin Luther King, while, in the wake of the Watergate scandal, the Senate had already formed the Select Committee to Study Governmental Operations with Respect to Intelligence Activities (known as the Church Committee).

It is also in this context that *Newsweek* journalist Edward Jay Epstein published in the *Reader's Digest* (then in his book *Legend: The Secret World of Lee Harvey Oswald*, 1978) an interview of George De Mohrenschildt, a Russian geologist and consultant to Texan oilmen, who had befriended Oswald and his Russian wife in Dallas in 1962. De Mohrenschildt admitted that Oswald was introduced to him at the instigation of Dallas CIA agent J. Walton Moore.[61] That piece of information is dubious for several reasons. First, Moore was officially FBI rather than CIA. Second, it rests on a printed interview given by De Mohrenschildt to journalist Edward Epstein a few hours before his death. So De Mohrenschildt was in no position to confirm or deny the words that Epstein ascribed to him. In fact, De Mohrenschildt's published interview contradicts his own manuscript account of his relationship to Oswald, revealed after his death.[62] Moreover, Epstein's main source for his book *Legend: The Secret World of Lee Harvey Oswald* (1978) is James Jesus Angleton, who was actively spreading disinformation at the time of the HSCA, defending the theory that Oswald was a KGB agent with CIA connections.

De Mohrenschildt's death was ruled a suicide. The Sherriff's report mentions that in his last months he complained that "the Jews" and "the Jewish mafia" were out to get him.[63] Needless to say, Epstein doesn't recall De Mohrenschildt mentioning this fear.

The "Jewish mafia" is taboo, in Kennedy research as well as in mainstream news. However, much has been said about the involvement of other "mafias": "MOBSTERS LINKED TO

---

[61] James Douglass, *JFK and the Unspeakable, op. cit.*, p. 46.
[62] George de Mohrenschildt, *I am a Patsy!* on jfkassassination.net/russ/jfkinfo4/jfk12/hscapatsy.htm.
[63] Read the Sheriff's Office report on mcadams.posc.mu.edu/death2.txt.

JFK DEATH," ran a *Washington Post* headline in 1977, after the HSCA report was released.[64] It is commonly admitted that Jack Ruby belonged to the underworld, but saying he belonged to the Jewish community is considered bad taste. His real name is hardly mentioned in the book by Jewish journalist Seth Kantor, *Who Was Jack Ruby?* (1978, retitled *The Ruby Cover-Up* in 1980). Note that Kantor, who was working for the *Dallas Times Herald* in 1963, had then given the Warren Commission false testimony about a conversation he had had with Ruby in front of Parkland Hospital in Dallas, where Kennedy had been taken, during which Ruby had appeared distressed by the death of his beloved president.[65]

All the above examples illustrate a fundamental principle of the propaganda destined to maintain Americans in the ignorance of the real nature of the forces that dominate the "deep state." This propaganda functions on two levels: on the surface is the official lie of the Warren Commission Report (Oswald the lone nut); below that are several lies or half-truths focusing on government and underworld complicity. The involvement of elements from the CIA, implicitly suggested by mainstream media and fully exploited by the controlled opposition, acts as a lure for all skeptics, and keeps most of the conspiracy sphere from going after Israel.

It is important to stress that investigators who focus their attention on the CIA and ignore Israel are not necessarily involved in conscious deception. I agree with Kevin Barrett that "a big part of this is the semi-conscious knowledge that if you 'go there' you will never get serious publishing and distribution." And in the early stage of the investigation, the CIA was the natural suspect for anybody considering the Warren Report as a fraud.

For some investigators, however, persistent self-deception may be linked to a deep-seated ethnic loyalty. It happens that the two most influential pioneers of JFK conspiracy theories are

---

[64] Gaeton Fonzi, *The Last Investigation: A Former Federal Investigator Reveals the Man Behind the Conspiracy to Kill JFK*, 1993, Skyhorse, 2013, k. 405–76.
[65] Listen to Kantor on YouTube, "Ruby at Parkland Hospital."

journalist Edward Jay Epstein with his book *Inquest* (1966), and lawyer Mark Lane (born Levin) with *Rush to Judgment* (1966), both indicting the CIA. They are the sole investigators mentioned in a "CIA Dispatch" dated January 1967, marked "PSYCH" and "Destroy when no longer needed," with the heading "RE: Concerning Criticism of the Warren Report." It is the earliest known use of the term "conspiracy theories," and it begins like this: "Conspiracy theories have frequently thrown suspicion on our organization, for example by falsely alleging that Lee Harvey Oswald worked for us. The aim of this dispatch is to provide material countering and discrediting the claims of the conspiracy theorists, so as to inhibit the circulation of such claims in other countries."[66] Indeed, years of reading through the whole spectrum of "JFK research" has convinced me that the evidence linking Oswald to the CIA is at best very weak, whereas there is hard evidence that he was on the payroll of the FBI. This is critically important for two reasons: first, it is well known that FBI and CIA have always been rivals (indeed, spying on each other); second, J. Edgar Hoover, the director of the FBI, was a longtime neighbor and friend of Johnson, and played a critical role in the JFK assassination cover-up by leaking his conclusions that Oswald acted alone even before the Warren Commission convened. (No one could contradict Hoover, who maintained himself at the head of the FBI for 48 years until his death at age 72, spanning nine presidents, thanks to his secrets files on just about everybody that counted in Washington.) This CIA Dispatch #1035–960 is important as the first government document mentioning "conspiracy theories" and as a propaganda program to discredit them. But it also shows that the CIA was forced to enter into damage control mode by dissenters such as Epstein and Lane who insisted on incriminating the CIA, while never mentioning evidence against Israel.

---

[66] CIA Dispatch #1035–960, on www.jfklancer.com/CIA.html, reproduced in Lance deHaven-Smith, *Conspiracy Theory in America*, University of Texas Press, 2013, kindle, k. 2785–2819.

That Israeli agents have been instrumental in spreading conspiracy theories targeting the CIA has become evident in regard to Oliver Stone's film *JFK* released in 1991. It starred Kevin Costner in the role of New Orleans District Attorney Jim Garrison, who opened an investigation into Kennedy's assassination in 1967. This film, which shook public opinion to the point of motivating the President John F. Kennedy Assassination Records Collection Act of 1992, was produced by Arnon Milchan, described in a 2011 biography as being from his youth "one of the most important covert agents that Israeli intelligence has ever fielded," involved in arms smuggling from the US to Israel.[67] In 2013 Milchan publicly revealed his extended activity as a secret agent of Israel, working in particular to boost Israel's nuclear program.[68]

It is therefore no wonder that Stone's film gives no hint of the Mossad connection that Garrison stumbled upon. So it appears that the confrontation between the official theory and the inside-job conspiracy theory is largely staged by Zionist interests, or at least serves the interest of Israel by keeping the public's attention away from any thought of Israeli participation. At the same time, the half-truth of the CIA's involvement serves as a constant threat of blackmail against American institutions, forcing the state to defend tooth and nail its impossible theory (magic bullet and all), knowing full well that, if this cover-up is ever revealed, it will be the first to be exposed (for both the operation and its cover-up). Such is the general operating mode by which Israel controls the US: it implicates elements of the US government in its black operations, in order to involve them in the cover-up, as the Zionist-controlled mainstream media serves as a sword of Damocles hanging over their heads.

The same strategy, of playing one lie against another in order to obscure the real issue, has been applied twice in the Kennedy affair. This was, in the very early stage, the strategy employed by Lyndon Johnson and his accomplice Edgar Hoover: while

---

[67] Meir Doron, *Confidential: The Life of Secret Agent Turned Hollywood Tycoon – Arnon Milchan*, Gefen Books, 2011, p. xi.

[68] Stuart Winer, "Hollywood producer Arnon Milchan reveals past as secret agent," *Times of Israel*, November 25, 2013, on www.timesofisrael.com.

Johnson was circulating within the government the dangerous theory of a communist plot, Hoover spread to the public, as a lid on this bombshell, the reassuring thesis of the lone gunman. The rumor of the communist plot was used as the argument to convince federal and state officials to settle for the lone nut theory as the public version, in the name of the national interest and for the sake of world peace (while the thesis of the communist plot occasionally resurfaces).[69] Once the risk of triggering a world war had disappeared, the conspiracy theory of the CIA plot took on the function of the new dangerous thesis that had to be smothered, lest the fire of popular outrage lead to a major crisis. The CIA theory invaded popular culture in the 70s, together with other false leads such as the mafia theory.

Besides this method of "triangulation," which consists of one camp staging a fight between two other camps while remaining invisible, the general strategy of controlled opposition can be summarized as "contain and contaminate." First, contain public opinion within strict limits to prevent Israeli involvement from ever being mentioned. Second, contaminate public opinion by a variety of false leads that, by their sheer number, generate a sort of learned helplessness, the sense that "the truth will never be known." And finally, promote the most bizarre theories that serve as a scarecrow to keep reasonable people away from alternative theories in general.

To summarize, a triple lie has been woven around the Kennedy assassination, each lie corresponding to a fake Oswald: there is the lone-nut Oswald, the Castro-agent Oswald, and the CIA-asset Oswald. None of them is the real Oswald, who has no relevance to the case anyway. So any investigation that focuses on Oswald is bound to lose itself in one of these three false trails. Even the CIA asset Oswald is largely bogus, since in reality, Oswald's connections to the world of intelligence and espionage mostly involved the Navy. Oswald was a Marine, and it was under the Secretary of the Navy John Connally that he was sent into Russia as a false deserter. Before that, he had been

---

[69] For example Gus Russo, *Live by the Sword: The Secret War Against Castro and the Death of JFK*, Bancroft Press, 1998.

based in Atsugi in Japan with the ONI (Office of Naval Intelligence). The ONI is the oldest American intelligence service (founded in 1881), the first to practice domestic surveillance, and the first to develop a relationship with organized crime, as documented by Professor Jeffrey Dorwart in his two-volume history of the ONI (Naval Institute Press, 1983).

In New Orleans, Oswald kept his post office box in the same building where the ONI had its local office. But while the CIA has always taken the heat for the assassination of President Kennedy, the ONI has managed to escape publicity. When CIA Director Richard Helms was asked by the HSCA about their interest in Oswald after his defection, he said that "it would have been considered a Navy matter," and recommended they talk to ONI Director Rufus Taylor—who happened to have died two weeks earlier. No wonder the Assassination Records Review Board, formed in the 1990s to reinvestigate Kennedy's murder, said in a final 236-page report that "the Office of Naval Intelligence (ONI) was described as a puzzle, if not a black hole." Johnson's close ties with the Navy are certainly not unrelated to this black hole.[70]

For fifty years, the Israeli trail in the Kennedy assassination has been covered up, and anyone who dares mention it is immediately ostracized from the community of respectable Kennedy conspiracy theorists. American congressman Paul Findley nevertheless had the courage to write in March 1992 in the *Washington Report on Middle East Affairs*: "It is interesting to note that in all the words written and uttered about the Kennedy assassination, Israel's intelligence agency, the Mossad, has never been mentioned." One single author has seriously examined the case against the Israeli underworld: Michael Collins Piper, in his 1995 book *Final Judgment: The Missing Link in the JFK Assassination Conspiracy*. Piper has been treated like the plague ever since. But his work has grown in influence. In 2013, in his edition of Kennedy's letters, including those to Ben-Gurion about Dimona, Martin Sandler writes of Piper's work: "Of all the

---

[70] jfkcountercoup.blogspot.fr/2011/10/oni-assassination-of-president-kennedy.html.

conspiracy theories, it remains one of the most intriguing."[71]
The Libyan leader Muammar Gaddafi should be counted among
those convinced by Piper. He declared in 2008: "Kennedy
decided to monitor the Dimona nuclear plant. He insisted on
doing so, in order to determine whether or not it produced
nuclear weapons. The Israelis refused, but he insisted. This crisis
was resolved with the resignation of Ben-Gurion. He resigned
so he would not have to agree to the monitoring of the Dimona
plant, and he gave the green light for the killing of Kennedy.
Kennedy was killed because he insisted on the monitoring of the
Dimona plant."[72] On September 23, 2009, Gaddafi had the guts
to demand a new investigation in a speech to the General
Assembly of the United Nations.[73]

Johnson, a "Jewish President"?

The assassination of President Kennedy was a hidden coup
d'état meant to replace an independent government with a
government subservient to Israel's interests. From the very next
day, all of Kennedy's policies hostile to Israel's agenda were
reversed, without the American people having the slightest idea
of what was going on. The American Zionist Council escaped
foreign agent status by renaming itself the American Israel
Public Affairs Committee (AIPAC). The consequence was that,
by 1973, as Senator William Fulbright would remark on CBS,
"Israel controls the Senate, [...] anything Israel wants, Israel
gets."[74]

Kennedy's death relieved Israel of all pressure (diplomatic or
otherwise) to stop its nuclear program, or even to be forced to
acknowledge it. Historian Stephen Green tells it better: "Perhaps
the most significant development of 1963 for the Israeli nuclear
weapons program, however, occurred on November 22: On a
plane flying from Dallas to Washington, D.C., Lyndon Johnson
was sworn in as the 36th President of the United States,

---

[71] Martin W. Sandler (ed.), *The Letters of John F. Kennedy*, Bloomsbury, 2013.
[72] YouTube, "Gaddafi says JFK assassinated by Israel."
[73] YouTube, "Gaddafi calls for investigation into JFK/MLK assassinations."
[74] Quoted in Paul Findley, *They Dare to Speak Out: People and Institutions Confront Israel's Lobby*, Lawrence Hill Books, 2003 (archive.org), p. 95.

following the assassination of John F. Kennedy." Green explains further: "In the early years of the Johnson administration the Israeli nuclear weapons program was referred to in Washington as 'the delicate topic.' Lyndon Johnson's White House saw no Dimona, heard no Dimona, and spoke no Dimona when the reactor went critical in early 1964."[75]

Faced with Johnson's complete lack of interest in that issue, John McCone resigned from the CIA in 1965: "When I cannot get the President to read my reports, then it's time to go." Israel acquired its first nuclear bomb around 1967, and the public had to wait until 1986 to know about it, thanks to the publication in the *Sunday Times* of photographs taken by Israeli technician Mordechai Vanunu inside the Dimona complex. (Vanunu was abducted by the Mossad, convicted of treason in Israel, and imprisoned for 18 years, including 11 in solitary confinement).

Under Johnson, military aid to Israel reached $92 million in 1966, more than the total of all previous years combined. Johnson even allowed the delivery of Phantom missiles capable of carrying nuclear warheads. As for US foreign policy, it took a decidedly pro-Israel turn, under the supervision of Myer Feldman, now promoted special counsel for the Middle East, with the help of Walt and Eugene Rostow, also sons of Jewish immigrants (the first acting as special counsel for national security, the second as under-secretary of state).[76]

In 2013, the Associated Press reported on newly released tapes from Johnson's White House office showing LBJ's "personal and often emotional connection to Israel." The tapes showed that during the Johnson presidency, "the United States became Israel's chief diplomatic ally and primary arms supplier." An article from the *5 Towns Jewish Times* "Our First Jewish President Lyndon Johnson?" recalls Johnson's continuous support of Jews and Israel in the 1940s and 50s, then his role in the crafting of pro-Israel UN Resolution 242 in November 1967. It concludes: "President Johnson firmly pointed American

---

[75] Stephen Green, *Taking Sides: America's Secret Relations With a Militant Israel*, William Morrow & Co., 1984, p. 166.
[76] Alan Hart, *Zionism: The Real Enemy of the Jews*, vol. 3: *Conflict Without End?*, Clarity Press, 2010, pp. 21–22.

policy in a pro-Israel direction. In historical context, the American emergency airlift to Israel in 1973, the constant diplomatic support, the economic and military assistance and the strategic bonds between the two countries can all be credited to the seeds planted by LBJ."

The article also mentions that "research into Johnson's personal history indicates that he inherited his concern for the Jewish people from his family. His aunt Jessie Johnson Hatcher, a major influence on LBJ, was a member of the Zionist Organization of America." And, in an additional note: "The facts indicate that both of Lyndon Johnson's great-grandparents, on the maternal side, were Jewish. [...] The line of Jewish mothers can be traced back three generations in Lyndon Johnson's family tree. There is little doubt that he was Jewish."[77] Johnson, the son of Rebekah Baines and Samuel Johnson, and grandson by his mother of Ruth Huffman, attributed his philo-Semitism to a family inheritance: "Take care of the Jews, 'God's Chosen People.' Consider them your friends and help them any way you can," he remembered his grandfather saying.[78] His wife, known as Lady Bird, would later testify: "Jews have been woven into the warp and woof of all his years." And is not Johnson the only American president ever to have inaugurated a synagogue—in Austin, a month after becoming President?[79] So there is ample ground for believing that Johnson was some kind of crypto-Jew. In any case, there can hardly be any doubt that he was a crypto-Zionist.

With Johnson in control of the White House, Israel could resume its plan of expansion without fear of US interference. Johnson ignored all of Khrushchev's overtures to pursue the peace process he had started with Kennedy, thus making sure the Cold War would continue to provide the necessary context

---

[77] Morris Smith, "Our First Jewish President Lyndon Johnson? – an update!!," *5 Towns Jewish Times*, April 11, 2013, on 5tjt.com.

[78] James Smallwood, "Operation Texas: Lyndon B. Johnson, The Jewish Question and the Nazi Holocaust," *East Texas Historical Journal*, vol. 50, 2, p. 89, on scholarworks.sfasu.edu/ethj.

[79] "Lyndon B. Johnson – A Righteous Gentile," lyndonjohnsonandisrael.blogspot.fr; Seymour Hersh, *The Samson Option, op. cit.*, p. 127.

for America's support of Israel's aggression against Egypt. Military involvement in Vietnam, which Kennedy had decided to reduce leading toward full withdrawal by 1965, was instead escalated by Johnson for that very purpose (and for the profit of the military-industrial complex, in which Johnson invested heavily).

In 1967 Israel tripled its area in less than a week, extending to the south, north, and east. It amputated the Gaza Strip and Sinai from Egypt, the Golan Heights from Syria, and the West Bank and East Jerusalem from Jordan. Having learned the lesson of its failure in 1956, Israel succeeded in creating the illusion that it was acting in self-defense. By poisoning Soviet espionage with false communications, Israel incited Nasser to begin troop movements in Sharm el-Sheikh near the Israeli border. On May 27, 1967, Nasser blocked access to the Straits of Tiran, cutting the Israeli Navy's access to the Red Sea. Israeli propaganda, disseminated in the United States, cast these defensive movements as preparations for aggression, justifying a preventive attack by Israel.

Such propaganda could not deceive American intelligence. But Johnson had given Israel a green light in a letter to Israeli Prime Minister Levi Eshkol, dated June 3: "I want to protect the territorial integrity of Israel […] and will provide as effective American support as possible to preserve the peace and freedom of your nation and of the area."[80] Johnson also asked the CIA to transmit to the Israeli army the precise positions of the Egyptian air bases to be destroyed.

Four days after the start of the Israeli attack, Nasser accepted the ceasefire request from the UN Security Council. It was too soon for Israel, which had not yet achieved all its objectives. It was then that, on June 8, 1967, the USS Liberty, an NSA spy ship, easily recognizable by its large American flag, covered by radar antennae and unarmed, was stationed in international waters off Sinai. For seventy-five minutes, the ship was bombed, strafed, and torpedoed by Israeli Mirage jets and three torpedo boats, with the obvious intention of sinking it

---

[80] State Department Archive: 2001-2009.state.gov/r/pa/ho/frus/johnsonlb/xix/28057.htm.

without leaving any survivors. (Even the lifeboats were machine-gunned.)

The spy activity of the USS Liberty, some analysts say, was to ensure that Israel would not go beyond the secret US permission to invade Sinai. But the Israeli military hierarchy, and Moshe Dayan in particular, intended to take full advantage of the situation, and as soon as the fighting in Egypt ceased, it redeployed its troops to the north to annex Syrian and Jordanian territories. The attack on the USS Liberty therefore had two objectives: it sought to neutralize US surveillance and with it the American ability to interfere; but it was also conceived as a false flag operation that would have been blamed on Egypt if it had succeeded, that is, if the ship had been sunk and its crew exterminated. Testimonials indicate that Johnson supported this option by intervening personally to prohibit the nearby Sixth Fleet from rescuing the USS Liberty after the crew, despite the initial destruction of its transmitters, had managed to send off an SOS. Everything suggests that the attack on the USS Liberty had been secretly authorized by the White House. Had the subterfuge of blaming the Egyptians worked, the United States would have used the pretext to intervene militarily alongside Israel, probably forcing the USSR to go to war.[81]

The USS Liberty affair was suppressed by a commission of inquiry headed by Admiral John Sidney McCain II, commander-in-chief of US Naval forces in Europe (and father of Arizona Senator John McCain III). The survivors received a medal in an unadvertised ceremony, accompanied by a formal order never to mention the incident. Only recently have some broken the silence.[82]

Johnson accepted Israel's spurious "targeting error" explanation. In January 1968 he invited the Israeli prime minister, Levi Eshkol, to Washington, and warmly welcomed him to his Texas ranch. What's more, Johnson rewarded Israel by lifting the embargo on offensive military equipment: US-

---

[81] Robert Allen, *Beyond Treason: Reflections on the Cover-up of the June 1967 Israeli Attack on the USS Liberty, an American Spy Ship*, CreateSpace, 2012.
[82] Watch the 2014 Al-Jazeera documentary *The Day Israel Attacked America*.

made tanks and aircraft immediately flowed to Tel Aviv. Under Nixon, military sales would reach $600 million in 1971 and $3 billion two years later, making Israel the biggest customer of the US defense industry.

At the end of the Six-Day War, Moscow contented itself with protesting against Israel's annexation of new territories by breaking diplomatic relations with Tel Aviv and stopping the emigration of its Jewish citizens, which had been accelerating in the previous months. The UN Security Council condemned Israel's "acquisition of territory by war" and called for "withdrawal of Israel armed forces from territories occupied in the recent conflict." This Resolution 242, which has since been frequently invoked in the peace negotiations in the Middle East, has still not been enforced.

On November 27, 1967, faced with Israel's refusal to comply, De Gaulle denounced in a press conference Israel's illegal occupation of the territories, "which cannot go without oppression, repression, expulsions. [. . .] Unless the UN itself tore up its own charter, a settlement must be based on the evacuation of the occupied territories." Some believe that this de Gaulle statement (accompanied by his famous description of the Jewish people as "cocky and domineering") was not unrelated to the destabilization of his government in May 1968, carried out mainly by Trotskyites with the main agitator being Daniel Cohn-Bendit.[83]

It bears repeating that the Cold War provided the indispensable context for the Israeli conquest of new territories and the accompanying ethnic cleansing, expanding Israel's borders and weakening its Arab enemies. Without the Cold War and its propaganda of fear and hatred, there would have been no chance of convincing the American people that Israel was their ally and Nasser their enemy. If we admit that this enterprise had been long premeditated, we may understand that Israel had a major reason to eliminate Kennedy, in addition to those already mentioned: with Kennedy re-elected in November 1964, and

---

[83] On the Jewish-led student uprising in Paris in 1968, read Yair Auron, *Les Juifs d'extrême gauche en Mai 68,* Albin Michel, 1998.

Khrushchev simultaneously in power in the USSR, the end of
the Cold War loomed before 1968. The monstrous absurdity of
the Vietnam War, which had no other purpose than to prolong
and intensify this global conflict, would never have taken place.[84]
With Kennedy and Khrushchev in office, given what is known
today of their secret rapprochement, Israel had no chance of
accomplishing the tripling of its territory resulting from the Six-
Day War. Khrushchev, let us not forget, was the architect of de-
Stalinization and the subsequent "thaw." He rehabilitated many
political prisoners, such as Alexander Solzhenitsyn, whom he
authorized to publish his first famous work, *A Day in the Life of
Ivan Denisovich* (1962). Bill Walton remembers that on November
19, 1963, after signing the first Nuclear Test-Ban Treaty,
Kennedy declared that "he intended to be the first President of
the United States to visit the Kremlin as soon as he and
Khrushchev reached another arms control agreement."[85]
Kennedy died three days later. Khrushchev, who was in the
same position as Kennedy in relation to his hawkish advisors,
lost his meager support. He was overthrown in 1964, his
country plunged back into the cold, and Solzhenitsyn was again
censured.

On August 7, 1970, Mark Lane wrote an article for the *Los
Angeles Free Press* entitled "CIA Killed JFK to Keep War
Going."[86] This cannot be true. Neither the CIA nor the
Pentagon wanted to "keep the war going." What the hawks
wanted was to quickly end the war by a full-scale American
victory. If there was one country that had an interest in keeping
and maximizing the tension while avoiding a decisive clash, it
was clearly Israel.

Serial Assassinations

On April 4, 1968, Reverend Martin Luther King Jr. was killed in
circumstances not unlike those surrounding the murder of the

---

[84] Watch the "alternate history" film by Koji Masutani, *Virtual JFK: Vietnam If Kennedy
Had Lived*, 2009.
[85] Douglass, *JFK and the Unspeakable, op. cit.*, p. 378.
[86] Michael Collins Piper, *False Flags, op. cit.*, p. 173.

late President Kennedy. The name, portrait, and profile of the alleged lone sniper were broadcast almost instantly. As William Pepper, King's friend and attorney, has shown in *An Act of State: The Execution of Martin Luther King* (2003), the mentally deficient James Earl Ray had been handled by some unidentified "Raul" (possibly connected to Jack Ruby), who had arranged for his housing in a room overlooking King's balcony at the Lorraine Motel in Memphis, and for a gun to be found under his window with his fingerprints on it. The lawyer appointed to defend Ray had no trouble convincing him to plead guilty in hopes of receiving leniency from the court. Nobody paid attention when Ray recanted three days later, maintaining his innocence thereafter until his death in 1998. Reverend King had embarrassed Johnson's government through his stance against the Vietnam War, and further through his project to gather "a multiracial army of the poor" in a "Poor People's Campaign" that would march on Washington and camp on Capitol Hill until Congress signed a "Declaration of the Human Rights of the Poor."

Since it is seldom pointed out, it is worth emphasizing that King had also strongly disappointed the Jewish-Zionist community, who felt he had never paid back an important debt. King had received strong support—in money, legal advice, media coverage, and other areas—from American Jews, leading to his receiving the Nobel Peace Prize in 1964. Many Jews had helped organize his march on Washington, DC, which culminated in his famous "I have a dream" speech of August 28, 1963, in front of the Lincoln Memorial. As Seth Berkman recalled on the fortieth anniversary of that historic landmark: "Arnie Aronson was a little-known but crucial organizer; Rabbi Uri Miller recited the opening prayer; Rabbi Joachim Prinz delivered a stirring speech just before King's historic words." It was the same Joachim Prinz who had in 1934 applauded the Nazi state for being "built upon the principle of the purity of nation and race," now claiming that Jews have always taught "that when God created man, he created him as everybody's neighbor."[87]

In return for their support, Zionists expected from King some friendly gesture toward Israel. He was officially invited more than once to Israel, but always politely declined ("too busy"). According to *Haaretz*, "Documents that have come to light 45 years after the assassination of Martin Luther King Jr. show Israel's efforts to woo the civil rights leader—a campaign that never came to fruition."[88] After 1967, black nationalists, such as SNCC's leadership, became increasingly critical of Israel. There was a rift within the civil rights movement, many resenting the disproportionate presence of Jews. King's visit to Israel would have broken the movement apart. Whether or not King was assassinated for failing to pay his debt, it is a matter of record that, after his death, Zionists abused his legacy by pretending he had expressed support for Israel in a letter written to an anti-Zionist friend, containing the following passage: "You declare, my friend; that you do not hate the Jews, you are merely 'anti-Zionist' [...]. And I say, let the truth ring forth from the high mountain tops, let it echo through the valleys of God's green earth: When people criticize Zionism, they mean Jews [...]. Anti-Semitism, the hatred of the Jewish people, has been and remains a blot on the soul of mankind. In this we are in full agreement. So know also this: Anti-Zionist is inherently anti-Semitic, and ever will be so."

This letter is a hoax. It first appeared in the book *Shared Dreams: Martin Luther King, Jr. & the Jewish Community* by Rabbi Marc Schneier (1999), an attempt to fight against rising black anti-Semitism, naively forwarded by Dr. King's son, Martin Luther King III. Although fully proven fake, it has since been reprinted in many books and web pages. The Anti-Defamation League's Michael Salberg used that very quote in his July 31, 2001, testimony before the US House of Representatives

---

[87] Seth Berkman, "The Jews Who Marched on Washington With Martin Luther King," Forward.com, August 27, 2013, on forward.com. Prinz's speech is on www.joachimprinz.com/images/mow.mp3.

[88] Ofer Aderet, "How Martin Luther King Jr. avoided visiting Israel," *Haaretz*, February 23, 2013.

International Relations Committee's Subcommittee on International Operations and Human Rights.[89] And so King provided, once dead, the very support to Israel that he had always refused to give when alive.

Two months after King's death, it was the turn of Robert Kennedy, John's younger brother and former attorney general— and a strong supporter of King—to be assassinated in a still more bizarre way. On March 16, 1968, Robert had announced his candidacy for the presidency. All those who had mourned John found hope that Robert would regain control of the White House and, from there, reopen the investigation into his brother's death. He was assassinated on June 6 in Los Angeles, just after winning the California primaries and thereby becoming the most likely Democratic candidate. The presumed assassin, Sirhan Sirhan, has always claimed, and continues to claim, that he has never had any recollection of his act: "I was told by my attorney that I shot and killed Senator Robert F. Kennedy and that to deny this would be completely futile, [but] I had and continue to have no memory of the shooting of Senator Kennedy." He also claims to have no memory of "many things and incidents which took place in the weeks leading up to the shooting."[90]

Psychiatric expertise, including lie-detector tests, have confirmed that Sirhan's amnesia is not faked. In 2008, Harvard University professor Daniel Brown, a noted expert in hypnosis and trauma-induced memory loss, interviewed Sirhan for a total of sixty hours, and concluded that Sirhan, who belongs to the category of "high hypnotizables," acted involuntarily under the effect of hypnotic suggestion: "His firing of the gun was neither under his voluntary control, nor done with conscious knowledge, but is likely a product of automatic hypnotic behavior and coercive control." During his sessions with Dr. Brown, Sirhan could remember having been accompanied by a sexy woman, before suddenly finding himself at a shooting

[89] Fadi Kiblawi and Will Youmans, "Israel's apologists and the Martin Luther King Jr. hoax," January 18, 2004, on electronicintifada.net.
[90] Frank Morales, "The Assassination of RFK: A Time for Justice!," June 16, 2012, on www.globalresearch.ca; YouTube, "Sirhan Sirhan Denied Parole."

range. According to Brown, "Mr. Sirhan did not go with the intent to shoot Senator Kennedy, but did respond to a specific hypnotic cue given to him by that woman to enter 'range mode,' during which Mr. Sirhan automatically and involuntarily responded with a 'flashback' that he was shooting at a firing range at circle targets." Months after Sirhan recalled these details, Dr. William Pepper found an entry in the police file that showed that Sirhan had visited a police firing range and signed the register just days before the assassination. He was handled by a man who did not sign the register.[91]

Available information is too sketchy to reconstitute entirely how Sirhan was programmed. We know that he had been treated by a neurosurgeon after a head injury, after which his behavior had changed, according to his mother. We also know he was interested in occultism and attended the Rosicrucian order AMORC, founded by Spencer Lewis. Sirhan may have fallen into the hands of an agent working for CIA MKUltra projects, supervised by the infamous Dr. Sidney Gottlieb (not a Nazi doctor, incidentally, but the son of Hungarian Jews whose real name was Joseph Scheider). Under Gottlieb's supervision, teams working on a research project named Bluebird had to answer such questions as: "Can a person under hypnosis be forced to commit murder?" according to a document dated May 1951.[92]

One person who may have been involved in Sirhan's programming, and who reportedly bragged about it to two prostitutes, is famed hypnotist Dr. William Joseph Bryan Jr. Bryan makes no secret of having worked for the Air Force in the "brainwashing section." His biggest claim to fame, which he bragged about all the time, was how he had hypnotized the Boston Strangler, Albert Di Salvo, into confessing to the crime. In the notebook found at his home, Sirhan Sirhan had written, in the same style reminiscent of automatic writing as other

---

[91] Jacqui Goddard, "Sirhan Sirhan, assassin of Robert F. Kennedy, launches new campaign for freedom 42 years later," *The Telegraph*, December 3, 2011, on www.telegraph.co.uk/search/.

[92] Colin Ross, *Bluebird: Deliberate Creation of Multiple Personality by Psychiatrists*, Manitou Communications, 2000, summary on www.wanttoknow.info/bluebird10pg.

incriminating words: "God help me . . . please help me. Salvo Di Di Salvo Die S Salvo." It is surmised he heard the name while under hypnosis.[93]

Other pages of the same notebook, which Sirhan recognizes as his own handwriting but does not remember writing, are also reminiscent of automatic writing: "My determination to eliminate R.F.K. is becoming more the more of an unshakable obsession . . . R.F.K. must die RFK must be killed. Robert F. Kennedy must be assassinated R.F.K. must be assassinated . . . R.F.K. must be assassinated assassinated . . . Robert F. Kennedy must be assassinated before 5 June 68 Robert F. Kennedy must be assassinated I have never heard please pay to the order of of of of of."[94]

Besides the question of Sirhan's programming, there are serious ballistic and forensic contradictions in the official explanation of Kennedy's murder. Evidence suggests that, in fact, none of Sirhan's bullets hit Kennedy. According to the autopsy report of Chief Medical Examiner-Coroner Dr. Thomas T. Noguchi, Robert Kennedy died of a gunshot wound to the brain, fired from behind the right ear at point blank range, following an upward angle. Noguchi restated his conclusion in his 1983 memoirs, *Coroner,* and his conclusion has been backed by other professionals. Yet the sworn testimony of twelve shooting witnesses established that Robert had never turned his back on Sirhan and that Sirhan was five to six feet away from his target when he fired. Moreover, Sirhan was physically overpowered by Karl Uecker after his second shot, and, although he continued pressing the trigger mechanically, his revolver was then not directed toward Kennedy. Tallying all the bullet impacts in the pantry, and those that wounded five people around Kennedy, shows that at least twelve bullets were fired, while Sirhan's gun carried only eight. On April 23, 2011, attorneys William Pepper and his associate, Laurie Dusek, gathered all this evidence and more in a 58-page file submitted

[93] William Turner and John Christian, *The Assassination of Robert F. Kennedy: The Conspiracy and Cover-up* (1978), Basic Books, 2006, pp. 225–229.
[94] Shane O'Sullivan, *Who Killed Bobby? The Unsolved Murder of Robert F. Kennedy,* Union Square Press, 2008, pp. 5, 44, 103.

to the Court of California, asking that Sirhan's case be reopened. They documented major irregularities in the 1968 trial, including the fact that laboratory tests showed the fatal bullet had not been shot from Sirhan's revolver, but from another gun with a different serial number; thus, instead of incriminating Sirhan, the ballistic test in fact should have proved him innocent. Pepper has also provided a computer analysis of audio recordings during the shooting, made by engineer Philip Van Praag in 2008, which confirms that two guns are heard.[95]

There are strong suspicions that the second shooter was Thane Eugene Cesar, a security guard hired for the evening, who was behind Kennedy at the time of shooting, and seen with his pistol drawn by several witnesses, one of whom, Don Schulman, positively saw him fire. Cesar was never investigated, even though he did not conceal his hatred for the Kennedys, who according to him had "sold the country down the road to the commies."[96]

Just hours after Robert's assassination, the press was able to inform the American people not only of the identity of the assassin, but also his motive, and even his detailed biography. Twenty-four-year-old Sirhan Bishara Sirhan was born in Jordan and had moved to the United States when his family was expelled from West Jerusalem in 1948. After the shooting, a newspaper clipping was found in Sirhan's pocket, quoting favorable comments made by Robert regarding Israel and, in particular, what sounded like an electoral commitment: "The United States should without delay sell Israel the 50 Phantom jets she has so long been promised." Handwritten notes by Sirhan found in a notebook at his home confirmed that his act had been premeditated and motivated by hatred of Israel. Jerry Cohen of the *Los Angeles Times* wrote, in a front page article on

---

[95] Frank Morales, "The Assassination of RFK: A Time for Justice!" June 16, 2012, on www.globalresearch.ca; watch on YouTube, "RFK Assassination 40th Anniversary (2008) Paul Schrade on CNN."

[96] Philip Melanson, *The Robert F. Kennedy Assassination: New Revelations on the Conspiracy And Cover-Up*, S.P.I. Books, 1994, p. 25. For a full overview, watch Shane O'Sullivan's 2007 investigative documentary *RFK Must Die: The Assassination of Bobby Kennedy*, or read his book *Who Killed Bobby? The Unsolved Murder of Robert F. Kennedy*, Union Square Press, 2008. See also Don Schulman's testimony in *The Second Gun* (1973), from 42 min.

June 6, that Sirhan is "described by acquaintances as a 'virulent' anti-Israeli," (Cohen changed that into "virulent anti-Semite" in an article for the *Salt Lake Tribune*), and that: "Investigation and disclosures from persons who knew him best revealed [him] as a young man with a supreme hatred for the state of Israel." Cohen infers that "Senator Kennedy […] became a personification of that hatred because of his recent pro-Israeli statements." Cohen further learned from Los Angeles Mayor Samuel Yorty that: "About three weeks ago the young Jordanian refugee accused of shooting Sen. Robert Kennedy wrote a memo to himself, […] The memo said: 'Kennedy must be assassinated before June 5, 1968'—the first anniversary of the Six-Day War in which Israel humiliated three Arab neighbors, Egypt, Syria and Jordan." In a perhaps cryptic final note, Cohen cited Prof. Joseph Eliash of UCLA, who remarked that "his middle name, Bashara, means 'good news'."[97]

In 2008, on the occasion of the 40th anniversary of Bobby's assassination, this tragic day was installed into the post-9/11 mythology of the Clash of Civilizations and the War on Terror. The *Jewish Daily Forward* wrote: "One cannot help but note the parallel between Kennedy's assassination and the terrorist attacks of September 11, 2001. In both tragic cases, Arab fanaticism reared its ugly head on American soil, irrevocably changing the course of events in this country." "Robert Kennedy was the first American victim of modern Arab terrorism." "Sirhan hated Kennedy because he had supported Israel." Writing for the *Boston Globe*, Sasha Issenberg recalled that the death of Robert Kennedy was "a first taste of Mideast terror." He quotes Harvard professor Alan Dershowitz, a former volunteer in Robert Kennedy's campaign (better known as Jonathan Pollard's lawyer), reflecting: "I thought of it as an act of violence motivated by hatred of Israel and of anybody

---

[97] Jerry Cohen, "Yorty Reveals That Suspect's Memo Set Deadline for Death," *Los Angeles Times*, June 6, 1968, pp. 1 and 12, on latimesblogs.latimes.com/thedailymirror /2008/06/june-6-1968.html. Jerry Cohen, "Jerusalem-Born Suspect Called An Anti-Semite," *Salt Lake Tribune*, June 6, 1968, on www.newspapers.com. See also Harry Rosenthal, "Senator Kennedy's support for Israel promoted decision declares Sirhan," *The Telegraph*, March 5, 1969, on news.google.com.

who supported Israel," "It was in some ways the beginning of Islamic terrorism in America. It was the first shot. A lot of us didn't recognize it at the time."[98] The fact that Sirhan was from a Christian family was lost on Dershowitz, who speaks of "Islamic terrorism." But the *Jewish Forward* took care to specify Sirhan's faith, only to add that Islam ran in his veins anyway: "But what he shared with his Muslim cousins—the perpetrators of September 11—was a visceral, irrational hatred of Israel. It drove him to murder a man whom some still believe might have been the greatest hope of an earlier generation."[99]

For the *Jewish Forward,* it seems, the point was to remind the Jews: "See, it's always the same eternal hatred of Jews and Israel." For the *Boston Globe,* the point was rather to tell Americans: "We are all Israelis." (the *Boston Globe* is owned by the *New York Times,* controlled by the Sulzberger family, although Dershowitz would dismiss such a remark as "nonsense" in a 2010 article, "Do Jews Control the Media?")[100]

If Sirhan was, like Oswald, a patsy, only of a more sophisticated type (a Manchurian candidate), the next question is: who had an interest in having people believe that Robert was killed by a fanatic Palestinian motivated by hatred of Israel? To raise the question is to answer it. But then, we are faced with a dilemma, for if Robert Kennedy was supportive of Israel, why would Israel kill him? The dilemma is an illusion, since it rests on a misleading assumption, which is part of the deception: in reality, Robert Kennedy was not pro-Israel. He was simply campaigning. As everyone knows, a few good wishes and empty promises to Israel are an inescapable ritual in such circumstances. And Robert's statement in an Oregon synagogue, mentioned in the May 27 Pasadena *Independent Star-News* article found in Sirhan's pocket, didn't exceed the minimal

---

[98] Sasha Issenberg, "Slaying gave US a first taste of Mideast terror," *Boston Globe,* June 5, 2008, on www.boston.com.

[99] Jeffrey Salkin, "Remember What Bobby Kennedy Died For," *Forward.com,* June 5, 2008. Also Michael Fischbach, "First Shot in Terror War Killed RFK," *Los Angeles Times,* June 02, 2003, on articles.latimes.com.

[100] Alan Dershowitz, "Do Jews Control the Media?," huffingtonpost.com, October 6, 2010.

requirements. Its author David Lawrence had, in an earlier article entitled "Paradoxical Bob," underlined how little credit should be given to such electoral promises: "Presidential candidates are out to get votes and some of them do not realize their own inconsistencies." As for the documentary aired on May 20, 1968, mentioning Robert's trip to Palestine in 1948, it was another campaign ad aimed at Jewish voters. When Robert Kennedy had visited Palestine, one month before Israel declared its independence, he was twenty-two years old. In the series of articles he drew from that trip for the *Boston Globe*, he praised the pioneer spirit of the Zionists, and expressed the hope that: "If a Jewish state is formed it will be the only remaining stabilizing factor in the near and far East." But he had also voiced the fears of the Arabs in quite prophetic terms: "The Arabs are most concerned about the great increase in the Jews in Palestine: 80,000 in 1948. The Arabs have always feared this encroachment and maintain that the Jews will never be satisfied with just their section of Palestine, but will gradually move to overpower the rest of the country and will eventually move onto the enormously wealthy oil lands. They are determined that the Jews will never get the toehold that would be necessary for the fulfillment of that policy."

Less than five years before his presidential bid, Robert Kennedy had not been, in his brother's government, a particularly pro-Israel attorney general: he had infuriated Zionist leaders by supporting an investigation led by Senator William Fulbright of the Senate Committee on Foreign Relations aimed at registering the American Zionist Council as a "foreign agent" subject to the obligations defined by the Foreign Agents Registration Act of 1938, which would have considerably hindered its efficiency. After 1963, the AZC escaped this procedure by changing its status and renaming itself AIPAC.[101] All things considered, there is no ground for believing that Robert Kennedy would have been, as president of the US, particularly Israel-friendly. His brother certainly had not been. The Kennedy family, proudly Irish and Catholic, was known for

---

[101] The Israel Lobby Archive, www.irmep.org/ila/forrel/.

its hostility to Jewish influence in politics, a classic theme of anti-Kennedy literature, best represented by the 1996 book by Ronald Kessler with the highly suggestive title, *The Sins of the Father: Joseph P. Kennedy and the Dynasty He Founded.*[102] Joe Kennedy had been notoriously critical of Jewish influence during World War II. While US Ambassador in London from 1938 to 1940, he supported Chamberlain's appeasement policy toward Hitler. When Roosevelt was about to enter the war, he resigned "to devote my efforts to what seems to me the greatest cause in the world today: to help the President keep the US out of the war." After the war, he reportedly said "the Jews have won the war."[103]

All things considered, it can only be by an outstanding hypocrisy that the *Jewish Daily Forward* wrote, on June 6, 2008: "In remembering Bobby Kennedy, let us remember not just what he lived for, but also what he died for—namely, the precious nature of the American-Israeli relationship."[104] Robert Kennedy's death had not been a bad thing for the precious "American-Israeli relationship." As a US president, would he have saved Israel from disaster in 1973, as had Nixon and Kissinger by providing it with unlimited military support against Egypt? Nothing is less sure.

But let us assume, for the sake of argument, that Robert Kennedy was perceived as pro-Israel in 1968. All the same, Israel would have had a compelling motive to eliminate him, for the simple reason that Robert was, above all else, his brother's heir and avenger.

All of his biographers have stressed his total commitment and loyalty to his brother John, whom he idolized. In return, John had come to trust his judgment on almost every issue, and had made him, not only his attorney general, but also his closest adviser. Robert didn't have John's charisma, nor his ambition. He felt that his brother's coat, which he had literally worn

---

[102] Ronald Kessler, *The Sins of the Father: Joseph P. Kennedy and the Dynasty He Founded,* Hodder & Stoughton, 1996.
[103] Quoted in Herbert Druks, *John F. Kennedy and Israel,* Praeger Security International, 2005, p. 10
[104] Jeffrey Salkin, "Remember What Bobby Kennedy Died For," *op. cit.*

during his first months of mourning, was too big for him. If he finally decided to run for president in 1968, it was under the pressure of destiny. As a lover of Greek tragedies, Robert believed in fate. And he knew that he was, in the eyes of millions of Americans, the legitimate heir to the murdered king—as well as his avenger, even if the thought was rarely voiced. His public appearances led to displays of fervor never seen before for a presidential candidate, and his total lack of concern for his own security made him look all the more genuine.

This exceptional brotherly friendship between John and Robert has an obvious implication for the investigator into Robert's death. And the fact that this is seldom mentioned is a cause for wonder. As Lance deHaven-Smith has remarked in *Conspiracy Theory in America*, "It is seldom considered that the Kennedy assassinations might have been serial murders. In fact, in speaking about the murders, Americans rarely use the plural, 'Kennedy assassinations'. [...] Clearly, this quirk in the Kennedy assassination(s) lexicon reflects an unconscious effort by journalists, politicians, and millions of ordinary Americans to avoid thinking about the two assassinations together, despite the fact that the victims are connected in countless ways."[105]

John and Robert were two brothers united by an unshakable love and loyalty,. What is the probability that their murders are unrelated? Rather, we should start with the assumption that they are related. For there is a good chance that their solution resides in the link between them. In fact, common sense naturally leads to the hypothesis that Robert was prevented from becoming president because, obsessed with justice as he was, he had to be prevented from reaching a position where he could reopen the case of his brother's death. Both murders have at least two things in common: Johnson and Israel. First, consider the fact that they precisely frame the presidency of Lyndon Johnson, who controlled both investigations: Johnson became president the day of John's death, and he retired a few months after Robert's death. As for Israel's implication, the plot to blame an anti-Israel Palestinian gives it away in Robert's case. In John's

---

[105] Lance deHaven-Smith, *Conspiracy Theory in America, op. cit.*, k. 284–292.

case, Israel's fingerprints are even more unmistakable, and one must wonder why most investigators make so much effort not to see them.

Was there, in 1968, any reason to believe that Robert intended to reopen the investigation into his brother's death, once in the White House? The answer is yes. From November 22, 1963, Robert was alienated and closely monitored by Johnson and Hoover. Although still attorney general, he knew he was powerless against the forces that had killed his brother. Yet he lost no time beginning his own investigation. He first asked CIA director John McCone, a Kennedy friend, to find out if the plot had anything to do with the agency. In March 1964, he had a face-to-face conversation with mobster Jimmy Hoffa, his sworn enemy, whom he had battled for ten years, and whom he suspected of having taken revenge on his brother. Robert also asked his friend Daniel Moynihan to search for any complicity in the Secret Service, which had been responsible for the president's security in Dallas.[106] And of course Robert suspected Johnson, whom he had always despised and mistrusted. "Johnson lies all the time," he is reported saying. "I'm just telling you, he just lies continuously, about everything. In every conversation I have with him, he lies. As I've said, he lies even when he doesn't have to."[107]

In fact, a week after JFK's death, November 29, 1963, Bill Walton, a friend of the Kennedys, went to Moscow and handed to Georgi Bolshakov (the agent who had already carried secret communications between Khrushchev and Kennedy) a message for Khrushchev from Robert and Jacqueline Kennedy. According to the memo found in the Soviet archives in the 90s by Alexandr Fursenko and Timothy Naftali (*One Hell of a Gamble*, 1998), they wanted to inform the Soviet premier that they believed John Kennedy had been "the victim of a right-wing conspiracy," "that only RFK could implement John Kennedy's

[106] David Talbot, *Brothers, op. cit.*, 2007, pp. 21–22.
[107] Jeff Shesol, *Mutual Contempt: Lyndon Johnson, Robert Kennedy, and the Feud that Defined a Decade*, WW Norton & Co., 1997, 2012, p. 95.

vision, and that the cooling that might occur in U.S.-Soviet relations because of Johnson would not last forever."[108]

Johnson had several cards in his hand to keep Robert quiet. One of them was his Cuban-Soviet conspiracy theory, which could be reactivated at any time. Its purpose was twofold: it made it possible to silence *all* conspiracy theories under the veiled threat of nuclear war, but it was also designed to silence Robert Kennedy, for it came with the accessory theory that Castro had killed John Kennedy in retaliation for Robert Kennedy's attempts on his life. In 1967, in an effort to stop Robert from running for president, Johnson leaked the idea to *Washington Post* columnist Drew Pearson, who spread the rumor. Hundreds of newspapers reported in March: "President Johnson is sitting on a political H-bomb, an unconfirmed report that Senator Robert Kennedy may have approved an assassination plot [against Castro] which then possibly backfired against his late brother."[109] The obvious implication was that Robert was responsible for his brother's death. This theory still occasionally surfaces, for example in Gus Russo, *Live By the Sword: The Secret War Against Castro and the Death of JFK* (1998), which even suggests that Oswald had been originally trained to assassinate Castro.

When the Warren Commission report was released, Robert Kennedy had no choice but to publicly endorse it, but "privately he was dismissive of it," as his son Robert Kennedy, Jr. remembers.[110] To friends who wondered why he wouldn't voice his doubt, he said: "there's nothing I can do about it. Not now."[111] Yet Robert contacted an MI6 officer friend of the Kennedy family (dating back to the days when Joe Kennedy was the US ambassador to England), who made arrangements for two French intelligence operatives to conduct, over a three-year period, a quiet investigation that involved hundreds of

---

[108] David Talbot, *Brothers, op. cit.*, pp. 25–27.

[109] Max Holland, "The Assassination Tapes," *The Atlantic*, June 2004, on www.theatlantic.com; David Talbot, *Brothers, op. cit.*, p. 348.

[110] Associated Press, "RFK children speak about JFK assassination," January 12, 2013, on www.usatoday.com.

[111] David Talbot, *Brothers, op. cit.*, pp. 278-280, 305.

interviews in the United States. One of them was André Ducret, head of the security for French President Charles De Gaulle. Over the years, these French secret agents hired men to infiltrate the Texas oil industry, the CIA, and Cuban mercenary groups in Florida. Their report, replete with innuendo about Lyndon Johnson and right-wing Texas oil barons, was delivered to Bobby Kennedy only months before his own assassination in June of 1968.

After Bobby's death, the last surviving brother, Senator Ted Kennedy, showed no interest in the material. The agents then hired a French writer by the name of Hervé Lamarr to fashion the material into a book, under the pseudonym of James Hepburn.[112] The book was first published in French under the title L'Amérique brûle, and translated into eleven languages. No major US publisher was willing to print it, but it nevertheless circulated under the title Farewell America: The Plot to Kill JFK. Its conclusion is worth quoting: "President Kennedy's assassination was the work of magicians. It was a stage trick, complete with accessories and fake mirrors, and when the curtain fell, the actors, and even the scenery disappeared. [...] the plotters were correct when they guessed that their crime would be concealed by shadows and silences, that it would be blamed on a 'madman' and negligence."[113]

Robert Kennedy had planned to run for the presidency in 1972, but the horrors of Vietnam and the realization of the urgency of the time precipitated his decision to run in 1968. Another factor may have been the opening of an investigation by New Orleans District Attorney Jim Garrison in 1967. Garrison was privileged to see Abraham Zapruder's amateur film, confiscated by the FBI on the day of the assassination, whose images show that the fatal shot came from the grassy knoll well in front of the president, not the School Book Depository located behind. Garrison's investigation, however,

---

[112] Gus Russo, Live by the Sword: The Secret War Against Castro and the Death of JFK, Bancroft Press, 1998, pp. 574–575.
[113] James Hepburn, Farewell America: The Plot to Kill JFK, Penmarin Books, 2002, p. 269.

suffered a smear campaign and the mysterious deaths of his two main suspects and witnesses, Guy Banister and David Ferrie.

When talk of the investigation began, Kennedy asked one of his closest advisors, Frank Mankiewicz, to follow its developments: "I want you to look into this, read everything you can, so if it gets to a point where I can do something about this, you can tell me what I need to know." He confided to his friend William Attwood, then editor of *Look* magazine, that he, like Garrison, suspected a conspiracy, "but I can't do anything until we get control of the White House."[114] He refrained from openly supporting Garrison, believing that since the outcome of the investigation was uncertain, it could jeopardize his plans to reopen the case later, and even weaken his chances of election by construing his motivation as a family feud. Garrison claims that Robert sent him a message through a mutual friend: "Keep up the good work. I support you and when I'm president I am going to blow the whole thing wide open." But Garrison rightly feared that Robert would not live long enough, and thought that speaking out publicly would have protected him.[115]

In conclusion, there can be no doubt that, had he been elected president, Robert Kennedy would have reopened the case of his brother's assassination, in one way or another. This certainly did not escape John's murderers. They had no other way to stop him than by killing him.

History seems to replay indefinitely the mythical struggle of Seth against Osiris. The story of the Kennedy brothers and their nemesis Lyndon Johnson is an Osirian tragedy, with two Irish-Catholic siblings as Osiris and, playing Seth, a crypto-Jewish Texan who, having seized the throne by murder, hastened to tie the destiny of America to that of Israel. This time, Seth did not give Horus a chance: John John (JFK Jr.), who had turned three on the day of his father's funeral, was eliminated in a suspicious plane crash on July 16, 1999, in the company of his pregnant wife and sister-in-law.

---

[114] David Talbot, *Brothers, op. cit.*, pp. 312–314.
[115] Garrison, quoted in David Talbot, *Brothers, op. cit.*, p. 333.

At the age of 39, JFK Jr. was preparing to enter politics. In 1995 he founded *George* magazine, which seemed harmless until it began to take an interest in political assassinations. In March 1997, *George* published a 13-page article by Guela Amir, the mother of Yigal Amir, the assassin of Israeli Prime Minister Yitzhak Rabin, who had offended the Israeli right-wing by agreeing to a "land for peace" exchange with the Palestinians. Guela Amir revealed that her son operated under the guardianship of a Shin Bet agent opposed to the peace process.[116] Thus, John Jr. was eliminated while following in the footsteps of his father, entering politics through the door of journalism and taking an interest in the crimes of the Israeli deep state.

In 1968, the death of Robert Kennedy benefited Republican Richard Nixon, who won the presidency eight years after being beaten by John F. Kennedy. Nixon made Henry Kissinger his national security advisor. Secretary of State William Rogers, who was trying to reduce US military involvement around the world, went head-to-head with Kissinger on the issue of Palestine, finally resigning in 1973 while complaining that Kissinger was sabotaging his efforts for a just and equitable peace. Kissinger replaced Rogers, filling both positions simultaneously for the first time in history, giving him total control over foreign policy. Thus, when Egypt and Syria launched the Yom Kippur War on October 6, 1973, with the aim of recovering the territories illegally occupied by Israel, Nixon responded to the call of Golda Meir and saved Israel from disaster by ordering an airlift supplying the Zionists with almost unlimited weapons. After the war, US military assistance to Israel intensified.

In April 1974, however, Nixon attempted to regain control, and sent the deputy director of the CIA, General Vernon Walters, to a secret meeting with PLO leaders without informing Kissinger. Walters returned convinced of the legitimacy and good faith of Yasser Arafat. In July 1974, Nixon himself traveled to Egypt, Saudi Arabia, Syria, Israel, and Jordan and criticized

---

[116] "A Mother's Defense, by Guela Amir on the Rabin Assassination," *George,* March 1997, on groups.google.com.

Israel's intransigence. On August 6, 1974, Nixon announced to Kissinger that he intended to cut off all military and economic aid to Israel if it refused to comply with the UN resolutions.[117] Just three days later, Nixon was forced to resign by the intensification of the Watergate scandal. Bob Woodward, the journalist who broke the scandal, had a rather curious background, revealed by Len Colodny and Robert Gettlin in *Silent Coup* (1991): he had been hired by the *Washington Post* on the recommendation of its president Paul Ignatius, the former Navy secretary appointed by Johnson in 1967. Woodward had worked five years for the Navy in the communications sector with a top-secret security clearance.[118]

Nixon was replaced by his vice-president Gerald Ford, a former member of the Warren Commission, known for his pro-Israel positions. One of his first decisions was to recognize Jerusalem as capital of the Jewish state, in violation of UN resolutions. Under Ford, the infiltration of Israel into the heart of the American state apparatus entered a new stage, which we will explore in the next chapter.

The Triumph of Zionist Propaganda

During the period studied in this chapter, the United States plunged into a deep, covert war, most of which remains completely hidden from an American public who nevertheless confusedly feels that American democracy died in Dallas on November 22, 1963. The lie about Kennedy's assassination infected the national psyche, as a repressed secret festering in the unconscious of America and making it vulnerable to other lies. Every lie creates a predisposition to falsehood, and even the need for other lies to cover it. Conversely, the unveiling of a lie may unravel other lies, perhaps even the whole fabric of untruth out of which twentieth-century American history is woven. That

---

117 Alan Hart, *Zionism*, vol. 3, *op. cit.*, pp. 198–203.
118 Read Len Colodny and Robert Gettlin, *Silent Coup: The Removal of a President*, St Martin's Press, 1991, and Jim Hougan, *Secret Agenda: Watergate, Deep Throat, and the CIA*, Ballantine Books, 1986.

is why we still see today, on the part of the government, a fierce desire to perpetuate the lie about Kennedy's death.

The Johnson years also mark a turning point in American Jewish public opinion. Until the middle of the twentieth century, the majority felt that Jews were doing very well in the Diaspora. Few had any desire to emigrate to Palestine as required by the Zionist creed. Many also feared that the creation of a Jewish state would lead to accusations of dual loyalty. Theodor Herzl had replied in advance to this fear by asserting that, on the contrary, assimilated Jews who did not wish to live in Palestine would be freed from the suspicion of double loyalty by their very choice: "They would no longer be disturbed in their 'chromatic function,' as Darwin puts it, but would be able to assimilate in peace, because the present anti-Semitism would have been stopped for ever."[119]

Yet even before the creation of Israel, the Zionists, through the Yiddish press in particular, were demanding of American Jews that if they did not emigrate to Israel, they should at least be loyal and generous to Zionism. This moral requirement became even stronger during the first two decades of the post-war period, by which time the Jews had become "the most prosperous, educated, politically influential, and professionally accomplished ethnoreligious group in the United States," in Yuri Slezkine's words.[120] Zionist pressure tore the fabric of the American Jewish community. "It is not Palestine alone that has been partitioned. A vast number of American Jews were split in two by the same political act," wrote Alfred Lilienthal in his book *What Price Israel?* (1953).[121] Another anti-Zionist Jewish journalist, William Zukerman, was also subjected to violent attacks for denouncing in 1934 "the threat of Jewish fascism" and then in 1955 "the wave of hysteria currently unleashed among American Jews" by "a propaganda campaign on the part of a foreign government."[122] This quarrel remained essentially

---

[119] Theodor Herzl, *The Jewish State,* on www.jewishvirtuallibrary.org.

[120] Yuri Slezkine, *The Jewish Century,* Princeton University Press, 2004, kindle, k. 5529.

[121] Alfred Lilienthal, *What Price Israel?,* (1953), Infinity Publishing, 2003, pp. 175, 102–112.

[122] William Zukerman, "The Menace of Jewish Fascism," *The Nation,* April 25 and June 27, 1934, on www.zundelsite.org/archive/french/rhr/Zuker.pdf.

internal to the Jewish community, and the voices of the anti-Zionist Jews were largely stifled in the public debate. In the 1960s they became increasingly rare, so that gradually the mass of American Jews was encouraged to feel Israeli at heart.

However, until 1967, American Jews remained discreet about their support for Israel, knowing perfectly well that this support amounted to a dual loyalty. What could it mean to be a Zionist in the United States after 1947, if not allegiance to a foreign power? It was only after the Six-Day War of 1967 that American Jews began to support Israel more actively and openly. Many American Jews could recognize themselves in Rabbi Abraham Joshua Heschel's comment that until June 1967, "I had not known how Jewish I was."[123]

There were two reasons for this change of mind. First, Zionist control of the press had become such that American public opinion was easily persuaded that Israel had been the victim and not the aggressor in the Six-Day War. The mainstream media took seriously the statement of Prime Minister Levi Eshkol to the Knesset on June 12, 1967, that "the existence of the State of Israel was hanging by a thread, but the hopes of the Arab leaders to exterminate Israel have been wiped out."[124] Israel's victory was a divine miracle, according to the storytelling propagated in the United States. It was pure propaganda, as several Israeli ministers and high-ranking officials later disclosed: "I do not believe that Nasser wanted war. The two divisions which he sent into Sinai on May 14 would not have been enough to unleash an offensive against Israel. He knew it and we knew it," confided chief of staff and future prime minister Yitzhak Rabin (*Le Monde*, February 28, 1968). "The claim that the danger of genocide was hanging over our heads in June 1967, and that Israel was fighting for its physical existence was only a bluff," revealed General

---

[123] Quoted in Kevin MacDonald, *Separation and Its Discontents: Toward an Evolutionary Theory of Anti-Semitism*, Praeger, 1998, kindle 2013, k. 6343–50.
[124] Quoted in Roger Garaudy, *Le Procès du sionisme israélien*, Éditions Vent du Large, 1998 (archive.org), p. 40.

Matetiyahu Peled, head of the logistics command (*Le Monde*, June 3, 1972).[125]

Secondly, after 1967, the crushing deployment of Israeli power against Egypt, a nation supported diplomatically by the USSR, enabled the Johnson administration to elevate Israel to a strategic asset in the Cold War. "For American Jewish elites, Israel's subordination to US power was a windfall," Norman Finkelstein explains. "Jews now stood on the front lines defending America—indeed, 'Western civilization'—against the retrograde Arab hordes. Whereas before 1967 Israel conjured the bogey of dual loyalty, it now connoted super-loyalty. [...] After the 1967 war, Israel's military élan could be celebrated because its guns pointed in the right direction—against America's enemies. Its martial prowess might even facilitate entry into the inner sanctums of American power." Therefore "After the June war, mainstream American Jewish organizations worked full time to firm up the American-Israeli alliance."[126] The *New York Times* and the *Washington Post*, which until then had remained relatively restrained, became openly pro-Israel.

Israeli leaders, for their part, stopped blaming American Jews and recognized the legitimacy of serving Israel while residing in the United States. In very revealing terms, Benjamin Ginsberg writes that already in the 1950s, "an accommodation was reached between the Jewish state in Israel and the Jewish state in America"; but it was after 1967 that the compromise became a consensus, as anti-Zionist Jews were marginalized and silenced.[127] Thus was born a new Israel, whose capital was no longer only Tel Aviv but also New York; a transatlantic Israel, a nation without borders, delocalized. It was not really a novelty, but rather a new balance between two realities, one old and the other beginning in 1947. Let us not forget that until the foundation of the Jewish state, "Israel" was a common designation of the international Jewish community, as when the

---

[125] Other examples in Alan Hart, *Zionism*, vol. 3, *op. cit.*, pp. 16–17.
[126] Norman Finkelstein, *The Holocaust Industry: Reflections on the Exploitation of Jewish Suffering*, Verso, 2014, p. 6.
[127] Benjamin Ginsberg, *Jews in American Politics: Essays*, dir. Sandy Maisel, Rowman & Littlefield, 2004, p. 22.

British Daily Express of March 24, 1933, printed on its front page: "The whole of Israel throughout the world is united in declaring an economic and financial war on Germany."[128]

In May 1947, the Zionists gave the name Israel to the new "Jewish nation" they proclaimed in Palestine, giving the word a different meaning. The two notions (national Israel and international Israel) are made inseparable by the fact that every Jew in the world is virtually a citizen of Israel, since all he has to do is ask. In the 1970s, the hearts of an increasing number of American Jews began to beat secretly, and then more and more loudly, for Israel. Reform Judaism, which until then had declared itself to be exclusively religious, soon rationalized this new situation by a 1976 resolution affirming: "The State of Israel and the Diaspora, in fruitful dialogue, can show how a People transcends nationalism while affirming it, thus establishing an example for humanity."[129]

It is important to emphasize that the commitment of an international Jewish elite capable of influencing foreign governments has been necessary not only for the foundation of Israel, but also for its survival. Even today, Israel's survival is entirely dependent on the influence of the Zionist network in the United States and Europe (euphemistically called the "pro-Israel lobby"). Again, the parallel with the post-exilic period is valid, since for many centuries the kingdom of Israel was virtually ruled by the Babylonian exiles, with Nehemiah himself retaining his principal residence there. Is it not written in the Book of Baruch that the Babylonian exiles collected money to send to the Jews who remained in Jerusalem? After the destruction of Jerusalem by the Romans, Babylon remained the center of universal Judaism (and the place where the Talmud was written).

The American Jewish community (New York, for short) now fulfills the same function, as has been pointed out by many prominent Zionists such as Jacob Neusner in *A History of the Jews*

---

[128] Alison Weir, *Against Our Better Judgment: The Hidden History of How the U.S. Was Used to Create Israel*, 2014, k. 3280–94.

[129] Quoted in Kevin MacDonald, *Separation and Its Discontents, op. cit.*, k. 5463–68.

in Babylonia (1965), and, before him, Max Dimont in *Jews, God and History* (1962). The American Jews who prefer to remain in the United States rather than emigrate to Israel are, Dimont argued, as essential to the community as the Babylonian Jews who declined the invitation to return to Palestine in the Persian era: "Today, as once before, we have both an independent State of Israel and the Diaspora. But, as in the past, the State of Israel today is a citadel of Judaism, a haven of refuge, the center of Jewish nationalism where dwell only two million of the world's twelve million Jews. The Diaspora, although it has shifted its center through the ages with the rise and fall of civilizations, still remains the universal soul of Judaism."[130] In other words, New York is to Tel Aviv what Jewish universalism is to Jewish nationalism: two sides of the same reality. Although its theoretical vocation is to welcome all the Jews of the world, the State of Israel would collapse if it achieved this goal. It is unsustainable without the support of international Jewry, mobilized by such groups as AIPAC and B'nai B'rith (in Hebrew, "sons of the covenant," founded in New York in 1843).

Broadly, among the Jewish community, Israel brings together all those who, through their family origins, feel "eternally" or "unconditionally" attached to it. Israel is thus a country of the heart and not just an administrative citizenship. In this sense, the fifty-two American Jewish representative organizations, as well as the Conference of Presidents of Major American Jewish Organizations, which has been coordinating them since 1956, are part of Israel, insofar as they are openly devoted to Israel's defense—for example when they fight anti-Zionism by calling it anti-Semitism. From this point of view, Israel has two world capitals: Tel Aviv and New York. Over the years, pushed by their representative elites, American and European Jews have forged such a personal and intimate connection with the State of Israel that the defense of this state has become for them a sort of second nature, a self-preservation

---

[130] Quoted in Michael Collins Piper, *The New Babylon: Those Who Reign Supreme*, American Free Press, 2009, p. 27.

instinct. It would seem that Zionism has succeeded in transforming each Jew into an Israeli at heart, even a sleeper agent of Israel. As a result, the phenomenon announced by Alfred Lilienthal in 1953 has been realized: "In contemporary Judaism, the worship of the State of Israel is crowding out the worship of God."[131] Israel has become what Yahweh once was: the soul or god of the Jewish community. Basically, Israel substituted itself for its national god in the same way that Humanity had substituted itself for its universal God during the Enlightenment. The phenomenon can be regarded as indirect proof that Yahweh has never ceased to be for the Jews the god of Israel.

But Israel is not the only divinity of contemporary Jews. For "The State of Israel is God's answer to Auschwitz," wrote Abraham Herschel in 1969, in a Trinitarian formula that summarizes the relationship between Yahweh, Israel, and Holocaust.[132] The memorial cult of "the Holocaust" (the term refers to a religious sacrifice and is intimately linked in the book of Ezra to the reconstruction of the Temple) is today inseparable from support for Israel; the two form a single amalgamated bond holding the global Jewish community together. The cult was inaugurated during the trial of Adolf Eichmann in Israel (abducted in 1960 in Argentina, tried in 1961, and hanged in 1962)—a formidably effective global communications operation, staged by Ben-Gurion "to educate our youth. In addition, this trial is needed because the world has started to forget the Nazi horrors." He admitted: "The fate of Eichmann, the person, has no interest for me whatsoever. What is important is the spectacle." The Eichmann trial, declared Mapai's general secretary in an electoral speech, was intended as "the trial of the Jewish people against eternal anti-Semitism in all nations and through all generations."[133] At the same time, it was necessary to scrub away the still-fresh stain of the collaboration between Zionism and Nazism: it was bad taste to remind the

---

[131] Alfred Lilienthal, *What Price Israel?*, *op. cit.*, p. 144.
[132] Abraham Herschel, *Israel: An Echo of Eternity*, Doubleday, 1969, p. 115.
[133] Idith Zertal, *Israel's Holocaust and the Politics of Nationhood*, Cambridge University Press, 2005, pp. 97, 107, 110.

world that Adolf Eichmann, an admirer of Herzl, had visited Palestine for the first time in 1937 under the Haavara Agreement, and had met on this occasion Ben-Gurion's assistant, Teddy Kollek, future mayor of Jerusalem.[134]

The Holocaust, the avatar of Yahweh, escapes history to join the category of myth, which is why "it is not within reach of historians."[135] This sacralization of the Holocaust through permanent media brainwashing fulfills two complementary functions: guilt in the Gentiles, fear among the Jews. Through guilt, the Gentiles are kept in check and all their criticisms are neutralized under the threat of passing for potential gas chamber operators. Through fear, the Jewish community is kept under control and their loyalty to Israel strengthened, Israel being presented to them as an "insurance policy," a fortress (preferably well armed) in which to take refuge in the event of a new Holocaust. The spiritual power of this cult is such that the trauma of the Holocaust has now been proven to be passed from generation to generation on the genetic level, via what is called "epigenetic inheritance" according to a research team at New York's Mount Sinai Hospital, led by Rachel Yehuda.[136]

Every religion has its priests. It was in the late 1960s that Elie Wiesel became an international star of the Holocaust. His book *Night*, published in 1958 with a preface by François Mauriac, was translated into German in 1962 with, as if by magic, the "crematory ovens" (intended to incinerate the dead) systematically transformed (11 times) into *Gaskammer*, or "gas chambers," which thus make their appearance in force in Holocaust mythology. As Alain Soral put it, "As founding sacrifice, the gas chamber has replaced the cross of Christ."[137]

Shortly after Elie Wiesel's Nobel Peace Prize in 1986, controversy erupted. Wiesel was denounced as an impostor by

---

[134] Alison Weir, *Against Our Better Judgment, op. cit.*, k. 565–633.

[135] Declaration of Jewish representative Henry Bulawko, Oxford, July 1988, quoted in Anne Kling, *Menteurs et affabulateurs de la Shoah*, Éditions Mithra, 2013, p. 11.

[136] "Study of Holocaust survivors finds trauma passed on to children's genes," *The Guardian*, August 21, 2015, on www.theguardian.com/science/2015/aug/21/study-of-holocaust-survivors-finds-trauma-passed-on-to-childrens-genes.

[137] Alain Soral, "Pour le droit au blasphème," 2008, on www.egaliteetreconciliation.fr.

Miklos Grüner, a friend and fellow prisoner of the real Lazar Wiesel at the camps of Auschwitz and Buchenwald.[138] But what does it matter? Elie Wiesel remains to this day "the consummate narrator of the death and resurrection of the Jewish people."[139] In the writings of Wiesel and company, the Holocaust has become an initiatory mystery, as ironically illustrated by Norman Finkelstein, himself the son of two survivors of the Warsaw ghetto and the camps, who quotes from Wiesel's book *Against Silence*: "Wiesel intones that the Holocaust 'leads into darkness,' 'negates all answers,' 'lies outside, if not beyond, history,' 'defies both knowledge and description,' 'cannot be explained nor visualized,' is 'never to be comprehended or transmitted,' marks a 'destruction of history' and a 'mutation on a cosmic scale.' Only the survivor-priest (read: only Wiesel) is qualified to divine its mystery. And yet, The Holocaust's mystery, Wiesel avows, is 'noncommunicable'; 'we cannot even talk about it.' Thus, for his standard fee of $25,000 (plus chauffeured limousine), Wiesel lectures that the 'secret' of Auschwitz's 'truth lies in silence.'"[140]

As an "ideological representation," Norman Finkelstein explains, "The Holocaust" is "a coherent construct" whose dogmas "sustain significant political and class interests. Indeed, The Holocaust has proven to be an indispensable ideological weapon. Through its deployment, one of the world's most formidable military powers, with a horrendous human rights record, has cast itself as a 'victim' state, and the most successful ethnic group in the United States has likewise acquired victim status." As a matter of fact, "organized Jewry remembered The Holocaust when Israeli power peaked, [and] when American Jewish power peaked. [...] Thus American Jewish elites could strike heroic poses as they indulged in cowardly bullying."[141]

The sacralization of the Holocaust, while sealing the exceptionality of the Jewish people as unsurpassable victim of history, allows it to universalize its enemy. Ben-Gurion had

138 Anne Kling, *Menteurs et affabulateurs de la Shoah, op. cit.*, pp. 203–223.
139 Andrew Heinze, *Jews and the American Soul: Human Nature in the Twentieth Century*, Princeton University Press, 2006, p. 329.
140 Norman Finkelstein, *The Holocaust Industry, op. cit.*, p. 47.
141 Norman Finkelstein, *The Holocaust Industry, op. cit.*, pp. 7, 41.

already, speaking of the imminent war in Palestine in 1947, warned that the Arabs were "the disciples and even teachers of Hitler, who know only one way of solving the Jewish problem: total destruction." But it was during preparations for the Six-Day War that what Idith Zertal calls the "Nazification of the Arabs" began. Equating Nasser with Hitler became a common theme of Israeli propaganda. *Haaretz* led the campaign with such articles as "The Return of the Hitlerite Danger," where the paper's military correspondent claimed that Israel must "crush the machinations of the new Hitler right away, while it is still possible to do so." Even Ben-Gurion, the head of state, joined in: "I have no doubt that the Egyptian dictatorship is being instructed by the large number of Nazis who are there."[142]

The Holocaust is universal and polymorphous. After being incarnated in Nazi Germany, it can return in the guise of a new enemy. For there are, forever, only two camps: Israel and the rest of the world. The enemy changes identity but remains the same, universal and timeless: Hitler was himself only an avatar of Nebuchadnezzar, and the Holocaust the latest biblical episode. In the Bible itself, moreover, the enemies follow and resemble each other: Egypt, Babylon, and Persia form a series, completed by Rome, but at bottom they are one in the Jewish imagination. They are all Esau. They are interchangeable: the story of Esther could just as well happen in Babylon, and that of Daniel in Persia.

---

[142] Idith Zertal, *Israel's Holocaust and the Politics of Nationhood,* Cambridge University Press, 2005, pp. 173, 196, 120, 98.

Chapter 9

THE VICIOUS CABAL

> "O Lord, You made the world for our sakes. As for the other people, which also come of Adam, You have said that they are nothing, but like spittle."
>
> Fourth Book of Ezra 6:55–56

Neoconned

As we have seen, the end of the 1960s marked a decisive turning point in the United States' relationship with Israel. One key factor was the emergence of a new American Jewish elite who, under the misleading name of "neoconservatives," was gradually gaining considerable influence over American foreign policy. The neoconservative movement was born in the editorial office of the monthly magazine *Commentary*, the press organ of the American Jewish Committee. "If there is an intellectual movement in America to whose invention Jews can lay sole claim, neoconservatism is it," writes Gal Beckerman in the *Jewish Daily Forward*, January 6, 2006. "It is a fact that as a political philosophy, neoconservatism was born among the children of Jewish immigrants and is now largely the intellectual domain of those immigrants' grandchildren."[1]

The founding fathers of neoconservatism (Norman Podhoretz, Irving Kristol, Donald Kagan, Paul Wolfowitz, Adam Shulsky) are disciples of Leo Strauss. Born into a family of German Orthodox Jews, Strauss taught mainly at the University of Chicago and was a specialist in Thomas Hobbes. Strauss's thought is often elliptical because he believes that truth is harmful to the common man and the social order and should be reserved for superior minds (while religion is for the rest, as the necessary opium of the people). For this reason, Strauss

---

[1] Quoted in Stephen Sniegoski, *The Transparent Cabal: The Neoconservative Agenda, War in the Middle East, and the National Interest of Israel*, Enigma Edition, 2008, p. 26.

rarely speaks in his own name, but rather expresses himself as a
commentator on such classical authors as Plato or Thomas
Hobbes. Though Strauss is difficult to read, three basic ideas can
easily be extracted from his political philosophy. First, nations
derive their strength from their myths, which are necessary for
government and governance. Second, national myths have no
necessary relationship with historical reality, but rather are socio-
cultural constructions that the state has a duty to disseminate.
Third, to be effective, any national myth must be marked by a
clear distinction between good and evil, for it derives its
cohesive strength from the hatred of an enemy nation.[2]

Strauss greatly admired Machiavelli, the fifteenth-century
political philosopher who rejected the classical tradition that
sought to make virtue the foundation of power, and asserted
that only the appearance of virtue counts, and that the
successful prince must be a "great simulator" who "manipulates
and cons people's minds." In his *Thoughts on Machiavelli*, Strauss
parts from the intellectual trend of trying to rehabilitate the
author of *The Prince*, and instead agrees with the "simple
opinion" that regards his political theory as immoral, for it is
precisely in this immorality that resides "the intrepidity of his
thought, the grandeur of his vision, and the graceful subtlety of
his speech." Machiavelli, writes Strauss, "is a patriot of a
particular kind: He is more concerned with the salvation of his
fatherland than with the salvation of his soul."[3]

Strauss, like his disciples, could be qualified as a meta-
Zionist in the sense that, while he is an ardent supporter of the
State of Israel, he rejects the idea that Israel as a nation should
be contained within borders; Israel must retain her specificity,
which is to be everywhere. In his 1962 lecture "Why We Remain
Jews," Strauss quotes, as "the most profound and radical
statement on assimilation that I have read," Nietzsche's *Dawn of
Day* aphorism 205, a sort of prophecy of the Jews' conquest
through integration: "It only remains for them either to become
the lords of Europe or to lose Europe [...] at some time Europe

---

[2] Shadia Drury, *Leo Strauss and the American Right*, St. Martin's Press, 1999, pp. 1–29.
[3] Leo Strauss, *Thoughts on Machiavelli*, University of Chicago Press, 1995, pp. 10–13.

may fall like a perfectly ripe fruit into their hand, which only casually reaches out. In the meantime it is necessary for them to distinguish themselves in all the areas of European distinction and to stand among the first, until they will be far enough along to determine themselves that which distinguishes."[4]

Second, the neoconservatives of the first generation mostly came from the left, even the extreme Trotskyist left for some luminaries like Irving Kristol, one of the main editors of *Commentary*. It was at the end of the 60s that *Commentary* became, in the words of Benjamin Balint, "the contentious magazine that transformed the Jewish left into the neoconservative right."[5] Sexual liberation, which they had largely supported, suddenly seemed decadent; and pacifism, irresponsible. Norman Podhoretz, editor-in-chief of *Commentary* from 1960 to 1995, changed from anti-Vietnam War activist to defense budget booster, leading the rest of the magazine along with him. He gave the explanation of this turning point in 1979: "American support for Israel depended upon continued American involvement in international affairs—from which it followed that an American withdrawal into the kind of isolationist mood [. . .] that now looked as though it might soon prevail again, represented a direct threat to the security of Israel."[6] Since the survival of Israel depends on American protection and help, US military might and global involvement must be reinforced. This is why Irving Kristol committed members of the American Jewish Congress in 1973 to fight George McGovern's proposal to reduce the military budget by 30 percent: "This is to drive a knife into the heart of Israel. [. . .] Jews don't like a big military budget, but it is now an interest of the Jews to have a large and powerful military establishment in the United States. [. . .] American Jews who care about the survival of the state of Israel have to say, no, we don't want to cut the military budget, it is important to keep that military budget big, so that we can

---

[4] Leo Strauss, "Why We Remain Jews," in Shadia Drury, *Leo Strauss and the American Right, op. cit.*, pp. 31–43.
[5] Benjamin Balint, *Running Commentary: The Contentious Magazine That Transformed the Jewish Left into the Neoconservative Right*, Public Affairs, 2010.
[6] Norman Podhoretz, *Breaking Ranks: A Political Memoir*, Harper & Row, 1979, p. 336.

defend Israel."[7] It is therefore good for Israel that American Jews become, as American citizens, ardent interventionists. But it was also necessary that this interventionism should appear on the national public scene as American patriotism. This explains why the neoconservatives take such special care to forbid any public mention of their Jewishness. Even Carl Bernstein, though a Jew himself, provoked a scandal by citing, on national television, the responsibility of "Jewish neocons" for the Iraq war.[8] The truth is that the neoconservatives are crypto-Zionists. The "neoconservative" label they have given themselves is a mask. (Most "neo" things are fake).

Crypto-Zionism is a phenomenon that goes far beyond neoconservatism, and can even be compared to the crypto-Judaism of the sixteenth century. If, after June 1967, as Norman Podhoretz recalls, Israel became "the religion of the American Jews,"[9] it goes without saying that this religion should remain discreet, if possible even secret, since it was incompatible with American patriotism, at least as conceived by those who, in a similar way, consecrate an almost religious worship to America. The loyalty of American Jews to Israel, of course, naturally engendered the fear of being accused of allegiance to a foreign state, and thus aroused in them, as protective camouflage, increased patriotism in their public proclamations. The more American Jews became Israelis, the more they felt the need to be American in the public square. It was not just about being a Jew in the tent and a man in the street, according to the saying of the Haskalah, but of being "an Israeli within the Jewish community, and an American on the public goy stage."

For most of today's American Jews, this dual identity has become almost an unconscious reflex, as the interests of Israel and the United States seem to coincide in their mind. But to get there, it was necessary that this habit of thought be inculcated into them by their ruling elites. The neoconservatives were the spearhead of this ideological struggle, gradually dragging along

---

[7] Philip Weiss, "30 Years Ago, Neocons Were More Candid About Their Israel-Centered Views," May 23, 2007, on mondoweiss.net/2007/05/30_years_ago_ne/.

[8] April 26, 2013, on MSNBC, watch on YouTube.

[9] Norman Podhoretz, *Breaking Ranks, op. cit.,* p. 335.

with them almost all the Jewish representative elites of America. They highlighted a new form of US patriotism profitable to Israel, just as the sixteenth-century crypto-Jews had encouraged a new pro-Judaism form of Christianity (Calvinism).

The Hijacking of the Republican Party

The neoconservatives initially operated in the Democratic camp because, until the 1980s, interventionism was a Democratic tradition, linked to a "progressive" utopian discourse. It was Woodrow Wilson who had declared in 1912, "We are chosen and prominently chosen to show the way to the nations of the world how they shall walk in the path of liberty."[10] Richard Perle, one of the most influential and most Machiavellian neocons, was from 1969 to 1980 parliamentary assistant to Senator Henry "Scoop" Jackson, who succeeded Johnson as the leader of the militarist and pro-Israel wing of the Democratic Party. In 1970, Perle was caught red-handed by the FBI while transmitting to the Israeli embassy classified information obtained from Hal Sonnenfeldt, a member of the National Security Council.[11]

Perle skillfully took advantage of the Watergate hurricane to bring his two associates, Donald Rumsfeld and Dick Cheney, into the Republican camp. The two would remain the main mercenaries or "Sabbath goys" of the neoconservatives, placed in strategic posts to open the doors of the kingdom. After succeeding Nixon, Gerald Ford (who had been a member of the Warren Commission) appointed Donald Rumsfeld as his chief of staff; Rumsfeld then chose Dick Cheney as his deputy. Having inspired Ford in the cabinet reshuffle that became known journalistically as the "Halloween Massacre," Rumsfeld then seized the position of secretary of defense, while Cheney replaced him as chief of staff. Thus there appeared for the first time the explosive combination of Rumsfeld at Defense, Cheney in the White House.

---

[10] Wilson Center, www.wilsoncenter.org/about-woodrow-wilson.
[11] Patrick Buchanan, "Whose War? The Loudest Clique Behind the President's Policy," *The American Conservative*, March 24, 2003, www.theamericanconservative.com.

After America evacuated its troops from Vietnam in 1973, the Cold War calmed down, partly thanks to the diplomatic initiatives of Nixon and Kissinger. The CIA produced reassuring analyses of the USSR's military capabilities and ambitions. It was then that, with the help of a powerful lobby financed by weapons manufacturers—the Committee on the Present Danger—Rumsfeld and Cheney persuaded Ford to appoint an independent committee, known as Team B. Its mandate was to revise upward the CIA estimates of the Soviet threat, and reactivate a war atmosphere in public opinion, Congress, and the administration. Team B was composed of twelve experts chosen from among the most fanatical cold warriors. It was chaired by Richard Pipes and cochaired by Paul Wolfowitz, two protégés of Perle. The committee produced a terrifying report claiming Moscow possessed not only a large and sophisticated arsenal of weapons of mass destruction, but also the will to dominate all of Europe and the Middle East—and the readiness to start a nuclear confrontation. Pointing to a "window of vulnerability" in the US defense system, Team B's report advocated a broad and urgent increase in the defense budget, which began under Carter and then accelerated under Reagan.

Thus those who were later called the neoconservatives entered the state apparatus for the first time—in the baggage of Rumsfeld and Cheney—and bound their fate to the Republican party. Those previously called "conservatives," who were non-interventionists, were gradually pushed to the margins and described as paleo-conservatives, while the neoconservatives took over the reins of the Republican Party. During the parenthesis of Democratic president Jimmy Carter (1976–80), the neoconservatives reinforced their influence within the Republican Party. In order to unify the largest number of Jews around their policies, they founded the Jewish Institute for National Security Affairs (JINSA), which became the second-most powerful pro-Israel lobby after AIPAC. One of its stated aims was: "To inform the American defense and foreign affairs community about the important role Israel can and does play in bolstering democratic interests in the Mediterranean and the Middle East."[12]

Mimicking true conservatives, neoconservatives built their reputations for defending American traditional values. The best-known example is that of Allan Bloom, a disciple of Leo Strauss, who published *The Closing of the American Mind* in 1988. This moralistic posture, along with their warlike anti-communism, allowed the neocons to rally the Christian right. In 1980 evangelical Christians became for the first time a major electoral force mobilized to support Israel in the name of the struggle against communism. They had the advantage of being extremely manipulable, quaffing as "gospel truth" the inflamed sermons of the stars of their mega-churches, who assumed ever-more-assertive pro-Israel positions. Exemplifying this trend, televangelist Jerry Falwell received the Jabotinsky Centennial Medal from Menachem Begin in 1980 for services rendered to Israel, declaring "he who stands against Israel stands against God."[13]

Pastors such as Falwell help influence US foreign policy in a pro-Israel direction. But even more importantly, they serve as camouflage for the neoconservatives. The obtrusive presence of Christians makes Jewish influence less visible. In reality, evangelical Christians do represent an electoral force, but have no coherent political agenda and therefore no direct political power. When, in 1980, the evangelical Christians voted overwhelmingly for Ronald Reagan, none of their representatives acceded to any position of responsibility.

On the other hand, the neoconservatives were paid with a dozen posts in national security and foreign policy: Richard Perle and Douglas Feith to the Department of Defense, Richard Pipes at the National Security Council, and Paul Wolfowitz, Lewis "Scooter" Libby, and Michael Ledeen in the State Department. They helped Reagan escalate the Cold War, showering billions of dollars on the military-industrial complex. Thanks in particular to the Strategic Defense Initiative, a space

---

[12] Official website: www.jinsa.org/about.
[13] Robert Ajemian, "Jerry Falwell's Crusade," *Time*, September 2, 1985.

shield better known as "Star Wars," the defense budget
exploded, reaching for the first time the landmark of a trillion
dollars. Reagan created CENTCOM, the US military command
center in the Middle East, and consolidated the American
alliance with Israel, declaring: "Israel has the democratic will,
national cohesion, technological capacity and military fiber to
stand forth as America's trusted ally."[14] In 1981, the two
countries signed their first military pact, then embarked on
several shared operations, some legal and others not, as
evidenced by the network of arms trafficking and paramilitary
operations embedded within the Iran-Contra affair. Militarism
and Zionism had become so linked in their common cause that
in his 1982 book *The Real Anti-Semitism in America*, the director
of the Anti-Defamation League, Nathan Perlmutter, could
portray the pacifism of the "peacemakers of Vietnam vintage,
transmuters of swords into plowshares," as a new form of anti-
Semitism.[15]

It was in this context that Israeli strategists planned the next
stage of the project for a Greater Israel extending "from the
Nile to the Euphrates" according to the promise of Yahweh to
Abraham (Genesis 15:18), and to the vision of the founding
fathers of Zionism, including Theodor Herzl.[16] One of the most
explicit documents on this project, known through its
translation from Hebrew into English by Israel Shahak, is a text
entitled "A Strategy for Israel in the Eighties," written for the
World Zionist Organization in February 1982 by Oded Yinon, a
former senior official in the Ministry of Foreign Affairs and
contributor to the *Jerusalem Post*. The author presents the pluri-
ethnic character of Middle Eastern states as offering "far-
reaching opportunities for the first time since 1967" for opening
"a new epoch in human history." He advocates a strategy of
control of the Middle East by fragmenting all of Israel's

---

[14] Alan Hart, *Zionism: The Real Enemy of the Jews*, vol. 3: *Conflict Without End?*, Clarity
Press, 2010, p. 222.
[15] Andrew and Leslie Cockburn, *Dangerous Liaison: The Inside Story of the U.S.-Israeli
Covert Relationship*, HarperCollins, 1991, p. 189.
[16] *The Complete Diaries of Theodor Herzl*, edited by Raphael Patai, Herzl Press & Thomas
Yoseloff, 1960, vol. 2, p. 711.

neighbors on the model of what was partially accomplished in Lebanon by a "civil war" which, from 1975 to 1990, ravaged that nation of seventeen religious communities plus Palestinian refugees—a country, in other words, that formed an inverted reflection of the mono-confessional and endogamic nation that is Israel: "The total disintegration of Lebanon into five regional localized governments is the precedent for the entire Arab world including Egypt, Syria, Iraq, and the Arab peninsula, in a similar fashion. The dissolution of Egypt and later Iraq into districts of ethnic and religious minorities following the example of Lebanon is the main long-range objective of Israel on the Eastern Front. The present military weakening of these states is the short-term objective. Syria will disintegrate into several states along the lines of its ethnic and sectarian structure, as is happening in Lebanon today." In this process, "Every kind of inter-Arab confrontation will assist us in the short run."[17]

But it wasn't happening fast enough. The fate of Lebanon, home of the Palestinian resistance since the occupation of the West Bank and Gaza in 1967, had not yet been sealed. In June 1982, Minister of Defense Ariel Sharon launched the invasion of Lebanon (Operation "Peace in Galilee") and pulverized the prestigious capital, Beirut, under a carpet of bombs that had been graciously furnished by the United States, killing 10,000 civilians and creating half a million refugees. The massacre of more than 1,500 women, children, and old people in the two Palestinian refugee camps of Beirut gave Sharon the nickname "the Butcher of Sabra and Shatila." Israel's aggression brought new chaos to Lebanon, but after the retreat of Israeli troops, Syrian and Iranian influence in the region grew stronger. Though the PLO was militarily weakened, another resistance group was born: Hezbollah, a Shi'ite movement financed by Iran and calling for the destruction of the State of Israel.

Under the Israel-friendly presidency of Reagan, America could only respond with feeble gestures. What is euphemistically called the "Israeli lobby"—actually a gargantuan power machine using corruption and blackmail against the US elite—kept the

---

[17] Read on www.globalresearch.ca/greater-israel-the-zionist-plan-for-the-middle-east.

number one global power on a tight leash. The 1988 election of George Bush Sr., Reagan's vice president, changed things slightly. Bush was less a friend to Israel than to Saudi Arabia, where he had business ties since the 1970s. James Baker, his campaign manager appointed secretary of state, used economic pressure to force Israeli Prime Minister Yitshak Shamir to participate in the Madrid Conference in November 1991, and appeared receptive to Arab proposals during the Conference.[18]

Bush mostly purged neoconservatives from his government, but nonetheless accorded the secretary of defense post to Dick Cheney, who brought along Scooter Libby and Paul Wolfowitz. The latter was then able to strengthen his position at the Pentagon, where he had already served as deputy assistant secretary of defense under Carter before migrating to the State Department under Reagan. When Bush unleashed Operation Desert Storm in January 1991, he did it to liberate Kuwait, protect Saudi Arabia, and annihilate the Iraqi army. He held to his UN Security Council mandate, resisting demands from the neoconservatives—he called them "the crazies"—to invade Iraq and overthrow Saddam Hussein's regime. On March 6, 1991, he stood before Congress and declared the war had ended. When he mentioned in his speech "the very real prospect of a new world order," it was for the purpose of underlining his trust in the mission of the United Nations organization. What he called for was "a world where the United Nations, freed from the Cold War stalemate, is poised to fulfil the historic vision of its founders."

This was when a competing doctrine, the so-called "Wolfowitz doctrine," was formulated in a secret report dated February 1992 and fortuitously "leaked" to the *New York Times*, which published extracts on March 7. Under the title *Defense Planning Guidance*, the report, written by Wolfowitz and Libby, vaunted American hegemony: "Our first objective is to prevent the re-emergence of a new rival," and to enforce "the sense that the world order is ultimately backed by the U.S." In opposition to Bush's public discourses, the Wolfowitz report advocated

---

[18] Alan Hart, *Zionism*, vol. 3, *op. cit.*, p. 361.

unilateralism, denigrating the role of the United Nations and stating the US cannot "allow our critical interests to depend solely on international mechanisms that can be blocked by countries whose interests may be very different from our own." Therefore, "we should expect future coalitions to be ad hoc assemblies." Finally the report, which would become official policy under Bush Jr. in 2001, promotes the need for preemptive war "for deterring potential competitors from even aspiring to a larger regional or global role." The document also makes a specific commitment to the security of Israel.[19]

Bush's opposition to the neoconservative agenda probably caused his defeat in the 1992 elections, just as the Democrat Jimmy Carter paid for his dovish policies and his critiques of Israel in 1980. It is a disconcerting fact that, since the end of World War II, the only American presidents deprived of a second term in office (including the partially deprived Nixon) were those who resisted Israel the most. The only exception is Johnson, whose unpopularity was irreversible.

Setting the Stage for the Clash of Civilizations

The Clinton Administration (1993–2000) was itself "full of warm Jews," in the words of an influential rabbi quoted by the Israeli newspaper *Maariv*. He deemed that the United States no longer possessed "a government of goyim." In the National Security Council, for example, "7 out of 11 top staffers are Jews."[20]

The clan of the neoconservatives, for their part, entrenched themselves in the opposition. They reinforced their influence on the Republican party and on public opinion, thanks to a press more and more subservient to their crypto-imperial version of American patriotism. They indirectly influenced foreign policy in the Middle East by creating or taking control of a large number of think tanks: the Washington Institute for Near East Policy

---

[19] Read full report on www.archives.gov/declassification/iscap/pdf/2008-003-doc9.pdf.
[20] Avinoam Bar-Yosef, "The Jews Who Run Clinton's Court," *Maariv*, September 2, 1994, translated by Israel Shahak in *Open Secrets: Israeli Nuclear and Foreign Policies*, Pluto Press, 1997.

(WINEP), where Richard Perle has served since 1985; the Middle East Forum (MEF) founded in 1990 by Daniel Pipes (son of Richard); and the Middle East Media Research Institute (MEMRI), founded by Meyrav Wurmser in 1998. William Kristol, son of Irving, founded in 1995 a new magazine, the *Weekly Standard*, which immediately became the dominant voice of the neoconservatives thanks to funding from the pro-Israel Rupert Murdoch. In 1997 it would be the first publication to call for a new war against Saddam Hussein. The neocons also flooded the book market with propaganda portraying Saddam Hussein as a threat to America. Besides *Tyranny's Ally: America's Failure to Defeat Saddam Hussein* by David Wurmser (1999), let us mention Laurie Mylroie's *Study of Revenge: Saddam Hussein's Unfinished War Against America* (2000), which is about "an undercover war of terrorism, waged by Saddam Hussein," that is nothing more than "a phase in a conflict that began in August 1990, when Iraq invaded Kuwait, and that has not ended." Richard Perle has described this book as "splendid and wholly convincing."[21]

In Israel, Benjamin Netanyahu succeeded Shimon Perez as Prime Minister in 1996. Netanyahu is the grandson of a Lithuanian rabbi who immigrated to Palestine in 1920. His father, like many settlers in Eastern Europe, traded his original name for a local one: Benzion Mileikowsky became Benzion Netanyahu. Benzion, whom we have already quoted in earlier chapters, was from 1940 onward the assistant to Zeev Jabotinsky, whose heroic portrait he painted in his book *The Founding Fathers of Zionism* (alongside Leo Pinsker, Theodor Herzl, Max Nordau, and Israel Zangwill). Jabotinsky, creator of the first Israeli armed forces and inspirer of the Irgun, is also the founder of "revisionist Zionism," a current that broke with Weizmann's World Zionist Organization in 1925. Convinced that the Zionist project could never be achieved by diplomacy alone, he wrote in 1923, in an article entitled "The Iron Wall": "All colonization, even the most restricted, must continue in defiance of the will of the native population. Therefore, it can

---

[21] Stephen Sniegoski, *The Transparent Cabal, op. cit.*, p. 98.

continue and develop only under the shield of force, comprising an Iron Wall that the local population can never break through. This is our Arab policy. To formulate it any other way would be hypocrisy. […] Zionism is a colonizing adventure and therefore it stands or it falls by the question of armed force."

Hypocrisy was the strategic choice of Weizmann as well as Ben-Gurion. The latter was reserved in his public statements, but privately expressed his desire to expel the Arabs from Palestine; whereas revisionist Zionism, an unrepressed movement that wears its violence on its sleeve, is more honest. The coming to power of Benjamin Netanyahu in 1996 thus marked the hardening of Israeli policy toward the Palestinians. In 2009, Netanyahu appointed as minister of foreign affairs and deputy prime minister Avigdor Lieberman, the founder of the Yisrael Beiteinu party, which presents itself as "a national movement with the clear vision to follow in the brave path of Zev Jabotinsky."[22] During the assault on Gaza in January 2009, Lieberman advocated "fighting Hamas just as the United States fought the Japanese during the Second World War."[23]

Benjamin Netanyahu also symbolizes the increasingly important role played by neoconservatives and American Jews in general concerning the fate of Israel, which currently enjoys unprecedented support from American Jewish billionaires. He himself lived, studied, and worked in the United States from 1960 to 1978, between his 11th and his 27th year—except during his military service—and again after the age of 33, when he was appointed deputy ambassador to Washington and then permanent delegate to the United Nations. His political destiny was planned in the United States; in that sense, Netanyahu is a creature of the neoconservatives. The only thing that distinguishes him from them is that, for public relations reasons, he does not possess American nationality. Indeed, a significant number of neoconservatives are Israeli citizens, have family in Israel, or have resided there themselves. Elliott Abrams wrote in

---

[22] Official site: www.yisraelbeytenu.com.
[23] "Lieberman: Do to Hamas what the US did to Japan," *Jerusalem Post*, January 13, 2009, www.jpost.com/Israel/Lieberman-Do-to-Hamas-what-the-US-did-to-Japan.

1997, before becoming deputy national security adviser in the Bush II administration: "Outside the land of Israel, there can be no doubt that Jews, faithful to the covenant between God and Abraham, are to stand apart from the nation in which they live. It is the very nature of being Jewish to be apart—except in Israel—from the rest of the population."[24]

In 1996 the neoconservatives threw all their weight behind their ultimate think tank, the Project for the New American Century (PNAC), directed by William Kristol and Robert Kagan. PNAC recommended taking advantage of the defeat of communism to reinforce American hegemony by preventing the emergence of any rival. Their *Statement of Principles* vowed to extend the current *Pax Americana*, which entailed "a military that is strong and ready to meet both present and future challenges."[25] In its September 2000 report entitled *Rebuilding America's Defenses*, PNAC anticipated that US forces must become "able to rapidly deploy and win multiple simultaneous large-scale wars." This required a profound transformation, including a new military corps, the "US Space Forces," to control both space and cyberspace, and the development of "a new family of nuclear weapons designed to address new sets of military requirements." Unfortunately, according to the authors of the report, "the process of transformation […] is likely to be a long one, absent some catastrophic and catalyzing event—like a new Pearl Harbor."[26]

PNAC's architects played the American hegemony card by draping themselves in the super-patriotic discourse of America's civilizing mission. But their duplicity is exposed in a document brought to public knowledge in 2008: a report published in 1996 by the Israeli think tank Institute for Advanced Strategic and Political Studies (IASPS), entitled *A Clean Break: A New Strategy for Securing the Realm*, written specifically for the new Israeli prime minister, Benjamin Netanyahu. The team responsible for the report was led by Richard Perle, and included Douglas Feith and

---

[24] Elliott Abrams, *Faith or Fear: How Jews Can Survive in a Christian America*, Simon & Schuster, 1997, p. 181.

[25] On PNAC's website, www.newamericancentury.org/statementofprinciples.htm.

[26] PNAC, www.newamericancentury.org/RebuildingAmericasDefenses.pdf.

David Wurmser, who figured the same year among the signatories of PNAC. As its title suggests, the *Clean Break* report invited Netanyahu to break with the Oslo Accords of 1993, which officially committed Israel to the return of the territories it occupied illegally since 1967. The new prime minister should instead "engage every possible energy on rebuilding Zionism" and reaffirm Israel's right to the West Bank and the Gaza Strip.[27]

One thing has not changed since the time of Ezra: Israel needs a foreign empire. Since its founding in 1948 and even more so since its expansion in 1967, Israel's security and sustainability have depended totally on American support. America must therefore remain imperial. But the fall of communism meant the end of the Cold War. And the end of the Cold War would inevitably trigger a refocusing of the United States on internal politics, a return to the founding principles defended by the traditional conservatives (fallen to the rank of "paleoconservatives"). These principles include this famous warning from George Washington during his farewell speech: "The nation which indulges towards another a habitual hatred or a habitual fondness is in some degree a slave. It is a slave to its animosity or to its affection, either of which is sufficient to lead it astray from its duty and its interest. [...] Sympathy for the favorite nation, facilitating the illusion of an imaginary common interest in cases where no real common interest exists, and infusing into one the enmities of the other, betrays the former into a participation in the quarrels and wars of the latter without adequate inducement or justification. [...] And it gives to ambitious, corrupted, or deluded citizens (who devote themselves to the favorite nation), facility to betray or sacrifice the interests of their own country, without odium, sometimes even with popularity."[28]

Israel needed to prevent at all costs an isolationist turn by the United States, which would lead to the abandonment of its "passionate attachment" for Israel. It was therefore necessary to

---

27 Full text on the IASPS website: www.iasps.org/strat1.htm.
28 Former under secretary of state George Ball borrows from this speech the title of his book *The Passionate Attachment* (1992), on US-Israel relationship.

boost the imperialistic spirit of the United States, relying on internal forces already predisposed to such a mission. These historically tended to be on the Democratic side, among the members of the Council on Foreign Relations, notably Zbigniew Brzezinski, Carter's national security adviser and member of the influential Council on Foreign Relations. Brzezinski was basically Russophobic due to his Polish origins. He was the figurehead of the geostrategic current advocating a modern version of the Great Game, which he summarizes in his book *The Grand Chessboard: American Primacy and Its Geostrategic Imperative* (1998). His vision, inherited from the British theorists of the end of the nineteenth century, consists essentially of preventing Russia from allying itself with Europe by digging a "blood trench" between the Slavic and Latin peoples and controlling everything from Central Asia to Ukraine. Afghanistan has always played an important role as a buffer state, and it was Brzezinski who, under Carter, had instigated the destabilization of the pro-Soviet secular regime through the financing and arming of the mujahideen (favoring the radical Islamic allies of Pakistan over the moderates like the pro-Iranian Ahmed Massoud).[29] However, Brzezinski was far from sharing the neoconservative passion for Israel; he even spoke out against Bush Sr.'s Gulf War I. In any case, he remained on the sidelines of the Clinton government and no longer had much influence in Washington in the 1990s.

The alliance of Brzezinski and his friends at the Council on Foreign Relations was therefore far from sufficient to bring America into a major military adventure in the Middle East. For this, the United States needed an enemy. Just as the First and Second World Wars were necessary to found Israel, the Cold War (or Third World War) provided the necessary context for the implementation of the Zionist program; the 1967 annexations would never have been possible without this context. After the dislocation of the Communist bloc, Israel needed a new world war, or at least a new threat of world war,

---

[29] "Les révélations d'un ancien conseiller de Carter," *Le Nouvel Observateur*, January 15, 1998.

to retain the support of the United States. So a new enemy, perfectly fitted to Israel's needs, magically appeared. The new paradigm developed by the masters of hasbara (Israeli propaganda) is summarized in two slogans: the "war on terror" and the "clash of civilizations."

The first was already widely disseminated since the 1980s, especially by Benjamin Netanyahu himself. During his years at the Washington embassy and the United Nations, Netanyahu contributed more than anyone else to introducing into the American consciousness the idea that Arab terrorism not only threatened Israel, but also the United States and the democratic world in its entirety. It is the central message of his books, *International Terrorism: Challenge and Response* (1982); *Terrorism: How the West Can Win* (1986); and *A Place Among the Nations: Israel and the World* (1993). In the latter, he drew a systematic analogy between Arafat and Hitler, and introduced the farfetched claim that the Mufti of Jerusalem, Haj Amin Al-Husseini, had been "one of the initiators of the systematic extermination of European Jewry" by advising Hitler, Ribbentrop, and Himmler (a claim without historical substantiation, but already current in Israeli propaganda). He also wrote: "Violence is ubiquitous in the political life of all Arab countries. [...] International terrorism is the quintessential Middle East export and its techniques are those of the Arab regimes and organisations that invented it."[30] In *Fighting Terrorism: How Democracies Can Defeat Domestic and International Terrorists* (1995), he coined the term "war on terror."

Netanyahu appeared regularly on CNN in the early 1990s, contributing to the transformation of the world's leading news channel into a major Zionist propaganda tool.[31] As Kevin Barrett explains, "The effect of the ubiquitous *terror* trope is to delegitimize the exercise of power by Muslims, and to legitimize the exercise of power against them. Above all, it delegitimizes any Muslim resort to violence—even in self-defense—while

---

[30] Binyamin Netanyahu, *A Place Among the Nations: Israel and the World*, Bantam, 1993, pp. 193, 102–103.
[31] Max Blumenthal, *Goliath*, Nation Books, 2013, pp. 28–31.

offering carte-blanche legitimacy to violent aggression against Muslims."[32]

The term "clash of civilizations," which refers to a broader process encompassing "the war on terror," was used for the first time by one of the most influential thinkers of the neoconservative current, Bernard Lewis (holder of Israeli, British, and American passports) in an article in the September 1990 issue of *Atlantic Monthly*, entitled "The Roots of Muslim Rage." The concept was taken up in a manifesto by Samuel Huntington in *Commentary* magazine in the summer of 1994 and then in a book by the same author published by the Olin Foundation, a neoconservative think tank. After the Soviet peril, prophesied Huntington, here comes the Islamic peril. And do not be mistaken: "The fundamental problem for the West is not Islamic fundamentalism. It is Islam, a different civilization whose people are convinced of the superiority of their culture and are obsessed with the inferiority of their power." Huntington functioned as a liaison between Brzezinski (with whom he co-wrote articles) and the neoconservatives. He shared Brzezinski's pragmatism and vision of the Great Game: "The West won the world not by the superiority of its ideas or values or religion, but rather by its superiority in applying organized violence. Westerners often forget this fact, non-Westerners never do."[33] This was music to the ears of the neoconservatives, who make Huntington a true intellectual star.

Never in history has a book of geopolitics been the subject of such international media hype. Between 1992 and 1994 a parody of intellectual debate was acted in the press, opposing, on one side, Francis Fukuyama and his prophecy of the "end of history"—meaning "the universalization of Western liberal democracy as the final form of human government"—and, on the other side, Samuel Huntington and his vision of the "clash of civilizations." Interestingly, like Brzezinski, Fukuyama and Huntington are members of the Trilateral Commission, and

[32] Kevin Barrett, "Toward a Civil Global Dialogue on Blasphemy vs. Free Speech: A Muslim View," in Kevin Barrett (ed.), *We Are Not Charlie Hebdo*, pp. 1–36 (p. 7).
[33] Samuel Huntington, *The Clash of Civilizations and the Remaking of World Order*, Simon & Schuster, 1996, pp. 217, 51.

Fukuyama is a member of PNAC. Both were token goys, with Fukuyama playing the role of Huntington's stooge, until the attacks of September 11, 2001, validated the latter's prophecy in an appallingly dramatic way. Huntington's book, meanwhile, has been translated into fifty languages and commented on by the entire world's press. At the same time, the "clash of civilizations" has been implanted in mass consciousness by Hollywood, as Jack Shaheen explains in *Real Bad Arabs: How Hollywood Vilifies a People* (Olive Branch Press, 2012), based on the analysis of more than a thousand films over thirty years.[34]

The neocons pressured the Clinton administration to intervene in Iraq, helped by a network of Zionist moles within the FBI and other secret services. On February 26, 1993, a bomb exploded under the World Trade Center in New York City, killing six people, injuring more than a thousand and causing $300 million damage. In the course of the trial it was revealed that an FBI informant, a former Egyptian army officer named Emad Salem, had been asked to supply the conspirators with explosives he believed to be fake and destined for a sting operation. As reported in the *New York Times,* October 28, 1993: "Law-enforcement officials were told that terrorists were building a bomb that was eventually used to blow up the World Trade Center, and they planned to thwart the plotters by secretly substituting harmless powder for the explosives, an informer said after the blast. The informer was to have helped the plotters build the bomb and supply the fake powder, but the plan was called off by an F.B.I. supervisor who had other ideas about how the informer, Emad A. Salem, should be used, the informer said."[35]

The neocons nevertheless called for a global war on terrorism, but Clinton did not relent. In a possibly unrelated incident, on September 11, 1994, a drunken pilot by the name of Frank Eugene Corder crashed his Cessna 150 L into the White

---

[34] Watch also the documentary: "Real Bad Arabs: How Hollywood Vilifies a People."
[35] Ralph Blumenthal, "Tapes Depict Proposal to Thwart Bomb Used in Trade Center Blast," October 28, 1993, on www.nytimes.com.

House lawn two floors below Clinton's bedroom, killing himself in the process.

Next came the Oklahoma City bombing of April 19, 1995. It was, according to investigator Michael Collins Piper, orchestrated or perhaps simply monitored and diverted by the Mossad: "The Mossad's intent was for the tragedy to be linked to the Iraqi government of Saddam Hussein and that this 'false flag' could be used to force then-president Bill Clinton to invade Iraq and bring down Saddam, Israel's hated enemy." But "President Bill Clinton refused to go along with the Zionist agenda and directed those responsible for the investigation— namely the Justice Department and the FBI—to cover up the false flags."[36]

As late as 2004, a book by former television journalist Jayna Davis, *The Third Terrorist*, acclaimed by pro-Zionist elements in the monopoly media, purported to demonstrate that Saddam and bin Laden were involved in a highly unlikely alliance to blow up the Murrah Building in Oklahoma City and blame it on American white supremacists. It is in this context that Monica Lewinski was hired as a White House intern, and has sex with President Clinton from November 1995 to March 1997. After the Clinton administration successfully thwarted the Israeli psychological operation, on January 17, 1998, the first revelation of the President's affair with 22-year-old Monica Lewinsky appeared in *Newsweek*. Lewinsky, the daughter of Zionist east European immigrants, and a graduate of Lewis & Clark College, was a Queen Esther of a new kind. She had confided in her coworker Linda Tripp, who then proceeded to secretly record her torrid phone conversations with Clinton, while Lewinsky kept, unwashed for two years, her blue dress with the incriminating sperm stains. Syrian newspaper *Tishrin Al-Usbu'a* speculates that "her goal was to embarrass President Clinton, to blackmail him and weaken his status before Netanyahu's government."[37]

---

[36] Michael Collins Piper, *False Flags: Template for Terror*, American Free Press, 2013, pp. 128, 15.
[37] *Tishrin Al-Usbu'a*, August 24, 1998, as quoted by the Anti-Defamation League, on archive.adl.org/syria_media/syria_monica.asp.

Indeed, on January 21, 1998, while the *Washington Post* published an article on the Lewinsky case, Clinton urgently received Israeli prime minister Benjamin Netanyahu for an unannounced 90-minute interview. On January 26, 1998, Clinton received a real ultimatum, in the form of a letter signed by Elliott Abrams, Robert Kagan, William Kristol, Richard Perle, Paul Wolfowitz, and other neoconservatives urging him to use his State of the Union address to make removal of Saddam Hussein's regime the "aim of American foreign policy" and to use military action because "diplomacy is failing." Were Clinton to do that, the signers pledged to "offer our full support in this difficult but necessary endeavor."[38] Clinton did nothing: his speech was entirely centered on the economy (the central theme of his election campaigns and his presidency). In the months that followed, the "Monicagate" scandal became an ordeal for Clinton, who was charged with perjury and threatened with impeachment.

The "New Pearl Harbor"

In November 2000, Bush Jr. was elected under conditions that raised protests of electoral fraud. Two dozen neoconservatives took over key positions in foreign policy. The White House spokesman, Ari Fleischer, was a neocon, as was the president's main speechwriter David Frum, who co-authored in 2003 a book with Richard Perle, *An End to Evil: How to Win the War on Terror*. Dick Cheney, after leading the victorious Bush campaign, chose for himself the vice presidency, picked Scooter Libby as his deputy, and took the leading role in forming Bush's government. He entrusted the State Department to Colin Powell, but surrounded him with neocon aides such as David Wurmser. Another "Sabbath goy" was National Security Adviser Condoleezza Rice, a Russia specialist with no expertise in the Middle East, which made her entirely dependent on her neocon adviser Philip Zelikow. William Luti and Elliott Abrams, and later Eliot Cohen, were also tasked with steering Rice. But it was mainly from within the Defense Department under Donald

---

[38] Patrick Buchanan, "Whose War?," *op. cit.*

Rumsfeld that the most influential neocons were able to fashion US foreign and military policy. Richard Perle occupied the crucial position of director of the Defense Policy Board, responsible for defining military strategy, while Paul Wolfowitz became the "soul of the Pentagon" as deputy secretary with Douglas Feith as under secretary. As for President Bush, he once declared to journalists: "If you want a glimpse of how I think about foreign policy, read Natan Sharansky's book, *The Case for Democracy*. It's a great book." Sharansky is a radical Zionist, founder of the party Yisrael Ba'aliya ("Israel for aliyah") and chairman of One Jerusalem, which advocates Israeli sovereignty over a unified Jerusalem.[39]

After eight months in the presidency (almost half of them on vacation) Bush was confronted with the "catastrophic event" that PNAC had called for a year earlier. The culprit was immediately identified as Osama bin Laden. It was a real "Hanukkah miracle" for Israel, commented *Haaretz* journalist Aluf Benn: "Osama bin Laden's September 11 attacks placed Israel firmly on the right side of the strategic map with the US, and put the Arab world at a disadvantage as it now faces its own difficult decisions about its future." On the day of the attacks, acting Prime Minister Ariel Sharon announced at a press conference: "The war against terror is an international war. A war of a coalition of the free world against all of the terror groups...This is a war between the good and the bad, between humanity and those who are bloodthirsty. The criminal attack today on innocent civilians in the United States, is a turning point in war against international terror."[40] As for Netanyahu, he commented: "It's very good [...] it will generate immediate sympathy [...], strengthen the bond between our two peoples, because we've experienced terror over so many decades, but the United States has now experienced a massive hemorrhaging of terror."[41]

---

[39] Brandon Martinez, *Grand Deceptions: Zionist Intrigue in the 20th and 21st Centuries*, k. 323–7.

[40] Brandon Martinez, *Grand Deceptions, op. cit.*, k. 692, 496.

[41] James Bennet, "Spilled Blood Is Seen as Bond That Draws 2 Nations Closer," *New York Times*, September 12, 2001.

The first to publicly announce the name of bin Laden was Ehud Barak, the outgoing Israeli prime minister (1999–2001), in an interview with the BBC just one hour after the destruction of the Twin Towers of the World Trade Center (and again the following day). He concluded: "It's a time to launch an operational, complete war against terror."[42] The world's media proclaimed the new era of the clash of civilizations and the war on terrorism. "It is the day that will change our lives. It is the day when the war that the terrorists declared on the US [. . .] has been brought home to the US," proclaimed Lewis Paul Bremer, chairman of the National Commission on Terrorism, on NBC the same day, pointing to bin Laden as "a prime suspect."[43]

The message was hammered day after day into the minds of traumatized Americans. On September 21, Netanyahu published an op-ed in the *New York Post* entitled "Today, We Are All Americans," in which he delivered his favorite propaganda line: "For the bin Ladens of the world, Israel is merely a sideshow. America is the target." Three days later the *New Republic* responded with a headline on behalf of the Americans: "We are all Israelis now." Americans experienced 9/11 as a product of anti-US hatred from an Arab world engendered by terrorist Islamism, and they felt an immediate sympathy for Israel, which the neoconservatives relentlessly exploited. One of the goals was to encourage Americans to view Israel's oppression of the Palestinians as part of the global fight against Islamic terrorism.

It was a great success. In the years preceding September 11, Israel's reputation on the international stage had bottomed out; condemnations had been raining from around the world for its policy of apartheid and annexation, and increasing numbers of American voices questioned the merits of the special relationship between the United States and Israel. Only a few hours after the attacks, former CIA analyst George Friedman could write on his website stratfor.com: "The big winner today, intended or not, is the state of Israel. Israel has been under siege

---

[42] See on YouTube, "Ehud Barak, interviewed on BBC an hour after attacks"; see him also on the BBC News talk show "Hard Talk" on September 12.
[43] YouTube, "Paul Bremer interview, NBC, 12:46, 9/11."

by suicide bombers for more than a year. It has responded by waging a systematic war against Palestinian command structures. The international community, particularly the United States, has pressured Israel heavily to stop its operations. The argument has been made that the threat of suicide bombings, though real, does not itself constitute a genuine threat to Israeli national security and should not trigger the kind of response Israel is making. Today's events change all of this. [...] There is no question, therefore, that the Israeli leadership is feeling relief."[44] As Americans now intended to fight Arab terrorists to the death, they would stop demanding from Israel more proportionate retaliation.

The signatories of the PNAC letter to President Bush on April 3, 2002, (including William Kristol, Richard Perle, Daniel Pipes, Norman Podhoretz, Robert Kagan, and James Woolsey) went so far as to claim that the Arab world hates Israel because it is a friend of the United States, rather than the reverse: "No one should doubt that the United States and Israel share a common enemy. We are both targets of what you have correctly called an 'Axis of Evil.' Israel is targeted in part because it is our friend, and in part because it is an island of liberal, democratic principles—American principles—in a sea of tyranny, intolerance, and hatred."[45] Once again, it was a matter of writing history upside down: in reality, America had no enemy in the Middle East before its alliance with Israel in the late 1960s. But this big lie became the heart of Israel's new strategy for controlling the West. It would be repeated and illustrated as often as necessary: "Extremist Islam does not hate the West because of Israel; it hates Israel because Israel is an integral part of the West and its values of freedom," asserted Benjamin Netanyahu in Paris after the *Charlie Hebdo* attack of January 2015, an event that bore the marks of a staged terror attack designed to illustrate precisely this message.[46]

---

[44] Quoted in Michael Collins Piper, *False Flags: Template for Terror,* American Free Press, 2013, pp. 165–168.

[45] PNAC, www.newamericancentury.org/Bushletter-040302.htm.

[46] See my analysis in Kevin Barrett (ed.), *We Are Not Charlie Hebdo: Free Thinkers Question the French 9/11,* Sifting & Winnowing Books, 2015, pp. 91–101.

The secondary objective of September 11 and the other pseudo-Islamist attacks perpetrated on American and European soil is to persuade as many Jews as possible that they are not safe in the West and that they would do well to settle in Israel. Zionist propaganda making Israel a refuge for the Jews of the world is finding a second wind. Israeli writer Yossi Klein Halevi echoed this view in the October 15, 2001, issue of the pro-Israel *New Republic*: "In the last year, it had become a much-noted irony that Israel was the country where a Jew was most likely to be killed for being a Jew. For many, the United States had beckoned as the real Jewish refuge; in a poll taken just before the bin Laden attacks, 37 percent of Israelis said their friends or relatives were discussing emigration. That probably changed on September 11. I was among the thousands of Israelis who crowded Kennedy Airport on the weekend after the attack, desperate to find a flight to Tel Aviv. 'At least we're going back where it's safe,' people joked."[47]

Thanks to a few skeptical and courageous investigators, many anomalies in the politicians' and media's explanation of the events of 9/11 were transmitted on the internet during the following months, providing evidence that this was a false flag operation, and that Osama bin Laden was innocent, as he repeatedly affirmed in the Afghan press and on Al Jazeera.[48] The proofs of this appalling fraud have been accumulating ever since, and are now accessible to anyone who takes the trouble to spend a few hours of research on the internet. The scientific evidence is unimpeachable: for example, the Architects and Engineers for 9/11 Truth (AE911Truth.org) have demonstrated that it was impossible for plane crashes and jet fuel fires to trigger the collapse of the Twin Towers. The so-called pancake collapse theory initially invoked by the government institutes in charge of the investigation—like the completely different subsequent official theories—was a farce. It is enough to carefully watch the destruction of the Towers to see that they do

---

[47] Quoted in Michael Collins Piper, *False Flags, op. cit.*, pp. 210–211.
[48] Philippe Broussard, "En dépit des déclarations américaines, les indices menant à Ben Laden restent minces," *Le Monde*, September 25, 2001.

not collapse, but literally explode, pulverizing concrete and projecting pieces of steel beams weighing several hundred tons hundreds of meters laterally at high speeds. The pyroclastic dust that flooded through the streets at high speed after the collapse, not unlike the dust from a volcano, indicates a high temperature mixture of hot gasses and relatively dense solid particles, an impossible phenomenon in a simple collapse.[49] It is also impossible that WTC7, another skyscraper (47 stories), which had not been hit by a plane, collapsed into its own footprint at near free-fall speed, unless by "controlled demolition."[50] "No steel building has ever been destroyed by fire," noted Bill Manning, editor of *Fire Engineering* magazine in the January 2002 issue, calling the government investigation "a half-baked farce."[51]

From their side, members of Firefighters for 9/11 Truth protest that the fires in the Twin Towers were of low intensity and cannot explain their collapse. In 2005, the New York Fire Department (FDNY) released 503 recorded oral testimonies given by firefighters shortly after the events. One hundred and eighteen of them describe sequences of synchronized explosions just before the collapse, well below the zone of impact.[52] Firemen were fighting fires at ground zero for ninety-nine days after September 11. The presence of molten metal in the wreckage, observed by countless witnesses for more than three weeks after the attack, is inexplicable within the framework of the official theory, but is easily explained by the presence of incompletely burned explosives, their combustion slowed by lack of oxygen. Firefighter Philip Ruvolo testified before Étienne Sauret's camera for his film *Collateral Damages* (2011): "You'd get down below and you'd see molten steel—molten

---

[49] See the photos published by the website 9-11 Research, "Twin Towers' Dust Clouds," 911research.wtc7.net/wtc/evidence/photos/dust.html.
[50] The documentary *The Mystery of WTC7* by Architects & Engineers for 9/11 Truth, on Dailymotion, is a good introduction to these technical issues.
[51] Bill Manning, "$elling Out the Investigation," *Fire Engineering*, January 1, 2002.
[52] "Witnesses to the Towers' Explosions," *9-11 Review*, 911review.com/coverup/oralhistories.html.

steel running down the channelways, like you were in a foundry—like lava."[53]

Aviation professionals from the group Pilots for 9/11 Truth also report many impossibilities in the official thesis. And then there are the Shanksville and Pentagon sites: anyone who examines the available photos can see that no crashed jetliners are visible. As for the Twin Towers, opinions differ, but it is in any case established that the charted speeds of the two aircraft, 443 mph and 542 mph respectively, and the precision of the strikes exclude Boeing 767s, because these speeds are virtually impossible near sea level. In the unlikely event such speeds could be attained without the aircraft falling apart, the planes could not be flown accurately, especially by the "terrible pilots" blamed for the attacks. Recall that neither of the black boxes of the jetliners alleged to have hit the World Trade Center was ever found, an incomprehensible situation.

Alleged telephone calls from passengers are equally problematic. Two calls were allegedly made from AA77 by Barbara Olson to her husband Ted Olson. The Olsons are both public figures: Barbara was a well-known CNN reporter, and Ted had been solicitor general during the first Bush term (after defending Bush in the disputed 2000 election, and then Dick Cheney when he refused to submit to Congress Enron-related documents during that investigation). Barbara Olson's calls, reported on CNN in the afternoon of September 11, contributed to crystallizing some details of the official story, such as the "box cutters" used by the hijackers. Repeatedly invited on television shows, Ted Olson frequently contradicted himself when questioned about the calls from his wife. In a 2006 report, the FBI attributed only one call from Barbara Olson, and it was an unconnected call lasting 0 seconds. Barbara Olson, born Kay Bracher of Jewish parents, had studied at Yeshiva University School of Law. After her studies she was hired by the legal firm WilmerHale, of which Jamie Gorelick, a future member of the 9/11 Commission, was a member, and whose clients include many Israeli firms, such as Amdocs, one of the

---

[53] YouTube, "Molten Metal Flows at Ground Zero."

two digital communications companies (with Comverse Infosys) involved in Israeli espionage in the United States.[54]

The two phone calls from airline flight attendant Amy Sweeney of AA11 also deserve scrutiny. In a first call, oddly passed to the American Airlines reservation service, air hostess Amy Sweeney identified "the" hijacker as the passenger in seat 9B, before correcting herself in a second call to designate the passenger in 10B instead. Seat 9B was that of Daniel Lewin, a former officer in Sayeret Matkal, a special unit in the Israel Defense Forces specializing in counterterrorism—in other words a professional assassin. The official story claims that the passenger in 10B was the terrorist Satam Al Suqami (whose famous passport would miraculously escape from the plane to be found on a street in Lower Manhattan) and that Al Suqami killed Daniel Lewin, who was sitting immediately in front of him. It should be remembered that, unlike Lewin, Suqami was not included in the flight manifest published by the airlines. Indeed, none of the four passenger lists included a single Arab name.

Researchers who believe Israel with its American Zionist supporters orchestrated 9/11 cite the behavior of a group of individuals who have come to be known as the "dancing Israelis" since their arrest. Their aim was to pass themselves off as "dancing Arabs." Dressed in ostensibly "Middle Eastern" attire, they were seen by various witnesses on the roof of a van parked in Jersey City, cheering and taking photos with the Twin Towers in the background, at the very moment the first plane hit the North Tower. Alerted by witnesses, the police immediately issued an all-points bulletin. The van was intercepted around 4 pm, with five young men inside: Sivan and Paul Kurzberg, Yaron Shmuel, Oded Ellner, and Omer Marmari. The Kurzberg brothers were formally identified as Mossad agents, and all of them officially worked for a moving company (a classic cover for espionage) named Urban Moving Systems, whose owner, Dominik Otto Suter, quickly fled the

---

[54] Watch the documentary series by Carl Cameron, *Fox News Series on Israeli Spying on US Telecommunications* (erased from the site of Fox, but available on YouTube).

country for Tel Aviv.[55] These five Israelis, the only suspects arrested on the very day of the attacks, were undoubtedly part of a vast network.

Indeed, on that date, the federal police were busy dismantling the largest Israeli spy network ever uncovered on American soil. An official report by the Drug Enforcement Agency (DEA) reported that 140 spies had been apprehended since March 2001, most of them posing as art students selling cheap "made in China" reproductions. Aged from twenty to thirty years old and organized in twenty teams of four to eight members, they visited at least "36 sensitive sites of the Department of Defense." Many of them were identified as members of the Mossad, and six were in possession of phones paid for by a former Israeli vice consul. Sixty arrests occurred after September 11, bringing the total number of Israeli spies arrested to 200. "A majority of those questioned have stated they served in military intelligence, electronic signal intercept, or explosive ordnance units. Some have been linked to high-ranking officials in the Israeli military. One was the son of a two-star general, one served as the bodyguard to the head of the Israeli Army, one served in a Patriot mission unit." Another, Peer Segalovitz, officer in the 605 Battalion of the Golan Heights "acknowledged he could blow up buildings, bridges, cars, and anything else that he needed to."[56] Yet all were finally released. These young Israelis probably played only subordinate roles, but their numbers testify to the important logistics put in place by Israel.

The DEA report also mentions that "the Hollywood, Florida, area seems to be a central point for these individuals."[57] More than 30 out of the 140 fake Israeli students identified before 9/11 lived in that city of 140,000 inhabitants. And this city also happens to be the place where fifteen of the nineteen alleged 9/11 Islamist hijackers had regrouped (nine in

---

[55] Christopher Bollyn, *Solving 9-11: The Deception That Changed the World*, C. Bollyn, 2012, pp. 278–280.
[56] Christopher Bollyn, *Solving 9-11, op. cit.*, p. 159.
[57] Justin Raimondo, *The Terror Enigma: 9/11 and the Israeli Connection*, iUniverse, 2003, p. 3.

Hollywood, six in the vicinity), including four of the five supposed to have hijacked Flight AA11. What was the relationship between the Israeli spies and the Islamist terrorists? We were told by mainstream media that the former were monitoring the latter, but simply failed to report suspicious activities of these terrorists to American authorities. From such a presentation, Israel comes out only slightly tainted, since a spy agency cannot be blamed for not sharing information with the country it is spying in. At most, Israel can be accused of "letting it happen"—a guarantee of impunity. In reality, the Israeli agents were certainly not just monitoring the future "hijackers," but financing and manipulating them, before disposing of them. We know that Israeli Hanan Serfaty, who rented two flats near Mohamed Atta, had handled at least $100,000 in three months. And we also learned from the *New York Times* on February 19, 2009, that Ali al-Jarrah, cousin of the alleged hijacker of Flight UA93 Ziad al-Jarrah, had spent twenty-five years spying for the Mossad as an undercover agent infiltrating the Palestinian resistance and Hezbollah since 1983.[58]

Artist cover seems popular with Israeli spies. Shortly before September 11, a group of fourteen "artists" under the name of Gelatin installed themselves on the ninety-first floor of the North Tower. There, as a work of "street art," they removed a window and extended a wooden balcony—a piece of scaffolding posing as an art work. To understand what role this balcony may have played, it must be remembered that the explosion supposedly resulting from the impact of the Boeing AA11 on the North Tower took place between the ninety-second and the ninety-eighth floors. It should be added that floors ninety-three to one hundred were occupied by Marsh & McLennan, whose CEO was Jeffrey Greenberg, son of wealthy Zionist (and financier of George W. Bush) Maurice Greenberg, who also happens to be the owner of Kroll Inc., the firm in charge of security for the entire World Trade Center complex on 9/11. The Greenbergs were also the insurers of the Twin Towers and,

---

[58] Robert Worth, "Lebanese in Shock Over Arrest of an Accused Spy," *New York Times*, February 19, 2009.

on July 24, 2001, they took the precaution of having the contract reinsured by competitors.

In November 2000, the board of directors of Marsh & McLennan was joined by Lewis Paul Bremer, the chairman of the National Commission on Terrorism, who, on September 11, 2001, would appear on NBC to name bin Laden as prime suspect. In 2003, Bremer would be appointed administrator of the Coalition Provisional Authority in Iraq to level the Iraqi state to the ground and oversee the theft of almost a trillion dollars intended for its reconstruction. With the only film of the impact on the North Tower being that of the Naudet brothers, who are under suspicion for numerous reasons, many researchers are convinced that no aircraft hit this tower, and that the explosion simulating the impact was provoked by pre-planted explosives inside the tower.

It is still impossible to precisely name the masterminds of the operation. But it should be noted that both Netanyahu and Ehud Barak were temporarily out of the Israeli government in September 2001, just like Ben-Gurion at the time of Kennedy's assassination: Barak replaced Netanyahu as prime minister in July 1999, but stepped aside in March 2001 in favor of Ariel Sharon, who brought back Netanyahu as minister of foreign affairs in 2002 (with Netanyahu again becoming prime minister in 2009). A few months before 9/11, Barak, the former head of Israeli military intelligence (Salait Makal), had been "recruited" as a consultant to a Mossad front company, SCP Partner, specializing in security and located a few kilometers from Urban Moving Systems.[59]

A large number of influential Jewish personalities, working inside or outside the government, were important contributors to the operation's orchestration or subsequent manipulation. I shall cite here only two representative examples. The first is Larry Silverstein, the real estate shark who, with his partner Frank Lowy, leased the Twin Towers from New York City in the spring of 2001. The head of the New York Port Authority, who granted Silverstein and Lowy the lease, was none other than

---

[59] Christopher Bollyn, *Solving 9-11, op. cit.*, pp. 278–280.

Lewis Eisenberg, another member of the United Jewish Appeal Federation and former vice president of AIPAC. It appeared that Silverstein had made a very bad deal, because the Twin Towers had to be decontaminated for asbestos. The decontamination process had been indefinitely postponed since the 1980s because of its cost, estimated at nearly $1 billion in 1989. In 2001, the New York Port Authority had been all too happy to shift responsibility to Silverstein.[60]

Immediately after acquiring the Twin Towers, Silverstein renegotiated the insurance contracts to cover terrorist attacks, doubling the coverage to $3.5 billion, and made sure he would retain the right to rebuild after such an event. After the attacks, he took his insurers to court in order to receive double compensation, claiming that the two planes were two separate attacks. After a long legal battle, he pocketed $4.5 billion.[61] A leading member of the United Jewish Appeal Federation of Jewish Philanthropies of New York, the biggest fundraiser for Israel (after the US government, which pays about $3 billion per year in aid to Israel), Silverstein also maintained "close ties with Netanyahu," according to Haaretz (November 21, 2001). "The two have been on friendly terms since Netanyahu's stint as Israel's ambassador to the United Nations. For years they kept in close touch. Every Sunday afternoon, New York time, Netanyahu would call Silverstein."[62]

The second example is Philip Zelikow, executive director of the 9/11 Commission created in November 2002. Thomas Kean and Lee Hamilton, who officially led the commission, revealed in their book *Without Precedent: The Inside Story of the 9/11 Commission* (2006), that the commission "was set up to fail" from the beginning. Zelikow had already written a synopsis and a conclusion for the final report before the first meeting. Zelikow controlled all the working groups, prevented them from

---

[60] "Towers' Destruction 'Solved' Asbestos Problem," on 911research.wtc7.net/wtc/evidence/asbestos.html.

[61] Tom Topousis, "WTC Insure War Is Over," *New York Post*, May 24, 2007, on nypost.com.

[62] Sara Leibovich-Dar, "Up in Smoke," *Haaretz*, November 21, 2001, on haaretz.com/up-in-smoke-1.75334.

communicating with each other, and gave them the singular mission to prove the official story; Team 1A, for example, was tasked to "tell the story of Al-Qaeda's most successful operation—the 9/11 attacks." All information, and any request for information, had to pass through him.

Zelikow is a pure Straussian, a self-proclaimed specialist in terrorism and the creation of "public myths" by "'searing' or 'molding' events [that] take on 'transcendent' importance and, therefore, retain their power even as the experiencing generation passes from the scene."[63] In December 1998, he co-signed with John Deutch an article for *Foreign Affairs* entitled "Catastrophic Terrorism," in which they speculated on what would have happened if the 1993 WTC bombing (already arbitrarily attributed to bin Laden) had been done with a nuclear bomb: "An act of catastrophic terrorism that killed thousands or tens of thousands of people and/or disrupted the necessities of life for hundreds of thousands, or even millions, would be a watershed event in America's history. It could involve loss of life and property unprecedented for peacetime and undermine Americans' fundamental sense of security within their own borders in a manner akin to the 1949 Soviet atomic bomb test, or perhaps even worse. [...] Like Pearl Harbor, the event would divide our past and future into a before and after. The United States might respond with draconian measures scaling back civil liberties, allowing wider surveillance of citizens, detention of suspects and use of deadly force."[64] Such is the man who controlled the governmental investigation on the 9/11 terror attacks.

The Controlled Opposition

A majority of conspiracy groups and sites avoid discussing the role of Israel in 9/11 and prefer to point the finger at President Bush and his clan. Yet the situation in which the president found himself at the time of the attacks—reading *The Pet Goat* with primary schoolchildren in Florida—dramatically illustrates

63 "Philip Zelikow," Wikipedia.
64 David Ray Griffin, *9/11 Contradictions*, Arris Books, 2008, pp. 295–296.

how he was removed from direct control of ongoing operations. In my view, the interminable eight minutes during which Bush remains unresponsive after learning that the second WTC tower had just been hit, made famous by Michael Moore's film *Fahrenheit 9/11*, are to 9/11 what the Zapruder film is to the Kennedy assassination: the moment when Bush was turned into a dummy—the next best thing to a corpse—while Cheney was taking over the real government (as Lou Dubose and Jake Bernstein have shown in *Vice: Dick Cheney and the Hijacking of the American Presidency*).[65]

If the president was taken by surprise on the day of the attacks, why did he cover for the real culprits by validating the bin Laden-Al Qaeda thesis? It was necessary that a means of blackmail against the president and, more generally, against the American state, be prepared in advance. Indeed, as with the JFK assassination, the difficulty was not so much the logistics of the operation itself as the obstruction of the investigation. A large number of very high-ranking people needed to be sufficiently implicated to have an interest in the truth not seeing the light, and to understand instantly that lying (the false flag) also served to cover for them. The best way to create such a situation is the "hijacked conspiracy." This is the hypothesis I developed in my previous book *JFK-9/11*: that decision-makers in the US deep state had planned a false flag attack on a limited scale (for example, fake aircraft events at the Pentagon and Shanksville) with the limited purpose of justifying the invasion of Afghanistan; but that they were taken over by the infiltrated Zionist network, whose goal was much more ambitious. The invasion of Afghanistan to liquidate the Taliban regime, which had become an obstacle to the UNOCAL (Union Oil of California) pipeline project, was prepared in July 2001 after the failure of the final negotiations (it could not have been launched just one month after the 9/11 attacks without having been planned long before). A false attack blamed on Osama bin Laden, a friend and guest of the Taliban, was ordered to justify

---

[65] Lou Dubose and Jake Bernstein, *Vice: Dick Cheney and the Hijacking of the American Presidency*, Random House, 2006.

this intervention on the international scene and in public opinion. In this way the invasion could be disguised as a manhunt.

But this goal did not in itself interest the neoconservatives. What did they care about Afghanistan? What they wanted was a new war against Iraq and then a general conflagration in the Middle East leading to the crumbling of all the real or potential enemies of Israel. So, with the help of their New York super-sayanim (with Larry Silverstein in the lead), they outbid everyone and gave the operation the scale they wanted, taking everyone by surprise. To trigger a war of civilization against the Middle East, there needed to be something visually dramatic and traumatic, like the explosion of the Twin Towers and several thousand deaths. I cannot address here the technical investigation of these attacks, and would encourage the reader to view the documentary by Ace Baker entitled *9/11: The Great American Psy-Opera*[66] and to read my articles.[67]

Thanks to the complicity of the mainstream media, the neoconservatives won the game against small players like George W. Bush, Colin Powell, and Condoleezza Rice, who, unintentionally embroiled in geopolitical machinations of global scope, only had to save face. On September 19 and 20, Richard Perle's Defense Policy Board met in the company of Paul Wolfowitz and Bernard Lewis (inventor of the self-fulfilling prophecy of the "clash of civilizations") but in the absence of Colin Powell and Condoleezza Rice. Those assembled agreed on the need to overthrow Saddam Hussein at the end of the initial phase of the war in Afghanistan. They prepared a letter to Bush, written on PNAC letterhead, to remind him of his historic mission: "Even if evidence does not link Iraq directly to the attack, any strategy aiming at the eradication of terrorism and its sponsors must include a determined effort to remove Saddam Hussein from power in Iraq. Failure to undertake such an effort will constitute an early and perhaps decisive surrender in the war

---

[66] See chapters 6 and 7 on www.youtube.com/playlist?list=PLEA05F393EC843D80.
[67] Especially www.veteransnewsnow.com/2014/08/31/the-911-triple-cross.

on international terrorism."[68] This, again, was an ultimatum. Bush was certainly aware of the leverage that the neocons had acquired over the major print and television media. He was obliged, under penalty of ending in the proverbial trash bin of history, to endorse the invasion of Iraq that his father had refused the Zionists ten years earlier.

As for Brzezinski and other US imperialists, their support for the invasion of Afghanistan made their timid protests against the Iraq war ineffective. It was a little late in February 2007 when Brzezinski denounced before the Senate "a historical, strategic and moral calamity [...] driven by Manichaean impulses and imperial hubris." Anxious to stop the infernal machine he helped set in motion, the former national security advisor publicly worried that the failure in Iraq would soon be "followed by accusations of Iranian responsibility for the failure; then by some provocation in Iraq or a terrorist act in the U.S. blamed on Iran; culminating in a 'defensive' U.S. military action against Iran that plunges a lonely America into a spreading and deepening quagmire eventually ranging across Iraq, Iran, Afghanistan, and Pakistan."[69] In 2012 he declared, regarding the risk of conflagration with Iran, that Obama should stop following Israel like a "stupid mule."[70]

After 9/11, the media played the same double game as after the JFK assassination. Most of the major newspapers and television channels presented the official thesis as verified and incontestable. But some people simultaneously voiced an indirect suspicion of possible complicity of George W. Bush and his father, questioning their relations with the major Saudi families. It was the *New York Times* of July 26, 2003, that first revealed President Bush had requested that a section of 28 pages be classified secret and withdrawn from the report of the 9/11 Commission—a section detailing possible involvement of specific Saudi officials. One of the key men in this blackmail operation was Senator Bob Graham (brother of Philip Graham,

---

[68] Stephen Sniegoski, *The Transparent Cabal, op. cit.*, p. 144.
[69] SFRC Testimony by Zbigniew Brzezinski, February 1, 2007, on foreign.senate.gov /testimony/2007/BrzezinskiTestimony070201.pdf.
[70] YouTube, "Brzezinski: US won't follow Israel like a stupid mule."

son-in-law and successor to the founder of the *Washington Post* Eugene Meyer), who as president of the Senate Intelligence Committee was a member of the Joint Congressional Inquiry on 9/11. In his book *Intelligence Matters: The CIA, the FBI, Saudi Arabia, and the Failure of America's War on Terror* (2004), and in articles, interviews, and conferences, Graham claimed that these 28 pages contained "proofs" that members of the Saudi royal family financed Al-Qaeda, and that they had been censored because of "the special personal friendship between the [Saudi] royal family and the highest levels of our national government [meaning the president]." Graham made his first revelation on *Democracy Now*, the Pacifica network show founded by Amy Goodman,[71] who, according to Wikipedia, is "of Orthodox Jewish heritage; her maternal grandfather was an Orthodox rabbi." *Democracy Now*, which regularly invites Noam Chomsky, is a typical example of controlled opposition whose aim is to maintain dissent within the dominant paradigm (bin Laden's guilt) while giving the illusion of adversarial debate. But the threat of disclosing the classified pages, which have since been regularly mentioned by the press, also maintained the pressure on Bush and his clan and prevented them from pointing the finger at Israel.

Simultaneously, the neoconservatives blackmailed the Saudi dynasty. Speaking in an interview with PBS in December 2002, Graham sent a message to Saudi Arabia with his "evidence that foreign governments have helped to facilitate the activities of at least some of the terrorists in the United States." David Wurmser had already opened hostilities with an article in the *Weekly Standard* of October 29, 2001, entitled: "The Saudi Connection: Osama bin Laden's a Lot Closer to the Saudi Royal Family Than You Think." In June 2002, the *Hudson Institute*, a bastion of neoconservative doctrine, sponsored a seminar on the theme "Discourses on Democracy: Saudi Arabia, Friend or Foe?"—most guests suggesting that "foe" is the correct answer—then promoted the book *Hatred's Kingdom: How Saudi Arabia Supports the New Global Terrorism* by Dore Gold, who has

---

[71] "Bob Graham on Democracy Now about the Sauds and 9/11," on YouTube.

served as advisor to Netanyahu and Sharon as well as ambassador to the United Nations. On July 10, 2002, the Franco-American neoconservative Laurent Murawiec, a member of the Hudson Institute and the Committee on the Present Danger, appeared before Richard Perle's Defense Policy Board to explain that Saudi Arabia is "the kernel of evil, the prime mover, the most dangerous opponent" and recommend that the United States invade, occupy, and fragment the state. He summarized his "Grand Strategy for the Middle East" with these words: "Iraq is the tactical pivot, Saudi Arabia the strategic pivot, Egypt the prize."[72] In their book published in 2003, *An End to Evil: How to Win the War on Terror*, Richard Perle and David Frum, Bush's speechwriter, argue that "the Saudis qualify for their own membership in the axis of evil," and implore President Bush to "tell the truth about Saudi Arabia," namely that the Saudi princes finance Al-Qaeda.[73] These repeated threats were highly effective, judging by the evolution of Saudi policy, which in the following decades played Israel's game by redirecting its jihadist networks against Libya and Syria.

In the quest for the truth about September 11 as in the Kennedy case, controlled opposition operates on many levels, and many honest scholars now realize that the 9/11 truth movement itself is largely channeled to hide the role of Israel. The half-truth of the exclusively "inside job" thesis, which denounces 9/11 as a false flag operation perpetrated by the American state on its own citizens, functions like a secondary false flag, insofar as it protects the real masters of the operation, who are in fact agents in the service of a foreign nation. One of the aims of this "inside job" maneuver is to force American leaders to maintain the "bin Laden did it" masquerade, knowing that raising the mask would reveal the features of Uncle Sam. No longer controlling the media, they would not have the means to raise this second veil to reveal the face of the real culprit. Any effort to get at the truth would be political suicide. Everyone

---

[72] Thomas E. Ricks, "Briefing Depicted Saudis as Enemies; Ultimatum Urged to Pentagon Board," *Washington Post*, August 6, 2002.

[73] Stephen Sniegoski, *The Transparent Cabal, op. cit.*, p. 204.

understands the issue: if one day, under mounting pressure from public opinion or for some other strategic reason, the mainstream media abandons the official bin Laden story, the well-rehearsed slogan "9/11 was an inside job" will have prepared Americans to turn against their own government, while the neocon Zionists will remain untouchable. And God knows what will happen, if the government has not by then succeeded in disarming its citizens through Sandy Hook-type psy-ops. Government officials have little choice but to stick to the Al-Qaeda story, at least for the next fifty years.

After reaching this conclusion, which I defended in a long Internet article,[74] I had the satisfaction of finding that Victor Thorn, in a book that had eluded me, had expressed it much earlier, and in harsher terms:

"In essence, the '9-11 truth movement' was created *prior* to Sept. 11, 2001 as a means of suppressing news relating to Israeli complicity. By 2002–2003, 'truthers' began appearing at rallies holding placards that read '9-11 was an inside job.' Initially, these signs provided hope for those who didn't believe the government and mainstream media's absurd cover stories. But then an awful realization emerged: The slogan '9-11 was an inside job' was quite possibly the greatest example of Israeli propaganda ever devised. [...] The mantra, '9-11 was an inside job' is only partially true and is inherently damaging to the 'truth movement' because it shifts all attention away from Israel's traitorous assault against America. [...] Leaders of these fake 9-11 groups know the truth about Israel's 9-11 barbarity. Their willingness to perpetuate or cover it up ultimately makes them as guilty and vile as those who launched the attacks. There are no degrees of separation in this matter. It's a black-and-white issue. Tell the entire truth about Israel's Murder, Inc. cabal, or sleep in the same infected bed as these murdering dogs lie in. [...] Faux conspiratologists complain about the government and news

---

[74] Laurent Guyénot, "The 9/11 Triple Cross," Aug. 31, 2014, veteransnewsnow.com.

sources not telling the truth, yet they've erected an utter blackout on data regarding Israel and 9-11."[75]

There is evidence that the 9/11 truth movement was infiltrated and infected very early in order to divert it from the Mossad job track and fix it on the inside job track: the possible forgery of a top-secret memorandum entitled Operation Northwoods, the blueprint for a false flag operation conceived to serve as a *casus belli* against Cuba in 1962. General Lyman Lemnitzer, chairman of the Joint Chiefs of Staff, is said to have presented it to Kennedy's defense secretary Robert McNamara, who rejected it. The project consisted of a wave of terrorist acts falsely attributed to Cuba, culminating in the explosion over Cuban waters of a plane allegedly carrying vacationing American students. The explosion would have been preceded by distress signals indicating an attack by a Cuban fighter. The actual passengers would be secretly transferred to another plane, and a state funeral would be held in their remembrance. This planned operation was revealed to the public by James Bamford in May 2001 in his book *Body of Secrets*,[76] then immediately reported on *ABC News*, so it was fresh in the public mind on 9/11. The film *Loose Change* (2005), the most widely watched dissident documentary in the world, opens with a presentation of Operation Northwoods, making its thesis of a plot emanating from the US government extremely compelling. Operation Northwoods is sufficient to prove that in 1962 the US military had the will and the capacity to organize a false flag attack to trigger a war, and that such an operation would have involved the use of drones and fictitious victims.

It should be noted that the three young Jews who produced this film (Dylan Avery, Corey Rowe, and Jason Bermas), associated with Alex Jones, hitched their whole thesis to an operation that was never carried out. They failed to mention the attack on the USS Liberty, which actually took place. They did not breathe a word about the double loyalty of the

---

[75] Victor Thorn, *Made in Israel: 9-11 and the Jewish Plot Against America*, Sisyphus Press, 2011, on www.pdf-archive.com/2014/06/06/made-in-israel/.

[76] James Bamford, *Body of Secrets: How America's NSA and Britain's GCHQ Eavesdrop on the World*, Century, 2001, pp. 84–90.

neoconservatives, and treated anyone who cited the Israeli role in 9/11 as anti-Semitic. The Operation Northwoods revelations killed two birds with one stone. The scandal was also picked up by recent books on the Kennedy assassination incriminating the CIA, the Pentagon, and the military-industrial complex, thus illustrating the Machiavellianism of the military elites and their conflict with the president, who ostensibly sacked Lemnitzer for daring to imagine Operation Northwoods.[77]

There is even a reasonable chance that the document is a forgery, as Carol Valentine has suggested by pointing out a few anachronistic British colloquialisms.[78] When asked about it in 2006, at a time when he spoke openly of many other dark secrets, Robert McNamara, to whom the Northwoods memo was supposedly given, declared: "I have absolutely zero recollection of it."[79] Moreover, in 1962, Lemnitzer was not dismissed but promoted to supreme commander of NATO forces in Europe. The Northwoods document is not listed on any government site. It is apparently Bamford who provided it to the National Security Archive Project at George Washington University, where it is searchable.[80] Random House informs us that, to write his book, Bamford—an ex-Navy employee gone into journalism after Watergate, just like Bob Woodward—was granted "unprecedented access to Crypto City (the NSA campus in Ft. Meade, MD), senior NSA officials, and thousands of NSA documents," by none other than NSA director Michael Hayden.[81]

In other words, it was Hayden who supplied Bamford with his sources, including, presumably, the Northwoods memorandum. We do not know where he found it since this memo is supposed to be the copy found in the personal papers of Lemnitzer (who, we are told, destroyed all his archives at the

---

[77] For example, James Douglass, *JFK and the Unspeakable: Why He Died and Why It Matters*, Touchstone, 2008, pp. 95–97.

[78] Read Carol Valentine's "Operation Northwoods: The Counterfeit," www.public-action.com/911/northwds.html.

[79] David Talbot, *Brothers: The Hidden History of the Kennedy Years*, Simon & Schuster, 2007, p. 107.

[80] National Security Archive: www.gwu.edu/~nsarchiv/news/20010430/.

[81] www.randomhouse.com/features/bamford/author.html.

Pentagon himself). After moving to the CIA, Hayden retired as a principal at the Chertoff Group, the security consultancy founded by Michael Chertoff.[82] Chertoff, son of a rabbi and a pioneer of Mossad, is one of the key moles placed to obstruct any genuine inquiry into 9/11. For example, it was Chertoff who stopped the FBI's investigation into the five "dancing Israelis," repatriating them back to Israel for mere "visa violations." So we should reasonably consider the possibility that Operation Northwoods was invented four months before 9/11 for the purpose of predisposing truth seekers toward the hypothesis of a US rather than Israeli false flag operation, and toward the hypothesis of US military drones crashing into the WTC.

In my opinion, the Northwoods memo, which appeared out of nowhere four months before September 11, is one of the false clues planted before and after the event in order to put skeptics on the trail of an American conspiracy rather than an Israeli one. It was probably with the same aim of preconditioning the protest movement that the Fox TV channel (a sounding board for neoconservative-Zionist propaganda) broadcast on March 4, 2001, the first episode of *The Lone Gunmen* TV series, seen by 13 million Americans, in which computer hackers working for a secret cabal within the government hijack a jet by remote control with the intention of crashing it into one of the Twin Towers, while making it appear to have been hijacked by Islamic terrorists, with the purpose of triggering a global war on terrorism.[83]

The Fourth World War

In the days that followed 9/11, the president's speeches (written by the neoconservative David Frum) would characterize the terrorist attack as the trigger for a world war of a new type, one fought against an invisible enemy scattered throughout the Middle East. First, vengeance must come not only against bin Laden, but also against the state harboring him: "We will make

---

[82] Seamus Coogan, "Addendum: Who Is James Bamford? And What Was He Doing with ARRB?," August 2010, on www.ctka.net.
[83] YouTube, "The Lone Gunmen Pilot – 9/11 Predictive Programming."

no distinction between those who committed these acts and those who harbor them" (September 11). Second, the war extends to the world: "Our war on terror begins with Al Qaeda, but it does not end there. It will not end until every terrorist group of global reach has been found, stopped and defeated" (September 20). Seven countries were declared "rogue states" for their alleged support of global terrorism: Iran, Iraq, Syria, Libya, Sudan, Cuba and North Korea (September 16). Third, any country that does not support Washington will be treated as an enemy: "Every nation, in every region, now has a decision to make. Either you are with us, or you are with the terrorists" (September 20).[84] These new rules would provide a pretext for endless aggression against any and all Muslim countries: it would be enough to claim that they harbor terrorists. By equating the "war on terrorism" with a "crusade" (September 16), Bush validated the concept of a war between civilizations.

In an article in the *Wall Street Journal* dated November 20, 2001, the neoconservative Eliot Cohen dubbed the war against terrorism as "World War IV," a framing soon echoed by other American Zionists. In September 2004, at a conference in Washington attended by Norman Podhoretz and Paul Wolfowitz entitled "World War IV: Why We Fight, Whom We Fight, How We Fight," Cohen said: "The enemy in this war is not 'terrorism' [...] but militant Islam." Like the Cold War (considered to be WWIII), this imminent Fourth World War, according to Cohen's vision, has ideological roots, will have global implications, and will last a long time, involving a whole range of conflicts. The self-fulfilling prophecy of a new World War centered in the Middle East has also been popularized by Norman Podhoretz, in "How to Win World War IV" (*Commentary*, February 2002). It was followed by a second article in September 2004, "World War IV: How It Started, What It Means, and Why We Have to Win," and finally in 2007 in a book called *World War IV: The Long Struggle Against Islamofascism*.[85]

---

84 Bush's speeches on www.presidentialrhetoric.com/.
85 Stephen Sniegoski, *The Transparent Cabal, op. cit.*, p. 193.

General Wesley Clark (son of Benjamin Jacob Kanne and proud descendant of a lineage of rabbis), former commandant of NATO in Europe, writes in his book *Winning Modern Wars* (2003) that one month after September 11, 2001, a Pentagon general showed him a memo from neoconservative strategists "that describes how we're gonna take out seven countries in five years, starting with Iraq, and then Syria, Lebanon, Libya, Somalia and Sudan and finishing off with Iran."[86] In his September 20 speech, President Bush also cited seven "rogue states" for their support of global terrorism: Iran, Iraq, Syria, Libya, Sudan, Cuba, and North Korea. It is curious to note in this list the presence of Cuba and North Korea, which replace Lebanon and Somalia on Clark's list. One possible explanation is that Bush or his entourage refused to include Lebanon and Somalia, but that the number seven was retained for its symbolic value, perhaps as an encrypted signature. Indeed, the motif of the "Seven Nations" doomed by God forms part of the biblical myths instilled in Israeli schoolchildren. According to Deuteronomy, Yahweh says that he will deliver to Israel "seven nations greater and mightier than [it]," adding: "you must utterly destroy them; you shall make no covenant with them, and show no mercy to them. You shall not make marriages with them..." (7:1–2). It is further prophesied to Israel: "And he will give their kings into your hand, and you shall make their name perish from under heaven" (7:24). In the twelfth century, Maimonides affirmed in his *Book of Commandments* that the injunction to "let not a single Canaanite survive" was binding for all time, adding: "Putting the seven nations to the sword is a duty incumbent on us; indeed, it is an obligatory war."[87]

Iraq was the first nation attacked by the Anglo-American coalition. The justification given by the government and the media was the stock of "weapons of mass destruction" held by Saddam. CIA director George Tenet was reluctant to confirm this threat. He knew that Saddam no longer had any such arms, thanks to information provided by his son-in-law Hussein

---

[86] Wesley Clark, *Winning Modern Wars*, Public Affairs, 2003, p. 130.
[87] André Gaillard, *Les Racines judaïques de l'antisémitisme*, AMG Éditions, 2012, p. 84.

Kamel who fled Iraq in 1995 after being in charge of Iraq's military industry. But the CIA, accused of incompetence for not being able to prevent September 11, was under intense pressure; Britt Snider, a close professional associate of Tenet's, had already been forced to resign as staff director of the joint House and Senate Intelligence Committee investigation of the 9/11 attacks, due to the claim of a conflict of interest made by Frank Gaffney Jr., president of the Center for Security Policy (CSP) founded by William Kristol. Cheney and Rumsfeld could then renew their winning Team B strategy, essentially overtaking the CIA with a parallel structure set up to produce the alarmist report they needed: the Office of Special Plans (OSP), a special unit within the Near East and South Asia (NESA) offices at the Pentagon. Nicknamed "the Cabal," the OSP was controlled by neoconservatives William Luti, Abram Shulsky, Douglas Feith, and Paul Wolfowitz. Lieutenant Colonel Karen Kwiatkowski, who worked for the NESA at this time, testified in 2004 to the incompetence of members of the OSP, whom she saw "usurp measured and carefully considered assessments, and through suppression and distortion of intelligence analysis promulgate what were in fact falsehoods to both Congress and the executive office of the president."[88] Either convinced or pretending to be, the president then announced to the nation, on October 7, 2002, that Saddam Hussein could at any time "provide a biological or chemical weapon to a terrorist group or individual terrorists." Bush further claimed that Saddam also possessed the aircraft and drones necessary to "disperse chemical or biological weapons across broad areas [. . .], targeting the United States"; even worse, "the evidence indicates that Iraq is reconstituting its nuclear weapons program." Time was running out, for Saddam "could have a nuclear weapon in less than a year. And if we allow that to happen, a terrible line would be crossed. [. . .] Facing clear evidence of peril, we cannot wait for the final proof, the smoking gun that could come in the form of a mushroom cloud."[89]

---

[88] Stephen Sniegoski, *The Transparent Cabal, op. cit.*, p. 162.
[89] Stephen Sniegoski, *The Transparent Cabal, op. cit.*, p. 155.

Despite his initial reluctance, Secretary of State Colin Powell pleaded for war before the United Nations General Assembly on February 5, 2003. In 2005, after resigning to give way to Condoleezza Rice, he publicly regretted his speech to the UN, calling it "a blot on my record" and claiming to have been deceived.[90] His chief of staff, Colonel Lawrence Wilkerson, likewise would confess in 2006, soon after resigning: "My participation in that presentation at the UN constitutes the lowest point in my professional life. I participated in a hoax on the American people, the international community and the United Nations Security Council."[91] In 2011, Wilkerson openly denounced the duplicity of neoconservatives such as David Wurmser and Douglas Feith, whom he considered "card-carrying members of the Likud party. […] I often wondered if their primary allegiance was to their own country or to Israel. That was the thing that troubled me, because there was so much that they said and did that looked like it was more reflective of Israel's interest than our own."[92]

The fact that the invasion of Iraq and the destruction of all its state structures was carried out on behalf of Israel is now widely accepted. Even the best liars betray themselves sometimes, and Philip Zelikow let slip the secret during a conference at the University of Virginia on September 10, 2002: "Why would Iraq attack America or use nuclear weapons against us? I'll tell you what I think the real threat is and actually has been since 1990: it's the threat against Israel. And this is the threat that dare not speak its name, because the Europeans don't care deeply about that threat, I will tell you frankly. And the American government doesn't want to lean too hard on it rhetorically, because it is not a popular sell."[93]

---

[90] Steven Weisman, "Powell Calls His U.N. Speech a Lasting Blot on His Record," *New York Times,* September 9, 2005, on www.nytimes.com.
[91] Transcript on www.pbs.org/now/politics/wilkerson.html.
[92] Stephen Sniegoski, *The Transparent Cabal, op. cit.,* p. 120.
[93] Noted by *Inter-Press Service* on March 29, 2004, under the title "U.S.: Iraq war is to protect Israel, says 9/11 panel chief," and repeated by *United Press International* the next day, on www.upi.com.

And thus did Israel get rid of its worst enemy without losing
a single human life or spending a single penny. The cost to
Americans was valued at $3 trillion in 2008 by economist Joseph
Stiglitz, and would likely exceed $5 trillion.[94] The resulting
impoverishment was not felt until 2008, and then with extreme
violence, because Americans had been artificially immersed in a
bubble of economic euphoria. Such was the contribution of
Alan Greenspan, president of the Federal Reserve from 1987 to
2006, who, through excessive deregulation, favored the growth
of subprime mortgage companies and caused the overall rate of
individual property ownership to explode. It was, according to
the relevant analysis of Gilad Atzmon, a crucial aspect of the
neoconservative plan: "These figures led Americans to believe
that their economy was indeed booming. And when an economy
is booming nobody is really interested in foreign affairs, certainly
not in a million dead Iraqis."[95]

The Iraq War represented, for the crypto-Zionists who
launched it, a decisive step toward the ever-closer goal of
Greater Israel. It was in this context that the October 2003
"Jerusalem Summit" was held in the symbolically significant
King David Hotel. It was meant to forge an alliance between
Zionist Jews and evangelical Christians around a "theopolitical"
project. This project would consider Israel, in the words of the
"Jerusalem Declaration" signed by its participants, "the key to
the harmony of civilizations," replacing the United Nations that
had become "a tribalized confederation hijacked by Third World
dictatorships": "Jerusalem's spiritual and historical importance
endows it with a special authority to become a center of world's
unity. [. . .] We believe that one of the objectives of Israel's
divinely-inspired rebirth is to make it the center of the new unity
of the nations, which will lead to an era of peace and prosperity,
foretold by the Prophets." Three acting Israeli ministers spoke at
the summit, including Benjamin Netanyahu. Richard Perle, the

---

[94] Joseph Stiglitz, *The Three Trillion Dollar War: The True Cost of the Iraq Conflict*, WW
Norton & Co., 2008.
[95] Gilad Atzmon, *The Wandering Who? A Study of Jewish Identity Politics*, Zero Books,
2011, p. 29.

guest of honor, received on this occasion the Henry Scoop Jackson Award.[96]

The evangelical Christian support for this project should not come as a surprise. With more than fifty million members, the Christians United for Israel movement, founded by John Hagee, had become a considerable political force in the United States. Its president, Pastor John Hagee, author of *Jerusalem Countdown: A Prelude to War* (2007), called without hesitation for "a preemptive military strike against Iran."

Iran, in fact, is the ultimate target of the neoconservatives. An Iran armed with the atomic bomb is indeed the nightmare of Israel. "Never let an enemy country acquire nuclear weapons" is a fundamental principle formulated since the 60s by the leaders of Israel. Netanyahu has for ten years demonized Tehran by accusing it of the darkest designs, before the General Assembly of the UN (September 27, 2012) and before the US Congress (May 24, 2011 and March 3, 2015). "The United States should drop a nuclear bomb on Iran to spur the country to end its nuclear program," proposed American billionaire Sheldon Adelson in 2013. Adelson is one of the biggest donors to both the American Republican party and the Israeli Likud. In 2015 he threatened to use all his money to humiliate and prevent the re-election of any Congressional representative who boycotted Israeli Prime Minister Benjamin Netanyahu's speech in the US Congress.[97]

The second fundamental principle of Israel's foreign policy is known as "the Samson Option." Formulated in the 1970s, when Israel had acquired a sufficient stock of atomic bombs, it is summarized by Ron Rosenbaum in *How the End Begins: The Road to a Nuclear World War III* (2012): "Abandonment of proportionality is the essence of the so-called Samson Option in all its variants. A Samson Option is made possible by the fact that even if Israel has been obliterated, it can be sure that its Dolphin-class nuclear missile submarines cruising the Red Sea,

---

[96] Official website: www.jerusalemsummit.org/eng/declaration.php.
[97] Jim Wall, "Good Morning America, Bibi is Coming to Town," February 15, 2015, on mycatbirdseat.com.

the Indian Ocean, and the Persian Gulf at depths impervious to detection, can carry out a genocidal-scale retaliation virtually anywhere in the world." Israel could easily "bring down the pillars of the world (attack Moscow and European capitals, for instance)" as well as the "holy places of Islam."[98]

A third, tacit principle determines the character of twenty-first-century Israeli proxy wars in the Middle East: the abandonment of the distinction between soldiers and civilians through the category of "terrorist"—which justifies, moreover, contempt for all the "laws of war" by which men have attempted to civilize barbarism. Inhuman treatment in Abu Ghraib prison in Iraq will remain in history as one of the most sinister symbols of this total degradation. Is it a coincidence that, according to the great reporter Robert Fisk of *The Independent* of London: "The head of an American company whose personnel are implicated in the Iraqi tortures [at Abu Ghraib], it now turns out, attended an 'anti-terror' training camp in Israel and, earlier this year, was presented with an award by Shaul Mofaz, the right-wing Israeli defense minister."[99]

"Color revolutions" are regime changes that give the appearance of a revolution, in that they mobilize large segments of the people, but are actually coups d'état, in that they do not aim at changing structures, but rather at substituting one elite for another to lead a pro-US economic and foreign policy. In 2009 the first "green revolution" was launched against Iran. It was puppeteered by Washington and led by expatriated Americanized bloggers. Though a failure, carbon copies succeeded two years later with the "Arab Spring" in Tunisia and Egypt. In 2011 it was revealed that several of the Algerian, Moroccan, Tunisian, Yemeni, Syrian, and Egyptian internet users who triggered the disturbances had taken a training course in 2009 on techniques of peaceful revolutions offered by CANVAS, the Center for Applied Nonviolent Action and Strategies, funded by Freedom House. Freedom House is an

---

[98] Ron Rosenbaum, in *How the End Begins: The Road to a Nuclear World War III*, Simon & Schuster, 2012, pp. 141–142, 21–22.
[99] Robert Fisk, "The Re-writing of Iraqi History Is Now Going On at Supersonic Speed," *The Independent*, May 26, 2004.

organization funded 75 percent by the federal government (via the National Endowment for Democracy and the State Department), which according to its statutes "assists the development of freedoms in the world," on the assumption that "The American predominance in international affairs is essential for the cause of human rights and freedom." Led by James Woolsey, director of the CIA between 1993 and 1995, it has included the famous "philanthropists" Samuel Huntington, Donald Rumsfeld, Paul Wolfowitz, and Zbigniew Brzezinski.

After Egypt it was Libya's turn. Dictator Muammar Gaddafi had committed the double mistake of trying to get closer to Europe and the United States while refusing any compromise with Israel. Tribal, ethnic, and religious rivalries are the Achilles heel of the countries of the Middle East, as a result of their arbitrarily drawn borders on the ruins of the Ottoman Empire. The strategy of destruction consists of encouraging, arming, and financing the groups opposed to the regime, augmented by fanatics and mercenaries of various types, and then casting the resulting disturbances as "repression" in the eyes of Western public opinion. This then justifies armed intervention to "support the rebels." The decisive role played by the French government in convincing the UN Security Council to validate such aggression will remain an indelible stain on the history of France. The former chief of staff of the French Armed Forces, Admiral Édouard Guillaud, declared on January 26, 2014, one week before his retirement: "The South of Libya has become a real black hole [. . .] a place for the regeneration of terrorism, of supplying arms to terrorists, it is the new center of gravity for terrorism."[100]

The hordes of jihadists recruited to destroy Libya (many of them from Iraq) would then be redirected toward Syria to launch the same type of "Arab Spring." Threatened with destruction, Syria was offered as an alternative a puppet government whose president, Burhan Ghalioun, promised in 2011 to "end the military relationship to Iran and cut off arms

---

[100] Hassan Hamadé, "Lettre ouverte aux Européens coincés derrières le rideau de fer israélo-US," May 21, 2014, on www.voltairenet.org/.

supplies to Hezbollah and Hamas, and establish ties with Israel."[101] The true nature of the Syrian "rebels"—stateless barbarians, drug addicts, and Al Qaeda allies—could not be hidden for long from the public. They had to be supported discreetly, as for example by delivering them weapons by way of phantom "moderate rebels," or directly but "by mistake." Meanwhile Israel was taking care of their wounded and sending them back into combat, while occasionally bombing Syrian government positions. As an additional bonus, the image of black-masked medieval butchers served to demonize Islam in the eyes of a public opinion paralyzed by confusion.[102]

Such is the contribution of this new genre of "Marranos." Consider the case of Adam Pearlman, grandson of an administrator of the Anti-Defamation League, who under the pseudonym Adam Yahiye Gadahn, unconvincingly bearded and beturbaned, broadcast anti-American Islamic diatribes in 2009 before being unmasked; or Joseph Leonard Cohen, member of the Revolution Muslim group under the name of Youssef al Khattab.[103] Meanwhile, the FBI and other Zionist-infiltrated secret services continue to foster terror attacks on American soil under the pretext of thwarting them.[104]

---

[101] Joe Quinn, "Syria's Fake Color Revolution," in *ISIS Is US: The Shocking Truth Behind the Army of Terror*, Progressive Press, 2016, p. 26.

[102] Watch "Adam Curtis – Oh Dearism" on YouTube.

[103] "American al Qaeda member acknowledges Jewish ancestry," June 13, 2009, on edition.cnn.com; watch "Fake Al Qaeda Actors EXPOSED!" on YouTube.

[104] Glenn Greenwald, "The FBI again thwarts its own Terror plot: Are there so few actual Terrorists that the FBI has to recruit them into manufactured attacks?," *Salon*, September 29, 2011, on www.salon.com.

Chapter 10

THE GREAT GAME OF ZION

> "A man whose testicles have been crushed or whose male member has been cut off must not be admitted to the assembly of Yahweh. No half-breed may be admitted to the assembly of Yahweh; not even his descendants to the tenth generation may be admitted to the assembly of Yahweh."
>
> Deuteronomy 23:2–3

Darwinism, Racism, and Supremacism

We have discussed in chapter 6 the deleterious influence of Thomas Hobbes, the seventeenth-century founder of a new conception of man and the "social contract." We also mentioned his direct heir Adam Smith, who proposed a mercantile utopia that would allegedly transform the sum of individual egoists into a happy community through the free market alone. Soon after Smith there appeared, in the same ideological lineage, Thomas Malthus. The "law of Malthus," enunciated in his *Essay on the Principle of Population* (1798), postulates that any period of prosperity creates an exponential increase in population that, if not stopped, eventually exceeds food production capacity, resulting in famines, wars, and excess mortality. Malthus therefore opposed social protection legislation, for "these laws create the poor whom they assist." Therefore: "If a man cannot feed his children, they must die of hunger." Malthusianism, well-adapted to the Victorian mental climate, inspired Herbert Spencer, who formulated the natural law of "survival of the fittest" in *Progress: Its Law and Cause* (1857) and denounced the absurdity of socialist initiatives aimed at protecting weak individuals from the harsh laws of natural selection.

Spencer's theory, often called "social Darwinism," is now stigmatized as an abusive misappropriation of Charles Darwin's biological evolutionary thought. But it was actually Spencer who prepared the scene for Darwin; Spencer's book appeared two years before Darwin's *On the Origin of Species* (1859). So it is really Darwinism that should be called "biological Spencerism."

Darwin was well received by the Victorian bourgeoisie because he blended the "natural sciences" with the Spencerian law of "survival of the fittest," which was already in embryo in the thought of Thomas Hobbes. Darwin's cousin Francis Galton, author of *Hereditary Genius: An Inquiry Into Its Laws and Consequences* (1869), invented "eugenics" to correct the perverse effect of civilization, which "diminishes the rigour of the application of the law of natural selection and preserves weakly lives that would have perished in barbarous lands." Apparently, Spencer's laissez-faire was not enough; the state must intervene, not to help the weak, but to prevent them from reproducing themselves. It was Leonard Darwin, Charles's son, who led the fight as president of the British Eugenics Society from 1911 to 1928.

Karl Marx, after having for some time shared his friend Friedrich Engels's enthusiasm for Darwin's *Origin of Species* as "the natural-history foundation of our viewpoint," had second thoughts when he recognized that Darwin had merely projected the rules of British capitalism onto the animal kingdom. "It is remarkable," Marx wrote to Engels on June 18, 1862, "how Darwin rediscovers, among the beasts and plants, the society of England with its division of labour, competition, opening up of new markets, 'inventions' and Malthusian 'struggle for existence.' It is Hobbes' *bellum omnium contra omnes* [the war of all against all] and is reminiscent of Hegel's *Phenomenology*, in which civil society figures as an 'intellectual animal kingdom,' whereas, in Darwin, the animal kingdom figures as civil society."[1]

Indeed, the enthusiasm for Darwinism cannot be explained by its scientific merits, and it was not naturalists who first welcomed it. Let us recall that the idea of evolution, that is to say a genealogical kinship between animal species, had been

---

[1] Mehmet Tabak, *Dialectics of Human Nature in Marx's Philosophy*, Palgrave Macmillan, 2012.

popular long before Darwin. Darwin's originality was to suppose that evolution resulted from a blind process of "natural selection" of the Malthusian type, that is, based essentially on competition for resources. From the reasonable hypothesis of the adaptation of species to their environment by natural selection (the common sense hypothesis justified by his observations), Darwin drew up the bold and forever unprovable hypothesis that natural selection is also responsible for the emergence of new species. (A species is defined as a group of individuals capable of breeding among themselves, but not with individuals of another species.) The idea is simple and easily illustrated: When food available to leaf browsers becomes scarce, short-necked browsers die first; and this process, repeated over a very long time scale, produces giraffes. For this to happen requires that some animals be accidentally born with a neck longer than others, and that such accidents accumulate a sufficient number of times to create a new species. By this simple mechanism, Darwin explained how, over a few hundred million years, bacteria became homo sapiens, by way of fish and monkeys.

It is important to understand that, according to Darwin, "natural selection" is not creative in itself, but destructive; it acts only negatively by eliminating the least able individuals. It allows only the preservation of accidental variations, when they are advantageous to the individual under the conditions of existence in which he is placed. Darwin had no idea of the nature and causes of these "accidentally produced variations," and did not exclude factors yet unknown. (As is generally the case, the master was less dogmatic than his students.) It was not until the genetic discoveries of the 1940s that accidental variations were determined to be mistakes in the reproduction of the DNA code.

However, experiments show that genes are replicators and hence stabilizers, and that their accidental mutations only produce degenerations, which are generally sterile, and in no case carry any "selective advantage" that could be passed down. In other words, natural selection tends to preserve the genetic heritage by eliminating individuals who deviate too much from the standard. It has room for maneuver and may eventually produce some adaptation to changes in the environment, but in general it prevents evolution rather than encouraging it. It is true that "artificial selection" in the long run makes it possible to "improve" a domestic animal species from the point of view of a particular criterion (yield of milk or meat, for example) and thus create a new "race." But not a new species; even modern genetic technology does not allow us to take this step.

Genetic discoveries and common sense should therefore have caused the extinction of Darwinism among the credible theories of evolution. Yet this was not the case. On the contrary, since it was less a scientific theory than a theology of the death of God, a new form of speculative Darwinism was coined under the name "the synthetic theory of evolution." It relies entirely on the idea that man has developed purely accidentally from the first bacteria, without the intervention of any intelligent design, by the simple combination of "chance and necessity."[2] Darwinism today synthesizes the idea that modern man is supposed to have of himself and that is inculcated by orthodox education. It is both a doctrine of the essence of man and a myth of the creation of man. Darwinism is the heart of nihilist theology. For this reason, it will probably also resist the new challenge of epigenetics, which proves the genetic inheritance of acquired characteristics, as Jean-Baptiste de Lamarck had theorized.

In 1920, the English writer Bernard Shaw saw in Darwinism (or rather the dogmatic form elaborated by August Weismann and popularized at the time under the name of neo-Darwinism) a new secular religion whose philosophical foundation is the denial of any other reality than matter, alongside the ethical principle of competition for the survival of the fittest. In ten years, Shaw wrote, "Neo-Darwinism in politics had produced a European catastrophe of a magnitude so appalling, and a scope so unpredictable, that as I write these lines in 1920, it is still far from certain whether our civilisation will survive it." But Shaw, who was a proponent of the theory of "creative evolution" or

---

[2] Jacques Monod, *Le Hasard et la nécessité. Essai sur la philosophie naturelle de la biologie moderne* (1970), Points, 2014.

vitalism, like Henri Bergson in France (*Creative Evolution*, 1907), also understood that Darwinism's appeal was linked to the growing disgust that rational thought feels for the capricious and genocidal demiurge of the Old Testament: "What made it scientifically intolerable was that it was ready at a moment's notice to upset the whole order of the universe on the most trumpery provocation."[3] Even today, Darwinian ideology remains in power by fraudulently presenting itself as the only alternative to biblical "creationism." Darwin or the Bible, such is the ridiculous alternative proposed to the docile intelligence of the schoolchildren and students of the West.

The paradigm of Malthus, Spencer, Darwin, and Galton deserves the name "Darwinian paradigm" for three reasons. First, it is the Darwinian idea of "selection" that best summarizes the paradigm. Secondly, this paradigm is now firmly rooted in the supposed Darwinian (actually pre-Darwinian) idea that "man descends from the ape." And finally, Darwin is now the venerated prophet of this secular religion. By convention, therefore, let us call the processes of natural or artificial selection "Darwinian mechanisms" or "Darwinian strategies." This is an abuse of language, since these very real mechanisms do not validate Darwin's speculative theory on the appearance of species; but the terms are justified by usage.

The Darwinian paradigm goes beyond left-right divisions; Spencer's "laissez-faire" is rather right-wing, but Galton's eugenics, which valorizes state interventionism, is historically left-wing.[4] Nonetheless, the latter is merely a more sophisticated version of the former, claiming to support the "survival of the fittest" by the sterilization of the less able. In its classical form, "social Darwinism" is a faithful ally of Smith's economic liberalism. "Millionaires are the product of natural selection, acting on the whole social body to choose those who meet the requirements of a given task," enthused the American William Graham Sumner in 1907.

---

[3] Bernard Shaw, preface to *Back to Methuselah* (1921), on www.gutenberg.org.
[4] André Pichot, *L'Eugénisme ou les généticiens saisis par la philanthropie,* Hatier, 1995.

Darwin is the direct descendant of Hobbes, via Malthus and Spencer. In fact, he only made literal what was still a metaphor in Hobbes: Man is an animal. Not only is the civilized man descended from the savage, but the savage himself descends from the ape. Darwinism soon imposed itself as the metaphysical framework of all "human sciences," and the foundation of a new idea of man, who is no longer distinguished from the animal kingdom by a qualitative leap. Sigmund Freud, among others, owed his success to having re-founded psychology on Darwinian principles, that is to say, on the premise that the creative spirit of man was only a by-product of his (repressed) animal instincts: "The development of man till now seems to me to require no other explanation than that of animals" (*Beyond the Pleasure Principle*, 1920); "It is merely the principle of pleasure [. . .] which from the outset governs the operations of the psychic apparatus" (*Civilization and Its Discontents*, 1929). Since, according to Darwinian logic, procreation determines selective advantage, it was naturally in the sex drive that Freud found the key to the human psyche.

Darwinism scientifically condoned racism, the ideological justification for colonialism, slavery, and ethnic cleansing. Darwin had extended his theory from animal species to human races in his second work, *The Descent of Man, and Selection in Relation to Sex* (1871), in which he predicted that in a few centuries, "the civilized races of man will almost certainly exterminate, and replace, the savage races throughout the world." Darwin brought to this idea the stamp of natural science, and above all, by linking it to his theory of the origin of species, he implicitly placed this genocidal process in the continuity of a positive evolution that had earlier produced the savage from the monkey.

The English and the Americans found in Darwin the confirmation of the superiority of the "Anglo-Saxon" or "Nordic" race: "a race of leaders, organizers and aristocrats," according to the American Madison Grant. In *The Passing of the Great Race* (1916) Grant advocated limiting the immigration of other European races ("Alpine" and "Mediterranean") and maintaining segregation between black and white because "once raised to social equality their influence will be destructive to themselves and to the whites." The worst danger was that whites and blacks would "amalgamate and form a population of race bastards in which the lower type ultimately preponderates."

Judaism as Darwinian Strategy

The Darwinian paradigm has a strong resonance among Jewish supremacists. Harry Waton wrote in his *Program for the Jews,* published in 1939: "Since the Jews are the highest and most cultured people on earth, the Jews have a right to subordinate to themselves the rest of mankind and to be the masters over the whole earth. Now, indeed, this is the historic destiny of the Jews."[5]

In fact, the notion of natural selection among human races came to Jewish thinkers long before it dawned on Spencer and Darwin. As mentioned in chapter 5, the Marrano Isaac de la Peyrère can be considered as a precursor, with his Talmudic theory of the Adamic origin of the Jews and pre-Adamic origin of the Gentiles (*Præadamitæ*, 1655). Seven years before Darwin's *The Origin of Species*, it was Disraeli who developed a proto-Darwinian vision of the struggle of the races: "It is in vain for man to attempt to baffle the inexorable law of nature which has decreed that a superior race shall never be destroyed or absorbed by an inferior" (*Lord George Bentinck,* 1852). Shortly thereafter, the inventors of the first Darwinian racialist theories were Jewish authors, such as Ludwig Gumplowicz, professor of political science in Graz for twenty years and author of *The Struggle of Races* (1883).

Many of the most enthusiastic disciples of Spencer, Darwin, and Galton were Jewish. Lucien Wolf, a well-known journalist, editor-in-chief of the *Jewish World,* but also a politician and historian, was one of the first to develop a "Darwinian" theory of Jewish racial superiority, in an 1884 article entitled "What Is Judaism? A Question of Today," published in the *Fortnightly Review,* one of the most popular and influential British magazines. Jewish superiority, he wrote, "constitutes almost a

---

[5] Harry Waton, *A Program for the Jews and an Answer to All Anti-Semites: A Program for Humanity,* 1939 (archive.org), pp. 99–100.

stage in evolution" (unlike the followers of Mohammed, who "are among the rotting branches of the great tree of humanity"). This superiority is the result of eugenic principles enshrined in Jewish law, and encouraged by tradition: "The natural impulse to reject all further infusions of alien blood, as soon as the consciousness of superiority was reached, found every support in their national legends and traditions, and became accentuated by the hostility of their neighbours." The key to Jewish superiority is, therefore, consanguinity: "Jewish separatism, or 'tribalism,' as it is now called, was invented to enable the Jews to keep untainted for the benefit of mankind not only the teachings of Judaism but also their physical results as illustrations of their value."[6] Like many thinkers of his time, Wolf was actually more Larmarckian than Darwinian, since he did not speak of "selection" and thus suggested that Talmudic eugenics produces acquired traits that are transmitted. But let us not forget that Darwin himself did not exclude this Lamarckian factor.

On the other hand, Wolf refers here only to a process internal to "race." His contemporary and friend Joseph Jacobs, who worked with Francis Galton, emphasized the competitive relationship between races, thus introducing a factor of selection. In his *Studies in Jewish Statistics: Social, Vital and Anthropometric* (1891), a collection of articles first published in the *Jewish Chronicle*, Jacobs suggests that persecution has brought out the best of Jewish potentialities: "The weaker members of each generation have been weeded out by persecution which tempted them or forced them to embrace Christianity, and thus contemporary Jews are the survival of a long process of unnatural selection which has seemingly fitted them excellently for the struggle for intellectual existence."[7] This perception of persecution as a selective factor—a Spencerian mechanism ensuring the "survival of the fittest" by way of the expulsion of "soft" Jews from the gene pool—is a commonplace in the

---

[6] Daniel Langton, "Jewish evolutionary perspectives on Judaism, antisemitism, and race science in late nineteenth-century England: a comparative study of Lucien Wolf and Joseph Jacobs," *Jewish Historical Studies*, volume 46, 2014, pp. 37–73, on www.escholar.manchester.ac.uk.

[7] Daniel Langton, "Jewish evolutionary perspectives on Judaism," *op. cit.*

Jewish community's discourse about itself. Theodor Herzl, among many others, evoked this idea without bothering to argue for it, since it went without saying among those he was addressing: "Jew-baiting has merely stripped off our weaklings; the strong among us were invariably true to their race when persecution broke out against them."[8]

Jewish literature about the Jews is full of "Darwinian" explanations of the uniqueness of the Jewish people. Here is an example from the Zionist Nahum Goldmann: "One of the great prodigies of Jewish psychology, which explains to a large extent the extraordinary survival of our people in spite of two thousand years of dispersion, has consisted in creating an absolutely brilliant defense mechanism against the politico-economic situation in which the Jews found themselves—against persecution and exile. This mechanism can be explained in a few words: The Jews have regarded their persecutors as an inferior race."[9] In other words, persecution reinforced the community's sense of superiority.

Here is how Yuri Larin, a close associate of Lenin, explained the overrepresentation of Jews "in the apparatus of public organizations": "The Jewish worker, because of the peculiarity of his past life and because of the additional oppression and persecution he had to endure for many years under tsarism, has developed a large number of special traits that equip him for active roles in revolutionary and public work. The exceptional development of the special psychological makeup necessary for leadership roles has made Jewish revolutionary workers more capable of gaining prominence in public life than the average Russian worker, who lived under very different conditions." According to Larin, the economic "struggle for survival" in overcrowded shtetls had created above-average individuals. "In other words, the conditions of everyday life produced in urban Jews a peculiar, exceptional energy," unlike "the bulk of our Russian workers [who] were of peasant origin and thus hardly

---

8 Theodor Herzl, *The Jewish State*, on www.jewishvirtuallibrary.org.
9 Nahum Goldmann, *Le Paradoxe juif. Conversations en français avec Léon Abramowicz*, Stock, 1976 (archive.org), p. 9.

capable of systematic activity." Moreover, because of the discrimination against Jewish workers under the tsarist regime, "there developed, among this segment of the Jewish people, an unusually strong sense of solidarity and a predisposition toward mutual help and support." Finally, because education had always been the main path of Jews toward emancipation, "tens of thousands of Jewish laboring youth used to spend long years, night in night out, bent over their books, in an attempt to break out of the narrow circle of restrictions. It rarely worked [...], but the higher cultural level acquired in this manner went on to benefit the revolutionary struggle."[10] Jews, in other words, are closer than others to the proverbial New Man that Revolution aimed at creating.

Whatever factors one invokes (persecution, valorization of intellectual work), the consensus result is that the Jews are on average more intelligent than the Gentiles, and therefore well suited for holding power over them. "Superior Jewish intelligence is part of the Jewish self-stereotype," writes Raphael Patai, a Hungarian Jew who taught in Israel before emigrating to the United States, in his book *The Jewish Mind* (1977). "The same rumor is mooted by Gentiles as well. Those of them who are free of the taint of anti-Semitism simply refer to it as a fact, without any emotional overtones, unless it be a twinge of envy or a note of grudging admiration. The anti-Semite will find it possible to speak of Jewish intelligence only in terms of negative connotations such as shrewdness, sharpness, craftiness, cunning, slyness, and the like. [...] All people who know Jews, whatever their reaction to them otherwise, subscribe to the rumor of their intelligence." The rumor is based on fact: studies have shown that Jews have, on average, an IQ well above 100 (the general average), especially, but not exclusively, in the field of "verbal intelligence" (as opposed to "performance intelligence"). Among common Darwinian explanations, Patai mentions the well-known contrast between the Christian tradition of clerical celibacy versus the strong competitiveness of Talmudic scholars

---

[10] Quoted in Yuri Slezkine, *The Jewish Century*, Princeton University Press, 2004, kindle, k. 4402–4417.

in the matrimonial market. In the Middle Ages, intellectually superior men were deprived of progeny if they were Christians, but obtained wives of choice and a large number of descendants if they were Jews.[11]

The assumed intellectual superiority of the Jews acts as a Darwinian filter in the cultural sphere, which tends to Judaize itself almost automatically through co-optation. Andre Gide noted this phenomenon with some irritation in his diary in 1914: "It seems to me that this tendency to constantly emphasize the Jew, preferring him and taking a special interest in him, this predisposition to recognizing in him talent, even genius, stems from the fact that a Jew is particularly sensitive to Jewish qualities."[12] And thus are mediocre thinkers and creators, even plagiarists, raised atop Mt. Parnassus, their works immortalized, canonized, and deemed mandatory reading. They, in their turn—convinced that genius comes more naturally to Jews—lionize and favor their Jewish brethren.

Blood, Race, and Genes

The term "group solidarity," mentioned by Yuri Larin, refers to what Charles Darwin wrote in *The Descent of Man, and Selection in Relation to Sex* (1871): "A tribe including many members who, possessing in a high degree the spirit of patriotism, fidelity, obedience, courage, and sympathy, who were always ready to aid one another, and to sacrifice themselves for the common good, would be victorious over most other tribes; and this would be natural selection."[13] This principle, called "group selection," introduces an internal contradiction in Darwin's theory: insofar as individuals who are willing to sacrifice themselves for the group have less chance of survival, altruism should not be transmitted as a genetic trait in the group. This contradiction does not concern us, since the validity of the Darwinian theory

---

[11] Raphael Patai, *The Jewish Mind*, Wayne State University Press, 1977 (on books.google.fr), pp. 287, 305–306; on IQ, read Kevin MacDonald, *A People That Shall Dwell Alone: Judaism as a Group Evolutionary Strategy*, Praeger, 1994, kindle 2013, chap. 7.
[12] André Gide, *Œuvres complètes*, Gallimard, 1933, tome VIII, p. 571.
[13] Charles Darwin, *La Descendance de l'homme et la sélection sexuelle*, 1891 (on darwin-online.org.uk), p. 143.

of the evolution of species is irrelevant here. We are interested only in Darwinian mechanisms capable of explaining the superiority of the Jews in their competitive relations with the Gentiles.

Nonetheless, it is worth mentioning Richard Dawkins's effort to resolve the contradiction of "group selection" in his best-selling book *The Selfish Gene*. Dawkins believes he can do it by taking the standpoint of the "gene," defined as "any portion of chromosomal material that potentially lasts for enough generations to serve as a unit of natural selection." From that standpoint, "we and all other animals, are machines created by our genes," allowing them to replicate indefinitely.[14] This view seems to correspond fairly well to the Deuteronomic ideology. The insistence of the Jewish tradition on the law of endogamy from the Bible to the present day makes it possible to consider Judaism as a strategy of preservation, even improvement, of a genetic heritage. It is better understood by reading what Benzion Netanyahu, father of the Israeli prime minister, writes about transgressions against endogamy: "Only by intermarriage can a person uproot himself from a nation, and then only in so far as his descendants are concerned. His individuality, which is an extract and an example of the qualities of his nation, may then be lost in future generations, dominated by qualities of other nations. Quitting a nation is, therefore, even from a biological point of view, an act of suicide."[15] Golda Meir, prime minister of Israel from 1969 to 1974, found a more modern formulation: "To marry a non-Jew is to join the six million [exterminated Jews]."[16] Indeed, in Jewish Orthodox communities, the Jew who marries a goy is considered dead, and even given a symbolic funeral by his family.

This obsession with endogamy is the central theme of the book of Ezra, which lists the genealogies of the pure lines worthy of reproduction. These lines obviously refer to an elite class rather than a people. And still today, within the Jewish

---

[14] Richard Dawkins, *The Selfish Gene*, Oxford University Press, 1976, 2006, pp. 28, 2.
[15] Benzion Netanyahu, *The Founding Fathers of Zionism* (1938), Balfour Books, 2012, k. 2203–7.
[16] Quoted in Edgar Morin, *Le Monde moderne et la question juive*, Seuil, 2006.

community, endogamy is all the more valued as one moves up the social hierarchy. The almost caricatural illustration of this principle is the Rothschild dynasty: the most powerful Jewish family in the world is also the most endogamous. Of the 58 marriages contracted by the descendants of Mayer Amschel Rothschild, half were between cousins. In the space of a little more than a hundred years, they married each other 18 times, 16 times between first cousins.[17] The rule, written down by Mayer Amschel in his last will, is for Rothschild boys to marry Rothschild girls, while also admitting a few handpicked goyish aristocrats to the lineage. Such unions enrich the Rothschild gene pool, since their offspring are Jewish on the principle that Jewishness is transmitted through the mother.[18]

In the world of the Jewish super-rich, genetic heritage and financial heritage are closely intertwined. Corporate mergers are consecrated by marriages: Solomon Loeb and Abraham Kuhn of Kuhn, Loeb & Co. (founded in 1867) married each other's sisters, while Jacob Schiff married the daughter of Solomon Loeb to become boss of the bank in 1875. Similarly, the two Sachs sons married two Goldman daughters, forming the bank Goldman Sachs (founded in 1869). Conversely, marriages with non-Jews, amounting to genetic defections, are most frequent among the less well-off sections of the Jewish community—a phenomenon that, from the Judeo-Darwinian point of view, is tantamount to expelling the weak from the group.

We have shown in chapter 3 that the core teaching of the Hebrew Bible deprives the individual of any other life after death than through his progeny. Man's only destiny beyond his earthly life is the survival of his people. It is as if the Jewishness in each Jew were a piece of a collective soul. Therefore renouncing Jewishness, for a Jew, is like tearing away part of his soul. In his *Essay on the Jewish Soul* (1929), Isaac Kadmi-Cohen described Judaism as "the spiritualized deification of the race," and his God as "the exaltation of the entity represented by the

---

[17] Kevin MacDonald, *A People That Shall Dwell Alone, op. cit.,* k. 5044–53.
[18] Kevin MacDonald, *Separation and Its Discontents: Toward an Evolutionary Theory of Anti-Semitism,* Praeger, 1998, kindle 2013, k. 3975–4004.

race."[19] This may be why many Jews who seemed detached from their community, even critical of it, suddenly begin to feel late in life—at the age when ordinary Christians begin to ponder the hereafter and the salvation of their souls—to become intensely Jewish, as if their only perspective beyond their earthly existence was to join their souls to that of the chosen people, adding another stone to the edifice. The power of this tribal rootedness is well summed up by the Jewish proverb: "You can take the boy out of Israel, but you can't take Israel out of the boy."[20]

This Jewish focus on genetic heritage, which is tantamount to creating a tribal psyche or group soul, also explains why we often see people who seem unconcerned with their Jewish origins suddenly becoming fervent defenders of the Jewish community. At the raising of the slightest alarm, involving any perceived criticism or threat to the community, they react as if, deep down inside, they themselves were gravely and personally threatened. An ethnic ego—an *anima judaica* that had been asleep inside them—suddenly seizes control of their being. A good example is the Hollywood scriptwriter Ben Hecht, son of Jewish immigrants, who recounts in his autobiography *A Child of the Century* (1954) how, after writing the 1931 bestseller *A Jew in Love* deemed insulting to Jews, he "turned into a Jew" in 1939: "The German mass murder of the Jews, recently begun, had brought my Jewishness to the surface." He then became a fervent Zionist and converted the gangster Mickey Cohen to the cause of the Irgun, whose terrorism against the British he supported in his May 1947 letter to the *New York Post* entitled "Letter to the Terrorists of Palestine": "My Brave Friends, The Jews of America are for you [. . .] Every time you blow up a British arsenal, or wreck a British jail, or send a British railroad train sky high, or rob a British bank, or let go with your guns and bombs at the British betrayers and invaders of your

---

[19] Isaac Kadmi-Cohen, *Nomades: Essai sur l'âme juive,* Felix Alcan, 1929 (archive.org), p. 98.
[20] Gilad Atzmon, *Du tribalisme à l'universel,* Kontre Kulture, 2015, p. 129.

homeland, the Jews of America make a little holiday in their hearts."[21]

The Hebrew Bible itself is the most striking achievement of this special collective genius of the Jewish people, capable of working "as one person" (Ezra 3:1). For the Bible is not the work of an individual genius, but of several lines of priests whose contributions are spread over centuries. No other known literary work has such a collective character. It is this supra-individual origin that gives the Bible a superhuman aura and justifies its sacred character, helping make the biblical Yahweh the collective soul of the Jewish people. We can say almost as much of the Talmud, which is the result of an accumulation of comments by generations of rabbis. Zionism provides another illustration of the Jews' ability to link their individual destinies to the collective destiny of their people. No other people, it seems to me, are capable of such perseverance toward a single and unwavering goal, pursued step by step over several generations—even over a hundred generations if we trace the Zionist project back to the period of Exile.

The national orientation of the Jewish soul infuses all collective action with a spiritual force that no other community can compete with. It is this spiritual or animistic connection that explains the exceptional capacity of the Jews to work in networks. Their absolute loyalty to the national goals they set makes these networks frighteningly effective, because they are based on a tacit confidence that requires no written contract. We see this type of network at work throughout history. Neoconservatives have recently demonstrated the formidable effectiveness of this esprit de corps: in two generations, a network of a few hundred people penetrated the nerve centers of the American state with the precise aim of seizing the levers of its foreign and military policies.

In an article in the *Jewish World Review* of June 7, 1999, the neoconservative Michael Ledeen, disciple of Leo Strauss and founding member of the *Jewish Institute for National Security Affairs*

---

[21] Stuart Schoffman, "A Stone for His Slingshot," *Jewish Review of Books*, Spring 2014, jewishreviewofbooks.com/articles/735/a-stone-for-his-slingshot/.

(JINSA), assumes that Machiavelli, the son of a papal financier, must have been a "secret Jew," since "if you listen to his political philosophy you will hear Jewish music."[22] The affinity between Judaism and Machiavellianism can be understood by reading Leo Strauss's *Thoughts on Machiavelli*. Strauss believes Machiavelli is a patriot of the highest degree because he understood that only the nation is immortal and has a soul, and that the best leaders are those who have no fear of damning their individual soul, since they have none.[23] One understands better modern Zionism of the neoconservative kind when one has grasped this affinity between Judaism and Machiavellianism: Judaism, like Machiavellian politics, is seen as a superior kind of patriotism, because it totally subordinates the immortality of the individual to that of the nation.

On a more pragmatic level, the *esprit de corps* that characterizes the Jewish community and gives it this extraordinary capacity to move as a single person, sometimes scattering like a school of fish and then reconstituting itself, rests on a profound internalization of discipline and submission to the authority of the elites—in the last instance, to Yahweh, the soul of the group. Although theoretically devoid of central authority since the destruction of the Temple, the Jewish community is organically structured in concentric circles. This was noted in the 1970s by Daniel Elazar (*Community and Polity: Organizational Dynamics of American Jewry*, 1976): in the center is the core 5–8 percent for whom Jewishness is a permanent concern; on the periphery are Jews who are totally assimilated and who play an important role in public relations while remaining mobilizable under the banner of the fight against anti-Semitism.[24] There are currently about 300 national Jewish organizations in the United States, with an annual budget of $6 billion. These organizations do not all share the same sensibilities, yet the most important ones speak with one voice

---

22 Michael Ledeen, "What Machiavelli (A Secret Jew?) Learned from Moses," *Jewish World Review*, June 7, 1999, on www.jewishworldreview.com/0699/machiavelli1.asp.

23 Leo Strauss, *Thoughts on Machiavelli*, University of Chicago Press, 1978, p. 42.

24 Kevin MacDonald, *Separation and Its Discontents, op. cit.*, k. 6668–91.

through the 52 members of the Conference of Presidents of Major American Jewish Organizations.[25]

Nomads and Refugees

An often-advanced explanation of the specificity of the Jewish people is their supposed nomadic origin. This is the thesis of Yuri Slezkine, who notes, for example, that "All service nomads are endogamous, and many of them observe dietary restrictions that make fraternizing with their neighbors/clients impossible." Or that "All nomads defined themselves in genealogical terms; most 'service nomads' persisted in doing so in the midst of dominant agrarian societies that sacralized space. They were people wedded to time, not land." The sedentary peasant is rooted in the land, while the nomadic pastoralist is rooted in his genealogy. Ask a peasant where he comes from, and he will name his village; ask a nomad and he will name his tribe.[26] There is exaggeration and reductionism in such stereotypes. Do they apply to the Indians of the American plains, for example? We may doubt it, and find many other counterexamples.

As early as 1929 Isaac Kadmi-Cohen explained Jewish tribalism by nomadic origin. He saw in Judaism the purest product of nomadism. "If nomadism has been the precious guardian of the unity of the race, it is because it has preserved it from lengthy contact with the same land, from a continuous fixation on the same soil, a sedentary rootedness which inevitably transforms, through adaption and selection, the variegated products of the wild meadow into a wheat field. It detaches man from the earth." Kadmi-Cohen also attributes the Jews' utilitarian spirit to their nomadic heritage. The peasant gains his subsistence from the earth, but his relation to the earth is transgenerational: he belongs to the earth more than the earth belongs to him. Love of the land is the basis of peasants' patriotism, unlike the nomad; "In the (nomadic) Jew, patriotism for the homeland, like its microcosmic expression in the love of

[25] Jonathan Goldberg, *Jewish Power: Inside the American Jewish Establishment*, Addison-Wesley, 1997, pp. 38–39.
[26] Yuri Slezkine, *The Jewish Century*, Princeton University Press, 2004, pp. 12, 9.

a parcel of earth, does not exist." Consequently, land is not seen as an end in itself, but "through the prism of self-interest, through the advantage that can be derived from it."[27]

There may be some truth in this explanation of the Jewish character by primordial nomadism. But it has its weaknesses. Kadmi-Cohen applies it to all the Semites, dividing them into two branches, Arabs and Jews. But he does not address the question of what distinguishes Arabs from Jews. He confines himself to this remark: "Of the two main branches of the Semitic tree, only the Jewish branch has preserved its original purity."[28] But the Arab Bedouins have remained nomadic much longer than the Jews, making it difficult to see how their nomadism could be less pure. Moreover, the nomadism of the first Hebrews is not as obvious as it seems. Genesis does not describe them as functional nomads whose migrations were regulated by the seasons, the need for game or pasture, or trade. The Hebrews, obviously, were perpetually in search of a land where they could settle permanently. As we have seen, the etymology of "Hebrew" (*habiru*) reminds us that they were originally *refugees*—migrants rather than nomads.

These considerations help us better understand the paradoxical character of Hebrew "nomadism." "Unlike sedentary peoples, the nomad did not pay homage to the land," writes Kadmi-Cohen. But how can we describe the Jews' attachment to their Promised Land? And especially their peculiar way of appropriating it? Most conquering peoples borrow the place-names of the people they have conquered. Even the European pioneers of the New World adopted the Amerindian names of many of the rivers, mountains, and territories of the American continent. Not so the Israelis who, from 1947 onward, erased the Arab names of bulldozed villages, renaming them in Hebrew. The ideology of the "Redemption of the Earth" demanded no less.[29] Here is the expression of an odd

---

[27] Isaac Kadmi-Cohen, *Nomades: Essai sur l'âme juive*, Felix Alcan, 1929 (archive.org), pp. 14, 89.

[28] Isaac Kadmi-Cohen, *Nomades, op. cit.*, p. 124.

[29] Israel Shahak, *Jewish History, Jewish Religion: The Weight of Three Thousand Years*, Pluto Press, 1994, p. 8.

sort of possessiveness, radically different from the nomad's freedom from attachment to the soil.

This brings us to another paradoxical aspect of the "nomadism" of the Jews: their relationship to property. The Jew, like the nomad, is not interested in landed property. But no other nomadic people has developed an interest in movable property comparable to that of Diaspora Jews. An ancient example is the theft of gold from the Egyptians before the flight from Egypt. The looting of precious metals also featured in the conquest of Canaan: "All the silver and all the gold, everything made of bronze or iron, will be consecrated to Yahweh and put in his treasury" (Joshua 6:19). Moreover, the Jews were undoubtedly the first to have regarded money not as a means of exchanging goods, but as a commodity. We can see, with Jacques Attali, the increasing dematerialization of money as the triumph of nomadism (that is, of the Jewish type by Darwinian selection). But we must recognize that such "nomadism" has little to do with the normal anthropological use of the term.

In conclusion, the explanation of Judaism by nomadism is not entirely convincing. The Jewish people have never defined themselves as nomads, but rather as wanderers. And their forty years of wandering in the desert are hardly a paradise lost. Jews' obsession with the Promised Land, and their taste for mobile, transportable property, have little to do with the freedom of the nomad exalted by Kadmi-Cohen. The Jew, moreover, is atavistically urban. Let us not confuse nomadism and cosmopolitanism.

Assimilation, Dissimulation

Keeping in mind that we are talking about cultural not genetic transmission, the Darwinian dialectic remains enlightening in understanding the mechanisms by which the Jewish community ensures its survival as a group and its competitiveness among other human groups.

The preservation of the group means the struggle against assimilation into other groups, through a cult of ethnic identity that begins at an early age. Referring to the Hebrew school of his childhood, which he attended after regular school hours like all American Jewish schoolchildren of his time, Samuel Roth explained: "The preservation of Jewish religion and culture are merely excuses for something else, a smoke-screen. What the Jew really wants and expects to achieve through the instrumentality of the Hebrew school is to cultivate in his son the sharp awareness that he is a Jew and that as a racial Jew—apart from all the other races—he is waging an old war against his neighbors. The young Jew must learn to remember that before anything else he is a Jew, that, before any other allegiance, comes his allegiance to the Jewish People."[30] What he learns in the synagogue, with the ritual of Kol Nidre, is that disloyalty toward non-Jews is blessed by God.

Competitiveness with non-Jews involves strategies that can be described in Darwinian terms as "crypsis" and "mimicry." The former, also called camouflage, is defined as "the faculty of a species to merge with its environment"; the second, as "the faculty of one species to resemble another." These are adaptive strategies conventionally attributed to the Jews, and rightly so. The Jew has an extraordinary capacity "to conform externally to his temporary surroundings," wrote Hilaire Belloc in 1922; "a Jew takes on with inexplicable rapidity the colour of his environment." But this must not be confused with actual assimilation. Such crypsis is an adaptive strategy for security in a potentially hostile environment. By no means is it a renunciation of Jewish identity: "while he is, within, and through all his ultimate character, above all things a Jew; yet in the superficial and most immediately apparent things he is clothed in the very habit of whatever society he for the moment inhabits." Another commonly expressed grievance against the Jews involves their propensity for secrecy. They are accused of hiding behind borrowed Gentile names, working in occult networks, and so on. Such mimicry is often suspected of serving concealment, not assimilation.[31]

---

[30] Samuel Roth, *Jews Must Live: An Account of the Persecution of the World by Israel on All the Frontiers of Civilization*, 1934 (archive.org).
[31] Hilaire Belloc, *The Jews*, Constable & Co., 1922 (archive.org), pp. 32–35.

In *A People That Shall Dwell Alone*, social psychology professor Kevin MacDonald argues that Judaism is a "group evolutionary strategy among peoples." He sees it as remarkably effective, providing the Jewish community with a decisive selective advantage. From his Darwinian perspective, Kevin MacDonald naturally sees crypto-Judaism as "an authentic case of crypsis quite analogous to cases of mimetic camouflage in the natural world." This also applies, according to MacDonald, to the sincere converts who nevertheless maintain group separatism—those who, while willingly accepting the water of baptism, believe that it has not changed the nature of the blood flowing in their veins, and who feel the need to maintain the purity of this Jewish blood. "Indeed, one might note that New Christians who maintained group separatism while sincerely accepting Christianity were really engaging in a very interesting evolutionary strategy—a true case of crypsis entirely analogous to crypsis in the natural world. Such people would be even more invisible to the surrounding society than crypto-Jews, because they would attend church regularly, not circumcise themselves, eat pork, etc., and have no psychological qualms about doing so. [...] Psychological acceptance of Christianity may have been the best possible means of continuing Judaism as a group evolutionary strategy during the period of the Inquisition."[32]

From the same Darwinian perspective, MacDonald analyzes Reform Judaism, which mimics Christianity in defining itself as a religion. This allows the Jewish community to maintain its cohesion and endogamy. In other words, Judaism serves as the religious mask of ethnic Jewry. Thus in 1897, at the height of the immigration of Jews from Eastern Europe, the Central Conference of American Rabbis adopted the following resolution: "Resolved that we totally disapprove of any attempt for the establishment of a Jewish State. [...] We reaffirm that the object of Judaism is not political nor national, but spiritual, and addresses itself to the continuous growth of peace, justice and love of the human race, to a messianic time when all men will recognize that they form 'one great brotherhood' for the

---

[32] Kevin MacDonald, *Separation and Its Discontents, op. cit.*, k. 5876–82.

establishment of God's kingdom on earth."[33] Zionism is a reaction against this trend, which Moses Hess already condemned as the repression of one's inner nature: "Those of our brethren who, for purposes of obtaining emancipation, endeavor to persuade themselves, as well as others, that modern Jews possess no trace of a national feeling, have really lost their heads." A Jew is a Jew "by virtue of his racial origin, even though his ancestors may have become apostates."[34] According to Benzion Netanyahu, defining Jewishness as religion rather than nationality "was the fruit of self-deception rather than of hypocrisy."[35]

I am inclined to believe that unconscious self-deception plays a major role, since the unconscious is the seat of the group soul, as the group thinks through the individual. But the distinction between self-deception and hypocrisy is of little importance from a Darwinian perspective. It does not matter what Nahum Goldmann really means when he writes: "Even today it is hardly possible to say whether to be a Jew consists first of belonging to a people or practicing a religion, or the two together."[36] Deliberately or unconsciously, these statements serve to maintain a misunderstanding, a strategic ambivalence. Religion and race are two different things, and Wolf's assertion has no logical meaning unless we admit that Judaism is a religion seen from the outside and a "race" (ethnicity) from the inside: "The best strategy for Judaism is to maximize the ethnic, particularistic aspects of Judaism within the limits necessary to prevent these aspects from resulting in anti-Semitism."[37] The religious facade makes it possible to benefit from the religious tolerance of an open society. But the ethnic definition is also useful in a multicultural society, and helps to disarm critics through the "anti-Semite" label.

---

[33] Quoted in Naomi Cohen, *The Americanization of Zionism, 1897–1948*, Brandeis University Press, 2003, p. 43.

[34] Moses Hess, *Rome and Jerusalem: A Study in Jewish Nationalism*, 1918 (archive.org), pp. 71, 27.

[35] Benzion Netanyahu, *The Founding Fathers of Zionism, op. cit.*, k. 157–66.

[36] Nahum Goldmann, *Le Paradoxe juif, op. cit.*, p. 9.

[37] Kevin MacDonald, *Separation and Its Discontents, op. cit.*, k. 4935–37.

Unfortunately, this strategy, once the Gentiles see through it, is one of the main sources of recurrent Judeophobia. Recognizing that the Jewish people everywhere form "a state within the state," Adolf Hitler wrote in *Mein Kampf* (1923): "It was one of the most ingenious tricks that was ever invented to let this State sail under the flag of 'religion,' thus securing for it the tolerance that the Aryan is always ready to grant to a religious denomination. Actually the Mosaic religion is nothing but a doctrine of the preservation of the Jewish race."[38]

As the American rabbis suggested in their statement, the notion of religion, in its modern sense, presupposes a universal vocation. This vocation is unambiguous in Christianity and Islam. In the case of Judaism, on the other hand, universalism is essentially a message addressed to the Gentiles, even though it is internalized by many Jews. Universalism is interpretable in Darwinian terms as another form of crypsis by which the Jewish people of the Diaspora seek to minimize the hostility of the host peoples and maximize their sympathy. Again, it does not matter whether the double game is deliberately deceptive, or an instinctive, spontaneous way of adjusting communication according to whether one is addressing a family member or a stranger. After all, in the vast majority of people, ideas and opinions are like clothes. They are merely ways of appearing in public. One can have one opinion at home and another for social life, without necessarily feeling hypocritical. Moses Hess, addressing himself mainly to his fellow Jews, defended the national character of Judaism and denounced the assimilationist Jew's "beautiful phrases about humanity and enlightenment which he employs as a cloak to hide his treason."[39] We are reminded of the double language of the book of Ezra, where Yahweh is "the God of heaven" for the Persian kings, but "the God of Israel" in the rest of the book. The book of Ezra is a key to understanding Judaism, since the Yahwist ideology with its tribal-universal ambiguity crystallized during this period. Put simply, it seems that Yahweh is the tribal god of the Jews that

---

[38] Adolf Hitler, *Mein Kampf*, Reynal & Hitchcock, 1941 (archive.org), p. 196.
[39] Moses Hess, *Rome and Jerusalem, op. cit.*, p. 74.

the rest of humanity takes for the universal God. This is why, although the Tanakh of the Jews and the Old Testament of the Christians are practically identical, they are two totally different books according to how they are read.

The duplicity of modern Judaism has been discussed by Gilad Atzmon, who grew up in Israel in a family of Zionist militants (his grandfather was an Irgun official), but later became a severe critic of this legacy. To him, the Haskalah insight, "Be a Jew at home and a goy on the street" (formulated by the poet Judah Leib Gordon but often attributed to Moses Mendelssohn) is fundamentally dishonest: "The Haskalah Jew is destined to live in a dual, deceptive mode, if not practically a state of schizophrenia. [...] The Haskalah Jew is deceiving his or her God when at home, and misleading the goy once in the street. In fact, it is this duality of tribalism and universalism that is at the very heart of the collective secular Jewish identity. This duality has never been properly resolved."

Zionism began as an effort to resolve this contradiction, so that a Jew could be a Jew both at home and in the street. But the result is that "there is no trace of universalism in either the Zionist's 'street' or in his 'home'." However, since Israel has a vital need for support from the international community, the Zionist Jew still has to don the mask of universalism and humanism, not so much in the streets of Tel Aviv, but in those of New York, London, and Paris. For historical reasons, Zionism is today a global and not just a national project. Jews of the Diaspora participate in it at least as actively as Israelis do. "Within the Jewish framework, the Israelis colonize Palestine and the Jewish Diaspora is there to mobilise lobbies by recruiting international support."[40] Zionism is no longer a nationalism but a globalism, a project for a new world order.

But has it ever been anything else? Theodor Herzl and Max Nordau no doubt thought of Zionism on the model of the nationalisms of the eighteenth and nineteenth centuries. "Early Zionist thinkers were apparently galvanized by a deep revulsion

---

[40] Gilad Atzmon, *The Wandering Who? A Study of Jewish Identity Politics,* Zero Books, 2011, pp. 55–56, 70.

for the diaspora Jews," writes Gilad Atzmon. "They preached for a radical metamorphosis of the Jew. They promised that Zionism would civilize the diaspora Jew by means of a manufactured homecoming. [...] They vowed to change, striving to become a 'people like all other people.'" Atzmon cites Aaron David Gordon, founder of Labor Zionism: "We are a parasitic people. We have no roots in the soil, there is no ground beneath our feet. And we are parasites not only in an economic sense, but in spirit, in thought, in poetry, in literature, and in our virtues, our ideals, our higher human aspirations."[41]

However, in retrospect, Zionist nationalism may have masked a very different project. No other nationalist movement has ever viewed the concept of a people in such exclusively genetic terms—not even Nazism. "Zionism is a form of racism and racial discrimination," as Resolution 3379 of the United Nations General Assembly so aptly put it on November 10, 1975.[42] Blood takes precedence over land. That is why Israel has never ceased to mean, for the Jews themselves, a world community rather than a national community. And that is why the ultimate goal of Zionism cannot be just Israel, as Gilad Atzmon stresses: "In fact, there is no geographical centre to the Zionist endeavor. It is hard to determine where Zionist decisions are made." The strength of modern Zionism rests on an organic rather than hierarchical link between Jews. "While the organism functions as a whole, the particular organ fulfills an elementary function without being aware of its specific role within the entire system."[43] It is the ideology, internalized by each individual, that is the center. And this ideology, in the last analysis, is that of biblical Yahwism. Naturally there must be a cognitive elite to perpetually pump the ideology throughout the organism.

This ideology is epitomized by the book of Esther, which Atzmon illustrates by quoting an article by Rafael Medoff titled "A Purim Lesson: Lobbying Against Genocide, Then and

---

[41] Gilad Atzmon, *Being in Time: A Post-Political Manifesto*, Skyscraper, 2017, pp. 66-67.
[42] Resolution abrogated in 1991 by Resolution 46/86.
[43] Gilad Atzmon, *The Wandering Who?*, *op. cit.*, p. 21.

Now." From the story of Esther and her cousin Mordecai, Medoff draws as a lesson the importance of infiltrating power (which he euphemistically calls "lobbying"): "The holiday of Purim celebrates the successful effort by prominent Jews in the capitol of ancient Persia to prevent genocide against the Jewish people." So, Atzmon comments, "To internalise the message of the *Book of Esther* is to aim for the most influential centres of hegemony, to collaborate with power and bond with rulers." And the Esther-Mordecai tandem is the perfect illustration of the organic complementarity of the different levels of Jews. "Medoff's reading of the *Book of Esther* provides a glaring insight into the internal codes of Jewish collective survival dynamics, in which the assimilated (Esther) and the observant (Mordechai) join forces with Jewish interests on their minds." Esther not only incarnates the assimilated Jew, but the most assimilated of all, the crypto-Jew, since the king and the people are unaware that she is Jewish. In the organic onion-layer structure of the Jewish community, even "anti-Zionists of Jewish descent [...] are there to portray an image of ideological plurality and ethical concern."[44]

The Mission Theory

Modern Zionism is a global project because it is the child of Yahwism—a rebellious child in its youth, but loyal in maturity. Jewishness itself is a global project, for what does election mean if not a universal mission? This universal mission, too, has a double face. There are many Jews who associate this mission with a priesthood for the salvation of mankind. Jabotinsky quotes in *The War and the Jew* (1942), in a mocking tone, a Parisian friend who adhered to the theory "that it was the sacred mission of the Jews to live scattered among the Gentiles and help them rise to higher ethical levels."[45] The Italian rabbi Elijah Benamozegh, author of *Israel and Humanity* (1914), is one of the most famous representatives of this "mission theory": "The

---

[44] Gilad Atzmon, *The Wandering Who?, op. cit.*, pp. 159–160, 70.
[45] Vladimir Jabotinsky, *The War and the Jew*, Dial Press, 1942 (archive.org), pp. 116–117.

constitution of a universal religion is the ultimate goal of Judaism," he writes. This entails a sense of Israel's superiority: "In Heaven, one God of all men, and on earth a single family of peoples, among whom Israel is the eldest, responsible for the priestly teaching function and the administration of the true religion of humanity." Universal religion therefore implies "the recognition that humanity must accept the truth of the doctrine of Israel." This universal religion will not be Judaism proper, but an inferior form, founded on the laws God gave to Noah and not on the more demanding ones given to Moses. The universal religion of the Gentiles will be Noachism. "The special cult of Israel is safeguarding the means of realization of the true universal religion, Noachism."[46] This conception deviates significantly from the Bible, whose only universalist message is that the nations (goyim) must pay tribute to Yahweh in his Jerusalem Temple. It is therefore legitimate to ask whether the fraud of Noachism and all the other versions of the "mission theory" are not simply skillful rationalizations of Jewish supremacism. The same question may be asked about the attempt of Joseph Salvador, in his book *Paris, Rome and Jerusalem* (1860), to outline a universal religion based on a fusion of Judaism and Christianity. He believed that the natural center for this syncretistic religion would be Jerusalem, and therefore advocated the establishment of a new state, a bridge between the Orient and the Occident, encompassing the borders of ancient Israel.[47]

Yet it would be wrong to suspect conscious hypocrisy in most of the countless Jewish thinkers who have echoed the Jewish people's global "humanitarian mission." There is certainly none in Alfred Nossig, a Jewish artist and activist who, before working for the emigration of selected Jews to Palestine by collaborating with the Gestapo in the Warsaw ghetto, wrote in *Integrales Judentum* ("Integral Judaism"), published in Berlin in 1922: "The Jewish community is more than a people in the

---

[46] Élie Benamozegh, *Israël et l'humanité* (1914), Albin Michel, 1980, pp. 28–29, 40, 365.
[47] Joseph Salvador, *Paris, Rome et Jérusalem, ou la question religieuse au XIXᵉ siècle,* Michel Lévy, 1860 (archive.org).

modern political sense of the word. It is the repository of a historically global mission, I would say even a cosmic one, entrusted to it by its founders Noah and Abraham, Jacob and Moses. [. . .] It forms an unconscious nucleus of our being, the common substance of our soul. [. . .] The primordial conception of our ancestors was to found not a tribe but a world order destined to guide humanity in its development. This is the true meaning, the only meaning of the election of the Hebrews as a chosen people."[48]

In its secular formulation, the mission theory naturally substitutes superiority for chosenness: "I believe in our moral and intellectual superiority, in our capacity to serve as a model for the redemption of the human race," declared David Ben-Gurion. "This belief of mine is based on my knowledge of the Jewish people, not some mystical faith."[49] But this "mission" has many broad, even contradictory interpretations. The rabbi Daniel Gordis, vice president of the Jewish University of Los Angeles, offers one variant in *Does the World Need Jews?* "Jewish tradition has always claimed that Jews need to be different in order that they might play a quasi-subversive role in society [. . .] the goal is to be a contributing and respectful 'thorn in the side' of society."[50] And so the "mission theory" can never be refuted: Whether it is constructive or subversive, the Jewish contribution is always a gift to mankind. It is positive both in bringing the One God to humanity, and in dragging religion through the mud; positive both in raising humanity's moral level, and also in undermining moral values. Everything that the chosen people do, by definition, is a "humanitarian mission." So the mission theory is in reality only a posture aimed at compelling respect and demanding gratitude. What it disguises as a "mission," in the minds of the Gentiles but also of progressive Jews, is nothing but chauvinism and Jewish separatism. The ultimate purpose of

---

[48] Alfred Nossig, *Integrales Judentum*, 1922, pp. 1–5.
[49] Quoted in Arthur Hertzberg, *The Zionist State*, Jewish Publication Society, 1997, p. 94.
[50] Daniel Gordis, *Does the World Need Jews? Rethinking Chosenness and American Jewish Identity*, Scribner, 1997, p. 177.

the mission theory is to explain that Jews must remain a separate nation, in order to fulfill their universal mission.

Implicit in the mission theory in all its forms is the inferiority of non-Jewish cultures. The Jewish historian Albert Lindemann observes in his co-religionists an instinctive propensity "to view surrounding Gentile society as pervasively flawed, polluted, or sick. The belief of Jews in premodern times that they, God's chosen people, had been condemned by their god, because of their own sins, to live in subjugation in the polluted lands of the uncircumcised, the brutal, the unclean, the eaters of filth—of the reviled Children of Esau—took on new forms in a modern context." So it does not astonish Lindemann "that many Jews have been, since the early nineteenth century, powerfully attracted to those modern secular ideologies that managed to reaffirm indirectly, with a new language, an older sense of the tainted qualities of prevailing Gentile life."[51] According to Andrew Heinze in *Jews and the American Soul*, "the story of American ideas about the mind and soul is one in which Jews have been central actors," with the preoccupation "to purge the evils they associated with Christian civilization."[52]

From the 1930s, Freudianism gained considerable influence in the United States, thanks to the immigration of a large number of members of the Berlin Psychoanalytic Institute, almost all Jews. This current swarmed into a multitude of schools, and the 1960s produced the so-called Freudo-Marxists, equally inclined to diagnose the ills of society and the traditional family.

According to the psychoanalytic diagnosis, Christian societies suffer from sexual repression. The cure, therefore, is sexual liberation. Jewish intellectuals were the spearheads of the attack on moral and Christian values and the fight against the censorship of pornography. Norman Podhoretz pointed this out

---

[51] Albert Lindemann, *Esau's Tears: Modern Anti-Semitism and the Rise of the Jews*, Cambridge University Press, 1997, pp. 13–15.
[52] Andrew Heinze, *Jews and the American Soul: Human Nature in the Twentieth Century*, Princeton University Press, 2006, pp. 3, 352.

in an August 1995 *Commentary* article,[53] and professor Nathan Abrams of the University of Aberdeen goes further in an article in the *Jewish Quarterly* (reprinted in the collection *Jews and Sex*): "Jews in America have been sexual revolutionaries. A large amount of the material on sexual liberation was written by Jews. Those at the forefront of the movement which forced America to adopt a more liberal view of sex were Jewish. Jews were also at the vanguard of the sexual revolution of the 1960s. Wilhelm Reich, Herbert Marcuse and Paul Goodman replaced Marx, Trotsky and Lenin as required revolutionary reading."[54] The sexual revolution, like the drug culture, arrived just in time to depoliticize youth during the Lyndon Johnson era, when Israel's parasitism of America was gaining critical mass.

Hijacking Christianity

"The Jews are not merely out of step with Christian civilization, they hold it in utter contempt," explains Michael Wex in his essay on Yiddish culture, *Born to Kvetch*.[55] But the Haskalah strategy requires paying obsequious respect to Christianity. It consists not only in imitating Christianity in order to enjoy the same rights and dignity as a universal religion, but also in asserting paternity in order to absorb it. "What gave birth to the Christian gospel," Rabbi Benamozegh claims, "is this faith in the universal religion that the Jews believed was born by their ancient doctrine and whose reign they were to establish one day." But Christianity, like Islam, is an imperfect expression of this ideal, the true form of which should be Noachism, the universal law "which Judaism has preciously preserved and which was the starting point and impetus of Christian preaching in the world."[56] Benamozegh therefore exhorts Christianity to

---

[53] Quoted in Kevin MacDonald, *The Culture of Critique: Toward an Evolutionary Theory of Jewish Involvement in Twentieth-Century Intellectual and Political Movements,* Praeger, 1998, kindle 2013, k. 12545–48.

[54] Nathan Abrams, "Nathan Abrams on Jews in the American Porn Industry," *Jewish Quarterly,* winter 2004, www.jewishquarterly.org/issuearchive/articled325.html?article id=38.

[55] Michael Wex, *Born to Kvetch: Yiddish Language and Culture in All of Its Moods,* Harper Perennial, 2006, p. 24.

[56] Élie Benamozegh, *Israël et l'humanité, op. cit.,* p. 29.

acknowledge its errors and return to its sources. The source is Jesus the Jew, while responsibility for Christian anti-Semitism is blamed on St. Paul, the first self-hating Jew, who wrote that the Jews "do not please God, they are enemies of all men" (1 Thessalonians 2:15–16).[57] Heinrich Graetz writes in his *History of the Jews*: "Jesus made no attack upon Judaism itself, he had no idea of becoming the reformer of Jewish doctrine or the propounder of a new law; he sought merely to redeem the sinner, to call him to a good and holy life, to teach him that he is a child of God, and to prepare him for the approaching Messianic time." And so, he "fell a victim to a misunderstanding. How great was the woe caused by that one execution! How many deaths and sufferings of every description has it not caused among the children of Israel!"[58]

This process can be described as a superficial "Christianization of Judaism": Judaism not only mimics the universalist message of Christianity, but also claims Jesus as one of its honorable representatives. Better yet, the crucifixion of Christ becomes the symbol of the martyrdom of the Jews. In 1918, Rabbi Kaufmann Kohler, a leading figure of American Reform Judaism, wrote in his *Jewish Theology*: "Israel is the champion of the Lord, chosen to battle and suffer for the supreme values of mankind, for freedom and justice, truth and humanity; the man of woe and grief, whose blood is to fertilize the soil with the seeds of righteousness and love for mankind. [...] Accordingly, modern Judaism proclaims more insistently than ever that the Jewish people is the Servant of the Lord, the suffering Messiah of the nations, who offered his life as an atoning sacrifice for humanity and furnished his blood as the cement with which to build the divine kingdom of truth and justice."[59]

---

[57] Hyam Maccoby, *The Mythmaker: Paul and the Invention of Christianity,* HarperCollins, 1986.

[58] Heinrich Graetz, *History of the Jews,* Jewish Publication Society of America, 1891 (archive.org), pp. 155, 165.

[59] Kaufmann Kohler, *Jewish Theology, Systematically and Historically Considered,* Macmillan, 1918 (on www.gutenberg.org), pp. 378–380.

This aping of Christian soteriology (doctrine of salvation) culminates in the religion of the Holocaust, with Auschwitz replacing Calvary. And because absolute good needs its enemy absolute evil, one understands the importance of transforming Hitler into a quasi-metaphysical principle, with titles like *Explaining Hitler: The Search for the Origins of His Evil* by Ron Rosenbaum (1998), which became in the French translation: *Pourquoi Hitler? Enquête sur l'origine du mal* ("Why Hitler? An Inquiry into the Origin of Evil"). The forelock and mustache of the Führer have replaced the horns of the devil in folk iconography.

While mimicking Christianity, Judaism also seeks to transform it. And so the counterpart of the Christianization of Judaism is the Judaization of Christianity. According to the historian of Judaism Daniel Lindenberg, "the Jewish Reformation does not only want to 'assimilate' unilaterally into the modern Christian world. In a way, it aims to 'reform' it, too. [...] It is really about awakening the Hebrew 'root' of a Christianity reconciled with Human Rights."[60]

In fact, it is really about eradicating all traces of anti-Judaism from Christianity—from the Gospel if it were possible—in order to turn Christianity into a Judeophilic religion, that is, a branch of Judaism. Jules Isaac, founder of the Jewish-Christian Friendship group in 1948, began this task in the years preceding Vatican II. He called on Catholics to renounce their anti-Judaism and to recognize Jews as their "elder brothers" on the basis of a vision of Jesus identical to that of Graetz: "The originality of Jesus did not consist of innovating in matters of faith and breaking with the religion of his fathers, but simply of extracting from Scripture and the whole Jewish oral tradition the elements of a truly pure faith and universal morality." On December 15, 1959, Isaac delivered a lecture at the Sorbonne entitled "The Necessary Redress of Christian Teaching about Israel," later published as *L'Enseignement du mépris* ("Teaching Contempt"). To satisfy him, John XXIII appointed Cardinal Bea

---

[60] Daniel Lindenberg, *Figures d'Israël. L'identité juive entre marranisme et sionisme (1649–1998)*, Fayard, 2014, p. 17.

to head the Secretariat for the Unity of Christian Religions, which also deals with relations with Judaism. Bea's two immediate assistants, Bishop Baum and Monsignor Oesterreicher, were converted Jews, and Bea was considered to be of Marrano origin (his real name would have been Behar). These assertions were supported in a *Look* magazine article of January 25, 1966, referring to secret meetings between Bea and the American Jewish Committee.[61]

The protagonists in this drama include the Congregation of Our Lady of Sion, founded in 1843 by two Jewish brothers in Strasbourg, Théodore and Alphonse Rastisbonne, "to testify in the Church and in the world of the faithfulness of God to his love for the Jewish people, and to work at fulfilling the biblical promises revealed to the patriarchs and prophets of Israel for all mankind." Although initially devoted to the conversion of the Jews, it contributed to the Church's renunciation of that mission under Vatican II.

The result of all these combined actions was the birth of a new ostensibly Judeophilic Christianity, promoted by personalities such as the Archbishop of Paris Aron Jean-Marie Lustiger. In his book *The Promise*, whose cover shows Pope John Paul II praying at the Wailing Wall, Lustiger explains why "though Christian by faith and baptism, [he is] as Jewish as the apostles were," and why Jesus's message is the continuation of the law of Moses and a confirmation of the election of the Jewish people: "One can only receive the Spirit of Jesus on the strict condition of sharing the hope of Israel," since "the figure of the Messiah is at the same time the figure of Israel."[62]

Today's Judeophiles and crypto-Jews in the Roman Curia are, of course, ardent Zionists. The casual admission of the prelate David-Maria Jaeger, the principal architect of diplomatic relations between Israel and the Vatican, speaks volumes about the extent of this phenomenon. Born in Tel Aviv of Jewish parents and converted to Catholicism, but defining himself

---

[61] Martin Peltier, *L'Antichristianisme juif: L'enseignement de la haine*, Diffusion Internationale Édition, 2014, pp. 197–209.
[62] Jean-Marie Lustiger, *La Promesse*, Parole & Silence, 2002, pp. 99, 57.

primarily as an "Israeli Jew," Jaeger told a journalist from the Israeli daily *Haaretz* in 2011: "I'm just like any Israeli citizen who works for an international organization situated outside the country—just like there are Israelis at the International Monetary Fund in Washington, the United Nations in New York or UNESCO in Paris."[63]

The Judaization of Christianity culminates in American Evangelical Christianity, the direct descendant of Calvinist Puritanism. A few decades of skillful manipulation has succeeded in transforming Evangelicals into powerful allies of Zionism. The initial impulse can be traced back to Methodist pastor William Eugene Blackstone. His book *Jesus Is Coming* (1878) sold millions of copies and was translated into forty-eight languages. It became the key reference of what is called "dispensationalism," the doctrine that the gathering of Jews in Palestine is the precondition for the Return of Christ on Earth (after which, of course, the Jews will finally recognize Christ). In 1890 Blackstone organized a conference of Christian and Jewish leaders. The following year he launched a petition signed by 413 Christian leaders and a handful of Jewish ones. This petition, known as the Blackstone Memorial, proposes "Why shall not the powers which under the Treaty of Berlin, in 1878, gave Bulgaria to the Bulgarians and Servia to the Servians now give Palestine back to the Jews?"[64]

The Judaization of American Christianity, and English Christianity to a lesser extent, has not been a spontaneous process, but rather one controlled by skillful manipulation. An example is the Scofield Reference Bible, published in 1909 and revised in 1917. It is characterized by dubious and highly tendentious footnotes. For example, the promise of Yahweh to Abraham in Genesis 12:1–3 merits a two-thirds-page footnote explaining that "God made an unconditional promise of blessings through Abram's seed to the nation of Israel to inherit a specific territory forever," accompanied by "a curse laid upon

---

[63] Tomer Zarchin, "Israeli Jew Turned Catholic Priest Named Head of Papal Court," *Haaretz*, June 03, 2011, www.haaretz.com/.
[64] Yaakov Ariel, *On Behalf of Israel: American Fundamentalist Attitudes toward Jews, Judaism, and Zionism, 1865–1945*, Carlson Publishing, 1991, pp. 70–72.

those who persecute the Jews," or "commit the sin of anti-Semitism." In reality, at this point Jacob, who would receive the name of Israel and beget the Jewish people, was not even born yet, nor was his father. The same note explains that "Both O.T. and N.T. are full of post-Sinaitic promises concerning Israel and the land which is to be Israel's everlasting possession."

How was Cyrus Scofield, a lawyer without theological training, capable of publishing such a work with the prestigious Oxford University Press? The mystery has been solved: Scofield was only a front man for a project whose real sponsor was Samuel Untermeyer, a Wall Street lawyer, Federal Reserve co-founder, devoted Zionist, and close associate of Woodrow Wilson. As noted in chapter 7, Untermeyer called for a "holy war" against Germany in 1933.[65]

Israel's technique for manipulating history can be interpreted in Hegelian terms. Since he formulated the dialectical law of history in the early nineteenth century, Hegel has had two kinds of disciples: those who examine the past to verify the law, and those who apply the law to shape the future. Marx belonged to the second category: although he claimed to merely predict an inevitable revolution, he contributed to hastening it. Marx may have understood this better than Hegel, because such laws were long known in his Jewish social environment. Manipulating history, rather than saving souls, has been from the start the great concern of Judaism. And it has never been so successfully done as during the "Jewish century," as Yuri Slezkine names the twentieth century.

It is through dialectical oppositions that the great Jewish movements of the nineteenth and twentieth centuries have been able to bend history. The three major Jewish movements were hatched around the same time: Reform Judaism, the fruit of eighteenth century Haskalah; Bolshevism, based on Marxism, which fed on earlier socialist ideas before smothering them; and Zionism. Reform Judaism and Zionism appeared in Western Europe almost simultaneously, in the same intellectual milieu

---

[65] Joseph Canfield, *The Incredible Scofield and His Book*, Ross House Books, 2004, pp. 219–220.

that produced Heinrich Graetz's *History of the Jews*. Both used the victimization of the Jews as a springboard for their ascent to positions of power. While Reform Judaism was crafting a new image of the Jews as the collective suffering Messiah, Zionism was capitalizing on the Russian pogroms to advance its claim for the Jews to have "a nation of their own, a nation like others." While originally affirming their mutual incompatibility and competing for the hearts of Jews—wealthy and destitute alike—these two movements finally joined hands and congratulated each other on their marvelous common achievement: a nation like no other, with both a national territory and an international citizenry. Except for a few unreformed orthodox Jews, most Jews today see no contradiction between Reform Judaism and Zionism. The question of whether such dialectical machinery is engineered by Yahweh or by B'nai B'rith is open to debate. But most Jews involved in such movements are certainly not aware of the full picture. The process rests on an ambiguity that is the very essence of Jewishness: the impossibility of deciding whether it is a religion or a nationality.

The dialectical opposition between Zionism and communism is another case in point. Both originated, again, in the same milieu, and the very nature of their opposition is perhaps best represented by the friendship between Karl Marx and Moses Hess. Theodor Herzl, we remember, used the threat of communism in his Zionist diplomatic overtures to the Russian and German leaders: "Support my movement, and I will rid your cities of their revolutionaries." Churchill, also on the Zionist side, dramatized the opposition between the "good Jews" (Zionists) and the "bad Jews" (communists) in his 1920 article "Zionism versus Bolshevism."

Similar dialectical machinery can be found in all levels of Jewish movements. Consider, for example, the opposition between pro-Nazi Zionists and anti-Nazi Zionists in the 1930s. The Hegelian synthesis between the two is best embodied by Joachim Prinz, who in 1934 expressed sympathy for the Nazi racial laws, and in 1958 was elected president of the *American Jewish Congress*, the very organization that in 1933 had called for total economic war on Germany.

Reshaping the Cultural Environment

The manipulation of the Christian mind to make it favorable to the Jews and to Israel is one aspect among others of a general strategy of modifying the cultural environments of host nations to make them more conducive to the Jewish community. This strategy differs from the Darwinian crypsis by which the community blends into the environment to make its ethnic character less visible. Here, on the contrary, it is a question of modifying the environment to make it more tolerant of ethnic communities, or to diffuse the ethnic problem and thus divert Gentile hostility toward other ethnic communities. The Jews are then able, using the strategy of "triangulation," to pose as mediators of conflicts

This, for Kevin MacDonald, explains why "transforming the United States into a multicultural society has been a major Jewish goal since the 19th century."[66] The project entails both increasing national tolerance toward ethnic communities, and increasing the numerical importance and diversity of ethnic communities through massive immigration, celebrating multiculturalism, and fostering ethnic pluralism. One of the emblematic figures of this cultural movement was Israel Zangwill, the successful author of the play *The Melting Pot* (1908), whose title has become a metaphor for American society. The hero is a Jew who emigrated to the United States to flee the pogroms that decimated his family in Russia. He falls in love with a Christian Russian immigrant, who turns out to be the daughter of the Russian officer responsible for the death of his family. The father of the bride repents, and the couple lives happily ever after. The hero makes himself the bard of assimilation by mixed marriages, through which God gives birth to a new man: "America is God's Crucible, the great Melting-Pot where all the races of Europe are melting and reforming." The paradox is that when he was writing this play, Zangwill was a committed Zionist leader, that is, the leader of a movement affirming the impossibility of Jews living among Gentiles, and

---

[66] Kevin MacDonald, *The Culture of Critique, op. cit.*, k. 10975–76.

demanding that they be ethnically separated. Zangwill is the author of another famous formula: "Palestine is a land without people for a people without land." There is no better illustration of the Jewish community's double language and double game, which advocates cross-breeding among the Gentiles and ethnic purity among the Jews. The neoconservative Douglas Feith said it bluntly in a speech delivered in Jerusalem in 1997: "There is a place in the world for non-ethnic nations and there is a place for ethnic nations."[67]

In the United States, the 1924 Johnson-Reed Act severely restricted immigration, especially from Asia and Eastern Europe. The lifting of this restrictive legislation was a high-priority political struggle for practically all Jewish organizations. They won in 1965, with a new immigration law that forced the doors of immigration wide open. To weaken the ethnic homogeneity of the host nation is to weaken what Ludwig Gumplowicz called its "syngeneic feeling," of which anti-Semitism seems to be an almost inevitable by-product. A satisfying situation was achieved around 1993, according to Jewish activist Earl Raab, associated with the Anti-Defamation League, writing in the *Jewish Bulletin*: "The Census Bureau has just reported that about half of the American population will soon be non-white or non-European. And they will all be American citizens. We have tipped beyond the point where a Nazi-Aryan party will be able to prevail in this country. We [Jews] have been nourishing the American climate of opposition to bigotry for about half a century. That climate has not yet been perfected, but the heterogeneous nature of our population tends to make it irreversible—and makes our constitutional constraints against bigotry more practical than ever."[68]

In addition, Jews played a prominent role in the organization of the African-American Civil Rights Movement. From the founding of the National Association for the Advancement of Colored People (NAACP) in 1909, all of its presidents were

---

[67] Stephen Sniegoski, *The Transparent Cabal: The Neoconservative Agenda, War in the Middle East, and the National Interest of Israel,* Enigma Edition, 2008, p. 119.
[68] Quoted in Kevin MacDonald, *The Culture of Critique, op. cit.*, k. 246–7.

Jews until 1975. After the Second World War, the majority of Jewish organizations were involved in the Civil Rights Movement. Jews provided its financial, legal, strategic, and even ideological support. (By contrast, no African-American has been admitted to the major Jewish organizations, much less been allowed to run them).

As was pointed out earlier, Jews contributed massively to the success of Martin Luther King Jr.'s 1963 march on Washington, DC, which led to his being awarded the Nobel Peace Prize. The introductory remarks of Rabbi Joachim Prinz, then chairman of the *American Jewish Congress,* before King's famous "I have a dream" speech on August 28, 1963, offer a telling example of Jewish opportunism: "I speak to you as an American Jew," Prinz begins. "As Jews, we bring to this great demonstration in which thousands of us proudly participate a twofold experience: one of the spirit, and one of our history. In the realm of the spirit, our fathers told us thousands of years ago that when God created man, he created him as everybody's neighbour [...]. From our Jewish experience of three and a half thousand years, we say: Our ancient history began with slavery and the yearning for freedom." There followed a brief reminder of Jewish suffering from the ghettos of the Middle Ages to the recent Holocaust. Then, just when we would expect a word about the condition of black Americans, Prinz brushes away the issue: Americans "must speak up and act," he says, "not for the sake of the negro, not for the sake of the black community, but for the sake of the image, the dream, the idea, and the aspiration of America itself."[69]

Some Black American leaders like Louis Farrakhan believe that the Jews championed their cause out of self-interest, essentially hijacking it.[70] Charles Silberman seemingly agrees, while extending the analysis to other battles: "American Jews are committed to cultural tolerance because of their belief—firmly rooted in history—that Jews are only safe in a society that

---

[69] Seth Berkman, "The Jews Who Marched on Washington with Martin Luther King," Forward.com, August 27, 2013. Prinz's speech is on www.joachimprinz.com/images /mow.mp3.
[70] Kevin MacDonald, *The Culture of Critique, op. cit.,* k. 10865–10918.

welcomes a broad spectrum of attitudes and behaviors, as well as a diversity of religions and ethnic groups. It is this belief, for example, and not approval of homosexuality, that leads an overwhelming majority of American Jews to support the rights of homosexuals."[71] And so, thanks to the "Jewish identity merchants," as Gilad Atzmon call them, "We are transformed into a matrix of a manifold of Jew-like tribal groupings defined largely by biology (color, gender, sexual preferences, race, etc.). However, it is hardly surprising that Jewish identity merchants are way better than anyone else in being Jews. Jews have been practicing Jewish tribal survival strategies (identity politics and ethnocentrism) for 3000 years."[72]

Throughout the twentieth century, cinema has been a powerful means of shaping American culture. Hollywood was founded by newly immigrated Jews from Eastern Europe in the 1920s: the Warner brothers, Carl Laemmle, William Fox, Harry Cohn, Samuel Goldwyn, Louis B. Mayer, Irving Thalberg, Adolph Zukor, and others. They built empires whose names became mythical: Twentieth-Century Fox, Columbia, MGM, Universal. These "giants [...] dared invent their own vision of the American Dream. Even to this day, the American values defined largely by the movies of these émigrés endure in American cinema and culture."[73] Their dream factory gradually became a nightmare. In *Hollywood vs. America*, an angry Michael Medved asks: "Why does our popular culture seem so consistently hostile to the values that most Americans hold dear? Why does the entertainment industry attack religion, glorify brutality, undermine the family, and deride patriotism?" Medved asserts that "Hollywood ignores—and assaults—the values of ordinary American families, pursuing a self-destructive and

---

[71] Charles Silberman, *A Certain People: American Jews and Their Lives Today*, Summit Books, 1985, p. 350.
[72] gilad.co.uk, June 02, 2015.
[73] Neal Gabler, *An Empire of Their Own: How the Jews Invented Hollywood*, Anchor, 1989 (publisher's presentation).

alienated ideological agenda that is harmful to the nation at large."[74]

Never mentioned in Medved's book is the Jewish influence on Hollywood. This is not surprising, given that Medved was born of German and Ukrainian Jewish parents, and presides over an Orthodox synagogue engaged in proselytism among liberal Jews in Southern California, not far from Hollywood. Like all neoconservatives of his kind, Medved plays the patriot by denouncing the "self-destruction" of the nation by liberal values. Hollywood is like bolshevism: if it is good, it is Jewish; but if it is bad, Jews have nothing to do with it.

More candid is Joel Stein, who defines himself as a "proud Jew," and replied in a 2008 *Los Angeles Times* article to Abe Foxman, who believes that talking about Jews' power over Hollywood is "dangerous": "I don't care if Americans think we're running the news media, Hollywood, Wall Street or the government. I just care that we get to keep running them."[75] Only a Jew can say such a thing without suffering the wrath of the ADL. In June 2014, the British actor Gary Oldman had to apologize to the Jewish community for having affirmed, in an interview with the magazine *Playboy*, that Hollywood is "run by the Jews."

Hollywood subversion exemplifies the thorn-in-the-side version of the "theory of mission," according to which the attack on moral values is a service to society. It has largely been Jewish intellectuals who, possessed by this mission, have waged a war of attrition against Christian moral values, as Nathan Abrams noted in the article quoted earlier. It has also been Jews, beginning with the founder of *Playboy* Hugh Heffner, who, in pornography and erotica, have broken all the moral barriers one by one. "There's no getting away from the fact that secular Jews have played (and still continue to play) a disproportionate role throughout the adult film industry in America. Jewish involvement in pornography has a long history in the United

---

[74] Michael Medved, *Hollywood vs. America: Popular Culture and the War on Tradition*, Harper Perennial, 1993 (publisher's presentation).
[75] Joel Stein, "Who Runs Hollywood? C'mon," *Los Angeles Times*, December 19, 2008, on articles.latimes.com/2008/dec/19/opinion/oe-stein19.

States, as Jews have helped to transform a fringe subculture into what has become a primary constituent of Americana." The testimony of its producers, cited by Abrams, suggests that pornography for them is not only a lucrative business, but also "a way of defiling Christian culture": "The only reason that Jews are in pornography is that we think that Christ sucks. Catholicism sucks," explains Al Goldstein.[76]

Changing the cultural environment of a nation requires the control of the screen and the press—the dream factory and the manufacture of opinion. The first is centered in Hollywood, on the West Coast, while the second is traditionally concentrated in the East, its two historic landmarks being the *Washington Post* and the *New York Times*. The news media act as a Darwinian mechanism of "cultural selection." They do not really create new ideas, but instead decide whether an idea, a bit of news, an opinion, a book, or an artist is or is not admissible. In this way they indirectly determine our conceptions of truth, beauty, and goodness. In a society blessed with a truly free and independent press, a wide variety of opinion, values, and tastes will find expression. But since the end of the nineteenth century, the press has grown ever-more concentrated in the hands of Jewish owners and publishers. These media barons have a natural tendency to showcase the contributions of their own community. And they have grown more and more involved in the defense of the interests of their community and of Israel.

The *Washington Post* was purchased in 1933 by Eugene Meyer, who was close to both Harry Truman (who appointed him the first president of the World Bank in 1947) and the very Zionist American Jewish Committee. In 1952, the committee stated as its mission to "continue to stimulate pro-Israel sentiments among the American people, particularly on radio and television." The other leading American newspaper, the *New York Times*, was bought in 1896 by Adolph Simon Ochs, whose son-in-law Arthur Hays Sulzberger became director of

---

[76] Nathan Abrams, "Nathan Abrams on Jews in the American Porn Industry," *Jewish Quarterly*, Winter 2004, on www.jewishquarterly.org/issuearchive/articled325.html ?articleid=38.

publication in 1938, and was succeeded by his son and then his grandson. Sulzberger denounced in 1946 the "coercive methods of the Zionists" influencing his editorial line. But from the creation of Israel to the present day, the newspaper he founded has produced singularly unbalanced coverage of Palestine.[77] The two other top-selling daily newspapers, the *Wall Street Journal* and *USA Today*, are also owned by Jews, as are the three main weekly magazines (*Time, Newsweek, US News & World Report*) as well as most political reviews (*National Review, New Republic, Weekly Standard*). Alongside the defense of Israel, they all promote the religion of the Holocaust.

The television industry has followed a similar path, and the concentration of Jewish power there is even more extreme. "Today, seven Jewish Americans run the vast majority of US television networks, the printed press, the Hollywood movie industry, the book publishing industry, and the recording industry," writes John Whitley.[78] The major news channels—ABC, NBC, CBS, and CNN—are naturally included in this category, as well as Rupert Murdoch's FOX empire, a mainstay of neoconservative propaganda. Murdoch, while not Jewish, is close to Ariel Sharon and Likud. In 2004 he directly or indirectly owned more than 175 print titles (40 million newspapers sold weekly) and 35 television channels, reaching 110 million spectators on four continents.

Given the pro-Israel bias of these media moguls, when the US Department of Justice investigates foreign groups that brought $36 million into the US to plant stories in the US media promoting Israeli foreign policy objectives, it is only pointing at the tree concealing the forest.[79]

In such a situation, everything Middle East-related is very carefully filtered and spun. But what is perhaps even more important is that the media has become the most important

---

[77] Alfred Lilienthal, *What Price Israel?* (1953), Infinity Publishing, 2003, pp. 134–135, 95, 143.

[78] John Whitley, "Seven Jewish Americans Control Most US Media," November 21, 2003, on www.rense.com.

[79] *Russia Today* interviews Grant Smith of the Institute for Research: Middle Eastern Policy, on www.youtube.com/watch?v=kureFeGmoDI.

power, after money, in American democracy. The press makes
and unmakes reputations, and thus elections, while maintaining
the illusion of popular choice. In a conference in Israel, Haim
Saban, a media magnate and multimillionaire, gave his recipe for
influencing US politics: "Donations to political parties, think-
tanks and media control." Gilad Atzmon suggests this is why
"democracy today, especially in the English speaking world, is a
political system that specialises in positioning inadequate,
unqualified and dubious types in leadership positions."[80]

But what makes the power of the Jewish elite unique is the
taboo that surrounds it. As the editorial writer Joseph Sobran
wrote: "Survival in public life requires that you know all about it,
but never refer to it. A hypocritical etiquette forces us to pretend
that the Jews are powerless victims; and if you don't respect
their victimhood, they'll destroy you."[81] Actually, you may refer
to Jewish power if you are Jewish, like Joel Stein as quoted
above, but not if you are a Gentile: star presenter Rick Sanchez
was dismissed in 2010 for having said that CNN and the other
media networks were all run by Jews.[82] Gilad Atzmon therefore
correctly characterizes Jewish Power as "the capacity to silence
criticism of Jewish Power."[83]

---

[80] Gilad Atzmon, *The Wandering Who?, op. cit.,* p. 171.

[81] *Sobran's,* March 1996, quoted in Kevin MacDonald, *Separation and Its Discontents, op. cit.,* k. 2161–72.

[82] "Rick Sanchez: Jon Stewart a 'Bigot,' Jews Run CNN & All Media," huffingtonpost.com, October 1, 2010.

[83] www.gilad.co.uk/writings/2015/2/9/jewish-power-political-correctness-and-the-left.

Chapter 11

CHILDREN OF THE MAD GOD

"By my own self I swear it; what comes from my mouth is saving justice, it is an irrevocable word: All shall bend the knee to me, by me every tongue shall swear."

Isaiah 45:23

Yahweh, the Levites, and the People

In chapter 2, I drew the portrait of Yahweh as a "sociopath among the gods," based on his raging extermination of his peers. I also hypothesized that this little tribal god's self-styled status as the only true God and sole creator of the universe exemplifies sociopathic narcissism. In this chapter I will discuss Yahweh not in his relationship to other gods, but to his chosen people.

From a Feuerbachian point of view (see chapter 3), Yahweh could be regarded as a personification of Jewishness, "the objectified Jewish essence," just as the universal God of Christianity is, for Feuerbach, "the objectified human essence." From this point of view, the "character" and "mentality" of Yahweh would be the projection of those of the Jewish people. But that is not accurate. For in the Bible, it is not the Jewish people but its religious elites who incarnate Yahweh and who speak, legislate, and rage in his name. "Yahweh" is nothing more than the voice of the priests. The prophets themselves, who speak in God's name, are really the spokesmen of the priests, or of some priestly clan or another.

The people, on the other hand, are almost always rebels against Yahweh's authority. The main theme of biblical history is the "alliance" between Yahweh and his people, and its leitmotiv is the alternance of submission, insubordination, and punishment.

Consider chapter 42 of the book of Jeremiah, whose ideology is so typically Deuteronomic that some biblical historians speculate that Jeremiah and his scribe Baruch were the main authors of Deuteronomy and the six following books.[1] After the fall of Jerusalem, the people of Judah come to Jeremiah asking him to intercede before God, "so that Yahweh your God may show us the way we are to go and what we must do." The prophet Jeremiah answers them: "I hear you; I will indeed pray to Yahweh your God as you ask; and whatever answer Yahweh your God gives you, I will tell you, keeping nothing back from you." The Judeans promise to "obey the voice of Yahweh our God to whom we are sending you." "Ten days later the word of Yahweh came to Jeremiah," who then summons "all the people from least to greatest" and reports that Yahweh has told him to tell them not to take refuge in Egypt, lest they "will die by sword, famine and plague: not a single one of them will survive or escape the disaster I [Yahweh] shall inflict on them." But a few clever ones challenge Jeremiah and doubt whether he has really consulted with Yahweh. "When Jeremiah had finished telling all the people all the words of Yahweh their God, which Yahweh their God had sent him to tell them—all the words quoted above—Azariah son of Hoshaiah, and Johanan son of Kareah, and all those arrogant men, said to Jeremiah, 'You are lying. Yahweh our God did not send you to say, 'Do not go to Egypt and settle there.' It was Baruch son of Neriah, who keeps inciting you against us, to hand us over to the Chaldaeans so that they can put us to death or deport us to Babylon'" (43:1–3). Finally, none of the leaders followed Yahweh/Jeremiah's order. They took refuge in Egypt, and Jeremiah actually went with them. Every reader may ponder in his heart if, in the same situation, he would have been among the "arrogant" or the gullible, and thus clarify his relationship to prophetic authority and the Bible in general.

Here, as throughout biblical history, the people are presented as rebelling against the authority of Yahweh, whether it is incarnated by Moses, the priests, or the prophets. Consequently, the Jewish national character or mentality cannot be deduced directly from the character or mentality of Yahweh.

---

[1] Richard Elliott Friedman, *Who Wrote the Bible?*, Summit Books, 1997.

What interests us is the cognitive mechanisms that Yahweh induces in his people. To study Jewish collective psychology, we must consider how the believer or ethnic Jew cognitively internalizes the foundations of his religion and identity inscribed in the Bible. This is difficult for Christians, who are not used to reading the Bible as Jews do: Christians do not identify with the Jewish people, nor do they feel directly concerned with the relationship between Yahweh and Israel. They tend to rationalize Yahweh's behavior in the Old Testament by the notion that he was dealing with a hardened people.

In this chapter, I will suggest that Yahweh, as the sociopathic or psychopathic god, has inculcated in the Jewish people the syndrome of the "psychopath's son." Philip Roth has formulated this very idea through the character of Smilesburger in *Operation Shylock*: "A Jew knows God and how, from the very first day He created man, He has been irritated with him from morning till night. [...] To appeal to a crazy, irritated father, that is what it is to be a Jew. To appeal to a crazy, *violent* father, and for three thousand years, that is what it is to be a crazy Jew!"[2]

This approach makes it possible to give a dialectical account of sociopsychological tensions in the Jewish community as a whole, and in each Jew individually insofar as he identifies with that community. The son of a psychopath, unless he escapes early on from his father, has no choice but to structure his personality by mimicking the paternal psychopathy. But his psychic autonomy also drives him to free himself from this father who lives in him, at the cost of terrible suffering.

What Is a Psychopath?

Psychopathy is a syndrome of traits classified among the personality disorders. Some behaviorally oriented psychiatrists prefer the term sociopathy. In an effort to get everyone to agree, the *Diagnostic and Statistical Manual of Mental Disorders*, the American psychiatric bible, has decided on "antisocial personality disorder." I prefer the term psychopathy, which is still more commonly used, but we need to keep in mind that we

---

[2] Philip Roth, *Operation Shylock: A Confession,* Simon & Schuster, 1993, p. 110.

are talking fundamentally of a disorder of sociability. Since our personality is what connects us to society, psychopathy is the archetypal personality disorder, of which all others can be considered partial manifestations or variations.

Canadian psychologist Robert Hare, in the wake of Hervey Cleckley's *The Mask of Sanity* (1941), has defined the diagnostic criteria of psychopathy on the basis of a cognitive checklist that is now widely adopted.[3] The most striking traits of the psychopath are lack of empathy and conscience. Other traits are common to narcissism: Psychopaths have a grand vision of their own importance. In their minds, everything is owed to them because they are exceptional. They are never wrong, and failures are always the fault of others. They often show megalomania, but some learn to hide their arrogance under false modesty. If the psychopath pretends to rise to the universal level, it is because he confuses it with his personal interests, and the truth with his own opinions. However, the psychopath is distinguished from the simple narcissist by his appetite for power, which makes him much more destructive. Moreover, his capacity for harm is not inhibited by any scruples or remorse: he is incapable of feeling guilt. Although he imagines himself a hero, and in some cases looks like a hero, the psychopath is, on the human spectrum, the polar opposite of the hero who sacrifices himself for his community. He has no qualms about sacrificing the people around him, and, when he knows he is lost, he consoles himself by causing as many people as possible to fall.

Basically, the psychopath perceives others as objects. He has a mechanical view of people and human relationships (and, in some way, of himself as well). Although devoid of conscience, he often has a keen perception of the law, which he, as a mechanic of the social engine, overestimates. He has not internalized moral law and in this sense is not socialized, but he has mastered the rules of the game and cheats without qualms if he can. For the same reason, the psychopath almost always

---

[3] Robert Hare, *Without Conscience: The Disturbing World of the Psychopaths Among Us*, Guilford Press, 1993.

develops an immoderate taste for money. He idealizes it as the epitome of power, the very essence of the social; he thinks that people can be bought and sold like things, and life often proves him right.

The diagnostic criteria for psychopathy also include pathological lying, cunning, and manipulative behavior. The psychopath feels only very superficial emotions and has no real feelings for anyone; but he has developed a great ability to deceive. He can be charming to the point of being charismatic. He typically shows highly developed verbal intelligence and lies with disconcerting aplomb. He is unable to feel empathy, but learns to simulate it, sometimes with a tendency to histrionism (Latin *histrio*, "theater actor"). But the psychopath is more than what psychoanalyst Helene Deutsche has called the "as-if personality," endowed with purely mimetic "ungenuine pseudo emotions": he is a manipulator. It is through his extraordinary ability to feign, trick, trap, and capture that the psychopath draws his power. Although he himself is immunized against guilt, he becomes a master in the art of using guilt to dominate others.

In any situation, the psychopath projects a *persona*, which can vary according to circumstances. The opinions he holds in public are all disguises that he tailors to his own advantage. However, lying is so deeply embedded in his nature that the question of his "sincerity" is almost irrelevant: the psychopath can beat a lie detector. The truth has no value in his eyes, or merges with the version of events that suits him. The psychopath is unable to put himself in the place of others, and thus to view himself critically. Confident in any circumstance of being right and innocent (and superior), he considers the resentment of his victims as irrational and pointless.

According to Hervey Cleckley: "The psychopath presents a technical appearance of sanity, often one of high intellectual capacities, and not infrequently succeeds in business or professional activities." But this appearance of sanity is misleading, for the psychopath suffers from a profound underlying disorder Cleckley calls "semantic aphasia," characterized by a disconnection between language and emotion.[4] Although those close to the psychopath—at least those who learn the hard way his true nature—can judge him raving mad, the psychopath is not "sick" because he does not "suffer." He is innocent of neurosis, and never requests psychiatric care (except as a strategic calculation). He is not psychotic, and cannot be regarded as maladapted to social life. On the contrary, he is, in a certain sense, over-adjusted. (That is why the real mystery, from a Darwinian point of view, is not the existence of psychopaths, but their low proportion in the population.)

Unfortunately, there have been few studies on the psychopath's behavior as a father. Yet it is easy to understand that, if the psychopath likes to dominate, manipulate, and mentally enslave, he will find easy prey in his own children. Since we are reflecting on the relationship of Yahweh to his chosen people, what interests us specifically is the experience of the favorite son of a psychopathic father, whom the father chose as an extension of his own narcissistic self. We must also imagine a family unit whose mother is absent or erased. Let us go further: the most illuminating example might be that of a psychopath who, for one reason or another, finds himself incapable of realizing his ambitions except through his chosen or only son.

Such a father idealizes himself as God creating man in his own image. His son is his creature, and therefore he recognizes in him only what he has shaped in him. All that the son accomplishes serves to nourish the narcissism of the father, who claims credit and expects recognition. On the other hand, he makes his son pay dearly for what he considers his failures: they are proof that, left to himself, the son is a loser. The psychopathic father demands the submission of his son, and if he wills his son's success, it is only to feed his own ego.

The fusional love that the psychopathic father feels for his son should not be confused with empathy. It is the exact

---

[4] Hervey Cleckley, *The Mask of Sanity* (1941), quoted in Paul Babiak and Robert Hare, *Snakes in Suits: When Psychopaths Go to Work*, HarperCollins, 2007, p. 20.

opposite, even if the father, in his narcissistic self-heroization, confuses them. Far from seeking to promote the psychic autonomy of his son, the psychopath seeks to control him by any means, to keep him dependent. Consciously or not (it is always difficult to say, for the psychopath does not reflect on his own motivations), he will set up the mechanisms for his son's enslavement by lowering his psychological defenses. These mechanisms often have an incestuous dimension. Though himself devoid of moral conscience, he does not hesitate to play on his son's guilt, accusing him of ingratitude. Everything he gives is secretly conditional and serves to create a moral debt. The "double bind," which deeply confuses the child and hinders his cognitive development, can be a deliberate strategy used by the psychopathic father.

The psychopath isolates his victims and seeks to undermine their confidence in others. The psychopathic father will typically prevent his son from building nurturing bonds with others, especially family members who are aware of his psychological issues. An uncle who feels a particular affection for his nephew—or, worse, worries about him—will be repulsed as a dangerous rival. The psychopathic father is a jealous god: he must secure control over any relationship that his son establishes with others. If he is sufficiently vigilant, his son will find no comfort, no substitute parent figure, and therefore no lever of resilience. He will be trained to perceive all generous attention as a threat, any gesture of sympathy as an aggression. All around him he will see only potential enemies. One of the psychopath's favorite means of manipulation is the "triangulation" of relationships, which gives him indirect and therefore less perceptible control.

The Psychopathic God

The behavior of Yahweh toward his people, as presented in biblical history, can be examined through the psychological prism we have just described. Yahweh is a father to his people, but a father who, to keep his son under his tight control, prevents him from forming any empathic alliance with other peoples. He convinces the Jews that all those who wish to be their friends are in fact their worst enemies, that all confidence in Gentiles leads only to disaster. The Jews must place their entire trust in Yahweh alone. The cultic and food prohibitions are there precisely to prevent all socialization outside the tribe: "I shall set you apart from all these peoples, for you to be mine" (Leviticus 20:26); "you, out of all peoples, shall be my personal possession, for the whole world is mine. For me you shall be a kingdom of priests, a holy nation" (Exodus 19:5–6). This last sentence is often cited out of context as evidence that the Jewish people are divinely commissioned to be the spiritual guide of humanity. It is a misunderstanding: what Yahweh wants is a people consecrated to his worship, just as the psychopathic father seeks, in the devotion of his son, the exaltation of his own narcissism.

It is often claimed that Yahweh demands that his people exhibit moral superiority. The claim is nonsensical. Let us repeat: there is no trace in the Torah of any struggle between good and evil, in the metaphysical sense. The only criterion of Yahweh's approval is obedience to his arbitrary laws. The fate of the Jewish people is linked exclusively to this criterion, so that every reversal of fortune is explained by a breach of contract on the part of the people, and serves to strengthen the submission of the people. When a people attacks the Hebrews, it is never because of what the Hebrews did to it, but because of the infidelity of the Hebrew people to Yahweh. For other peoples are but vulgar instruments in the hands of Yahweh. The guilt that the Jewish people should feel about failing to obey Yahweh obliterates self-reflection and self-criticism, and prevents them from being able to even consider the grievances of the Gentiles. In Kevin MacDonald's words: "The idea that Jewish suffering results from Jews straying from their own law occurs almost like a constant drumbeat throughout the Tanakh—a constant reminder that the persecution of Jews is not the result of their own behavior vis-à-vis Gentiles but rather the result of their behavior vis-à-vis God."[5] If the Jewish people have sinned, it is

---

[5] Kevin MacDonald, *Separation and Its Discontents: Toward an Evolutionary Theory of Anti-Semitism*, Praeger, 1998, kindle 2013, k. 6187–89.

against God, never against other peoples. And if they have sinned against God, it is precisely by sympathizing with other peoples, by "assimilating" with them. A terrible double bind has seized the chosen people: it is caught between the exalting glory of the Election and the exorbitant price of the Covenant; between promises of world domination and threats of extinction. Note that when Yahweh refrains from destroying his people who "rebelled against me," it is out of concern for his own reputation: "I then resolved to vent my fury on them in the desert and destroy them. But respect for my own name kept me from letting it be profaned in the eyes of the nations, before whom I had brought them out" (Ezekiel 20:13–14).

In his book *Der jüdische Selbsthaß* ("Jewish Self-Hatred") published in Berlin in 1930, Theodor Lessing wrote: "To the question: 'Why do not we love ourselves?' Jewish doctrine answers since the beginning of time: 'Because we are guilty' [...] In every Jewish man there is a deeply buried tendency to interpret any misfortune that strikes him as the atonement for a fault he has committed." The Jews, says Lessing, are "the first and perhaps the only ones" to have developed such an attitude. He sees this as the origin of a "self-hatred" that affects all Jews in varying degrees.[6]

There is a deep truth in this diagnosis, but Lessing's formulation is confusing. If to seek in oneself the causes of the violence of others means the capacity to examine oneself by putting oneself in the place of others, then it is an empathic process, based on the premise that the other shares with oneself the same humanity and therefore a comparable way of seeing and feeling things. This is not at all what Judaism teaches. And that is the problem Lessing has not grasped. As we have just seen, Judaism (biblical Yahwism as well as Talmudic rabbinism) teaches the Jews that all their misfortunes are explained by their disobedience to Yahweh, and that their most serious fault is to fraternize with the non-Jews. The biblical message, in essence, is: "Do not frequent idolaters (non-Jews), despise their traditions, and—if possible—exploit them, enslave them, and exterminate

---

6 Théodor Lessing, *La Haine de soi: ou le refus d'être juif* (1930), Pocket, 2011, pp. 46–47.

them. If, after that, they violate you, it is your fault: you have not obeyed scrupulously enough." Such is the insane cognitive logic, internalized over a hundred generations, that encloses the Jews in the infernal cycle of chosenness and persecution. This mode of thought is based on the denial of the other's humanity, which is indeed the essence of psychopathy. It does not occur to the psychopath to question the feelings of the other in order to try to understand his anger, because the other is fundamentally an object and not a person: his actions are events whose motivation is irrelevant. Thus, after the war that decimated the Jewish community of Alexandria between 115 and 117 CE, the fact that it was the culmination of numerous clashes between Jews and non-Jews (Greeks and Egyptians) did not lead Jews to reflect on the reasons that led the Alexandrians to collaborate with the Roman armies against them. According to the Talmudist of the second century Rabbi Simeon ben Yohai, the Roman emperor was only the instrument of divine justice to punish the Jews for remaining in Egypt.[7] Never, ever, has the Jewish community taken into account the grievances of its persecutors. Its elites forbid it.

Whoever cannot bear to see himself in others' eyes has not learned to love himself. This answers Lessing's question: "How is it that all peoples love themselves, while the Jew is the only one who has so much trouble loving himself?"[8]

Of course, in speaking here of "Yahweh" as a psychopathic or sociopathic father, and of the election he confers as a curse, I am speaking metaphorically and abstractly. I do not believe in the objective existence of such a mad god. But if Yahweh is imaginary, that does not change his psychological stranglehold. Yahweh is the persona (the mask) invented by the Levitical elites; the relationship between the people and Yahweh in the Bible is in fact only a projection of the relationship between the people and their Levitical elites. Judaism, which has the nature of an alliance—that is, a contract—between the Jews and their

---

[7] *Jerusalem Talmud*, Sukkah V, 1, 55b, quoted in Joseph Mélèze Modrzejewski, *The Jews of Egypt, From Rameses II to Emperor Hadrian*, Princeton University Press, 1995, p. xvii.
[8] Théodor Lessing, *La Haine de soi: ou le refus d'être juif, op. cit.*, p. 74.

god, is a dictatorship based on a more or less arbitrary set of laws whose object is less the well-being of the people than the mere exercise of divine power. And since control always needs to be reinforced, the evolution of Judaism is marked by uninterrupted legalistic escalation: after Deuteronomy come the laws of Leviticus, then the innumerable laws of the Pharisees that give rise to rabbinic Judaism. According to the consecrated expression, the Talmudic laws are conceived as "a barrier around the barrier of the Torah." Maimonides, the medieval Talmudic scholar, established a catalogue of 613 authoritative commandments (365 bans and 248 obligations).

For a non-religious Jew, the Jews are not God's chosen people, but his "inventors." As David Ben-Gurion put it, it was not Yahweh who chose the Jewish people, but the Jewish people who chose Yahweh. So the covenant between Yahweh and his people is really only an alliance between Jews, whose elites dictate terms. Paradoxically, this hardly affects the religious conception of chosenness. In fact, there is even more arrogance in the profane conception, for being chosen by God at least leaves room for a sacrificial interpretation, which would imply a higher moral requirement and a vocation to suffer for humanity—a conception mostly put forward in apologetic literature for non-Jews. In contrast, the secular Jews' concept of self-election is accompanied by an exaltation of the superiority of the Jewish people, including superiority in suffering. It is no longer disobedience to God that provokes misfortunes but the eternal hatred of the Gentiles. For Nathan and Ruth Perlmutter, anti-Semitism stems from "the jealousy of the Gentiles and their fury at seeing the Jews surpass them. [...] The Gentiles, more numerous and less evolved, are annoyed to see the Jews, fewer and more evolved."[9] Alternatively, in Jacques Attali's conception, anti-Semitism stems from humanity's ingratitude for what the Jews gave it, namely God and money.[10] Thus from within this cognitive straitjacket that prevents all self-criticism,

[9] Nathan and Ruth Perlmutter, *The Real Anti-Semitism in America,* Arbor House Publishing Company, 1984, pp. 36, 40.
[10] Watch Attali, "Le Nouvel Ordre Mondial et Israël," on YouTube.

anti-Semitism seemingly confirms the superiority and generosity of the Jews. The Holocaust, the culmination of anti-Semitism, becomes "a distasteful secular version of chosenness," according to Ismar Schorsch, chancellor of the Jewish Theological Seminary.[11] The divine—diabolical—figure of the Holocaust has replaced a Yahweh who is losing authority. But it is always the same elite that uses this divinity for its own purposes. After all, in good old-fashioned Yahwist theology, it is always Yahweh who strikes Israel, using the hands of its enemies, to punish it for its infidelity.

Killing Yahweh

As the son of a psychopath builds his own personality under the influence of his pathological parent, he can never be fully individualized or socialized. His psychological development will depend on his father's investment in him, his natural capacity for resilience, his access to other meaningful relationships, and factors still unknown to psychology. To simplify, we may say that during adolescence the psychopath's son faces a stark choice between submission or self-destruction. If he submits, he will eventually internalize the father's psychopathy (without necessarily renouncing the desire to kill him). Psychiatrists note a hereditary factor in psychopathy, but the explanation is probably less genetic than cognitive or epigenetic: when the child's psychic tension is resolved by surrender, the child integrates the cognitive structure of the father. In effect, he becomes his father. If, on the other hand, the son chooses the second alternative, self-destruction, he will wander in the limbo of psychosis, awaiting an improbable miracle, a rebirth he may find in faith or love. Between these two extremes lies the vast domain of neuroses and unresolved Oedipus complexes, minor personality or developmental disorders, all of which are characterized by deficiencies in the capacity for sociability.

Every Jew finds himself in such a situation, to the extent that he identifies himself as a Jew. He is torn by opposite and

---

[11] Quoted in Norman Finkelstein, *The Holocaust Industry: Reflections on the Exploitation of Jewish Suffering*, Verso, 2014, p. 50.

partly unconscious wills, which have their ultimate source in his ambivalent relationship to his ethnic god—who is, on the psychological level, merely the internalized symbolic representation of the tribal elites' power over him. Every Jew, insofar as he believes himself to be Jewish, feels this schism, this inner tension, which is at bottom the struggle between his Jewishness and his humanity. This is the most probable explanation for the high rate of neuroses among Jews. The neurotic Jew is not just a Hollywood stereotype created by Woody Allen or the Coen brothers. The 1906 *Jewish Encyclopedia* wrote: "The Jews are more subject to diseases of the nervous system than the other races and peoples among which they dwell. Hysteria and neurasthenia appear to be most frequent."[12] Isaac Kadmi-Cohen speaks of "a congenital neurosis characterized by a lack of balance between objective data and judgment [...] a nervous excitability, a chronic exaltation of passion."[13] This anomaly, often attributed to endogamy, has been a concern for many Jewish doctors and psychiatrists, including Sigmund Freud. Research by Leo Srole in the 1960s shows that the Jewish rate of neuroses and character disorders was about three times as high as that of Catholics and Protestants.[14] Neurosis results from psychic tension that threatens the integrity of the self, and that can degenerate into psychosis when the tension reaches a point of rupture. Freud wrongly reduced this tension to a conflict between the id (sexual instinct) and the superego, but his schema nevertheless has the merit of emphasizing the role of the castrating image of the father. For the Jews, the symbolic image of the father internalized in the superego is superimposed on that of Yahweh.

At the first Zionist Congress (1897), Max Nordau offered Zionism as the solution to this inner schism that undermines the psyche of the "emancipated Jew," whose "best powers are exhausted in the suppression, or at least in the difficult

---

12 "Nervous diseases," by Joseph Jacobs and Maurice Fishberg, on www.jewishency clopedia.com/articles/11446-nervous-diseases.
13 Isaac Kadmi-Cohen, *Nomades: Essai sur l'âme juive, op. cit.*, p. 36.
14 Nathan Agi, "The Neurotic Jew," *The Beacon*, December 5, 2011, on thebeaconmag .websitesbyrafi.com.

concealment of his own real character. For he fears that this character might be recognized as Jewish, and he has never the satisfaction of showing himself as he is in all his thoughts and sentiments. He becomes an inner cripple, and externally unreal, and thereby always ridiculous and hateful to all higher feeling men, as is everything that is unreal."[15] But Nordau's diagnosis is incomplete. Such alienation stems not only from the effort to be "a Jew at home and a man in the street," but more deeply from the contradictions between Jewish tribalism and Jewish supposed universalism.

Whatever role a mature Jew may play in the community, each Jew experiences during his youth an inner rupture between his Jewishness and his humanity, and for better or worse must manage this paradoxical double identity. As sociologist Daniel Bell explains: "I was born in galut [exile] and I accept—now gladly, though once in pain—the double burden and the double pleasure of my self-consciousness, the outward life of an American and the inward secret of the Jew. I walk with this sign as a frontlet between my eyes [Deuteronomy 11:18], and it is as visible to some secret others as their sign is to me." Like many other fully assimilated Jews who have achieved social success in their host nation, Bell feels ever-more-acutely with age "that one does not stand alone, that the past is still present, and that there are responsibilities of participation even when the community of which one is a part is a community woven by the thinning strands of memory."[16]

Anyone who finally submits to the communal sociopathic mentality becomes a vector of it in his turn. Although the transmission is not exclusively generational, we observe among the elites a propensity to pass this mentality from father to son. The neoconservatives, one of the most sociopathic elites in history, are a case in point: Irving Kristol was succeeded by his son William, Donald Kagan by his son Robert, Richard Pipes by his son Daniel, and Norman Podhoretz by his son John and

---

[15] Quoted in Gilad Atzmon, *The Wandering Who? A Study of Jewish Identity Politics,* Zero Books, 2011, p. 59. Nordau's full text on www.jewishvirtuallibrary.org.

[16] Daniel Bell, "Reflections on Jewish Identity," *Commentary,* June 31, 1961, quoted in Kevin MacDonald, *Separation and Its Discontents, op. cit.,* k. 6316–22.

son-in-law Elliott Abrams. The champion of the second generation, Benjamin Netanyahu, is himself the son of Benzion Netanyahu, a paranoid Zionist who in February 2009, the day before his son's election, declared: "Today we are facing, plain and simple, a danger of annihilation. This is not only the ongoing existential danger to Israel, but a real danger of complete annihilation. People think that the Shoah [Holocaust] is over but it's not. It is continuing all the time."[17]

There has always been a minority of Jews who, by self-examination (often under painful circumstances) succeed in escaping from the mental shackles of their Jewishness. They are stigmatized as suffering from "self-hatred," and the anathema or persecution they endure only makes their emancipation more heroic. They have symbolically killed the father. The "murder of the father" is one of Freud's most fertile intuitions, but Freud has mistakenly generalized: only the son of the destructive and manipulative father needs to "kill the father." This is why Freudian psychoanalysis, born of the "self-cure" of its founder, is indeed, if not a "Jewish national affair" as Freud said, at least a theory deeply marked by the Jewish collective psyche.[18] For the Jewish father is the representative of the Jewish collective superego, whose other name is Yahweh, and every Jew aspires to the depths of his soul to free himself from Yahweh.

But we must also understand what is meant by "killing the psychopathic father" (as representative of the collective Jewish sociopathy). Anyone who simply hates the father is in danger of unknowingly absorbing his inheritance. He resembles him in his very rejection. Jewish revolt often assumes this character; the Jewish revolutionaries of Russia who rejected the Talmud, the synagogue, and the Kahal were, in their internationalism, just as petrified with hatred of "the nations" as their rabbis. The metaphysical revolt of the emancipated Jew sweeps away

---

[17] Quoted in Alan Hart, *Zionism: The Real Enemy of the Jews*, vol. 3: *Conflict Without End?*, Clarity Press, 2010, p. 364.

[18] Freud told how he became aware of the need to "kill the father" after his own father, Jakob, had been humiliated by a Gentile; so it is the Jewish father whom he sought to "kill." Read John Murray Cuddihy, *The Ordeal of Civility: Freud, Marx, Levi-Strauss, and the Jewish Struggle with Modernity*, Basic Books, 1974, pp. 52–54.

everything in its path. Perpetually on the run, he does not find the rest he aspires to, but carries away those he meets in his flight, recreating wherever he passes the disenchanted world of his native prison. To kill the sociopathic and destructive father, in the sense of true emancipation, must be understood as transcending the hatred of the father. For hatred is still a manifestation of his grip. To extirpate the toxic father from one's soul presupposes having identified his nature and influence: an eminently perilous, almost superhuman undertaking, since the son thus emancipated finds himself without a father at all. Perhaps such emancipation is impossible without an encounter with the transcendent.

It goes far beyond family roots and uprootings. To renounce his Jewishness, for a Jew, is like tearing himself from that collective part of his soul of which we have spoken. Ideas do not flow in the blood, but each person carries within himself his ancestors, in a mysterious and largely unconscious way. In other words, ideas are not simply a question of choice, for no one chooses the way in which he structures his vision of the world and of himself, his relation to the group and to men outside the group, from early childhood onward, beginning even before the acquisition of language. Our cultural heritage is deeply rooted in an unconscious whose deepest layers are ancestral. From this point of view, tribal endogamy creates a hermetically sealed chamber that is mental and not merely genetic.

To understand this human reality, one must appeal to transgenerational psychology, one of the most enriching developments in depth psychology. Based on a few observations by Freud, Nicolas Abraham and Maria Török introduced the notion of the "phantom," defined as "a formation of the unconscious which has the peculiarity of never having been conscious [...] and resulting from transmission, the mode of which remains to be determined, from the unconscious of a parent to the unconscious of a child."[19] Ivan Boszormenyi-Nagy speaks of "invisible loyalties" that unconsciously connect us

---

[19] Nicolas Abraham and Maria Török, *L'Écorce et le Noyau*, Aubier-Flammarion, 1978, p. 429.

with our ancestors. Such loyalties, which shape our destiny largely unconsciously, are based on value systems that vary from one culture to another: "The development of loyalty is determined by the history of the family, by the type of justice that the family practices, and by family myths. It finds resonance in each member of the family. Upon each one falls on the one hand, obligations, according to position and role; and on the other hand, a sense of debts and merits, along with a personal style and manner of compliance."[20] Vincent de Gaulejac evokes "sociopsychic knots" and "genealogical impasses," paradoxical and neurotic situations of the type: "I do not want to be what I am." In seeking to escape from a painful family situation that has helped form his identity, the individual is led to reproduce it. "While wanting to break away at any cost, he remains attached without understanding why. In attempting to construct himself in an elsewhere, he remains overdetermined by a filiation which imposes itself on him even if he thinks he is escaping from it. These unconscious inscriptions lead us to postulate the existence of a genealogical past that imposes itself on the subject and structures his psychic functioning."[21]

Such considerations help us understand the psychological tensions that seize every person in the Jewish community who seeks to move away from it; no community cultivates a more powerful sense of ancestral loyalty. Consider the case of Robert, the son of a deportee to the concentration camps who was interviewed by Claudine Vegh for her collection of testimonies *I Didn't Say Goodbye* (first published in French in 1979). Robert was fourteen when his father was deported to Auschwitz. When he was torn from his son, he shouted: "'Robert, never forget, you are Jewish and you must remain Jewish!' These were his last words, I hear them as if it were yesterday. He did not say to me: 'I love you, do not fear anything, take care of yourself,' but this one sentence. [...] I resent them, you understand? Yes, I resent the dead who have paid for their lives with mine! It's

---

[20] Ivan Boszormenyi-Nagy, *Invisible Loyalties: Reciprocity in Intergenerational Family Therapy*, Harper & Row, 1973, p. 56.
[21] Vincent de Gaulejac, *L'Histoire en héritage. Roman familial et trajectoire sociale*, Payot, 2012, pp. 141–142, 146–147.

unbearable! [...] My eldest daughter, who is a student, is leaving to settle permanently in Israel! She told me she had to do what I had not been able to accomplish [...] The buckle is closed, he adds, the torch is passed on ... Suddenly very tired: 'My father would have been proud of her.'"[22] This kind of personal testimony helps us understand the power of this invisible loyalty that the funeral cult of Auschwitz crystallizes in a whole generation of Jews.

When considering the traumatic essence of Judaism, we must consider the issue of ritual circumcision performed on eight-day-old infants as commanded by the Biblical God to Abraham (Genesis 17:9-14). It must be distinguished from the circumcision practiced in ancient Egypt on fourteen-year-old boys as a kind of rite of passage, or from Islamic circumcision, which is not done before the age of five, generally later. Unlike the child or teenager, the infant is psychologically incapable of giving any positive meaning to the violence done to him. Eight days after emerging from his mother's womb—a trauma in itself—what he needs most of all is to develop trust in the benevolence of those who welcomed him into this world, starting with his mother.

Because infants cannot speak, rabbis who justify the tradition speak in their place to minimize their physical pain and psychological plight. But according to Professor Ronald Goldman, author of *Circumcision, the Hidden Trauma*, scientific studies prove the neurological impact of infant circumcision, for which there exists no effective anesthetic. Behavioral changes observed after the operation, including sleep disorders and inhibition in mother-child bonding, are signs of a post-traumatic stress syndrome. The loss of trust in the mother is the potential source of a future unconscious hatred of women, the social consequences of which can be tremendous.[23]

During the Jewish ceremony, the mother is normally kept away from the scene, and the baby's screams are partly covered

---

[22] Claudine Vegh, *Je ne lui ai pas dit au-revoir*, Gallimard (1979), 2014, pp. 169–182.
[23] Ronald Goldman, *Circumcision, the Hidden Trauma: How an American Cultural Practice Affects Infants and Ultimately Us All*, Vanguard, 1997.

by the loud cheers of the men surrounding it—a clear message to the baby if it could think about it. But mothers who happen to witness the ritual empathize with the trauma of their child, and suffer enduring trauma themselves: "The screams of my baby remain embedded in my bones and haunt my mind," says Miriam Pollack. "His cry sounded like he was being butchered. I lost my milk." Nancy Wainer Cohen: "I will go to my grave hearing that horrible wail, and feeling somewhat responsible." Elizabeth Pickard-Ginsburg: "I don't feel I can recover from it. [...] We had this beautiful baby boy and seven beautiful days and this beautiful rhythm starting, and it was like something had been shattered! ... When he was first born there was a tie with my young one, my newborn. And when the circumcision happened, in order to allow it I had to cut off the bond. I had to cut off my natural instincts, and in doing so I cut off a lot of feelings towards Jesse. I cut it off to repress the pain and to repress the natural instinct to stop the circumcision." These testimonies, and more, can be found on the Circumcision Resource Center web page "Mothers Who Observed Circumcision."[24] They illustrate the repressed guilt that lies behind the stereotype of the Jewish mother.

Sigmund Freud, that great explorer of infantile traumas, is rather discreet on the subject—though he didn't have his own children circumcised. He broaches it in his latest books, but only in the context of his anthropological speculations, without delving into the psychological implications. In *New Introductory Lectures on Psychoanalysis*, we read: "It is our suspicion that during the human family's primeval period castration used actually to be carried out by a jealous and cruel father upon growing boys, and that circumcision, which so frequently plays a part in puberty rites among primitive people, is a clearly recognizable relic of it."[25] Freud touches again on the subject in *Moses and Monotheism*, published a few months before his death: "Circumcision is a symbolical substitute of castration, a

---

[24] www.circumcision.org/mothers.htm.

[25] Sigmund Freud, *New Introductory Lectures on Psychoanalysis* (1933), Hogarth Press, 1964, p. 86.

punishment which the primaeval father dealt his sons long ago out of the awfulness of his power, and whosoever accepted this symbol showed by so doing that he was ready to submit to his father's will, although it was at the cost of a painful sacrifice."[26] Among Freud's disciples, almost all of them Jewish, the only one to have reflected upon the trauma of infantile circumcision is Sándor Ferenczi, whom Freud long considered his most gifted acolyte, but who was ostracized when he started defending the veracity of his patients' memories of infantile sexual abuses, rather than following the Freudian theory that these memories were mere repressed fantasies.[27]

The link between circumcision and paternal violence is also recognized by Jewish tradition, which has always related God's two commands to Abraham—to circumcise his sons, and to sacrifice Isaac—although they are separate events in the Bible. Infantile circumcision physically impresses on every Jew, and on all Jews collectively, Yahweh's abusive and traumatic domination. It is like a genetic mark, passed on from father to son, to engrave the Yahwist covenant in pain and in sexuality. It is also the ultimate sign of separation: the uncircumcised are deemed impure and the Torah forbids socializing with them, let alone marrying them. Circumcision is the lock of the "Jewish prison."

Jewishness and Selective Empathy

The most optimistic low-end estimate of the proportion of psychopaths in the Western population is 1 percent. They should not be confused with the proverbial 1 percent who own half the world's wealth. Yet a study among senior executives of large companies, published under the title *Snakes in Suits*, shows that psychopathic traits are widespread among them.[28] This is

---

[26] Sigmund Freud, *Moses and Monotheism*, Hogarth Press, 1939, p. 192.

[27] On Ferenczi and Freud's denial of his patients' real traumas, read Jeffrey Masson, *The Assault on Truth: Freud's Suppression of the Seduction Theory*, Farrar Strauss & Giroux, 1984.

[28] Paul Babiak and Robert Hare, *Snakes in Suits, op. cit.* The authors appear in the documentary *I Am Fishead* (2011).

not surprising, since modern society values psychopathic traits and favors the upward mobility of psychopaths.

The fact that Jews today are disproportionately represented among the elite ("though barely 2% of the [American] nation's population is Jewish, close to half its billionaires are Jews," remarks Benjamin Ginsberg in *The Fatal Embrace*)[29] should not lead us to conclude that psychopathy is more prevalent among the chosen people. In a way, quite the opposite is the case: Jews demonstrate among themselves an extraordinary capacity for empathy, or at least familiarity, that breeds exceptional solidarity to the point of self-sacrifice. The anti-Semitic stereotype that Jews are more egotistical, less loyal, less courageous, and less generous than non-Jews is totally unfair, as Hilaire Belloc pointed out in 1922. On the contrary, their loyalty, courage, and generosity often far outstrip those of their neighbors. However, these qualities tend to be oriented selectively toward themselves, and it is perhaps for this reason that they are more intense.[30] It is true that Otto Weininger (a self-hating Jew according to Lessing) argued against the notion of "solidarity" among Jews: "When some accusation is made against some unknown member of the Jewish race, all Jews secretly take the part of the accused, and wish, hope for, and seek to establish his innocence. But it must not be thought that they are interesting themselves more in the fate of the individual Jew than they would do in the case of an individual Christian. It is the menace to Jewry in general, the fear that the shameful shadow may do harm to Jewry as a whole, which is the origin of the apparent feeling of sympathy."[31]

The selective nature of this empathy suggests that it is addressed less to the humanity of others than to their Jewishness. Here is what happens when two New York Jews meet: "We have never met before, but I instantly know him. One look, one phrase, and I know where he grew up, how he grew up, where he got his drive and his sense of humor. He is

---

[29] Benjamin Ginsberg, *The Fatal Embrace: Jews and the State*, University of Chicago Press, 1993, p. 1.
[30] Hilaire Belloc, *The Jews*, Constable & Co., 1922 (archive.org), pp. 73–80.
[31] Otto Weininger, *Sex and Character* (1903), A.L. Burt (archive.org), p. 310 (translation corrected).

New York. He is Jewish. He looks like my uncle Louis, his voice is my uncle Sam. I feel we've been together at countless weddings, bar mitzvahs, and funerals. I know his genetic structure. I'm certain that within the last five hundred years—perhaps even more recently—we shared the same ancestor."[32] This is Secretary of Labor Robert Reich's memory of his first meeting with Alan Greenspan, chairman of the Council of the Federal Reserve, two very influential Americans, about whom we would like to believe that such familiarity does not affect their judgment of the American national interest.

As Tacitus suggested two thousand years ago, there seems to be a correlation between the intensity of solidarity with kinsmen and the lack of it with others: "Among themselves they are inflexibly honest and ever ready to show compassion, though they regard the rest of mankind with all the hatred of enemies" (*Histories* V.5). The relationship between these two contrary attitudes can be understood with the help of Freud. The founder of psychoanalysis studied the psychopathology of religion in three books: *Totem and Taboo*, *Civilization and Its Discontents*, and *The Future of an Illusion*, in which he describes religion as "the universal obsessional neurosis of humanity." Freud was not here talking about neurosis in the strict sense. On the contrary, by adopting the cognitive framework of religious faith, "devout believers are safeguarded in a high degree against the risk of certain neurotic illnesses; their acceptance of the universal neurosis spares them the task of constructing a personal one."[33] Expressed in a less polemical way, the idea is that religion makes it possible to sublimate the neurotic tendencies. Freud was mainly concerned with the majority religion of the Viennese bourgeoisie he rubbed shoulders with: Catholicism. We can adopt a similar approach to Judaism, but then must turn from neurosis to psychopathy or sociopathy. In certain essential aspects, Judaism is a form of "collective sociopathy." This does not mean that "the Jews" are sociopaths, but rather that they are

---

[32] Robert Reich, *Locked in the Cabinet*, Scribner, 1997, quoted in Kevin MacDonald, *Culture of Critique: Toward an Evolutionary Theory of Jewish Involvement in Twentieth-Century Intellectual and Political Movements*, Praeger, 1998, kindle 2013, k. 9222–27.
[33] Sigmund Freud, *The Future of an Illusion*, Hogarth Press, 1928, p. 76.

victims of a mental trap inherited from their ancestors and imposed by their elites. The difference between collective sociopathy and individual sociopathy is the same as between collective neurosis and individual neurosis according to Freud: participation in a collective sociopathic mentality allows members of the community to channel sociopathic tendencies toward the outside of the community, and to maintain within it a high degree of sociability.

The idea is easy to illustrate: The individual who feels exceptional and surrounded by hostile people is a megalomaniac and a paranoiac; but the English Jew of Romanian origin Maurice Samuel speaks acceptably on behalf of his community when, in his 1924 book *You Gentiles*, he shares his "belief that we Jews stand apart from you gentiles, that a primal duality breaks the humanity I know into two distinct parts; that this duality is a fundamental, and that all differences among you gentiles are trivialities compared with that which divided all of you from us." The individual possessed by the passion to destroy is considered dangerously insane, but Samuel is simply a communitarian Jew when he writes: "We Jews, we, the destroyers, will remain the destroyers forever. [...] We will forever destroy because we need a world of our own, a God-world, which it is not in your nature to build."[34] Maurice Samuel was undoubtedly a charming and quite sane man. It is only when the Jews think and act as representatives of the Jews and in the name of the Jews—when they say "we Jews . . ."—that their behavior toward non-Jews and their conception of relations with non-Jews betrays a sociopathic structure.

Empathy could be defined as the ability of individual souls to temporarily merge. Now, as we have seen, the Jews feel united by a kind of collective or ethnic soul that occupies a greater or lesser part of their individual souls, according to individuals and circumstances. The Jewish ethnohistorian Raphael Patai, author of *The Jewish Mind,* posits "consciousness of belonging as the ultimate criterion of Jewishness."[35] This is

---

[34] Maurice Samuel, *You Gentiles,* New York, 1924 (archive.org), pp. 12, 155.
[35] Raphael Patai, *The Jewish Mind,* Wayne State University Press, 1977, p. 25.

indeed how many Jews recall their Jewishness. "Being Jewish to me," says French philosopher Alain Finkielkraut, "is to feel involved, concerned, sometimes compromised by what other Jews do. It's a feeling of belonging, affiliation; and in this affiliation, there is, for example, the tortured link to Israel."[36] This powerful "sense of belonging" is the undisputed strength of the Jewish community; every Jew experiences himself as part and parcel of the chosen people, and those who speak for the community relentlessly reinforce this feeling. Whatever commendable act a Jew achieves reflects on the community. When a Jew is a victim, the Jewish people as a whole is victimized. By contrast, if he is guilty, his Jewishness is repressed because it would implicate the whole people in his guilt: everyone knows Albert Einstein was a Jew, but who knows that Jack the Ripper was, too?[37] Jewishness is in some sense a latent sentiment capable of being activated by the slightest alarm. "The feeling of Jewishness remains in me something dark, abyssal, and above all, unstable. Both powerful and labile. Nothing is as important to me as my Jewishness which, however, in many respects, has so little importance in my life," writes Jacques Derrida.[38]

The self-hatred label, applied to any Jew who apostatizes or criticizes his community of origin, betrays a conception of Jewishness as a central and ineradicable element of individuality. Consider how Benzion Netanyahu analyzes the situation of the Jew who marries a non-Jewess: "His individuality, which is an extract and an example of the qualities of his nation, may then be lost in future generations, dominated by qualities of other nations. Quitting a nation is, therefore, even from a biological point of view, an act of suicide. It shows that the individual does not value his own special qualities."[39] Thus, according to

---

[36] "Juif? Selon Alain Finkielkraut," on YouTube.

[37] This serial killer operating in London in 1888 has been identified by his DNA as being Polish immigrant Aaron Kosminski. Hollywood is no longer interested.

[38] Jacques Derrida and Elisabeth Roudinesco, *De quoi demain… Dialogue*, Fayard, 2001, p. 310, quoted in Hervé Ryssen, *Les Espérances planétariennes*, Éditions Baskerville, 2005, p. 183.

[39] Benzion Netanyahu, *The Founding Fathers of Zionism* (1938), Balfour Books, 2012, k. 2203–7.

Netanyahu, it is not Jewishness that is a part of the Jew's individuality, but his individuality that is a manifestation of Jewishness. Such remarks make it possible to understand how the high degree of empathy and sociability—that is to say, in practice, mutual aid—in the Jewish community is linked to the paradigm of the Jewish group soul.

The obsessional memory of the Holocaust is also rooted in this same paradigm; for the group soul connects each Jew to the millions of Jewish victims of Nazism, with an intensity not found in any other national memorial cult. Every Jew, even the offspring of Sephardim from North Africa who never saw a Nazi uniform, feels victimized by the Holocaust, and traumatized for life as a survivor. This kind of blurred boundary between personal memory and collective memory is one of the striking symptoms of Jewishness. The phenomenon is simple to understand in the light of the sociological theory of memory of Maurice Halbwachs, who writes in *Les Cadres sociaux de la mémoire* ("The Social Frames of Memory," 1925): "Most often, if I remember, it is that others give me incentive to remember, that their memory comes to the aid of mine, that mine relies on theirs."[40] This explains in part the number of "false memories" contained in the testimonies of survivors of the camps: the mythologizing of some becomes, forty years later, the memories of others.[41]

Another consequence: any aggression against a Jew awakens in him, and among the other members of his community, the trauma of the Holocaust. Any anti-Semitic, Judeophobic, or simply Judeo-critical speech brings to mind the fear of "the darkest hours" in history. Any injustice against a Jew is a little Auschwitz. Every Jew killed is a potential genocide; whoever kills a Jew kills the Jewish people. Such is the mental pattern of the Zionist Claude Ranel when he evokes the Israeli perception of Palestinian resistance in *Moi, Juif palestinien* (1970): "What the fedayeen did not understand [...] is that any terrorist act will

---

[40] Maurice Halbwachs, *Les Cadres sociaux de la mémoire* (1925), Albin Michel, 1994, p. 2.
[41] e.g., Schlomo Venezia, *Sonderkommando. Dans l'enfer des chambres à gaz*, written in 2006, prefaced by Simone Veil and translated in 19 languages, and Binjamin Wilkomirski, *Fragments. Une enfance 1939–1948*, published in 1997.

always be automatically interpreted by Israel as the simulacrum on a small scale of the generalized massacre of an entire population."[42] Here, I think, we have a psychological key to understanding the nature of the Israeli-Palestinian conflict.

Universalism and the Chosenness Complex

The association of Judaism and universalism is endlessly harped upon. Politically correct goyim assimilate the message. "We are all Jews insofar as we care about the universal," Jean Hyppolite is reported saying to his students at the École Normale Supérieure.[43] Judaism, we are told, invented the universal God, and humanism with it. We have seen what lies behind the first proposition: the universal God invented by the Jews is actually a particularly jealous tribal god seized with an exterminating rage against all other gods, and his universalism is only a disguise hiding supremacism and contempt for all non-Jewish particularisms.

Jewish universalism is artificial. It is a posture, a persona. Johann Gottlieb Fichte, writing in 1793, was not mistaken: "The Jew who overcomes the difficult, one may say insurmountable, barriers which lie before him, and attains a love of justice, mankind, and truth—that Jew is a hero and a saint. I do not know whether such Jews ever existed or exist today. I shall believe it as soon as I meet such Jews. But dare you not sell me beautiful appearances for the real thing."[44] Jewish universalism is a fable intended to obfuscate reality and confuse the goy. Aaron David Gordon, founder of the Zionist party Hapoel Hatzair (Young Worker), puts it this way: "We always shout the word Humanity louder than all others, not because we have an ethics superior to others but because Humanity is an abstraction, an ethereal notion: In life there are only peoples (*Völker*)."[45]

Such an understanding is not given to everyone. Most Jews probably do not bother to question the paradoxical character of

---

[42] Claude Ranel, *Moi, Juif palestinien*, Robert Laffont, 1970, p. 106.

[43] Quoted in Maurice-Ruben Hayoun, *Maïmonide ou l'autre Moïse*, Pocket, 2013.

[44] In *The Jew in the Modern World: A Documentary History*, ed. Paul Mendes-Flohr and Jehuda Reinharz, 2nd edition, Oxford University Press, 1995, p. 309.

[45] Aaron David Gordon, *Briefe aus Palästina*, Berlin, 1919 (archive.org), pp. 19–20.

Jewish universalism. The paradox is repressed in the recesses of the psyche. Universalism could be seen as an unconscious compensation for tribalism; the Jew absolves himself of his atavistic tribalism by an ideal image of himself as a universalist humanist. This psychological consideration is also important for understanding the phenomenon of crypto-Jewishness, which cannot be reduced to conscious duplicity. The following remark by the historian of Judaism Daniel Lindenberg illustrates the psychological dimension of these contradictions: "Anyone who has known Communist Jews, ex-Kominternists, or even some prominent representatives of the 1968 generation will know what frustrated crypto-Jewishness means: Here are men and women who, in principle, according to the 'internationalist' dogma, have stifled in themselves all traces of 'particularism' and 'petty-bourgeois Jewish chauvinism,' who are nauseated by Zionism, support Arab nationalism and the great Soviet Union—yet who secretly rejoice in Israel's military victories, tell anti-Soviet jokes, and weep while listening to a Yiddish song. This goes on until the day when, like a Leopold Trepper, they can bring out their repressed Jewishness, sometimes becoming, like the Marranos of the past, the most intransigent of neophytes."[46] The role of the unconscious in this duplicity must be relativized. There is undoubtedly a very deliberate intention on the part of many cognitive elites to bluff the goyim, but also to deceive the Jews themselves about the nature of the solidarity demanded of them.

Jewish universalism is a part of the Jews' self-image, and amounts to an expression of limitless ethnic narcissism. Remember: the best deceivers are self-deceivers, and the psychopath typically ends up believing in his own lies, for he ignores the value of truth. There is no need to question the sincerity of Jewish thinkers claiming that the Jewish people is "the seed that is germinating the humanity of the future" (Jacob Kaplan, chief rabbi of France), or "the living ladder that meets the sky" (Emmanuel Levinas), or that "Israel equals humanity"

---

[46] Daniel Lindenberg, *Figures d'Israël. L'identité juive entre marranisme et sionisme (1649–1998)*, Fayard, 2014, p. 10.

(Emmanuel Levinas),[47] or that "The Jew is closer to humanity than any other," so that "the enemy of the Jews is the enemy of humanity" and therefore killing Jews is "murdering all mankind" (Elie Wiesel).[48] Worse, "Hitting a Jew is hitting God Himself," according to Cardinal Aron Jean-Marie Lustiger,[49] taken almost verbatim from the Talmud (Sanhedrin 58b: "Hitting a Jew is like slapping the face of God himself").

This explains why the strange notion of "crimes against humanity" was created specifically to describe the massacre of Jews (at the Nuremberg trials in 1945), while the term "genocide" was coined for the same purpose by Raphael Lemkin in 1944. Their extension to other victims of history led to the choice of yet another term, the Holocaust—hard to beat. According to Abraham Foxman, chairman of the Anti-Defamation League, the Holocaust is "not simply one example of genocide but a near successful attempt on the life of God's chosen children and, thus, on God himself."[50] Using strangely circular reasoning, Jean Daniel puts forward as proof of the incomparable character of Jewish suffering the fact that no one has ever questioned another human drama as did the (Jewish) thinkers by wondering "how to think after Auschwitz" (Emil Fackenheim) or what became of "The Concept of God after Auschwitz" (Hans Jonas). It follows that "meditating on the Jewish question amounts to meditating [...] on the human condition."[51] What Daniel does not see is that the phenomenon he underlines demonstrates not the incomparable character of Jewish suffering but the incomparable character of Jewish ethnocentrism.

---

[47] Quoted in Hervé Ryssen, *La Guerre eschatologique*, Éditions Baskerville, 2013, p. 23, and *Les Espérances planétariennes, op. cit.*, p. 189.

[48] Quoted in Roger Garaudy, *Le Procès du sionisme israélien*, Vent du Large, 1998 (archive.org), p. 17.

[49] Daniel Rondeau, "Pourquoi Lustiger dérange," *L'Express*, November 21, 2002, on www.lexpress.fr.

[50] *Frontline*, January 1994, quoted in Kevin MacDonald, *Culture of Critique, op. cit.*, k. 1247–48.

[51] Jean Daniel, *La Prison juive. Humeurs et méditations d'un témoin*, Odile Jacob, 2003, pp. 30–31.

Yahweh, the Jewish universal God, is only a narcissistic tribal god, in the clinical sense of the term. Jewish universalism is only a hypertrophied ethnocentrism. For if the Jew is the essence of humanity, it follows implicitly that the non-Jew is a little less than human. Many rabbis have made the idea explicit. Abraham Isaac Hacohen Kook, known as Rav Cook, first Ashkenazi chief rabbi in the Land of Israel until his death in 1935, explained: "The difference between a Jewish soul and souls of non-Jews—all of them in all different levels—is greater and deeper than the difference between a human soul and the souls of cattle."[52] Isaac Kadmi-Cohen reminds us that "in ancient Hebrew, the verb 'to die' applies to all living things, human or beast. For Hebrews, one uses the euphemism 'rejoin one's people' (*Héasef léamo*)."[53]

It is almost always in reference to their Jewishness that Jews feel and proclaim themselves universalist. In other words, the universalism of the Jews is almost always a Jewish universalism, that is, in reality, a tribal narcissism. It is fake. Using an oxymoron, Jewishness can be defined as universalist tribalism, or tribal universalism. The Judeo-centric mode of thought is immune to the cognitive dissonance that may result from the contradiction between the universalist discourse and the tribalistic practice. If the Jew is the essence of humanity, what is good for the Jews is good for mankind, on principle: "Judaism considers only the salvation of the house of Israel, which alone will permit the salvation of the seventy nations of the universe" (Rabi, *Anatomie du Judaisme français*, 1962).[54] The Jews are the indispensable people. "I believe in our moral and intellectual superiority, in our capacity to serve as a model for the redemption of the human race," proclaimed Ben-Gurion, the founding father of Israel.[55] It is by remaining a separate people

---

[52] Israel Shahak and Norman Mezvinsky, *Jewish Fundamentalism in Israel*, Pluto Press, 1999, p. 176.

[53] Isaac Kadmi-Cohen, *Nomades: Essai sur l'âme juive, op. cit.*, p. 141.

[54] Quoted in Martin Peltier, *L'Antichristianisme juif. L'enseignement de la haine*, Diffusion Internationale Édition, 2014, p. 250.

[55] Arthur Hertzberg, *The Zionist State*, Jewish Publication Society, 1997, p. 94.

that the Jews will help unify humanity. And so their separatism is supposedly necessary for their universalism.

The double ethnic-religious nature of Judaism helps streamline the paradox that the Jews should remain a separate people in order to spread their universal religion. This is, for example, the thesis of Felix Adler (1851–1933): When the Jewish people has fulfilled its mission of dissolving the ethnicity of the rest of humanity, then it will be allowed to disappear. And so the world's most ethnically oriented community succeeds in masquerading as the champion of universalism. Thus when Martin Buber called for a state for the Jews, it was so they could serve humanity. For it is only by fulfilling its messianic dream of a national home, he said, that the Jewish religion can lead humanity toward the messianic age.[56] This argument, developed by Reform Judaism, is intended primarily for goyim but also for "soft" Jews, in order to convince them that their commitment in favor of the group is a service to humanity.

The ethnocentrism of communal Jewish thinkers is particularly apparent in their vision of universal history. Israelis, "the most separatist people in the world" according to Nahum Goldmann (former president of the World Jewish Organization and founder of the World Jewish Congress), "have the great weakness of thinking that the whole world revolves around them."[57] Another fervent Zionist, Josef Kastein, acknowledges in his *History and Destiny of the Jews* (1933): "The Jewish world was Judeocentric, and the Jews could interpret everything that happened only from the standpoint of themselves as the center."[58] Josué Jehouda illustrates this perfectly in *Antisemitism, Mirror of the World*: "He who plumbs the depths of universal history, to gain an overall vision, finds that from ancient times until today two opposing currents are fighting over history, penetrating and shaping it constantly: the messianic current and the anti-Semitic current. [...] messianism and anti-Semitism are

---

[56] Kevin MacDonald, *Culture of Critique, op. cit.*, k. 9983–10008, and *Separation and Its Discontents, op. cit.*, k. 5485–91.
[57] Nahum Goldmann, *Le Paradoxe juif. Conversations en français avec Léon Abramowicz*, Stock, 1976 (archive.org), pp. 6, 31.
[58] Josef Kastein, *History and Destiny of the Jews*, Garden City, 1936, p. 127.

the two opposite poles of the journey of humanity."[59] Such expressions of extreme ethnocentrism only confirm Karl Marx's view that "the Jew [...] can behave towards the state only in a Jewish way—that is, [...] by deeming himself justified in separating himself from mankind, by abstaining on principle from taking part in the historical movement, by putting his trust in a future which has nothing in common with the future of mankind in general."[60]

Judeocentrism is not only a way of learning history, but also a way of writing it and using it as a weapon of domination rather than as a search for truth. The founder of sociology Emile Durkheim (1858–1917), quite critical of his Jewish community, wrote: "The Jew [...] seeks to learn not in order to replace his collective prejudices by reflective thought, but merely to be better armed for the struggle. [...] he superimposes this intellectual life upon his habitual routine with no effect of the former upon the latter."[61] Quite often the search for truth becomes a smokescreen, the only important question being, "Is it good for the Jews?"[62] But the communal pride of certain Jewish intellectuals is so outrageous that it cannot be interpreted as purely demagogic. It often appears downright pathological, as when Bernard-Henry Levy, who is accustomed to such ethnocentric delusions, declares: "The French language is perhaps one of the most precious things in this country; and it is a Jew—and what a Jew, Rashi—who deserves credit for having almost invented it."[63]

Jewishness seems to induce a blind spot among some high-level intellectuals: they become irrational as soon as they approach a subject with any relationship to their community, as if an unconscious imperative—some programmed subroutine in the superego—suddenly short-circuited their objectivity. I

[59] Josué Jehouda, *L'Antisémitisme, miroir du monde*, Éditions Synthesis, 1958, p. 185.

[60] Karl Marx, *On the Jewish Question*, 1843, on www.marxists.org/archive.

[61] Quoted in Kevin MacDonald, *Separation and Its Discontents, op. cit.*, k. 5403–10.

[62] Jonny Geller made it the title of his humorous book *Yes, But Is It Good for the Jews?*, Bloomsbury, 2006.

[63] In February 2016 on "La Radio de la Communauté Juive" (RCJ), on YouTube, "Invité du 12/13 Bernard-Henry Levy."

recently came across an astonishing example of this phenomenon while opening a book by the psychiatrist Simon Baron-Cohen, *The Science of Evil: On Empathy and the Origins of Cruelty*. Here is how the author begins his book: "When I was seven years old, my father told me the Nazis had turned Jews into lampshades. Just one of those comments that you hear once, and the thought never goes away. To a child's mind (even to an adult's) these two types of things just don't belong together. He also told me the Nazis turned Jews into bars of soap. It sounds so unbelievable, yet it is actually true. I knew our family was Jewish, so this image of turning people into objects felt a bit close to home. My father also told me about one of his former girlfriends, Ruth Goldblatt, whose mother had survived a concentration camp. He had been introduced to the mother and was shocked to discover that her hands were reversed. Nazi scientists had severed Mrs. Goldblatt's hands, switched them around, and sewn them on again so that if she put her hands out palms down, her thumbs were on the outside and her little fingers were on the inside. Just one of the many 'experiments' they had conducted. I realized there was a paradox at the heart of human nature—people could objectify others—that my young mind was not yet ready to figure out. [...] Today, almost half a century after my father's revelations to me about the extremes of human behavior, my mind is still exercised by the same, single question: How can we understand human cruelty?"[64] I had to read this passage twice to make sure I understood correctly, and to finally admit the obvious: Baron-Cohen doesn't doubt the stories told him by his father. And nowhere in the book does he wonder about the motivation of those who invent such stories or those who relate them to their children. The story serves only to introduce his theme: how can human beings commit such acts? This book was written in 2011 by a physician of great reputation—although not a specialist in hand surgery—whose works are, in general, models of scientific rigor.

---

[64] Simon Baron-Cohen, *The Science of Evil: On Empathy and the Origins of Cruelty*, Basic Books, 2011, k. 108–150.

The Holocaust Attitude

The psychopath is unable to see the other person's point of view, and criticism strikes him as irrational aggression. He does not know the feeling of guilt, and constantly plays innocent: those who have crossed his path are solely responsible for their own destruction. Their reproaches are baseless, and their anger an irrational hatred. This is the reaction of the Jewish elites to criticism: to them it can be nothing other than the expression of visceral anti-Semitism, an atavistic goyish disease. "Judeophobia is a variety of demonopathy, with the distinction that it is not peculiar to particular races but is common to the whole of mankind," writes Leon Pinsker, a medical doctor. It is "a psychic aberration. As a psychic aberration it is hereditary, and as a disease transmitted for two thousand years it is incurable." By way of consequence, the Jews are "the people chosen for universal hatred."[65] This curious formula could be the credo of secular Zionism, and reflects pretty well a widespread feeling among Jews and Israelis, as is well documented in Yoav Shamir's excellent film *Defamation* (2009).

In their own eyes, the Jews have no responsibility for the hostility of the Gentiles toward them. There are certainly exceptions that confirm the rule: Thus, in a deliberately provocative way, Samuel Roth wrote (in 1934): "There is not a single instance when the Jews have not fully deserved the bitter fruit of the fury of their persecutors."[66] By such remarks, Roth has marginalized himself in his community. The politically correct point of view of a leading Jewish intellectual such as André Neher is the exact opposite: "One thing that Judaism has which other spiritualities lack is innocence. We are innocent, and we feel even more deeply that we are innocent when we are accused. [...] It is this innocence that we must be aware of at present, and that we must never deny, never, in any

---

[65] Leon Pinsker, *Auto-Emancipation: An Appeal to His People by a Russian Jew* (1882), on www.jewishvirtuallibrary.org/jsource/Zionism/pinsker.html.
[66] Samuel Roth, *Jews Must Live: An Account of the Persecution of the World by Israel on All the Frontiers of Civilization*, 1934 (archive.org). For a more balanced point of view, read Bernard Lazare, *L'Antisémitisme, son histoire et ses causes* (1894), Kontre Kulture, 2011.

circumstance."[67] And it works: "You will understand nothing of anti-Semitism," wrote Jean-Paul Sartre, "if you fail to remember that the Jew, that object of so much hatred, is perfectly innocent, nay harmless" (*Réflexions sur la question juive,* 1946).[68] Anti-Semitism is so universal and sneaky that it is there even when one does not see it: "In their great majority, Christians— or those recognized as such—are anti-Semites. For even in the best of them, the very ones who have engaged the most generous combat against Nazi anti-Semitism, it is easy to detect the traces of more or less unconscious anti-Semitism" (Jules Isaac, *L'Enseignement du mépris,* 1962).[69] We can detect here what Yiddish writer and 1978 Nobel Prize nominee Isaac Bashevis Singer describes as a monomaniac tendency of the Jew: "When he gets an idea into his head it becomes so strong that he forgets about everything else. Let's consider the Jew who fights anti-Semitism. He will find anti-Semitism everywhere, even on an empty island or in the Sahara. The obsessed person becomes funny because he cannot see the exception to the rule, or he creates nonexistent rules."[70] In the final analysis, this obsessive fear is only a side effect of chosenness, since the destiny of the chosen one is to be misunderstood and rejected. From the psychological point of view, chosenness leads directly to the persecution complex.

And persecution is the dominant theme of Jewish history. Michael Walzer remembers: "I was taught Jewish history as a long tale of exile and persecution—Holocaust history read backwards."[71] Persecution is also the central theme of the liturgy and Jewish feasts: Passover, Hanukkah, Purim, Yom Kippur. Persecution is so essential to the Jewish identity that, when it does not exist, there is an urgent need to invent it. An obsessive fear of anti-Semitism must be maintained in the minds of the

---

[67] Quoted in Hervé Ryssen, *Les Espérances planétariennes, op. cit.,* p. 319.

[68] Jean-Paul Sartre, *Réflexions sur la question juive* (1946), Gallimard, 1985, p. 183.

[69] Quoted in Martin Peltier, *L'Antichristianisme juif, op. cit.,* p. 206.

[70] Isaac Bashevis Singer and Richard Burgin, *Conversations With Isaac Bashevis Singer,* Doubleday, 1985, p. 45.

[71] Michael Walzer, "Toward a New Realization of Jewishness," *Congress Monthly,* Vol. 61, No. 4, 1994, p. 4, quoted in Kevin MacDonald, *Separation and Its Discontents, op. cit.,* k. 4675–86.

Jews, for it is the glue that holds the community together, the only thing capable of resisting the dissolving effect of assimilation. Toward the end of his life, Jewish writer Ilya Ehrenburg repeated that he would consider himself a Jew "as long as there was a single anti-Semite left on earth."[72] (One should take him seriously: As a Soviet propagandist during WWII, Ehrenburg's leaflets urged Red Army soldiers to "kill! kill! kill!": "The Germans are not human beings. [...] There is nothing more amusing for us than a heap of German corpses. [...] Kill the Germans—that is your grandmother's request. Kill the German—that is your child's prayer. Kill the German—that is your motherland's loud request. [...] Kill, Red Army men, kill! No fascist is innocent, be he alive, be he as yet unborn.")[73] When real Judeophobia is in decline, it becomes necessary to raise the specter of imaginary anti-Semitism. Even asleep, even invisible, the beast must remain a permanent threat in everyone's mind.

The incantatory cult of the Holocaust, developed in the 1960s, is part of the same strategy. It could be considered a sort of cannibalizing the dead, if the dead were really at the center of this cult. But that is not the case. Only their number and the power it confers are important. Recent polls indicate that being Jewish is increasingly defined as the funeral cult of the Holocaust: a 2013 Pew Research poll on the theme "A Portrait of Jewish Americans" shows that, to the question "What's essential to being Jewish?" "Remembering the Holocaust" comes first for 73 percent of respondents. Next comes "Caring about Israel," then "Observing Jewish laws" (not to mention those whose first reaction is to congratulate themselves by ticking "Leading an ethical and moral life").[74] The Jewish people is no longer defined as the chosen people. It is now the exterminatable people. "The Jewish religion died 200 years ago. Now there is nothing that unifies the Jews around the world apart from the Holocaust," once remarked Yeshayahu

---

[72] Kevin MacDonald, *Culture of Critique, op. cit.*, k. 3176–78.
[73] Thomas Goodrich, *Hellstorm: The Death of Nazi Germany, 1944–1947*, CreateSpace, 2014, p. 94. Watch the documentary of the same title.
[74] "A Portrait of Jewish Americans," on www.pewforum.org.

Leibowitz, professor at the Hebrew University in Jerusalem.[75] If the Holocaust has supplanted Yahweh as the new god of Israel, it is because its primary function is the same: separate the Jews, exile them into their exceptionality, foster a new morbid form of the chosenness complex. For if the whole Western world is now "remembering the Holocaust," not all men are equal in this cult. Just as Yahweh divided humankind into the chosen people and the rest of the nations, the Holocaust separates the victims and their tormentors. And so the Holocaust, the absolute Evil, turns out to be functionally interchangeable with Yahweh.

The Holocaust is a jealous god: there is no museum or commemoration for the genocide of American Indians (not even a name for this unspeakable crime for which Americans are collectively responsible, while they are innocent of the Holocaust). To the Ukrainians who wished to commemorate the "Holodomor"—the death of 7 to 8 millions of them in 1932–1933 by a deliberately provoked famine against the kulaks resisting collectivization—Israeli president Shimon Peres advised, during a visit to Kiev on November 25, 2010: "Forget History."[76] The Holocaust is eternal, "It is continuing all the time," declared Benzion Netanyahu in 2009.[77] In reality, according to Israeli philosopher Gilad Atzmon, biblical Yahwism was from the start a religion of the Holocaust: "the Holocaust is actually engraved in the Jewish culture, discourse and spirit. [...] To be a Jew is to see a threat in every goy, to be on constant alert."[78]

The sacralization of the Holocaust and its media liturgy fulfills two complementary functions: guilt among the Gentiles, fear among the Jews. Through guilt, the Gentiles are kept in check, and all their criticisms are neutralized by equating them to gas chambers. Through fear, the Jewish community is kept under control, and its loyalty to Israel strengthened, as Israel is

---

[75] Reported by Uri Avnery in 2005, quoted in Gilad Atzmon, *The Wandering Who?, op. cit.*, pp. 161–162.

[76] Alexander Motyl, "Ukrainians and Jews…," April 15, 2011, worldaffairsjournal.org.

[77] Quoted in Alan Hart, *Zionism: The Real Enemy of the Jews*, vol. 3: *Conflict Without End?*, Clarity Press, 2010, p. 364.

[78] Gilad Atzmon, *The Wandering Who?, op. cit.*, p. 162.

depicted as an "insurance policy," a fortress (preferably well-armed), and a refuge in the event of a new Holocaust. The quasi-miraculous power of this cult is such that "the trauma of the Holocaust is transmitted genetically" by "epigenetic heredity," according to a study by a team of researchers at Mount Sinai Hospital in New York under the direction of Rachel Yehuda.[79]

With its many museums and incessant media liturgy, the Holocaust cult has now replaced the worship of Christ. Remembering the martyrdom of the chosen people has become the civic religion of Western Europe. It has the added advantage of stifling the cries of the Palestinian people, Gazans in particular, who are being crucified with increasingly demonic violence. According to historian Zygmunt Bauman, Israel uses the Holocaust "as the certificate of its political legitimacy, as safe-conduct pass for its past and future policies, and, above all, as advance payment for the injustices it might itself commit."[80]

The Holocaust is not only the Jews' worst memory, it is their ever-possible future. The Israelis' greatest fear is of another Holocaust, this time on Israelis, as *Haaretz* journalist Yair Sheleg explained in 2006: "It is hard to believe, but just 60 years after the Holocaust the Jewish people is again in danger of extermination." Each anti-Semitic act, every expression of Judeophobia, is a small Holocaust, capable of prefiguring a new catastrophe. Israeli musician and philosopher Gilad Atzmon speaks of a "Pre-Traumatic Stress Syndrome (Pre-TSS)" to characterize the fundamental mood of Jewish and Israeli culture, induced by the political and cultural elite, who, through constant reminders of the last Holocaust, keep the population under permanent expectation of the next one.[81] For example, "young Israelis are brought to Auschwitz by various Zionist organizations with the aim of turning them into traumatized Jewish adults."[82] The conviction that Jew-hatred is inherent in

---

[79] Tori Rodrigues, "Descendants of Holocaust Survivors Have Altered Stress Hormones," *Scientific American*, March 1, 2015, on www.scientificamerican.com.
[80] Kevin MacDonald, *Separation and Its Discontents, op. cit.*, k. 4674–86.
[81] Gilad Atzmon, *The Wandering Who?, op. cit.*, pp. 130–131.
[82] Gilad Atzmon, *The Wandering Who?, op. cit.*, pp. 179–180, 223–224.

Gentiles is so intimately linked to modern Jewish identity that the Jew who renounces Jewishness—or criticizes it too severely, like Gilad Atzmon—is treated as a self-hating Jew, that is to say, accused of having internalized the goyim's hatred of him.

The liturgy of the Holocaust is accompanied by a perpetually alarmist discourse on anti-Semitism. A survey conducted in 1985 indicated that one-third of the Jews in the San Francisco Bay Area believed that a Jew could not be elected to Congress, even though three of the four local representatives in Congress were Jews, as were the two Senators from California and the mayor of San Francisco. A 1990 survey shows that eight out of ten American Jews are concerned about anti-Semitism and believe it is increasing, while 90 percent of non-Jews believe that anti-Semitism is residual. The discrepancy between perception and reality suggests a form of self-deception aimed at maintaining a fantasized self-image as oppressed outsider. The need to feed the fear of anti-Semitism has led Jewish organizations to characterize as anti-Semitic attitudes such as indifference to Jewish concerns or discomfiture at the overrepresentation of Jews among cultural, intellectual, financial, and political elites.[83]

Ultimately, like most traits of Jewish collective psychology, the inability to accept any responsibility for the hostility of the goyim is a lesson learned in the Bible, especially in the story of Jacob and Esau, who in the rabbinic tradition symbolize respectively Israel and the nations, or Judaism and Christianity. When Jacob usurps the birthright of Esau by deceiving his father Isaac, he gains the divine blessing. Esau's resentment, like Cain's for Abel, is presented without a shred of sympathy. In the short book of Obadiah, Yahweh chastises Esau: "For the violence done to your brother Jacob, shame will cover you and you will be annihilated forever!" (Obadiah 1:10); "The House of Jacob will be a fire, the House of Joseph a flame, and the House of Esau like stubble. They will set it alight and burn it up, and no one of the House of Esau will survive" (1:18), "and sovereignty will be Yahweh's!" (1:21). Thus nations that dare protest against Israel's below-the-belt punches, which are always automatically

---

[83] Kevin MacDonald, *Separation and Its Discontents, op. cit.,* k. 4687–99.

legitimate, deserve to be annihilated. In the words of Henry Makow, "Organized Jewry (Neocons, Zionists, B'nai Brith) has the self-consciousness of a snake devouring a mouse. It regards the death spasms of the mouse as 'hatred.'"[84]

The Sociopathic State

Victimization has become the essence of Israeli national identity, according to Idith Zertal, professor at the Hebrew University in Jerusalem: "Israeli society nationalized the memory of the Holocaust." "The Holocaust is inserted directly and metaphorically into everyday life in Israel, which is loaded, in this fashion, with meaning beyond itself, as are power and the ideology of power." By this process, Israel has been transformed "into an ahistorical and apolitical twilight zone, where Auschwitz is not a past event but a threatening present and a constant option. By means of Auschwitz—which has become over the years Israel's main reference in its relations with a world defined repeatedly as anti-Semitic and forever hostile—Israel rendered itself immune to criticism, and impervious to a rational dialogue with the world around her."[85]

With regard to the Palestinians, "Israeli Jews' consciousness is characterized by a sense of victimization, a siege mentality, blind patriotism, belligerence, self-righteousness, dehumanization of the Palestinians, and insensitivity to their suffering," in the words of journalist Akiva Eldar (writing after Operation Cast Lead against Gaza in 2008–2009).[86] Many lucid Israelis are worried about their country's plunge into collective pathology. Yehoshafat Harkabi, deputy director of military intelligence, wrote: "Dazzled by its self-righteousness, Israel cannot see the case of the other side. Self-righteousness encourages nations no less than individuals to absolve themselves of every failing and shake off the guilt of every mishap. When everyone is guilty

---

[84] Henry Makow, *Illuminati: The Cult that Hijacked the World*, CreateSpace, 2008, kindle, k. 268–69.

[85] Idith Zertal, *Israel's Holocaust and the Politics of Nationhood*, Cambridge University Press, 2010, pp. 5, 169, 4.

[86] Quoted in Max Blumenthal, *Goliath: Life and Loathing in Greater Israel*, Nation Books, 2013, p. 16.

except them, the very possibility of self-criticism and self-improvement vanishes…"[87] The Israeli journalist Gideon Levy wrote in *Haaretz* in 2010 that "Only psychiatrists can explain Israel's behavior," suggesting as a possible diagnosis, "paranoia, schizophrenia and megalomania."[88] Sociopathy is probably a better guess. If any nationalism is a collective egoism, Israel's is more like a collective sociopathy.

What can be said of a state that, having received from the community of nations, by an exceptional privilege, a land whose indigenous inhabitants were thus dispossessed, bases its foreign policy on the following principle, expressed by its leader (Ben-Gurion) ten years later: "We must wean ourselves from the preposterous and totally unfounded and baseless illusion that there is outside the State of Israel a force and a will that would protect the life of our citizens. Our own capacity for self-defense is our only security"?[89] What is to be said of a country that, having made the Holocaust the universal, eternal, and ultimate crime, and seeing only potential and interchangeable enemies around it, behaves as if it wanted to punish the Palestinians for the crimes committed by Europeans (as Palestinian spokeswoman Hanan Ashrawi often remarks)?

Our diagnosis should take into account Israel's extraordinary manipulative capacity on the world stage via corruption and propaganda—the bank and the press. The relationship between Israel and the United States is akin to the bond between a typical psychopath and the impressionable bully he has decided to manipulate. Israel's control of the American mind is achieved on the mass level through the press and the entertainment industry, on the governmental level through the irresistible influence of the neocons and AIPAC, and on a still deeper level through wide-scale spying and the infiltration and hijacking of intelligence and secret services. As *Haaretz* recently revealed, two

---

[87] Alan Hart, *Zionism: The Real Enemy of the Jews*, vol. 2: *David Becomes Goliath*, Clarity Press, 2009, pp. 42–49.

[88] Gideon Levy, "Only Psychiatrists Can Explain Israel's Behavior," *Haaretz*, January 10, 2010, on www.haaretz.com.

[89] David Ben-Gurion, *Vision and Fulfilment*, 1958, vol. 5, p. 125, quoted in Alan Hart, *Zionism: The Real Enemy of the Jews*, vol. 2, p. 130.

Israeli high-tech firms (Verint and Narus) with ties to Mossad, have provided the spy software for the NSA, thus securing for Israel access to all collected data. Other Israeli software "front companies" have likewise infiltrated the US administration and military-industrial sector. And, as James Petras comments, "because of the power and influence of the Conference of Presidents of the 52 Major American Jewish Organizations, Justice Department officials have ordered dozens of Israeli espionage cases to be dropped. The tight Israeli ties to the US spy apparatus serves to prevent deeper scrutiny into Israel's operations and political goals—at a very high price in terms of the security of US citizens."[90]

The golden rule of manipulation formulated by Colonel Mandell House (who was the intermediary between the Zionist network and President Woodrow Wilson) applies generally to Israel's manipulation of the United States: "With the President [. . .] it was invariably my intention to always to make him believe that ideas he derived from me were his own."[91] Such is also the essence of Israel's strategy with the US; behind the mask of American patriotism, the neocons have managed to lead America into a Middle East policy that only serves Israeli interests, by pretending to the American people that it serves their interests. The psychopath tries to interfere in all the human relationships of his prey, so as to prevent any alliance that could allow him to be unmasked. Isolate and divide-and-rule are the essence of this strategy. This is precisely what Israel and its neoconservative moles have done, by trying to split the United States from its historic allies in the Middle East, with the aim of one day remaining the only ally of the United States in the area. The demonization of all heads of state in the Arab world is part of this strategy. One of Israel's great successes has been to ensure that its own enemies, the Arab peoples, today have a fierce hatred for the United States.

---

[90] "What Was the Israeli Involvement in Collecting U.S. Communications Intel for the NSA?" *Haaretz*, June 8, 2013, quoted in James Petras, *The Politics of Empire: The US, Israel and the Middle East*, Clarity Press, 2014, p. 50.
[91] Arthur Howden Smith, *The Real Colonel House*, 1918, quoted in Aline de Diéguez, *Aux Sources du chaos mondial actuel*, aline.dedieguez.pagesperso-orange.fr.

The power of the Zionist manipulation of the United States, based on quasi-total control of the mainstream media alongside large-scale psychological operations such as September 11, is truly bewildering. But it becomes understandable in light of what Robert Hare names the "psychopathic bond." It even becomes predictable to some extent, if we keep in mind that the psychopath has no ability to question, no limits to his appetite for power, and no remorse about leading humanity into ruin to save his skin. Nothing better illustrates the psychopathic nature of Zionism than the apocalyptic nuclear blackmail Israel perpetually exercises over the West, with its policy of the "Samson Option," which Golda Meir summed up in 1974 as "Israel's willingness in a doomsday situation to take the region down with it."[92] Using this threat, Meir blackmailed Kissinger and Nixon into coming to Israel's rescue during the Yom Kippur War.

By drawing a parallel between psychopathy as a personality disorder and the attitude of Israel, I do not mean, of course, the Jews in general. They are the first to be manipulated by their elites, and they are part of this collective psychopathy only to the extent of their submission to those elites. Jewishness, we must not forget, is whatever idea the Jews make of it; and the idea the Jews make of it is, almost entirely, the one imposed on them by their elites. What is at issue is the prevailing ideology of Israel, and (more discreetly) of international Jewry. Dominant discourse is always shaped by the elite. Sometimes a strong current of popular thought emerges to challenge the dominant way of thinking, but nothing of this kind is yet observable in the Jewish community; it is overwhelmingly docile to its elite, which currently dominates the media and the entertainment industry and therefore enjoys considerable mind-control powers. Their ruse is to maintain in the Jews an absolute conviction of the immaculate innocence of their people, and simultaneously to inculcate a paranoid fear of anti-Semitism, this "disease transmitted for two thousand years, incurable" (Leon Pinsker).

---

[92] Alan Hart, *Zionism: The Real Enemy of the Jews*, vol. 2, *op. cit.*, p. 194.

In *The Corporation: The Pathological Pursuit of Profit and Power*, Joel Bakan noted that large companies behave like psychopaths, insensitive to the suffering of those they crush in their pursuit of profit: "Corporate behavior is very similar to that of a psychopath."[93] Yet a company's culture, while involving every employee to one degree or another, is driven by its ruling elite. The Enron scandal has shown the world the tremendous damage that can be done by a company run by people of high intelligence and perverse ideology.[94] My analysis here of the Jewish community is based on exactly the same reasoning. Like it or not, the character of a nation is exemplified and largely determined by its leaders, whether legitimate or illegitimate.

Not all elites deserve to be put in the same bag. Many Zionist leaders have had the courage to confront the monster they created, and to try to undo the damage. Moshe Sharett, foreign minister from 1948 to 1956 and prime minister from 1954 to 1955, advocated a moderate Zionism respectful of international rules, in contrast to the methods of Ben-Gurion, Pinhas Levon, Moshe Dayan, and Shimon Peres, the clan bent on "setting the Middle East on fire." Yet men like Sharett have always remained isolated and never had a chance to overcome the psychopathic ideological power machine of Zionism. Israel seems destined to be directed by the most extremist, openly racist, paranoid, and Machiavellian elements—the most lacking in all inhibitions normally imposed by empathy and respect for other peoples.

In the final analysis, was not this destiny blueprinted in the Bible? If Israel seems bewitched by a sociopathic destiny, is it not the fault of its evil genius Yahweh? Does not the Zionist manipulation go back to the creation by the ancient Levites of this particularly xenophobic tribal egregore that has usurped the title of "Creator of the Universe" and "Father of Humanity"?

---

[93] Joel Bakan, *The Corporation: The Pathological Pursuit of Profit and Power*, Free Press, 2005. Watch also the documentary of the same title.

[94] Read Bethany MacLean and Peter Elkind, *The Smartest Guys in the Room: The Amazing Rise and Scandalous Fall of Enron*, Penguin, 2004, and watch the documentary of the same title (2005) on YouTube.

As a collective entity, the Jewish people has always behaved like a sociopath among other peoples. Many Jews, of course, have resisted that collective mind frame. But most have been bred into it for generations—not just by their parents, but by their tribal god, the fake Yahweh. Today's Jews cannot be blamed for having inherited as sacred text the most extraordinary hoax in all human history. As children of a psychopathic god, they are his first victims. But although no one is responsible for the faith he has grown up with, everyone, at some stage, should take responsibility for it.

We must hope that Jewish revolt against the divine sociopath will one day take on a collective character. The Jewish community has always been torn between an assimilationist tendency and a separatist tendency, between genuine thirst for universality and tribal particularism. All the tragedies it has experienced stem from the maneuvers of its elites opposing majoritarian aspirations to integration. These elites endlessly revive the tribal spirit from which they derive their power. It is under the double banner of the Holocaust and Israel that Jews are today called upon to strengthen their communal solidarity.

Only when the biblical Yahweh is correctly diagnosed and publicly exposed as a sociopathic myth will the Jews have a chance to collectively break away from his psychopathic bond, renounce the curse of being the chosen people, and learn to empathize with the rest of humankind. Until then, courageous Jews, from Jesus and Paul to Shlomo Sand and Gilad Atzmon, will continue to pave the way in solitude, vilified as self-hating Jews by those they wish to liberate.

Made in the USA
Las Vegas, NV
29 December 2020